South Wales Sport Climbs

Mark Glaister
Roy Thomas
Goi Ashmore
Gary Gibson

Text, crag photography and topos by Mark Glaister
Additional text and route information Roy Thomas,
Goi Ashmore, Gary Gibson
Action photography as credited
Edited by Alan James
Printed in Europe by LF Book Services
Distributed by Cordee (cordee.co.uk)

Maps by Alan James
Contains OS data © Crown copyright
and database right 2024

Published by ROCKFAX in December 2024
© ROCKFAX 2024

All rights reserved. No part of this publication may be reproduced, stored in a retrieval system, or transmitted in any form or by any means, electronic, mechanical, photocopying or otherwise without prior written permission of the copyright owner. A CIP catalogue record is available from the British Library.

We only use paper made from wood fibre from sustainable forests and produced according to ISO 14001 environmental standard

Fax69 - ISBN 978 1 873341 14 8

Cover: Marti Hallett on *Silver Sixpence* (7a) - *p.140* - in the Tooth Fairy Area, Third Sister on Gower.
Photo: Mark Glaister.

This page: Chris Davies on *Retrobution* (7b) - *p.103* - at the Trial Wall on Gower. Photo: Andy van Kints.

This book belongs to:

Contents — South Wales Sport Climbs

Introduction..........4
Coverage..........6
Rockfax Digital..........8
Symbols, Map and Topo Key..........9
Previous Guidebooks..........10
Acknowledgements..........12
Rockfax Publications..........14

South Wales Sport Logistics..........16
When to Go..........18
Getting Around and Map..........20
Accommodation..........22
Pubs..........24
Cafes, Gear Shops and Walls..........26

South Wales Sport Climbing..........28
Access..........30
Gear..........32
Bolting..........34
Grades..........36
Graded List..........38
Destination Planner..........42

Carmarthenshire..........46
Telpyn Point..........48
Morfa Bychan..........56
Pendine..........66

Gower..........74
Rhossili Beach..........76
Trial Wall Area..........98
Third Sister Area..........116
Free Luncher's to Fetlock Zawn..........142
Port Eynon..........150
Oxwich..........151
Utopia Area..........154
Watch House..........158
Foxhole..........164
Minchin Hole..........174
Bowen's Parlour Area..........178
Bosco's Gulch Area..........184
Pwlldu Bay..........192
Rams Tor..........194
Barland Quarry..........196

Inland and Coastal Limestone..........198
Dinas Rock..........200
Darren Fawr..........216
Taff's Well..........222
Taff's Well West..........240
Gilwern East..........250
Gilwern West..........268
Witches Point..........284
Temple Bay..........296
Castle Upon Alun..........306
Costa del Major..........312

The Valleys Sandstone..........324
Craig Cwm..........328
Dyffryn..........336
Abbey Buttress..........342
Pen Pych..........346
Space Mountain..........348
Treherbert Quarry..........358
Gelli..........366
Ferndale..........372
Blaenllechau..........380
Dan Dicks..........384
Trebanog..........386
Glynfach..........390
Trehafod..........392
The Darren..........396
Cwmaman..........402
Mountain Ash..........408
Mount Pleasant..........418
The Gap..........424
Navigation Quarry..........436
Abertysswg..........446
Deri..........448
Bargoed..........450
Ridgeway..........456
Llanbradach..........458
Sirhowy..........470
Cox's Quarry..........480
Cross Keys Quarry..........482
Cwmcarn..........486
Tyle y Coch..........490
Tirpentwys..........494

Route Index..........502
General Index..........512

South Wales Sport Climbs   Introduction

South of the Brecon Beacons (Bannau Brycheiniog) and spanning the land and sea cliffs from the River Wye on the Welsh border to the green rurality of Pembrokeshire lies a wealth of sport climbing. South Wales sport climbing pretty much covers the full catalogue of grades ranging from easy going 3s and 4s through to some state-of-the-art upper end grade 8s. There is plenty on offer to keep both local and visitor busy for a very long time, with currently around 2700 fully bolted sport climbs now developed and with the potential for lots more to come.

South Wales sport climbing takes place on limestone and sandstone cliffs both natural and quarried. The multitude of venues are located in environments that vary from sea-cliff to mountainside, and in post industrial to world heritage settings.

Whether you are local, studying at Cardiff or Swansea, travelling to or from Pembroke's trad sea cliffs or just on a quick trip from London down the M4 corridor, the amount of sport climbing on offer is vast and provides huge potential to enjoy well equipped climbs in some superb and diverse locations.

The climbing is easily split into four main areas - The Valleys Sandstone, Gower, the Inland and Coastal Limestone crags and Camarthenshire's sea cliffs.

Gower's stunning beaches and cliffs will be a main draw for holidaying visitors and locals alike, whilst nearby Camarthenshire's remote sea-cliifs will reward those prepared to try somewhere off of the beaten track.

South Wales Sport Climbs

Introduction — page 5

The inland limestone and coastal cliffs close to Cardiff and Swansea have been long established and well used by locals but have not been recognised by many from further afield despite quick access and lots of routes throughout the grade spectrum.

Finally, the sandstone quarries that line the sides of the valleys stretching up towards the Brecon Beacons bring another dimension to the area. The ambience may not be what some come for but lurking in the confines of these little-known venues are some truly memorable routes that will test technique and finger strength to the max.

Mark Glaister, October 2024

Rhossili Beach and Worm's Head. Photo: Keith Sharples

South Wales Sport Climbs — Introduction

Aaron Martin tackling the classic sandstone wall pitch *Propaganda* (7a+) - *p.404* - at Cwmaman in The Valleys. The image pretty much sums up the extremely fingery climbing experience to be had on the sandstone quarried faces that pepper the hillsides which lead up from the coast to the foothills of the Brecon Beacons (Bannau Brycheiniog). Photo: Elis Rees

Introduction — South Wales Sport Climbs

Coverage

This is the second edition of South Wales Sport Climbs from Rockfax. It covers virtually all of the worthwhile sport climbing to be found on the limestone and sandstone natural crags and quarries of South Wales. The area is geographically diverse and encompasses many landscapes that range from tidal sea cliffs to inland quarries set high up in the industrial valleys that lead up toward the mountains of the Brecon Beacons. There are around 2700 routes to go at; enough to keep both the occasional visitor and local enthusiasts busy for many years.

The Valleys Sandstone quarries and the spectacular sea-cliffs of Gower have been climbed on for decades the former being responsible for many steely fingered locals and the later for its wealth of stunning trad sea cliffs. However since the 1990s it has been the rapid development of sport climbing that has been the major source of action in the area - firstly on the sandstone quarries and now across the inland limestone and limestone sea cliffs.

The styles and difficulty of climbs available is remarkable for such a compact area, access is easy with a good road network and workable options for those who want to use public transport. Staying in the area is easily arranged with the popular 'climbers' options of camping or modern hostel accommodation being widely available. Non climbing options are more than well catered for with stunning mountain walking in the Brecon Beacons National Park and state-of-the-art mountain biking set alongside some world class beaches.

So if you have enjoyed the sport climbing at Portland, North Wales, The Peak District or Yorkshire give South Wales a punt - rock up at Foxhole, Rhosilli, Rams Grove, Third Sister, Dinas Rock, Witches Point, Sirhowy, Navigation Quarry, Tirpentwys or Gilwern and you might well be in for a pleasant surprise?

South Wales Sport Climbs — Rockfax Digital

Rockfax Digital brings together 50 guides from 4 publishers covering over 80,000 routes on 1600+ crags and presents it in a user-friendly package for use on mobile devices.

The heart of Rockfax Digital is the crag and route information covering 'areas' which roughly correspond to the printed guidebooks. The main data is sold by subscription so that you purchase access to everything for a period of time, from a month to a year. Once you are subscribed, you will have everything on Rockfax Digital for the duration. You can download the main data and store it on your device so you don't need any signal to be able to read the descriptions and see the topos and maps. There is plenty of free content available without a subscription, enabling you to get a really good impression of what Rockfax Digital is like without shelling out any money.

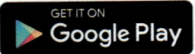

Rockfax Digital is available as an app which is free to download and incredibly useful in its own right. It contains a detailed crag map linked to the UKClimbing crags database with basic information and route lists for crags worldwide. The map also displays all the 3,800+ listings from the UKClimbing Directory of climbing walls, outdoor shops, climbing clubs, outdoor-specific accommodation and instructors and guides, amongst others.

How to Subscribe to Rockfax Digital
Go to **rockfax.digital** to find links to download the app and create an account. New users can subscribe and get 7 days free.

Scan to find out more

UKC Logbooks
A popular method of logging your climbing is to use the **UKClimbing.com** logbooks system. This database has 645,000+ routes on over 24,400+ crags. So far, over 66,900 users have recorded more than 10.8 million ascents! To set up your own logbook, just register at **UKClimbing.com** and click on the logbook tab. You will be able to record every ascent you make, when you did it, what style you climbed it in and who you did it with. Each entry has a place for your own notes. You can also add your vote to the grade/star system which is used by guidebook writers to get opinions on grades and quality of routes. The logbook can be private, public or restricted to your own climbing partners only.

Rockfax Digital can be linked to your **UKClimbing.com** user account and logbook so that you can record your activity while at the crag. To do this you will need a 3G/4G/5G data connection. You can also look at the UKC logbooks to see if anyone has climbed your chosen route recently to check on conditions.

Symbols, Map and Topo Key — South Wales Sport Climbs

Route Symbols

 A good route which is well worth the effort.

 A very good route, one of the best on the crag.

 A brilliant route, one of the best in the area.

 Technical climbing requiring good balance and technique, or complex and tricky moves.

 Powerful climbing; roofs, steep rock, low lock-offs or long moves off small holds.

 Sustained climbing; either lots of hard moves or steep rock giving pumpy climbing.

 Fingery climbing with significant small holds on the hard sections.

 Fluttery climbing with long fall potential or a scary run-out.

 A long reach is helpful, or even essential, for one or more of the moves.

 Some loose rock may be encountered.

 Graunchy climbing - wide cracks or awkward and thrutchy moves.

 A trad route requiring gear on a crag which is predominantly sport routes.

Crag Symbols

 Angle of the approach walk to the crag with the approximate approach time.

 Approximate time that the crag is in the sun (when it is shining).

 The crag is exposed and may be cold especially if the wind is blowing.

 The crag can offer shelter from the wind. Can be a suntrap - good in winter, bad when hot.

 A buttress with some multi-pitch routes.

 A buttress where some, or all, of the routes are affected by the tide. Check the details carefully.

 The buttress suffers from seepage. It may be wet and unclimbable after prolonged periods of rain.

 A buttress that requires an abseil approach.

 The crag/buttress has a restriction due to nesting birds - check the crag information.

 The crag/buttress has either restricted or special access requirements. Check the details carefully.

 Deserted - Currently under-used and usually quiet. Fewer good routes or remote and smaller areas.

Quiet - Less popular sections on major crags, or good buttresses with awkward approaches.

Busy - Places you will seldom be alone, especially at weekends. Good routes and easy access.

 Crowded - The most popular sections of the most popular crags which are always busy.

Topo Key

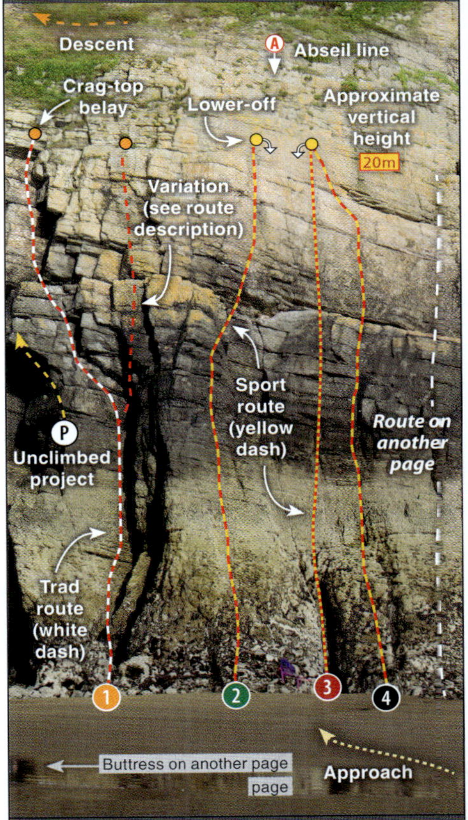

Descent • Abseil line • Crag-top belay • Lower-off • Approximate vertical height 20m • Variation (see route description) • Sport route (yellow dash) • Route on another page • P Unclimbed project • Trad route (white dash) • Buttress on another page • Approach

Map Key

Scan QR code for parking • A crag in different chapter page • Sandy beach • Rocky shore • A crag page • Minor path • Main path • GPS Coordinates of parking • Town/village • Main map symbols See page 20 • Track • Additional parking • Traffic lights • A Roads • Junction number • Trees • Motorway • B Roads

Previous Guides and Route Information Sources

The traditional and sport climbing on the sandstone and limestone crags of South Wales has been documented since the 1970s. We are very grateful to all those who have worked on previous guidebooks and those who have taken the trouble to record their endeavours. The key books and web based information sites are listed below.

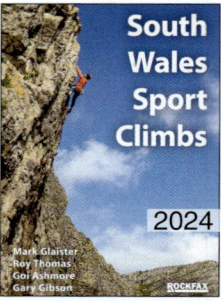

Guides

Gower - J.O.Talbot (West Col 1970)

South East Wales - J.C.Horsfield (SWMC 1973)

South East Wales - J.Harwood (SWMC 1978)

Gower and South East Wales
- M.Danford, T.Penning (SWMC 1983)

Gower & S.E.Wales - A.E.Richardson (SWMC 1991)

South East Wales Sandstone
- G.Ashmore, A.Senior (JDMEL 1991)

South East Wales Sandstone - G.Ashmore (JDMEL 1995)

Gower Sport Climbs - A.Berry (1997)

South East Wales Sandstone, Limestone & Gower Sports Topos
- G.Gibson (Climb High 1997)

Gower & S.E.Wales - G.Ashmore, R.Thomas (SWMC 2003)

South Wales Sport Climbs
- M.Glaister, R.Thomas, G.Ashmore, G.Gibson (Rockfax 2016)

The Gilwern Area
- G.Percival, G.Jenkin, M.Davies (Great Western Rock 2020)

Gower Rock - S.Llewellyn, M.Woodfield (Pesda Press 2020)

Gower Trad - M.Woodfield, M.Glaister (Rockfax Digital 2024)
Pembroke and Gower Trad print guide coming in 2025

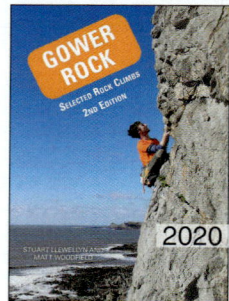

Websites

South Wales Climbing Wiki swcw.org.uk - A big online Wiki that covers all of the trad and sport climbing in the area. A good spot to look for new developments.

UKClimbing ukclimbing.com - Online route database for all areas (including trad) covered in this guidebook.

South Wales Bouldering Guide swbg.co.uk - Online guide to bouldering in the area.

Guidebook Footnote

The inclusion of a climbing area in this guidebook does not mean that you have a right of access or the right to climb upon it. The descriptions of routes within this guide are recorded for historical reasons only and no reliance should be placed on the accuracy of the description. The grades set in this guide are a fair assessment of the difficulty of the climbs. Climbers who attempt a route of a particular standard should use their own judgment as to whether they are proficient enough to tackle that route. This book is not a substitute for experience and proper judgment. The authors, publisher and distributors of this book do not recognise any liability for injury or damage caused to, or by, climbers, third parties, or property arising from such persons seeking reliance on this guidebook as an assurance for their own safety.

David McLean pulling past the overhang midway up the popular *This God is Mine* (7b+) - *p.288* - at the Stone Wings Cliff, Witches Point. Witches Point is a fantastic seaside sport crag that has some classy pitches in the 6th, 7th and 8th grades. Photo: Keith Sharples

Andy Collins fully committed on the powerful upper bulge of *Serpent's Tooth* (6b+) - *p.131* - at Third Sister - Bottom. This crag is a relatively new addition to the sport climbing on offer at Gower and is a smart choice if it is unpleasantly windy on the higher crags hereabouts. Photo: Mark Glaister

Acknowledgements — South Wales Sport Climbs

Rockfax is very grateful to the following advertisers who have supported this guidebook:

Awesome Walls - *Inside front cover*
awesomewalls.co.uk

Beta Climbing Designs - *Page 33*
betaclimbingdesigns.com

BMC - *Page 31*
thebmc.co.uk

DMM - *Page 35*
dmmwales.com

Up and Under - *Inside back cover*
upandunder.co.uk

Overhang Climbing Centre - *Page 2*
overhangcarmarthen.co.uk

Petzl - *Back cover flap*
petzl.co.uk

We would like to thank all the people who have helped put together this edition of South Wales Sport Climbs.
Eben Muse, Al Rosier, Rob McAllister, Andy Sharp, Dean Howard, John Bullock, Danny McCarroll, Arlo Rogers, Marti Hallett, Matt Woodfield, Aaron Martin, Joe Jones, Bridget Glaister, Bethan Cox, Daniel Sadler, Becky Athay, Myles Jordan, Mike Dunk, Kat Lumby, Ben Tiffin, Corie Jones, John Warner, Jen Warner, Jeremy Wilson, Paul Cox, James Eves, Andy Collins, Charlotte Macdonald, Tom Skelhon, John Adams, Stella Adams, Rosy Klinkenburg, Jay Astbury, Rhys Evans.

We would like to extend a special thanks to Tim Hoddy, who maintains the South Wales Climbing Wiki, a vital online source of the routes and development in the area covered by this book.

A huge thanks to all those who have taken and been the subjects of the portfolio of shots that go toward making a huge contribution to the appeal of the book. Carl Ryan, Keith Sharples, Elis Rees, Simon Rawlinson, Marsha Balaeva, Tom Skelhon, Dave Simmonite, Sam Brown, Al Rosier, Katherine Woolley, Aaron Martin, Rhys Allen, Andy van Kints, Amy Chitty, Jacob Isaac, Mike Hutton, Cat McKenna, Sam Parsons, Eben Muse.

It has as ever been a pleasure to work with Alan James and the UKC/Rockfax team on the production of this guidebook.

Mark Glaister, Roy Thomas, Gary Gibson, Goi Ashmore - October 2024

Rockfax Publications

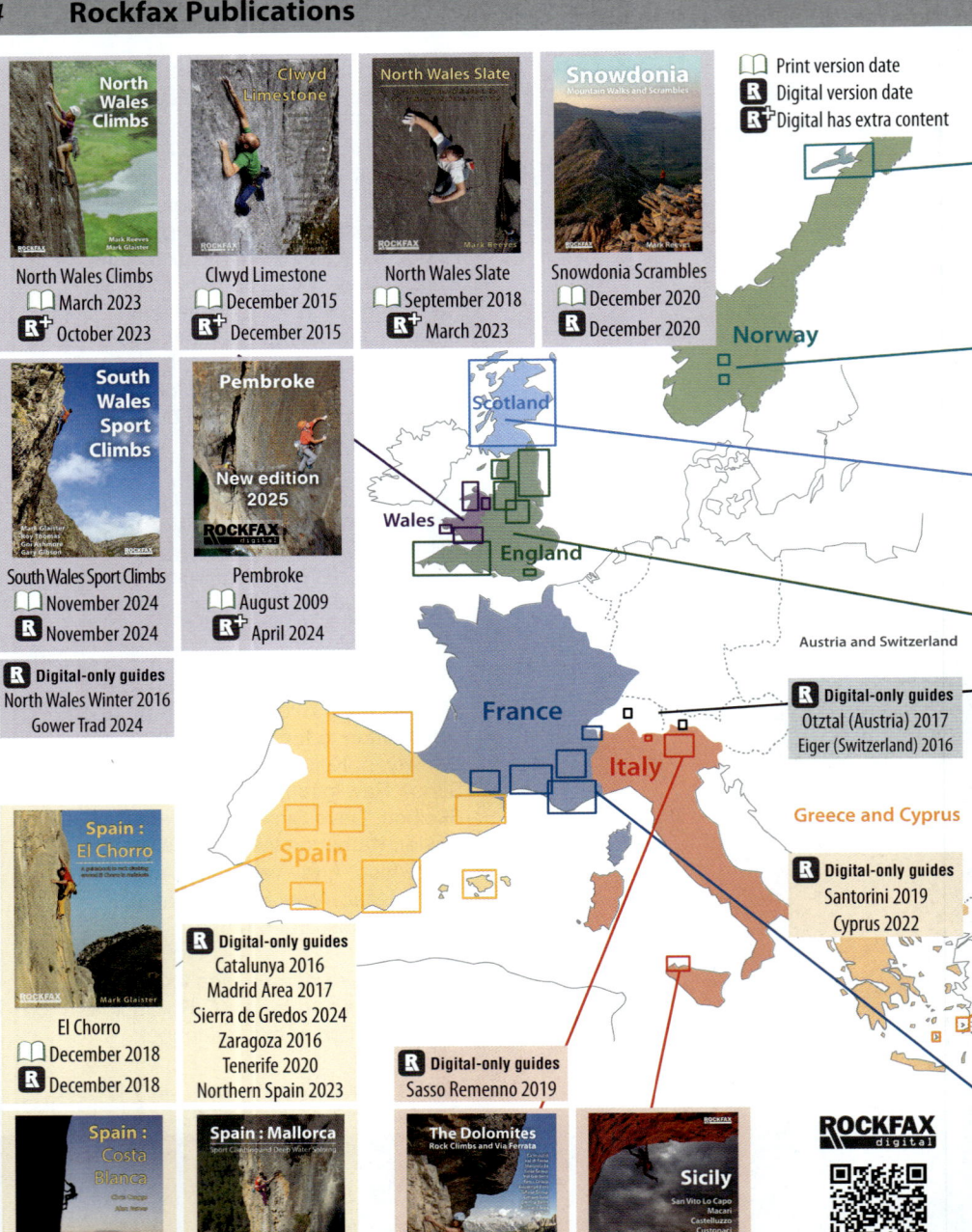

Rockfax Publications

Lofoten Climbs
📖 May 2024
® May 2024

® Digital-only guides
Rjukan 2016
Nissedal 2016

SMC Digital-only guides
Scottish Rock Climbs 2024
Scottish Winter Climbs 2019
Highland Scrambles 2020
Available on the Rockfax App

Lake District Climbs
📖 November 2019
R+ October 2023

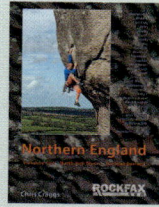

Northern England
📖 February 2008
® February 2008

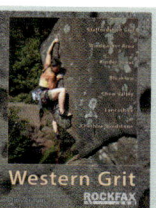

Western Grit
📖 April 2009
® June 2023

Northern Limestone
📖 January 2015
R+ June 2023

Eastern Grit
📖 May 2022
R+ August 2022

Peak Limestone
📖 June 2020
R+ October 2023

Peak Bouldering
📖 August 2023
R+ October 2023

West Country Climbs
📖 December 2022
R+ April 2023

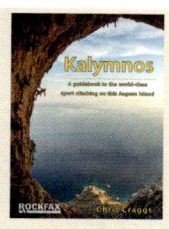

Kalymnos
📖 May 2018
R+ April 2023

Southern Sandstone
📖 September 2017
R+ May 2023

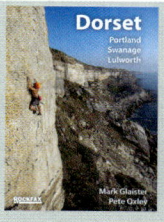

Dorset
📖 July 2021
® June 2023

Dorset Bouldering
📖 May 2014
R+ January 2020

Devon Bouldering
📖 January 2024
® January 2024

® Digital-only guides
Ailefroide 2021
Maurienne 2021

For all trade printed book orders please direct enquiries to Cordee
Telephone: +44 145 561 1185   Email: info@cordee.co.uk
Trade Sales: sales@cordee.co.uk   Web: cordee.co.uk

France : Ariege
📖 December 2012
R+ April 2021

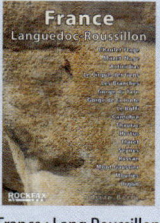

France : Lang.Roussillon
📖 November 2011
® November 2011

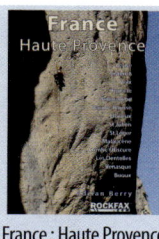

France : Haute Provence
📖 December 2009
R+ November 2022

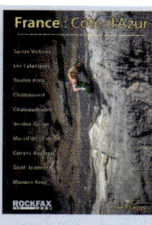

France : Côte d'Azur
📖 February 2017
® February 2017

Chamonix
📖 July 2022
® July 2022

Sam Clarke on the severely overhanging *Achilles' Wrath* (8b) - *p.84* - at Shipwreck Cove, Rhossili Beach, Gower. Since the first sport routes were established at Rhossili Beach in 2012, the area has become very popular with Shipwreck Cove being a beacon for hard climbing in the upper grades and the other sectors a magnet for teams looking for beach-side grade 4s, 5s and 6s. Photo: Keith Sharples

South Wales Sport Logistics

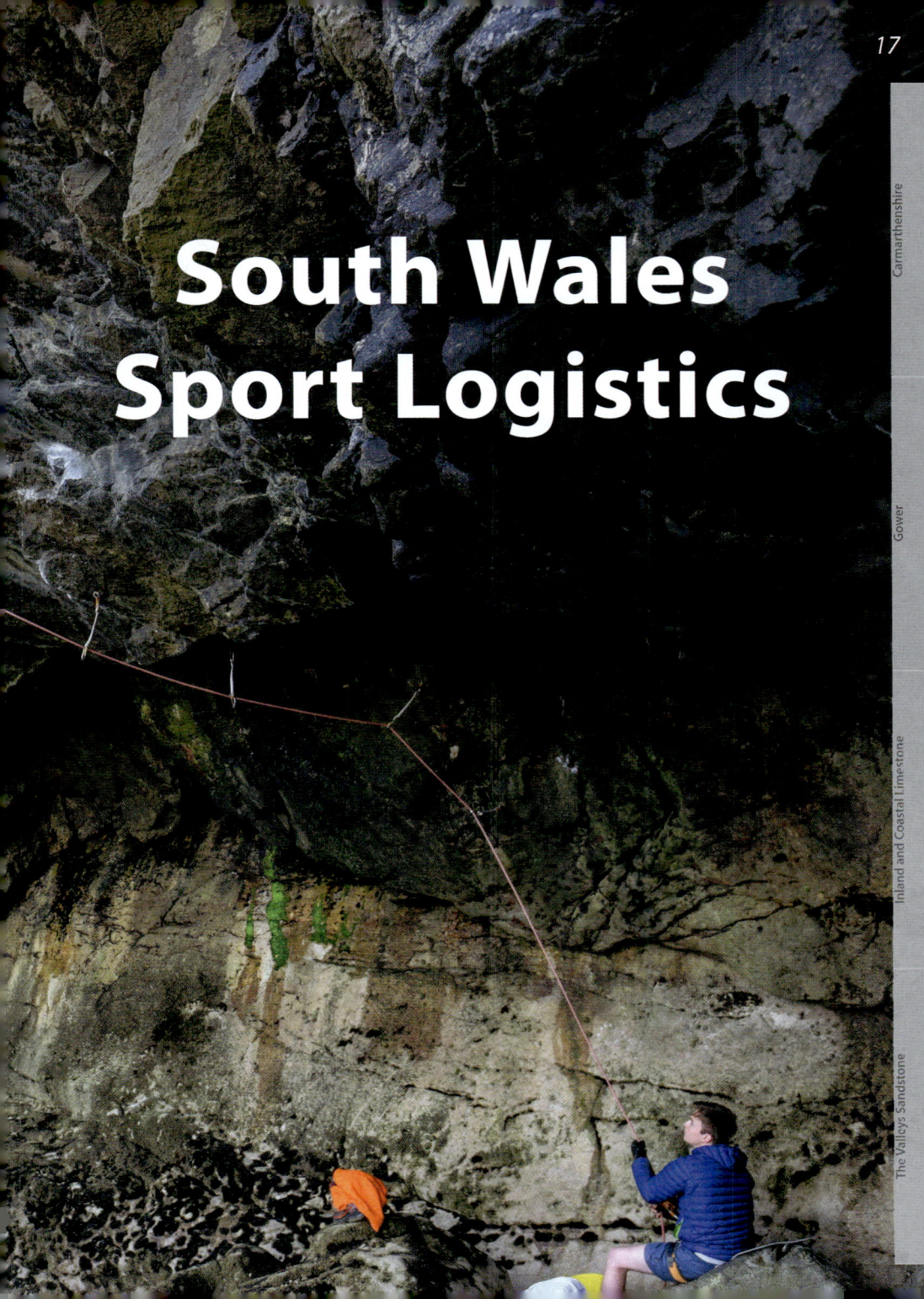

Mountain Rescue
In the event of an accident requiring the assistance of Mountain Rescue:
Dial 112 and ask for
'POLICE - MOUNTAIN RESCUE' or 'COASTGUARD'
This is very important since just asking for 'Police' will redirect you to a switchboard which could be a long way from your current location. This can cause delays in the rescue procedure as the authorities try and track down where the injured party is. Asking for 'Mountain Rescue' or 'Coastguard' will redirect you to people who know the area well.

When to Go
The climbing sites covered in this guide are geographically diverse, ranging from exposed mountain tops to sheltered seaside sun-traps. As a result there is scope for climbing in good conditions throughout the year. The climate data given below is for Gower and it is here that the most reliable conditions are to be found during the cooler months. The other areas are best climbed on from Spring until Autumn, heading to the higher crags such as Treherbert and Gilwern for fresher conditions when things become very hot lower down.

Temperature °C	Jan	Feb	Mar	Apr	May	Jun	Jul	Aug	Sep	Oct	Nov	Dec
Average Max Temp (°C)	5	6	7	10	13	16	18	18	15	11	7	5
Average Min Temp (°C)	1	1	2	3	6	8	10	11	9	6	3	1
Average Rain Days/month	10	6	9	7	6	8	7	8	7	9	8	9

Bethan Cox making a late afternoon autumnal ascent of *Snap Crackle 'n' Pop* (6a) - *p.277* - at Sector Hindu Kush, Gilwern West. The Gilwern crags, both East and West, have seen a lot of new routing and re-equipping since the previous Rockfax guide was published in 2016. The approach to the crag has also been radically altered following a landslip damaging the old road. Nevertheless, although the walk to the western crags is now longer, it is a very pleasant walk and pretty flat. Photo: Mark Glaister

When to Go South Wales Sport Logistics

South Wales Sport Logistics — Getting Around and Map

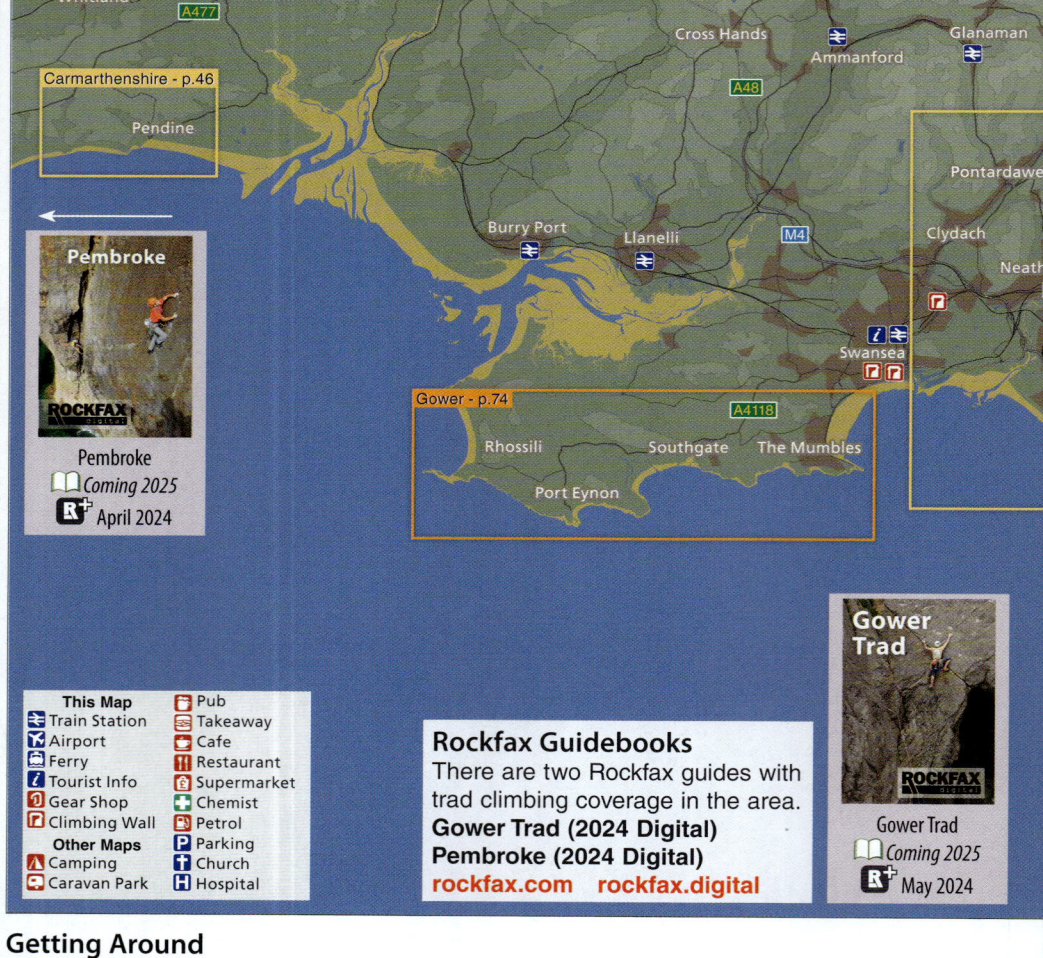

Getting Around
The starting points for approaches to the crags are all easily reached by car and the approach descriptions are written assuming you have access to a car.

Public Transport
If you doi wish to use public transport then the crags in this area are generally easy to get to. Gower, the Valleys Sandstone, Witches Point and Dinas Rock are all easily reached from either Cardiff, Bridgend or Swansea by rail and bus. Nearly all the Valleys Sandstone crags are within striking distance of train stations. Gower is well serviced by bus from Swansea and it is possible to camp within walking distance of the crags.

Buses - The best website is **traveline.info**.
Trains - For timetable information go to **thetrainline.com**

Getting Around and Map — **South Wales Sport Logistics**

Satellite Navigation

 The parking spots on the close-up maps are indicated with a precise GPS location and QR code (right). Just point your phone at the QR code and open in your chosen navigation app to take you direct to the parking spots.

Tourist Information

For general information for a visit contact the tourist information websites listed below:

breconbeacons.org
visitabergavenny.co.uk
visitablaenavon.co.uk
visitcardiff.com
visitcrickhowell.wales
visitwales.com

More information on all areas and travel tips are at **information-britain.co.uk** and **visitwales.com**

South Wales Sport Logistics — Accommodation

Charlotte Macdonald on *Fiesta* (6b) - *p.137* - at Third Sister - Upper, Gower. This crag was one of the first to have some popular lower grade lines bolted and has now been joined in recent times by many more close by, the majority containing routes in the 6th and 7th grades. Photo: Andy van Kints

Accommodation

Useful for all types of accommodation:
ukclimbing.com/listings

Camping

The Valley Campsite - *map p.48*
Amroth Road, Llanteg, Narberth.
thevalleycampsite.co.uk
Basic site for Carmarthenshire crags.

Pitton Cross Camping - *map p.117*
Rhossili, Gower. pittoncross.co.uk
Great site that is well positioned for Gower crags. Book at busy times. Can walk to crags.

Eastern Slade Barn
Eastern Slade Farm, Oxwich, Gower.
easternsladebarngower.co.uk
Superb accommodation plus a basic camping field. Book ahead for the bunkhouse.

Lone Wolf Campsite
Glyn y Mul Farm, Aberdulais.
glynymulfarm.co.uk
Out of the way site. No groups. Well placed for Dinas Rock. Must book ahead.

Acorn Camping - *map p.312*
Ham Lane South, Llantwit Major.
acorncamping.co.uk
Well positioned for Witches Point, Costa del Major and crags just off of the M4. No groups allowed. Book ahead at busy times.

Pyscodlyn Farm
Pyscodlyn Farm, Abergavenny.
pyscodlyncaravanpark.com
Excellent facilities. Close to Abergavenny and Crickhowell for food and pubs. Good for Gilwern crags and dropping over into the sandstone crags. Handy for Brecon Beacons.

Cwmcarn Forest Camping - *map p.482*
Crosskeys. cwmcarnforest.co.uk
Good camping with camping pods also available. Mountain bike opportunities. Good for the sandstone especially the eastern valleys. Possible to walk to a couple of crags.

Aaron Martin getting to grips with the typical Costa del Major bands of horizontally bedded limestone on the route *S'Not Yours* (6a+) - *p.320* - at The Nose, Costa del Major. Photo: Carl Ryan

Pubs

Springwell Inn - *map p.56*
Pendine, Carmarthen. Nice spot close to the beach and friendly.

Worm's Head Hotel - *map p.192*
Rhossili, Gower. Fine location overlooking the beach and Worm's Head. Decent food and great outside terrace. Can be busy.

King Arthur Hotel
Reynoldston, Gower. Excellent venue. Good food and beer garden. Not particularly close to the coast but worth the effort to get to.

The Joiners Arms - *map p.192*
Bishopston. Handy spot for crags at the eastern end of Gower.

Gwaelod y Garth Inn
Taff's Well, Gwaelod-y-Garth. Close to Taff's Well area crags, nice rustic and homely.

The Bear Hotel
Crickhowell. Hotel bar with good atmosphere and food. Close to Gilwern.

The Three Golden Cups - *map p.284*
Southerndown, Bridgend. Small pub close to Witches Point and the beach.

The Pelican - *map p.284*
Ogmore-by-Sea. Upmarket venue with food and a lively atmosphere. Near Witches Point.

Prince of Wales
Ton Kenfig, Bridgend. Good pub with food midway between Witches Point and Abbey Buttress.

Glantaff Inn - *map p.418*
Quakers Yard, Treharris. Good friendly spot central to many of the Valleys crags. Good food and beer.

Greenhouse Inn
Newport Road, Llantarnam. On the western side of the Valleys and a good spot post Tirpentwys.

The Worm's Head Hotel by the parking in Rhossili. Photo: Mark Glaister

South Wales Sport Logistics

Eleri Clarke on the super-steep *Pioneers of the Hypnotic Groove* (7b) - *p.171* - at Foxhole, Gower. Foxhole is the most popular of the harder venues on Gower being a year-round option having no tidal problems, a line-up of brilliant routes and multiple link-ups. Photo: Elis Rees

Cafes

Amorth/Pendine - Lots of options on the seafront.

The View Cafe - *map p.76*
Rhossili, Gower. Great views out over the beach and close to the parking. Good coffee.

Three Cliffs Coffee Shop - *map p.164*
Southgate, Gower. Great Cafe next to parking. Also has a shop with Post office and cashpoint.

Cafe at Book-ish
High Street, Crickhowell. Close to Gilwern. Good coffee and atmosphere.

Dunraven Beach Cafe - *map p.284*
Southerndown. Seasonal cafe by Witches Point.

Valleys Sandstone area has lots of cafes and fast food outlets in the towns and villages.

Climbing Shops

Up and Under
490 Cowbridge Road East, Victoria Park, Cardiff, CF5 1BL. Tel: 02920 578579
upandunder.co.uk
Specialist climbing and outdoor gear retailer in Cardiff with online ordering.
See inside back cover, map page 21.

Crickhowell Adventure - High Street, Crickhowell.

More shops at -
ukclimbing.com/listings/outdoor_shops/

Climbing Walls

Overhang Climbing Centre
Churchill House, Picton Terrace, Carmarthen SA31 3DF. Tel: 01267 237981
overhangcarmarthen.co.uk
Indoor climbing centre with a 12m lead wall and 2 bouldering areas. Cafe with snacks.
See page 2, map page 20.

Rock UK, Old Drift Mine, Trelewis, Treharris.
Dynamic Rock, Hebron Road, Swansea.
The Climbing Hangar - Castell Close, Swansea.
Flashpoint Swansea - Parc Tawe, Swansea.
Boulders - Culverhouse Cross, Cardiff.
Flashpoint Cardiff - Penarth Road, Cardiff.
Boulders - St. Catherines Park, Cardiff.

More walls and information at -
ukclimbing.com/listings/climbing_walls/

The View cafe at Rhossili. Photo: Mark Glaister

Bridget Glaister on *F*uc*ose* (6b) - *p.123* - at Rams Grove Crag, Gower. Photo: Mark Glaister

A climber moves up to the headwall of *Supertramp* (7a) - *p.499* - at Tirpentwys. Since the publication of the previous Rockfax guidebook to the sport climbing available in South Wales, the pecking order of popular venues has firmed up and in The Valleys particularly Tirpentwys and Navigation Quarry have become highly regarded alongside the older go-to spots such as The Gap and Sirhowy. Photo: Mark Glaister

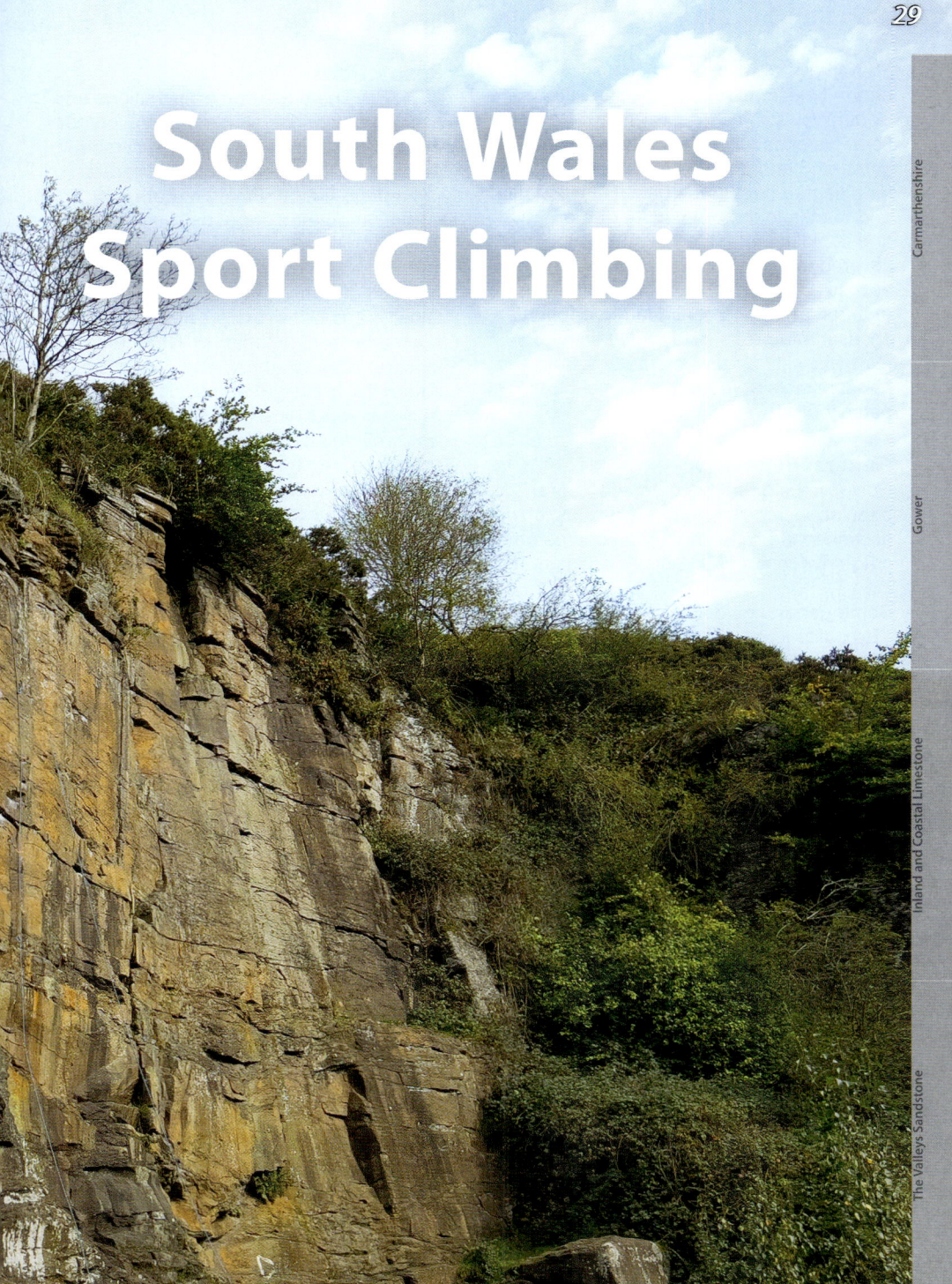

South Wales Sport Climbing

There have always been access issues on the limestone and sandstone cliffs of South Wales. Clashes over nesting birds, flora, historical sites, land ownership, gardening and dogs have all been causes for disagreement in the past. Despite this, and thanks to the great work of the BMC and its volunteers, the majority of the crags covered in this book currently have good access arrangements. Usually all that is required to ensure continued freedom of access to the cliffs, and to maintain good relations with landowners and stewards, is a responsible approach and level of general behaviour.

General Behaviour

Rock climbing has become ever more popular, increasing numbers of people want access to the cliffs and the pressures on the crag environment have never been greater.

Some general guidelines:
- Be polite to other countryside users
- Don't light fires or use barbecues
- Close gates after you go through them
- Park sensibly as described in this book
- Don't stray from the popular paths
- Don't disturb animals especially sea birds
- Use less chalk
- Don't use wire brushes
- Take your litter home
- Go before you go!

Parking

All the crags in this book have parking areas which are indicated with GPS coordinates and QR codes on the maps (see right - just scan with your phone).

Please use these parking areas. If there is one thing above all others that annoys landowners, it is having their drive/field blocked by someone's car. In some cases parking may involve you spending some money in one of the Pay and Display parking areas.

Restrictions

There are some restrictions and warnings so keep a look out for the red 'Restrictions' and 'Birds' symbol (above). The restricted dates generally range from the beginning of February to the end of July. Signs are usually erected on the crag approaches where there is new or updated information on the extent or duration of a restriction.

Other crags have very precise parking and approach requirements, whilst others have strict rules on what can and cannot be done due to the presence of historic artefacts. At some sandstone quarries access is less well defined (often due to liability concerns) and has led to signs being erected that state that climbing is not allowed. In these cases climbing has often gone on unhindered for many years but, should you be asked to leave, please do so politely and send details of the owner and circumstances to the BMC.

BMC RAD App

Access arrangements can change and we recommend that, when unsure, you use the BMC Regional Access Database (RAD) to check what the current situation is. You can check the RAD here -
thebmc.co.uk/modules/RAD/
or install the BMC RAD app from your iOS or Android app store.
If you do encounter problems, contact the BMC Access and Conservation representative. They are always happy to discuss problems and often their involvement at an early stage can defuse a situation before it escalates into a serious access dispute.

British Mountaineering Council,
177-179 Burton Road,
Manchester, M20 2BB.
Tel: 0870 010 4878
Web: thebmc.co.uk
Email: office@thebmc.co.uk

RAD APP [REGIONAL ACCESS DATABASE]

▲BMC

The source of the most up to date access advice for climbers in England and Wales

thebmc.co.uk/rad

Gear

Most of the sport routes described in this book have good solid bolts and lower-offs in place. For the vast majority of routes a 60m rope and 14 quickdraws is sufficient to climb them. However there are a number of routes that will require a longer rope to get down (and probably more quickdraws). **To avoid any doubt, always tie a stopper knot in the dead end of the rope to ensure that it will not pass through the belay device.**

A clip-stick is a very useful piece of kit as some initial bolts are high and the landings not ideal, especially on the sea cliffs.

On a small number of the sea cliffs an abseil rope will be needed to access the base of the crag.

If you intend to climb any of the trad routes described then you will need a full rack of wires and cams and double ropes.

Rhoslyn Frugtniet on *Palace of Swords Reversed* (8a) - *p.171* - at Foxhole, Gower. Photo: Simon Rawlinson.

BETASTICKevo

BetaClimbingDesigns.com

Bolting

The work of maintaining the bolts has been carried out by many individuals. It has been a huge task and is ongoing. If you come across any routes that need re-equipping then please submit your comments to the databases on - **ukclimbing.com**.

South Wales Bolt Fund

The South Wales Bolt Fund was formed to help with the replacement of protection bolts and lower-offs throughout South Wales. More details, and a link to donations, is available on the website - **southwalesboltfund.co.uk**

If you enjoy the sport routes in this book then consider donating an evening's beer money to the South Wales Bolt Fund.

Proceeds from some of the sales of this guidebook will go towards this fund.

Matt Woodfield on *Any Old Iron* (6c) - *p.248* - at The Outer Pit, Taff's Well West. Photo: Mark Glaister

Photo: Aaron Martin

climb now
work later

shaped for climbing

ALPHA SPORT

Will Bosi, Meconi (8a), Margalef, Spain
Band of Birds

The Alpha Sport is the ultimate sport climbing quickdraw. Shaped for success with a confidence inspiring gate action, the rest is up to you. A durable and easy to grab nylon sling reduces the effort of working routes. For sport climbers who prize positive handling and quick clipping.

dmmwales.com

South Wales Sport Climbing Grades

Most of the routes in this book are sport routes which are given a **Sport Grade**. A sport route is defined as one where all the major protection comes from gear fixed in the rock (bolts).

There are a few trad routes covered where the majority of the gear is carried by the lead climber and is hand-placed. These are given a **British Trad Grade** and a red and white dotted line on the topo (instead of the normal red and yellow dotted line).

Sport Grade
The sport grade is a measure of how hard it is going to be to get up a certain section of rock. It makes no attempt to tell you how hard the hardest move is, nor how scary a route is.

British Trad Grade
1) Adjectival grade (Diff, VDiff, Severe, Hard Severe (HS), Very Severe (VS), Hard Very Severe (HVS), E1... to E10).
The trad grade gives an overall picture of the route including how well protected it is, how sustained and a general indication of the level of difficulty of the whole route.
2) Technical grade (4a, 4b, 4c... to 7b).
The difficulty of the hardest single move, or short section.

More information on grades:
rockfax.com/publications/grades.html

Sport Grade	British Trad Grade (for well-protected routes)	UIAA	USA
2a	Mod (Moderate)	I	5.1
2b		II	5.2
2c	Diff (Difficult)		5.3
3a	VDiff (Very Difficult)	III-	5.4
3b		III	
3c	Sev (Severe) HVD (Hard Very Difficult)	III+	5.5
4a	HS (Hard Severe) 4a	IV-	5.6
4b	VS (Very Severe) 4c	IV	5.7
4c		IV+	5.8
5a	HVS (Hard Very Severe) 5b	V- / V	
5b	E1 5a	V+	5.9
5c		VI-	5.10a
6a	E2 5b	VI	5.10b
6a+		VI+	
6b	E3 5c	VII- / VII	5.10c / 5.10d
6b+		VII+	5.11a
6c	E4 6b		5.11b
6c+		VIII-	5.11c
7a	E5 6a	VIII	5.11d
7a+		VIII+	5.12a
7b	E6 6b	IX-	5.12b
7b+			5.12c
7c	E7 6c	IX	5.12d
7c+		IX+	5.13a
8a	E8 7a	X-	5.13b
8a+			5.13c
8b	E9 7a	X	5.13d
8b+		X+	5.14a
8c	E10 7b	XI-	5.14b
8c+		XI	5.14c
9a	E11 7b		5.14d
9a+		XI+	5.15a

Colour Coding
The routes are given a colour-coded dot corresponding to a grade band.

● **Green Routes** *Beginners* - everything at grade **4c** (up to **Severe**) and under. Good routes to start out your climbing career on.

● **Orange Routes** *Experienced* - **5a** to **6a+** inclusive **(HS to HVS)**. General ticking routes for those with more experience. There are many excellent routes available across this band.

● **Red Routes** *Advanced* - **6b** to **7a** inclusive **(E1 to E3)**. For the experienced and keen climber. Anyone operating at this level can attempt some of the best climbing in the area.

● **Black Routes** *Expert* - **7a+** to **7c+** inclusive **(E4 to E6)**. If you are up to it then this band has some major national testpieces.

○ **White Spots** *Elite* - **8a** and above **(E7)**. The hardest routes for the world's best climbers.

Olli Burrows moving up to the twin bulges on *Altered Carbon* (7a+) - *p.355* - at Space Mountain. Photo: Alan Rosier

South Wales Sport Climbing — Graded List

This graded list has been assembled from the votes on UKClimbing Logbooks. If you disagree strongly with the list then register your route online at ukclimbing.com/logbooks/

8c
- *** Importunity 146

8b+
- *** Helvetia 84
- *** Hell Dagger 84
- ** Surplomb de Ray 171

8b
- *** Achilles' Wrath 84
- *** Euro Fighter 84
- *** Mortal Kombat 211

8a+
- ** Delta Dagger 84
- ** Air Show. 84
- ** Masada 288

8a
- *** Palace of Swords Reversed . . . 171
- *** Kestrel 176
- *** Salva Mea 171
- *** Methuselah 288
- *** H1N1 213
- *** Vennerne 84

7c+
- *** The Dai Vinci Coed 288
- *** Senser 193
- *** Outta Time 213
- *** Super Size Me 289
- *** Hayabusa 213

7c
- *** Powers That Be 213
- *** One Ton Depot. 83
- *** Mad at the Sun 431
- *** Chives of Freedom 213
- ** Contraband 465
- ** Smashed Rat 209
- ** Ultimatum 146
- ** Skin Ed 203
- ** Pegasus 183
- ** Help, Help Me Rhondda 288
- ** Skull Attack 103
- ** Turkey Lurking 173

7b+
- ** World in Action 136
- ** Rose-Line 209
- ** Still Life 213
- ** Wide Eyed and Legless 138
- ** A Momentary Lapse of Reason 431
- ** Poultry in Motion 173
- ** Sharpy Unplugged 399
- ** This God is Mine 288
- ** Sangreal 209
- ** Edge-Hog 291
- ** Department of Correction . . 139
- ** Encore Magnifique 431
- ** Power Struggle 173

- ** Harlem 214
- ** Streaming Neutrinos 245
- ** Strawberry Jam 499
- ** Face 471
- ** Loctite 431
- ** Capstan 398
- ** The Basildon Slapper 398

7b
- ** Pleasant Valley Sunday 431
- ** Mother of Pearl 404
- ** Retrobution 103
- ** Butcher Heinrich 471
- ** G.L.C SAF 247
- ** The Sharp Cereal Professor . . . 214
- ** Anything You Can Do 431
- *** Pioneers of the Hypnotic Groove . . . 171
- ** Staple Diet 289
- ** Skanderbeg 471
- ** Trailblazer 247
- ** Watchmen 209
- ** Rat on a Hot Tin Roof 20
- ** The Future Holds 412
- ** Rise 398
- ** 'King Ada 471
- ** Straining at the Leash 290
- ** Wrecking Ball 82
- ** Berlin Extension 213
- ** Orion 183
- ** Crime and Punishment 103
- ** No Chips Round Here 414
- ** Fowl Play 172
- ** Wet Afternoon 234

7a+
- ** Urban Development 344
- ** King Zog 471
- ** Rob Roy 202
- ** Scared Seal Banter 434
- ** Crawling King Snake 176
- ** Scream for Cream 247
- *** Cointreau 410
- ** Get Flossed 431
- ** Jezebel 193
- ** Altered Carbon 355
- ** Berlin 213
- ** Galactus 354
- ** Marine Layer 83
- ** Propaganda 404
- ** Slip into Something Sexy . . . 469
- ** Lyddite 455
- ** Outspan 410
- ** Jump the Sun 175
- ** Sink or Swim 247
- ** Eastern Bloc Rock 442
- ** Ducky Lucky 173
- ** Round are Way 398
- ** Pump Action 163
- ** Kings of New York 231
- ** It's a Black World 245
- ** King George vs the Suffragettes 85
- ** When I'm 64 180
- ** Sheer Heart Attack 476
- ** The Raven 177
- ** Food for Parasites 468
- ** Fe 500 344

- ** The Connecticut Connection . . 231
- ** Pastis on Ice 410
- ** Sinner Man 113

7a
- ** The Hant 103
- ** Promises 228
- ** A Cleft Stick 492
- ** Valleys Initiative 417
- ** Look Over Yonder 234
- ** Sign of the Times 344
- ** The World-v-Gibson 290
- *** Western Front Direct 442
- ** Foxy Lady 172
- ** Normal Norman 247
- ** Joy de Viva 173
- ** Killer Queen 476
- ** Palm 244
- ** You Never Can Tell 246
- ** Paradise Row 492
- ** Debbie Reynolds 138
- ** Nosepicker 363
- ** King Prawn 53
- ** The Hooker 173
- *** Mawr, Mawr, Mawr 471
- ** Liassic Lark 288
- ** Banog's Barmy Army 388
- *** Melting Man 232
- ** Bolder Boulder 138
- ** Marmalade Skies 171
- ** Hail Mary 500
- ** Tragic Moustache 289
- ** Misadventure 416
- ** Too Many Fingers 163
- ** Salmon Running, Bear Cunning 431
- ** Diagnosis Made Easy 274
- ** One Track Mind 432
- ** Wisdom 140
- *** Jacky Fisher's Phobia 68
- ** Cybernetic Sex Samurai 354
- ** Silver Sixpence 140
- ** Supertramp 499
- ** Minnesota Nice 232

6c+
- ** Double Dutch 197
- *** Blockiness 86
- ** Swim With The Sharks 175
- ** Five O'Clock Shadow 289
- ** Lucky Lizzy 171
- ** Tidal Rush 61
- ** El Camino Del Roy 215
- ** Great Expectations 442
- *** Blackman's Pinch 102
- ** Fairies Wear Boots 492
- ** Stump Stroker 345
- ** The Constant Gardener 195
- ** White Noise (Trial Wall A) . . 109
- *** Open Wide Please 140
- ** There's Life in the Old Dog Yet 291
- *** Genghis Khan 232
- ** Thin Lizzy 295
- ** Uprising 135
- ** Ulrika Ka Ka Ka 235
- ** Wages of Sin 113
- *** Goose in Lucy 171

Carmarthenshire · Gower · Inland and Coastal Limestone · The Valleys Sandstone

Alan Cassidy on *Helvetia* (8b+) - *p.84* - one of many hard pitches at the magnificent Shipwreck Cove, Rhossili Beach, Gower. Photo: Elis Rees

South Wales Sport Climbing — Graded List

6c

- ** Wij zitten nog in een sneeuwstorm 197
- ** Operation Moonshot 354
- ** The Quiet Earth 219
- ** Asthmanaut 355
- ** The Daughters of Lear 131
- ** The Grout of San Romano . . . 434
- ** Long Awaited 298
- ** Angel of Mons 236
- ** Hostility Suite 472
- ** Clip Joint 163
- ** Deus Ex Machina 442
- ** Book End Rib 261
- ** Organised Chaos 231
- ** Black Adder 80
- ** Decades Apart 193
- ** The Relaxed Ladybird 442
- ** Nouveau Cuisine 123
- ** Arab Spring 135
- ** Vanity of Small Differences . . 260
- *** Hanging by a Thread 291
- ** Vladimir and the Pearl 52
- ** Glucosamine and Chondroitin . 276
- ** Leave it to Me (The G) 431
- *** Twilight World 137
- ** Sophie's Wit Tank 72
- ** Battle of the Bulge 274
- ** Miss You 197
- ** Daggers 234
- *** Asset Manager 61
- ** Water 135
- ** Any Old Iron 248
- ** Par 3 86
- ** Out of Pocket 311
- ** Academy Awards 215
- ** On the Road 333
- ** The Road to Mandalay 332
- ** Power Vacuum 135
- ** Nine Green Bottles 377
- *** Strange Little Girl 471
- ** Closed Road 333
- ** Controlled Emission 432
- ** Dream Academy 215
- ** Oh Man 124

6b+

- ** Blinded by Love 463
- ** Pubic Enema 308
- ** Litigious/Fergie's Folly 255
- ** John's Route 86
- ** You are What You Is 464
- ** Tarus Bulbous 232
- ** Mouse Trap 444
- *** Rising Sap 412
- ** Straining Pitch 163
- ** Magic Carpet 255
- ** The Cragmeister 499
- ** Peachy 492
- ** Tread Gently 160
- ** No Epoxy au Oxley 172
- ** Rock Bottom 145
- ** Credit Squeeze 60
- ** Drone On 334
- ** Sleeping Dogs Lie 430
- ** Writings on the Wall 345
- ** Croeso I Gymru 290

- *** Selling Short 61
- ** Queens of the Stone Age . . . 476
- ** Away With The Mixer 383
- ** Slipping into Luxury 469
- ** Red Square 231
- ** Cheesy Rider 202
- ** Rag and Bone 248
- *** Al-Tikrit 120
- ** Jaded Locals 161
- ** Beware the Burly Butcher of Bargoed 455
- *** Off the Peg 145
- ** The Intensity of Spring 219
- *** GAZ 316 344
- ** Nematode 144
- *** Killer Arete 391
- ** Craxsploitation 442
- ** Bye Dad 95
- ** Twisted Logic 500
- ** Slip into the Queen 476
- ** Flakes and Chips 501
- *** Crock Licker 364
- ** Crimp Paddle 94
- ** Road Kill 333
- ** Between the Lines 463
- ** Reaction Series 183
- ** Gwest y Gymru 7 Inch Mix . . 234

6b

- ** A Freem of White Horses 308
- ** Id-iot 235
- ** Hot Flush 145
- ** Chock a Block 145
- ** Feud For Thought 183
- ** The Burning Glass 303
- ** Rattle Those Tusks 431
- ** Fiesta 137
- ** Good Gear, Good Cheer 235
- ** Land of the Dinosaurs 431
- *** Nappy Rush 462
- ** Dan'ds-Inferno 385
- ** California Freeming 308
- ** Great Expectorations 294
- ** Siege of Syracuse 303
- ** Black Magic 442
- ** Central Integrator 65
- ** Lundy Boy 499
- ** Flow Job 274
- ** Decimus Maximus 236
- ** Soapy Dahl 71
- ** Smoke and Mirrors 294
- ** Magic Touch 289
- ** A Little Something I Prepared Earlier 370
- ** Tea Leaves 274
- *** Fatal Reflection 412
- ** Lateralus 478
- ** Terry Forkwit 364
- ** Blood, Sweat and Beers 441
- ** Orangutanarium 419
- ** Gwyn's Road 333
- ** A Poxy Queen 476
- ** Bluster 428
- ** Magic Circle 294
- * Bottom Drawers 88
- ** Sunni Daze 120
- ** Dirty as a Dog 463

- ** Sorry Lorry Morry 400
- ** Cold Inconvenience 144
- ** One More for Me 123
- ** Threadbare 144
- ** I Am what I Am 464

6a+

- ** F*uc*ose 123
- ** Iron to Defeat Napoleon 260
- ** No Beer, No Fear 235
- * Lips Of My Shofarot 302
- ** Discount Included in the Price . 395
- ** Knackers Yard 248
- ** All Things Bright and Beautiful 274
- ** Southeast Wall 137
- * Mr Softy 255
- ** Fear Inoculum 219
- * Pelagic Mush 289
- * Drag Queen 476
- ** Full Metal Jacket 248
- * Poker in the Eye 430
- * No Bear, No Fear 235
- * Fluster 428
- *** Don't Sit on My Sofa 197
- ** The Two Hundred Year Echo . 260
- ** Marlin on the Wall 428
- ** Hung Over 144
- ** Parlour Vous le Sport 183
- ** Terrordactyl 487
- * First Handout 86
- ** Bending Sickle 161
- ** All For Nothing 63
- ** Hooker with a Penis 478
- * Grey Wall 254
- ** Las Mariposas 130
- ** The Clot Thickens 89
- ** Galvanised 369
- *** Jubilee Step Sister 127
- ** Hawk's Cheep 455
- ** Under the Mattress 96

6a

- ** Heading South 61
- ** Pocket Battleship 338
- * The White Stuff 261
- * Whatever Floats Your Boat . . . 275
- ** Abra-Ker-Fucking-Dabra 294
- * Pwll Du Crack 275
- ** Up Yours 434
- *** Groping for Jugs 455
- ** Death Twitch 441
- ** Bowen to the Inevitable 183
- ** Blow Me Another One 299
- * Sister Mary's Blessed Finger . 137
- * Them's Be Barnacles 92
- * Mental Mantels 500
- * Spit it Out 107
- ** Black Night's Rein 254
- * Lamisil 90
- * The Pervasive Grey 264
- * Zoo Time 406
- ** Mr Potatoe Head 203
- ** Rocky 499
- * Snap, Crackle and Pop 277
- * Spoilt Bastard 362
- * Dolphin Snoggin' 257
- *** Lemon Soul 95

Graded List — South Wales Sport Climbing

5c

	Route	Page
**	The Enema Affair	137
*	Fromage Frais	202
	Mega Mix	234
*	Filial Duty	95
	A Paddock Full of Ponies	275
**	Scurvy Dog	94
*	Little Queen	476
	Monica's Dress	107
	Lone Road	333
*	Buckets of Bubbly	102
*	The Great Satan	263
**	Gojira	377
*	Nietzche's Niche	303
**	Dicky Dyson	382
*	Put Your Back Into It	263
**	Angry Pirate	226
*	Galena Puts Lead in your Pencil	310
**	Excavation Right	160

5b

	Route	Page
**	Dawsons Creek	95
**	The Plumb	256
*	A Mermaid's Tale	95
*	All Aboard My Dingy	275
*	Purple Sue	263
*	Golden Plover	187
*	Seaman in the Groove	92
**	Holds May Spin	96
*	Descartes' Dithers	303
**	Cash in the Attic	96

5a

	Route	Page
***	Dawson's Corner	95
**	Utopia	155
*	White Noise	277
	Lara	92
*	Pleiades	131
*	The Road to Nowhere	277
*	Groovy Baby	132

4c

	Route	Page
**	Holy Sister	127
*	Crack Me Up	275
*	Nosey Parcour	320
*	Smeghead	204
**	S'not on Your Nellie	320
*	Brittle Biscuit	277
*	Basil Brush	171
**	Down Under	369
*	Vulpix	171
***	Fistful of Tenners	96

4b

	Route	Page
*	Pure Cino	91
*	Border Control	91
*	Lock 'n' Roll	484
*	Devilment	113
*	Dreaming of Cleaner Things	314
*	Leopard Prints	168
*	Fat End of the Veg	108
*	Me Harty's	92
*	Catapult	91

4a

	Route	Page
*	Whispering Whelks	92
*	Julie's Delight	155

Paul Cox on the continually steep climbing encountered on the classy line of Killer Arete (6b+) - p.391 - at Glynfach. Photo: Mark Glaister

Destination Planner

Region	Area	Routes	up to 4c	5a to 6a+	6b to 7a	7a+ to 7c+	8a up
Carmarthenshire	Telpyn Point	46	1	21	20	4	-
Carmarthenshire	Morfa Bychan	62	2	27	26	7	-
Carmarthenshire	Pendine	62	1	18	25	17	-
Gower	Rhossili Beach	131	23	53	31	9	15
Gower	Trial Wall Area	107	7	43	47	9	1
Gower	Third Sister Area	155	7	50	71	24	3
Gower	Free Luncher's to Fetlock Zawn	33	-	8	22	1	2
Gower	Port Eynon	3	-	1	2	-	-
Gower	Oxwich	25	-	7	16	2	-
Gower	Utopia Area	22	5	11	6	-	-
Gower	Watch House	39	5	11	19	4	-
Gower	Foxhole	43	10	9	11	9	4
Gower	Minchin Hole	19	-	1	7	8	3
Gower	Bowen's Parlour Area	32	1	11	12	8	-
Gower	Bosco's Gulch Area	67	5	25	29	8	-
Gower	Pwlldu Bay	12	-	-	5	6	1
Gower	Rams Tor	14	-	-	5	9	-
Gower	Barland Quarry	14	-	4	8	2	-
Inland and Coastal Limestone	Dinas Rock	109	1	11	44	45	8
Inland and Coastal Limestone	Darren Fawr	32	-	6	25	1	-
Inland and Coastal Limestone	Taff's Well	90	8	22	49	9	-
Inland and Coastal Limestone	Taff's Well West	55	3	16	18	18	-
Inland and Coastal Limestone	Gilwern East	116	14	53	42	7	-
Inland and Coastal Limestone	Gilwern West	110	8	59	35	8	-
The Valleys Sandstone	Witches Point	82	3	19	36	21	3
The Valleys Sandstone	Temple Bay	76	4	43	28	1	-
The Valleys Sandstone	Castle Upon Alun	45	6	16	22	1	-
The Valleys Sandstone	Costa del Major	76	6	44	20	6	-

Approach	Sun	Shelter	Dry in rain	Seepage	Access	Abseil	Tidal	Summary	Page	
10 min	Sun and shade			Seepage			Tidal	A remote but friendly sea cliff, composed of hard vertical sandstone within easy reach of Pembroke trad crags.	50	Carmarthenshire
2 - 10 min	Sun and shade	Sheltered		Seepage			Tidal	A good, although slightly tidal cliff. Easy access and with many interesting routes in the mid-grades.	58	
10 min	Morning						Tidal	Restricted access due to a tight tide window. Substantial climbs that take strong lines on good quality limestone.	67	
12 - 14 min	Sun and shade		Dry in the rain	Seepage			Tidal	Many routes straight off of one of Wales's finest beaches. The crags are tidal and conditions are not always ideal.	80	
10 - 14 min	Afternoon			Seepage	Access			A collection of walls set high above Rhossili beach. A wide ranging appeal from grades 5 to 8. Reliable conditions.	102	Gower
20 - 40 min	Afternoon	Windy		Seepage				A stunning section of coast dotted with some fine sport crags that offer plenty of routes in the mid and higher grades.	120	
30 - 35 min	Morning	Sheltered	Dry in the rain	Seepage			Tidal	A collection of zawn walls the most popular being Free Luncher's which is an excellent venue for grade 6s. Some buttresses are tidal.	144	
20 min	Afternoon			Seepage			Tidal	A small, tidal and remote crag that might be useful if staying locally.	150	
15 min	Not much sun	Sheltered		Seepage	Restrictions		Tidal	A long low wall that is tidal and hidden amongst trees. Lots in the mid-grades but often dirty and can be humid. Tidal access.	152	
22 - 23 min	Lots of sun	Sheltered		Seepage				A collection of non-tidal crags that has some popular lower grade routes. The approach is a scramble not on a path and needs care.	155	
16 min	Sun and shade			Seepage			Tidal	A varied set of crags. The slab has some fierce pitches whilst Watch House East has more conventional fare and is tidal.	159	
12 min	Afternoon	Sheltered	Dry in the rain	Seepage			Tidal	Superb sport crag that offers some of the best steep climbing in the area on excellent rock. Short approach and sheltered.	168	
12 min	Sun and shade				Restrictions			An unusual setting in a large sea-level cave/zawn with a number of atmospheric lines. Some important restrictions.	175	
15 - 17 min	Sun and shade	Sheltered	Dry in the rain	Seepage			Tidal	A collection of walls, overhangs and small zawns with a good spread of grades. Some sections are tidal. Awkward approach.	179	
17 - 20 min	Afternoon				Access		Tidal	An interesting set of tidal cliffs with a range of routes across the grades. A little awkward to navigate around the cliffs.	185	
23 min	Morning	Sheltered						One good hard section of quarried cliff with a number of tough 7s. The right side of this crag is covered with mud.	193	Inland and Coastal Limestone
10 min	Evening					Abseil		A wide crag that has bands of fierce overhangs running across it. The best access is via abseil.	195	
5 min	Early morning	Sheltered			Restrictions			A rather gloomy inland old quarry working that has some intense slab climbs. Access problems - check first.	197	
2 - 12 min	Morning	Sheltered	Dry in the rain	Seepage	Restrictions			One of South Wales's premier crags that has lots of hard climbs on excellent limestone and is set in a quiet valley.	202	
30 min	Afternoon	Windy						A limestone escarpment with lots of mid-grade climbs. Exposed and on the slopes of the Brecon Beacons. The approach is long.	218	
1 - 5 min	Afternoon	Sheltered		Seepage				Impressive walls close to Cardiff. A good number of long face routes on generally good rock. Road noise level is high.	226	
10 - 13 min	Not much sun	Sheltered	Dry in the rain	Seepage				Two sections of cliff, one steep and the other slabby. The dense tree canopy shelters some of the cliff from rainfall.	244	
10 - 16 min	Morning	Sheltered		Seepage				A secluded series of quarried bays. Quick to approach and with lots in the low-to-mid grades. Good in hot weather.	254	
20 - 23 min	Afternoon	Windy						A popular spot for teams of mixed abilities with many routes in the low-to-mid grades. Exposed and high up.	272	The Valleys Sandstone
5 - 6 min	Evening			Seepage			Tidal	A steep, high standard cliff set next to a fine surf beach. Many excellent routes. Only marginally tidal at its landward end.	288	
15 min	To mid afternoon						Tidal	A long line of low walls. Many steep and sharp lines on solid rock. Tidal and next to a quiet beach.	298	
15 min	To mid afternoon	Sheltered						A hidden quarried wall of good, steep slabs. It is prone to getting dirty and the approach path can be overgrown.	308	
20 min	Lots of sun			Seepage			Tidal	An unusual sea cliff of horizontally banded walls. Extensive with many routes in the mid-grades. Mildly tidal.	314	

Faded symbol means only some of the routes are affected by the symbol characteristic

Destination Planner

	Crag	Routes	up to 4c	5a to 6a+	6b to 7a	7a+ to 7c+	8a up
Carmarthenshire	Craig Cwm	57	2	28	27	-	☐
	Dyffryn	45	1	27	17	-	☐
	Abbey Buttress	26	-	7	15	4	☐
	Pen Pych	12	-	2	7	3	☐
	Space Mountain	40	1	9	24	6	☐
	Treherbert Quarry	37	2	21	11	3	☐
Gower	Gelli	53	9	27	16	1	☐
	Ferndale	60	3	25	29	3	☐
	Blaenllechau	17	7	4	6	-	☐
	Dan Dicks	14	-	2	8	4	☐
	Trebanog	17	1	6	9	1	☐
	Glynfach	11	-	5	5	1	☐
	Trehafod	19	-	8	11	-	☐
The Valleys Sandstone	The Darren	23	-	3	12	8	☐
	Cwmaman	29	-	14	9	6	☐
	Mountain Ash	59	-	21	24	13	☐
	Mount Pleasant	60	1	42	15	2	☐
	The Gap	68	1	26	31	10	☐
	Navigation Quarry	51	4	17	25	5	☐
Inland and Coastal Limestone	Abertwssyg	11	-	6	3	2	☐
	Deri	17	-	2	10	5	☐
	Bargoed	27	-	6	18	2	☐
	Ridgeway	9	-	3	6	-	☐
	Llanbradach	90	3	7	64	16	☐
	Sirhowy	53	-	19	27	7	☐
The Valleys Sandstone	Cox's Quarry	8	-	3	5	-	☐
	Cross Keys Quarry	31	7	14	9	1	☐
	Cwmcarn	26	-	13	13	-	☐
	Tyle y Coch	22	8	2	9	3	☐
	Tirpentwys	30	2	17	10	1	☐
	TOTALS (full book)	2699	172	975	1156	351	40

Approach	Sun	Shelter	Dry in rain	Seepage	Access	Abseil	Tidal	Summary	Page
5 - 8 min	Morning							A lovely series of small sandstone buttresses set in a pleasant location. Lots of grade 5s and 6s. Easy approach.	332
20 min	Morning	Sheltered						A good local spot with lots of short but interesting lower-grade lines in a quiet location. A longish approach.	338
10 min	Afternoon	Windy						An old quarry with plenty of climbs close to the M4 and overlooking the steelworks at Port Talbot.	344
25 min	To mid afternoon			Seepage				A small crag in a gorgeous location next to a waterfall. A long but fine walk in. A popular tourist spot.	347
20 min	To mid afternoon				Access			An extensive series of walls and stacked overhangs in a stunning position high up at the end of the Rhondda Valley.	352
20 min	Afternoon	Windy						A quiet venue with some good climbs. Has the feeling of a mountain cliff and therefore is a warm weather venue.	362
10 min	Evening							Lots of lower-grade routes. The approach is a bit grotty initially, but the crag itself is quiet and pleasant.	368
4 - 10 min	Morning	Sheltered		Seepage				A series of vertical walls in a quarry high above the valley. Also a smaller lower level quarry good for a quick hit.	374
10 min	Afternoon	Sheltered						A good little quarry for some easier lines. A quiet spot with a good view. Alternative approach if main path overgrown.	382
10 min	Morning	Sheltered			Access			An easily accessed crag with some impressive lines, but prone to becoming vegetated. Bird restrictions.	385
1 min	Sun and shade	Windy						A small local spot good for a workout. Plenty of sun in winter and dries quickly. A quick approach.	388
13 min	Afternoon	Windy						A small quarry high on the hillside with a limited number of routes. Worth a look for the climbs on Killer Arete Buttress.	391
1 min (Roadside)	Afternoon	Sheltered	Dry in the rain					A small cliff with some stiff problems that is only a minute from the railway station platform. Nice evening venue.	394
5 min	Not much sun	Sheltered	Dry in the rain					Good local training crag that has a wall of super-steep climbs in the 7th grade.	398
10 min	Afternoon	Sheltered		Seepage				A vertical blank wall that is home to some finger searing classic testpieces. Some easier lines on adjacent walls.	404
5 min	From mid morning	Sheltered		Seepage				A collection of quarried walls shrouded by trees and quick to get to. Many decent routes across the grades.	410
13 min	Afternoon							A two tiered quarry that has been developed over many years. A good place spoiled by some fly tipping on the approach.	419
2 - 4 min	Not much sun							An old forcing ground of hard climbing in the Valleys. Still gets plenty of attention which keeps it in good condition.	428
15 min	Lots of sun	Sheltered		Seepage	Access			A lovely spot with good sport routes and also some trad. Sunny aspect and with excellent rock.	440
10 min	From mid morning	Windy						A section of exposed escarpment perched above a quarried slope with a small number of pitches in the 5 to 7b range.	447
7 min	Evening		Dry in the rain		Access			A fine little crag with a steep wall of grade 7s. Restriction due to nesting birds early in the year.	449
1 min	Afternoon			Seepage				A small quarry, set in woods, with lots of routes and a very swift approach Something here for most climbers.	454
2 min	Morning	Sheltered						An old quarry, the best section of which is a small wall of good rock that is quick to approach from the parking.	457
10 - 20 min	Morning	Sheltered		Seepage				A massive quarry with impressive walls. Good routes. The Upper Tier is impressive and well worth a look.	462
1 - 5 min	Afternoon	Sheltered						One of the Valleys's best. A lovely spot with brilliant climbs on its two best walls. A very quick approach.	471
20 min	Morning	Sheltered						A tiny wall of excellent well bolted rock located within a huge quarry. Good intense lines set in a sheltered dell.	481
5 min	Afternoon	Sheltered						Very convenient and sheltered small quarry with lots of grade 6s. Open and gets lots of sun even in cooler months.	483
10 min	From mid morning	Sheltered						Tree shrouded quarry that has lots of routes. Best when dry and leaves are off of the trees.	487
4 min	Morning	Sheltered	Dry in the rain	Seepage	Restrictions			A small fierce little crag with good routes. Seepage can be a problem. Minor access issue.	492
12 min	Lots of sun	Sheltered						An excellent quarry. Lots of good lines on clean and well-bolted rock. A very pleasant spot to hang out and climb.	498

Faded symbol means only some of the routes are affected by the symbol characteristic

Carmarthenshire

Tom Skelhon starting up the fine thin cracks of *Vladimir and the Pearl* (6c) - *p.52* - on The Mollusc Wall at Telpyn Point, Carmarthenshire. The three sport crags in Carmarthenshire are tidal sea cliffs which gives the climbing a more committing feel and the need for planning ahead. The area lies between Gower and Pembroke and is much less visited although some of the climbs are well worth searching out, or popping by on the way past if you are heading to Pembroke. Another plus is the opportunity to call in at some little known spots such as Pendine Sands the location for early land speed records, and the village of Laugharne the former inspirational home of Dylan Thomas. Photo: Mark Glaister

Telpyn Point

Grade Spread | 1 | 21 | 20 | 4 | -

Set between Pembroke and Gower is this surprising sport climbing sea cliff venue. Telpyn Point, like its nearby neighbours Morfa Bychan and Pendine, offers plenty of sport climbs on well-equipped rock in a beautiful setting. The rock is a hard sandstone and provides both technical and strenuous lines. The routes close to the descent scramble are excellent and provide a good range of mid-to-hard grade routes that will appeal to many. Lurking around the corner is a wall with a totally different feel - radically steep, covered with stacked overhangs and only really appealing to those who like their sport climbing with a heavy dose of adventure.

Approach

From the roundabout on the A40 at St Clears, take the A477 to Tenby. After 8 miles turn left signed to Amroth. From the seafront at Amroth, follow the road east towards Pendine for around 1.5 miles to a parking layby (with a large coastguard warning sign) on the right, just before the Carmarthenshire border sign, and opposite two gates. Follow a footpath down towards the sea, and as the path veers right, go down steps on the left to a small footbridge and over a stile. Continue along the coast path for 200m until a small path on the right leads through gorse to the cliff top. The crag lies below this point. Walk down right to good rock ledges on the cliff edge and scramble down below these (easiest to the right, looking out) to ledges at sea level.

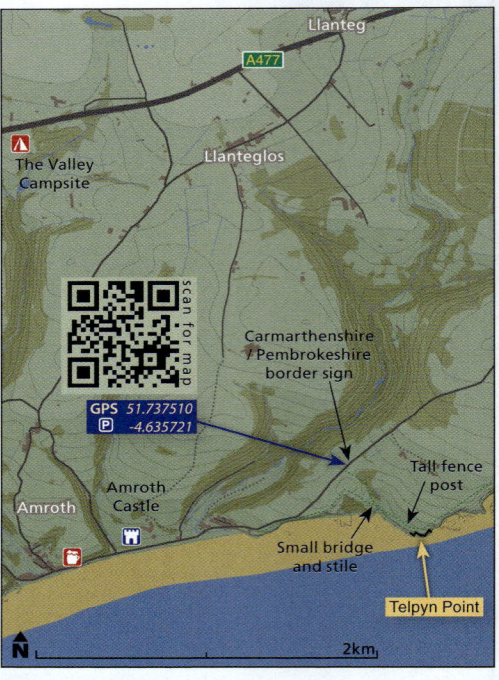

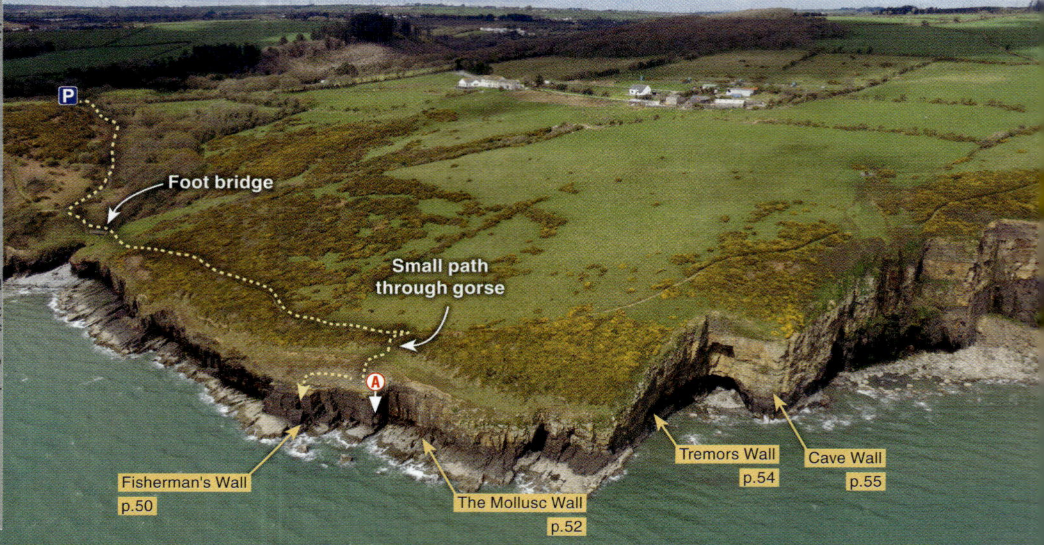

- Fisherman's Wall p.50
- The Mollusc Wall p.52
- Tremors Wall p.54
- Cave Wall p.55

Telpyn Point

Tom Skelhon beginning the excellent wall climbing on *King Prawn* (7a) - *p.53* - at The Mollusc Wall, Telpyn Point. Photo: Mark Glaister

Tides
The base is tidal and can only be accessed 4 hours either side of low tide. The Mollusc Wall can be reached by abseil and its base is usually above high tide in calm sea conditions.

Conditions
The cliff gets plenty of sun from midday onwards and is clean although seepage can be a problem after prolonged rainfall. The gently sloping rock platform at the base is extremely slick when wet and walking over it requires great care.

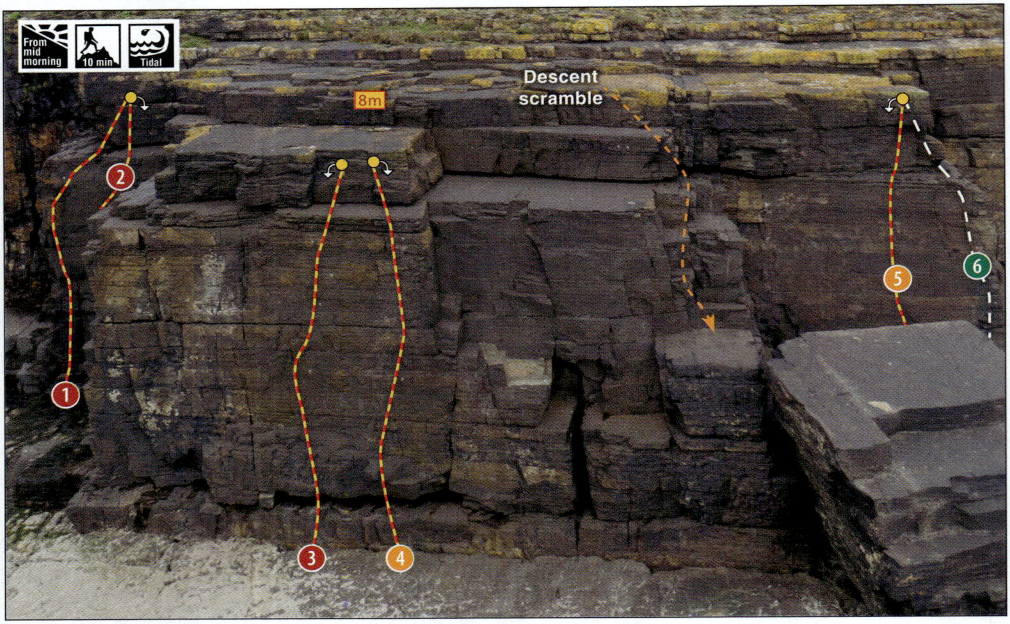

Telpyn Point — Fisherman's Wall

Fisherman's Wall

A couple of short bolted faces, composed of perfect rock. The walls are situated above a tidal platform, which although only gently sloping is treacherously greasy when wet and requires great care when crossing it.

Approach (map and overview p.48) - Either abseil directly into the wall or, just as easily, scramble down ledges on the right (facing out).

Tides - The ledge under the wall is only accessible for 4 hours on either side of low water.

Conditions - The walls face southwest and dry very quickly after rain. They take little seepage.

❶ Damp Cod Piece  6b+
Takes the left arete of the short set-back wall via a complex move right from arete to reach the ledge. Often seeps at the top.
FA. R.Thomas, H.May 2023

❷ Cod Father  6b
The centre of the wall and upper flake to the right of the arete taken by *Damp Cod Piece*.
FA. R.Thomas, H.May 2023

❸ Signal Crayfish 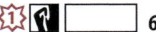 6b
Follow some fragile flakes up the centre of the wall.
FA. R.Thomas, H.May 2023

❹ Fishmonger 6a
Climb left of bolts at **6b**, or climb to their right using hands on the arete at **6a**. Two for the price of one!
FA. R.Thomas 5.2023

❺ Little Shrimp 6a+
A very short isolated wall with two hard moves.
FA. R.Thomas, G.Gibson 27.8.2006

Fisherman's Wall — Telpyn Point

⑥ Sand Eel 4c
The arete, climbed on its left to a shared lower-off on ledge.
FA. R.Thomas 2007

⑦ Get Your Cod Out 5c
The short wall on the left above a raised ledge. Trickier than it looks if climbed direct
FA. M.Davies 2020s

⑧ For Cod's Sake 5b
The short wall and ledges on the right above the raised ledge.
FA. R.Thomas 2007

⑨ Small Fry 6a
A tight line that takes the corner-crack up to a ledge on the left and then finishes direct up the wall.
FA. R.Thomas, M.Hirst, N.O'Neill 28.7.2008

⑩ Cure for Crabs 5c
The vague crack-line on the left-hand side of the wall passing an old peg. A stiff pull over the overhang above the ledge is needed.
FA. R.Thomas, G.Gibson 26.8.2006

⑪ Wrasse .... 6b+
A short fingery wall that leads to a shallow juggy groove above. Much harder if you cannot span to the ledge (6c+).
FA. G.Gibson, R.Thomas 26.8.2006

⑫ Cast Adrift .... 6a+
A very good little route. A stiff pull left of the cave gains the juggy upper wall.
FA. G.Gibson, R.Thomas 25.6.2006

⑬ Hook, Line and Stinker .. 6a+
Start just to the right of the low cave. Steep climbing but with superb hidden holds.
FA. G.Gibson, R.Thomas 26.8.2006

⑭ A Fisherman's Tackle 6b
A shallow jagged groove-line that has a hard move to pass the overlap.
FA. G.Gibson, R.Thomas 26.8.2006

⑮ Sprats from the Captain's Table .. 5c
Two tricky moves below the low ledge to the left. Pleasant and easier climbing lies above.
FA. R.Thomas, G.Gibson 26.8.2006

⑯ Kipper Ripper 6a
The right-hand side of the wall via ledges and crux small roof.
FA. R.Thomas 2023

The narrow wall to the right of the arete has suffered a large rockfall and the routes have all been lost, although the lower-offs are still in place.

Telpyn Point — The Mollusc Wall

The Mollusc Wall

A very good wall of sheer rock with routes that are sustained and fingery - the crux moves are nearly always in the final few metres. The walls are situated above a tidal platform, which although only gently sloping is treacherously greasy when wet and requires great care when crossing it.

Approach (map and overview p.48) - Either abseil in, or walk across the platform from below the Fisherman's Wall.

Tides - The approach to the wall is tidal and can only be accessed for around 4 hours on either side of low water. The base of the wall is not tidal, and in calm seas can easily be reached via abseil, even at high tide.

Conditions - The walls face southwest and dry relatively quickly. They do suffer from seepage, most surprisingly in humid weather when it really makes the routes significantly harder.

❶ Tough Carapace .... VS 4c
The corner. Use the lower-off on the right or escape left and top-out. This line may have been affected by rockfall.
FA. R.Thomas 2006

❷ Barnacles at Dawn 6c
A technical, balancy start with better holds on the upper section. Suffers from seepage.
FA. G.Gibson 27.8.2006

❸ Pray for the Cray .... 7a+
The left-trending crack-line has a final difficult pull.
FA. G.Gibson 25.6.2006

❹ Lobster Bisque 7b
Another vague crack-line which is reasonable until the desperately fingery finale.
FA. G.Gibson 25.6.2006

❺ Oyster Party 7a
A super little wall climb with technical moves away from the bolt at the top.
FA. G.Gibson, R.Thomas 18.6.2005

❻ Vladimir and the Pearl .. 6c
The central line of the wall leftwards via a prominent crack-line.
Photo p.46.
FA. G.Gibson, R.Thomas 18.6.2005

Area of large rockfall - routes unclimbable, lower-offs still in place

The Mollusc Wall — Telpyn Point

7 Shellin' Out 7b
A sustained affair with, as usual, a sting in the tail.
FA. G.Gibson 24.6.2006

8 King Prawn 7a
A fine series of thin cracks with good holds until the last move.
Photo p.49.
FA. G.Gibson, R.Thomas 18.6.2005

9 Man or Mollusc 7b
The final route of the wall once again saves the hardest to last.
FA. G.Gibson 24.6.2006

10 Telpyn Corner .... HVS 5a
The prominent corner proves a little unnerving.
FA. N.O'Neill, R.Thomas 2006

11 Mussel Man 5c
The arete on the right-hand side of the wall.
FA. R.Thomas, G.Gibson 24.6.2006

12 Moule Mariniere 6a
Start up a left-facing corner.
FA. R.Thomas, G.Gibson 24.6.2006

13 Ma Moule Don't Like U Laffin 5c
The wall, moving left from the last bolt to the lower-off.
FA. R.Thomas, G.Gibson 24.6.2006

The next four routes are on a south-facing wall in a small zawn/cave 30m to the right. Not shown on the topo.

14 Taxi to the Ocean 7a
Tackle the arete full on, finishing via some bizarre moves on its right-hand side.
FA. G.Gibson 27.8.2006

15 Diving for Pearls 6b
The fine overlapped wall. Short but excellent on lots of jugs.
FA. G.Gibson, R.Thomas 27.8.2006

16 Sea Fairer .... 6a+
Start up a groove and continue up the overlaps above it.
FA. G.Gibson, R.Thomas 27.8.2006

17 Glug, Glug, Glug .... 6a+
The wall to the right to a shared lower-off with *Sea Fairer*.
FA. G.Gibson, R.Thomas 27.8.2006

Telpyn Point — Tremors Wall

Tremors Wall

A big imposing wall with an intimidating atmosphere. It is composed of a series of slim grooves split by some hostile-looking overhangs. The current routes tackle the weaknesses in the roofs at relatively amenable grades. Any future additions are likely to be much harder. This is sport climbing with a large dose of adventure thrown in and is not a playground for the weak of spirit or those not used to handling loose rock.

Approach (map and overview p.48) - Continue round the corner from The Mollusc Wall and down some ledges to the base of the cliff.

Tides - The base of the wall is tidal and can only be accessed for around 3 hours on either side of low water.

Conditions - The wall can sport a little seepage towards its right-hand side which takes a while to dry. The climbs here can be very greasy in humid weather.

❶ Hullabaloo 6a
The left-facing groove line. Exit right and up at the roof.
FA. G.Gibson, R.Thomas 6.5.2007

❷ Crest of a Wave 6c
The right arete of the groove gives a few excellent moves.
FA. G.Gibson, R.Thomas 6.5.2007

❸ Keelhaul .... 6b+
Difficult moves through the right-hand side of the overlap.
FA. G.Gibson, R.Thomas 6.5.2007

❹ Plankwalk .... 6a+
The thin crackline springing from the right-hand side of the ledge is difficult to get established in. An airy pull and long reach gains the belay above it.
FA. G.Gibson, R.Thomas 22.6.2007

❺ The Richter Scale 6b
Start up *Plankwalk* and move right to a crack. The final overhang proves slightly easier than its neighbour.
FA. G.Gibson, R.Thomas 22.6.2007

❻ Tremors 6c
Intimidating moves but all of the holds are there - just keep cranking!
FA. G.Gibson, R.Thomas 5.5.2007

❼ Dead Man's Shoes 7a
The tiered overlaps provide a stern proposition. The final overlap is solved by passing it to the right.
FA. G.Gibson, M.Richardson 5.5.2007

❽ Spectre of Love .... 6c+
A classic of its type and very intimidating. The shallow groove is gained direct with no hard moves - just plenty of them!
FA. G.Gibson, M.Richardson 5.5.2007

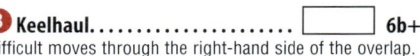

Cave Wall — Telpyn Point

Cave Wall

This wall surrounding the cave at the right-hand side of the Tremors Wall offers a handful of easier grade routes, together with one big pumpfest up the edge of the brooding cave. The rock quality here is better than on Tremors Wall but still requires care and is often dirty.

Approach (map and overview p.48) - Traverse the platform below Tremors Wall to the routes.

Tides - The base of the wall is tidal and can only be accessed for around 3 hours on either side of low water.

Conditions - The main cave takes seepage but the routes described are usually unaffected. The cliff faces west and gets some afternoon sunshine, but the routes can be greasy in humid conditions.

9 The Ego Sanction 7a
The right-hand side of the cave gives a jug-filled experience (the hollow block is locked in place) to reach its right-hand lip. The headwall is an endurance exam.
FA. G.Gibson 23.6.2007

10 Mental Message 6b
The shallow groove line to a steep upper wall passing a mid-height lower-off.
FA. R.Thomas, G.Gibson 4.5.2007

11 Men From Boys E2 5b
A trad line up the lower groove system to a belay ledge on the right (**5a**). Then the fine hand-jamming crack to the top (**5b**).
FA. R.Thomas, S.Llewelyn 6.2008

12 Safe Connection 5c
The centre of the wall via a thin crack system.
FA. R.Thomas, G.Gibson 23.6.2007

13 Innocents Abroad 6a
Branch right from *Safe Connection* to climb the wall.
FA. R.Thomas, S.Llewelyn 6.2008

Morfa Bychan

| Grade Spread | 2 | 27 | 26 | 7 | - |

Morfa Bychan is a limestone sea cliff tucked away in a tranquil cove and adjacent to a nice beach. It has some good quality rock and climbing and makes a worthwhile venue within easy reach of the Pembrokeshire crags, or when combined with a visit to the nearby Telpyn Point or Pendine. The cliff has a good grade mix and is very steep in parts, which initially makes it feel quite intimidating but on closer inspection it all feels quite friendly.

Approach

From the roundabout on the A40 at St Clears, take the A477 to Tenby. After 8 miles turn left signed to Amroth. From the seafront at Amroth, follow the road east towards Pendine, for around 4 miles. Turn right opposite some standing stones (signs saying access only). Go down a rough unmade road which leads to a tranquil cove in 1.5 miles. The crag is easily seen from here. The beach can also be reached via the coast path from Pendine.

Tides

The crag is tidal. The right-hand side of the Main Cliff can only be accessed for 4 hours on either side of low tide. It is possible to climb on the left-hand side when the tide is in (although access and escape is cut-off). Due to the steep vegetated slopes above the cliff, an abseil approach is not recommended. Sunnyside is accessible for 2 to 3 hours on either side of low tide and Zero Zawn for 1.5 to 2 hours on either side of low tide.

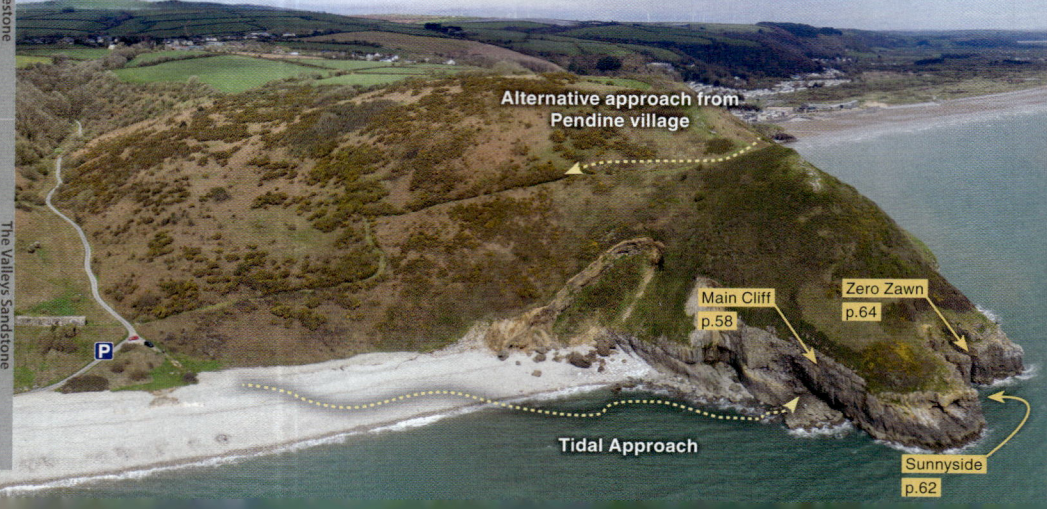

Morfa Bychan

Conditions

The Main Cliff faces west and gets the sun from mid-afternoon onwards making it an ideal summer venue. Sunnyside and Zero Zawn have a southerly aspect. The Main Cliff takes relatively little seepage, except in winter, and can be climbed upon even after a light shower. The rock can feel soapy in humid weather before the sun has moved onto the face to dry it out.

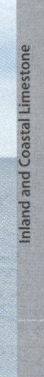

John Warner getting to grips with the mid-height layback feature of *Credit Squeeze* (6b+) - *p.60* - at the Main Cliff, Morfa Bychan. Photo: Mark Glaister

Morfa Bychan — Main Cliff

Main Cliff
A well-equipped cliff set in a lovely cove. The routes are steep and sustained and on good rock on the whole - some sections on the steeper lines are a little fragile.

Approach (map and overview p.56) - From the parking, walk along the pebble and sand beach to the rocky platform at the base of the cliff.

Tides - The base of the crag is tidal and can only be accessed for 4 hours on either side of low water.

Conditions - The rock can feel soapy in humid weather or before the sun has moved onto the face. It is possible to climb in showery weather. It is exposed to westerlies.

1 Best Possible Taste 6b
Short but intense lower wall leading to left side of *Sid Snot* starting ledge.
FA. R.Thomas, R.Phillips 9.8.2017

2 Another Cupid Stunt .... 6a+
The short wall under the ledge of *Sid Snot*.
FA. R.Thomas, R.Phillips 10.8.2017

3 Above the Stupid .... 6b+
A rubbly wall left of *Sid Snot* to a shared lower-off.
FA. R.Thomas 2017

4 Sid Snot .... 6b+
The left side of the platform starting off of a narrow ledge.
FA. R.Thomas, G.Ashmore 11.6.2017

5 Cut Through the Crap .... 6a+
The line almost at the end of the platform.
FA. R.Thomas, N.O'Neill, G.Ashmore 2.1.2017

6 Tasty Protein Supplement ..... 6a+
The wall and groove.
FA. R.Thomas, R.Phillip, E.Travers-Jones 28.12.2016

7 Dish the Dirt 6c
A fingery and powerful lower bulge is followed by much easier pleasant moves above.
FA. G.Gibson, R.Thomas 28.6.2008

8 Less is More .... 7a+
Complicated moves through the lower bulge precedes another tricky sequence via the short arete higher up.
FA. G.Gibson 15.8.2008

9 More than Enough 7a
A challenging stamina exercise. The upper section is often dirty..
FA. G.Gibson 29.6.2008

10 More More More 7a
Very overhanging with a tough central section.
FA. G.Gibson, R.Thomas 24.5.2009

11 Moreland .... 7a+
A stamina climbing exercise via a mid-height hanging corner.
FA. G.Gibson 24.5.2009

Morfa Bychan

Having conquered the overhung start the climber is tackling the fine wall climbing on *She's Slipping Away* (7a) - *p.60* - at the Main Cliff, Morfa Bychan
Photo: Mark Glaister

Morfa Bychan — Main Cliff

12 Burn After Reading — 6c+
Fine climbing from bottom to top with an amenable finale.
FA. G.Gibson, R.Thomas 7.6.2008

13 Morfa, Morfa, Morfa — 7a
At present the pillar under the top roof is dangerously loose. A tough and draining sequence through the lower bulge. The upper overlap has a good rest just before it.
FA. G.Gibson 8.6.2008

14 Listing Badly — 7a
A demanding start leads to an easier middle section and difficult finale through the capping overlap.
FA. G.Gibson 7.6.2008

15 Wreckage — 7a+
A very complex start, easier middle and then an even more difficult finish requiring a big wingspan.
FA. G.Gibson 6.6.2008

16 She's Slipping Away — 7a
A butch lower overhang complements a complex finale. A good taster for the harder routes. *Photo p. 59.*
FA. G.Gibson, R.Thomas 6.6.2008

17 Credit Squeeze — 6b+
A gem of a route with excellent moves that are deceptively pumpy. The initial corner is sometimes damp. *Photo p.57.*
FA. R.Thomas, G.Gibson 8.6.2008

18 The Pinch is On — 7a+
Direct up the leaning headwall above the start of *Credit Squeeze* with a hard finale.
FA. G.Gibson 24.5.2009

Main Cliff Morfa Bychan

19 Selling Short .... 6b+
A fine sister route to *Credit Squeeze* that breaks right after its initial corner.
FA. R.Thomas, G.Gibson 7.6.2008

20 Tidal Rush .... 6c+
Superb varied moves through the overhang and up the technical wall above.
FA. G.Gibson 8.6.2008

21 Asset Manager 6c
One of the best on the crag up the smooth looking wall. Start direct up the pushy initial wall.
FA. R.Thomas, G.Gibson 6.6.2008

22 Heading South 6a
The shallow groove system with enjoyable climbing throughout.
FA. R.Thomas, G.Gibson 6.6.2008

23 Insider Dealer .... 6b+
A hard sequence on the upper wall after easier preliminaries.
FA. R.Thomas, G.Gibson 28.6.2008

24 Bull Market 6a
Take the prominent break. Hardest at the top.
FA. R.Thomas, G.Gibson 28.6.2008

25 Crash and Dash 5b
A short exercise on the small wall above the ledge.
FA. R.Thomas, G.Gibson 29.6.2008

26 Pump and Dump .... 6a+
A hard sequence right from the start.
FA. R.Thomas, G.Gibson 29.6.2008

27 Toxic Assets 4c
The short wall.
FA. R.Thomas 2008

28 Green Shoots of Recovery 5a
The final route, on the arete.
FA. R.Thomas 2008

Approach and descent scramble for any tide access to Sunnyside and Zero Zawn

Low tide access to Sunnyside and Zero Zawn

Morfa Bychan — Sunnyside

Sunnyside

An isolated bay with some smart little sport pitches on good rock. Careful timing of the approach and exit with regard to the tides is needed to get the best from a visit.

Approach (map and overview p.56) **and Tides** - The cliff can be gained at very low tide along the beach from the base of the Main Cliff but, in order to get plenty of climbing time in, the best access is via the higher approach. From the seaward end of the Main Cliff, scramble up cracks, ledges and walls to the top of the cliff and walk around to abseil bolts above the cliff edge. To exit, climb up the easy *Get Out Claws* and reverse the scramble back to the Main Cliff.

Conditions - It faces roughly south and gets plenty of sun but can be greasy in humid weather.

❶ **Squeeze that Lemon** 6a
Climb the pillar via the vague arete.
FA. R.Thomas, G.Ashmore 12.5.2016

❷ **The Golden String** 6a
Start up the enclosed deep crack then head directly up the pillar.
FA. R.Thomas, G.Ashmore 26.7.2014

❸ **Noah's Arse** 5b
Climb the wall to a steepening, then step right to a shared lower-off with *Knee Jerk*.
FA. R.Thomas, E.Travers-Jones 24.8.2014

❹ **Knee Jerk** 6a
Contains some amusing moves to pass the overlap
FA. R.Thomas 27.7.2014

❺ **Euler's Number** .... 6c+
Shiny often damp wall to a large horizontal break. Pull out over the roof to finish.
FA. A.Bowman, M.Robinson 18.6.2015

❻ **Lucas Numbers** 6c
An awkward start gains a groove and roof. The line goes directly up to the first bolt, via a slot to a hand rail. Starting up the groove to the left is far easier and doesn't qualify for a tick.
FA. G.Ashmore 31.5.2014

❼ **Bonacci's Sequence** .. 7b
The overhanging right wall of the arete of *Lucas Numbers*. Technical with a huge lurch to finish.
FA. G.Ashmore 27.7.2014

Line of higher approach from Main Cliff

Sunnyside **Morfa Bychan**

⑧ Mistaking Cassini's Identity .... 7a+
The groove between *Bonacci's Sequence* and *All For Nothing*. Oddball climbing that involves a powerful lock off on a sloper.
FA. G.Ashmore 29.9.2014

⑨ All For Nothing .... 6a+
Start at the base of the ramp and climb the red wall and overlap.
FA. R.Thomas, E.Travers-Jones 5.7.2014

⑩ Get Out Claws 2c
The staircase right of *All For Nothing*.
FA. R.Thomas 28.7.2014

⑪ Zero Inclination .... 6a+
The faint rib and groove is quite tricky.
FA. R.Thomas, G.Ashmore 6.7.2014

⑫ Recurring Nightmare........... 5a
Left of *A Question Of Rabbits* a short stapled wall leads to the ledge of the following routes and a shared ring lower-off.
FA. R.Thomas, G.Ashmore 5.7.2014

⑬ A Question of Rabbits .... 6b+
The short wall. Start left of the arete and move into the centre of the face before heading upto the ledge.
FA. R.Thomas 27.7.2014

⑭ My Slice of Pie.................. 6a
The arete, big ledge and high groove.
FA. R.Thomas, G.Ashmore 6.2014

⑮ Sad Little Nutter............ HVS 5b
The thin crack in the left side of the pillar.
FA. R.Thomas, G.Ashmore 6.2014

⑯ Off at a Tangent .... 6a+
The wall to the right of the thin crack. Joins the other routes after the ledge.
FA. R.Thomas 6.2014

⑰ Smart Keas 6a
Left of the crack of *Daft Nutter*, take the sidewall then stick to the arete until tricky moves gain the ledge.
FA. R.Thomas, N.Goile, G.James 9.2014

⑱ Daft Nutter .... HVS 5b
The thin crack up the wall left of *You Sane Bolter* has good rock and a couple of hard moves.
FA. R.Thomas 5.2013

Zero Zawn

An impressive gash in the cliff that abuts the right-hand end of the Sunnyside crag The routes take time to come into condition but once climbable are excellent.
Approach (map and overview p.56) and Tides - The cliff can be gained at very low tide along the beach from the base of the Main Cliff but, in order to get plenty of climbing time in, the best access is via the higher approach. From the seaward end of the Main Cliff, scramble up cracks, ledges and walls to the top of the cliff and walk around to abseil bolts above the cliff edge. To exit, climb up the easy *Get Out Claws* and reverse the scramble back to the Main Cliff.
Conditions - Shady and needs a dry spell to come into condition. The bed of zawn has a pool in it.

1 You Sane Bolter .... (1 star) ☐ **6a+**
The groove on the right-hand side of the central pillar leading to a pedestal and lower-off above the break. Interesting moves.
FA. R.Thomas, G.Ashmore 6.2014

2 Bolus Feed .... (2 stars) ☐ **6b**
The pillar on the left-hand side of the zawn.
FA. R.Thomas, G.Ashmore 6.2014

3 Nil By Mouth .... (1 star) ☐ **6a+**
A tricky start off of the ledge at the start of the zawn.
FA. R.Thomas, G.Ashmore 6.2014

Afternoon | 10 min | Sheltered | Seepage | Tidal | Abseil in

4 Continued Nursing Care .... ☐ **6a+**
A short hard section.
FA. R.Thomas 31.5.2014

5 P.E.G Feed .... ☐ **5c**
The groove has an awkward start.
FA. R.Thomas, G.Ashmore, E.Travers-Jones 6.7.2014

6 Labrynthitis .... ☐ **6a+**
Deep inside the dark confines of the zawn. Usually wet.
FA. R.Thomas, G.Ashmore 8.2015

7 The Quest for the Origins of Place Holder Notation
.... (2 stars) ☐ **6b+**
The left-hand line on the right wall of the Zawn. Start as for *Turing's Sum* and take a rising traverse in.
FA. R.Thomas 27.7.2014

8 Disraeli's Curl .... (2 stars) ☐ **7a**
The vague groove towards the left of the wall, reached via the rising traverse from *Turing's Sum*.
FA. G.Ashmore 6.6.2014

9 Disraeli's Curl Direct............ ☐ **7a**
The awkward left-hand groove leading up into *Disraeli's Curl* is much harder than first appearances suggest. Very rarely dry - only seen dry to date on midwinter spring tides when the angle of the sun is low enough to dry it out.
FA. G.Ashmore 21.2.2015

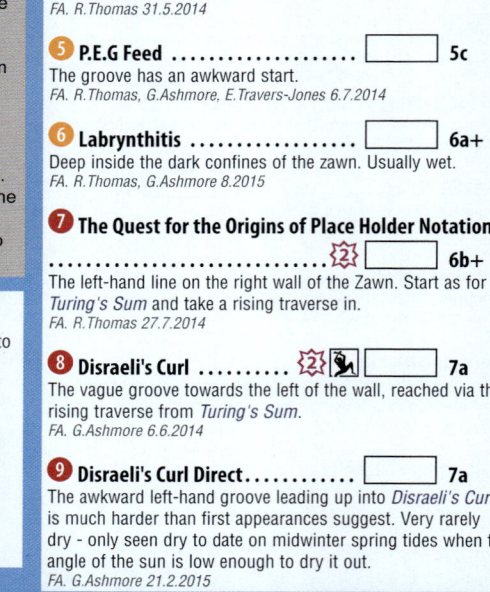

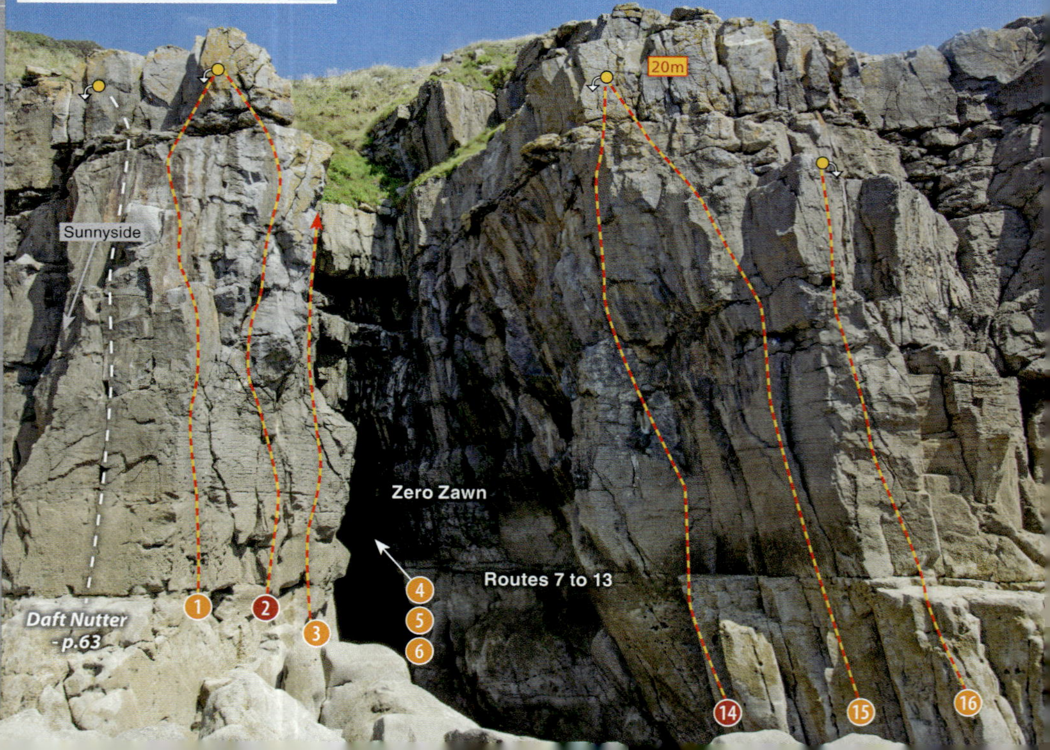

Zero Zawn **Morfa Bychan**

⑩ Kitchener's Nabla .... 7a+
The start is usually wet so either use the first bolt as an aid point, or gain the upper section from *Turing's Sum*.
FA. G.Ashmore 5.7.2014

⑪ Turing's Sum .... 6c+
The bomb bay chimney and harder-than-expected continuation groove. The start is feasible in wet conditions which is why it is used to reach the upper sections of the routes to the left.
FA. G.Ashmore 6.7.2014

⑫ Blank Dark Thirty 6b
The hanging set of grooves split by sloping shelves.
FA. R.Thomas, G.Ashmore 22.4.2015

⑬ Joys of a Tethered Goat .. 6b
Climb the pocketed rib left of the start of *Central Integrator*, and then head leftwards to gain and finish up *Blank Dark Thirty*.
FA. R.Thomas, G.Ashmore 22.5.2015

⑭ Central Integrator 6b
Start up a short corner to a ledge and then follow the groove.
FA. R.Thomas, R.Phillips 5.2014

⑮ Dismal Differentiator .... 6a+
The flake crack before heading left to a lower-off shared with *Central Integrator*.
FA. R.Thomas G.Ashmore 15.04.2014

⑯ Napier's Bones 6a
A short line up the pillar to the right of the zawn entrance.
FA. R.Thomas, E.Travers-Jones 8.2.20

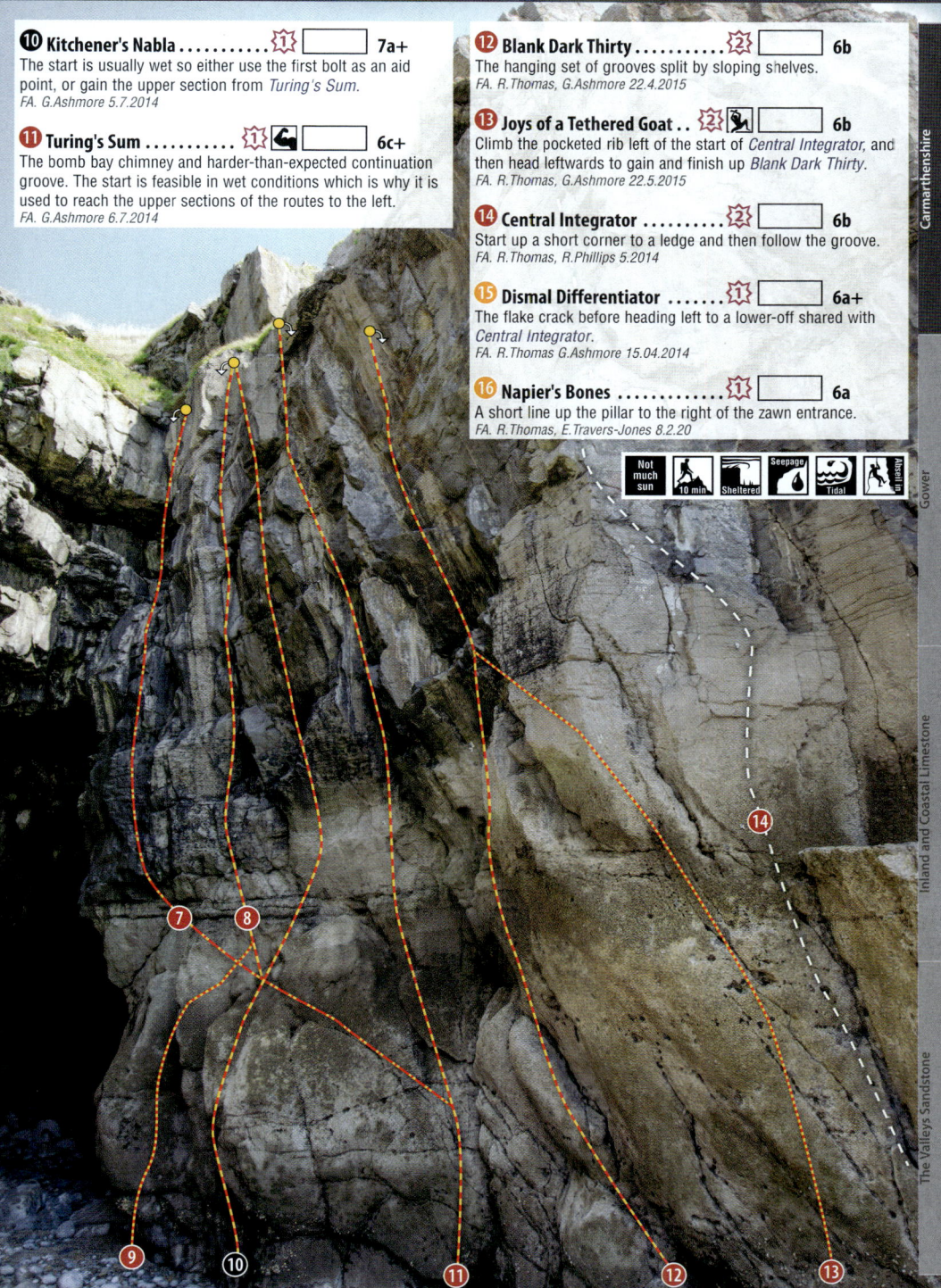

Pendine

| Grade Spread | 1 | 19 | 25 | 17 | - |

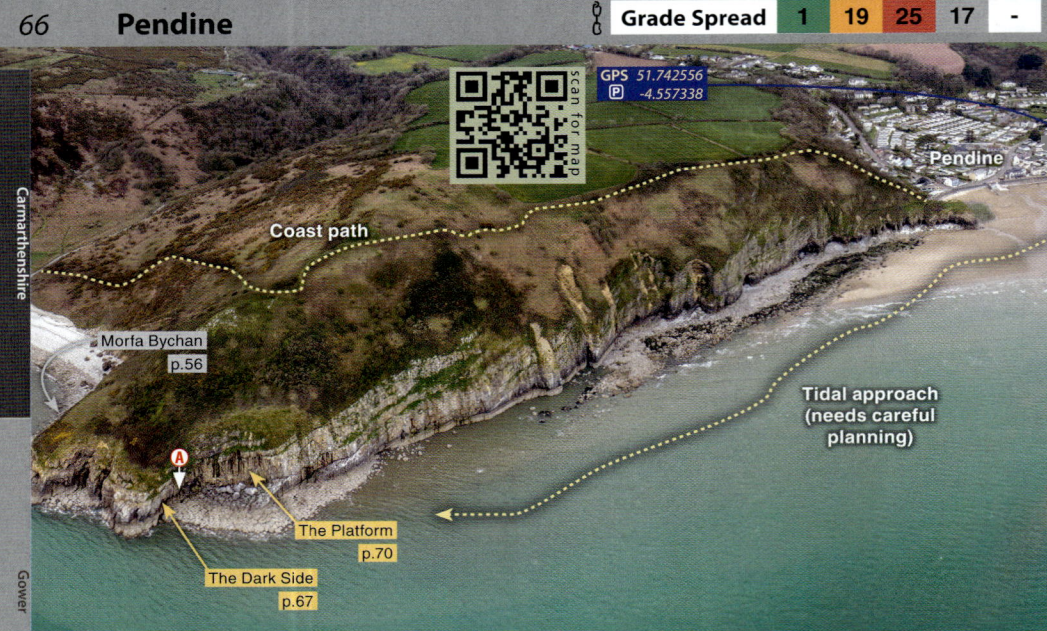

To the west of the tiny resort of Pendine, and its famous expanse of sand, is an excellent little sport cliff which has some of the area's best routes. The rock is excellent, the lines appealing and the location fabulous, however the approach needs careful planning to ensure that as much climbing as possible can be squeezed out of a visit. The left-hand crag, known as the Dark Side, is a long wall covered with narrow overhangs and has plenty of quality climbing in the 7s. The right-hand cliff called The Platform is taller but less steep and has numerous grade 6s that tackle some fine grooves, thin cracks and overlaps.

Approach   Map p.56
From the roundabout on the A40 at St Clears, take the A477 towards Tenby. After 6 miles turn left onto the B4314 (signed Red Roses) and follow it to Pendine. Park in the centre of the seaside village (roadside parking or car parks). Walk down onto the beach and head west for 10 minutes until the cliff is reached just before the headland.

Tides
Careful planning is needed. The simplest approach is to walk in as soon as you can as the tide goes out, climb for four hours, then walk out. Another option is to walk in at low tide and climb on the Platform Area as the tide comes back in (the platform is above high water level in calm seas) and walk out during the following low tide, although this makes for quite a long day. Another option for those familiar with the area is to approach via Morfa Bychan (p.56). Follow the approach to the abseil point for Sunnyside (p.62) but continue along the cliff edge above Zero Zawn and onward to an abseil point above the route *Before Planck's Time* - this allows access for around 4 hours either side of low water. To exit, climb out and reverse the approach.

Conditions
The cliff gets plenty of sun until mid afternoon and dries quickly. Seepage can be a problem after rainfall.

The Dark Side **Pendine** 67

The Dark Side
The roof-dotted wall that dips towards the sea is a fine section of cliff with some excellent grade 7s. The routes give powerful, technical and sustained climbing on excellent well-bolted rock.
Approach (map p.56) - Walk along the beach and then over boulders to below the cliff, or abseil in.
Tides - The base of the wall is uncovered for around 2 hours on either side of low tide.
Conditions - The cliff gets the sun until early afternoon.

❶ **Gizzard Puke** 4c
The prow above the escape chimney of The Dark Side.
FA. R.Thomas 11.6.2017

❷ **Short Sharp Sock** 6b
The short finger biting wall.
FA. R.Thomas, G.Ashmore 1.10.2015

❸ **Juice Runs Down My Leg** . 5c
Another short and fingery wall right of a crack.
FA. R.Thomas, G.Ashmore 25.3.2016

❹ **Straight as a Dai** 6b
Make some difficult moves up the barnacle band before the good stuff arrives.
FA. R.Thomas, G.Ashmore 16.4.2014

❺ **Central Deviator** 6b
Similar to *Straight as a Dai*. Keep your eyes peeled off line for the best sequence.
FA. R.Thomas, G.Ashmore 17.4.2014

❻ **The Tedium of a Long Distance Redpointer**
.... 6c+
The groove above the boulder.
FA. R.Thomas 2017

❼ **Silver Surfers Sermon** .... 6c+
A broken looking line that takes the pillar and crack.
FA. E.Travers-Jones 6.7.2015

❽ **Before Planck's Time** .... 7a+
The seam and hanging groove has a distinct crux. The lower-off is well above the band of vegetation.
FA. G.Ashmore, E.Travers-Jones 5.6.2015

❾ **Salisbury's Crowd** .... 7b+
Where the bolt lines split, keep up and left into the groove. Difficult to work out although reasonable to redpoint.
FA. G.Ashmore 10.7.2015

❿ **Gladstone's Deficit** 7b
Climb *Salisbury's Crowd* past its first overhang before stepping right to gain a break with difficulty. A further difficult couple of moves leads to good holds above the overlap and an easier finish up the flake. High in the grade.
FA. G.Ashmore 14.6.2015

Pendine — The Dark Side

11 Seven Thirty at Arras 7b
A long diagonal line that joins and finishes up the final section of *Badgers Out!*. Fantastic rock and climbing.
FA. G.Ashmore 20.5.2015

12 Quantum of Lydon's Future
.... 7b
Excellent. Some vicious undercutting leads to a shrill and awkward crux in the centre. Big jugs lead through the overlaps to finish.
FA. G.Ashmore, D.Emanuel 25.5.2015

13 Quantum of Lydon's Feelings
.... 7b+
Start up *Seven Thirty At Arras* and finish up *Quantum of Lydon's Future*.
FA. G.Ashmore 28.8.2015

14 Badger's Out! .... 7a+
The hanging chimney and vague groove.
FA. G.Ashmore 22.4.2015

15 Vera Figner's Lost List .... 7a+
Climb an arete to a chimney at the roof. Pull out left and make some very unlikely moves left to a good flake. Finish up the flake to a lower-off on the right.
FA. G.Ashmore, E.Travers-Jones 16.8.2014

16 Jacky Fisher's Phobia 7a
Start up *Vera Figner's Lost List* and climb direct out over the roof above the chimney. Finish up the slab to a shared lower-off with *Vera Figner's Lost List*.
FA. G.Ashmore, E.Travers-Jones 16.8.2014

17 Thousand Bomber Raid ...... 7b+
Take the pillar right of *Jacky Fisher's Phobia* to baffling moves left through the roof.
FA. G.Ashmore, R.Thomas 4.8.2016

18 Your Future, Our Clutter! . 7b+
The right-hand line up the pillar, turning mean at the roof.
FA. G.Ashmore 19.7.2016

The Dark Side — Pendine

19 Float Like a Butterfly, Sting Like a Bee ... 7b+
From a huge boulder climb the powerful groove to a blunt arete. Move left around the blunt arete to the start of some hard moves through the roof.
FA. G.Ashmore. G.Morris 4.6.2016

20 Z-Cars ... 7c
A forceful link-up, with a couple of new moves. Start up *Float Like a Butterfly* and then make powerful moves up from a pocket to gain the jug on the lip of *Becalmed on Dirac's Sea*. Finish up *Becalmed on Dirac's Sea*.
FA. G.Ashmore, G.Morris 9.7.2017

21 Adrift on Dirac's Sea ... 7b+
Start from the top of the large boulder right of *Float Like a Butterfly*. Head straight up the wall on slots to the line of undercuts in the roof. Follow the undercuts to a big pinch jug on the lip, then make a baffling series of moves up and left to the lower-off of *Float Like a Butterfly*.
FA. G.Ashmore, E.Travers-Jones 25.6.2017

22 Becalmed on Dirac's Sea ... 7b+
From the top of the large boulder, climb the wall right of *Adrift On Dirac's Sea* to gain a line of undercuts leading leftwards to the lip. Turn the lip with difficulty, and then using some crossly rock move up the wall above to gain the lower-off.
FA. G.Ashmore, E.Travers-Jones 25.6.2017

23 Seagull Stuka Strike ... 7b+
Climb the blunt rib then make a powerful traverse left to gain the left-hand hanging groove.
FA. G.Ashmore, R.Thomas 10.6.2016

24 Beer Coracle ... 7b
The right-most groove on the Dark Side. Difficult moves up into the groove, lead to a hard exit into the top groove.
FA. E.Travers-Jones 25.6.2017

25 Dog Head ... 6c+
The roof left of *Dog Leg* to a shared finish and lower-off.
FA. R.Thomas 2018

The Platform

A very good wall that has a large choice of worthwhile grade 6s. The rock is generally excellent and the routes follow subtle lines of corners and grooves.

Approach (map p.56, overview p.66) - Walk along the beach and up over boulders.
Tides - The base of the wall is above high tide in calm seas, but the approach is cut off.
Conditions - The cliff gets sun until late afternoon.

1 Dog Leg 1   6a
The left most bolt line moving leftwards up a ramp.
FA. R.Thomas, G.Ashmore 9.7.2015

2 Dog Wuff 2   6b
Climb a crack and finish direct on suoerb rock.
FA. R.Thomas, G.Ashmore 9.7.2015

3 Doggy Style Deviant 1   6a+
Start up *Doggy Style* and finish up the ramp on left.
FA. R.Thomas, E.Travers-Jones 21.7.2015

4 Doggy Style 6b
A fine bit of climbing starting up a crack
FA. R.Thomas, R.Phillips 18.7.2015

5 Doggy Bag 1   6a
Take the crack left of the large block that leans against the face - 'The Tombstone' - and continue up bubbly holds.
FA. R.Thomas, R.Phillips 18.7.2015

6 Litter Runt 6a
From the top of the 'Tombstone', make difficult moves up wall.
FA. R.Thomas, N.O'Neill, E.Travers-Jones 2.8.2015

7 Table Scraps 6a
From the top of the 'Tombstone', climb wall left of crack - dirty.
FA. R.Thomas, G.Gibson 6.9.2015

Lots of sun | 10 min | Tidal

The Platform Pendine

8 Give the Dog a Bone 5c
Start just to the right of the 'Tombstone' and climb the arete and its left side to a lower-off.
FA. R.Thomas, G.Gibson, H.Gibson 6.9.2015

9 Salty Dog 5c
Move up the technical groove to steeper ground. Big holds lead up left to a shared lower-off.
FA. H.Gibson, R.Thomas 8.6.2015

10 Bitch 6b
The smooth depression leads to steep pulling in upper section.
FA. G.Gibson, H.Gibson 8.6.2015

11 Snuffle Hound .... 6b+
Technical climbing past the mid-height slab.
FA. G.Gibson, H.Gibson 9.6.2015

12 Unleashed 6b
Excellent varied moves but can be muddy.
FA. G.Gibson, H.Gibson 9.6.2015

13 3D Dog .... 6a+
Make a difficult pull to enter the steep and technical groove.
FA. G.Gibson, H.Gibson 9.6.2015

14 Soapy Dog 6a
Start up groove of *Soapy Dahl*. At half height, bear left and finish up *3D Dog*.
FA. R.McAllister 15.5.2016

15 Soapy Dahl 6b
A striking line. The smooth groove with a diversion right.
FA. G.Gibson, H.Gibson 7.6.2015

16 Man Machine .... 6c+
The corner groove has some perplexing moves midway.
FA. G.Gibson, R.Thomas, H.Gibson 7.6.2015

17 Cross Country Booty Call . 7a+
The arete to a big round pocket and low lower-off.
FA. A.Rosier, R.McAllister 15.5.2016

Pendine The Platform

18 Sophie's Wit Tank 6c
Brilliant climbing up thin cracks on the face of the buttress.
FA. R.Thomas, G.Gibson, H.Gibson 8.6.2015

19 Perfect Prude .... 6b+
Bridge and layback up the corner right of *Sophie's Wit Tank*.
FA. R.Thomas 6.2015

20 Stroking the Lizard .... 6a+
The pillar, corners and exposed roof. A long pitch.
FA. R.Thomas, E.Travers-Jones 6.7.2015

21 Milking the Snake 6a
Follow corners to a roof. Pull over and move left to join and finish as for *Stroking the Lizard*.
FA. R.Thomas, G.Ashmore 10.7.2015

22 Stroke of Good Luck. 6c
Climb the short arete and its left wall direct.
FA. R.Thomas, R.Phillips 24.6.2015

23 Rubble Escalator........... 5b
The chimney.
FA. R.Thomas 18.6.2015

24 Blood Spunker .... 6a+
The crack and wall. Finish via a hand traverse right.
FA. D.Emanuel 2015

25 Dishonourable Discharge 5c
Layback up to join *Spunk Welder*.
FA. R.Thomas, R.Phillips 8.2015

26 Spunk Welded.............. 6a
The technical steep crack and slab.
FA. Dai Emanuel 2015

27 Stuck up Bitch........... 6c
Take the groove to a strenuous crack in the headwall.
FA. R.Thomas 1.10.2015

The Platform **Pendine**

Down and right of The Platform are some more routes.

33 Wristlock 6b
The wall and roof to a to a lower-off.
FA. R.Thomas, G.Ashmore 2.9.2016

34 Alpha Blocker .... 6a+
Climb the wall starting at a pointy handhold. Move directly over the small roof and head on up to join *Beat a Block, Ha!*.
FA. R.Thomas, G.Ashmore 7.2016

35 Beat a Block, Ha! 6b
Climb the short wall to a ledge and steep crack. Move up to gain a stacked block pillar before launching up the final wall.
FA. R.Thomas 7.2018

36 Hypertension .... 6a+
Start up *Beat A Block, Ha!* and then take the hanging groove and diagonal crack to a shared lower-off.
FA. R.Thomas, E.Travers-Jones 10.7.2016

37 ACE Inhibitors .... 6b+
Follow *Beat a Block, Ha!* to a ledge and then take the orange wall on the right.
FA. R.Thomas, G.Ashmore 23.7.2016

28 Waxing Lyrical............. 6b+
Move right from *Stuck up Bitch*. A single bolt lower-off.
FA. R.Thomas, E.Travers-Jones 1.11.2015

29 Mary Hinge's Close Shave .. 6b+
The corner/groove is very steep.
FA. R.Thomas 20.5.2015

30 Nothing in it 6b
The groove/crack to the left of the arete.
FA. R.Thomas 21.2.2015

31 McGoohan Loses Six .... 6c+
The arete is technical low down. A great line and position.
FA. G.Ashmore 21.7.2014

32 The Amount of Fun to be had by a Bear with a Broken Baculum 6a
The slab right of an arete on pockets and reinforced flakes.
FA. R.Thomas, E.Travers-Jones, G.Ashmore 22.3.2015

Gower

Jeremy Wilson on the fabulous wall of *Blackman's Pinch* (6c+) - *p.102* - the Trial Wall, Gower. The sport climbing on Gower is on limestone, more often than not with a magnificent seascape as the backdrop. Photo: Mark Glaister

Rhossili Beach

Grade Spread | 22 | 54 | 31 | 9 | 15

The development of the sport climbing potential on the beach-side sea cliffs at Rhossili has led to it becoming one of South Wales' most popular climbing destinations in recent years. The climbing is excellent, diverse and spans the grades from easy to desperate, but it is its situation next to one of Wales' finest beaches that really ramps up its appeal - get the tides right, some decent summer weather and a fantastic day of climbing, swimming and relaxation is guaranteed.

Approach and Tides

From the National Trust car park entrance, take the signed footpath down to the beach. Once on the beach head left. This is a tidal venue and care needs to be taken to ensure that you don't get caught out. The high water level varies considerably during neaps and springs and can shorten the times for access. The state of the sea and air pressure can have an influence, and in rough seas access is sometimes impossible.

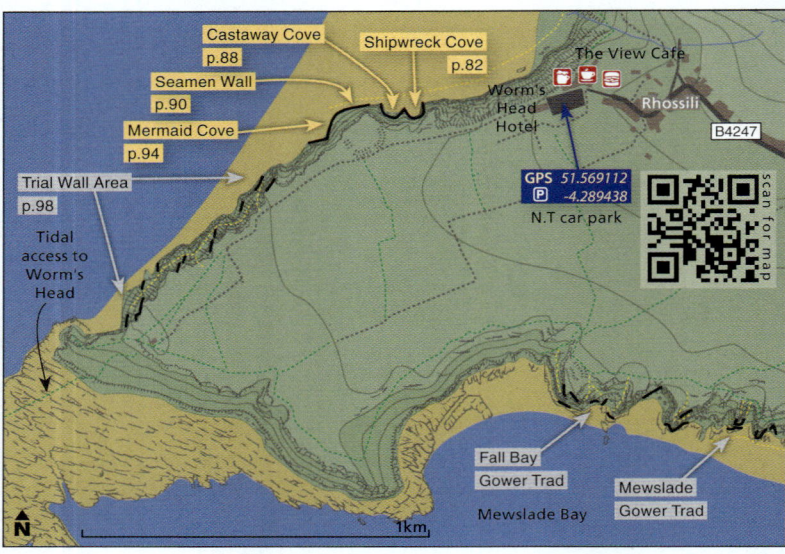

Black Wall and Shipwreck Cove - Accessible for around 3 hours either side of low water.
Castaway Cove and Seamen Wall - Accessible for around 2.5 hours either side of low water.
Mermaid Cove - Accessible for around 2 hours either side of low water.

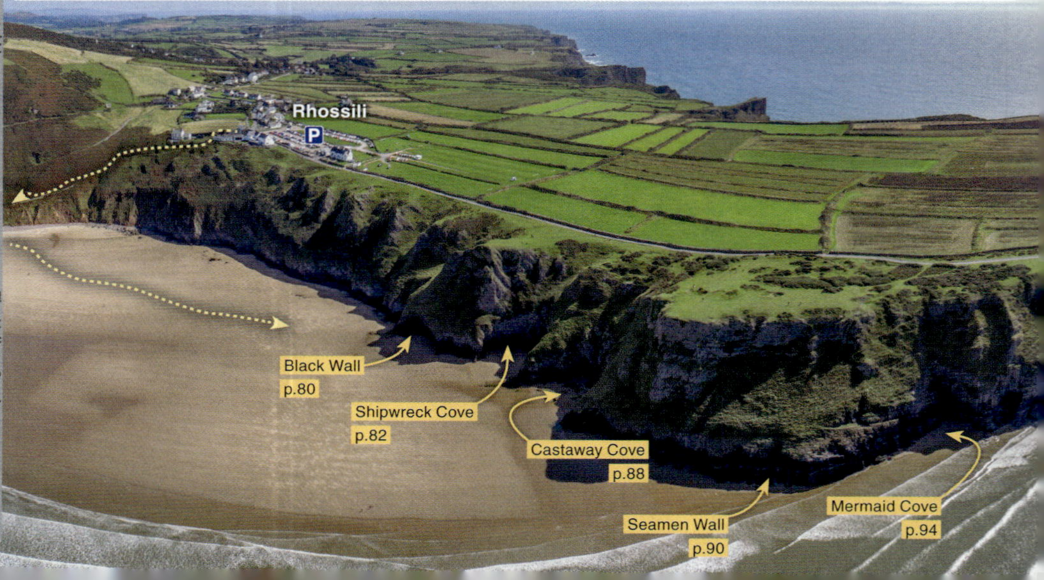

Rhossili Beach

Naomi Buys on *Air Show* (8a+) - *p.84* - at Shipwreck Cove, Rhossili Beach. Shipwreck Cove has been extensively developed and is now the focal point of hard sport climbing on Gower. Photo: Keith Sharples

Access
Be aware that this is a busy beach - make sure other users are aware of the dangers of falling rock and please watch your language.

Conditions
Sandy bases at all the crags means that a rope bag and mat are very useful. First bolts are high and the sand level varies so a clip-stick is very handy. At times it can be helpful to allow time for the sun to dry the rock and eradicate any lingering moisture.

Rhossili Beach

Royston Thomas on the upper section of *Holds May Spin* (5b) - *p.96* - at Mermaid Cove, Rhossili Beach. Mermaid Cove is the best of the Rhossili Beach crags for those looking for plenty of climbing in the lower and mid grades. The location is sublime as long as the weather and tides aline, however keep a watchful eye out for the incoming tide as a dry-footed walk back to the car is quickly cut-off! Photo: Mark Glaister

Rhossili Beach — Black Wall

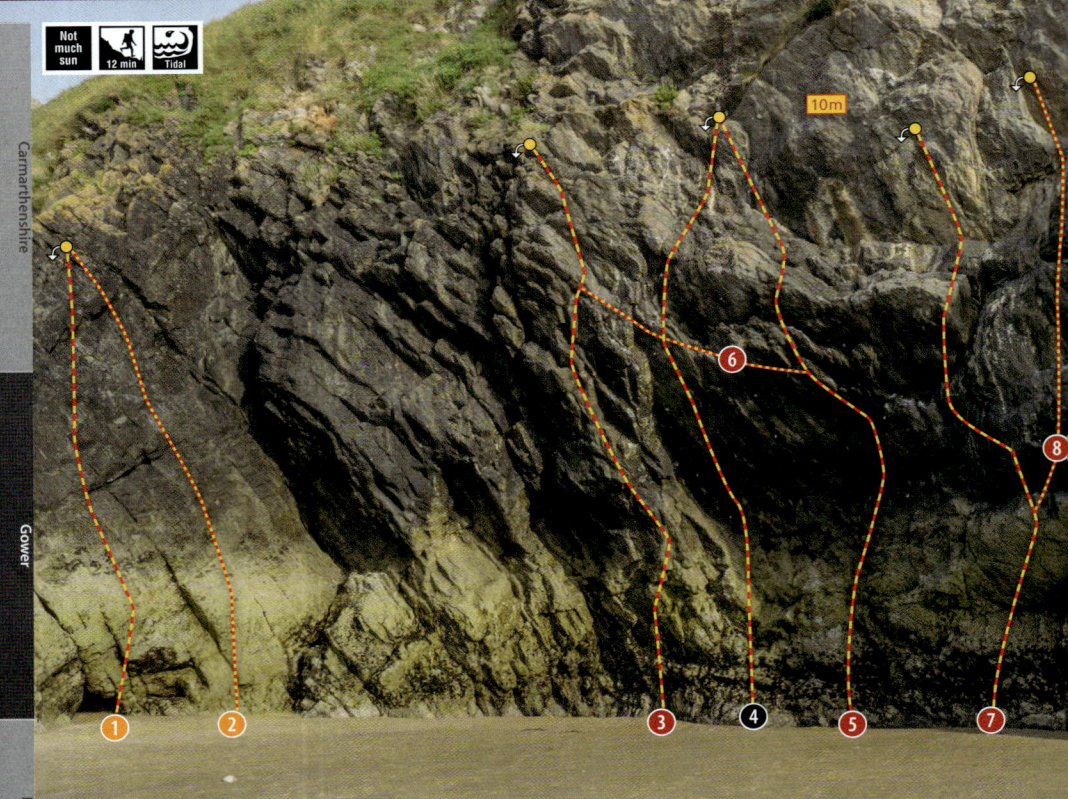

Black Wall
A short overhanging wall with some tough lines. It is the first of the beach crags to be clear of water, so is useful if waiting for the tide to retreat.
Approach (map and overview p.76) and Tides - Accessible for 3 hours either side of low water.
Conditions - The wall gets little sun except very early and late in the day during summer months. There is some possibility of climbing during rain, but the routes are harder in humid/greasy conditions.

1 Thieving Little Parasites — 6a
The left-hand line on the angled wall. Start steeply up diagonal breaks and then head more easily up right to a lower-off.
FA. R.Thomas 5.2014

2 Wittle Thieving Lankers — 5a
The right-hand line on the angled wall to the shared lower-off.
FA. R.Thomas 5.2014

3 Fats Waller — 6c+
The slim leaning corner is a fine but short-looking line. However, its bite is tougher than its bark!
FA. R.Lamey 26.8.2012

4 The Route with Two Pockets — 7b
Easy climbing leads to the steep wall that has only two pockets to cover a large distance.
FA. S.Rawlinson 8.2012

5 Black Adder — 6c
Small edges lead to a steep finale, which thankfully delivers large holds when they are needed. Easy once you know how, but harder for the short. *Photo opposite*.
FA. S.Rawlinson 8.2012

6 This ain't Pretty — 6c+
A link-up. From near the end of *Black Adder* traverse left along the rail to finish up *Fats Waller*.
FA. S.Rawlinson 10.3.2014

7 The Strongbow Flyer — 6b
An awkward start leads to some less-than-brilliant climbing. Much harder if the sand level is low.
FA. S.Rawlinson 8.2012

8 Rum Thieves — 6b+
Much better than its neighbour. Move directly up the smooth shield on good edges and side-pulls. Much harder if the sand level is low.
FA. S.Rawlinson 8.2012

Nicola Taylor on *Black Adder* (6c) - *opposite* - at Black Wall. As with all the sectors at Rhossili Beach, sandy bases are the norm and a plastic sheet or rope-bucket are useful additions to your climbing paraphernalia. Photo: Simon Rawlinson

Rhossili Beach — Shipwreck Cove

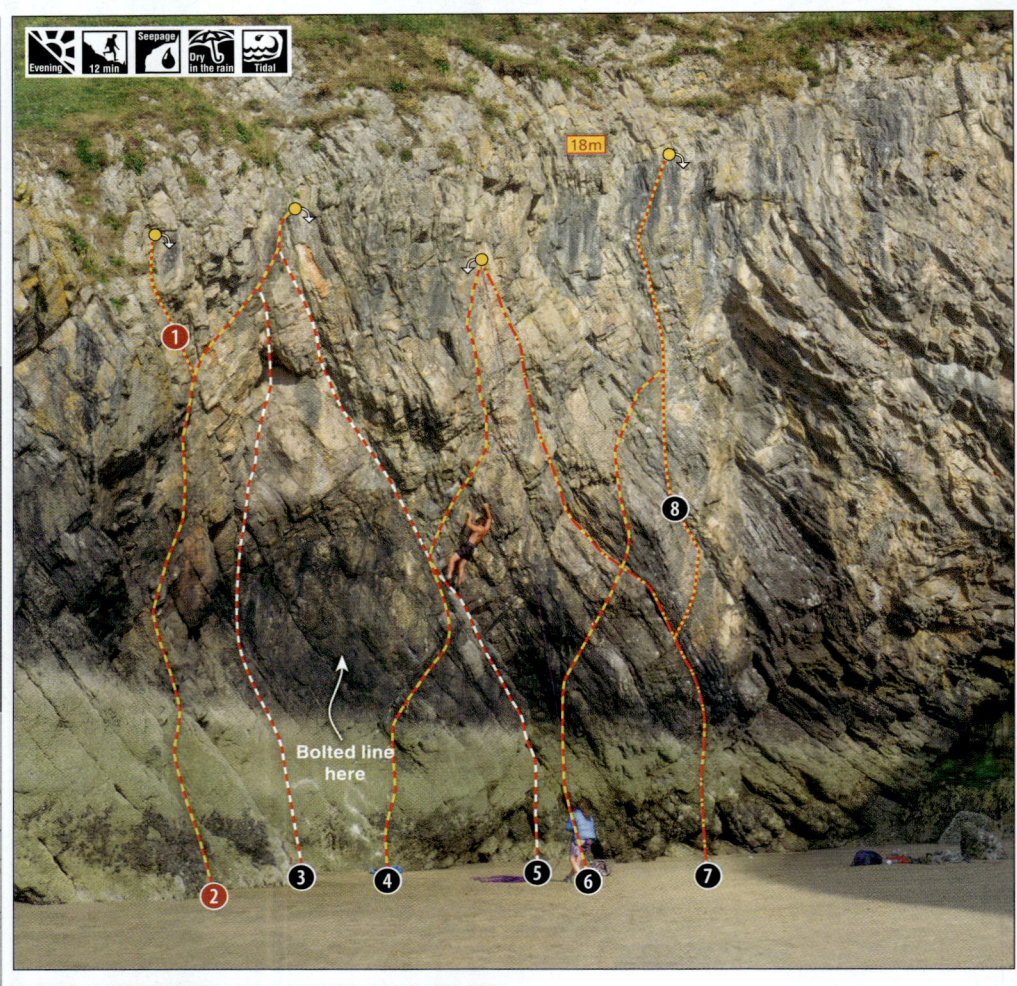

Shipwreck Cove

Shipwreck Cove is a brilliant sport climbing destination with some excellent routes from the mid grade 7s to high 8s. Most of the rock is sound, clean and STEEP! The far side of the cove has some good routes in the 6s that are best attempted in non-humid conditions or in the early morning sun. Some of the lines can be a touch sandy. Although tidal, the amount of time that access is possible will normally be longer than your arms will last out!

Approach (map and overview p.76) and Tides
- Accessible for 3 hours either side of low water. Wading in gives a little more time at the crag as the sand level in the cove is slightly higher than that crossed on the approach.

Conditions - The cove sees sun in the morning and evening and is often in condition during the drier months. It does seep after prolonged rainfall. Climbing during rainfall is possible. It can retain greasiness in some damp weather and is best if there is a light breeze to dry it out.

❶ **Stuart's Line Left Finish..** 6c
The left-hand finish to *Where Has Stu Gone?* takes the final sting out of the mother line. Not quite as good but more balanced.

❷ **Where Has Stu Gone?.** 6c+
A good introduction to the style of climbing on this wall, with a tough final few moves to reach the lower-off.

❸ **Mutiny Crack** E4 5c
The overhanging crack and niche is a butch mission. Some threads require long slings.
FA. S.Rawlinson 11.2012

❹ **Wrecking Ball** ... 7b
A pitch of three parts - a fingery thin crack followed by some steep pulls to a puzzling finish. *Photo opposite*.
FA. R.Lamey 1.9.2012

Rhossili Beach 83

Steve Marsh embarking on the steep pulls to leave the ramp on *Wrecking Ball* (7b) - *opposite* - at Shipwreck Cove, Rhossili Beach Photo: Elis Rees

❺ Attrition......... **E5 6a**
The long right-to-left leaning crack-line builds to a very steep ending and lower-off.
FA. P.Littlejohn 1997

❻ Bootneck.......... **7c**
Head up steep ground crossing *Marine Layer* to join and finish as for *One Ton Depot*. A good **7b** variant is to finish just before the final wall. Lower-off from the bolt.
FA. M.Richards 27.8.2017. FA. (Variant) A.Sharp 2017

❼ Marine Layer........ **7a+**
An unusual pitch - strenuous and with some varied sequences along the way.
FA. R.Lamey 25.5.2013

❽ One Ton Depot........ **7c**
A big line that saves its crux for the very top, though there are some good rests on the way. Start up *Marine Layer*.
FA. R.Lamey 9.8.2012

Rhossili Beach — Shipwreck Cove

⑨ Vennerne 8a
A superb pitch named after the wreck of the ship 'Vennerne', the remains of which are visible in Castaway Cove.
FA. R.Lamey 11.8.2012

⑩ Air Show .... 8a+
An incredibly sustained line with a few tricky moves thrown in. Start as for *Vennerne* and head right. *Photo p.77*.
FA. A.Berry 7.7.2013

⑪ Euro Fighter 8b
Climb *Air Show* past its crux (at half height), then move right into the finish of *Helvetia*.
FA. D.Pickford 2014

⑫ Helvetia .... 8b+
Not your typical British hard route, more European in style. A hard crux guards the upper wall which is unrelenting in difficulty. The route is named after the shipwreck on the main beach. *Photo p.39*.
FA. B.West 19.8.2014

⑬ Hellshow 8b
Climb *Helvetia* to its the twin undercuts. Move left from here and finish up *Airshow*.
FA. L.Jones 28.7.2021

⑭ Gunshow .... 8a+
Start up *Helvetia*, moving left to join *Air Show* at its fourth bolt. Now follow *Air Show* to below the final overlap before traversing out left to finish as for *Vennerne*.
FA. D.Pickford 2014

⑮ Armada 8b
Climb *Helvetia* to its large side pull, from where a powerful rightwards traverse gains two pinches and a blind slap for the jug at the end of the *Delta Dagger* crux. Finish up *Delta Dagger*.
FA. S.Clarke 2.6.2022

⑯ Delta Dagger .... 8a+
Steep! Upgraded following hold loss. *Photo p.87*.
FA. D.Pickford 15.8.2014

⑰ Fata Morgana 8b
Climb *Delta Dagger* to its fifth bolt and then break left into *Helvetia*, which is climbed to the rest before its final crux on two undercuts. Now move left again to finish up *Air Show*.
FA. D.Pickford 5.2016

⑱ Hell Dagger .... 8b+
Climb *Fata Morgana* to the knee-bar rest on *Helvetia*, finish as for *Helvetia*.
FA. S.McClure 2016

The route Cannonade has suffered a rock fall and is unstable.

⑲ Achilles' Wrath 8b
The central line through the super-steep wall is a wrestling match from start to finish! Knee bars and heel hooks are just some of the trickery required for success! *Photo p.16*.
FA. S.Rawlinson 11.2012

⑳ Hector Protector............... 8b
Climb easily up to a hole and then out over the roof. Traverse up left to finish as for *Achilles Wrath*. Rules are...Stay off the big resting holds/knee bar on *King George verses the Suffragettes*.
FA. S.Rawlinson 11.2012

Shipwreck Cove **Rhossili Beach**

Bolted lines here are not described owing to loose rock

㉓ King George verses the Suffragettes .... 7a+
A tricky start involving a wobbly jug leads through some impressive terrain. Move right to finish up the grey ramp.
FA. S.Rawlinson 2013

㉔ Cocky Black Chauffage 6c
A long rising traverse following the lower of two breaks which can only be stripped on a top-rope.
FA. A.Berry 2014

㉕ Cross Incontinents 6c
Continue along the upper of the two breaks. Can only be stripped on a top-rope.
FA. A.Berry 2014

㉖ Tsunami 8c
The massive rising traverse. Start up *King George*... and then *Hector Protector Right-hand* to the *Achilles' Wrath* undercut flake. Break left (do not gain the lip) to a jug on *Cannonade*, then turn the lip and span to the large hanging block above *Delta Dagger*. Layback along the block to twin pinches on *Armada* from where a hard traverse left joins *Helvetia* at its 'Spock' hold. Continue as for *Fata Morgana* and on past the crux of *Air Show*. Stay low and continue left to finish up *Gun Show*.
FA. S.Clarke 3.8.2024

Cannonade - unstable

㉑ Hector Rejector 8a
Start as for *Hector Protector*, but at its 5th bolt break right and finish as for *King George verses the Suffragettes*.
FA. S.McClure 1.8.2022

㉒ Hector Protector Right-hand Start 8a+
Start up *King George verses the Suffragettes*.

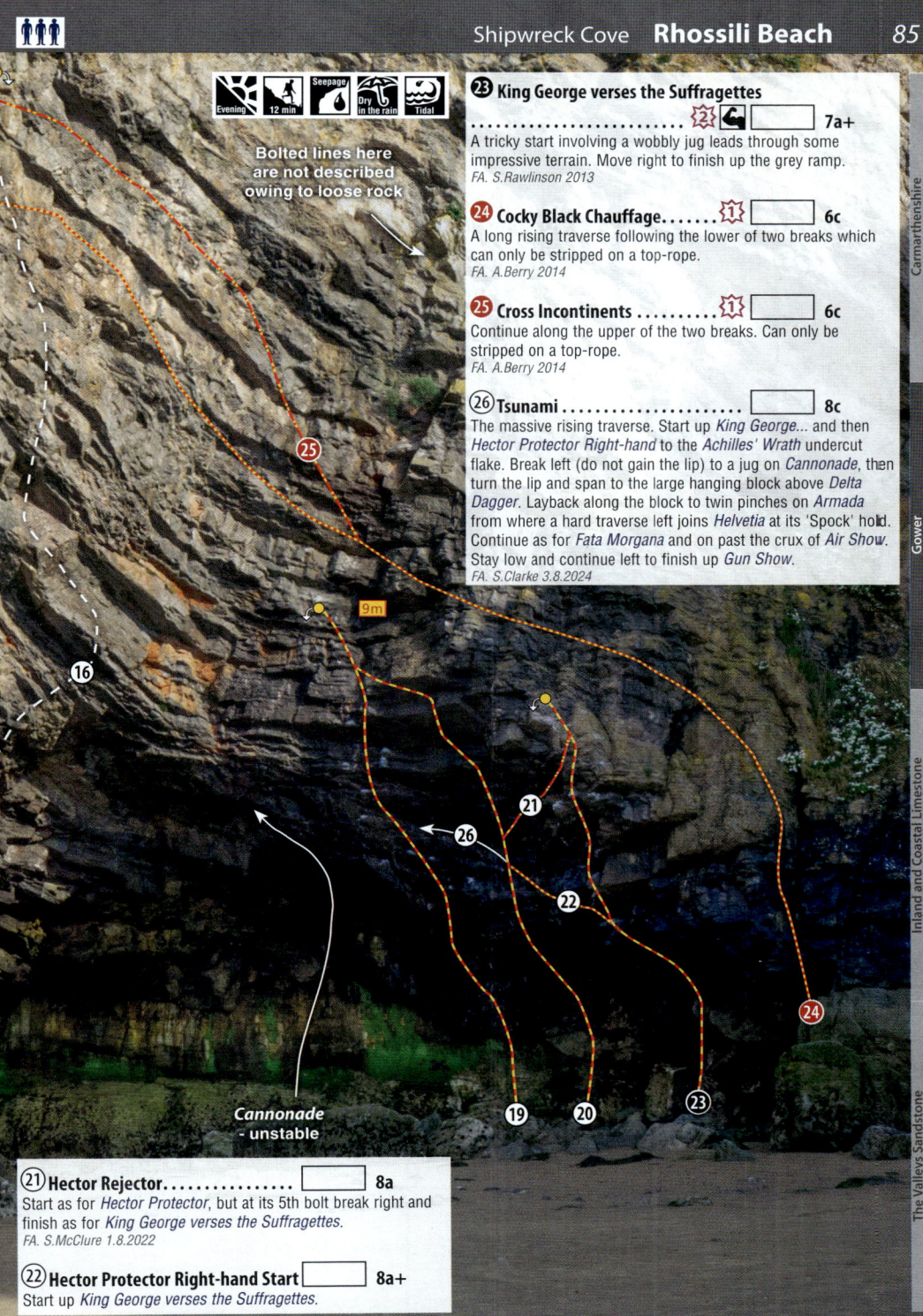

Rhossili Beach — Shipwreck Cove

㉗ Blockiness .... 6c+
Good and steep - especially at the start. Things become a little more technical higher up.
FA. R.Lamey 1.6.2013

㉘ Sand Man 6b
Climb up to the corners. It can be very sandy at times but, if clean, it is a good pitch.
FA. S.Rawlinson 2013

㉙ Par 3 .... 6c
Climb the lower wall to a steep mid-height section that leads to a final pull to the lower-off. A good route that stays free of sand.
FA. S.Rawlinson 2013

㉚ John's Route .... 6b+
Start up a ramp before heading up the wall and past the left side of the small cave. Sustained climbing.
FA. J.Bullock, R.Thomas 10.2013

㉛ First Handout .... 6a+
Pleasing climbing passing the ramp and niche to a lower-off out to the right and lower than that of *John's Route*.
FA. R.Thomas, J.Bullock 10.2013

㉜ Hand Shandy/Make a Splash .... 6a+
The right-hand line moving leftwards to a shared lower-off with *First Handout*.
FA. R.Thomas 2013

Ollie Torr cutting loose on the tough *Delta Dagger* (8a+) - *p.84* - at Shipwreck Cove, Rhossili Beach. Photo: Elis Rees

Rhossili Beach — Castaway Cove

Castaway Cove

The cove is adjacent to Shipwreck Cove and has some easier lines on generally good rock.

Approach (map and overview p.76) **and Tides**
- Accessible for 2.5 hours either side of low water.

Conditions - The climbs get sun in the morning on the right-hand side, and on summer evenings on the left. There is no possibility of climbing in the rain.

1 Top Drawer 5c
The left-hand side of the slab via a couple of small roofs.
FA. D.Emanuel, R.Thomas 10.2014

2 Bottom Drawers 6b
Follow the easy slab, then make harder moves to pass the overhang and finish at the same lower-off as *Top Drawer*. *Photo p.93*.
FA. R.Thomas, D.Emanuel 10.2014

3 Dirty Drawers .... 6b+
The right side of the slab past two small roofs. A steep start.
FA. R.Thomas, E.Rees 5.7.2015

4 Sticky Tissue Issue .... 7a+
The left-hand side of the wall over the bulge to a shared lower-off.
FA. Rossili Bolt Project c.2014

5 La Doux Parfum de la Lingerie Utilisé 6c
Cross the bulge to the right of *Sticky Tissue Issue*.
FA. D.Emanuel, R.Thomas 10.2014

6 Secret Drawers 5b
The corner is not recommended.
FA. D.Emanuel, R.Thomas 6.2014

7 Cast Me Away 6c
Climb the overhanging rib and shallow groove to an out-there and difficult finale.
FA. G.Gibson 3.6.2016

Castaway Cove — Rhossili Beach

⑧ Grazed and Transfused .... 6a+
The pleasant steep slab by a rib. Move right into *Dry Blood Beast* and finish up it.
FA. R.Thomas, G.Gibson 5.6.2016

⑨ Dry Blood Beast 6a
Climb the right side of the cave. Low in the grade.
FA. D.Emanuel, R.Thomas 6.2014

⑩ The Clot Thickens .... 6a+
The fine slab and wall via a prominent short crack.
FA. R.Thomas, G.Gibson 5.6.2016

⑪ Cracker Barrel .... 6b+
The short steep wall and shallow groove.
FA. G.Gibson 7.2016

⑫ Catching Fire .... 6c+
Follow the steep rib, overhanging wall and final overlap.
FA. G.Gibson 7.2016

⑬ Cinders Catch 6a
A nice pitch up the black rock on good but fairly spaced finger edges at first. Finish left of a small shattered corner.
FA. D.Emanuel, R.Thomas 6.2014

⑭ Dirty Innuendo 5c
Climb the black wall and then move left to join *Cinders Catch* just below its shattered corner.
FA. R.Thomas, D.Emanuel 6.2014

⑮ Geez Louise 5c
A teasing little exercise. Climb easily to the final wall and move up it before stepping right to the lower-off avoiding the ledge on the right.
FA. R.Thomas, D.Emanuel 6.2014

⑯ Mini the Minx 5a
A short but pleasant wall.
FA. R.Thomas, G.Gibson 3.6.2016

Rhossili Beach — Seamen Wall

Seamen Wall
A wide, short wall with some steep sections which runs between Castaway Cove and Mermaid Cove.
Approach (map and overview p.76) and Tides - Accessible for 2.5 hours either side of low water.
Conditions - The wall gets some early morning and late afternoon sun in the summer months. There is no possibility of climbing during rain.

1 Bored of Toad Hall 6a
An isolated line on the right-hand side of the first cave.
FA. D.Emanuel, R.Thomas 9.2014

2 The King's Shilling ... 6b
The overhanging crack in the bay.
FA. D.Emanuel, R.Thomas 10.2014

3 Captain Jacque Hoff ..... 6b+
A direct assault on the overhang via its right-hand side, finishing at the same lower-off as *The King's Shilling*.
FA. R.Thomas, D.Emanuel 27.9.2014

4 Concrete Cows 6a
Start up the corner via a roof with a hard start.
FA. R.Thomas, D.Emanuel 9.2014

5 Smeaton's Stump 5c
Enter the corner from the right more easily.
FA. R.Thomas, D.Emanuel 10.2014

6 Good Ship Venus 5c
Climb right of the crack, stepping left to the lower-off.
FA. D.Emanuel, R.Thomas 10.2014

7 Lamisil 6a
The pleasant face and juggy overhang.
FA. G.Gibson 7.2016

8 Zeuwit 6b
An easy start precedes a tricky black face.
FA. G.Gibson 7.2016

9 Atraumen 5b
The shallow black groove.
FA. G.Gibson 7.2016

Seamen Wall Rhossili Beach

10 El Cino 4b
The shallow groove.
FA. G.Gibson 7.2016

11 Frappacino 4b
A shallow groove and slab.
FA. G.Gibson 7.2016

12 Pure Cino .... ☆ 4b
The blunt rib and face.
FA. G.Gibson 7.2016

13 Giraffacino 5c
A steady black slab and final overlap.
FA. G.Gibson 7.2016

14 Elephantacino 6a
The black slab and overlaps.
FA. G.Gibson 7.2016

15 Catapult .... ☆ 4b
The square-cut rib is very good.
FA. G.Gibson, R.Thomas 5.6.2016

16 Schengen .... ☆ 4b
Climb direct via a shallow groove.
FA. G.Gibson, R.Thomas 5.6.2016

17 Border Control .... ☆ 4b
The pleasant wall right of *Schengen*.
FA. G.Gibson, R.Thomas 5.6.2016

18 Checkpoint Checkout ..... ☆ 5b
The shallow black groove.
FA. G.Gibson 5.6.2016

19 Ma Maid's Mermaid .... ☆ 5b
A shallow groove and pleasant finishing slab.
FA. G.Gibson 4.6.2016

20 Andre Marriner 5b
The black right-facing corner.
FA. G.Gibson 4.6.2016

21 Marinieri .... 6a+
The smooth looking black face.
FA. G.Gibson 4.6.2016

Rhossili Beach — Seamen Wall

㉒ Black Sea Shanty .... ☐ **5a**
Take the easy wall to gain and finish up a pleasant shallow groove.
FA. G.Gibson, R.Thomas 7.8.2016

㉓ Sea Shanty Rib .... ☐ **4b**
Climb up the blunt rib to a tricky clip at the lower-off.
FA. G.Gibson, R.Thomas 7.8.2016

㉔ Seaman's Sea Shanty .... ☐ **5a**
The arete and shallow groove.
FA. G.Gibson, R.Thomas 7.8.2016

㉕ Seaman in the Groove .... 🔒 ☐ **5b**
The groove gives an excellent little line.
FA. G.Gibson, R.Thomas 7.8.2016

㉖ Them's Be Barnacles, Them's Be .... 🔒 ☐ **6a**
The fine arete finishing at a lower-off on the right.
FA. G.Gibson, R.Thomas 7.8.2016

㉗ No Tar .... 🔒 ☐ **5a**
The right-hand finish to *Them's Be Barnacles, Them's Be*.
FA. G.Gibson, R.Thomas 7.8.2016

㉘ Operation Seaman .... ☐ **5a**
Climb the arete right of the deep chimney.
FA. G.Gibson, R.Thomas 7.8.2016

㉙ Me Harty's .... 🔒 ☐ **4b**
Follow the pleasant rib and fine black wall.
FA. G.Gibson, R.Thomas 7.8.2016

㉚ Seaman Limbo .... 🔒 ☐ **6a**
The excellent right arete of the wall.
FA. G.Gibson, R.Thomas 7.8.2016

㉛ Kickback Tar .... ☐ **4b**
The wall and shallow black groove.
FA. G.Gibson, R.Thomas 7.8.2016

㉜ Barnacle Bill .... 🔒 ☐ **6a**
Good climbing up the side-wall of the chimney.
FA. R.Thomas, G.Gibson 7.8.2016

㉝ Whispering Whelks .... 🔒 ☐ **4a**
The blunt rib is a nice outing.
FA. R.Thomas, G.Gibson 7.8.2016

㉞ Pump My Bilge .... 🔒 ☐ **6a**
The wall and overhang tucked into the back of the recess.
FA. R.Thomas, G.Gibson 7.8.2016

㉟ All Hands on the Sea Cocks ...... ☐ **3a**
Follow the easy wall and well-positioned rib above.
FA. G.Gibson, R.Thomas 7.8.2016

Rhossili Beach

Catrin Rose on the short but technical *Bottom Drawers* (6b) - *p.88* - at Castaway Cove. Beyond the hard routes at Shipwreck Cove, the Rhossili Beach sectors offer plenty of climbing in the lower grades and are a perfect destination for those who are just getting started or those who like mixing beach and climbing life. Photo: Marsha Balaeva

Rhossili Beach — Mermaid Cove

Mermaid Cove

A lovely isolated cove which features a fine line-up of lower-grade sport climbs on good rock. The right-hand wall of the cove is much steeper and the barnacles are more of a hindrance on the starts. It is probably best to climb on the right-hand side of the cove in the morning when the sun has been on the wall.

Approach (map and overview p.76) - Walk out across the beach and the cove is just beyond the Seamen Wall.

Tides - Accessible for 2 hours either side of low water. Keep an eye on the water level as access for those hoping to stay dry is quickly cut off!

Conditions - The wall gets the sun from mid-afternoon onwards.

Evening | 14 min | Tidal

❶ Crass Word Pizzle — 4a
A low-angled slab that is quite pleasant but has a run-out on easy ground to reach the lower-off out to the right.
FA. R.Thomas, N.O'Neill 4.2014

❷ Landlubber — 4a
Straightforward climbing direct to a shared lower-off.
FA. Rhossili bolt project 2014

❸ The Naughty Corner — 4a
The corner, moving right to the belay shared with *Ursula*.
FA. Rhossili bolt project 2014

❹ Ursula — 4a
Climb the wall right of *The Naughty Corner* to a shared lower-off.
FA. Rhossili bolt project 2014

❺ Ceasg — 4a
An independent line up the wall via large and thin cracks.
FA. Rhossili bolt project 2014

❻ Turtle Apocalypse — 4a
The wall right of the cracks of *Ceasg*.
FA. Rhossili bolt project 2014

❼ No Father Day — 5c
Follow the slab passing a hard move using a crystal pocket.
FA. R.Thomas R.Phillips 2014

❽ Lara — 5a
The edge right of the slender groove. A nice line.
FA. J.Squire, S.Rawlinson 2014

❾ Scurvy Dog — 5c
The centre of the pillar left of the first cut-out.
FA. J.Squire, S.Rawlinson 2014

❿ Crimp Paddle — 6b+
Start up *Paternal Love* and then pull out left onto the wall above.
FA. S.Rawlinson, J.Squire 2014

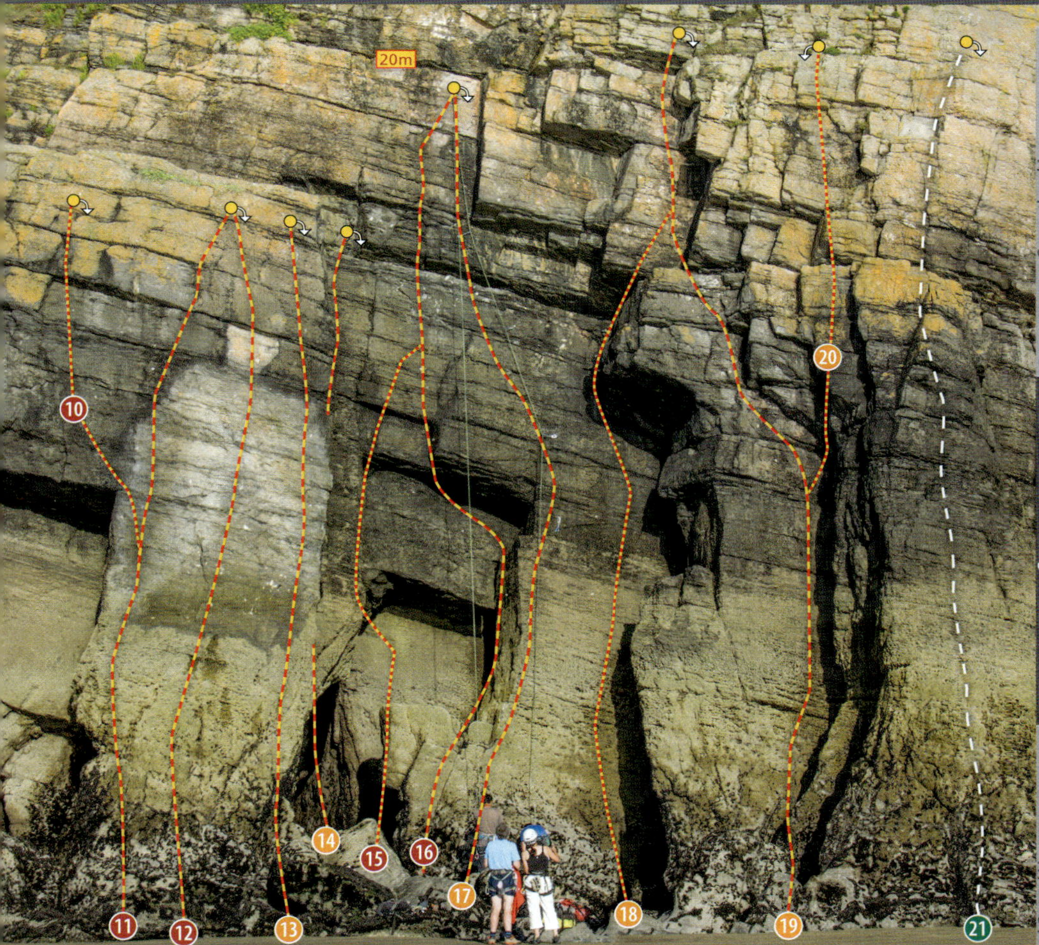

11 Paternal Love .... 1 star 6b
Follow the left edge of the pale pillar and wall above.
FA. R.Thomas, R.Phillips 2014

12 Bye Dad .... 2 stars 6b+
An excellent series of moves up the centre of the pillar.
FA. R.Thomas, R.Phillips 7.2014

13 Filial Duty .... 1 star 5c
A tough number that takes the right-hand arete of the pillar.
FA. R.Thomas, R.Phillips 7.2014

14 Fought to the End .... 1 star 5c
The hanging groove right of the pillar.
FA. R.Thomas, R.Phillips 2014

15 This Vicar's Tea Party .... 1 star 6b+
Mount the ledge then climb the sidewall via some tricky moves to join *Stingray* above its crux.
FA. R.Thomas 2014

16 Stingray .... 1 star 6c
Move up to and boulder through the block overhang.
FA. Rhossili bolt project 2014

17 Lemon Soul .... 3 stars 6a
A lovely pitch. Climb the arete and continue up the face before moving left to finish up a short groove.
FA. Rhossili bolt project 2014

18 A Mermaid's Tale .... 2 stars 5b
Climb left of the chimney, moving right to finish up a groove.
FA. A.Berry 2014

19 Dawson's Corner .... 3 stars 5a
Start up left of a chimney crack and then follow the exposed corner on superb holds.
FA. A.Berry 2014

20 Dawsons Creek .... 2 stars 5b
Start up *Dawson's Corner* and finish direct.
FA. G.Jenkin 2014

Rhossili Beach — Mermaid Cove

21 Fistful of Tenners 4c
The line of the cove. Climb the front of the narrow pillar and finish up the short tricky wall above.
FA. R.Thomas, E.Travers-Jones 2014

22 Under the Mattress .. 6a+
Climb to a high roof and pull onto the upper wall to finish at a lower-off on the right.
FA. R.Thomas, E.Travers-Jones 2014

23 Cash in the Attic 5b
Climb up to, and surmount a bulge to reach the upper wall.
FA. R.Thomas, E.Travers-Jones 2014

24 Holds May Spin 5b
Move up a corner to a break. Finish leftwards. *Photo p.78*.
FA. G.Jenkin 2014

25 Probate Pending............. 3b
Gain a ledge and finish up a slight left-facing corner and wall.
FA. R.Thomas, A.Howe 2014

26 Pysgodwibblywobbly 5a
Climb the short wall and arete. The name is Welsh for jellyfish.
FA. D.Emanuel 2014

27 Names from Roger's Profanisorous
.... 5b
Climb to the ledge and continue to a shared belay on the left.
FA. R.Thomas 2014

28 Al Perchino 4b
Climb the wall to a lower-off shared with *Scuttle*.
FA. D.Emanuel 2014

29 Scuttle 4b
A similar pitch to *Al Perchino*.
FA. D.Emanuel 2014

30 The Trevena Fish Hotel 4b
A longer slabby pitch left of the huge corner.
FA. D.Emanuel 2014

31 Scarfish 5c
A line on the upper wall, the belay of which is on a ledge best reached via *Al Perchino*.
FA. D.Emanuel 2014

Mermaid Cove — Rhossili Beach

32 The Naughty Step — 6a+
Start up *The Trevena Fish Hotel* and then move right and climb the sustained groove. Intimidating.
FA. R.Thomas, R.Phillips 16.8.2014

33 The Naughty Step Direct Start — 6b
The direct start is very bouldery.
FA. R.Thomas, R.Phillips 16.8.2014

34 A Mermaid's Footwork — 6b
The left-hand line up the pillar to the left of the wide crack.
FA. R.Thomas, R.Phillips 16.8.2014

35 Flounder — 6b
Climb just to the left of the wide crack to a shared lower-off.
FA. R.Thomas 16.8.2014

36 Somewhere in Her Smile She Knows — 6b+
The centre of the leaning pillar on pockets, then the face above.
FA. R.Thomas 16.8.2014

37 Besetting Fears — 6a
Follow the pocketed pillar to join *Somewhere in her Smile She Knows* close to the top.
FA. D.Emanuel, R.Thomas 6.2014

38 Horse Flavoured Shadows — 5c
Climb to a large ledge and then take the arete.
FA. D.Emanuel, R.Thomas 6.2014

39 Triton Left — 5b
The left-hand finish.
FA. D.Emanuel, R.Thomas 6.2014

40 Triton Right — 5b
The right-hand finish.
FA. D.Emanuel, R.Thomas 6.2014

Trial Wall Area

The Trial Wall Area encompasses a collection of crags located at the southwest tip of Gower. The venue is sandwiched between the intriguing geological feature of Worm's Head and the vast expanse of Rhossili Beach. The majority of the sport climbing is on excellent vertical rock, and spans the full grade range. The crags are non-tidal and can be climbed on throughout the year. This is a fine place to climb in its own right but makes a good alternative should the Rhossili Beach crags be out of condition or whilst waiting for the tide to allow the approach to be negotiated.

Approach
All of the Trial Wall Area cliffs are approached from the large National Trust car park (fee) at Rhossili village.

Tides
The Trial Wall Area cliffs are non-tidal and easily combined with the Rhossili Beach cliffs.

Conditions
The Trial Wall Area is a reliable year round destination with little in the way of seepage and receiving sun in the afternoon.

Trial Wall Area

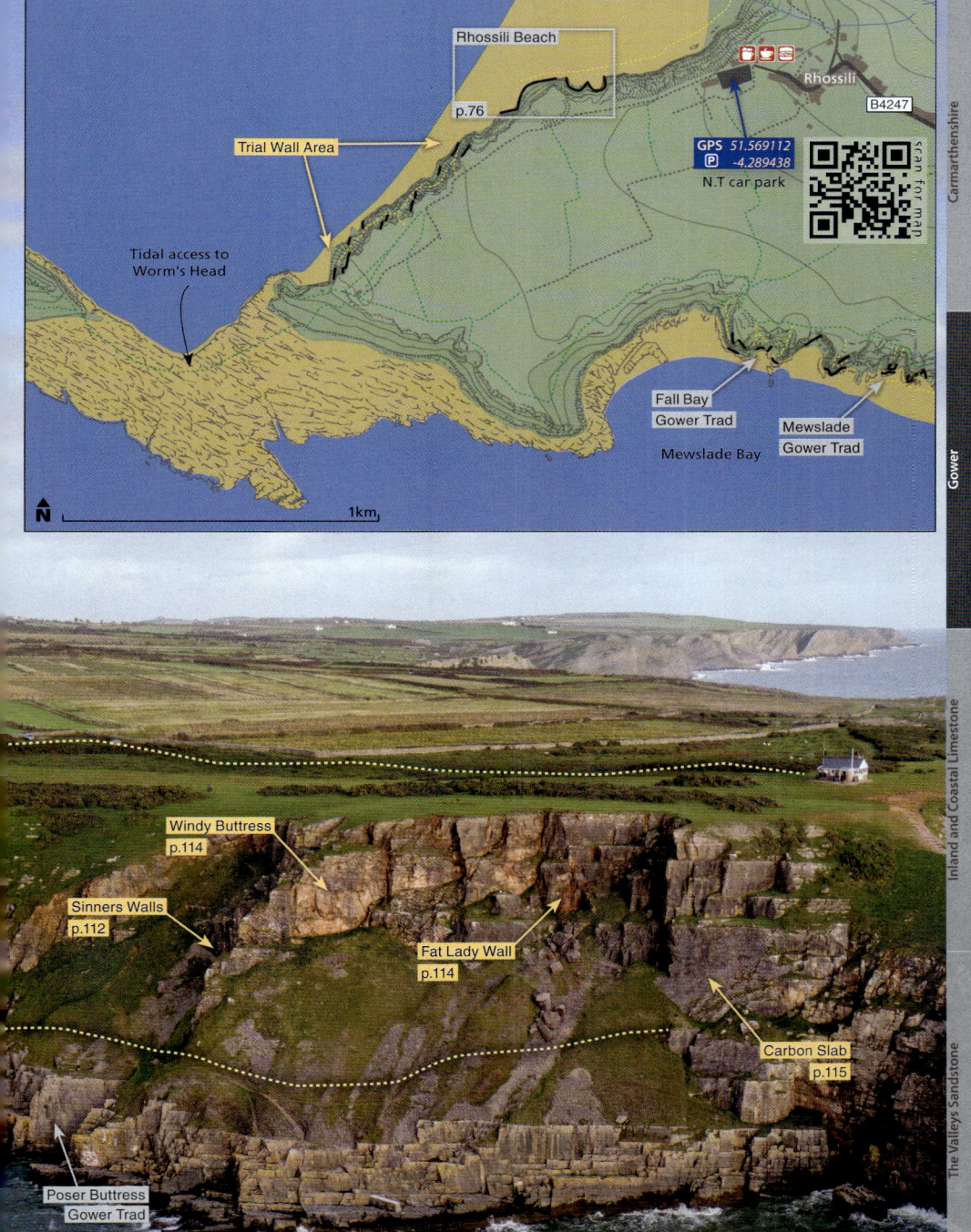

Trial Wall Area

James Eves beginning *Blockbuster* (5c) - *p.105* - on Lifebuoy Buttress at the Trial Wall Area. This area has been well developed in recent times. Not only are there more climbs, but the diversity in styles now also encompasses slabs, cracks and aretes enhancing what was previously just a wall climbing destination. Photo: Mark Glaister

Trial Wall and Retribution Wall

The Trial Wall is one of the older sport crags on Gower that has some tremendous pitches which require good technique and finger strength. Just to the left is the Retribution Wall that has some popular easier lines. Both walls are fairly sheltered facing northwest and there is little chance of staying dry in the rain.

Approach (map and overview p.99) - Leave the car park on the road/track towards Worm's Head. After about 10 minutes the track bends left. Head right, to the edge of the cliff and the wall can be seen down on the right. The Retribution Wall is just around the corner from the Trial Wall.

Access - There is usually a restriction here due to nesting birds. The dates may change, as may the extent, but it is usually from April to the end of July. Check signs at the crag and BMC RAD.

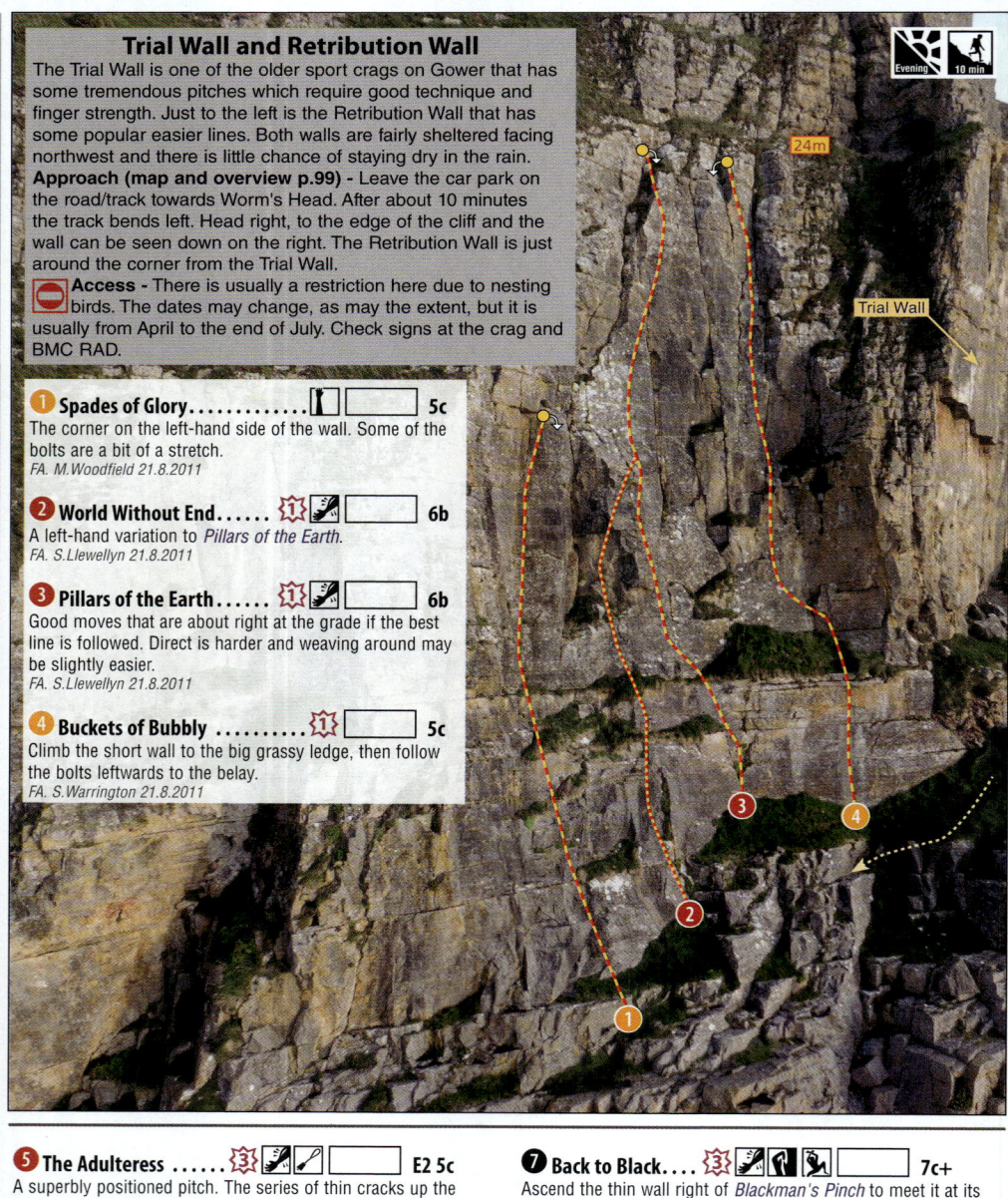

❶ Spades of Glory............ 5c
The corner on the left-hand side of the wall. Some of the bolts are a bit of a stretch.
FA. M.Woodfield 21.8.2011

❷ World Without End...... 6b
A left-hand variation to *Pillars of the Earth*.
FA. S.Llewellyn 21.8.2011

❸ Pillars of the Earth...... 6b
Good moves that are about right at the grade if the best line is followed. Direct is harder and weaving around may be slightly easier.
FA. S.Llewellyn 21.8.2011

❹ Buckets of Bubbly 5c
Climb the short wall to the big grassy ledge, then follow the bolts leftwards to the belay.
FA. S.Warrington 21.8.2011

❺ The Adulteress E2 5c
A superbly positioned pitch. The series of thin cracks up the left-hand side of the wall with a difficult section to pass the overhang. Above the overhang traverse right to finish up the bolted crack of *Blackman's Pinch*.
FFA. A.Sharp, J.Harwood 8.11.1981

❻ Blackman's Pinch .... 6c+
The wall, narrow overhang and crack is a tremendous pitch that features some thin pulls on the crux. *Photo p.74*.
FFA. A.Sharp, J.Harwood 5.12.1981

❼ Back to Black.... 7c+
Ascend the thin wall right of *Blackman's Pinch* to meet it at its narrow overhang. From the break after the crux of *Blackman's Pinch* move right and finishing up *Skull Attack*. Finishing up *Blackman's Pinch* is **7b+**.
FA. M.Richards, A.Sharp 14.4.2018

❽ Zealot.......... 7c+
From the third clip on *Back to Black* climb direct via a very thin set of holds (avoiding holds on *Blackman's Pinch*) or make a desperate rockover right to join *Skull Attack* at the overhang.
FA. D.Comley 25.5.2019

Trial Wall and Retribution Wall — **Trial Wall Area**

9 Under Attack .... 7a+
Begin up *Skull Attack* and traverse left under the overhang to join and finish up *Blackman's Pinch*.
FA. A.Sharp, S.Marsh 4.2017

10 Skull Attack 7c
The long thin wall and overlap is a stunning climb.
FA. A.Sharp, P.Lewis 15.4.1984

11 Retrobution 7b
A superb pitch of escalating difficulty that is high in the grade. Some thin moves link the initial groove of *Crime and Punishment* to the upper section of *Skull Attack*. Photo p.1.
FA. M.Richards, A.Sharp 5.1.2013

12 Crime and Punishment 7b
The natural line up the middle of the wall taking in some brilliant and varied climbing - classic. Upgraded due to hold loss.
FA. A.Sharp, J.Harwood 18.10.1981

13 Black Wall Direct 8a+
The blank wall and capping overhang is a fingery and powerful mission. The move to pass the overhang is the crux.
FA. A.Forster, A.Sharp 1988

14 Black Wall .... 7b+
The easier, right-hand finish to *Black Wall Direct*. Very good.
FA. A.Sharp 2011

15 Inch Pinch 7a
Finish direct above the start of *The Hant*.
FA. A.Sharp, P.Lewis 4.1987

16 The Hant 7a
Thin initial moves followed by some tricky climbing at the top.
FA. A.Sharp, P.Lewis 4.1987

17 Tribulations 7a
The balancy right edge of the crag via some techy moves.
FA. R.Thomas 20.9.1998

18 As You Were! .... 7b+
A rising leftward traverse. From the second bolt on *The Hant* move left to *Black Wall* and climb to its upper bulge. Move into *Crime and Punishment* at the bottom of its short wide crack, then make a tricky traverse left into the top groove of *Skull Attack*, and finish up it.
FA. M.Richards 14.10.2017

Trial Wall Area — Wedge Wall

Wedge Wall
A compact little wall of very good rock that gives brief but intense climbing on finger edges.

Approach (map and overview p.99) - Walk out of the National Trust car park on the road/track towards Worm's Head. After 10 minutes at a point where the track bends left head out right to the edge of the cliff and keep an eye out down on the right for the Trial Wall. Drop down to the Trial Wall and the Wedge Wall is 50m across the small scree slope in front of Trial Wall.

❶ The Fin End of the Wedge 5b
Deceptive. Balance up and left onto the arete. Climb the arete, move right and then pull up to a ledge and lower-off.
FA. S.Llewellyn 9.9.2011

❷ Wedgling 5c
Move up past a narrow ledge and either head up right to the lower-off (the tall persons way), or go up to the top of the wall and hand traverse right to the lower-off.
FA. S.Llewellyn 9.9.2011

❸ Wedge-egade Master 6a
Make a couple of insecure moves to gain and pass the second bolt, before better holds quickly lead to the lower-off.
FA. S.Llewellyn 9.9.2011

❹ Wedge Dew Bin...... 6a
The thin seam/crack is a pleasant line climbed via a series of crimps and ledges.
FA. M.Woodfield 9.9.2011

❺ Atomic Wedgie 5c
The right-hand line of bolts is a good wall climb. No bridging out right at the start.
FA. M.Woodfield 9.9.2011

Lifebuoy Buttress
A prominent fin of good rock that has an eye-catching arete. The sunless side of the fin also has some pitches.

Approach (map and overview p.99) - Walk out of the National Trust car park on the road/track towards Worm's Head. After 10 minutes at a point where the track bends left head out right to the edge of the cliff and keep an eye out down on the right for the Trial Wall. Drop down to the Trial Wall and the Wedge Wall is 50m across the small scree slope in front of Trial Wall. Continue for a further 100m to below the fin and the first line.

❻ Checking Lichen 4b
The arete of a moss covered wall.
FA. R.Thomas, T.Hoddy 4.10.2017

❼ Towers of Curon .... 6b+
A short bouldery start gains better holds in the crack (starting from the grass above a mossy slab) to a shared belay with *Whetstone*.
FA. R.Thomas 1.2018

Lifebuoy Buttress **Trial Wall Area**

8 **Whetstone**.................. 6b+
Left (flipside) of *The Axe* arete.
FA. R.Thomas, T.Hoddy 19.11.2017

9 **The Axe**............. E1 5a
The spectacular arete has little in the way of gear.
FA. T.Penning, A.Sharp, J.Harwood 26.5.1985

10 **Blockbuster**..... 5c
The bolt-line to the right of *The Axe* has some good moves in a fine situation. Single bolt lower-off. *Photo p.100*.
FA. N.Williams, P.Williams 1978

11 **Hatchet Man**.......... 6b+
The sustained wall to a shared lower-off with *Blockbuster*.
FA. R.Thomas, E.Rees 5.2011

Trial Wall Area — Black Buttress

Black Buttress

A collection of popular walls covered with worthwhile grade 5s and 6s. The walls have large grassy bases and share the same awesome views of all the other Trial Wall Area cliffs. The crag is sheltered from southwesterly winds and gets the sun from mid-afternoon onwards.

Approach (map and overview p.99) - Leave the car park on the road/track towards Worm's Head. After about 10 minutes the track bends left. Head right to the edge of the cliff and follow the edge for 200m to a path that leads down to the cliff base. The crag can also be easily reached from the Trial Wall/Lifebouy Buttress by following the cliff-base path.

❶ Left Line............... 6b+
Start at a square-cut corner and follow the left-hand line of bolts passing some hollow rock.
FA. S.Llewellyn 2011

❷ A Life Without Porpoise.. 6c+
Climb the arete to the right of the slim corner to a grassy ledge. Bypass the ledge and climb the intricate and crimpy wall to a break with a hard move to finish up the slab on the left. Avoid feet in corner for full tick.
FA. P.Blackburn, P.Tucker 2014

❸ Spittle and Spume 6c
The blunt technical rib right of the slim corner is climbed direct. An eliminate line that avoids the cracks on either side, but involves some good moves.
FA. G.Gibson, R.Thomas 5.2016

❹ Fiff and Faff........... VS 5a
The jamming crack.
FA. G.Gibson, R.Thomas 5.2016

❺ Footsie 6a
Short but pleasant climbing starting from the right side of the raised platform.
FA. G.Gibson, R.Thomas 5.2016

Black Buttress **Trial Wall Area**

⑥ Pied Noir 6b
The short corner and technical slab above.
FA. G.Gibson, R.Thomas 5.2016

⑦ Wonderful Land .... 6b+
A fine route direct up the slab with a tricky start. Easier if you wander off line.
FA. G.Gibson, R.Thomas 5.2016

⑧ Monica's Dress 5c
The exciting overhang and crack above. Luckily easier than it first appears.
FA. R.Thomas, G.Gibson 5.2016

⑨ Spit it Out 6a
The hanging corner complete with flake is a fine line and climb.
FA. R.Thomas, G.Gibson 5.2016

⑩ Black Friday 7a
The desperate face to the right requires a humongous reach. An eliminate has been recorded going right from the small pocket and climbing the wall right of the bolts **7b+**.
FA. G.Gibson 5.2016

⑪ Can't Swallow That 5b
The crack-line on the right trending left at the top to the lower-off.
FA. R.Thomas, G.Gibson 5.2016

⑫ Down in One 5b
The right-hand crack to a ledge. Finish up the arete.
FA. J.Squire 2012

⑬ The Beautiful People .... 6a+
The left-hand side of the arete is a very good little exercise.
FA. G.Morris, A.Berry 2000s

⑭ Spit'n Polish 6b
The right-hand side of the arete via a groove.
FA. R.Thomas, R.Phillips 2014

⑮ Spic'n Span .... 6a+
The slabby face and arete on the far right.
FA. R.Thomas, G.Gibson 5.2016

Trial Wall Area — Veggie Slabs

Veggie Slabs
A shady compact buttress of reasonable rock that has a number lower-grade lines that will be useful should the nearby crags be busy. The buttress is sheltered from southwest winds but sees little sun.

Approach (map and overview p.99)
- Leave the car park on the road/track towards Worm's Head. After about 10 minutes the track bends left. Head right to the edge of the cliff and follow the edge for 200m to a path that leads down to the cliff base. The crag is just left of Black Buttress (when facing out to sea). The crag can also be easily reached from the Trial Wall/Lifebouy Buttress by following the cliff base path.

❶ **Fat End of the Veg** 4b
The short arete on the left side of the buttress
FA. R.Thomas, T.Hoddy 20.5.2017

❷ **Vegemite** 4c
Climb the groove in between *Fat End of the Veg* and *Vegazalle* and then step left beneath a dodgy looking block to finish up *Fat End of the Veg*.
FA. R.Thomas, T.Hoddy 20.5.2017

❸ **Vegazzle**................... 5a
The longish slab.
FA. R.Thomas, T.Hoddy 20.5.2017

❹ **Meat and Two Veg** 5c
Tackle the slab leading to a corner.
FA. R.Thomas, T.Hoddy 5.2017

❺ **Veg? Ina** .... HS 4a
Short wall, veggie ledge then corner to junction with *Veginismus* resisting all bolts within reach.
FA. R.Thomas 2017

❻ **Veginismus** 6a
The thin and techy slab on right is climbed direct.
FA. R.Thomas, T.Hoddy 20.5.2017

Silent Walls Trial Wall Area

Silent Walls

An eye-catching tall rib is the main feature of the crag and provides its standout pitch. The buttress is sheltered from southwest winds but sees little sun. The impressive bay to its right is home to a number of trad climbs.

Approach (map and overview p.99) - Leave the car park on the road/track towards Worm's Head. After about 10 minutes the track bends left. Head right to the edge of the cliff and follow the edge for 200m to a path that leads down to the cliff base. The crag is 70m to the left (when facing out to sea).

7 Nick's Corner .... HVS 5a
The deep-set short corner is a trad line.
FA. N.O'Neill, R.Thomas 1.6.2017

8 OK Squire 6a
The short slab/wall just right of *Nick's Corner*.
FA. R.Thomas, N.O'Neill 1.6.2017

9 Freeloaders Arete .... 6a+
The neat little arete to a shared belay with *OK Squire*.
FA. R.Thomas, N.O'Neill 1.6.2017

10 It's Oh So Quiet .... 6b+
The excellent arete has a reachy initial move.
FA. G.Gibson, R.Thomas 2017

11 Noisiness 6b
From a raised ledge the corner gives some good bridging and technical climbing.
FA. G.Gibson, R.Thomas 2017

12 Bedlam 6b
Climb the tricky crack on the slab before stepping left into a corner and continuing up to a lower-off.
FA. G.Gibson, R.Thomas 2017

13 White Noise .... 6c+
Climb the arete on its left direct through an overhang and up the face of a hanging buttress.
FA. G.Gibson, R.Thomas 5.2017

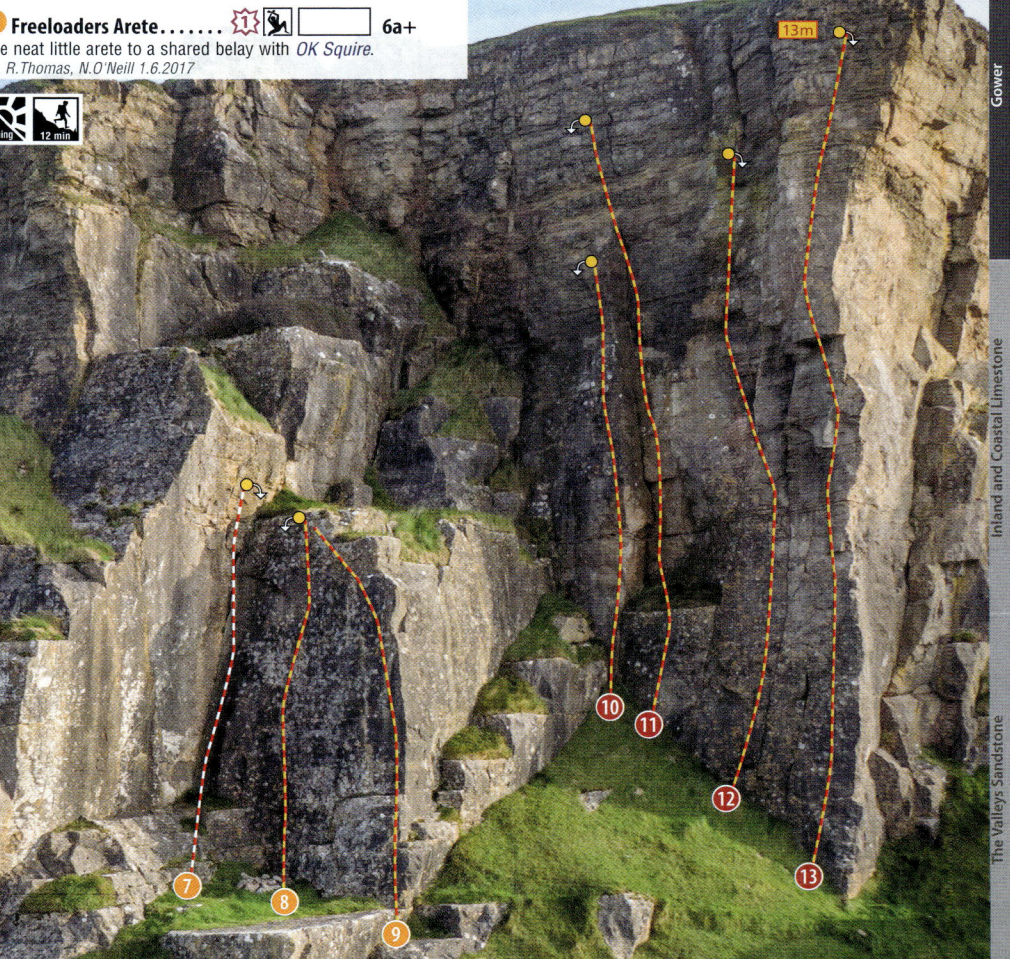

Trial Wall Area — Calcite Bay

Calcite Bay

A collection of faces that offer a variety of experiences on rock that should be handled with care. The buttress is sheltered from southwesterly winds but sees little sun on its right margin.

Approach (map and overview p.99) - Walk out of the National Trust car park on the road/track towards Worm's Head. After 10 minutes at a point where the track bends left head out right to the edge of the cliff and follow the edge for 200m to a path that leads down to the cliff base. Take the cliff base path left (facing out to sea) for 150m to below the bay.

1 Mutton Geoff .... 6b+
A line of big holds reaches some tough moves to get established on the headwall.
FA. G.Gibson, R.Thomas 2017

2 Lambs to the Slaughter .. 6c+
A similar but harder experience to *Mutton Geoff*.
FA. G.Gibson, R.Thomas 2017

3 Minnie Me 4c
The left-hand line on the little wall passed on the approached.
FA. G.Gibson, R.Thomas 2017

4 Minnie You 5b
The right-hand line on the little wall passed on the approached.
FA. G.Gibson, R.Thomas 2017

Calcite Bay **Trial Wall Area** *111*

⑤ Calcitron .... ⬜ **5b**
The left-hand line on the calcite wall itself passing a small ledge.
FA. R.Thomas, G.Gibson 16.6.2017

⑥ Calcite Crunch .... 🔖 ⬜ **6b+**
The surprisingly hold ridden wall gains a hard finishing sequence.
FA. R.Thomas, G.Gibson 15.6.2017

⑦ Calcite Punch.............. 🔖 ⬜ **6b+**
The right-hand alternative start to *Calcite Crunch*.
FA. R.Thomas, G.Gibson 15.6.2017

⑧ Crinoid Crimper................ ⬜ **5b**
The crinkly wall just to the left of a flake crack.
FA. R.Thomas, G.Gibson 15.6.2017

⑨ Just 2 Mohs .... ⬜ **5b**
The flake-line is a pleasant pitch.
FA. R.Thomas, G.Gibson 15.6.2017

⑩ Low on the Hardness Scale ...... ⬜ **5a**
The right-hand line on the wall of calcite has lots of good holds.
FA. R.Thomas, G.Gibson 15.6.2017

⑪ Calcite Crack'n Up .... 🔖 🔧 ⬜ **6a+**
The left-hand line on the shady right wall of Calcite Bay follows a thin crack to a lower-off
FA. G.Gibson, R.Thomas 7.2017

⑫ Drill Your Own .... 🔖 🔧 ⬜ **6b+**
The central line.
FA. G.Gibson, R.Thomas 7.2017

⑬ Calcitaclone............ 🔖 🔧 ⬜ **6b**
The right-hand line involves a number of thin tricky moves.
FA. G.Gibson, R.Thomas 7.2017

Trial Wall Area — Sinners Walls

Sinners Walls

An arc of walls and corners that has a good number of pitches on variable quality rock. The walls are sheltered from southwesterly winds but see little sun.

Approach (map and overview p.99) - Walk out of the National Trust car park on the road/track towards Worm's Head. After 10 minutes at a point where the track bends left head out right to the edge of the cliff and follow the edge for 200m to a path that leads down to the cliff base. Take the cliff base path left (facing out to sea) for 200m to below the walls.

❶ Devil May Care .... 6c+
The techy wall left of *Transgressor's Corner*.
FA. R.Thomas, G.Gibson 5.5.2017

❷ Transgressor's Corner 5a
The unusual calcite-lined corner crack.
FA. R.Thomas, G.Gibson 5.5.2017

❸ Butcher's Slab 6a
The slab to the right of the crack is hardest at the start.
FA. R.Thomas, G.Gibson 5.5.2017

❹ Repentance Arete Direct . 6c+
The direct start to *Repentance Arete*. Very balancy at the start, and then a pop to the break.
FA. S.Ferguson 20.10.2018

❺ Repentance Arete .... 6b+
Follow the right-hand side of the arete after moving out left from the crack.
FA. R.Thomas, G.Gibson 12.5.2017

❻ Stepped Corner 6a
The stepped corner has a tough initial few moves.
FA. R.Thomas, G.Gibson 5.5.2017

❼ Sin Bin .... 6a+
Some fragile calcite scabs lead to a slab with a tricky to clip lower-off for the short.
FA. R.Thomas, G.Gibson 6.5.2017

❽ Scintillate .... 6a+
Take the crunchy layback flake to meet and finish up *Sin Bin*.
FA. R.Thomas 2.7.2017

❾ Forgiveness 6b
The fragile calcite flake to join and finish as for *Sin Bin*.
FA. R.Thomas, T.Hoddy 2.7.2017

❿ Father Confessor .... 6a+
The pillar has some tricky final moves on sub optimal rock.
FA. R.Thomas, G.Gibson 6.5.2017

⓫ Sin Sear 4c
The corner, but beware of jammed blocks - do not use them.
FA. R.Thomas, T.Hoddy 2.7.2017

Sinners Walls **Trial Wall Area** 113

17 For Ye Who Has Sinned — 6c
The thin and techy slab leads to a steeper finish. The rock is poor near the top but the climbing low down is good.
FA. G.Gibson, R.Thomas 6.5.2017

18 The Seven Deadly Sins — 6b+
Balance up the thin scoop directly below the blunt rib clipping the first two bolts of *Wages of Sin*. Continue up the rib directly (two expansion bolts reported as rusty) to finish at the *For Ye Who Has Sinned* lower-off.
FA. G.Davis 17.7.2017

19 Wages of Sin — 6c+
A good technical wall climb.
FA. A.Sharp 1988

20 Sinner Man — 7a+
Hard thin climbing right of *Wages of Sin*.
FA. G.Gibson 7.2017

12 Cynical — 6b+
The bolted line to the right of *Sin Sear*.
FA. R.Thomas, T.Hoddy 4.2019

13 Sinbad — 6b
Begin up the shallow corner and pass the overhang on its right. Step left onto the hanging slab and follow this to the lower-off.
FA. G.Gibson, R.Thomas 6.5.2017

14 Sinus — 6b
The similar looking line to the right of *Sinbad* has a hard start.
FA. G.Gibson, R.Thomas 6.5.2017

15 Synthesizer Slab — 6b
The tricky slab is thin and technical.
FA. G.Gibson, R.Thomas 6.5.2017

16 Devilment — 4b
A pleasant climb up the short arete and easy stepped groove.
FA. R.Thomas, T.Hoddy 2.7.2017

Trial Wall Area — Windy Buttress and Fat Lady Wall

Windy Buttress
A wall of crunchy rock that is well-bolted.
Approach (map and overview p.99) - Walk out of the National Trust car park on the road/track towards Worm's Head. After 10 minutes at a point where the track bends left head out right to the edge of the cliff and follow the edge for 200m to a path that leads down to the cliff base. Take the cliff base path left (facing out to sea) for 230m to below the wall.

❶ Blow Me Down (Thar) — 6b+
The first line on the wall has a fragile start and a high first bolt.
FA. R.Thomas, T.Hoddy 2017

❷ Tha'r She Blows — 6b+
The central line of the buttress has a steep start.
FA. R.Thomas, T.Hoddy 19.8.2017

❸ A Stiff Blow — 6a
Crunchy crack and bulge above a ledge - take care with the rock.
FA. R.Thomas, G.Ashmore 29.9.2017

❹ Blow Up — 5c
Well bolted but watch the rock in places.
FA. R.Thomas, G.Ashmore 29.9.2017

Fat Lady Wall
A squat wall of compact rock with some decent pitches.
Approach (map and overview p.99) - Leave the car park on the road/track towards Worm's Head. After about 10 minutes the track bends left. Head right to the edge of the cliff and follow the edge for 200m to a path that leads down to the cliff base. Take the cliff base path left (facing out) for 230m to below the wall.

❺ Chubby Loving — 6a
Climb until a hand-jam is required to reach the top and a lower-off on the right.
FA. R.Thomas, T.Hoddy 29.7.2017

❻ Plumper Romp — 6b+
The wall just right of *Chubby Loving* to a shared lower-off.
FA. R.Thomas 8.2017

❼ Bosom Pals — 6b+
The thin wall passing a high initial bolt.
FA. R.Thomas 8.2017

❽ Butterball — 5c
Climb left of an earthy chimney to the short top arete.
FA. R.Thomas, G.Davis 4.8.2017

❾ It's Not All Over — 5c
The line right of the earthy chimney to a shared lower-off.
FA. R.Thomas, T.Hoddy 4.8.2017

Carbon Slab — Trial Wall Area

Carbon Slab
A very good dark grey slab of solid rock that is well-bolted. Take care belaying as the ground below is steep.
Approach (map and overview p.99) - Leave the car park on the road/track towards Worm's Head. After about 10 minutes the track bends left. Head right to the edge of the cliff and follow the edge for 200m to a path that leads down to the cliff base. Take the cliff base path left (facing out to sea) for 230m to the slab.

10 Wait for the Fat Lady's Thong. 5b
Begin in the corner and climb left of the arete to a lower-off.
FA. R.Thomas, G.Ashmore, E.Travers-Jones 8.2017

11 Carbonate 6a
A striking line up and left of the main slab routes. Starting in a grassy bay, gain and continue up the arete.
FA. R.Thomas, G.Gibson 18.7.2017

12 Carboniferous 5a
Follow the left arete of the slab itself.
FA. G.Gibson, R.Thomas 5.5.2017

13 Carbon Copy 6b
The second line on the slab. Can be climbed efficiently with a sequence of undercuts and side-pulls or with brute force pulling on crimps.
FA. G.Gibson, R.Thomas 5.5.2017

14 Carbon Dating 6b+
Start as for *Carbon Copy*, before moving right up the thin upper wall. Very good.
FA. G.Gibson, R.Thomas 5.5.2017

15 Carbon Era 6b
An appealing line.
FA. G.Gibson, R.Thomas 5.5.2017

16 Carbon Times 6b
The line above two grassy diagonal rakes.
FA. G.Gibson, R.Thomas 5.5.2017

17 Carbon Light 4b
The right-hand route steepens above the grassy rakes.
FA. G.Gibson 7.2017

Third Sister Area

Grade Spread | 7 | 50 | 71 | 24 | 3

A visually stunning section of coast dotted with many fine sport crags that offer plenty of routes in the higher grades as well as some lovely mid-grade routes. There has been a lot of development in this area with some fine new additions. The rock is excellent and the cliffs have the ambience of sea cliff climbing but the majority are not worried by tidal restrictions.

Approach

There are two separate approaches however it is possible to reach all crags from either, but expect to put in some miles on foot if this option is taken.

Saddam's Wall, Rams Grove Crag, Rams Grove Seaward Crag, First Sister, Second Sister, Sister 2.5, Third Sister - Bottom, Third Sister - Lower, Third Sister - Middle - From Scurlage drive 2.7miles and at the hamlet of Pitton turn left and park at Great Pitton Farm (fee). Turn left out of the car park and walk along the road for 150m and at a fork go left along a track (public footpath) uphill for 100m through two gates. Continue for 300m to another gate. Go through the gate and follow the signed footpath along the field margins to another gate. Go through the gate and meet the coast path a little further on at the head of the Rams Grove Valley. All the various approaches are described from here.

Third Sister - Upper, Deborah's Zawn, Tooth Fairy, Deborah's Overhang, TV Zawn - From Scurlage, drive 1.3 miles to parking on the right at Pilton Green (indicated by a small National Trust sign) opposite a sand-coloured house called 'Clifflands'. The parking is on the grass next to the track (can be boggy if wet). Cross the road and take a footpath on the left of the sandy-coloured house that heads across fields towards the coast. As the path nears the coast it dips into a small valley and the coast path is reached. From here each cliff's approach is described separately.

Conditions

Most of the crags apart from Deborah's Zawn and TV Zawn are high above the sea and are accessible at all states of tide. The majority of the crags dry quickly, but Deborah's Zawn and TV Zawn need time to dry out as well as crisp weather to be in the best condition.

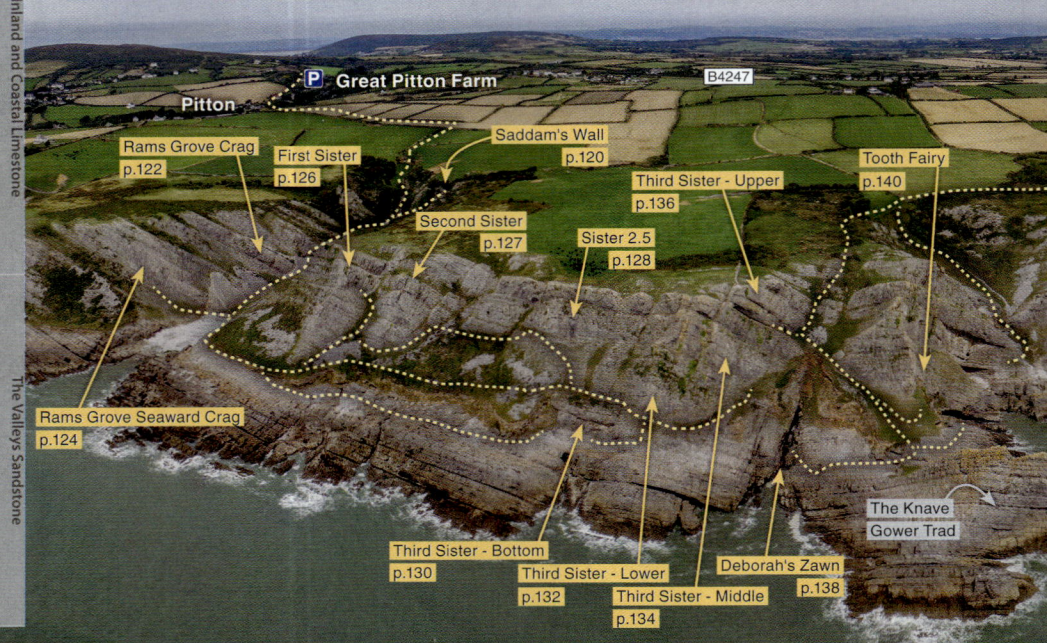

Third Sister Area 117

Third Sister Area

James Eves tackling fine rock at Rams Grove Crag on *Just One Cornetto* (6b) - *p.123* - Gower. This crag, and nearby Saddam's Wall, are set back from the coast and offer shelter from westerly winds. Photo: Mark Glaister

Third Sister Area — Saddam's Wall

Saddam's Wall

A secluded wall of good weathered rock that contains some interesting bolted lines. The base can get a bit vegetated at times. A very sheltered venue.

Approach (map and overview p.117) - From the coast path walk down the Rams Grove Valley for 120m and then cut back up left into an old quarry. Saddam's Wall is at the top of the rocky slope on the right.

❸ Al-Tikrit .... 6b+
A fine pitch on excellent rock. Well worth searching out.
FA. G.Gibson, R.Thomas 2018

❹ Sunni Daze. 6b
The right-hand edge of the pillar is followed direct via a series of overlaps to a belay at the very top of the pillar.
FA. R.Thomas, T.Hoddy 25.11.2018

❶ Chemical Ali. 4c
The first route on the left side of the wall moving right near the top to a to a lower-off.
FA. R.Thomas, G.Ashmore 17.2.2019

❷ Barzan Lost His Head 6a
A faint groove and wall on the left-hand side of crag.
FA. R.Thomas, T.Hoddy, E.Rees, R.Phillips, N.O'Neill 2.1.2019

Third Sister Area

Andy Collins exiting the tricky upper groove on the excellent *Open Wide Please* (6c+) - *p.140* - at Tooth Fairy Crag on Gower. Photo: Mark Glaister

Third Sister Area — Rams Grove Crag

Rams Grove Crag
A good crag with plenty of mid-grade lines which tackle the numerous bulges and grooves that line the face. This area is set back from the sea and fairly sheltered. The climbs are well bolted and the rock is generally solid although there are still some looser sections.
Approach (map and overview p.117) - From the coast path, walk down the Rams Grove Valley for 200m and the crag is immediately on the right.

① Stand at Ease .... 6a+
The open chimney at the left side of the crag. Gain the chimney with difficulty, and climb with care past a very large block.
FA. R.Thomas 2022

② Sh**storm 6c
Good steep climbing via the bulges right of the open chimney of *Stand at Ease*.
FA. R.Thomas, E.Chapman 2022

③ Lack Toes Intolerant.. 7a
Climb easily to the bulge from where some powerful climbing on undercuts and edges gain the upper groove and lower-off.
FA. P.Barwood 3.4.2022

④ LMN SQZY .... 6c+
The fine right-trending corner/groove is approached initially via bolts on its right wall and some tough moves.
FA. P.Barwood 19.2.2022

Rams Grove Crag — Third Sister Area

5 EZ PZ .... 7a+
Climb to under the bulges. Use a double pocket and undercut side-pull to gain a welded on rock. Continue steeply to good holds and then some off-balance climbing to the lower-off.
FA. P.Barwood 3.4.2022

6 Nouveau Cuisine 6c
Takes the alternating overlaps and squat walls above the steady lower wall. A smart pitch with a hard to see good hold above the first overhang.
FA. R.Thomas, N.O'Neill 12.2021

7 Beth .... 6b+
Excellent steep moves via some good but hard-to-spot holds.
FA. P.Thomas, J.Harwood 1.1.1989

8 Insatiable Appetite .. 6a+
The long right-leaning corner is a fine line that gives sustained moves on very good rock. A mix of glue-in and through bolts protect.
FA. N.Williams pre1991

9 One More for Me 6b
A bulge and wall right of the corner of *Insatiable Appetite*. A very worthwhile pitch on surprisingly good holds.
FA. R.Thomas, T.Hoddy 11.2021

10 Just One Cornetto 6b
Pleasing moves to pass the lower steep ground. Take the upper section on the right to avoid the unstable looking pillar. *Photo p.118.*
FA. R.Thomas, T.Hoddy 11.2021

11 F*uc*ose .... 6a+
The wall and arete gives a great little pitch featuring some fingery and technical manoeuvres. *Photo p.27.*
FA. R.Thomas, N.O'Neill 8.2021

12 Molasses 6b
A tough starting sequence up the narrow corner reaches easier but still good climbing.
FA. R.Thomas, N.O'Neill 8.2021

Third Sister Area — Rams Grove Seaward Crag

Rams Grove Seaward Crag
A lovely wall, perched a good distance above the sea. The face receives all the sun going and is fast drying with a line-up of mid-grade wall climbs. They are well bolted and the rock is generally solid although there are still some looser sections.

Approach (map and overview p.117) - From the coast path, walk down the Rams Grove Valley for 270m and the crag is on the right just before the coastline is encountered and is approach up a short scree slope.

❶ Phelan Man 6b
A gentle initial section reaches a much trickier finale.
FA. G.Gibson, R.Thomas 2.2018

❷ Grainger Man .... 6a+
Good climbing with a technical start over a small overhang. The rock high up needs care.
FA. G.Gibson, R.Thomas 2.2018

❸ The Peacock Guys 6b
A groove leads to some technical manoeuvres to pass overlaps.
FA. G.Gibson, R.Thomas 2.2018

❹ Mano a Mano 6c
Good climbing with a perplexing sequence to pass the overlap.
FA. G.Gibson, R.Thomas 2.2018

❺ Man Up .... 6a+
Interesting, sustained wall climbing. Care needed with the rock.
FA. G.Gibson, R.Thomas 2.2018

❻ Man Down 6b
At first techy and then much steeper but on good holds. Care needed with the rock.
FA. G.Gibson, R.Thomas 2.2018

❼ Oh Man 6c
Fine climbing with a hard mid section and steep finish.
FA. G.Gibson, R.Thomas 2.2018

❽ Playing the Pink Oboe ... 6a
Pleasant wall climbing to shared belay on right. *Photo opposite.*
FA. R.Thomas, G.Gibson 5.6.2018

❾ Ram Raiders 6b
The lower wall has some intricate sequences that gain a steep finish.
FA. R.Thomas, G.Gibson 2.2018

❿ Ram Bam Thank Ewe Lamb 6a
The thin crack proves a tough exercise. Easier above
FA. R.Thomas, G.Gibson 2.2018

⓫ Blowing the Horn .... 6a+
The wall to merge and finish as for *Ram Bam Thank Ewe Lamb.*
FA. R.Thomas, G.Gibson 2.2018

Third Sister Area   125

Bridget Glaister getting to grips with *Playing the Pink Obce* (6a) - *opposite* - at the sunny seaside venue of Rams Grove Seaward Crag on Gower. Photo: Mark Glaister

Third Sister Area — First Sister

First Sister
A good spot for checking out some steep routes in the 6c to 7b range. The crag dries quickly but seepage can be present after wet periods.

Approach (map and overview p.117) - Walk down the Rams Grove Valley to the coastline. Take the path on the left (looking out to sea) for 150m until the crag can be easily viewed and approached.

1 Ugly Stepsister 5a
The rib above a wall on a ramp is loose.
FA. R.Thomas, G.Morris, J.Bullock 12.6.2021

2 Eowyn .... 7a+
Crimpy climbing up the steepening wall leads into a tough sequence that heads past the bulge. The groove and final bulge above provides a testing finale.
FA. D.McCarroll, J.Bullock 2021

3 Sister of Mercy 7a
The clean, snaking groove in the centre of the buttress gives a fine pitch with a tough hard section.
FA. J.Bullock, G.Evans 6.1987 FFA A.Price September 1988

4 Arwen 7b
Powerful and technical. From the base of the corner move diagonally up leftwards to a shallow groove. Step left to finish.
FA. D.McCarroll, J.Bullock 2021

5 South East Wall 6c
Climb the corner/wall, left of the prominent rib to the overlap (as for *The Angst of Anti-Fashion*). Pull right onto the rib and finish direct.
FA J.Bullock, G.Evans 1984

6 The Angst of Anti-Fashion 7a
Weaves up the through the overhangs. Move up the corner/wall and then traverse left between the overhangs to a hanging groove. Head up the groove to final moves left to the lower-off.
FA. M.Crocker, J.Harwood 22.2.2015

7 Luthien 7a
As for *South East Wall* then directly through the steepest part of the crag on surprisingly good holds.
FA. J.Bullock, D.McCarroll 2022

8 Rosie 6b
Surmount the overhang just right of the diagonal crack and then head out left and up the wall. Good steep climbing.
FA. J.Bullock, D.McCarroll 2021

9 Ugly Cousin 5c
The wall at the far right-hand end of First Sister.
FA. J.Bullock, D.McCarroll 2021

Second Sister **Third Sister Area** 127

Second Sister

A visually appealing buttress with a small number of very interesting climbs on solid, well bolted rock. Quick drying but very exposed to the elements.

Approach (map and overview p.117) - Walk down the Rams Grove Valley to the coastline. Head along the path on the left (looking out to sea) for 180m until the crag can be easily viewed and approached.

10 Holy Sister 4c
The slabby west wall of Second Sister, lower off at the grassy descending ramp.
FA. R.Thomas, N.O'Neill 24.3.2020

11 Above Holy Sister 5b
Continue from the belay on the grass terrace
FA. R.Thomas, N.O'Neill 2020

Lots of sun | 25 min

12 Sisters of Pain 5c
The shattered groove, overhang, easy slab gains a burly finish.
FA. R.Thomas, N.O'Neill 1.2024

13 Jubilee Step Sister ...... 6a+
Faint rib trending left to a stiff pull over roof.
FA. R.Thomas, Gandalf, N.O'Neill, E.Chapman 3.6.2022

14 Scissor Sister .... 6a+
Climb the lower walls and corners to below the roof. Layback the crack over the roof and up the headwall to a lower-off.
FA. R.Thomas, Gandalf 10.2023

Narrow foot-ledge - take great care

Third Sister Area — Sister 2.5

Sister 2.5

A series of vertical and bulging walls with plenty of pitches in the 5s and 6s. Seepage can be a problem here after wet weather.

Approach (map and overview p.117) - Walk down the Rams Grove Valley to the coastline. Head along the path on the left (looking out to sea) for 180m until the crag can be easily viewed and approached.

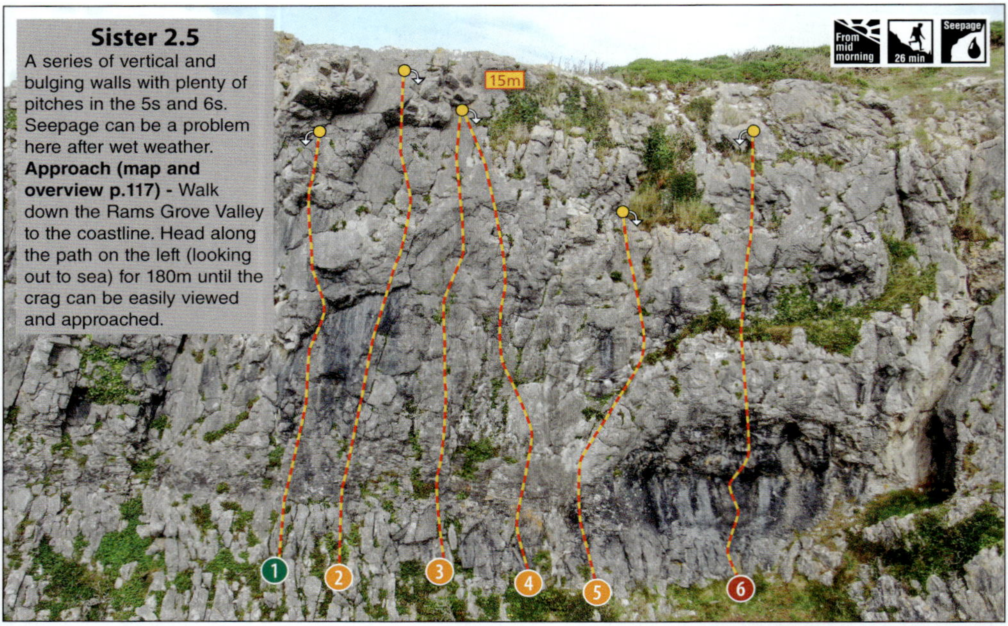

① **Pot Boiler** 4b
Pleasant climbing to a lower-off under the high overhang.
FA. R.Thomas, G.Gibson 1.2019

② **Hot off the Press** 5b
A worthwhile line to the right of *Pot Boiler*.
FA. G.Gibson, R.Thomas 8.1.2019

③ **Page Turner** 5a
The left-hand of two lines on the central section of wall.
FA. G.Gibson, R.Thomas 2019

④ **Final Draft** 5a
The right-hand central line is an excellent climb.
FA. G.Gibson, R.Thomas 2019

⑤ **Bodice Ripper** 5c
Fun jug pulling starting up the left side of the low bulging wall.
FA. R.Thomas, G.Gibson 8.1.2019

⑥ **Schmills and Boon** 6b
Head steeply through the tiered bulge.
FA. R.Thomas, G.Gibson 8.1.2019

⑦ **Scooby Doo** 4b
The far left edge of the lower section of the crag is short.
FA. R.Thomas, G.Gibson 3.2022

⑧ **Scobby Two Tokes** 5b
Line between *Scooby Do* and *Two Tokes on the Bong*.
FA. G.Gibson, R.Thomas 2022

⑨ **Two Tokes on the Bong** 4b
Curving line beginning up white rock and past two hollows.
FA. R.Thomas, G.Gibson 3.2022

Sister 2.5 Third Sister Area

10 La Ch Cha Cha .... ⬜ 5b
The clean line between ivy.
FA. G.Gibson 20.10.2023

11 Eat My Shorts .... ⬜ 5b
Steady climbing on the fringe of the main section of the crag.
FA. G.Gibson, H.Gibson 2018

12 Rikes Raggy .... ⬜ 6a
A few tricky moves that end at a shared lower-off.
FA. G.Gibson, H.Gibson 2018

13 Howdy Partner .... 💡 ⬜ 6a+
A steep start and wall reaches a lower-off above an overhang.
FA. G.Gibson, H.Gibson 2018

14 They Killed Kenny .... ⬜ 6a+
The brown crack-line moving left to a shared lower-off.
FA. G.Gibson, H.Gibson 2018

15 Suffering Succotash .... 💡 ⬜ 6b+
Puzzling moves lead to a hard move up onto the top slab.
FA. G.Gibson, H.Gibson 2018

16 Ridiculous is the Burden of Genius ⬜ 6b+
Steady moves to the overlap then it gets tough and steep.
FA. G.Gibson, H.Gibson 2018

17 What's Up Doc .... ⬜ 6c
Technical sequences on side-pulls and small edges.
FA. G.Gibson, H.Gibson 2018

18 Ay, Caramba .... 💡🧗🏁 ⬜ 6c+
Good wall climbing gains a problematic entry into a slim groove.
FA. G.Gibson, H.Gibson 2018

19 Drilling Beyond the Sea .... ⬜ 6c+
Climbs on the right side of the bolt line.
FA. G.Ashmore, G.Morrris 20.3.2022

20 Heavens to Murgatroyd ...... 💡 ⬜ 6c+
Thin wall climbing gains a series of difficult pulls on slopers.
FA. G.Gibson, H.Gibson 2018

21 It Stinks .... 💡 ⬜ 6c
A desperate series of moves leads onto the easier wall above.
FA. G.Gibson, H.Gibson 2018

22 It's Hero Time .... ⬜ 6a
The right margin of the wall moving leftwards to a lower-off.
FA. G.Gibson, H.Gibson 2018

Third Sister Area — Third Sister - Bottom

Third Sister - Bottom

Despite its rather diminutive appearance this is a very good spot that has a lot of action-packed pitches and is an extremely pleasant place to climb. Often sheltered from the wind and it dries quickly.

Approach (map and overview p.117) - Walk down the Rams Grove Valley to the coastline. Head along the path on the left (looking out to sea) for 320m until below Third Sister - Lower. Descend to the left (facing out) and then head back down a ramp rightwards to the base of the crag. The crag can also be approached along the rocky foreshore.

❶ Foam Under Sister 5b
The bolted edge of the wall at the far left end of the wall passing an orange rock scar.
FA. R.Thomas, G.Gibson 6.2019

❷ Prim .... 6a+
A good route with technicalities that ease with height.
FA. J.Bullock, D.McCarroll 2019

❸ The Haworth Lassies 6b
A pleasing line of techy wall climbing.
FA. D.McCarroll, J.Bullock 2019

❹ Las Mariposas .... 6a+
A varied little pitch that gains the hanging corner before moving left at the overhang to some final side-pulls on the upper wall.
FA. J.Bullock, D.McCarroll 2019

❺ Wierd and Wayward 6b
The slab, overhang and leaning wall just right of the corner of *Las Mariposas*. Good moves on better holds than first appears.
FA. J.Bullock, D.McCarroll 2019

❻ Moirai .... 6b+
A hard pull through the overhang on hard to see holds reaches the small hanging corner and lower-off.
FA. D.McCarroll, J.Bullock 8.2020

❼ Thankless Child .... 6b+
A tough sequence through steep ground. Finish rightwards.
FA. J.Bullock, D.McCarroll 2019

Third Sister Area — Third Sister - Bottom

⑧ Serpent's Tooth 6b
Reach the tooth and then climb forcefully to gain better holds as the angle eases. Continue to a shared lower-off. *Photo p.12*.
FA. J.Bullock, D.McCarroll 2019

⑨ The Daughters of Lear ... 6c
The biggest of the central bulges is overcome by a spectacular series of moves on pockets and side-pulls.
FA. D.McCarroll, J.Bullock 2019

⑩ The Underling .... 7a+
The steep bulge is immediately followed by technical moves onto a slabby section. Good bouldery moves.
FA. G.Gibson 6.2019

⑪ The Underling's Undercling ... 6b
The orange stained bulges are a stout proposition.
FA. G.Gibson 6.2019

⑫ Lost in Translation 6b
A steep series of pulls up the left side of the big overhang.
FA. D.McCarroll, J.Bullock 5.2021

⑬ I Don't Want to Dance ... 6c
Dance through the centre of the big overhang on some hard-to-see holds.
FA. B.McCarroll, D.McCarroll 9.2020

⑭ Ginny 5a
The corner is overcome by some steep manoeuvres midway.
FA. J.Bullock, D.McCarroll 5.2021

⑮ Pleiades 5a
The centre of the slab on good grey stone.
FA. J.Bullock, D.McCarroll 2019

⑯ Touching The Rusty Ring 6b
Climb directly up the steep right side of the wall then traverse left to the lower-off. Climbing left of the bolts is also a popular variation at **5b**.
FA. R.Thomas, G.Gibson 2019

Third Sister Area — Third Sister - Lower

Third Sister - Lower
A well-positioned section of crag that has good lines which need care with some of the rock in places.
Approach (map and overview p.117) - Walk down the Rams Grove Valley to the coast. Head along the path on the left (looking out) for 320m until the crag is reached.

1 Tower of Ecthelion .... 6b+
An isolated climb on good rock worth tracking down. Approach by a path that leads from the base of Sister 2.5 to a rope rail at its start. Gain the base of a crack and ascend it to meet some blind exposed climbing up the tower face.
FA. D.McCarroll, B.McCarroll 2022

2 Ramp It Up 5a
The pleasant ramp-line gives good climbing.
FA. R.Thomas, G.Gibson 4.2019

3 Teenage Rampage 6a
Climb to and directly over the bulge.
FA. G.Gibson, R.Thomas 2019

4 Groovy Baby 5a
The groove left of the dominating rib gives an excellent pitch.
FA. R.Thomas, G.Gibson 6.4.2019

5 Ballroom Blitz 5c
The slight groove system in the dominating rib.
FA. G.Gibson, R.Thomas 2019

6 Blockbuster .... 6b+
The front face of the rib has a devious move to pass the bulge.
FA. G.Gibson, R.Thomas 2019

Third Sister Area

Tom Skelhon on *Debbie Reynolds* (7a) - *p.138* - at Deborah's Zawn, an unusual coastal feature being narrow and inclined giving some steep and excellent hard climbing especially towards the rear of the zawn where the lines are heavily chalked in this image. Photo: Andy van Kints

7 Ugly Lovely Climb 5a
The chimney/crack right of the rib.
FA. G.Gibson, R.Thomas 4.2019

8 Amblimance 5b
The wall to the right of the chimney/crack is a pleasant pitch.
FA. G.Gibson, R.Thomas 5.2019

9 Two Nans and a Grandpa ..... 6a+
The pocketed intricate wall has some good moves.
FA. G.Gibson, R.Thomas 2019

10 Peruvian Marching Powder 5a
The final line on the wall is a nice wall pitch.
FA. G.Gibson, R.Thomas 2019

Third Sister Area — Third Sister - Middle

Third Sister - Middle

A large face that is home to lots of climbing but care is needed with the rock and when moving around the base which slopes down to a vertical drop.

Approach (map and overview p.117) - Walk down the Rams Grove Valley to the coastline. Head along the path on the left (looking out to sea) for 320m until below Third Sister Lower. Continue a short way further to below the crag. Do not access or approach via the fence on the right, it has been broken in the past and is in place to stop sheep escaping the farmers property.

Conditions - The crag is very exposed to the sun and wind but it does not seep and dries rapidly.

1 Like a Scorpion .... 6c+
1) 6c+, 27m. Take the left line of bolts to join *Gemini Spunk Wizard...* at its lower-off. Scramble to an accommodating ledge with a belay.
2) 6c+, 20m. Climb past a bouldery start to an arete which leads to the top of the crag.
FA. C.Wyatt, S.Topy 3.3.2023

2 Gemini Spunk Wizard and His Sexually Active Teapot
.... 6c+
Moves out left from *Harriet Harman and the Lehman Sisters*. Fourteen quickdraws required.
FA. D.Emanuel 2019

3 Harriet Harman and the Lehman Sisters
.... 6c+
A fine upper wall but the entry is now vegetated. Begin up a short slab and steeper wall which lead to a ledge, step right and follow the P-bolts to a lower off.
FA. G.Ashmore, R.Thomas 12.9.2009

Third Sister Area

4 Uprising 6c+
A sustained pitch with a tricky central bulge. A fine pitch.
FA. G.Gibson 6.2019

5 Water 6c
Superb sustained climbing with a crux move at the bulge.
FA. G.Gibson 6.2019

6 Arab Spring 6c
Fine climbing with a very fingery and tricky-to-read crux.
FA. G.Gibson 2019

7 Power Vacuum 6c
Intricate face climbing and a hard pull through the bulge.
FA. G.Gibson 2019

8 Gafsa 6c
Pleasant technical climbing to a bulge and easier upper face.
FA. G.Gibson 2019

9 Moshe Dayan is Coming to Get You 7a+
Climb *Mubarak* and traverse the lower diagonal break to gain *Gemini*.... at the top of its bulge.
FA. G.Ashmore, G.Morris 19.5.2021

10 Mubarak 6b
Fine techy climbing past a bulging nose to an easier upper wall.
FA. G.Gibson 2019

11 Bathroom Blitz 6a+
Climb *Gadhaffi Groove* to the prominent upper diagonal break. Follow this for 13m to join and finish as for *Harriet Harman and the Lehman Sisters*.
FA. G.Ashmore, G.Morris 28.8.2020

12 Gaddafi Groove 6a
Nice climbing on the right-hand side of the main section of wall.
FA. G.Gibson, R.Thomas 6.2019

13 Starting Block 5c
The left-hand line on the short wall just right of the main face.
FA. R.Thomas G.Gibson 6.2019

14 16KN Working Load 6a
The short wall to a shared lower-off with *Tricky Treat*.
FA. R.Thomas G.Gibson 6.2019

15 Tricky Treat 4a
The best of the lines at this end of the face.
FA. R.Thomas G.Gibson 6.2019

16 Tricksy or Treaty 4b
The short wall on the right is worh a look.
FA. R.Thomas G.Gibson 6.201

Midway up the exposed headwall of *The Enema Affair* (5c) - *p.137* - at Third Sister - Upper, Gower. This crag is a popular section of cliff that was one of the first to be equipped for sport climbing on Gower. More recently all three of 'The Sisters' have seen a great deal of development hugely expanding the number of sport routes available. Photo: Dave Simmonite

Third Sister Area — Third Sister - Upper

Third Sister - Upper

A great little crag set in a commanding position that has some intense pitches on excellent rock. A good spot on a sunny winter's day. There are also some trad routes on this wall which have not been described.

Approach (map and overview p.117) - At the coast path, go right through a green gate and follow the coast path (occasionally marked by wooden posts) through a further two gates. 100m past the second gate, take the left fork in the path out to the headland. A wide easy-angled grassy gully leads down to the sea. Descend the grassy gully and the Third Sister - Upper is on the right. The routes are on a narrow overhung ramp which becomes cramped and exposed to the left of *French Undressing*.

Conditions - The crag is very exposed to the sun and wind but it does not seep and dries rapidly.

❶ **Chilean Flame Thrower** .. 7b+
Start at the top of the ramp below a wedged boulder. Make bouldery moves up the severely overhung wall to easier ground.
FA. G.Ashmore 23.4.2010

❷ **Flaming Fingers** .... 7a+
Begin at a seat-like feature about 9m below the top of the terrace running up the crag. Make some powerful moves up the wall to the break. Step left, and make a tricky move up to finish.
FA. M.Crocker 21.8.1988

❸ **Sister Bliss** 7b
Follow a leftwards line from the start of *World in Action* into *Flaming Fingers* via a shallow groove. Clip the first two bolts of *World in Action*.
FA. M.Richards 6.5.2024

❹ **World in Action** ...... 7b+
A sequence of hard moves gains a rest at the break. Finish up the easier overhang and wall above.
FA. A.Sharp 1989

Third Sister - Upper Third Sister Area 137

5 Popped In, Souled Out
.... 7b
The third line of bolts to the left of the mid-height cave.
FA. A.Sharp, P.Lewis, J.Harwood 6.2.1988

6 Panorama 7c
A low level right-to-left line across flakes and a shallow groove. Start as for *Chilean Flame Flower*. Pull up and traverse left along a line of good holds, crossing *Popped In Souled Out* and *World in Action* to join and finish up *Sister Bliss*.
FA. M.Richards, A.Sharp 19.5.2024

7 Chilean Flame Flower 7b
A hard pitch up the leaning and reachy wall just right of *Popped In, Souled Out*.
FA. M.Crocker 21.8.1988

8 Leftism................... 7a
Climb the wall up a faint groove to the top bulge. Surmount this left of the last two bolts to a lower off. Clip the last bolt so the gate faces left to avoid the gate being loaded laterally in a fall.
FA. E.Jones, R.Thomas 2018

9 French Undressing ... 7a
Climb the wall to the small cave and huge nest at mid-height. Pull out of the cave and move steeply up and right to finish easily. The lower-off is in the upper wall.
FA. A.Sharp, P.Lewis 10.10.1987

10 Twilight World 6c
An exciting pitch. Move up to where the rock starts to bulge. Climb up through the bulge past a jug and finish up the less steep wall above.
FA. A.Sharp and team 10.10.1987

11 Southeast Wall .... 6a+
A deceptively steep exercise on good but sharp holds. Climb the crisp lower wall to some unexpected jug hauling to finish.
FA. J.Talbot, R.Corbett 1963. FFA A.Sharp, P.Lewis 1986

12 Fiesta 6b
Similar to *Southeast Wall* but more technical. The upper sect on can be climbed to the left or right of the bolts at the same grade.
Photo p.22.
FA. A.Sharp, P.Lewis, J.Harwood 10.10.1987

13 Bob's Your Uncle 6c
The thin bulging lower crack briefly joining *Fiesta* higher up.
FA. A.Sharp, R.Powles 6.10.1987

14 Fanny's Your Aunt....... 6a+
Exciting and sustained moves although care is required with some of the rock in places.
FA. R.Thomas, E.Jones 2018

15 Sister Mary's Blessed Finger
.... 6a
A worthwhile pitch with a spectacular upper wall. Climb the lower buttress direct with a tough move past the overlap. Move up to the steep headwall and climb it on (mostly) good jugs, moving right near the top to a lower-off.
FA. R.Thomas, G.Ashmore 2009

16 The Enema Affair 5c
Follow *Sister Mary's Blessed Finger* to the headwall and then follow the right-hand line of bolts steeply to a lower-off.
Photo p.135.
FA. R.Thomas, G.Ashmore 2009

Third Sister Area — Deborah's Zawn

Deborah's Zawn

A narrow zawn with some fine hard routes on excellent rock. Care is required on the routes at the back of the zawn due to the proximity of the opposing wall.

Approach (map and overview p.117) - At the coast path, go right through a green gate and follow the path (some wooden posts) through two gates. 100m past the second gate, bear left out to the headland. A wide easy-angled grassy gully leads down to the sea. Descend this (Third Sister - Upper on the right) leftwards until you can break back right on rock to the bed of the Zawn.

Tides - Climbing is possible for around 3.5 hours either side of low water.
Conditions - Good conditions can be elusive since it is both tidal and shady. It takes time to dry once the tide has retreated and sees little sun but is often at its best when the sun is low in the sky from autumn to spring. Seepage is only a problem after prolonged rainfall.

❶ **Debbie Likes it Wet** .... 6a+
The line on the far left of the zawn has some butch moves on very steep ground. The first bolt is best stick-clipped.
FA. R.Thomas, R.Phillips 9.2015

❷ **Silent Echo**.......... E1 5a
Climb the long left-to-right ramp-line starting on the left and finishing at a staple lower-off.
FA. A.Sharp, P.Lewis 1985

❸ **Charlie Barking**......... 7a
The short slim groove above the base of the ramp-line.
FA. M.Richards, A.Sharp. M.Shewring, D.Morris. 5.2011

❹ **Empty Your Pockets** 7b
A pocket pulling link up. From the second bolt on *Charlie Barking* span right into pockets on *Prison Bitch* and right again into the finish of *Debbie Reynolds*. Surprisingly pumpy!
FA. M.Richards 9.10.2022

❺ **Prison Bitch**......... 7b
The upper wall features some bouldery pocket pulling. Short-lived, but with some tough moves.
FA. A.Sharp, M.Richards 6.6.2015

❻ **Debbie Reynolds**............ 7a
The flake and wall. A good pitch with escalating difficulties.
Photo p.133.
FA. M.Crocker 21.8.1988

❼ **Happy Valley** .... 7a+
Climb *Debbie Reynolds* to the ramp-line, move right and climb the wall to gain the base of a crack/ramp which leads leftwards to join and finish as for *Debbie Reynolds*.
FA. M.Richards, A.Sharp 28.5.2017

❽ **Valley Uprising** .... 6c+
An interesting line crossing the diagonal ramp of *Silent Echo*.
FA. A.Sharp, M.Richards 6.6.2015

❾ **Bolder Boulder**... 7a
Start at a low arch. Make difficult moves up leftwards to better holds and continue to below the ramp of *Silent Echo*. Head steeply rightwards, keeping below the ramp-line, to a lower-off.
FA. A.Sharp, P.Lewis, J.Harwood 11.10.1987

❿ **Under Arrest** 8a
From just to the right of *Bolder Boulder*, climb up rightwards to meet *Wide Eyed and Legless*. Cross it via a hard sequence on pockets and crimps to good holds at a junction with *Resisting Arrest*. Move right to finish as for *Persistent Offender*.
FA. M.Richards, A.Sharp 25.9.2010

⓫ **Wide Eyed and Legless**
.... 7b+
The lower left-rising diagonal joining *Bolder Boulder* to finish.
FA. A.Sharp, P.Lewis, J.Harwood 1.10.1987

⓬ **Resisting Arrest** . 7b+
Climb the leftward rising line to finish up *Bolder Boulder*.
FA. A.Sharp, P.Lewis 1985

⓭ **Persistent Offender** .. 7c
Follow *Resisting Arrest* to a big hold at the top of its groove. Head rightwards to meet and finish up *Dog Days are Over*.
FA. M.Richards, A.Sharp 9.2014

⓮ **Underdog**........... 8a
From first bolt on *Resisting Arrest*, move up right into *Dog Days are Over* and finish up it.
FA. M.Richards, A.Sharp 18.6.2016

Deborah's Zawn — Third Sister Area

⑮ Department of Correction — 7b+
An awesome series of moves lead up the lower wall and into a prominent groove high up. Clip-stick the initial bolt.
FA. M.Richards, A.Sharp 28.2.2010

⑯ Deputy Dawg — 7b+
Start up *Support Your Local Sheriff* below a break. Pull up to the break and clip the second bolt then move leftwards along a line of undercuts to meet up with *Department of Correction* at its fourth bolt. Finish up this.
FA. M.Richards, A.Sharp 17.4.2010

⑰ Support Your Local Sheriff — 7b+
The impressive line on the far right of the wall has a powerful start and finish.
FA. A.Sharp, M.Richards 11.6.2010

⑱ Dog Days are Over — 8a+
A stunning diagonal line across the inner zawn's steepest and blankest territory. Start up *Support Your Local Sheriff* and follow it to its junction with *Department of Correction*. Hard moves to gain and then leave a two-finger pocket are followed by a pumpy finish that joins *Under Arrest* near the top.
FA. M.Richards, A.Sharp 5.6.2011

⑲ Line of Duty — 7c
A short line right of *Support Your Local Sheriff*. It has two bouldery sections. The lower-off is above the wide crack.
FA. M.Richards, A.Sharp 2.6.2018

Third Sister Area — Tooth Fairy

Tooth Fairy
Although only a small crag the quality of the climbing makes this a great venue. All the lines are gently overhanging and on good rock.

Approach (map and overview p.117) - At the coast path go right through a green gate and follow the coast path (occasionally marked by wooden posts) through a further two gates. 100m past the second gate, take the left fork in the path out to the headland. A wide easy-angled grassy gully leads down to the sea. Descend the grassy gully (Third Sister - Upper is on the right). For Tooth Fairy keep descending leftwards until it is possible to round the base of a buttress on the left and the base of the crag is immediately encountered.

Conditions - There is little in the way of seepage and the rock is quick drying although exposed to the elements.

❶ Dentist's Chair........ 6b
The first line on the left side of the buttress is difficult to get going past the initial overhang. Above move left into the upper groove and follow this to the lower-off.
FA. A.Sharp, P.Lewis, J.Harwood 24.10.1987

❷ Open Wide Please.... 6c+
A high quality pitch up the wall and slim groove above. The fingery lower wall gains an easing at the base of the tricky slim groove that is followed past a sharp pocket. *Photo p.121.*
FA. A.Sharp, P.Lewis 24.10.1987

❸ Silver Sixpence 7a
A worthy companion to its left-hand neighbour. Sustained and varied moves combine to give a pumpy experience.
Photo on cover.
FA. D.McCarroll, J.Bullock 5.2021

❹ Gnasher 7a
Follow the flake crack, finger traverse left and push on to a very steep finale.
FA. M.Crocker 1998

❺ Brass Farthing....... 7a
Good rock and climbing with a difficult to read upper wall.
FA. D.McCarroll, J.Bullock 5.2021

❻ Wisdom 7a
Begin 3m left of the end of the terrace and climb up to and over a bulge via some pressing moves.
FA. A. B.McCarroll, D.McCarroll 6.2021

❼ Dental Floss Tycoon 7a
Aim for the groove at the right side of the crag.
FA. G.Morris 2024

Deborah's Overhang and TV Zawn

Once the preserve of aid climbing, Deborah's Overhang is now the home of a few steep sport routes. At sea level below are some more steep routes in the tidal TV Zawn.

Approach (map and overview p.117) - At the coast path, go right through a green gate and follow the coast path (occasionally marked by wooden posts) through a further two gates. 20m past the second gate, head left down a valley (a small pinnacle on its right-hand side is a good landmark) to sea level. The crag is on the right. TV Zawn is at sea level below Deborah's Overhang. The lower section of the path is narrow, steep and above a big drop - great care needed. For 3 hours either side of low water the crags can be safely approached from under the Tooth Fairy crag.

Conditions - Deborah's Overhang is prone to seepage after wet weather but it is relatively sheltered.

Tides - TV Zawn is tidal and can be accessed for around 3 hours either side of low tide.

⑧ Going Down On Deborah. 6c
An unlikely start and a lurch gives access to the slim groove.
FA. R.Thomas, G.Ashmore 1997

⑨ Deborah .... 6c+
A powerful extended boulder problem.
FA. A.Sharp 1985

⑩ Hydraulic Lunch ..... 7c+
The original aid route from the 60s was hand-drilled with removable bolts. The modern result is a series of one-finger lock-offs, the top one requiring a little finger.
FA. G.Ashmore 3.5.1996

⑪ Three Minute Hero ...... 7a+
A short technical problem to gain the groove.
FA. A.Sharp 1985

⑫ Down Under Deborah 7a
The stepped overhang and groove is only partially bolted.
FA. R.Thomas 17.7 1999

⑬ Debauching Deborah 6c
The stepped overhang and wall is not bolted at present.
FA. R.Thomas 1997

⑭ New Zawn .... 6a+
The roof and slab to a single large staple lower-off.
FA. G.Ashmore 15.11.1996

⑮ Voyage of the Zawn Treader 5b
Pull over the roof and then head left to the staple lower-off.
FA. G.Ashmore 15.11.1996

Free Luncher's to Fetlock Zawn

Grade Spread - 8 22 1 2

This complex area has four zawns each with their own character. The approaches are slightly awkward but there is plenty on offer for the mid-grade climber looking for a bit of extra atmosphere. Zulu Zawn is an exception which only has three super-hard routes.

Approach
From Scurlage, drive 1.3 miles to parking on the right at Pilton Green (indicated by a small National Trust sign) opposite a sand coloured house called 'Clifflands' - the parking is on the grass next to the track (can be boggy if wet). Cross the road and take a footpath on the left of the sand-coloured house that heads across fields towards the coast. As the path nears the coast it dips into a small valley and the coast path is reached. From here each cliff's approach is described separately.

Conditions
The zawns are all very condition-dependent and can be greasy early in the day. It is usually best when the tide is low in the afternoon and there is a crisp onshore breeze to dry the rock out. At other times you may get lucky. Stalking Horse and Fetlock Zawn both require low tide. Free Luncher's Zawn and Zulu Zawn are both non-tidal but not good places in rough seas.

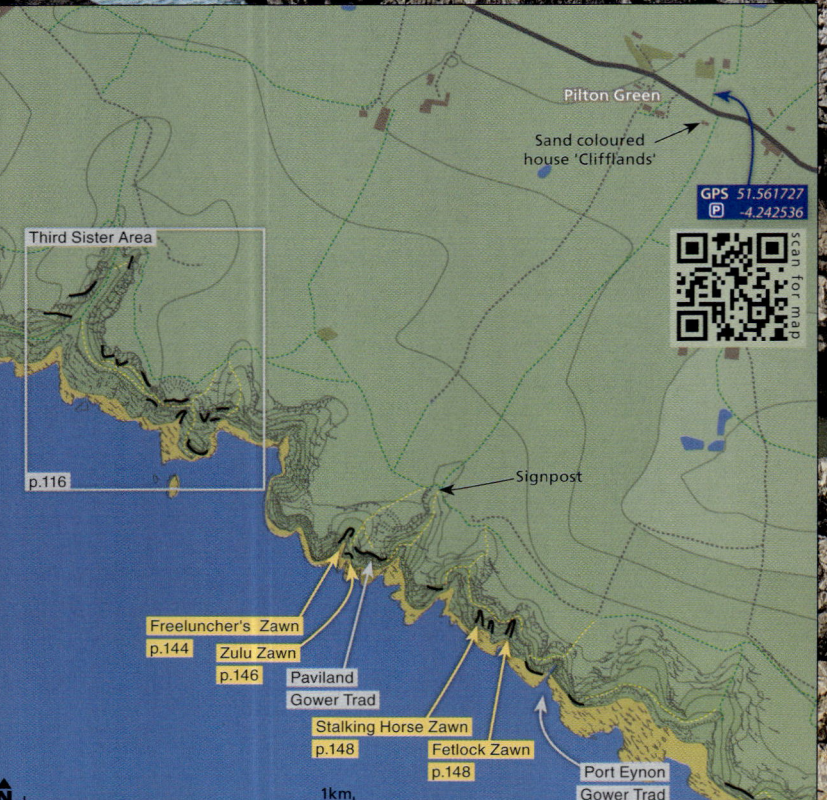

Free Luncher's to Fetlock Zawn

Sarah-Jane Barr on *Hung Over* (6a+) - *p.144* - at Free Luncher's Zawn, a really good place to spend a day ticking off some excellent mid-grade routes in a gorgeous setting. Photo: Tom Skelhon

Free Luncher's to Fetlock Zawn — Free Luncher's Zawn

Free Luncher's Zawn

An excellent venue with a quality set of mid-grade 6s. The rock is excellent and the zawn a nice place to spend a day. The base maybe inaccessible during heavy seas.

Approach (map p.142, overview p.146) - At the coast path, go right through a green gate. Walk up a short slope and then head out towards the cliff top. Between two headlands descend a wide easy-angled grassy depression and the slit of Free Luncher's Zawn is at the bottom on the right. Scramble down the left side (looking out to sea) and then back right to the base of the climbs.

Conditions - Can be cold if the sun is not out and there is a wind blowing. Suffers seepage in winter after rain.

❶ Dai's Route 5c
Slightly tidal at the start. Pull up and left steeply and then continue up the pleasant black wall to a lower-off.
FA. D.Emanuel 2011

❷ Cold Inconvenience .. 6b
Lean in from the right to clip the first bolt and then make some stiff pulls to get established on the wall. Finish up the leaning wall on surprisingly good holds.
FA. R.Thomas, G.Ashmore 2.2012

❸ Hung Over .... 6a+
A lovely pitch that gives a good introduction to the cliff. From the top left of the pinnacle, pull across onto the wall on jugs and then move up to and past a small overhang (with difficulty) to a smooth hole. Finish steeply on good holds. *Photo p.143.*
FA. R.Thomas, J.Bullock 4.1988

❹ Threadbare 6b
Pull onto the steep wall and climb it past pockets to a fingery right-hand move to finish.
FA. J.Bullock. G.Evans 15.2.1987

❺ Nematode .... 6b+
Pull onto the wall and make a sharp sequence over the square-cut overhang. Take the steep wall above on finger pockets and a good finger-flake.
FA. R.Thomas, J.Bullock, L.Moran 2.5.1988

Free Luncher's to Fetlock Zawn

Free Luncher's Zawn

6 Rock Bottom .... 6b+
Start above a wedged chockstone and step onto the apron of slabby rock. Move up to a shallow depression and a fingery exit.
FA. J.Bullock, G.Evans 24.4.1988

7 Chock a Block 6b
Follow the wall right of the slabby apron to steeper ground that is overcome on good holds.
FA. J.Bullock, L.Moran, R.Thomas 5.1988

8 Don't Look Down 6c
A project that has been climbed but the fixed gear is very old and spaced.
FA. C.Watkins, W.Calvert 7.3.2021

9 Off the Peg .... 6b+
An excellent sustained pitch. Climb the leaning lower wall to an overhung hole. Pull out and then left with difficulty to easier ground leading to a lower-off.
FA. J.Bullock, L.Moran, R.Thomas 5.1988

10 Scarface 6b
Climb the difficult initial wall to gain an easier corner/groove that holds some vegetation.
FA. J.Bullock, L.Moran, R.Thomas 5.1988

11 Hot Flush 6b
Make a hard sequence of moves up the steep lower wall to gain the base of a slim corner. Finish more easily up it.
FA. R.Thomas, G.Ashmore 12.4.2012

12 Stonewall .... 6b+
Move up steeply to reach the diagonal break and then continue up the fingery wall above it.
FA. J.Bullock, L.Moran, R.Thomas 5.1988

13 Ledger 6b
The last line of bolts on the wall is not easy to spot. Climb up to and past the diagonal break to finish at the lower-off shared with *Stonewall*.
FA. R.Thomas, J.Bullock, L.Moran 2.5.1988

Zulu Zawn

An extremely impressive and intimidating venue. The routes follow lines of weakness up the severely overhanging back wall of the zawn.

Approach (map p.142) - At the coast path, go right through a green gate. Walk up a short slope and then head out towards the cliff top. Between two headlands descend a wide easy-angled grassy depression and the slit of Free Luncher's Zawn is at the bottom on the right. As the scramble down steepens, Zulu Zawn lies down to the left. Either make an exposed scramble across the top of the zawn, and down to the base of the wall, or abseil in - gear needed to set up the abseil.

Tides - Non-tidal but needs calm conditions.

Conditions - The zawn is not a good place to be in heavy seas even at low tide. Seepage can be a problem.

① **Importunity** 8c
Begin up the corner on the left side of the wall (cam required) and at 6m move out right onto the wall and climb the bolted line via a scoop to a lower-off.
FA. A.Rogers 23.5.2024

② **Zulu Wall** 8a
An impressive natural line that tackles the central section of the severely overhanging back wall of the zawn. Follow a line of good holds to a high crux section.
FA. A.Berry 2010

③ **Ultimatum** 7c
A tricky sequence leads up the wall until a big flake is reached. From here launch rightwards with a beautiful drop knee (or a wild slap), to a ramp-line that leads to the lower-off.
Photo opposite.
FA. S.Rawlinson 3.6.2010

Simon Rawlinson on *Ultimatum* (7c) - *opposite* - at the intimidating Zulu Zawn. To the left are the chalked holds of the route *Zulu Wall* (8a) and between this and the corner is the recent addition *Importunity* (8c).
Photo: Rawlinson Collection

Stalking Horse and Fetlock Zawn

Two short but very steep venues that yield some tough pitches. Both zawns are tidal and need a bit of a breeze and/or sun for the best conditions.

Approach (map p.142) - Turn left at the coast path and walk east for 200m until above a wide valley leading down to the sea. Follow the valley down to the coast and go left until above Stalking Horse Zawn (the Stalking Horse itself is a rock outcrop just above the path). The base of the zawn can be approached via a scramble down either side or abseil. The Blowhole is 9m east of the zawn, descend by either abseil or short scramble. For Fetlock Zawn, walk below the Stalking Horse outcrop and scramble round and up to and across a fence. From the fence, head east a little way (40m) and find an easy point from which to descend to the rocks and then work your way back to the east side of the zawn. When just above the zawn, descend into it via an easy ramp situated towards the landward end.

❶ **Malopolski** .... 6b+
A direct line which crosses the diagonal crack of *Horse Wessel*.
FA. G.Ashmore, R.Thomas 1.5.2021

❷ **Cerbat Mustang** .... 6b+
Steep climbing up the wall to a shared lower-off.
FA. G.Ashmore, R.Thomas 25.4.2021

❸ **Suffolk Punch** .... 6c+
Gain the diagonal crack then climb steeply up the wall.
FA. G.Ashmore, R.Thomas 11.4.2021

❹ **Horse Wessel** .... 6b+
The diagonal crack is a fierce jamming exercise.
FA. G.Ashmore, R.Thomas 11.4.2021

❺ **Paso Fino** 6c
The steep wall left of the arete of the flaky corner.
FA. G.Ashmore, R.Thomas 5.2021

❻ **Frisky Foal** 5c
Climb right from the ramp and up the flaky corner, tricky to start. Pre-clipping the second bolt might preserve your ankles.
FA. R.Thomas, G.Morris 4.2021

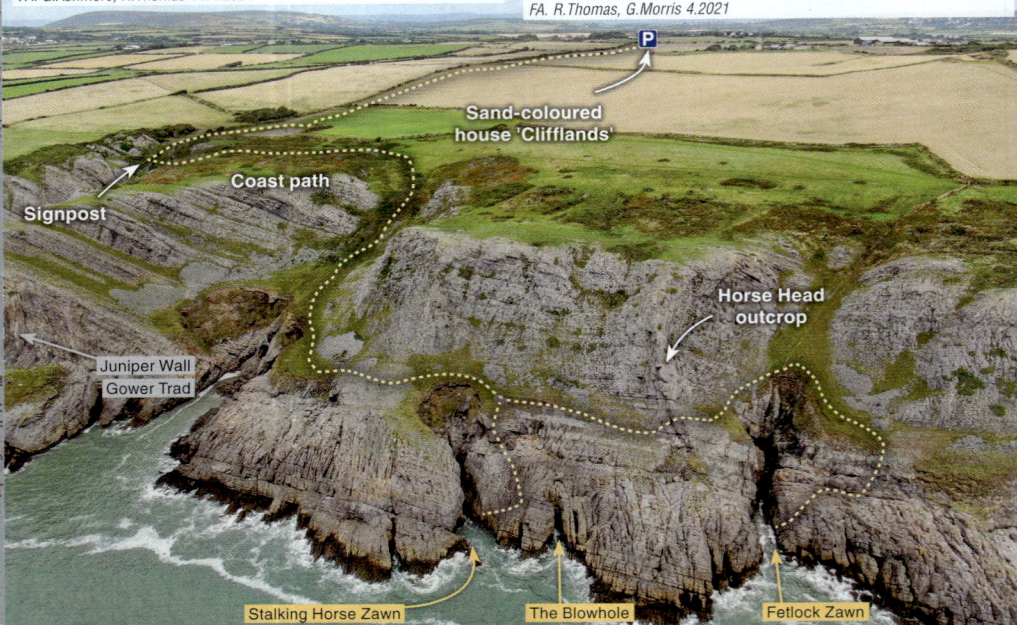

Free Luncher's to Fetlock Zawn

7 Filly Buster 5b
Climb the wall to the right of the flaky corner.
FA. R.Thomas, G.Morris 4.2021

8 Jockey Club 5c
Continue traversing right from *Filly Buster*. Either belay at a small spike or launch straight up steep flakes. Atmospheric.
FA. R.Thomas, G.Morris 4.2021

The Blowhole (no topo)

9 Pocket Universe 5c
A classic of the genre, squirm and back'n'foot up the chimney.
FA. G.Ashmore, R.Thomas, G.Morris 17.4.2021

10 Guth's Gut .... 6c+
3D climbing. Battle up the gaping rift to a shared lower-off.
FA. G.Ashmore, R.Thomas 1.5.2021

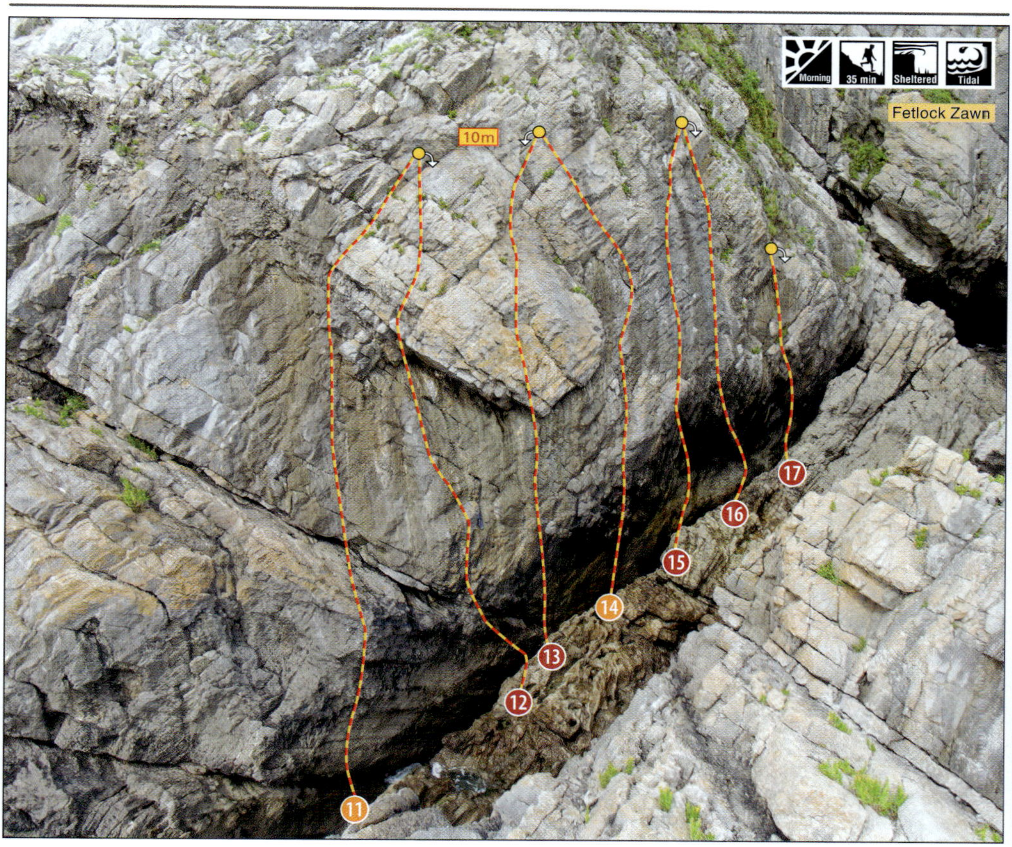

11 Brood Mare 6a
The left-hand line eases after the diagonal break is reached.
FA. R.Thomas 7.2020

12 Stud Farm 6b
From the base of the diagonal, climb the rib and overlap.
FA. R.Thomas 7.2020

13 Bareback Rider 6b
Climb the right side of a bulge, then the overlap via a thin seam.
FA. R.Thomas, T.Hoddy 7.2020

14 Pulling Back .... 6a+
The centre of the low bulge to a lower-off.
FA. R.Thomas, E.Chapman 7.2020

15 Crib Biter .... 6b+
A very steep start contrasts with a slabby section above.
FA. R.Thomas, G.Ashmore 5.2021

16 Stallions' Beans .... 6c+
Launch across the chasm and pull vigorously on pockets until easier moves are gained on the slab above.
FA. R.Thomas 8.2021

17 Saddle Sores 6b
A short route on the right that has a hard start.
FA. R.Thomas, Ed Chapman 8.2021

Port Eynon

Grade Spread - 1 2 - -

This small crag at the popular tourist area of Port Eynon is hidden in a secluded location below a conspicuous obelisk on the headland. This is not a major venue but useful if staying in the area or for those looking for something away from the more established spots.

Approach
From Scurlage, continue on the A4118 to Port Eynon. Go through the village and park in the large car park (Fee). Take the footpath through the caravan park to the Youth Hostel. Go right and then left on the footpath path which then climbs past some old quarries to the obelisk on the headland. Walk down left (facing out to sea) to the base of the cliff and then cut back right to the crag which is in the second inlet.

Tides
The crag is accessible for 3 hours either side of low water.

Conditions
The cliff is exposed to westerly winds and takes time for the base to dry out once the tide falls. Seepage maybe present.

❶ Humidor .... 6c+
Overcome the roof via two large pockets and a trying final move. Finish at a shared lower-off up on the right..
FA. G.Ashmore 28.9.2013

❷ Condenser .... 6b+
Gain and climb the roof to finish at the shared lower-off.
FA. G.Ashmore 28.9.2013

❸ Guillible Troubles 6a
Gain and climb the right side of the overhang then finish easily up left to the shared lower-off.
FA. R.Thomas, G.Ashmore 28.9.2013

Oxwich

Since the previous guidebook was published in 2016 the major crag of Oxwich's Sea Wall has mostly fallen down! A little further along the beach is the shy Oxwich in the Woods crag which has a good supply of grade 6s, though good conditions are not easy to find. There is plenty of bouldering on the huge boulders below the cliff that was the Oxwich Sea Wall.

Approach

From the A4118, turn left just after the village of Nicholston and follow the road across the marsh to Oxwich. On the left-hand side of the road is a parking area (fee). From the beach, contour the right edge for 500m until the remains of the Sea Walls are passed. Continue along the shore for another 300m and, at a low overhang, head up into the woods on a hidden path. The crag is 100m from the shore.

Tides

The crag is accessible for at least 3 hours either side of low water. It is actually above water at high tide so it is possible to walk in at low water, climb when the tide is in and then walk out again as the tide falls.

Conditions

Oxwich in the Woods is shaded by a dense tree canopy and is very greasy and unclimbable in humid conditions. It is also prone to getting dusty/dirty if traffic has been thin so may need to be cleaned.

Oxwich — In the Woods

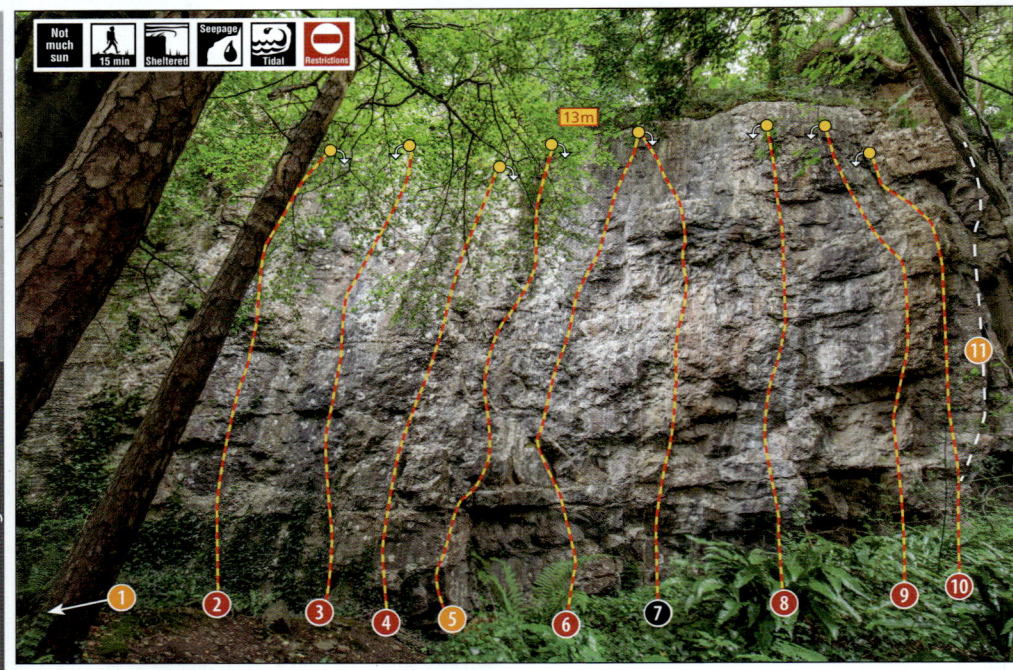

In the Woods

A compact wall of vertical and slightly leaning rock that gives some decent climbing when clean and dry.

Approach (map and overview p.151) - Walk a further 300m along the shoreline from the collapsed Oxwich Sea Wall and, at a low slit overhang in a section of cliff that juts out from the hillside, head up 100m into the woods.

Tides - The approach to the cliff is accessible for around 3 hours either side low water, though the base of the cliff is non-tidal.

Conditions - Only head to this crag in dry weather and bring a brush. The rock is prone to gathering dust and becomes very greasy and unclimbable when it is humid. The crag lies below a dense tree canopy which holds the moisture in.

Access - The cliff is in a SSSI and should not be approached from above.

❶ Load of Bullocks .... 6a+
20m to the left of the main crag is a route up a barrel-shaped buttress. Overgrown at the start.
FA. R.Thomas 2005

❷ Underneath the Larches ..... 6b+
Nice climbing with a tough initial sequence passing a thin crackline. Can get overgrown.
FA. G.Gibson 2005

❸ Life's Too Short 6c
Super fingery climbing up the right-hand side of the wall.
FA. G.Gibson 2005

❹ Snatched from the Cradle
.... 6b
Worthwhile fingery climbing. Keep out of *Cradle Snatcher*.
FA. G.Gibson 2005

❺ Cradle Snatcher 6a
Make hard pulls to gain the good looking groove above.
FA. G.Gibson 2005

❻ Baby Going Boing Boing
.... 6b+
Hard moves are needed to pass the low overhang which then accesses a smooth groove and awkward finish.
FA. G.Gibson 2005

❼ Laughing Boy .... 7b+
Powerful fingery pulls lead to a desperate twisting finale.
FA. G.Gibson 16.7.2005

❽ Baby Bouncer .... 6c+
A powerful undercut start gains good sustained climbing above.
FA. G.Gibson 17.7.2005

❾ Teenage Kicks .... 6c+
An impressive line. Start up the low hanging arete and then continue up the bulging rib above.
FA. G.Gibson 17.7.2005

❿ My Inheritance 6b
A tight line that is squeezed into the wall to the right, gained from the start of the groove of *Ox-Over Moon*.
FA. G.Gibson 17.7.2005

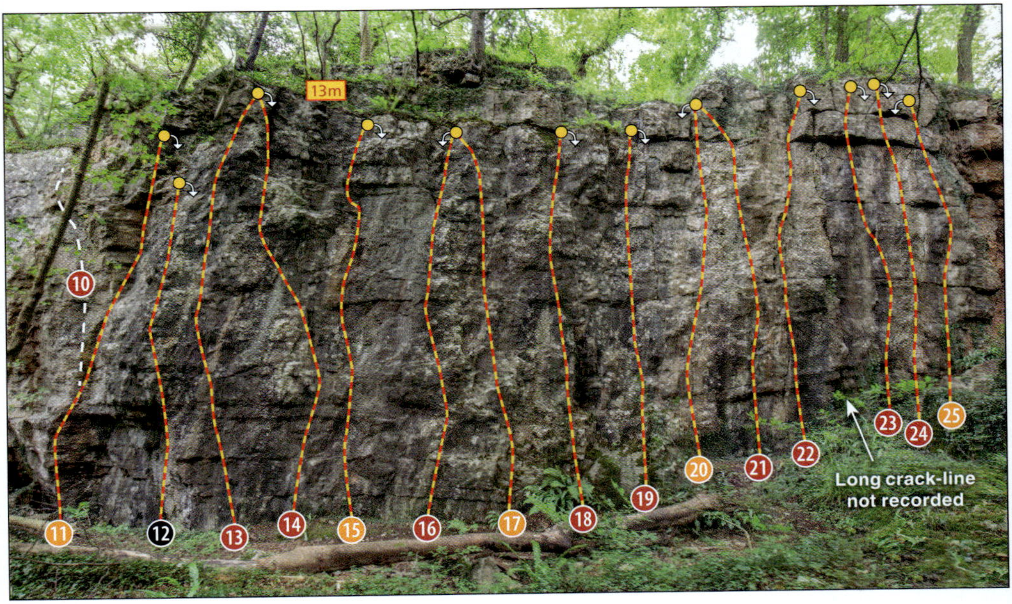

11 Ox-Over Moon .... 6a+
The open groove has a steep and tricky start.
FA. G.Gibson 17.7.2005

12 Dynamo Kiev .... 7b+
A powerful bouldery start that features a flying leap, is followed by fingery moves above.
FA. G.Gibson 17.7.2005

13 Grated Expectations 7a
Excellent thin moves following on from a fierce start.
FA. G.Gibson 17.7.2005

14 Anonymous Flare 6c
The left-leaning groove system.
FA. T.Dhallu 2004

15 Suppose I Try 6a
The shallow groove and thin crack-line.
FA. R.Thomas 2004

16 Anal Gesia 6b
Sustained and technical face climbing.
FA. R.Thomas 2004

17 Nice Groove .... 6a+
The groove is very nice when clean and dry.
FA. N.O'Neill 2004

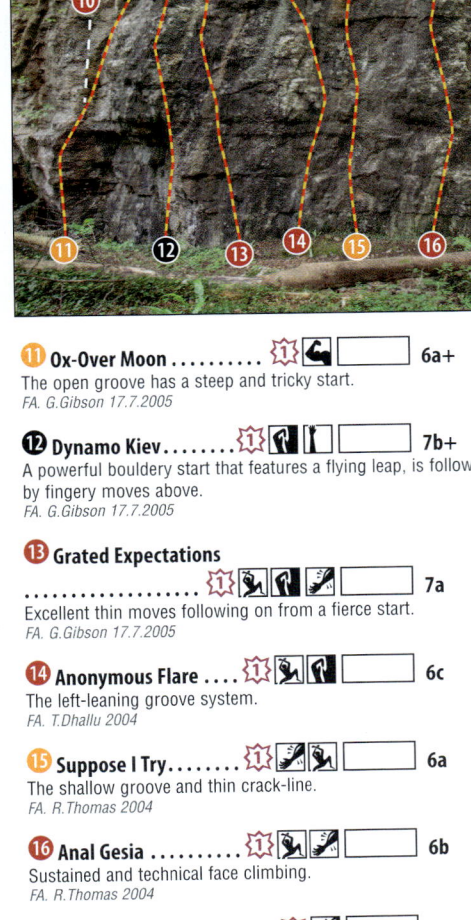

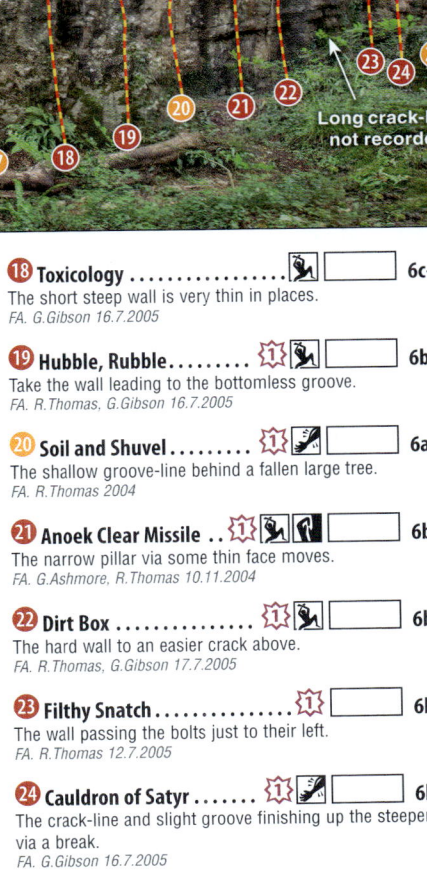

18 Toxicology .... 6c+
The short steep wall is very thin in places.
FA. G.Gibson 16.7.2005

19 Hubble, Rubble 6b
Take the wall leading to the bottomless groove.
FA. R.Thomas, G.Gibson 16.7.2005

20 Soil and Shuvel .... 6a+
The shallow groove-line behind a fallen large tree.
FA. R.Thomas 2004

21 Anoek Clear Missile .. 6b
The narrow pillar via some thin face moves.
FA. G.Ashmore, R.Thomas 10.11.2004

22 Dirt Box .... 6b+
The hard wall to an easier crack above.
FA. R.Thomas, G.Gibson 17.7.2005

23 Filthy Snatch 6b
The wall passing the bolts just to their left.
FA. R.Thomas 12.7.2005

24 Cauldron of Satyr 6b
The crack-line and slight groove finishing up the steeper wall via a break.
FA. G.Gibson 16.7.2005

25 Devil's Brew .... 6a+
The low bulge and thin crack-line to easier ground.
FA. R.Thomas 16.7.2005

Carmarthenshire
Gower
Inland and Coastal Limestone
The Valleys Sandstone

Utopia Area

| Grade Spread | 5 | 11 | 6 | - | - |

A popular area that is perfect for those operating in the low-to-mid grades. It is a reliable spot to head for during the cooler months being non-tidal, sheltered, having full sun all day and very little seepage. Most of the routes follow nicely featured slabs, but there are a number that have steep starts. The approach involves some exposed scrambling and care is needed to find the best line.

Approach   Map p.164

From the National Trust car park in Southgate, head west along the road. 50m before the road ends, follow the track on the left to where it meets more open ground; the distinct ridge of White Edge (a trad route) can be seen on the left. Cut down to the left in between gorse and the ridge to a col. On the opposite side of the col drop down 6m and then scramble on an indistinct line across the slope, descending slightly to an incised bedding plane that cuts back to ledges which lead around to below the Equal Opportunities Area. For Utopia Slabs continue on large ledges for 50m to the slabs.

Conditions

Sunny open and quick drying. Seepage is a problem in winter at Equal Opportunities.

Utopia Slabs

Utopia Slabs
A fine open cliff with some good low and mid-grade routes. The best climbing is on off-vertical slabs but some have steep starts.
Approach - Continue along from the Equal Opportunities area to the crag.
Conditions - The crag is sunny, open and quick drying.

① Julie's Delight 4a
A delightful nicely featured slab.
FA. J.Burrows, L.Burrows 2023

② Fools Rush In 4c
Begin up *Julie's Delight* and then break right and follow some accommodating big pockets to a lower-off.
FA. J.Burrows, L.Burrows 2023

③ Tom Foolery 5b
Begin in a groove then step left onto a ledge. Aim for the long crack-line and climb it. Sticking rigidly to the crack is **6a**.
FA. J.Bullock, D.McCarroll 2023

④ Ejit 4a
Head up the groove as for *Tom Foolery* and continue until it is possible to swing left onto a big flake. Follow the flake to the lower-off of *Tom Foolery*. Take care with the rock near the top.
FA. J.Bullock, D.McCarroll 2023

⑤ Meteor Storm 6a
Climb the steep groove left of the corner of *Utopia* to a bolt out left. Swing onto the arete and on up left to a shared lower-off. Do not continue up the loose top section of the groove.
FA. D.McCarroll, L.Burrows 2023

⑥ Utopia 5a
The beautiful full-height corner is a superb pitch.
FA. J.Bullock, D.McCarroll 2023

⑦ Michelinia 5a
A tricky pull through the overhang leads to pleasant slab climbing and the *Utopia* lower-off. Named for the spectacular fossil coral near the top.
FA. J.Bullock, D.McCarroll 2023

⑧ Xanadu 5b
Start as for *Michelinia* and move right along the lip of the overhang to good holds at the first arete. Continue up the slab above to a lower-off. *Photo p.157*.
FA. J.Bullock, D.McCarroll 2023

⑨ Xanadont 6a
The arete to the right of Xanadu can be accessed using the same start and traversing across the lip. Can be started by a steep and crimpy direct coming from the left (**6b+**) or a really crimpy and really steep from the right (**6c**).
FA. J.Bullock, D.McCarroll 2023

⑩ Elysium .... 6b+
A direct line through the steepest part of the arch. No sneaking off to either side at this grade.
FA. J.Bullock, D.McCarroll 2023

⑪ Erewhon 5b
Execute a tricky move to reach some jugs and then make a couple of steep pulls to gain a pleasant slab.
FA. J.Bullock, D.McCarroll 2023

Utopia Area — Equal Opportunities Area

Equal Opportunities Area

An overhung cave and small well-bolted slab that can be easily combined with the more extensive Utopia Slabs. The cave is also a popular bouldering venue.

Approach (map p.164 overview p.154) - From the National Trust car park in Southgate, head west along the road. 50m before the road ends follow the track on the left to where it meets more open ground; the distinct ridge of White Edge (a trad route) can be seen on the left. Cut down to the left in between gorse and the ridge to a col. On the opposite side of the col drop down 6m and then scramble on an indistinct line across the slope, descending slightly to an incised bedding plane that cuts back to ledges which lead around to below Equal Opportunities Area. This approach is an exposed scramble and needs care.

Conditions - The cave is sheltered but does seep at times. The slab dries rapidly.

1 Glamring 7a
Very steep climbing up the left edge of the cave.
FA. D.McCarroll 2024

2 Tom 6b
Jugs and side-pulls all the way.
FA. D.McCarroll, J.Bullock 2024

3 Bert .... 6a+
Breaks through the overhangs via the little corners. The holds are big and they need to be!
FA. D.McCarroll, J.Bullock 2024

4 Mandiba 6b
Good pockets lead the way through the bulges.
FA. J.Bullock, D.McCarroll 2024

5 Purgatory .... 6b+
Very steep ground via the sloping ledge.
FA. D.McCarroll, J.Bullock 2024

6 Godot 6c
Start in the corner, break right and then crimp through the bulge to jugs. Do not grovel into the loose corner. A direct line right of the bolts is 7a.
FA. D.McCarroll, J.Bullock 2024

7 Wait Here Please 6a
Aim for the slim leaning groove using the arete in places.
FA. J.Bullock, D.McCarroll 2024

8 Eirwyn 4c
The left edge of the slab passing right of the small overhang.
FA. J.Bullock 2024

9 Little White Dove 5c
The middle of the slab gives fine if escapable climbing.
FA. D.McCarroll, J.Bullock 2024

Utopia Area

Matt Woodfield on *Xanadu* (5b) - *p.155* - the Utopia Slabs. This area has been recently developed and, along with the nearby Equal Opportunities Area and adjoining slab, pretty much spans the grade range and even has some tough bouldering. Photo: Jacob Isaac

10 Egret........................ 4c
Hop over the left edge of the overlap and link the big holes.
FA. J.Bullock, D.McCarroll 2024

11 Archie........................ 6a
The central line through the overlap involves a steep pull.
FA. D.McCarroll, J.Bullock 2024

Watch House

Grade Spread | 5 | 11 | 19 | 4 | -

The Watch House crags offer differing climbing styles. Watch House Slab has some fierce pitches that should not be approached too casually, especially if out of practice on slabby territory! The overhanging Watch House East has more conventional fare, mostly featuring steep starts leading onto vertical walls.

Approach   Map p.164

From the National Trust car park (fee) at Southgate village, walk west along the small road on the edge of the houses for 250m, and at house number 9 break left across the field to the edge of the plateau. Descend a narrow path to the right of two grassy knolls to reach rocky ledges. Scramble right (looking out) over boulders to a ledge that leads to the Watch House Slab; or from the rocky ledges go left (looking out) for Watch House East. At lowish tide it is easy to walk between Foxhole and Watch House East - useful for taking a look at what is available or a quick change of venue.

Tides

Watch House Slab and The Shady Side are non-tidal. The Zawn is tidal and accessible for around 3 hours either side of low-water. During calm seas, climbing on Watch House East is possible on the landward lines at all times. The lines on the right are accessible for around 3.5 hours either side of low-water.

Conditions

Watch House Slab and the Shady Side are well above the sea. Watch House East and The Zawn are best avoided in rough weather. None of the crags offer the possibility of climbing whilst it is raining and all suffer seepage after prolonged rainfall.

Watch House

Shady Side and The Zawn

Opposite the main slab is a complex area of rock with a number of steep lines that need care with some of the rock. Underneath the approach ledge is a tidal zawn that has a couple of short, easy bolted routes.

Approach (map p.164 overview p.154 - Descend a narrow path to the right of two grassy knolls to reach rocky ledges. Scramble right (looking out) over boulders to a ledge that leads to the Watch House Slab area. The Zawn bed can be approached via a down-climb or short abseil.

Tides - The Zawn can be accesses for 3 hours either side of low water.

Conditions - There is some seepage after rain.

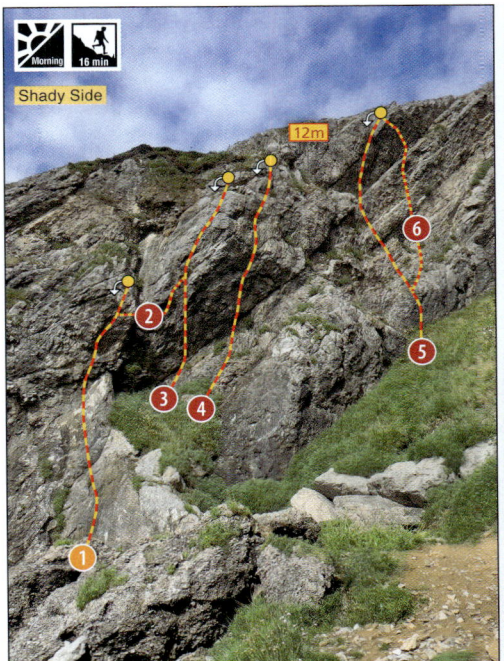

Shady Side

① **Solanum** 6a
Start on the ledge above the gully (belay bolt). Good steep climbing up the buttress left of the rubble-filled gully.
FA. D.McCarroll, J.Bullock 22.9.2021

② **One Step in the Shade** .... 6b+
Follow *Solanum* to its belay lower-off. Lean across the rubble-filled gap, clip a bolt and make an exciting step over on to the very overhanging wall using a good undercut which allows progress up and right. (DO NOT try to climb the slab instead of stepping onto the steep wall, you will pull a ton of rubble down on your second!)
FA. D.McCarroll 2018

③ **Bella Donna** 6c
Deadly. The hanging rib right of the rubble. Stay right of the bolts.
FA. D.McCarroll 2019

④ **Shadow Master** .... 6c+
The centre of the overhanging wall starting via the black slab. Nice moves on surprisingly good holds.
FA. D.McCarroll 2018

⑤ **Umbra** .... 6b+
Start up the slope beyond the triangular lower buttress (belay bolt). Climb the leaning wall with increasing difficulty to a distinct crux at the hanging crack. Step right into the niche.
FA. J.Bullock 2019

⑥ **Penumbra** 6b
Climb directly up the wall via two sloping ledges to finish right of the niche.
FA. J.Bullock, D.McCarroll 2019

The Zawn below is approached by a short abseil or down-climb.

⑦ **Ledger** 4c
Climb the zawn wall via the ledges.
FA. B.McCarroll, D.McCarroll 2018

⑧ **Raspberry Ripple** 4b
The slabby side of the zawn. Take the edge of the pink-rippled slab near the cave. No lower-off in place, belay required.
FA. B.McCarroll, D.McCarroll 2018

The Zawn

Watch House — Watch House Slab

Watch House Slab

A compact slab in a steep grassy gully. The rock is reasonable and the bolting good. The climbing is fierce and those not good at slabs should head elsewhere.

Approach (map p.164 overview p.154) - From Southgate car park, walk west along the small road on the edge of the houses for 250m. At house number 9, break left across the field to the edge of the plateau. Descend a steep narrow path right of two grassy knolls to rocky ledges just above sea level. Head right along rock ledges to the cliff.

Conditions - There is some seepage after rain.

1 Thorn 3b
The twisting rib at the top end of the slab.
FA. B.McCarroll 2017

2 Wynne 4b
Some varied climbing.
FA. D.McCarroll, B.McCarroll 2017

3 Excavation Left 6a
The blunt rib and slab with pleasant moves.
FA. J.Bullock, D.McCarroll 2008

4 Excavation Right 5c
Follow the smooth runnel until forced left onto the arete.
FA. D.McCarroll, J.Bullock 2023

5 Tickety-Boo 6a
A good little slab. Follow the high-angled slab just to the right of the right-facing shallow corner/groove. *Photo opposite*.
FA. D.McCarroll, J.Bullock 2023

6 Rise and Shine 5b
A useful easier hybrid. From the second bolt of *Tickety-Boo*, take the easiest line to the finish of *St.Vitus's Dance*.
FA. B.McCarrroll 6.2011

7 Sport Wars 6a
Begin just left of the bolt-line. A nice pitch.
FA. D.Cook, D.McCarroll 2008

8 Tread Gently .... 6b+
An intense and insecure start gains another tricky sequence that eventually relents to steadier climbing up the final wall.
FA. J.Bullock, D.McCarroll 2008

Watch House

9 St. Vitus's Dance — 6c+
A thin and technical lower wall eases above the white streaks.
FA. D.McCarroll, D.Cook 2008

10 The Drilling Fields — 7a
A tough slabby start gains much easier ground above.
FA. J.Bullock, D.McCarroll 2008

11 Anonymous Bosch — 6b
A good route up the overlapping walls.
FA. J.Bullock, D.McCarroll 2008

12 Jaded Locals — 6b+
The best pitch at the crag. Follow *Anonymous Bosch* to its second bolt and then head right and up through the bulges.
FA. J.Bullock, D.McCarroll 2008

13 I Bolt, Therefore I Am — 6c+
Climb the technical lower face to the bulge. Make some fingery pulls through the bulge to finish.
FA. J.Bullock, D.McCarroll 2008

14 Escapement — 6b
Step right at the top to reach the lower-off (rock straight above not suitable for bolting).
FA. J.Bullock, D.McCarroll 2018

15 Bending Sickle — 6a+
A right-to-left curving diagonal. Follow the pockets under the overhang until they run out. Clip the bolt above and keep going left, to join *St. Vitus's Dance* at the arch and finish up this.
FA. D.McCarroll, J.Bullock 5.2011

16 Trad Man V2 — 6c
Follow the right side of the calcite streak on pockets, avoiding the groove to the right.
FA. J.Bullock, D.McCarroll 2008

17 Non Binary — 5c
Start on the raised grassy ledge and follow the groove.
FA. D.McCarroll, J.Bullock 2020

18 Sport Girl — 5b
Steep, sharp and on big holds.
FA. D.McCarroll, J.Bullock 18.11.2018

19 Sportsman — 5b
The central line on the short steep wall has big holds and friendly bolting.
FA. D.McCarroll, J.Bullock 2024

20 Right Carfuffle — 3c
The right edge of the buttress, over the small overlaps.
FA. D.McCarroll, J.Bullock 2024

Fraser Norton on *Tickety-Boo* (6a) - *opposite* - at Watch House Slab, one of many good off-vertical pitches that are highly technical but thankfully not too strenuous. Photo: Matt Woodfield.

Watch House Watch House East

Watch House East

A steep crag down by the sea. Although tidal at its seaward end some of the routes can be climbed at all times in calm seas.

Approach (map p.164 overview p.154 - From Southgate car park, walk west along the small road on the edge of the houses for 250m. At house number 9, break left across the field to the edge of the plateau. Descend a steep narrow path right of two grassy knolls to rocky ledges just above sea level. Head left to the cliff.
Tides - During calm seas, climbing is possible at all times on the landward lines. The lines on the right are accessible for around 3.5 hours either side of low water.
Conditions - There is seepage after prolonged rainfall.

❶ **Left Wing Rebolt** 6b
Make some tough pulls to a ledge before moving left to the arete and following this to the top.
FA. D.McCarroll, J.Bullock 2009

❷ **Strain Drain** 7a
A direct line past a rail.
FA. J.Bullock, D.McCarroll 21.10.2012

❸ **Straining Pitch** .... 6b+
Start as for *Left Wing Rebolt* and continue via a steep crack and past a roof to the top. A good pitch.
FA. J.Bullock, G.Evans 1989

❹ **Touch and Go** .... 7a+
Climb the roof-infested line to the right of *Straining Pitch*.
FA. D.McCarroll, J.Bullock 10.2010

❺ **Jump to Conclusions**.. 7a
One tough move through the overlap, then some technical climbing remains up the wall and groove above. Start as for *Touch and Go*.
FA. J.Bullock, M.Kydd 2.9.1989

❻ **Pump Action** .... 7a+
Reach and climb a crack before some tricky moves gain an undercut and good pockets. Powerful climbing gains an arete and finishing groove above.
FA. J.Bullock, R.Thomas 1989

❼ **Clip Joint** 6c
A worthwhile pitch. The steep red groove has big holds at first and leads to a slab and arete.
FA. J.Bullock, G.Evans 16.5.1989

❽ **Chiropractor** 7b
Very steep pocket climbing off of the big boulder.
FA. D.McCarroll 2008

❾ **No Rest for the Wicked** 7a+
Start down behind the boulder - Use of the boulder should be avoided at this grade.
FA. A.Berry 1995

❿ **Too Many Fingers** 7a
A pumpy line avoiding the arete. From the belay it is possible to continue along *Nia Miss*. Moving out right from the steep ground lowers the grade to 6c+.
FA. D.McCarroll, J.Bullock 2008

⓫ **Nia Miss** 5c
An adventurous outing that requires careful route finding and some long slings. Start on the ledge at the right-hand side of the crag at a bolt belay. Step around the corner, and creep leftwards across the slab, then continue round to bridge up the corner.
FA. J.Bullock, D.McCarroll 2008

Foxhole

Grade Spread | 10 | 9 | 11 | 9 | 4

Gower's coastline is peppered with well-hidden bays. Foxhole is one of these with a back wall that lends itself both to climbing and isolation - a real gem. The left-hand side of the recess is formed by the roof of an old cave, whilst the right-hand side provides a fine wall of excellent fused limestone. There is a variety of climbing styles on offer here that ranges from some easy-angled slabs to super steep cave lines. All the routes are worth while but the best climbing is in the mid-to-higher grades. The crag is rainproof, very close to the parking and cafe, and can be climbed on all year round as long as it is not seeping.

Conditions

The cliff faces southwest and gets sunshine from mid-morning onwards. The overhanging nature means the crag can give shade, but it is not an ideal venue when the weather is hot and sunny. It does, however, make it an ideal spring and autumn venue. The crag suffers from seepage after spells of rain during the winter months, but when dry, it stays so for long periods and can even be climbed on in rain. The cliff is completely non-tidal.

Foxhole 165

Andy Sharp on *Turkey Lurking* (7c) - *p.173* - at Foxhole, Gower. This pitch along with a good number of other hard lines are popular long leftward traverses that cross some of the Main Crag's steepest ground. Photo: Elis Rees

Foxhole

Approach   Map p.164

Follow the road through Southgate village to the National Trust car park (fee). From here, walk west along the small road on the edge of the houses for 250m and at house number 9, break left across the field to the edge of the plateau. Descend to the left of two grassy knolls and when towards the bottom of the slope contour right on a path around the ridge and down to the crag. This is a different approach to that previously described.

Foxhole 167

Jordan Buys on *Goose in Lucy* (6c+) - *p.171* - at Foxhole. This route takes on some very steep ground at the left edge of the Main Crag and makes use of an unusual conglomerate rail on which the climber is moving along. Photo: Mike Hutton

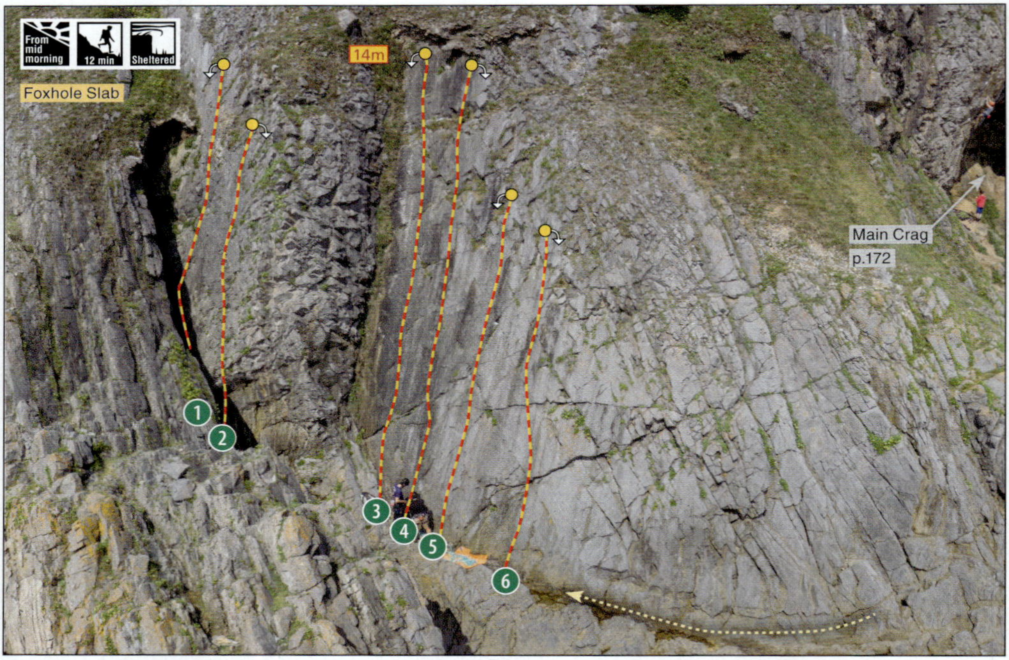

Foxhole — Foxhole Slab and Kitten Hole

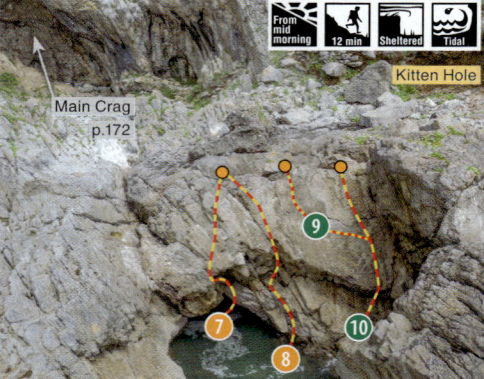

Foxhole Slab and Kitten Hole

On the left and to seaward of the main Foxhole crag are two other crags that contain a selection of easier lines, the easy-angled Foxhole Slab being particularly popular. Kitten Hole is a minor section of crag that is tidal.

Approach (map p.164 overview p.166) - From below the main crag head right (looking out to sea) for 60m to reach the base of Foxhole Slab. For Kitten Hole head right (looking out to sea) for 30m and descend a small promontory to the base of the crag - which is tidal.

Conditions - The slab faces southwest and gets sunshine from mid-morning onwards. Kitten Hole will need time to dry once the tide has fallen.

Tides - Kitten Hole is tidal and is accessible for around 4 hours either side of low water.

❶ Cleft a bit 4a
The left-most route past the easy slab and inside the deep cleft. Bridge up passing conglomerate to emerge onto the open slab
FA. R.McCarroll, B.McCarroll 2017

❷ Cleftomaniac 4b
In the cleft left of the main slab. Wide bridging or some steep pulling gains the clean slab which is climbed left of the bolts.
FA. B.McCarroll, D.McCarroll 26.4.2017

❸ Leopard Prints 4b
The pleasant slab just right of the corner. Excellent rock.
FA. S.Rusling, B.McCarroll 24.1.2017

❹ The Power of the Leopard Skin Leg Warmers
.... 3c
An enjoyable experience up the left side of the slab
FA. R.Frugtniet 3.2010

❺ A Leopard Cannot Change His Spots
.... 2c
The right-hand of the two shorter lines is fun.
FA. S.Rawlinson 4.5.2014

❻ Leopard Cub 2c
The rightmost line of glue-in bolts on the slab.
FA. N.Rocke 5.6.2022

Foxhole

Kitten Hole

7 Ninetails 6a
The very steep pillar right of the pool.
FA. B.McCarroll 2018

8 Kitten 5c
Fight up the jug-infested edge of the small cave.
FA. B.McCarroll 2018

9 Caninia 4b
Break out diagonally left from the slab of *Rugosa*.
FA. B.McCarroll 2018

10 Rugosa 3b
The right side of the slab is very pleasant.
FA. B.McCarroll 2018

Nicola Parkin on *Joy de Viva* (7a) - *p.173* - at Foxhole, Gower. The right-hand side of the Main Crag has a quartet of quality 7a's which culminate in exhilarating pulls to reach the lower-offs before the arms give up.
Photo: Marsha Balaeva

Main Crag

Foxhole is a real gem. The main crag is home to hard, high quality climbing on the roof of an old cave, and its right-hand side on a fine wall of excellent fused limestone.

Approach (map p.164 overview p.166) - Follow the road through Southgate village to the National Trust car park (fee). Walk west along the small road on the edge of the houses for 250m and, at house number 9, break left across the field to the edge of the plateau. Descend to the left of two grassy knolls and, when towards the bottom of the slope, contour right around the ridge and down to the crag.

❶ Never Out Fox the Fox 5a
Follow the black slab up left and then onward via steeper ground on good holds to the top.
FA. S.Llewellyn 10.6.2010

❷ Reynard 5c
Break right up good rock above the black slab at the start of *Never Out Fox the Fox*.
FA. D.McCarroll, J.Bullock 2022

Conditions - The main cliff faces southwest and gets sunshine from mid-morning onwards. The crag can give shade due to its steepness but it is not ideal when it is hot and sunny but it is an ideal spring and autumn venue. The crag suffers from seepage after rain but, when dry, it stays so for long periods and can even be climbed on in rain. The main cliff is non-tidal.

Main Crag Foxhole 171

3 Cunning Little Fox 5a
Head up the crack and ledges to a lower-off at a small overhang.
FA. S.Llewellyn 25.5.2010

4 Vulpes Vulpes 5b
The right-hand branch of *Cunning Little Fox* is worthwhile.
FA. D.McCarroll, J.Bullock 2018

5 Vulpix 4c
Pleasant bridging up the runnel left of *Basil Brush*.
FA. R.McCarroll 17.4.2017

6 Basil Brush 4c
The first climb on the main section of crag.
FA. D.McCarroll, J.Bullock 5.3.2013

7 Unholy Alliance .... 6a+
Steep climbing up the white pillar on the fringe of the main crag.
FA. M.Crocker, J.Harwood 1.5.1994

8 Marmalade Skies 7a
A tight line which follows the deceptively steep orange streak that features a tough pull just above mid-height.
FA. D.McCarroll, J.Bullock 2.3.201

9 Connard Canard 7b
A very steep route that follows the long grey streak with two bouldery sections.
FA. G.Gibson, M.Gouze 1.9.1998

10 Goose in Lucy .... 6c+
Popular and very good when dry. A bouldery start past some finger pockets leads onto a rail and jug-riddled upper wall. *Photo p.167*.
FA. R.Thomas, S.Coles 11.5.1996

11 Lucky Lizzy .... 6c+
Link *Goose in Lucy* to the prow of *Surplomb de Ray*.
FA. S.Rawlinson 23.4.2010

12 Surplomb de Ray .... 8b+
Make desperate bouldery moves to a good tufa jug and continue to finish up the much easier prow.
FA. S.Rawlinson 20.6.2010

13 Pioneers of the Hypnotic Groove
.... 7b
A brilliant exercise that tackles the severely leaning groove in the back of the cave. Can be extended up *Surplomb de Ray* (no change in grade). *Photo p.25*.
FA. G.Ashmore, S.Coles, J.Jewell 19.4.1996

14 Salva Mea 8a
Climb the short yellow wall and overhang. Continue via some powerful moves which gain a technical finish.
FA. S.Clarke 23.6.2018

15 L'Enigma et le Renard 8a
Begin up *Palace of Swords Reversed* and from its second bolt use some crimps, a sharp side-pulls and a dyno to reach and finish as for *Salva Mea*.
FA. P.Buchan 12.4.2019

16 Palace of Swords Reversed
.... 8a
The impressive bulging wall provides one of the testpieces of the area. *Photo p.32*.
FA. G.Ashmore 8.9.1996

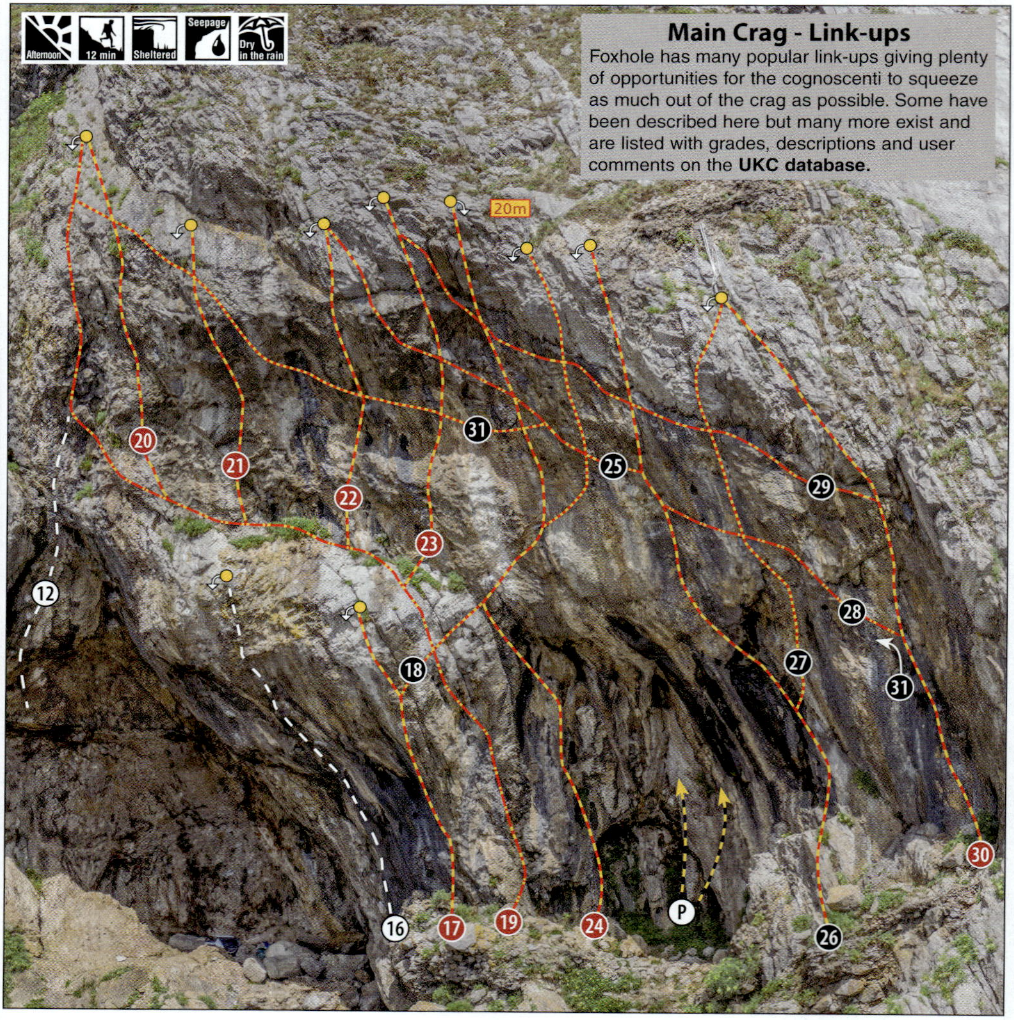

Foxhole — Main Crag

Main Crag - Link-ups
Foxhole has many popular link-ups giving plenty of opportunities for the cognoscenti to squeeze as much out of the crag as possible. Some have been described here but many more exist and are listed with grades, descriptions and user comments on the **UKC database**.

17 Chicken Licken 7a
A short, sharp mission just left of the arete to a mid-height easing and a lower-off.
FA. R.Thomas 19.7.1996

18 Fowl Play 7b
Some steep terrain. Climb *Chicken Licken* to its 4th bolt. Move right to a jug on *Joy de Viva*. Do the crux of this then move right again to some flat holds. Climb directly to jugs and a lower-off. Some long quickdraws are needed.
FA. M.Richards, A.Sharp 15.4.2010

19 No Epoxy au Oxley .... 6b+
Climb the steep cracks just right of the arete to the mid-height easing. Traverse leftwards and finish up the headwall as for *Surplomb de Ray*. Take some long slings to reduce rope drag.
FA. R.Thomas 1994

20 Gypsy Eyes .... 6b+
The headwall to the right of *No Epoxy au Oxley*. Take some long slings to reduce rope drag.
FA. S.Llewellyn 30.3.2013

21 Little Miss Lover 7a
The headwall 2m left of some conglomerate.
FA. M.Crocker 1.5.1994

22 Foxy Lady 7a
A superb route with plenty of good moves and climbing. Climb the leaning wall to a tough finishing sequence. A logical link-up of *Chicken Licken* into the upper section of *Foxy Lady* gives **Foxy Chicken, 7a+**.
FA. J.Bullock, R.Thomas 5.1990

Main Crag **Foxhole** *173*

㉓ The Hooker — 7a
Similar to its neighbour with great climbing. Start as for *Foxy Lady* and continue to some pushy moves up and left to finish.
FA. J.Bullock, R.Thomas 6.1990

㉔ Joy de Viva — 7a
Fine climbing that requires stamina and ingenuity. Climb to a hole then pull out right and up to some conglomerate. A further hard move gains better holds and a race for the lower-off.
Photo p.169.
FA. G.Gibson, R.Thomas 5.7.1997

㉕ Turkey Lurking — 7c
As for *Power Struggle* to the good holds after its 4th bolt, then make a hard move leftwards to a series of stiff pulls on good holds. Make a final rockover to gain the lower-off of *Foxy Lady*.
Photo p.165.
FA. E.Travers-Jones 10.8.1996

㉖ Power Struggle — 7b+
A tough and innocuous pitch on crisp little edges and side-pulls.
FA. M.Crocker, J.Harwood 1.5.1994

㉗ Ducky Lucky — 7a+
Superb climbing with a long reach or technical move.
FA. R.Thomas 10.8.1996

㉘ Poultry in Motion — 7b+
A rising traverse of the crag. Follow *The Day the Sky Fell in* to its 3rd bolt. Move left past *Ducky Lucky* and continuing along *Turkey Lurking* to finish.
FA. M.Richards, A.Sharp 6.2000

㉙ Where the Fox That? — 7b+
From the 4th bolt on *The Day the Sky Fell in*, take the upper break left with hard moves between *Power Struggle* and *Fowl Play*. From the jug in the bulge of *Fowl Play*, move leftwards past the final bolt of *Joy de Viva* to the finish of *The Hooker*.
FA. M.Richards, A.Sharp 15.4.2010

㉚ The Day the Sky Fell in... — 6b+
The steady looking groove on the right-hand side of the crag is more involved and strenuous that first impressions suggest.
FA. R.Thomas 18.5.1996

㉛ Motion Sickness — 7c+
The 'mega link' of the crag, traversing from the bottom right to the very top! Long, pumpy and great positions, 16 draws needed. Follow *Poultry in Motion* to the conglomerate shakeout jug on *Joy De Viva*. Stay low and span left to *The Hooker*. Cross through *Foxy Lady* (via a large sloper and sticking out stone below a large slot) until the glue-in bolts run out. Make crux moves upwards (via a small sloper) to join the last bolt of *Little Miss Lover* and reach the lip of the crag. Traverse the edge of the lip on good holds to finish as for *No Epoxy Au Oxley*.
FA. S.Clarke 17.6.2017

㉜ Easter Rising — 5a
The slab gains difficulty with height.
FA. R.McCarroll 2018

㉝ Evening Primrose — 5a
The steep line right of the slab. Care needed with some of the rock in places.
FA. J.Bullock, D.McCarroll 4.2022

Minchin Hole

An intriguing crag with some fine pitches in an unusual and atmospheric setting. Please pay close attention to the access notes.

Approach Map p.164

From the car park at Southgate, walk east along East Cliff Road for 300m to where a track comes in from the left. Head out towards the highest point of the cliff top (a rocky knoll) and then descend a steep path just to its right. Where the grass and scree turn to rock, a faint path leads left to the entrance of Minchin Hole.

Conditions

Minchin Hole does see sun on both walls and is often dry, but it is not a place to head for in cold weather or high seas. The base of the zawn is slightly tidal but only for a short time unless the sea state is rough.

Access

Remains of lions, spotted hyena and wild boar have been excavated here and it contains the remains of a rich fossil sequence. It is an SSSI and as such has some specific areas of concern.

> The 'stuck-on' conglomerate features are important from a conservation perspective and should be avoided.

> No loose rock is to be removed, the cave deposits go right up to the roof clinging to the sides outside as well as inside the cave.

> Gardening is not permitted and the cliff face must be left undisturbed.

> Bolt replacement on existing routes should be on a like-for-like basis only and no new routes should be added.

> Avoid the flying buttress of debris left of the start of *The Raven*. It is part of the bone-bearing 'cave earth' and has been left there to show how the sediments inside the cave link with those in the entrance.

> Should you see any fossils or bones (do not dislodge if partially buried) please notify the National Trust.

> Only the routes presented here should be climbed.

Minchin Hole

Fringe Benefits, 6a+ - de-bolted

Bolt belay

23m

❶ Beyond the Fringe — 6b
From a bolt belay, climb up the wall past a small tufa boss, to steeper climbing up the headwall to finish. A pleasant pitch.
FA. R.Thomas, G.Gibson 4.5.1998

❷ Triple Sigh — 6b+
Climb up right past the large conglomerate lump to gain the steep rib above.
FA. R.Thomas, G.Gibson 14.5.1998

❸ Swim With the Sharks — 6c+
An excellent pitch via a small overhang and leaning wall.
FA. R.Thomas 10.5.1998

❹ Fade to Black — 7a+
Follow *Swim With The Sharks* to its fifth bolt and then move out right to join and finish as for *Jump the Sun*.
FA. D.Howard, D.Howard 22.7.2024

❺ Until it Sleeps — 6c+
Climb the vertical wall of *Jump the Sun* to its roof and then move leftwards to meet and finish as for *Swim With the Sharks*.
FA. D.Howard, D.Howard 22.7.2024

❻ Jump the Sun — 7a+
A good climb up the wall and upper overhang to a some tough finishing moves. The lower staples are hard to spot.
FA. R.Thomas, G.Gibson 1.9.1998

Minchin Hole

7 Crawling King Snake .... 7a+
The leaning arete on the left side of the entrance to the back of the hole is a good pitch.
FA. G.Gibson, R.Thomas 1999

8 Kestrel 8a
Climb the vague arete with the hardest climbing in the lower half. Do not use the flying buttress of debris at the start.
FA. T.Nikonovas 2000s

9 Golden Eagle 8b
Start as for *Kestrel*. Follow *Kestrel* to its fifth bolt and then climb out right using a conglomerate crimp. Follow the glue-in bolts until a line of rightward leading undercuts are reached and finish as for *Way of the Warrior*.
FA. A.Rogers 1.6.2023

Minchin Hole

⑩ The Raven .... 7a+
A brilliant route with exhilarating climbing. Climb up good holds and make a stiff pull to gain the easier mid-height corner-crack. From its top, make some thin moves to better holds and a steep final couple of moves to the lower-off. *Photo this page*.
FA. G.Gibson, R.Thomas 1998

⑪ Skylark .... 8a+
Begin as for *Way of the Warrior* and where it heads out left finish direct via a painful pocket.
FA. A.Rogers 5.2024

⑫ Way of the Warrior ...... 7c+
Start as for *The Raven*. From the eighth bolt of *The Raven* head out left and up through some undercuts to finish at the lower-off of *Kestrel*.
FA. E.Rees 19.8.2022

⑬ Ravenclaw .... 7b+
A very worthwhile link from the last bolt of *The Raven* to the lower-off of *Kestrel* along the seam. Hands in the seam until the the flake of *Kestrel* is reached.
FA. E.Rees 8.8.2021

⑭ Merlin.................. 7c
A really nice long climb with some great moves. Climb *Voice From the Pulpit* to its upper lower-off, move left via the crux at the top of *The Raven* then struggle along the seam of *Ravenclaw*. Move up to finish at the lower-off of *Skylark*.
FA. S.Marsh, A.Sharp 26.8.2024

⑮ Voice From the Pulpit .... 7a+
Climb the stiff wall and steep conglomerate to a large ledge - intermediate lower-off in place here. Continue up the wall right of *The Raven* to a lower-off.
FA. G.Gibson 5.1998

⑯ Stuck on You .... 6c+
The vertical wall and bulging conglomerate to a lower-off.
FA. G.Gibson 5.1998

⑰ The Minchkins................. 6c
A similar line just to the right of *Stuck On You* to the same lower-off.
FA. G.Gibson 5.1998

⑱ Gary's Talking Climbs........ 6b
Good wall climbing to a lower-off at the top of a small pillar right of the conglomerate.
FA. G.Gibson 5.1998

⑲ Pinch a Minch 5c
The shallow left-facing corner/groove and less steep ground above to a lower-off.
FA. H.Gibson, G.Gibson 5.1998

High on *The Raven* (7a+) - *this page* - at the atmospheric Minchen Hole, Gower. Photo: Bridget Glaister

Bowen's Parlour Area

Grade Spread | 1 | 11 | 12 | 8 | -

Three sport crags lurk below the grass and scree slopes to the east of Minchen Hole. They all offer worthwhile climbing in the mid-grades including some steep grade 7s. There is a mix of both tidal and non-tidal sectors and sun and shade can be found throughout the day. A bit of forward planning will pay dividends here in order to squeeze the most out of a visit. It is worth noting that Minchen Hole cannot be reached safely without returning to the top of the approach slope.

Approach   Map p.164

Prawn Zawn and Bowen's Parlour - From the Southgate car park head east along East Cliff Road road for 700m until Bosco's Lane is reached. Face out to sea and head rightwards to a bench on the edge of the cliffs. Descend to above some inlets and scramble down, then right for Prawn Zawn or left for Bowen's Parlour.

The Pantheon - Traverse left above the inlets, past a massive hole in the ground. Then head down and back right to below the routes.

Conditions

The lower sector of Bowen's Parlour and Prawn Zawn are tidal. The Pantheon is set well back from the sea. Seepage does occur mainly during the winter months.

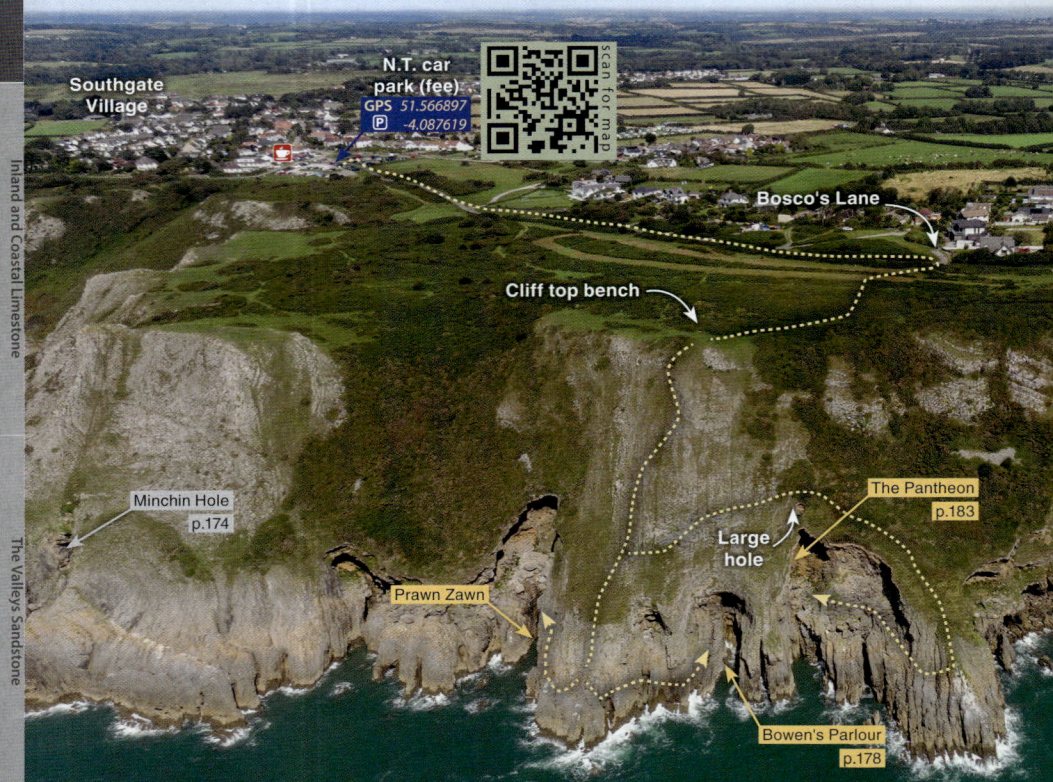

Prawn Zawn **Bowen's Parlour Area** 179

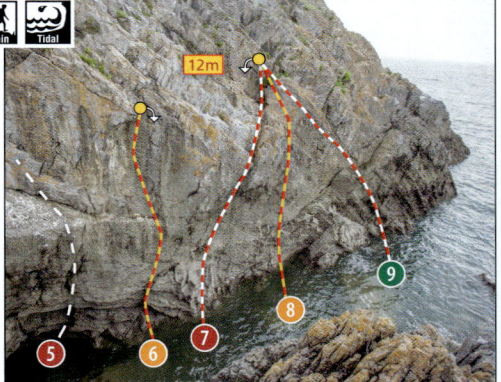

Prawn Zawn

A small inlet with some reasonable lines which are useful if it is busy at Bowen's Parlour.

Approach (map p.164) - The zawn is just west of Bowen's Parlour, reached by a scramble at the base of the main approach.

Tides - The zawn is tidal and is accessible for 2 hours either side of low water.

Conditions - The routes are west facing and get afternoon sun.

❶ Bull Fighter .... 7b+
A wild test of roof and mantel skills. You may need a spotter for the move around the lip!
FA. S.Rawlinson 12.5.2012

❷ Rush Hour .... 7b+
From the second bolt of *Bull Fighter*, move right and follow a parallel line.
FA. A.Wolsey-Heard 12.5.2012

❸ Prawn Star .... 6b+
A good pitch that takes the wall to the right of the overhang, moving right to the lower-off.
FA. R.Thomas, P.Hadley 1999

❹ Prawnsite 6b
The crack and groove.
FA. R.Thomas, P.Hadley 1999

❺ Hard Prawn .... 6c+
The harder direct version of *Prawnsite*.
FA. R.Thomas, P.Hadley 1999

❻ Soft Prawn .... 6a+
The flake and thin sharp wall above it.
FA. R.Thomas, P.Hadley 1999

❼ For King Trad Prawn E1 5a
Follow the crack up and right.
FA. P.Hadley 1999

❽ Prawn Cock Tale 6a
The wall with a barnacled start.
FA. R.Thomas, P.Hadley 1999

❾ Teen Prawn .... S 4a
Easy climbing leads left to the belay.
FA. R.Thomas, P.Hadley 1999

Bowen's Parlour Area — Bowen's Parlour

Bowen's Parlour

An impressive bowl of steep limestone and conglomerate provides some harder lines. Moving around on the ledge below the upper walls is a little tricky.

Approach (map p.164 overview p.178) - At sea level, head right (looking inland) to ledges below the upper walls and above The Zawn.

Conditions - Sun and shade can be found throughout the day.

1 Rudaceous Ramble ... 6a+
The rubble is more solid than it looks, and the corner much steeper than expected.
FA. J.Bullock, D.McCarroll 2009

2 Breccial Motion ... 6b+
Swing right to the delightful last few moves of *Parlour Games*.
FA. J.Bullock, D.McCarroll 2009

3 Parlour Games ... 7b
A direct line with a powerful crux.
FA. D.McCarroll, J.Bullock 2010

4 Parlour Français ... 7c
Start up *Parlour Games* and break through the overhang.
FA. M.Richards, A.Sharp 2010

5 Spider ... 6c
The arete gives a fine but short climb.
FA. J.Bullock, D.McCarroll 2009

6 Fly ... 6b
Unusual climbing using flowstone features.
FA. D.McCarroll, J.Bullock 2009

7 Still Nifty at Fifty ... 7a+
Move up the faint rib left of *When I'm 64* to where the good holds end. Break horizontally left to the lower-off.
FA. D.McCarroll 2010

8 When I'm 64 ... 7a+
The steepening diagonal is climbed on very positive holds to a wild finale off the 'house brick' hold.
FA. J.Bullock, D.McCarroll 2010

9 Aspidistra ... 6b+
Pull over the small roof using a high undercut.
FA. J.Bullock, D.McCarroll 2009

10 Maud ... 6b
Very steep climbing, but the holds are good. Some dodgy rock.
FA. D.McCarroll, J.Bullock 2009

Dean Howard completing the final moves up the headwall of *Pegasus* (7c) - *p.183* - at The Pantheon, Bowen's Parlour Area. Photo: Sam Brown

Bowen's Parlour Area — The Zawn

The Zawn

The Zawn is below the approach ledge of the main Bowen's Parlour area. The first two routes are on the east wall of the zawn.

Approach (map p.164 overview p.178) - At sea level, head right (looking inland) to ledges below the upper walls and above The Zawn. It is accessible for around 2 hours on either side of low water. Enter the zawn either by a scramble down or abseil. Keep an eye on the water level as it quickly floods the base of the zawn.

Conditions - Sun and shade can be found throughout the day although the majority of the lines get the sun in the afternoon.

1 Wisdom of Age 5a
The left line on the east-facing wall. Nice moves.
FA. D.McCarroll, J.Bullock 2010

2 Sallies of Youth 5c
The right line on the east-facing wall. Best in the sun otherwise it can be a bit greasy.
FA. D.McCarroll, J.Bullock 2010

3 All of a Quiver 6a
The steep cracks from the sloping platform left of *Bowen Arrow*.
FA. R.Thomas 7.2010

4 Bowen Arrow 6a
The corner and flake starting from the slippery slope.
FA. D.McCarroll, J.Bullock 2010

The Pantheon — Bowen's Parlour Area

5 Reaction Series .... 6b+
Layback up the big corner and attack the overlaps.
FA. D.McCarroll, J.Bullock 2010

6 Bowen to the Inevitable 6a
Great climbing up to and over the apex of the arch. Steeper than it looks.
FA. J.Bullock, D.McCarroll 2010

7 Parlour Vous le Sport .... 6a+
Straight up the steep ground right of the arch. It now has a hard start where there used to be a boulder - either clip-stick past this or come in from the left. There are also some perplexing moves before the final overlap.
FA. D.McCarroll, J.Bullock 2010

8 Feud for Thought 6b
Sustained climbing through the overlaps.
FA. J.Bullock, D.McCarroll 2010

9 Gentlemen Prefer Bolts.. 6c+
The steep wall via the 'boss'. The start is reachy and the difficulties continue above.
FA. J.Bullock, D.McCarroll 2010

10 Gentleman's Relish 6a
Follow the groove to a hard finish.
FA. R.Thomas, G.Ashmore 2010

11 Gentleman's Retreat 6a
Start just right of *Gentleman's Relish* and climb the wall to a belay on the upper ledge.
FA. R.Thomas, D.Emanuel 10.10.2010

The Pantheon
A compact section of very steep rock tucked away at the back of a boulder-filled cove.
Approach (map p.164 overview p.178) - Traverse left above Bowen's Parlour, past a massive hole in the ground, and head down and back right to below the routes.
Conditions - It is shady in the afternoon, non-tidal and also stays dry in rain. Seepage does occur but only after prolonged rainfall.

12 Pegasus 7c
Technical wall climbing on conglomerate holds leads to the first of three stepped roofs. Burly undercutting over these reaches the lower-off below the conglomerate cornice. *Photo p.181*.
FA. S.Rawlinson 9.2.2009

13 Orion. 7b
Start up *Pegasus* and move right to below a roof. Cross the roof using undercuts and a sharp two-finger pocket to gain good jugs under the second roof. Finish on more conglomerate holds to a gripping finale.
FA. S.Rawlinson 10.1.2009

Bosco's Gulch Area

Grade Spread 5 25 29 8 -

A collection of small zawns and walls with some good routes. It has a slightly more awkward approach than to the other crags hereabouts. Golden Temple, Golden Treasury, Golden Gulch and Golden Wall offer routes at either end of the grade spectrum, whilst Bosco's Gulch and Bucketland have plenty of good routes that see little attention and might need a brush before an ascent.

Approach and Tides   Map p.164

From the Southgate car park, head east along East Cliff Road road for 700m to Bosco's Lane. Face out to sea and head slightly right to the edge of the cliffs. Descend the slope to a small square-cut quarry. Bosco's Gulch is to the left and can be reached by a scramble down to sea level (2 hours either side of low water) or by abseiling from a prominent spike/bolts on the left rim of the quarry. If abseiling, leave a rope in place to allow an escape when the tide comes in. It is also worth checking that the base is clear of water when abseiling in as the abseil is free-hanging. Golden Temple, Golden Treasury, Golden Gulch and Golden Wall are on the right side of the quarry and accessed by a scramble down (3 hours either side of low water). Alternatively an easy scramble down from the base of the approach to The Pantheon is possible and useful if approaching from Bowen's Parlour - also 3 hours either side of low water.

Conditions

Bosco's Gulch is fairly sheltered but it takes time for seepage to dry out. Golden Temple, Golden Treasury, Golden Gulch and Golden Wall are more exposed to the elements.

Access

No climbing in the upper cave at the back of the zawn ('The Den') due to rare geology/artefacts. There is a bird restriction on the routes in The Cave from 1st March to 1st August.

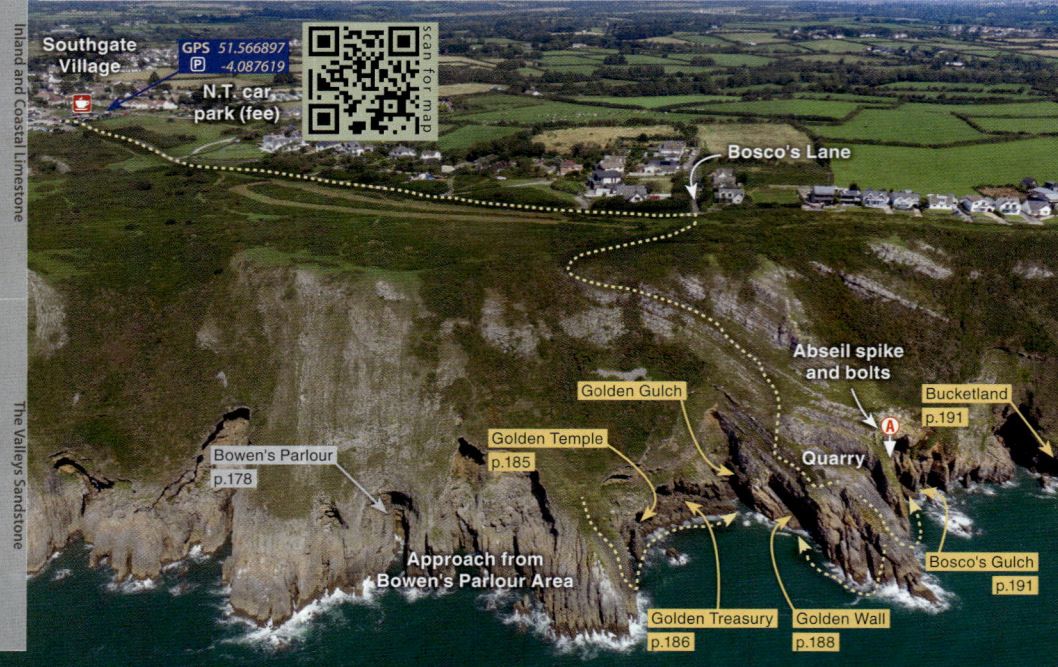

Bosco's Gulch Area

Golden Temple

A deceptively steep venue that has a number of short powerful lines centred around a cave. The routes are well-bolted and on good rock.

Approach (map p.164) - Scramble down from the quarry or use The Pantheon approach.

Tides - Access is possible for around 3 hours either side of low water.

Conditions - The back of the cave can take time to dry.

① Brexit Exit 4b
An escape/approach route on the left outside of the cave. The lower-off rings are in a big boulder set back to allow abseil entry if required.
FA. J.Bullock, D.McCarroll 2018

② First Order 5b
Broken line up the left wall outside the cave.
FA. J.Bullock, D.McCarroll 2018

③ Polynomial 6a
Good steep climbing on accommodating holds. Begin on the left wall of the cave and curve around the overhang.
FA. D.McCarroll, J.Bullock 2018

④ Meduseld .... 6c+
Steep and tricky moves. Start up *Polynomial* and then break right across the roof and headwall to a shared lower-off.
FA. D.McCarroll, B.McCarroll 2018

⑤ Gower Power 6a
A diagonal leftward line across the blank looking east wall of the cave, exiting through the large hole. A wonderful jug-fest and often bone-dry.
FA. D.McCarroll, J.Bullock 2019

⑥ Gower Gold 7a
Ascend the pillar on the right side of the cave entrance, then follow a witheringly steep line towards the central groove. Good holds and perfect rock all the way to the lower-off.
FA. D.McCarroll 2019

⑦ Amritsar .... 6b+
Climb up the steep pillar right of the cave entrance and curves left along the headwall of the cave. Steep stuff.
FA. D.McCarroll, G.Morris 2018

⑧ Palgrave 6c
Straight up the wall right of the cave entrance. Much tougher and steeper than first appearances would suggest.
FA. D.McCarroll 2018

Bosco's Gulch Area — Golden Treasury

Golden Treasury

A series of walls, pillars and large overhangs next to the Golden Temple. This section of cliff offers up plenty of well-bolted lines on good rock mainly in the 6s but also with some easier lines. Most of the routes are steeper than they first appear but to compensate aren't too long.

Approach (map p.164 overview p.184) - Scramble down from the quarry or use The Pantheon approach.
Tides - Access is possible for around 3 hours either side of low water.
Conditions - Quick drying and has a sunny aspect.

1 King Cnut 5b
The edge of the east-facing wall, just round the corner from Golden Temple. A useful escape if the tide is threatening.
FA. D.McCarroll, J.Bullock 2018

2 Pump and Dump 6a
The left-hand side of the east facing wall provides some deceptively steep climbing on hidden holds.
FA. J.Price, B.McCarroll 2018

3 Electrum 6a
The steep curving corner with big holds that disappear once the angle starts to ease.
FA. B.McCarroll, D.McCarroll 2018

4 Bold as Brass 6c
Head directly up the bulging orange wall to the upper lower-off rings. A very technical pitch.
FA. D.McCarroll, J.Bullock 2019

5 Copper Bottom 6a
Climb the curving crack at the right side of the east-facing wall until forced left and into the corner.
FA. J.Bullock, D.McCarroll 2019

6 Loud and Prowed 6c
The first route on the south-facing pillar to the right of the huge overhang. Make fingery moves up the severely overhanging buttress that leads to a puzzling sequence to pass the prow.
FA. D.McCarroll 2018

7 Slot Machine 6b
Unusual climbing up the slot infested wall. Some are better than others so choose your holds wisely.
FA. B.McCarroll, D.McCarroll 2018

8 Wish Bone .... 6a+
The left-hand arete of the conspicuous narrow gulch in the middle of the crag. Climb directly up the severely undercut arete, finishing to the right.
FA. J.Bullock, D.McCarroll 2019

Golden Treasury Bosco's Gulch Area

9 Goldfish 4c
The crack at the seaward end of the slab forming the left wall of the gulch.
FA. R.Waldron, B.McCarroll 2018

10 Pantomime Riposte 4c
The crack on the left wall further in towards the back of the narrow gulch. When it starts to get hard think about the name.
FA. D.McCarroll 2018

11 Copperopolis .... 6a+
The steep crozzly crack on the right wall of the gulch.
FA. D.McCarroll, J.Bullock 2018

12 Limonite .... 6a+
The shorter well-pocketed groove.
FA. D.McCarroll, J.Bullock 2018

13 Bre-X .... 6b+
Technical climbing up the hanging arete on the right edge of the gulch, with a steep pull to finish.
FA. B.McCarroll, D.McCarroll 2018

14 Gorilla Warfare 6b
A layback crack followed by wild climbing through the roof leads to jug pulling onto the ledge on the left.
FA. B.McCarroll 2018

15 King Louie 6c
Follow *Gorilla Warfare* but finish on the right up the arete and steep wall. Shares a lower-off with *Apricot Jam*.
FA. B.McCarroll 2018

16 Apricot Jam 6a
Climb the steep flake past a wobbly block to access the top jamming crack.
FA. J.Bullock, D.McCarroll 2018

17 Penny Falls 5c
Climbs the pocketed wall using the left edge at this grade. More like **6a+** if climbed direct.
FA. D.McCarroll, J.Bullock 2018

18 Golden Plover 5b
Delightful climbing up the wide crack with a steep start.
FA. D.McCarroll, J.Bullock 2018

19 Golden Gate 3b
Nice moves bridging up the walls onto the ledge.
FA. J.Bullock, D.McCarroll 2018

20 Golden Snitch 4b
Start on the boulder and step across to big holds on the steep wall. Shared lower-off with *Golden Gate*.
FA. J.Bullock, D.McCarroll 2018

Bosco's Gulch Area — Golden Gulch

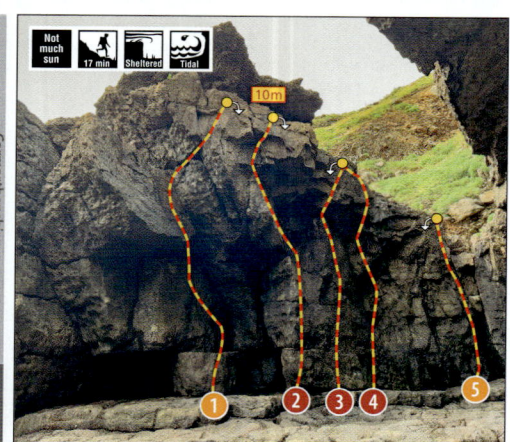

① Isambard's Bums .... 6a+
Start in a corner and climb up and left onto a stepped slab. Swing right to finish up the seriously overhanging arete.
FA. R.McCarroll 2018

② Dental Detour 6c
Start on the pillar and become horizontal, aiming for a jug. Getting into the upper groove is harder than it looks.

③ Fool .... 6b+
The shallow groove leads to a hard pull to pass the overhang.

④ Cheese Sandwich 6b
Tenuous climbing gains a slopey ledge then undercut and campus for the top.

⑤ Back Chimney 5b
The chimney at the very back of the zawn.

Golden Gulch

An interesting compact cliff that has some good short climbs on fine rock. Easily combined with Bosco's Gulch.
Approach (map p.164 overview p.184) - Scramble down from the quarry to the boulder beach, or via the Pantheon crag approach.

Tides - Accessible for 2 hours either side of low water.
Conditions - The routes on the right wall are west-facing so get afternoon sun, but those on the left see little sun.

Golden Wall — Bosco's Gulch Area

❻ The Gold Rush .... 7a+
A rising traverse finishing on the far left of the crag. There is a project that crosses the big overhangs.
FA. J.Bullock, D.McCarroll 1.9.2012

❼ Leftist Gold 7b
Start up *The Midas Touch* but break left before the roof. The longer-than-body-length roof is meaty.
FA. M.Barclay 2022

❽ The Midas Touch ..... 6c+
The wall and overlaps. Very good
FA. D.McCarroll, J.Bullock 10.2010

❾ A Starke Reminder 6b
A good pitch up the wall right of the big overhangs.
FA. D.McCarroll, J.Bullock 10.2010

❿ Aur of Glory .... 6a+
Enjoyable climbing on good holds.
FA. D.McCarroll, J.Bullock 10.2010

⓫ Aur of Need 6a
A similar route to *Aur of Glory* but a touch easier.
FA. D.McCarroll, J.Bullock 10.2010

⓬ Golden Boy 5c
The unusual runnel feature and upper wall.
FA. R.Thomas 2.2016

⓭ Golden Hour 5c
Make steep moves to easier and less steep ground.
FA. R.Thomas 2.2016

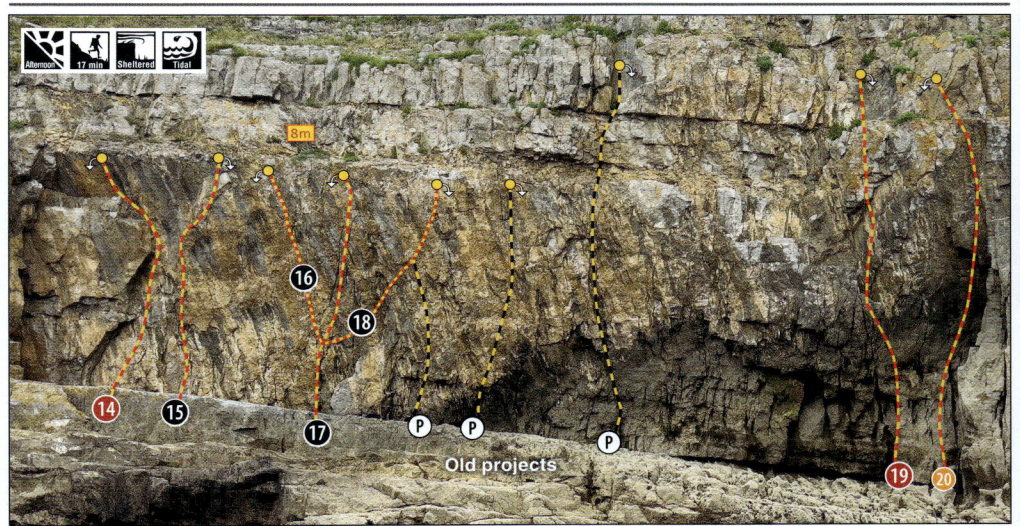

Golden Wall
The Golden Wall is a severely leaning and compact sheet of stone that has a collection of quite short (but very hard) routes strung across it.
Approach (map p.164 overview p.184) - Scramble down from the quarry to the boulder beach, or via the Pantheon crag approach.
Tides - The wall is accessible for 2 hours either side of low water. The routes are mostly non-tidal but the approach is tidal.
Conditions - The wall gets the afternoon sun.

⓮ Bye Bye Eddy .... 6b+
Super short, but good and powerful.
FA. S.Rawlinson 14.6.2010

⓯ All that Glitters is not Gold ... 7b+
Short and cruxy along the vague right-leading groove.
FA. S.Rawlinson 21.6.2010

⓰ Au .... 7c+
The left-hand line out of *Shining Dawn* is not bolted. This line was done on pre-placed wires to a lower-off.
FA. T.Starke 2000s

⓱ Shining Dawn 7c
Start up the diagonal flake and finish via a hard boulder problem.
FA. T.Starke 2000s

⓲ Golden Wonder 7b
Climb *Shining Dawn* to its second bolt, then move right and up.
FA. A.Sharp 2009

⓳ Gold Digger 6c
Great climbing starting up the steep line of weakness. A tough start leads to some good holds and a balancy finish.
FA. R.Thomas 2011

⓴ Gilded Cage 5b
The steep corner/groove at the seaward end of the wall.
FA. R.Thomas 1.2016

Bosco's Gulch Area — Bosco's Gulch

Bosco's Gulch
A long tidal wall of interesting rock and some harder pitches up in a shallow cave to the right.

Approach (map p.164 overview p.184) - The crag is accessed by a scramble from the small quarry. It is also possible to approach and retreat by abseil and leave a rope in place to allow escape up the final wall back to the abseil point. The Cave is reached via a scramble.

Tides - The crag is accessible for around 2 hours either side of low water.

Conditions - Fairly sheltered but takes time for seepage to dry out, especially in the back of the gulch.

🚫 **Access** - No climbing or access to the 'The Den' due to rare geology/artefacts. There is a bird restriction in the The Cave from 1 March to 1 August.

① Sam Can Do It 5b
A pleasant excursion up the crenelated wall.
FA. R.Thomas, S.Caan 4.2019

② Geoff's Nutcracker 5c
Climb just right of the scoop until it steepens then reach right on flakes to a lower-off.
FA. R.Thomas, T.Hoddy 3.2019

③ Simple Simon E2 5c
Climb straight up (2 bolts), move left and then climb rightwards following an unstable overlap to a lower-off.
FA. R.Thomas 29.5.1999

④ Clapham Injunction .. 6b
Start as for *Simple Simon*, and at the second bolt, move right and climb the wall. The direct start up a thin flake is **6c+** (one through-bolt at the start).
FA. R.Thomas 29.5.1999

⑤ Philandering Fillipino ... 6c
The flake and wall to the right have a powerful sequence to gain the overlap. Above the overlap, trend left to the lower-off.
FA. G.Gibson 2004

⑥ Gold Teeth in Them Thar Hills. 6a+
Climb juggy flakes and then make steep moves to gain the easier-angled (but still interesting) upper wall and lower-off.
FA. R.Thomas 29.5.1999

⑦ Hanger Them High .... 6a+
Start left of the prominent boulder. Move up and make some harder moves out right onto the grey upper wall. Finish up this more easily on excellent rock to a lower-off.
FA. R.Thomas 6.6.1999

Bucketland Bosco's Gulch Area

The Cave

10 The Clampetts 6c
Start right of the boulder and climb the wall trending leftwards to the lower-off.
FA. G.Gibson, R.Thomas 6.1999

11 Jump Over My Shadow 7a
Layback to the slab and up past the overlap to the headwall.
FA. G.Gibson 6.1999

12 Conglomeration 7a
Climb past a worrying-looking but sound block of conglomerate.
FA. G.Gibson 6.1999

13 Standing on a Beach 6c
An easy corner gains a ledge. From the ledge, move left onto the wall and follow the left-hand line of bolts to a lower-off.
FA. G.Gibson 6.1999

14 Reign of the Deer 7a
The right-hand finish on the upper wall to *Standing on a Beach*.
FA. G.Gibson 3.2000

The Cave up and right is reached by a short scramble. There is a bird restriction in the The Cave from 1 March to 1 August.

15 Snatch .... 6c+
The left-hand route in the upper cave is equipped with staples.
FA. G.Gibson, R.Thomas 2000

16 Starter for Ten 7c
The central crack/groove. Sustained climbing to the roof precedes a powerful crux and an easier finish.
FA. M.Richards, A.Sharp 6.2.2010

17 Squeal Like a Hog 6c
The impressive diagonal line is awkward, with spaced bolts.
FA. J.Bullock, G.Morris 2000

18 The Millennium Thug 7a
Crosses the previous route with some powerful moves.
FA. G.Gibson, R.Thomas 3.3.2000

8 Y'All Come Back Now .... 6a+
From the boulder climb up to and over the small overhang and then take the wall above slightly leftwards to the lower-off.
FA. R.Thomas 6.6.1999

9 Elffin Mermaid .... 6c+
Climb pockets and step left to the 2nd bolt. Go direct to the 3rd bolt on *The Clampetts* and continue past the grey roof to a ledge. Finish up the wall above to *The Clampetts* lower-off.
FA. D.Dyson, S.Brown 2.9.2021

Bucketland

Bucketland is a huge roof across the bay from the Gulch.
Approach (map p.164 overview p.184) - Cross the foreshore from the Gulch.
Tides - Accessible for 2 hours either side of low water.
Conditions - Fairly sheltered but takes time for seepage to dry out, especially in the back of the Gulch.
Access - No climbing or access to the 'The Den' due to rare geology/artefacts. There is a birdrestriction in the The Cave from 1 March to 1 August.

19 Eel Lips .... 7b+
The centre of the big roof. Pockets and stretches lead to a superb hold and just beyond an even better coral fossil. Some inventive heel-hooking is required to turn the lip, then a rock up leads to a static position and an easy finish.
FA. G.Ashmore, G.Morris 12.8.2017

Pwlldu Bay

Grade Spread - - 5 6 1

An old quarried wall of good limestone which is unfortunately blighted on its right-hand side by a coating of mud that forms every winter - these lines are not included here but details are available on **UKClimbing.com**. The steeper section on the left stays reasonably clean and gives some good hard pitches. The beach, sea and ambience are excellent. The site is an SSSI.

Approach
Park just off Pyle Road in Bishopston on one of the side roads and walk down Pwlldu Lane to the headland. Turn west (right looking out) and continue down to the bay, either by following the track all the way, or turn off on steps that lead to the east side of the bay. The crag is clearly visible on the west side of the bay.

Conditions
The crag gets the morning sun and is sheltered from the wind. During the winter, the crag is often wet.

Pwlldu Bay

1 Ashes to Ashes 7a
A good little route. Reaching the belay can be a bit hard/mucky at times - better to finish at the last bolt in these conditions **6c**.
FA. R.Thomas, J.Bullock, L.Moran 20.10.1986

2 Decades Apart 6c
Sustained, with long reaches between mostly good holds.
FA. G.Gibson, R.Thomas 2011

3 Bellerophon .... 7c+
An excellent line with a desperate finishing sequence. Up to the first lower-off is **Forty for Three, 7b+**.
FA. M.Richards, A.Sharp 7.8.2010 . FA. (FfT) M.Crocker, R.Thomas 1994

4 Senser .... 7c+
Great climbing up the centre of the buttress. To the first lower-off (widely-spaced staples) weighs in at **7b+**.
FA. M.Crocker 24.7.1994

5 Jezebel .... 7a+
Never desperate, but has some big moves. Superb climbing when clean. Top end of the grade.
FA. M.Crocker 9.7.1994

6 Crock Block 6c
The block has to be more secure than it looks.
FA. R.Thomas 7.1994

7 Old Slapper .... 7a+
The short groove and rib right of *Crock Block* succumbs to either a large number of slap attempts, or a stylish egyptian.
FA. R.Thomas 1994

8 Skedaddle .... 7a+
A bouldery little number up the groove an wall.
FA. M.Crocker 24.7.1994

The next routes are on walls to the right of the main quarry.

9 Cross the Rubicon .... 7b+
The left-hand line has no lower-off in place.
FA. M.Crocker 1990s

10 Fin 8a
The bouldery arete is worth tracking down.
FA. A.Berry 1994

11 4th Dimensional Melodies ... 6c+
From the left side of some boulders climb the pink hued, crystal covered wall. Clip-stick the second bolt.
FA. W.Calvert, D.Cook 28.6.2018

12 Young Fire, Old Flame 6c
About 100m right of *Fin*. Climb the cracked orange wall, sloping diagonal ramp and pocketed wall. Clip-stick the initial staple.
FA. W.Calvert, B.Gregory 4.2017

Rams Tor

Rams Tor is a wide sea cliff that has some ferocious square-cut overhangs guarding its base. Above the overhangs are thin walls which offer technical finishes in contrast to the burly starting moves.

Approach
Drive through Mumbles, past the 'Big Apple' (a kiosk) and the coastguard lookout, until the road ends at Bracelet Bay (ice cream parlour). Park here and follow the coast path west for 600m until it flattens out and the crag is visible down on the left. Either scramble down opposite (steep and often overgrown), or abseil from the belay of *Nostradamus* (there are also belay stakes).

Conditions
The crag faces west and gets afternoon and evening sun. It dries quickly and is usually sheltered from the wind. Although non-tidal, heavy seas will encroach up the ramp below some of the lines.

Rams Tor 195

① Rampage 7b
Pull into a niche and then to a projecting block. Head up and left to sloping holds on the lip and then go up and right to a roof. Traverse left until a stretch reaches a break and more long moves gain jugs. A stiff move to pockets and a stretch left to a sloping ledge brings the lower-off to hand.
FA. B.Gregory 17.10.2009

② The Constant Gardener .. 6c+
From a small cave trend left to a larger cave, below a stepped roof. Pull through the bulges and span leftwards past the final bolt and reach back right over the lip of the roof to gain good holds and the lower-off.
FA. B.Gregory 12.7.2009

③ Air Display .... 7a+
Climb a large flake and then move straight up to a corner on the left. Head rightwards to a hard finishing sequence.
FA. A.Rosier 25.7.2009

④ The Cool Crux Clan ... 7a
Never steep, but a few tricky bits to deal with and one very hard move at mid-height.
FA. A.Berry, G.Morris 1993

⑤ Ride the Funky Wave, Babe
.... 7a
The original route on this wall, and the most popular, with hard moves low down.
FA. N.Thomas 1992. FA. (Direct as described) A.Berry 1992

⑥ Rain Dance 7b
A good juggy start leads to a fingery pull onto the finishing slab.
FA. A.Berry 1993

⑦ Girdle Traverse E4 6b
Start up *Ride the Funky Wave, Babe* and then follow the break below the roof all the way past the sport routes until easy ground leads to the top.
FA. A.Berry 1996

⑧ Hypocritical Mass .... 7b+
A fingery boulder problem gains the break and is followed by another tough pull to turn the lip of the overhang.
FA. A.Berry 21.12.2008

⑨ Renaissance .... 6c+
Clip-stick the first bolt and use the rope to pull up to the jug. From here, follow good holds. The jug on the lip of the overhang is huge, but leaving it is not easy.
FA. A.Berry 1993

⑩ Captain Hook 7b
Start up *Nostradamus* and finish as for *Renaissance*.
FA. A.Berry 1993

⑪ Nostradamus .... 7b+
One of the best routes at the crag. Turning the lip is hard to read on the onsight.
FA. A.Berry, N.Thomas 1993

⑫ The Loneliness of the Long Distance Runner
.... 7b+
A seriously long reach around the roof at the start may prove insurmountable for some.
FA. A.Berry, J.Brown 1993

⑬ Totally Clips 7c
The first of the pure sport routes here, before the crag was re-bolted.
FA. A.Berry 1993

⑭ One Small Step E3 6a
The start is either a jump to the jug, or a fingery pull. Could possibly be a deep water solo on a high tide.
FA. A.Berry, J.Brown 1993

Barland Quarry

Grade Spread | - | 4 | 8 | 2 | -

An old disused quarry that is not very picturesque, but does have some quality hard slab routes. The rock and style of climbing is more akin to slate than limestone.

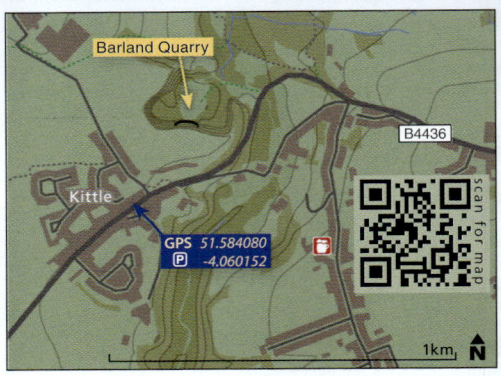

Approach
Barland Quarry is passed just before you reach the village of Kittle when travelling from the Swansea direction. Park in Kittle and walk back down the hill to find the quarry entrance on your left. Walk around the quarry along the wide track until you reach the base of the slabs. Do not park in the quarry entrance or in the large lay-by just up the hill.

Conditions
The slabs face northeast so do not get much sun, but this is an advantage in hot weather. It is worth noting that gear goes missing here from time to time but has recently been reequipped.

Access
The quarry is privately owned and climbing is not allowed by the owners. The information and descriptions presented here are only included for reasons of completeness. If asked to leave please do so immediately without fuss.

Barland Quarry 197

1 Jap's Eye .... 6a+
A tricky move to finish.
FA. R.Thomas 1.1998

2 Cheesy Flaps 5c
Slabby climbing on the left of the crag. A good starter.
FA. R.Thomas 20.3.1999

3 Double Dutch .... 6c+
A tricky start.
FA. G.Gibson, R.Thomas 1.1998

4 Mister Polite Goad ...... 6c+
Hard moves up to the first hole. Easier above.
FA. G.Gibson, H.Gibson 3.6.1998

5 Miss You 6c
Good quality climbing to an interesting finish best attacked with grit-esque technique.
FA. G.Gibson, R.Thomas 1998

6 Rotbeest .... 7b+
'Nasty animal'. The hardest route at Barland Quarry.
FA. G.Ashmore 25.8.1997

7 Wandelende tak 7a
'Stick insect'. Thin and technical climbing.
FA. G.Ashmore 17.8.1997

8 Geef onze fietsen terug.. 6c+
'Give Back our Bikes' - used to be chanted by Dutch football crowds at the Germans. Goes all the way up the face. To the first lower-off is 6c+ and then 6a+ to the top.
FA. G.Ashmore, J.Jewell 16.8.1997

9 Stoeipoesje 7a
Perhaps easier to climb than pronounce - stu-ee-poos-yuh.
FA. G.Ashmore 25.8.1997

10 Wij zitten nog in een sneeuwstorm
.... 6c
'We are still in a snowstorm'. Share a belay with *Stoeipoesje*.
FA. G.Ashmore 13.4.1998

11 Stinking of Fish 6b
A harder start to the following route.
FA. R.Thomas 7.6.1998

12 Telefunken U47 .... 5b
The line of weakness.
FA. R.Thomas 7.6.1998

13 Don't Sit on My Sofa ..... 6a+
A superb natural line that continues above *Telefunken U47*.
FA. R.Thomas 8.1998

14 I.K.M.E.N.K. .... 7a+
Ik kan mijn ei niet kwijt - 'I can't make my point'.
FA. G.Ashmore 14.9.1998

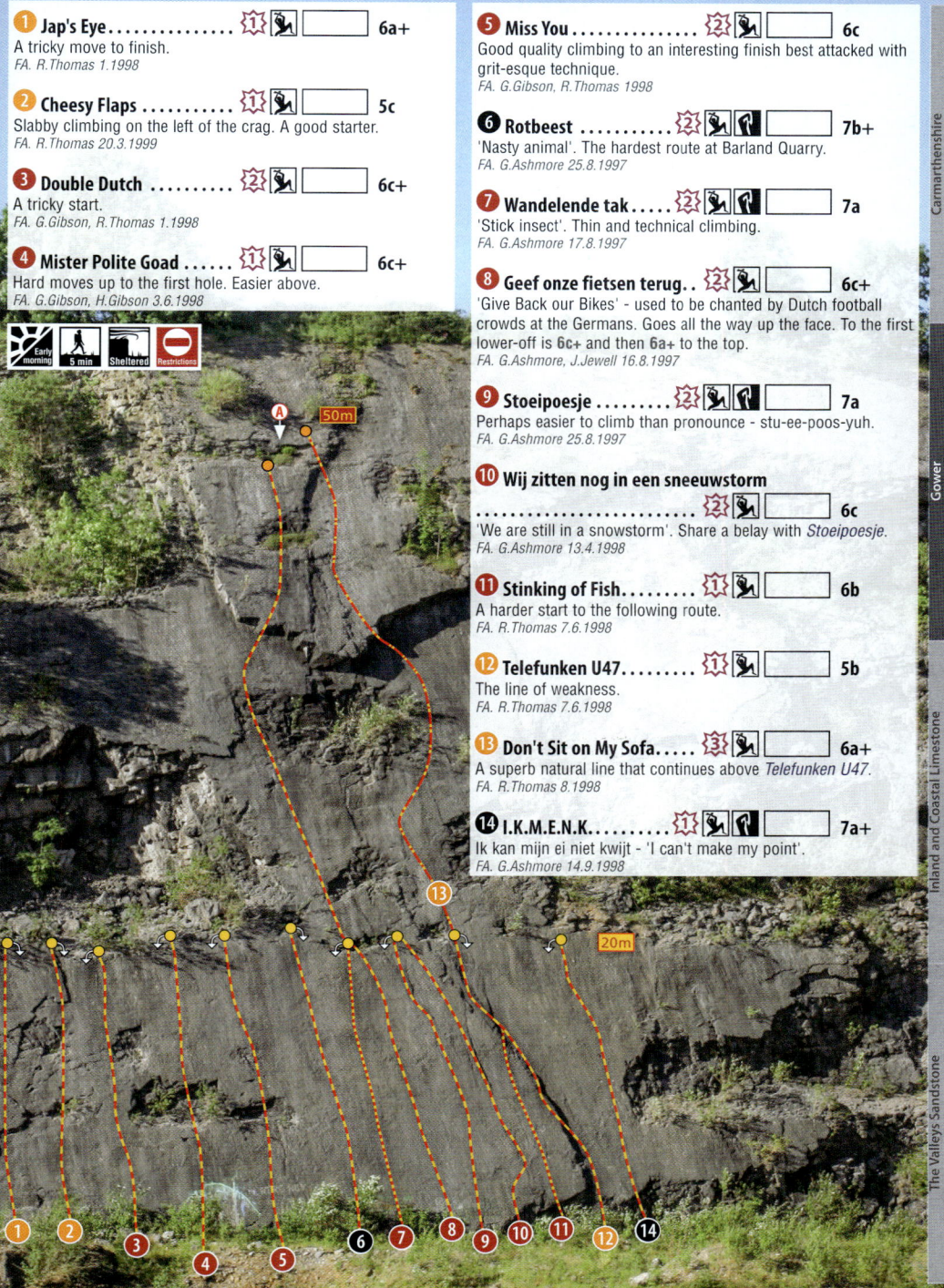

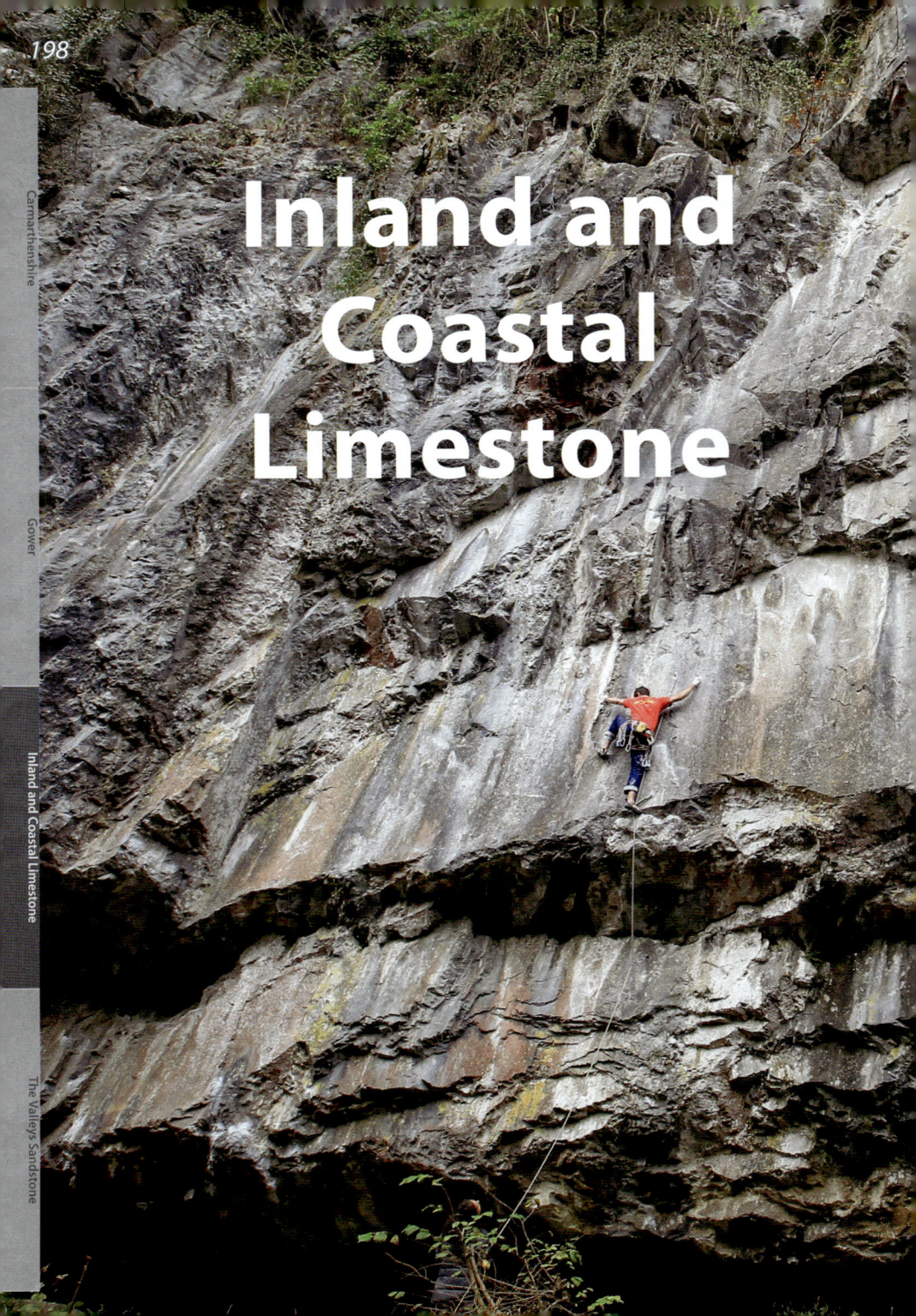

Inland and Coastal Limestone

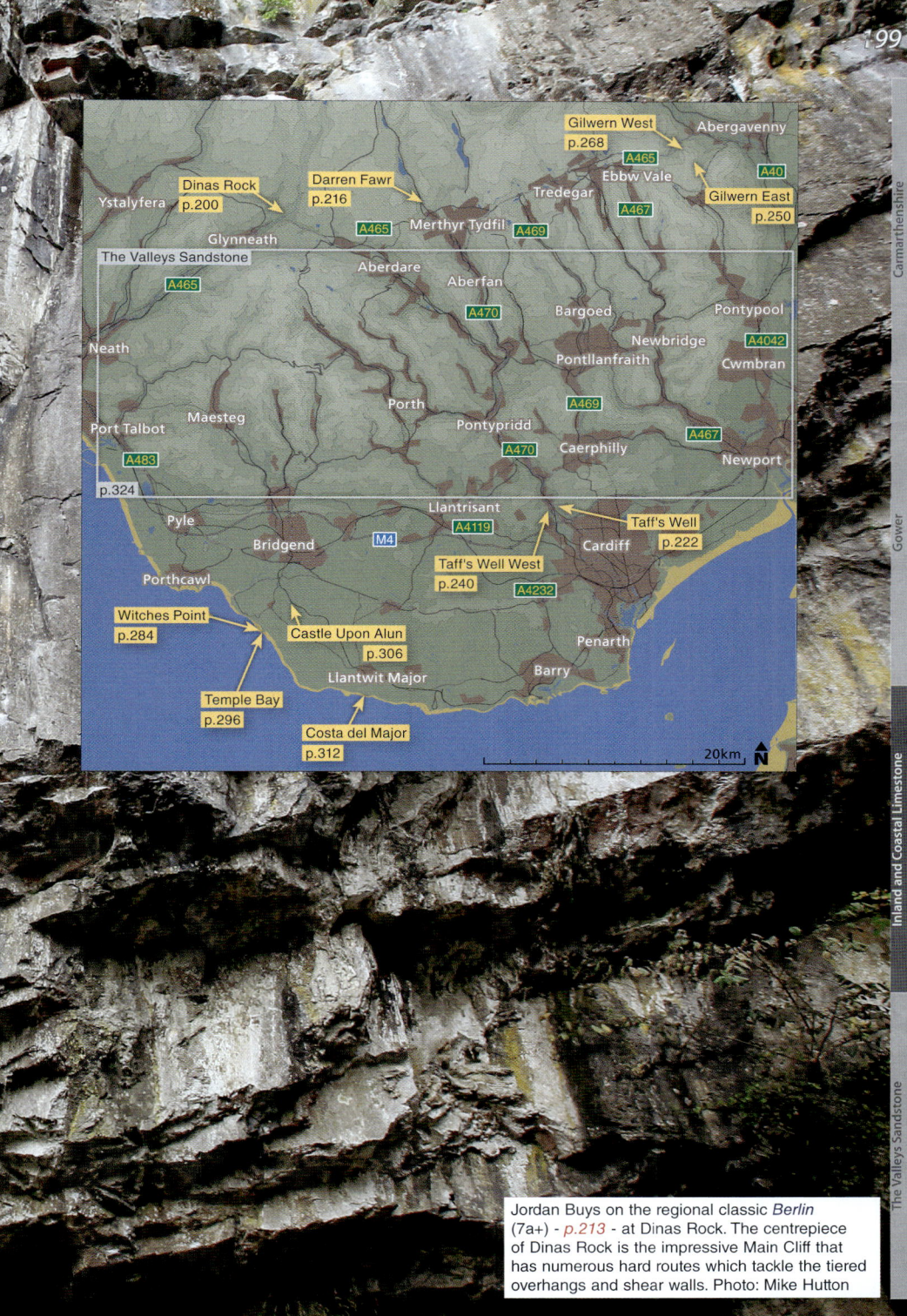

Jordan Buys on the regional classic *Berlin* (7a+) - *p.213* - at Dinas Rock. The centrepiece of Dinas Rock is the impressive Main Cliff that has numerous hard routes which tackle the tiered overhangs and shear walls. Photo: Mike Hutton

Dinas Rock

| Grade Spread | 1 | 11 | 44 | 45 | 8 |

Tucked away in a narrow gorge at the northern end of the Neath Valley, Dinas Rock is one of the best cliffs in South Wales. Its walls of high quality limestone are covered with overlaps, roofs, subtle grooves and water-worn features which combine to give some fine climbing. Technique and perseverance are needed as much as power and guile. Not all of the climbing is in the higher grades and the Roadside crags contain some very accessible routes in the lower and mid-grades.

Approach

Turn off the A465 into Glynneath (this is the second turning signed to Glynneath if approaching from Merthyr Tydfil). Turn right at the traffic lights and take the first turning left in 120m - the B4242, signed 'Pontneddfechan'. Follow this road until just before it begins to rise up

a hillside and turn right. The narrow road leads through the village and then turns abruptly right over a small bridge with a large car park in the quarry to the left - park here. The gates on the car park are locked at around 5pm, but it is always possible to exit over the one-way ramps. The Lower Cave is on private land. A small track leads off to the right alongside the river to reach the first area of rocks.

Conditions

Dinas Rock suffers seepage during the winter months and, unless it has been a reasonably dry, it can take a while to dry out in the spring. Once dry the crags stay dry for long periods and can be climbed on during showery spells, although in humid conditions will feel damp.

Naomi Buys on *Chives of Freedom* (7c) - *p.213* - at the Main Cliff. Dinas Rock is set in a picturesque tree-covered narrow valley that contains a fast flowing river which attracts large guided groups who descend its various waterfalls and pools. Photo: MIke Hutton

Dinas Rock — Roadside

Roadside

This is a pleasant spot and a popular destination, only a stone's throw from the parking. The routes cover a good grade range mainly in the 6s with one or two easier routes. It can be used as a destination in itself or as something to get going on before the bigger stuff is tackled to the right.

Approach (map and overview p.200) - Follow the track upstream from the car park and the first section of Roadside is encountered on the left after 100m.

Conditions - The crag faces southeast and gets the morning sun. It dries quickly after rain but it is not steep enough to offer any dry climbing when it is raining. Seepage can be a problem in the winter months, although it receives more sun when the leaves are off the trees.

❶ **Fromage Frais** 5c
An appealing line on the left-hand side of the wall. Move up to left-slanting ledges and follow the wall and right-trending flake/crack to a lower-off.
FA. R.Thomas, G.Gibson 1.2.1998

❷ **Rob Roy** .... 7a+
Good climbing up the centre of the wall with a low crux as you move up from the flake. Above the climbing is easier but still tricky until the finish of *Fromage Frais* is joined.
FA. S.Doerr 1995

❸ **Cheesy Rider** .... 6b+
A short difficult section leaving the ledge. The opinion on the grade varies - some finding it **6c** and others only **6b**.
FA. R.Thomas, G.Gibson 8.6.1995

❹ **Creme de Roquefort**..... 6b+
A series of long moves on generally good holds up the short wall and grey-coloured rock above.
FA. G.Gibson, R.Thomas 3.5.2009

❺ **Creme de Rockfall**........ 6b+
A shorter pitch that follows the rib right of *Cheesy Rider*.
FA. G.Gibson, R.Thomas 3.5.2009

❻ **Scraping the Barrel** ..... 6a+
Another short and bouldery line.
FA. R.Thomas, G.Gibson 1995

❼ **Tapping the Keg** 6c
The right-hand line is a much tougher proposition that features some thin climbing.
FA. R.Thomas 1998

Roadside **Dinas Rock**

The next section of the crag is just to the right where a wall of rock runs up leftwards from the path.

❽ Pinheads 6c
The grey wall provides an airy outing just about worth doing. Run out and ivy-covered at the time of writing.
FA. G.Gibson, R.Thomas 31.1.1998

❾ Skin Ed 7c
The smoothest part of the wall provides a stern test of finger strength and adhesive qualities.
FA. G.Gibson 30.3.1997

❿ The Inflated Roundhead . 7a+
A good face climb, a hard move over a bulge.
FA. M.Crocker, R.Thomas 14.4.1988. Direct G.Gibson 1997

⓫ Charlie's Rusks 6c
Easier but just as good as *The Inflated Roundhead*.
FA. G.Gibson 5.1.1997

⓬ The Deflated Dickhead .. 6b
A good direct line with a short crux.
FA. R.Thomas, G.Gibson 1997

⓭ Mr Potato Head .... 6a+
Follow the staples up the centre of the conglomerate, past a flake, to a ledge. From the ledge, climb past a niche and roof to moves right into a groove to finish.
FA. A.Rosier 3.5.2010

⓮ Pothead 5c
Climb just right of the tree.
FA. R.Thomas 9.5.2009

Dinas Rock — Roadside

17 Bonehead 5b
The arete of the rippled wall, just to the right of *Smeghead*.
FA. R.Thomas 9.5.2009

18 The Democatic Republic of Maesteg
.... 6a
Climb the scoop right of *Bonehead*.
FA. D.Emanuel 9.5.2009

The next buttress is 50m further along the track.

19 Connect One 6a
A short problematic bulge. Finish right from the last bolt.
FA. G.Gibson, R.Thomas 3.2.1997

20 Southwest Guru 6b
An even more problematic bulge.
FA. A.Sharp, P.Lewis 26.4.1988

21 Deadly Nightshade 6c
The compact, technical face gives good clean climbing.
FA. A.Price 10.1998

22 Screaming Lampshades .... 6c+
A hard boulder problem bulge. Move left to the lower-off.
FA. G.Gibson, R.Thomas 3.2.1997

23 Big Ears Takes Flight .... 6b+
The roof of the cave provides the difficulties but don't underestimate the finishing slab.
FA. R.Thomas, G.Gibson 28.3.1997

24 The Wake .... 6b+
Exit the right-hand side of the cave up onto the slab.
FA. R.Thomas, G.Gibson 28.3.1997

15 The Dumbfounded Dunderhead
.... 6b
After a hard start, the route is a little less interesting above.
FA. R.Thomas, G.Gibson 1997

16 Smeghead 4c
The rippled wall and flake right of *The Dumfounded Dunderhead*.
FA. R.Thomas 3.5.2009

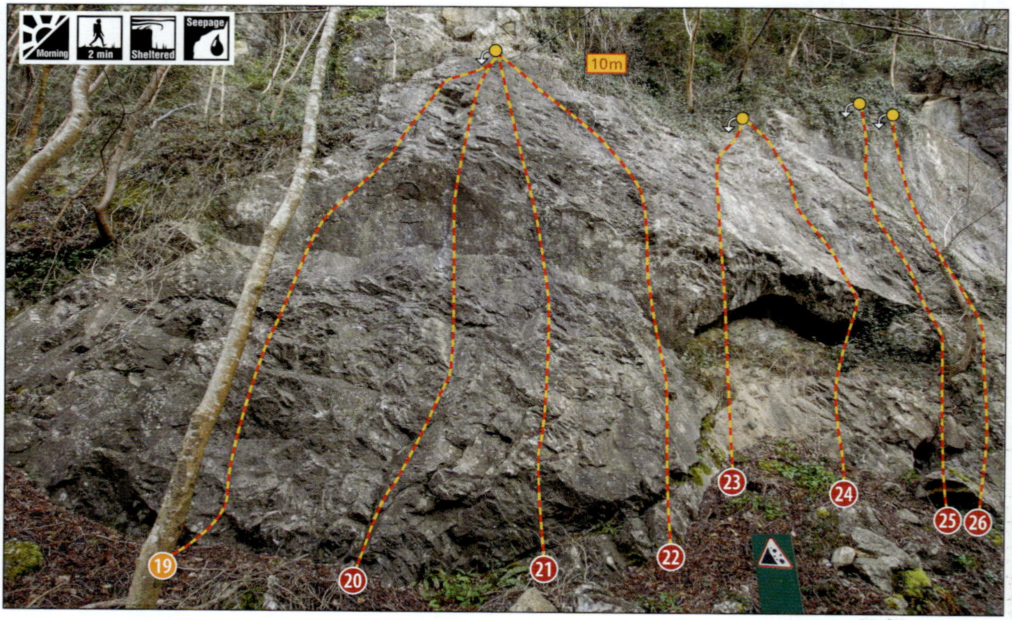

Dinas Rock

Al Rosier on *Beware of Poachers* (6c+) - *p.206* - at the Roadside crags, Dinas Rock. These crags are quickly approached along a pleasant level track from the parking. Photo: Carl Ryan

The next two routes start just right of the low arch/cave and can be overgrown but are good when clean.

25 Bob's Birthday Party 6b
The face gives good moves which are over far too quickly.
FA. B.Powles, A.Sharp, P.Lewis 1.10.1988

26 Cujo 6c
After an easy start tackle the smooth face above a flake.
FA. G.Gibson 3.2.1997

Dinas Rock — Roadside

27 Thinner 7a
Gaining the slab is straightforward, climbing it proves to be much harder. The start is overgrown so use the initial thin crack of *The Running Man* to access the base of the slab.
FA. G.Gibson, R.Thomas 29.3.1997

28 The Running Man 7a
Technical face climbing above a thin crack. The finish has been altered by rockfall and the lower-off is missing.
FA. A.Sharp 1.10.1988

29 Miss Alto 6b
The pleasant slab and steep hanging corner. This route is not affected by the rockfall.
FA. G.Gibson, R.Thomas, H.Gibson 28.3.1997

30 For the Love of Ivy .... HVS 5a
The impressive layback corner is sometimes choked in ivy. The finish has been altered by rockfall, but still goes at the grade.
FA. C.Connick, C.Smith 5.1979

31 The Regulators 7c
A short power-packed pitch with an airy finish. It is best to climb up the first two bolts of *The De-Regulators* to miss out a homemade hanger low down - the rest of the bolts are fine.
FA. G.Gibson 25.5.1997

32 The De-Regulators ... 7b
A super little route which tackles the upper wall just to the right of the hanging arete via some hard undercling moves.
FA. G.Gibson, R.Thomas 1.2.1998

33 Beware of Poachers ..... 6c+
Start up *The De-Regulators*. Good climbing with a technical move over a bulge to a flake. *Photo p.205*.
FA. A.Price, A.Long 1988

34 Open Roads .... 6b+
The slab and short wall, climbing direct through the overlap.
FA. G.Gibson, R.Thomas 5.1.1997

35 Squash the Squaddie .... 6b+
A pleasant face starting up a good wall and thin crack.
FA. A.Price, S.Elias 9.1988

36 Thousand Yard Stare . 6c+
Start at a very thin seam. An interesting sustained face climb through the left side of the overlap.
FA. A.Price, S.Thomas 10.1988

37 Pugsley 7a
Has a short, sharp crux low down.
FA. G.Gibson, R.Thomas 21.4.1995

38 Munsterosity 7a
Hard low down and all on awkward flat holds. A similar line to an old trad route *Herman Munster*. *Photo opposite*.
FA. G.Gibson 27.5.1995 FA. (HM) A.Sharp, T.Benjamin, A.Brown 1983

39 Morticia 7a
A steep line with good climbing that is run out between the first and second bolts.
FA. G.Gibson, R.Thomas 27.5.1995

Cat McKenna on *Munsterosity* (7a) - *opposite* - at the convenient Roadside crags that are a series of walls and buttresses which offer up some varied climbing styles in the grades ranging from 5b to 7c. Photo: Carl Ryan

Dinas Rock — Kennelgarth Wall

Kennelgarth Wall

A low and severely undercut wall of compact limestone that is a popular bouldering venue and home to a handful of fierce sport pitches. The lower section of the wall has a number of boulder problems that can be linked into the routes for those looking for even tougher challenges.

Approach (map and overview p.200) - Walk to where the track/path ends and the wall is on the left.
Descent - Not all of the lines have lower-offs but bolt belays are in place on the ledge above the wall.
Conditions - The wall gets some sun in the afternoon, and once dry stays dry. The lines might need a brush.

❶ Technitis. 6c
A short line on the left with a very technical move.
FA. P.Donnithorne, T.Meen 1988

❷ By Proxy. 7a
The wall just to the right of *Technitis*.
FA. G.Gibson, R.Thomas 30.3.1997

❸ Out Come the Freaks 7a+
Climb up past the arched overlap.
FA. A.Sharp 23.5.1988

❹ Fings Ain't What They Used To Be 7b+
Climb the seam and pockets to access a desperate sequence leftwards on the upper wall to finish.
FA. A.Sharp, P.Thomas, P.Lewis 15.5.1988

❺ Siberian Husky 7b+
From the triangular niche of *Kennelgarth*, follow the thin line left to join and finish as for *Fings Ain't What They Used To Be*.
FA. S.Rawlinson 30.4.2010

❻ Kennelgarth 7b+
Gain the triangular niche and then climb up left and then back right to finish.
FA. A.Sharp 1984. FFA. G.Ashmore 23.7.1994

❼ Eugene's High Point 7b+
The line to the right ends at the final staple - no one has made it to the top.
FA. E.Travers-Jones 1995

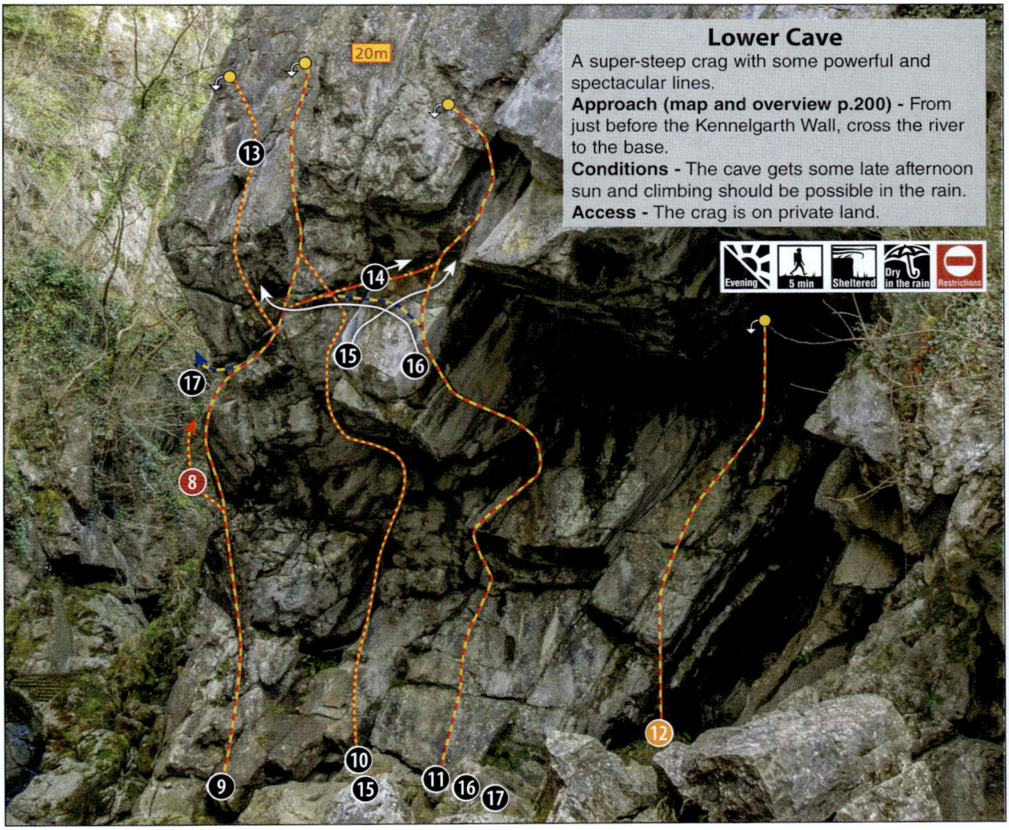

Lower Cave — Dinas Rock

Lower Cave
A super-steep crag with some powerful and spectacular lines.
Approach (map and overview p.200) - From just before the Kennelgarth Wall, cross the river to the base.
Conditions - The cave gets some late afternoon sun and climbing should be possible in the rain.
Access - The crag is on private land.

There are a number of good variations and link-ups.

❽ The Dandelion Slab 7a
The slab on the left.
FA. S.Rawlinson 5.6.2011

❾ Rose-Line .... 7b+
Take the hanging left arete to horizontal breaks and then move through a roof-crack to finish in a hanging groove.
FA. S.Rawlinson 3.6.2009

❿ Smashed Rat 7c
The long roof-crack to join and finish as for *Rose-Line*.
FA. M.Richards 24.6.2009

⓫ Rat on a Hot Tin Roof 7b
Move up steeply before a traverse can be made out to the front of the hanging block. To finish, pull out rightwards and up a rounded tube/crack - interesting.
FA. A.Sharp, P.Lewis (1pt) 1984. FFA. S.Rawlinson 26.3.2009

⓬ The First Step To Enlightenment . 5a
A hard start leads to easier ground and a weird trip into the belly of the cave. Worth taking a torch just to look around and beware - the caves that shoot off in all directions go a long way!
FA. S.Rawlinson 9.6.2011

⓭ Watchmen 7b
A direct finish to *Rose-Line*. From a spike at the horizontal breaks, finish direct up the crack. Variation - move up left and rock over onto the arete.
FA. S.Rawlinson 2009

⓮ Sangreal .... 7b+
From below the roof crack of *Rose-Line* keep traversing to join and finish as for *Rat on a Hot Tin Roof*.
FA. S.Rawlinson 6.6.2009

⓯ Sangria Finish .... 7b+
Link *Smashed Rat* to *Rat on a Hot Tin Roof*.
FA. S.Rawlinson 5.7.2009

⓰ Basilica .... 7b+
Link *Rat on a Hot Tin Roof* to *Rose-Line*.
FA. S.Rawlinson 6.6.2009

⓱ Tiger Cut .... 7c+
Start up *Rat on a Hot Tin Roof* and flip under the block into *Smashed Rat*. From halfway along the block break left into *Rose-line* and then *The Dandelion Slab*.
FA. S.Rawlinson 5.7.2009

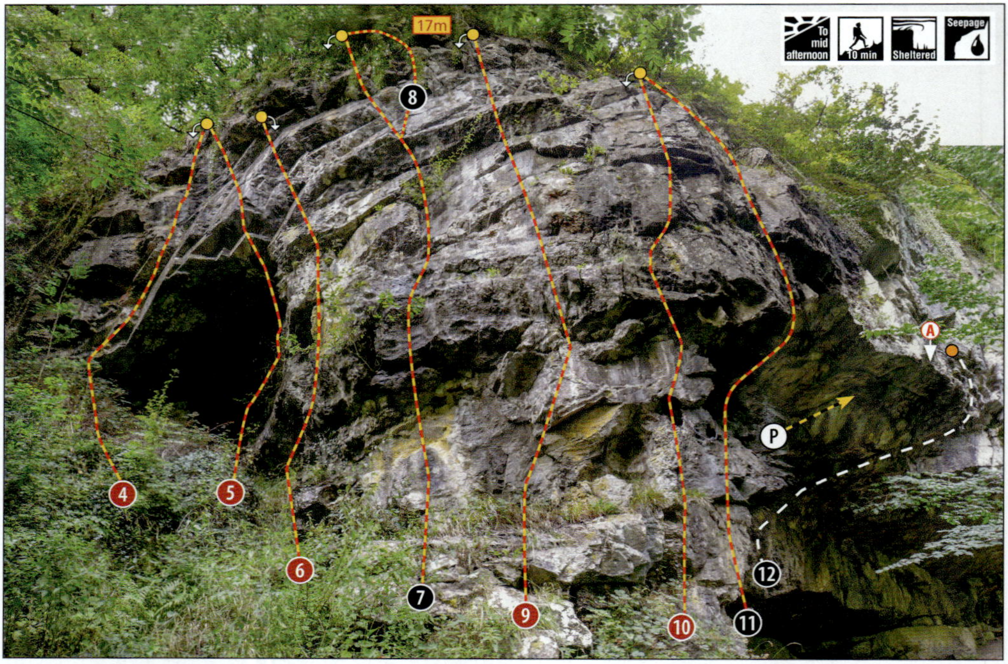

Dinas Rock — Main Cliff

Main Cliff

The showpiece section of Dinas Rock and one of the most important areas for hard sport climbing in South Wales. A series of overlaps and roofs, some of which are very large, guard the contrasting technical upper walls.

Approach (map and overview p.200) - Follow the riverside path past Kennelgarth Wall and scramble up the left-hand side of the river and the Main Cliff is just a little further on. Alternatively, should the river be in spate, take the path left of the car park. This rises steeply, levels out above the crag, then drops down to the river. Go downstream to the crag.

Conditions - The cliff faces southeast and receives sunshine until about midday. The face can seep after long periods of rain.

❶ Pis en Lit 6b
Climb direct just to the left of the arete. Stepping in from the right reduces the grade to **6a+**.
FA. R.Thomas, G.Gibson 15.2.1998

❷ Illegal Congress 6b
Takes on the wall to the right with some good moves.
FA. R.Thomas, G.Gibson 15.2.1998

❸ Family Values .... 6a+
The right-hand line on the buttress.
FA. R.Thomas, G.Gibson 1998

❹ Stray Cats............. 7a
Start in the cave. A long reach over the initial roof gains good holds that lead to a tricky finishing groove.
FA. P.Tilson, M.Danford 1972. FFA. A.Sharp, J.Harwood 9.8.1983

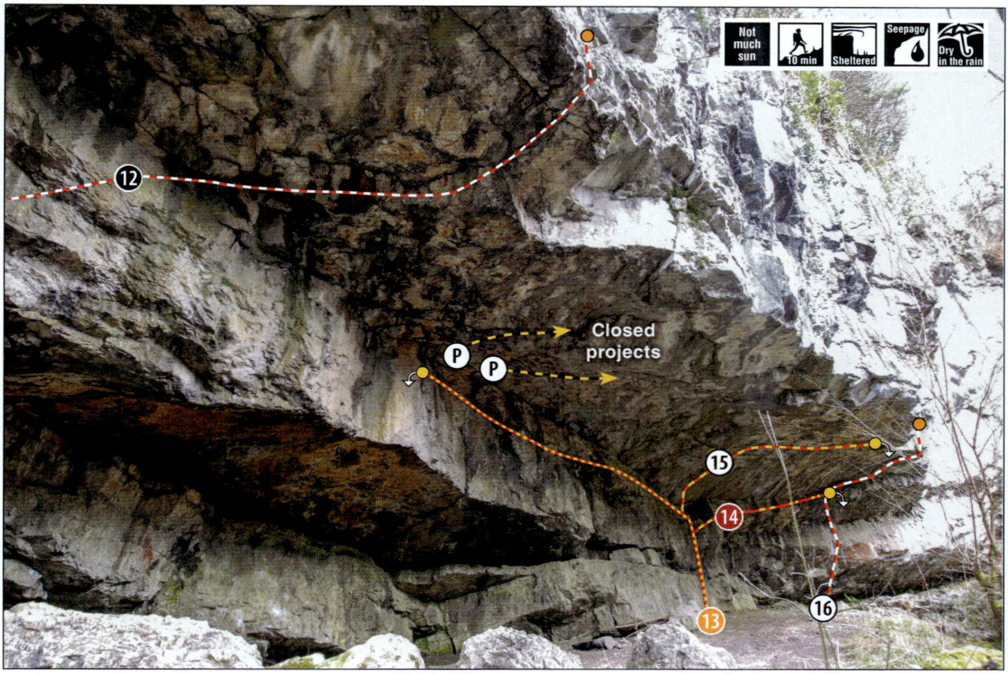

5 Puss Off .... 1★ 7a
The right-hand line out of the cave has a few powerful moves.
FA. G.Gibson, R.Thomas 22.3.1998

6 Each Way Nudger .... 1★ 6b+
Start on the left-hand side of the raised ledge. Move up over an overlap into a groove. Continue to a bulge, pass it on the left and finish over the final bulge, pulling left on good holds.
FA. G.Gibson and team 19.5.1985

7 When Push Comes to Shove .. 1★ 7a+
Climb to the half-height overhang and make some hard moves over it. Climb right of the bolt out on the left before swinging left for 3m to the lower-off on *Each Way Nudger*.
FA. G.Gibson, R.Thomas 15.2.1998

8 When Push Comes to Shove (Direct Finish)
.... 7b
Climb right of the last bolt on the normal line to good holds.
FA. G.Gibson 1990s

9 Call a Spade a Spade .... 1★ 6c
Climb direct from the raised ledge over the low bulge and then the mid-height overhang to finish up a short headwall.
FA. G.Gibson, R.Thomas 15.2.1998

10 Totally Radish .... 1★ 6c
Gain a large thread runner and then climb up over the overhang with difficulty. Finish up the arete on its left to gain the lower-off.
FA. G.Gibson, R.Thomas 22.3.1998

11 Durbin Two, Watson Nil .. 1★ 7c
The left-hand side of the roof provides a complicated sequence after a relatively easy start. Finish up the easier corner/groove.
FA. G.Ashmore 23.3.1997

12 Giant Killer .... 1★ E6 6a
The prominent diagonal roof crack is gained via a traverse in from the left. The crux is at the very lip. Abseil descent. The second pitch (which is **6a**) is overgrown.
FA. P.Littlejohn, T.Penning (1pt) 26.6.1983
FFA. M.Crocker, R.Thomas 14.4.1988

13 The Road to Eldorado.... 1★ 5a
Entertaining. Move up to the traverse line under the huge roof and follow it left to a lower-off.
FA. L.Collyer 12.6.2009

14 Gorilliant .... 1★ 7a
Move up to the break as for *The Road to Eldorado* and then head right along the break to a lower-off.
FA. A.Sharp 24.6.2009

15 Mortal Kombat ...... 3★ 8b
Tackles the massive roof above the start of *The Road to Eldorado*. Powerful and technical moves across the ceiling gain a lower-off station just under the lip. Stunning.
FA. S.Rawlinson 18.6.2011

16 Dina Crac .... 3★ E9 7a
Start up a bolted bouldery wall to meet *Gorilliant*. Climb the thin crack across the roof placing the gear as you go. **8b+** sport.
FA. T.Randall 8.2014

Carmarthenshire
Gower
Inland and Coastal Limestone
The Valleys Sandstone

Dinas Rock — Main Cliff

Main Cliff Dinas Rock

⑰ Sport Wars 8a
Move up to the roof and execute some powerful moves over it. Traverse leftwards to gain the base of a groove and climb the left-hand wall and arete above.
FA. G.Gibson (1pt) 27.8.1995. FFA. G.Ashmore 20.5.1997

⑱ Bloody Sport Climbers . . . 8a
Follow *Sport Wars* to the groove and then pull up right into it. Go right and finish up *Subversive Body Pumping*.
FA. M.Crocker, R.Thomas (1pt) 17.4.1988. FFA. G.Ashmore 20.5.1997

⑲ Captain Barbarossa 8a
A direct finish to *Sport Wars* up a steep prow.
FA. S.Rawlinson 9.10.2009

⑳ H1N1 . . . . 8a
Follow *Sport Wars* over its roof to a jug. Climb steeply direct to another jug on the right edge of a slab above. Move right into *Bloody Sport Climbers* and finish up *Subversive Body Pumping*.
FA. M.Richards 26.7.2009

㉑ The Black Pearl 8a
A good link-up. Climb *H1N1* to the edge of the slab and then finish as for *Captain Barbarossa*.
FA. S.Rawlinson 10.10.2009

㉒ Subversive Body Pumping 7b+
Start up *Sport Wars* and then make a hideous contorted entry into the bottomless groove - above things relent only slightly.
FA. M.Crocker, R.Thomas 6.3.1988

㉓ Powers That Be 7c
A rising connection of routes that gives good climbing. From just above the crux of *Subversive Body Pumping* move into *Berlin*, then onto *Still Life* to finish.
FA. M.Crocker, R.Thomas 30.4.1988

㉔ Dinasty 8a
A hard start over the lower overhangs gains the traverse line of *Powers That Be*. Move up to join and finish as for *Hayabusa*.
FA. M.Richards 14.6.2009

㉕ Berlin . . . . 7a+
A classic landmark route connecting a series of shallow grooves after a bouldery start. *Photo p.198.*
FA. G.Gibson, M.Ward, M.Crocker 18.5.1985

㉖ Berlin Extension 7b
Extend the upper section via a corner to finish as for *Still Life*.
FA. M.Richards, A.Sharp 1.6.2008

㉗ Hayabusa . . . . 7c+
A complex but fine climb that features lots of hard moves. Start up *Berlin* and head left and up to the beginning of a forearm-draining finale. Finish at the *Subversive Body Pumping* lower-off.
FA. M.Richards, A.Sharp 6.2008

㉘ Still Life . . . . 7b+
Technical wizardry throughout, particularly where the line departs *Berlin*. Save something in the tank for the finish.
FA. G.Gibson, R.Thomas 30.4.1994

㉙ Just in Time 7c
A hybrid route, linking up two great lines. Climb *Still Life* until a shattered pocket is reached, then move over to the arete and follow it as for *Outta Time* to finish.
FA. S.Robinson 29.5.2009

㉚ Chives of Freedom 7c
Pull through the roof to the base of the groove as for *The Big Time*. Make a desperate sequence through the bulges to reach the base of the central groove on *Still Life* and finish up this. *Photo p.201.*
FA. (as Angel Heart) Andy Sharp, Pete Lewis (1pt) 24.4.1988
FFA. G.Ashmore 5.6.1994

㉛ Outta Time . . . . 7c+
A good variation starting up *Chives of Freedom* and then taking the *The Big Time* groove until the arete to its left can be attained. Climb the arete and finish as for *Still Life*.
FA. M.Richards, A.Sharp 21.3.2009

㉜ The Big Time E6 6c
The long slim corner is the original line of this wall. The groove itself is bold and the direct finish over the roof highly entertaining. The original finish traversed off to the right.
FA. P.Littlejohn, T.Penning, J.Harwood (1pt) 7.5.1985
FFA. (with direct finish over roof) G.Gibson, R.Thomas 8.4.1995

Dinas Rock — Main Cliff

㉝ Crock of Gold 7c
A pumpy and dynamic roof is combined with a very technical and thin slab up the face to the right of *The Big Time* groove.
FA. M.Crocker, R.Thomas 17.4.1988

㉞ The Sharp Cereal Professor
.... 7b
A brilliant pitch. Climb steeply to the roof and pass it to grasp a good hold over the lip. Move up the slabby wall rightwards passing an overlap with some difficulty.
FA. G.Gibson, R.Thomas 1.5.1994

㉟ Salem's Lot .... 7b+
Climb the first section of *Crock of Gold* through the roof before move right to finish as for *The Sharp Cereal Professor*.
FA. A.Sharp, P.Lewis (2pts) 1985. FFA. M.Crocker, R.Thomas 15.4.1988

㊱ Muchas Maracas 7c
Climb *The Sharp Cereal Professor* and traverse the sandwiched wall rightwards to breach the overhang as for *Hawaiian Chance*.
FA. M.Richards 30.5.2009

㊲ Harlem .... 7b+
A classic with plenty of varied moves through the stepped overhangs to finish up a groove in the upper wall.
FA. A.Sharp, P.Lewis (2pts) 1985. FFA. M.Crocker, R.Thomas 15.4.1988

㊳ Hawaiian Chance 7c
A direct line with a hard sequence to leave *Spain* at mid-height.
FA. G.Gibson, R.Thomas 12.5.1991

㊴ Spain E4 6a
A traditional classic passing grooves, overlaps and slabs.
FA. G.Gibson 23.3.1985

㊵ Groovy Tube Day E2 5c
An unusual climb branching off right from *Spain* into the 'tube'.
FA. C.Connick, D.Hughes 1978

㊶ Dr Van Steiner .... 7a+
Cross *Groovy Tube Day* to meet and finish up *Spain*. Some gear is needed for the top section and abseil descent.
FA. G.Gibson 26.5.1991

Terrace Cliff Dinas Rock 215

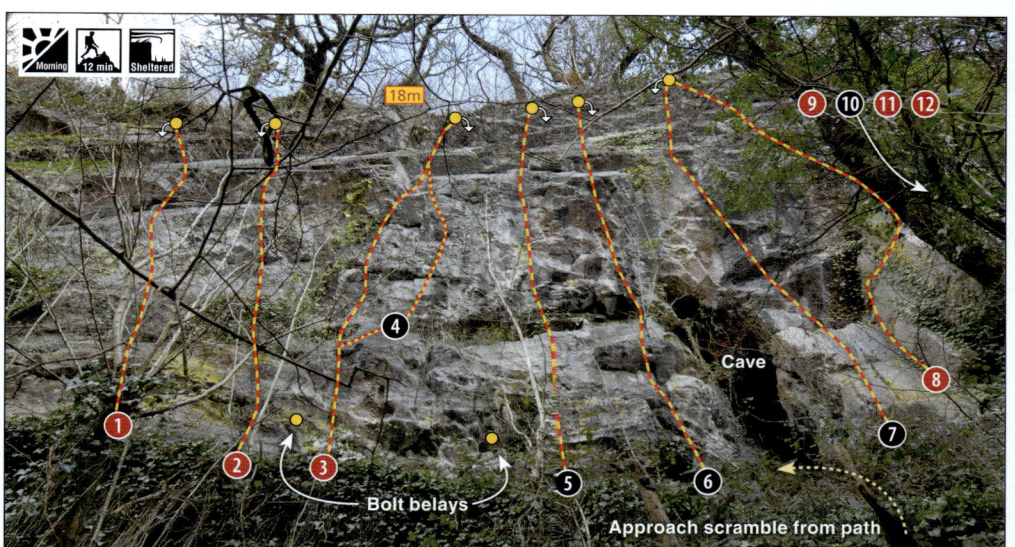

Terrace Cliff

At present this excellent section of cliff is losing the battle with the vegetation. However when clean it complements the Main Cliff having an easier selection of routes.

Approach (map and overview p.200) - Continue along the path below the Main Cliff and scramble up onto a small terrace by a cave.

Conditions - The walls face southeast and only get morning sunshine. They can suffer from seepage quite badly during the winter but, once dry remain so except in longer periods of rain.

The routes all start from a terrace at 7m that is gained by a diagonal scramble up from the path.

❶ Academy Awards 6c
The groove at the left end of the terrace. This line used to start from the main footpath and climb over a tough roof to gain the terrace, but is now overgrown.
FA. R.Thomas, G.Gibson 9.4.1995

❷ Dream Academy 6c
A classic slab and face climb with two technical cruxes.
FA. T.Penning, J.Harwood 14.5.1985

❸ El Camino del Roy .... 6c+
The hanging groove, with some fine and unusual moves to gain entry to it.
FA. R.Thomas, G.Gibson 14.5.1995

❹ Danny La Rue .... 7a+
Squeezed in but, not without interest.
FA. G.Gibson, R.Thomas 8.4.1995

❺ Incidentally X .... 7b+
A much changed route since the demise of a large flake. This has been resolved by a particularly trying rockover move.
FA. G.Gibson 23.3.1985 and also in 1995 after holds came off.

❻ Tortilla Flats 7b
Start just to the left of the cave. Unlikely terrain after a grubby start. Lower off the last bolt runner.
FA. G.Gibson 9.4.1995

❼ Pour Marcel 7b
Start just to the right of the cave. An unlikely looking pitch on pockets and slopers above the right arete of the cave.
FA. G.Gibson 14.5.1994

❽ Brazilian Blend .... 6c+
A little gem of a pitch with an airy and unusual crux sequence exiting the bulge.
FA. G.Gibson 19.5.1985

The next four routes start to the right.

❾ Sverige 7a
Two very technical sections with a good rest in-between.
FA. G.Gibson, T.Penning, M.Ward 19.5.1985

❿ Ma's Strict .... 7a+
Surprisingly difficult. Long reaches help, as does a sense of direction!
FA. G.Gibson, R.Thomas 25.3.1995

⓫ Breakout 6c
A fine upper section after an easy start.
FA. F.Sharp, J.Harwood 1.9.1983

⓬ Vitamin Z 7a
A harder right-hand version of *Breakout* on the upper walls.
FA. F.Sharp, P.Lewis 1985

Darren Fawr

Grade Spread | - | 6 | 25 | 1 | -

A west-facing escarpment of vertical limestone set high on the flanks of the Brecon Beacons. The escarpment where the climbing has been developed gives some long intricate wall climbs interspersed by the occasional overhang. The sectors are separated by sections of poorer rock and vegetation. The approach is long and the crag should only be considered on days of good calm weather.

Approach
From the A470 Merthyr Tydfil to Brecon road, the escarpment is visible above a massive scree slope. Turn off the A470 at a sign for Cefn Coed and, after 200m, park on the left by a gated track. Follow the track up past two metal gates and then on a less good track to a stile in a fence. Cross the stile and carry straight up and bear gently left to follow an old post and wire fence line (demarcating the golf course) shortly joining a quad track leading off to the left. Walk along the quad track for 10 minutes until a 1m high boulder is easily seen on the right. Drop down to the grassy edge of the scree slope and locate the narrow descent gully. The descent gully is the northerly gully NOT the gully with a fence above it. The descent gully requires a scramble and there is a fixed rope in place.

GPS 51.770876 -3.415915

Conditions
High and very exposed to the elements but quick drying and sunny from early afternoon. It is possible to climb here year round as long as the sun is out and it is not windy.

Nic Goile on *Rictus Grin* (6c) - *p.219* - at Darren Fawr. The exposed section of the escarpment, where the climbing is located, is set high on the hills that run up above the River Taff to the mountain tops of the Brecon Beacons. Photo: Alan Rosier

Darren Fawr — Left Side

Left Side
The Left Side is home to a collection of long pitches in the mid-grades that are well bolted and very exposed.
Approach (map and overview p.216) - From the base of the approach gully walk right (facing out). This is the furthest section from the base of the approach gully.
Conditions - High and very exposed to the elements but quick drying and sunny from early afternoon.

❶ Feeling Good is Good Enough 7a
At the second bolt shared with *Moonage Daydream* traverse left to an overhang and move up to a jug. Pull past the overhang and step left to the arete. Head up to a rest and a little higher move back right to finish up *Moonage Daydream*.
FA. A.Rosier, N.Goile 23.9.2023

❷ Moonage Daydream 6b+
The left-facing slim corner and flake gives a technical outing that increases in difficulty with height.
FA. A.Rosier 17.8.2023

Left Side Darren Fawr

❸ A Blue Sky Day 6c+
Fine climbing and positions. Begin to the left of the low strip roof. Head up the wall and connect two very slim left-facing overlap/corners. From the second go left and finish up the headwall.
FA. A Rosier, O.Burrows 2020

❹ Rainbow's End 6b+
Make hard moves to and past the low strip roof and then continue up the long fragile corner-line above.
FA. A.Rosier, R.Thomas 23.3.2020

❺ Three's the Charm 6b+
A well regarded pitch. Climb the tricky wall left of the large tree to pockets and flakes.
FA. A.Rosier, R.Thomas 23.3.2020

❻ Fear Inoculum 6a+
Good climbing with a tough start. From atop a pedestal head up and right to a groove with a capping overhang. Pull past the overhang and finish up the wall to the left of the continuation of the groove.
FA. A.Rosier, R.McAllister 1.9.2019

❼ The Intensity of Spring 6b+
Climb up past a low strip roof to a shallow angular niche. Step right to undercuts in the next strip roof from where a long reach gains a good hold. Finish up the compact walls above.
FA. A.Rosier, R.McAllister 2.10.2019

❽ Rictus Grin 6c
Take a sharp flake that leads to a long vertical slot. A series of side-pulls then gains a series of better holds and a bucket hold. Stand in the bucket and then move up to the lower-off.
Photo p.217.
FA. A.Rosier 20.10.2019

❾ The Quiet Earth 6c
A thin start and awkward slab accesses the mid-height overhangs. A hard rockover past the overhang gains a jug. Finish up the wall above on massive holds.
FA. R.McAllister, W.Calvert 9.6.2020

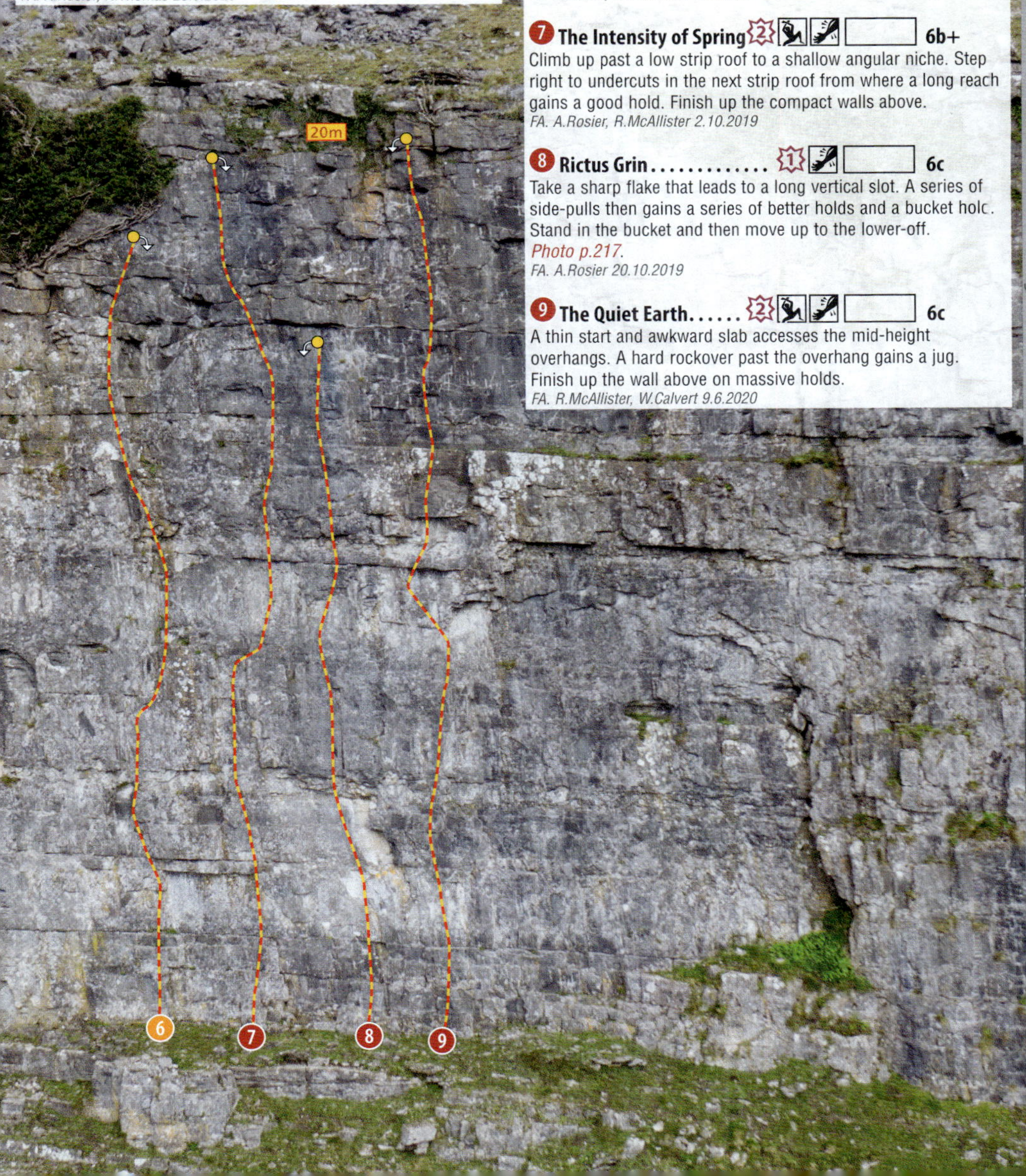

Darren Fawr Right Side

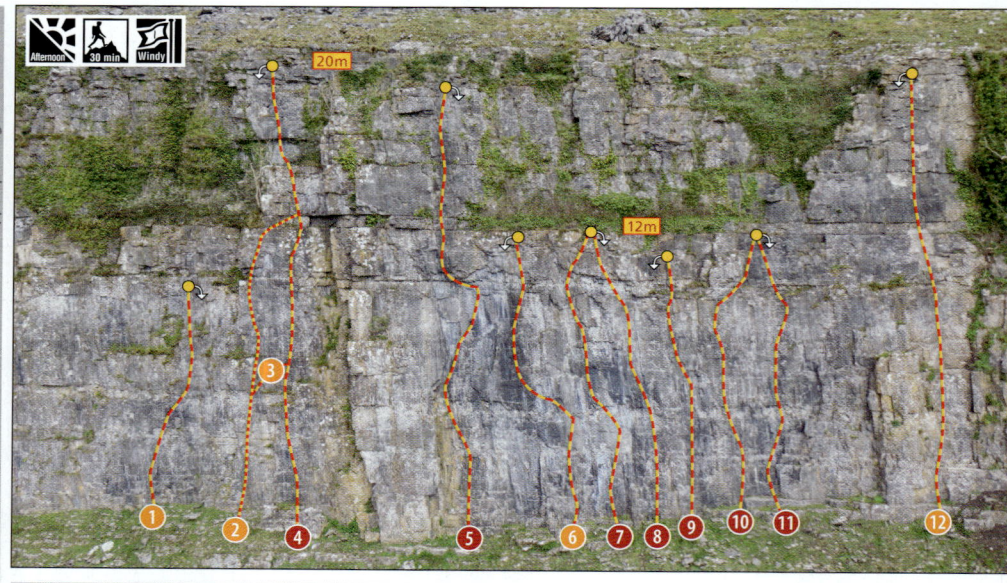

Right Side
The Right Side has plenty to keep teams interested in grade 6s very busy, with those centred around the route *Mannequins of Horror* being the best of the bunch.
Approach (map and overview p.216) - From the base of the approach gully walk right (facing out). This is the first section encountered.
Conditions - High and very exposed to the elements but quick drying and sunny from early afternoon.

❶ Liber Noctis 5c
A right-trending line on the wall left of *Starmageddon*.
FA. A.Rosier, C.Watkins 26.7.2024

❷ Starmageddon 5c
Head up to a faint arete, and at 14m move right at a narrow ledge to join and finish up *Red Wall*.
FA. A.Rosier 6.7.2024

❸ Tory-ectomy .... 6a+
Above the 3rd bolt *Starmageddon* move right to join *Red Wall*.
FA. A.Rosier 6.7.2024

❹ Red Wall .... 6b+
Climb left of an unstable tower. Do not stray from the line.
FA. A.Rosier 6.7.2024

❺ Vibrant Thing 6c
Climb a thin crack to a good ledge and continue to the upper roof. Pass the roof via a tricky move and finish easily.
FA. W.Calvert, W.Gregory 2017

❻ Dr. Finger Blaster .... 6a+
Climb easy ground to a difficult rock-over. Traverse delicately leftwards to a massive flake and ascend it to an awkward finish.
FA. A.Rosier, R.McAllister 2.10.2019

❼ Invincible 6c
The wall moving left at the first bolt. It has a shared lower-off with *Pneuma*.
FA. A.Rosier, W.Calvert 15.9.2019

❽ Pneuma 6b
Begin on the right arete of an open left-facing corner and follow a thin vertical seam to a big break. Take a thin flake to finish.
FA. A.Rosier, J.Westwood 8.9.2019

❾ Herding Cats .... 6b+
Strenuous moves are encountered at two long sharp side-pulls.
FA. A.Rosier, J.Westwood 8.9.2019

❿ Will of the People .... 6b+
A technical mid-section. Move right at the top to a shared lower-off with *Bongo Bongo Land*.
FA. A.Rosier, R.McAllister 2.10.2019

⓫ Bongo Bongo Land 6b
Climb the right-hand side of the wall, just left of stepped ramp.
FA. A.Rosier, R.McAllister 2.10.2019

⓬ Nazi Sheep .... 6a+
Two steps lead to a steepening wall with tough finishing moves.
FA. A.Rosier, R.McAllister 24.3.2024

⓭ Oumuamua .... 6b+
Begin left of a cave at ground level. Head up corner flakes until a step left gains a pocketed crack. Climb the crack with difficulty and pass the right side of a roof to finish up the headwall.
FA. R.McAllister, A.Rosier 1.9.2019

⓮ Weaponized Funk .... 6b+
At the third bolt make a tricky step left to good holds. Move back right and finish via the airy capping roof.
FA. A.Rosier, R.McAllister 24.3.2019

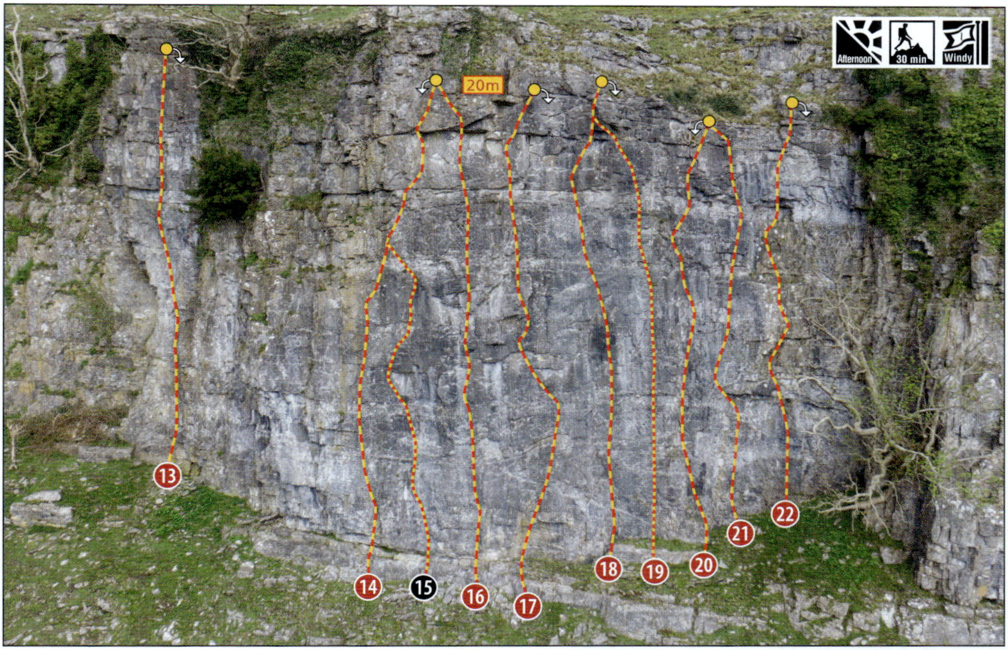

Right Side Darren Fawr

🔴15 Daisy Chainsaw......... 7a+
Climb a slab to a triangular roof and execute a difficult sequence of moves to pass it and reach a jug. Finish up *Weaponized Funk*.
FA. A.Rosier, W.Calvert, R.McAllister 9.6.2020

🔴16 Down and Out in Paris and London
.... 6c
An absorbing, intricate and wandering climb. Fortunately the top section has a good rest before the final roof.
FA. W.Calvert 15.11.2016

🔴17 Gladius................ 6c+
Begin at a low arch. Climb to a tough rock-over at 8m and finish up the easy corner/arete.
FA. A.Rosier, R.Brewer 24.3.2019

🔴18 Depression Cherry 6c
Climb into a shallow groove via a thin sequence. Finish to the right at the capping overhang.
FA. W.Calvert, B.Gregory 5.7.2016

🔴19 Mannequins of Horror 6b+
The front face has some tricky side-pull sequences. Head left near the top to a sloping ledge and weakness in the final roof.
FA. W.Calvert, B.Gregory 5.7.2016

🔴20 Dan's Dihedral.......... 6b+
The shallow corner and final bulge on good flakes.
FA. A.Rosier, O.Burrows 5.2020

🔴21 Ninja Worrier........... 6c+
A long low flake leads to good technical walls and a steep finish.
FA. R.McAllister, B.Brewer 24.3.2019

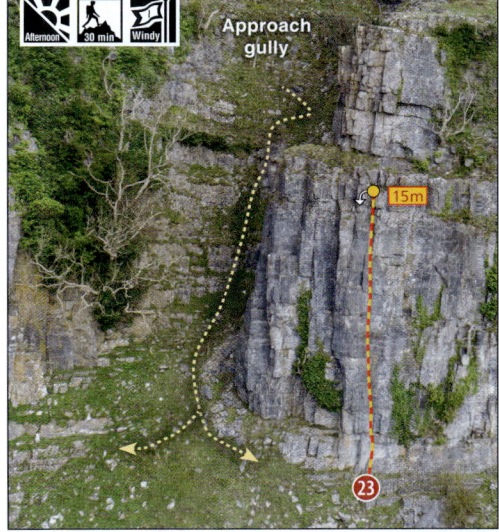

🔴22 The Fastest Horse in Town.... 6c+
Take on the butch, right-trending flake at 5m. Move out rightwards from the cave above it to reach big pockets.
FA. A.Rosier, O.Burrows 5.2020

🔴23 Tower of the Serpent........... 6b+
The front face of the tower right of the gully.
FA. A.Rosier, R.McAllister 9.6.2020

Taff's Well

| Grade Spread | 10 | 23 | 48 | 9 | - |

Taff's Well is a roadside crag on the outskirts of Cardiff, close to the M4 corridor. It consists of some big calcite walls mixed with areas of compact grey limestone. The climbs vary in style from short intricate face climbs through to longer routes - up to 35m in some cases - full of atmosphere and technical difficulties. Two other small crags close by have some less intimidating lower-grade lines and are further from the road and consequently quieter.

Approach
Exit the M4 at junction 32 onto the A470 north for Merthyr Tydfil. Take the first exit signed to Taff's Well and the crag can be seen on the right, immediately above the junction roundabout. Parking is possible in a small pull-off on the roundabout, directly below the cliff.
From Merthyr Tydfil, take the A470 south and take the exit signed for Tongwynlais. Once at the roundabout, the crag is immediately visible on the left above the small parking place. From the parking, a track leads directly to the main crag in 100m.
For Castle Coch, continue up the path past some steps on the left. In 40m head left on a small path, up the right-hand side of a small valley, to the crag which is below the castle.
For the Pinnacle, continue from the roundabout towards Taff's Well. After 300m, turn right, cross over the A470 and, in 350m, turn left onto Forest Road and park. Opposite the junction take a small path to the crag.

Conditions
The crag faces southwest and gets the sun from midday onwards. It dries very quickly and its open aspect gives for a pleasant atmosphere despite the noise from the road below.

Taff's Well 223

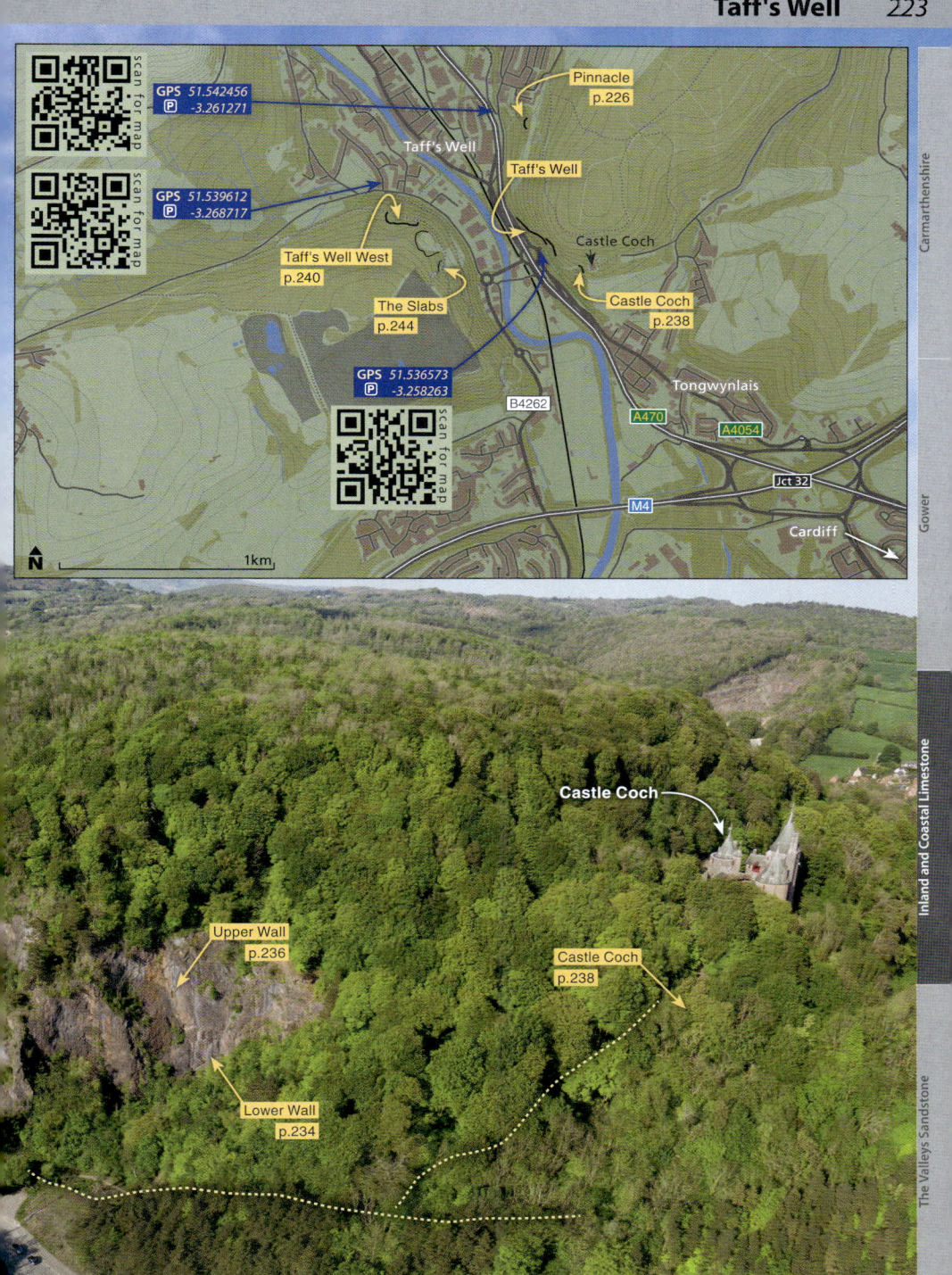

Becky Athay and Myles Jordan tackling the fine wall climbing to be had on *Red Square* (6b+) - *p.231* - on the left-hand side of the Calcite Wall at Taff's Well. The second is belayed at the top of a short approach pitch which allows access to this line and two other worthwhile wall pitches - *Organised Chaos* (6c) and *The Melty Man Cometh* (7a). Photo: Mark Glaister

Taff's Well 225

Taff's Well — Pinnacle

Pinnacle

A compact crag with some lower-grade lines on reasonable rock. The east-facing wall has three short but fun micro-routes. Keep noise to a minimum as there are residential houses close by.

Approach (map and overview p.223) - Continue from the roundabout below Taff's Well Main towards the village of Taff's Well. After 300m turn right, cross over the A470 and, in 350m, turn left onto Forest Road and park. Opposite the junction, take a small path through the woods to reach the crag in 50m

Conditions - The wall is open and gets plenty of afternoon sun. Seepage maybe a problem.

❶ Scurvy Rubber Ducky...Aaar! 4c
Climb direct past 4 bolts, then traverse right to reach the last bolt of *Crusty Barnacles* and finish up it to a shared lower-off.
FA. A.Rosier, R.McAllister, A.Rosier 25.4.2018

❷ Crusty Barnacles 5a
Start up a streak and continue via a mantelshelf onto a ledge.
FA. R.McAllister, A.Rosier 25.4.2018

❸ Poppin' in the Poop Deck 5c
The wall and groove/corner high on the face.
FA. A.Rosier, R.McAllister 23.4.2013

❹ Megalodon 6a
Move out right from *Poppin' on the Poop Deck* to a thin flake.
FA. A.Rosier, R.McAllister 23.4.2013

❺ Kiss the Gunner's Daughter 5c
Climb the bulge and tiny overhang before heading left.
FA. A.Rosier, R.McAllister 23.4.2013

❻ Angry Pirate 5c
Nice climbing up the wall to the left of the dirty central fault.
FA. A.Rosier, R.McAllister 25.4.2013

❼ Sharktopus vs Megapotamus 5c
Some tricky bouldery climbing at the start.
FA. A.Rosier, R.McAllister 25.4.2013

❽ Yar! 5a
Climb the groove direct after a bouldery start.
FA. A.Rosier, R.McAllister 25.4.2013

❾ Jurassic Shark 5c
The line on the far right of the main face.
FA. A.Rosier, R.McAllister 25.4.2013

The next three routes are to the right on the side-wall.

❿ Toxic Badger Dust 6a
Take the line up steep ground following the left-hand line of staple bolts to a lower-off.
FA. R.McAllister, A.Rosier 21.7.2020

⓫ Bermuda Tentacles 6a
A tricky start followed by easier climbing. Traverse left after clipping the final staple bolt to finish at a shared lower-off.
FA. R.McAllister, A.Rosier 21.7.2020

⓬ Slabasaurus 6a+
Ascend the slab and right-hand arete on the east-facing wall.
FA. R.McAllister, A.Rosier 21.7.2020

The Lower Wall at Taff's Well has a good selection of intricate and technical wall pitches that link slim corners and grooves via short walls and overlaps. Here Mike Dunk negotiates *Daggers* (6c) - *p.234* - at the Lower Wall. Photo: Mark Glaister

Taff's Well — The Shield

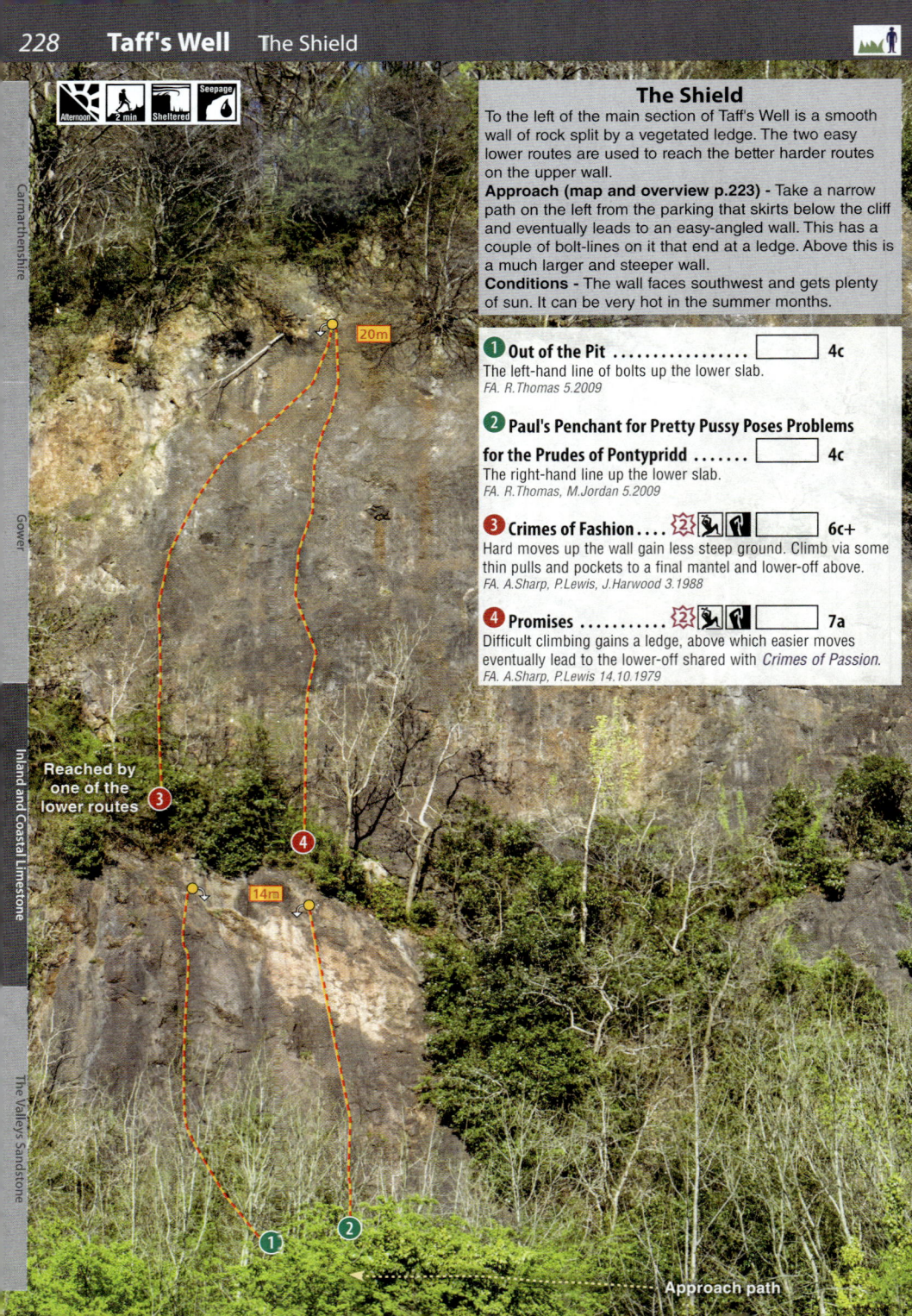

The Shield

To the left of the main section of Taff's Well is a smooth wall of rock split by a vegetated ledge. The two easy lower routes are used to reach the better harder routes on the upper wall.

Approach (map and overview p.223) - Take a narrow path on the left from the parking that skirts below the cliff and eventually leads to an easy-angled wall. This has a couple of bolt-lines on it that end at a ledge. Above this is a much larger and steeper wall.

Conditions - The wall faces southwest and gets plenty of sun. It can be very hot in the summer months.

❶ Out of the Pit 4c
The left-hand line of bolts up the lower slab.
FA. R.Thomas 5.2009

❷ Paul's Penchant for Pretty Pussy Poses Problems for the Prudes of Pontypridd 4c
The right-hand line up the lower slab.
FA. R.Thomas, M.Jordan 5.2009

❸ Crimes of Fashion .... 6c+
Hard moves up the wall gain less steep ground. Climb via some thin pulls and pockets to a final mantel and lower-off above.
FA. A.Sharp, P.Lewis, J.Harwood 3.1988

❹ Promises 7a
Difficult climbing gains a ledge, above which easier moves eventually lead to the lower-off shared with *Crimes of Passion*.
FA. A.Sharp, P.Lewis 14.10.1979

Taff's Well has some big pitches such as this one on the towering Calcite Wall *The Connecticut Connection* (7a+) - *p.231* - In this photo Mike Dunk is making some hard pulls to get established on the headwall of this 35m line. Photo: Mark Glaister

Calcite Wall — Taff's Well

Calcite Wall

An impressive and atmospheric wall with a big feel to it and plenty of good routes. Some of the rock is slightly friable, especially in the central section. Take a long rope and plenty of quickdraws (some routes need 18).

Approach (map and overview p.223) - On arriving at the base of the cliff, the wall is on the left.

Conditions - The wall faces southwest and gets plenty of sunshine. The cliffs can be very hot in the summer months. Seepage can occur in the central section during wet periods.

The first three routes share a common initial pitch to a ledge and optional intermediate belay The Red Organised Man.

❶ The Red Organised Man .... ☐ **6b**
The short tricky wall to attain the lower-off/belay ledge of the three routes that continue above.

❷ Red Square .... ⚄ 👤 ☐ **6b+**
The left-hand side of the wall above the intermediate belay with two technical sections. *Photo p.224.*
FA. A.Sharp, B.Powles 7.3.1988

❸ Organised Chaos ..... ⚄ 👤✏ ☐ **6c**
The central bolted line of the wall is well worth the effort. Sustained with a hard section midway up the wall above the intermediate belay.
FA. A.Sharp, P.Lewis, A.Swann 12.3.1988

❹ The Melty Man Cometh .. ⚀ 👤 ☐ **7a**
The right-hand of the trio that features three tricky sections all on good rock.
FA. G.Gibson, R.Thomas 17.5.2004

❺ Trebanog Calling .... ☐ **6a**
A micro-route that begins from a ledge not the grubby crack just right of the start of *The Red Organised Man.*
FA. R.Thomas 18.4.2018

❻ I'm Alright Jack .... 👤 ☐ **6b**
Climb from the right-hand side of the ledge to a shared lower-off with *Trebanog Calling.*
FA. R.Thomas 18.4.2018

The next set of sport routes take the centre of the huge face starting next to a rib that leads to a tree. There has been a small amount of de-bolting on this section of wall in order to restore the trad lines of Ye Old Campaigner, Painted Bird and Crowmar - not described. The easier initial walls of the longer routes are popular and have lower-offs in place and are described as routes in themselves.

❼ LA Confidential - Lower Wall .. ⚀ ☐ **5a**
The first wall of the full line is a good pitch in its own right.

❽ LA Confidential ..... 👤✏ ☐ **7a**
Unfortunately the block on the upper section of this line is unstable and in its current state this climb is dangerous.
FA. C.Gibson, R.Thomas 8.5.2004

❾ Kings of New York - Lower Wall
.... ⚀ 👤 ☐ **6b**
Start from the raised earth platform and climb the tricky lower section on to a scoop. From here weave your way up the wall to the shared half height lower-off.

❿ Kings of New York ⚄ 👤✏ ☐ **7a+**
A fine pitch with a relatively straightforward lower section and a fine sustained upper wall.
FA. C.Gibson 18.5.2004

⓫ The Connecticut Connection - Lower Wall
.... ⚀ 👤 ☐ **6a+**
The first section of the full pitch to a lower-off

⓬ The Connecticut Connection
.... ⚄ 👤✏ ☐ **7a+**
A huge line up the right side of the wall. A superb intricate top wall is the highlight of the pitch. *Photo p.229.*
FA. C.Gibson, R.Thomas 20.3.2009

⓭ Tainted Turd .... ⚀ ☐ **5c**
Move right at the second bolt of *The Connecticut Connection - Lower Wall* and then follow flakes past an overhang to the mid-height lower-off of *The Connecticut Connection.*
FA. F.Thomas, R.Phillips 21.4.2018

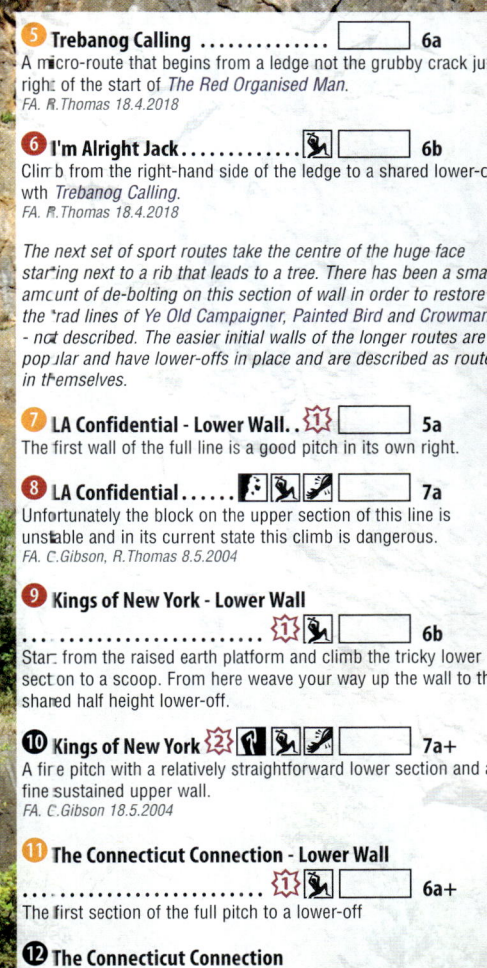

Approach path

Taff's Well — Calcite Wall

14 Minnesota Nice 7a
A worthwhile route taking the left edge of the wall on positive holds after a technical start.
FA. G.Gibson, R.Thomas 21.9.2003

15 Minnesota Spice .... 7b+
A short, thin and bouldery two bolt extension to *Minnesota Nice*.
FA. M.Richards 12.5.2018

16 Melting Man 7a
The centre of the face hidden behind the tree. A fine sustained exercise. *Photo opposite*.
FA. M.Crocker, J.Harwood 12.7.1992

17 Genghis Khan .... 6c+
A classic pitch with sustained face climbing. A tricky bulge at the start is taken on hidden in-cuts and pockets.
FA. A.Sharp, P.Lewis 1985. FA. (Direct start) G.Gibson 9.2003

18 Tarus Bulbous .... 6b+
Excellent face climbing via a techy bulge low down and a shallow rib above.
FA. G.Gibson, R.Thomas 9.6.2003

19 Bulbus Tara 4c
The faint groove-line above a prominent tree stump.
FA. R.Thomas, G.Gibson 20.9.2003

20 Hirsuit Ulvula 6a
The short technical arete and easy groove above.
FA. R.Thomas, 9.2003

Kat Lumby midway up the long wall climb of *Melting Man* (7a) - *opposite* - on the right-hand side of the Calcite Wall at Taff's Well. This section of the crag is one of its best having a number of cracking sustained face climbs. Photo: Mark Glaister

Taff's Well — Lower Wall

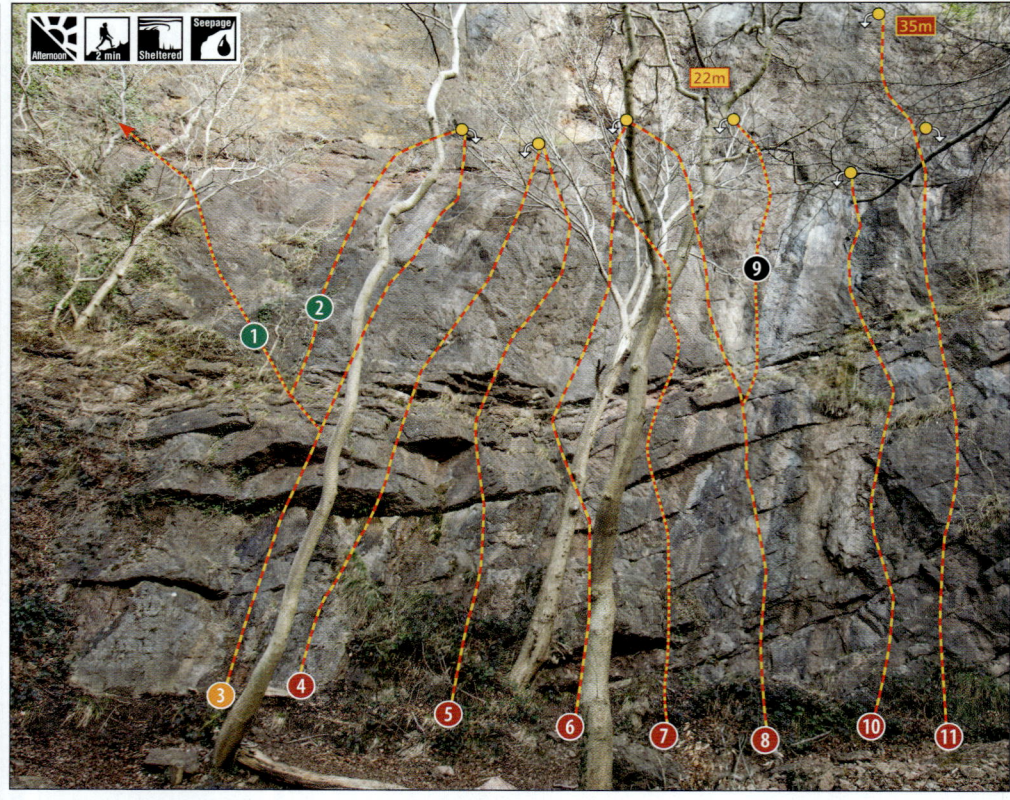

Lower Wall

The Lower Wall runs up diagonally right from the base of the Calcite Wall and has a lot of good pitches that are well shaded by the tree canopy. The routes tend to be of a technical and intricate nature.

Approach (map and overview p.223) - The base of the wall is just right of the point where the approach path arrives at the crag.

Conditions - Seepage can be a problem. The routes are well shaded in the summer months by the tree canopy.

① Pilgrim 4c
From the first bolt on *Mega Mix*, head up left to gain the ledge and lower-off at the start of the routes on the Upper Wall.
FA. M.Jordan 2016

② Tirpentwys Style. 4c
The slab left of *Mega Mix* to same lower-off.
FA. R.Thomas 1996

③ Mega Mix 5c
A gentle slab with a tough bulge near the top.
FA. G.Gibson, R.Thomas 3.8.2003

④ Gwest y Gymru 7 Inch Mix 6b+
The grey rib with sloping holds and technical moves.
FA. G.Griffiths 2001

⑤ The Twelve Inch Version! 7a
A difficult to read, short and bouldery route that features sloping holds and hidden edges.
FA. G.Gibson, R.Thomas 17.8.2003

⑥ Daggers 6c
An intricate face route with hidden holds and pleasant moves up a scoop. *Photo p.227*.
FA. M.Crocker, R.Thomas 22.1.1989

⑦ Gaze Over By There ..... 6b+
Start left of *Look Over Yonder*. Gain the ramp and follow it until a tricky step up leftwards to join *Daggers* and follow it past its last two bolts.
FA. R.Thomas 2018

⑧ Look Over Yonder 7a
Similar in style to *Daggers* but a notch harder in difficulty.
FA. M.Crocker, R.Thomas 22.1.1989

⑨ Wet Afternoon ... 7b
Start up *Look Over Yonder* and move right. Highly intricate face climbing with unusual moves and a scary fifth clip.
FA. G.Gibson, R.Thomas 28.6.1992

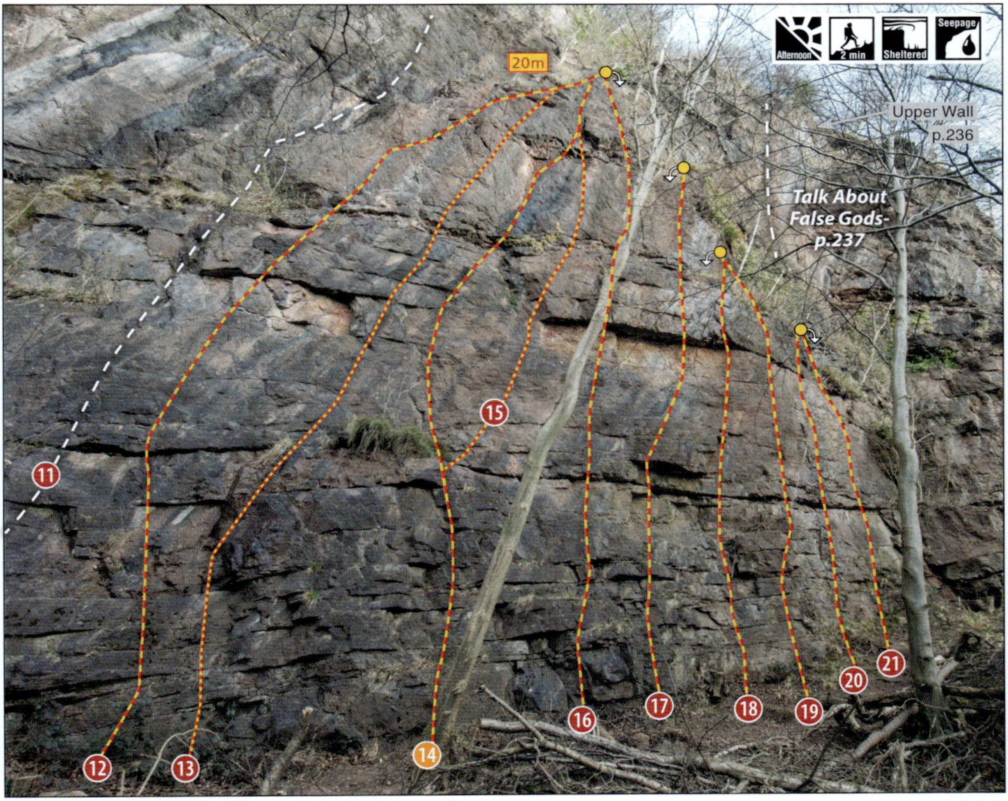

10 Open Groove .... 1 star 6b
The lower wall and open groove features some unusual moves.

11 Ulrika Ka Ka Ka .... 2 stars 6c+
A groove-line leads to an impressive blunt rib on the headwall. 70m rope required.
FA. G.Gibson, R.Thomas 16.8.2003

12 D'ya Hear Ma Dear ... 1 star 6b
The blunt, barrel-shaped rib to the right with the hardest moves at the top. Beware of a loose block midway.
FA. G.Gibson, R.Thomas 16.8.2003

13 Good Gear, Good Cheer .. 2 stars 6b
The pleasant blunt rib with one short hard section.
FA. R.Thomas, N.O'Neill 1.6.2002

14 No Beer, No Fear .... 2 stars 6a+
An enjoyable pitch aiming for the groove with a red left wall.
FA. R.Thomas, M.Learoyd 1990

15 Not My Fault! .... 1 star 6c+
Two boulder problems squeezed onto the wall and rib.
FA. G.Gibson, R.Thomas 3.8.2003

16 Id-iot .... 2 stars 6b
A technical lower move with fine climbing above.
FA. R.Thomas 2003

17 CJD .... 1 star 6b
A technical section in the middle is preceded by easier climbing.
FA. R.Thomas, G.Gibson 2003

18 Get Down on This .... 1 star 6c
Difficult moves through the upper overlap.
FA. R.Thomas, G.Gibson 2003

19 Get Thee Hence............. 6c+
Short but super technical climbing up a blunt rib.
FA. M.Crocker, R.Thomas 11.2.1989

20 Matt's Ice Bucket Challenge .. 6c
Technical moves up a faint crack.
FA. M.Hirst 7.2003

21 Tidy as Matt's Toolbox .... 6c+
The blank-looking wall.
FA. M.Hirst 7.2003

Taff's Well — Upper Wall

Upper Wall

The Upper Wall has some long well-positioned lines that see little action. Some of the rock is still friable in places.

Approach (map and overview p.223) - The first five routes are approached by starting up *Pilgrim* (p.234) and moving left to the belays, the rest are accessed by climbing routes from below on the Lower Wall.

Descent - Lower off or abseil with care.

Conditions - Seepage can be a problem.

1 Golgotha .... 6a+
The left-hand line moving right to finish via the last two bolts of *Jesus Wept*. Good climbing but prone to being dirty.
FA. R.Thomas, R.Phillips 19.4.2018

2 Jesus Wept 6c
A tricky start to an open slabby face with plenty of interest.
FA. G.Gibson, R.Thomas 21.9.2003

3 Christendom 7a
A long pitch with a delicate crux and easier climbing above.
FA. M.Crocker, R.Thomas 3.2.1989. FA. (Direct) G.Ashmore 26.5.2002

4 Angel of Mons 6c
A low crux and pleasant climbing above.
FA. G.Ashmore 28.5.2002

5 Decimus Maximus ... 6b
Pleasant climbing taking a rib and groove followed by an intricate slab.
FA. G.Gibson, R.Thomas 16.8.2003

Upper Wall — Taff's Well 237

Approach the next routes up *Jesus Wept* or *Golgotha* and move left to a belay below a steep wall.

6 Space Cowboys .... 6c+
The left-hand line with a low crux.
FA. G.Gibson, R.Thomas 6.9.2003

7 Heavenly 7a
The central line gives a sustained exercise in a great position.
FA. G.Gibson, R.Thomas 3.8.2003

8 Celestial Being .. 7b
Sustained with technical moves low down and thin ones high up.
FA. G.Gibson 19.9.2003

9 Maximus Extensicus 6c
The extension above the lower-off of *Decimus Maximus*.
FA. G.Gibson, R.Thomas 9.2003

The starts of the next lines are reached via *Gwest y Gymru...* and *Daggers* (p.234).

10 I'm Spartacus .... 7b+
Follow a snaking line up the black-streaked wall. Sustained and high in the grade. The rock is reported to be hollow in places.
FA. G.Gibson 8.4.2009

11 Sugar Bullets .... 7b+
An impressive route with an amenable lower half and impressive finale - with the crux being the last move.
FA. G.Gibson, R.Thomas 5.6.1993

12 Stray Bullets .... 6c+
The direct version of *Sugar Bullets* gives a fine sustained route.
FA. G.Gibson, R.Thomas 9.5.2004

13 Scram .... 7a+
Super-sustained face climbing with no single hard move but plenty of them. A bit crumbly but good.
FA. M.Crocker, R.Thomas 19.1.1989

14 New Day Today 7a
A hard sequence leads over a bulge then onto an easier face.
FA. G.Gibson, R.Thomas 11.5.1991

15 Rancho La Cha, Cha, Cha
.... 6c+
An arcing line with sustained climbing on crystalline holds.
FA. M.Crocker, R.Thomas 11.2.1989

16 Talk About False Gods .... 7b+
From above and right of the lower-off of *Get Thee Hence* (p.235), climb the weetabix-like thin wall.
FA. M.Crocker, R.Thomas 12.2.1989

Taff's Well — Castle Coch

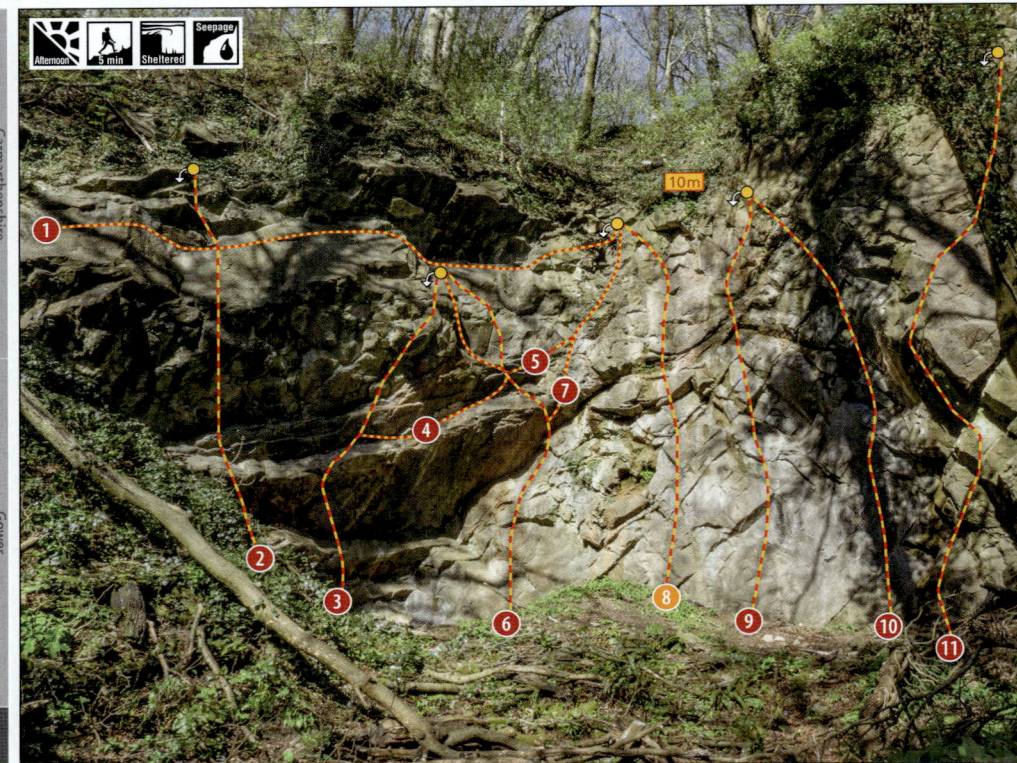

Castle Coch

A compact section of crag hidden in trees up and to the right of the main cliff. The routes are well bolted and range from powerful steep lines on the left to easier slabs on the right. The area is less noisy than the main areas, being further from the road. It may well be in condition when the Taff's Well main cliff is seeping.

Approach (map and overview p.223) - From the parking, a small track leads up rightwards below the main crag. Continue up the track past some steps on the left, and then 40m further on, head left up a small path. The path goes up the right-hand side of a small valley to the crag which is located just below the castle.

Descent - All routes have lower-offs in place - please do not top out.

Conditions - Sheltered and sunny in the afternoon but seepage can occur.

❶ The Slippery Lip Trip 6b
Start at the top of the bank on the left side of the crag, level with the narrow undercut slab. Traverse the slab to eventually reach the lower-off of *Games of Ambivalence* - lower off. This pitch is 25m long.
FA. A.Rosier, D.Emanuel 16.5.2009

❷ Lungworms 7a
The first line on left-hand side of the crag. Some steep pulls and undercutting past the overhang gains a delicate rock up onto the final slab and lower-off.
FA. R.McAllister, A.Rosier 14.7.2020

❸ The Crawling Chaos 7a
Climb up and right over the stepped overhang, passing a large rounded blob to a lower-off under the capping roof.
FA. A.Rosier 21.5.2009

❹ Escaping Chaos 6c
Begin as for *The Crawling Chaos* but, instead of moving over the bulge, traverse right along a rising ledge until some jugs are gained on *Play the Joker*. Take a direct line to the lower-off above, staying left of the bolt on *Play the Joker*.
FA. H.Brace 3.5.2019

❺ The Chaos Games 7a
Follow *Escaping Chaos* to the jugs on *Play The Joker*. Continue rightwards along the break to finish up *Games of Ambivalence*.
FA. H.Brace 8.2019

❻ Play the Joker .... 6b+
Climb to the low overhang and pull up left past a niche to a shared lower-off with *The Crawling Chaos*.
FA. R.Thomas 2009

Castle Coch **Taff's Well** 239

7 Games of Ambivalence 6b+
Start up *Play the Joker* but continue up the wall rightwards.
FA. J.Maddison, H.Andrews 5.4.2009

8 The Warmth of Man 6a
The line of bolts up the open angle in the back of the bay.
FA. D.Emanuel, R.Thomas 5.2009

9 Ass in the Hole 6b+
A difficult, steepening line to the left of *Royal Flush*.
FA. R.Thomas, D.Emanuel 2009

10 Royal Flush 6b+
The overhanging corner on the right side of the bay.
FA. R.Thomas, D.Emanuel 2009

11 Savant 6c+
A bouldery line with a reach dependant crux. Gain the leaning, rounded edge and use it to pull up and then right onto the slab. Climb easily rightwards to join and finish as for *Stalag Luft*.
FA. D.Emanuel. 25.5.2009

12 Stalag Luft 5c
Climb the pleasant slab rightwards passing a shot hole.
FA. K.Davies, D.Emanuel 21.2.2009

13 A Ride on the Chocolate Unicorn 5c
Climb the slab to a final difficult bulge and lower-off just above.
FA. D.Emanuel, K.Davies 21.2.2009

14 The Dark Art of Banana Magic 4a
The straightforward slab.
FA. D.Emanuel, D.Hannam 5.2009

15 R2 Sucking D2 Licking Deep
Inside a Half-Cooked Chicken 4a
The slab to join *The Dark Art of Banana Magic*.
FA. D.Emanuel 2009

16 For Fonting Friends 4a
The slabby line to the left of the stack of blocks - do not touch
FA. J.Maddison, H.Andrews 5.4.2009

17 Dissertation Distraction 4b
The steep wall just to the left of the jagged arete.
FA. M.Walter 11.5.2009

Taff's Well West

| Grade Spread | 1 | 15 | 18 | 15 | - |

On the other side of the valley and well hidden from the main crag at Taff's Well is a series of old quarried walls that contain some good sport climbs. The climbing style varies from slabs to slightly overhanging featured walls and all the routes are technical. Although most of the walls apart from the slabs are enclosed and shady, the climbing is well worth searching out in the right conditions.

Approach   Map p.223
Exit the M4 at junction 32 onto the A470 north for Merthyr Tydfil. Take the first exit signed to Taff's Well. The main crag can be seen on the right, immediately above the junction roundabout. For Taff's Well West, turn left at the roundabout signed to Radyr. Continue to another roundabout and turn right to Pentyrch. Drive a further 500m to Heol Berry - a minor road on the right - and park here. Cross the road and take a footpath into the woods (not the track just to its left). Follow the path rightwards until it meets a track. Go left on the track and follow this until Taff's Well West quarry is seen just right of the track. For The Slabs continue along the track until they come into view, close to the track on the right.

Conditions
The Slabs are open and not shaded by trees whilst the main quarry is shady and sees little sun. Seepage is often present on the Back Wall. The bases of a number of climbs can gather moss and will need a bit of a clean at times.

Access
The quarry is owned by the adjacent working quarry. Should any problems arise please report details to the BMC and Rockfax.

Taff's Well West

Aaron Martin moving through the steep ground of *It's a Black World* (7a+) - *p.245* - on the Diamond Wall at Taff's Well West. To the left is The Pinnacle a short pimple that in the past was known as the Matterhorn of Taff's Well. The Pinnacle is in fact the top of a huge spire that over the years has been in-filled with quarry waste. The ascent of the 'Matterhorn' in its original state was probably made in 1899 and is one of the earliest recorded climbs in South Wales.
Photo: Mark Glaister

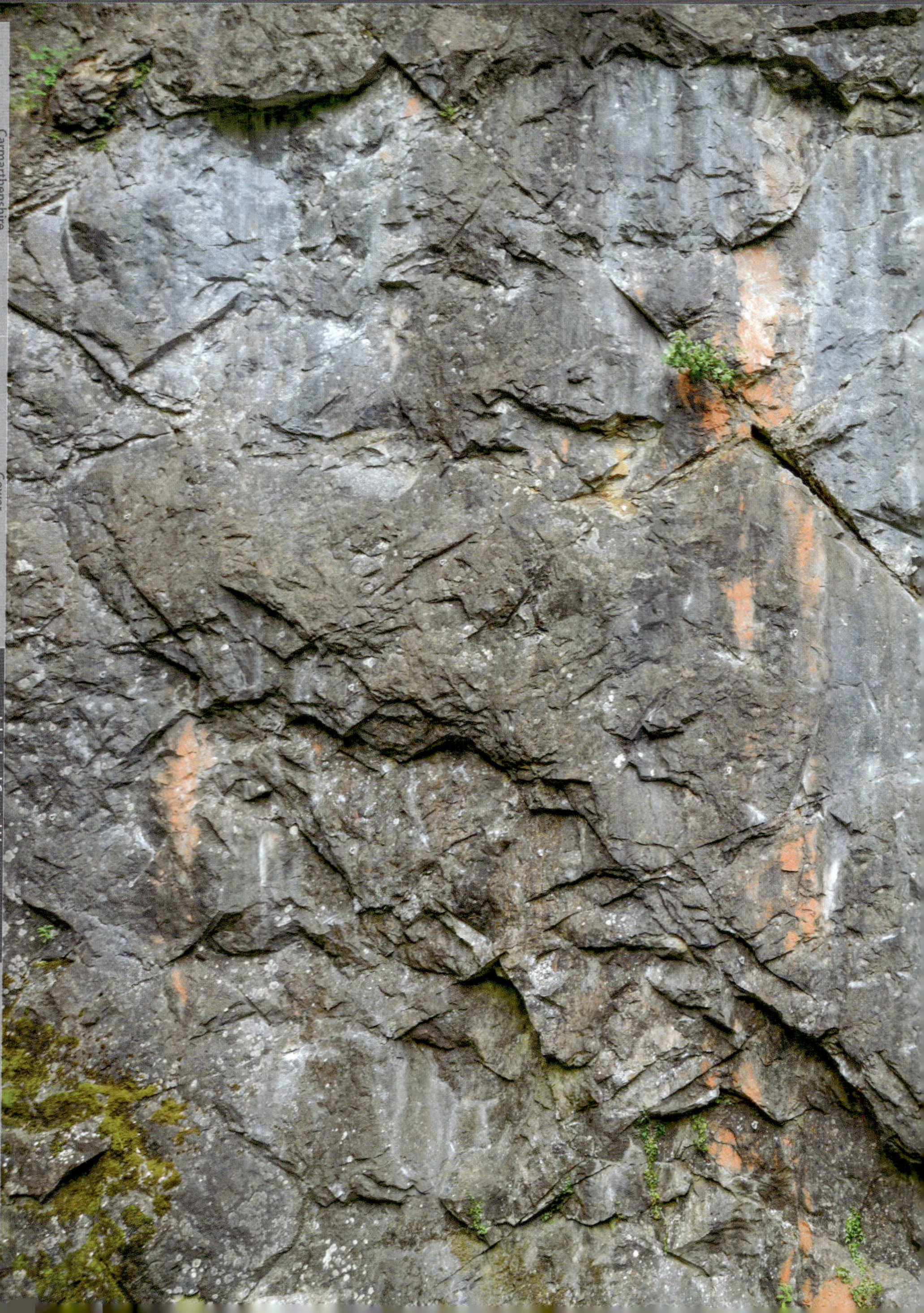

John Warner on the complex mid-height sequence of *Normal Norman* (7a) - *p.247* - on the North Wall at Taff's Well West. The various crags that make up Taff's Well West are extremely well concealed in amongst some dense woodland and offer up a good amount of technical and intense pitches in the mid grades. Photo: Mark Glaister

The Slabs

A large, slab which offers a number of intricate pitches. Some of the rock is a little brittle in places.

Approach (map p.223, overview p.242) - Continue along the track from the quarry for a few minutes, past a muddy section, and the slabs come into view on the right.

Conditions - Open and quick drying.

1 The Boney King of Nowhere Direct — 6a
There is an indirect version at 5a.
FA. G.Davis 30.5.2015

2 Once Upon a Time 6a
Climb between the ivy and the bush. Loose rock near the top.
FA. D.Emanuel 2010

3 Can the Can 6c
Climb leftwards to a point above a bush and finish direct.
FA. A.Sharp, P.Lewis 4.1987

4 Palm 7a
A fine and thin pitch. Start up *Can the Can* before stepping right up the sustained and technical wall.
FA. A.Sharp, P.Lewis 10.4.1987

5 Neil Kinnock's Last Stand 7a+
Climb the slabby wall just left of the mid-height depression. Hard and sustained in its upper reaches.
FA. G.Ashmore, R.Lawrence 10.7.1992

The Pinnacle and Diamond Wall — Taff's Well West

6 Chinese Whispers — 6c+
Start up *Neil Kinnock's Last Stand* and move right to a ledge. Climb up over a bulge and tackle the headwall on small holds.
FA. A.Sharp, P.Lewis 6.1987

7 Glenys Encounters Her First Limp Member — 6a
The far right-hand line of the slabs.
FA. R.Thomas, G.Ashmore 8.2009

The Pinnacle and Diamond Wall
Two narrow buttresses of good rock on the left-hand (south) wall of the main quarried bay. They stay in good condition longer than the North and Back Walls.

8 Clair de Lune — 6a
Follow pockets up the left-hand side of the pinnacle face.
FA. D.Emanuel, R.Phillips 21.6.2009

9 Mare Tranquilis — 5a
The short line right of the pockets.
FA. D.Emanuel, R.Phillips 21.6.2009

10 South East Wall (of the Pinnacle) — 3b
A two bolt line to lower-off on the back of The Pinnacle.

11 Bristol Beat — 7a
Step onto the wall and trend right past a pocket, before difficult moves up the blunt rib reach an easier traverse rightwards.
FA. A.Sharp, P.Lewis 3.4.1988

12 Streaming Neutrinos — 7b+
Climbs past the diamond-shaped niche in the centre of the face.
FA. M.Crocker, G.Gibson 13.12.1987

13 Doesn't Matter — 7b+
From the third bolt of *Dark Matter*, move up left into undercuts and follow these, clipping the 2nd and 3rd bolts of *Streaming Neutrinos*. Make a big move up into *Bristol Beat* to finish.
FA. M.Richards 16.7.2019

14 Singularity — 7c
Climb *Dark Matter* but stick to the prow above direct.
FA. S.Rawlinson 14.8.2018

15 Dark Matter — 7b+
Powerful moves on undercuts lead to a slim groove giving access to *It's a Black World* at it's crux.
FA. S.Rawlinson 31.7.2018

16 It's a Black World — 7a+
Trend rightwards then move up to a borehole and good holds on the left. Move left and pull over a bulge to better holds and continue directly to a ledge. *Photo p.241*.
FA. G.Gibson, R.Thomas, M.Ward 13.12.1987

17 Howling Hadrons — 6b
Start just right of *It's a Black World* and avoid sloping off right up the slab.
FA. R.Thomas, G.Gibson 12.5.2010

Taff's Well West — Back Wall

Back Wall

The impressive wall at the back of the quarry has good climbing but awkward access up its scrappy lower wall. This face seeps more than elsewhere in the quarry.
Approach (map p.223, overview p.242) - From the base of the quarry, use a fixed rope on the left or bolted lines on the right to reach the base of the main section of the Back Wall.

❶ Crooked Little Pinky............ 6b+
Climb flakes and pockets moving right to join *Raindogs*.
FA. R.Thomas, N.O'Neill 7.2010

❷ Raindogs............... 7a
Climb direct via flakes and some side-pulls to a hard section by a large flake. Finish on pockets to a ledge and lower-off.
FA. R.McAllister 22.7.2010

❸ The Quartz Bicycle.......... 7a
Gain a belay via the start of *Party Animal*. Head left then up to the overlap. Cross this to gain the left-hand end of the 'crystal ball niche' and finish up and slightly right. This line has suffered a rockfall, and is **7b** in its current form and still very dirty.
FA. G.Gibson, R.Thomas 20.4.1991

❹ Party Animal............. 7a+
Climb to below the headwall. Head up the rib and pockets before moving leftwards via more pockets to gain the 'crystal ball niche'. Take the right-hand line of bolts to a shared lower-off with *The Quartz Bicycle*.
FA. A.Sharp, P.Lewis 1987

❺ You Never Can Tell...... 7a
From good holds above the rib and pockets on *Party Animal* continue directly up the wall.
FA. G.Gibson, R.Thomas 14.10.1990

❻ Palm Springs............ 7b+
An old trad line that has now been bolted to give a good pitch. There is an optional belay below the headwall.
FA. M.Crocker, R.Thomas 30.5.1989

❼ A Million Destinies......... 7b
Start up an easy but grubby pitch to a belay. Climb the wall right of *Palm Springs* via pockets and then up a rib. A hard move rightwards leads to better crimps and lower-off.
FA. M.Crocker, R.Thomas 30.5.1989

❽ Stay Hungry............. 7b
Start up *A Million Destinies* to the belay under the headwall. Climb the tough crack-line in the headwall.
FA. A.Sharp, P.Lewis 1987

❾ Digitorum Brevis........... 7c
An easy start gains the base of the main wall. Move up left to pockets and climb the wall direct on more pockets to an undercut. Finish up the wall above.
FA. G.Gibson, R.Thomas 14.10.1990

North Wall   Taff's Well West   247

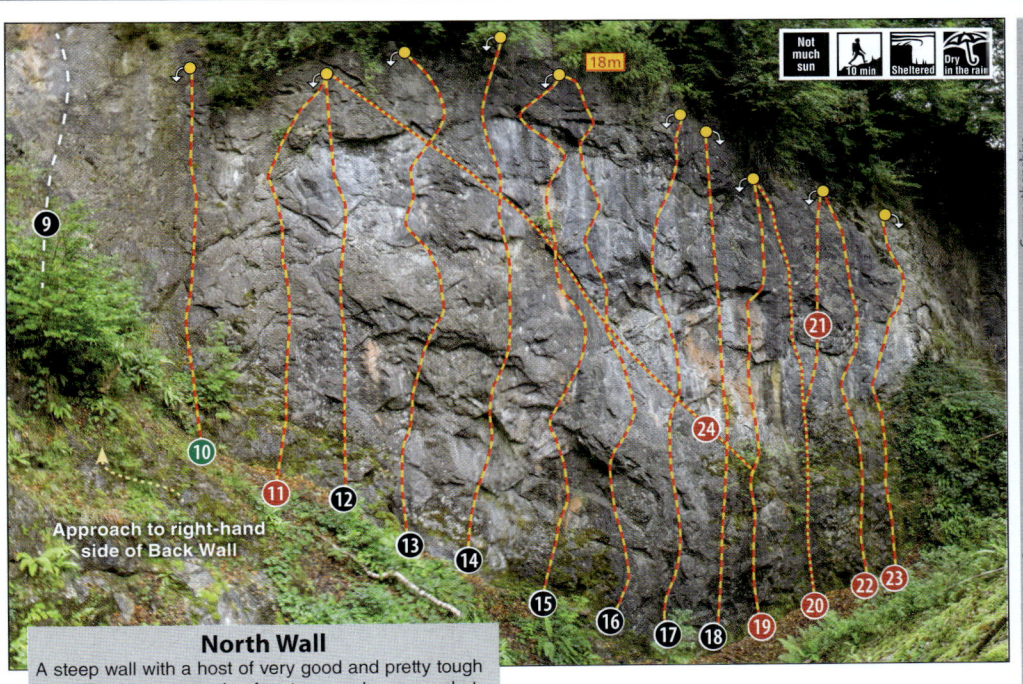

North Wall
A steep wall with a host of very good and pretty tough lines. The bottom couple of metres can be mossy, but is easily cleaned up. The tree canopy keeps the main section of the wall dry in rain during the summer.

⑩ Squeeze for Cream 4c
The far left line on the wall, starting from high up on the slope.
FA. R.Thomas 21.5.2010

⑪ The Creaming Dream 6c
Technical off-vertical wall moving right above the upper overlap.
FA. G.Gibson 21.3.1998

⑫ Ice Cream Sunday .... 7a+
Some hard climbing up to and over the mid-height bulge.
FA. G.Gibson, R.Thomas 14.10.1990

⑬ Scream for Cream .... 7a+
Move up to the bulge and use undercuts to break through it - hard. Finish direct above the top overlap.
FA. M.Ward, M.Crocker, G.Gibson 13.12.1987

⑭ G.L.C SAF 7b
A varied pitch that tackles the bulge, slab and upper wall.
FA. A.Rosier 15.6.2010

⑮ Trailblazer 7b
The route of the wall. Sustained and technical with a very difficult finish, first left then right, to reach the lower-off.
FA. M.Crocker, M.Ward, R.Thomas 6.12.1987

⑯ Sink or Swim .... 7a+
Sustained and airy climbing with a blind and powerful finish.
FA. G.Gibson 21.3.1998

⑰ Security Plus 7b
Strenuous climbing on undercut holds. An easy start but things become difficult and complicated above.
FA. G.Gibson, R.Thomas 20.9.1990

⑱ Give it Some Belly 7b
A steady lower wall leads to a desperate bulge and lunge.
FA. G.Gibson 3.2016

⑲ Normal Norman 7a
The wall and two overlaps. Some hollow rock. *Photo p.242*.
FA. G.Gibson, R.Thomas, M.Ward, M.Crocker 6.12.1987

⑳ Give it Some Wellie 6c
Climb up a shallow groove to a shared lower-off.
FA. G.Gibson, H.Gibson 5.6.2015

㉑ All's Well 6b
Climb the slab. At the overlap move up right to a groove and ledge at its end. Finish up the wall above.
FA. G.Gibson, R.Thomas, M.Ward, M.Crocker 6.12.1987

㉒ Bitter End 6c
Climb up to a flake. Above it, move right and up a slab to finish.
FA. R.Thomas 2000s

㉓ Adam Hussein's Nan 6b
The moss-covered slab and wall right of *Bitter End*.
FA. R.Thomas, G.Ashmore 27.6.2010

㉔ Taffy Duck 6c
A rising diagonal line that uses bolts on other lines.
FA. G.Gibson 28.4.1991

Carmarthenshire
Gower
Inland and Coastal Limestone
The Valleys Sandstone

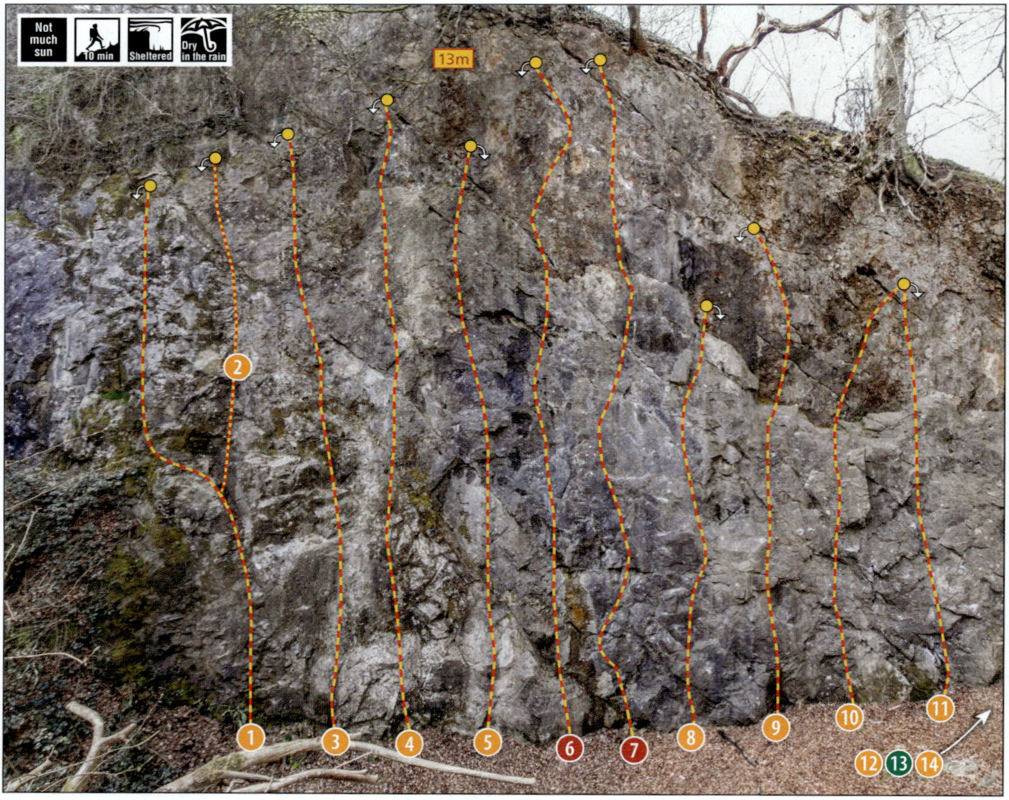

The Outer Pit

A rather gloomy wall, but it does have some good pitches that involve technical lower walls and strenuous overhanging upper sections. It is also shower-proof in the summer months due to the dense tree canopy that overhangs the crag.

Approach (map p.223, overview p.242)

Conditions - Mossy on its margins, but clean and sheltered from rain in its central section where the best routes are to be found. It is slow to dry once wet.

1 Affluenza 5c
Can be dirty. Best to start as for *Honeybucket Supreme* and then head left past a tree stump. Originally climbed direct.
FA. D.Emanuel, R.Thomas 11.6.2010

2 Honeybucket Supreme 5b
A dirty line past a mix of small and large bolts.
FA. D.Emanuel 6.6.2010

3 Faster! Pussycat 5c
Dirty at the start. Continue to join *Tinkers Dog* near the top.
FA. D.Emanuel, R.Thomas 6.6.2010

4 Tinkers Dog .... 1 star 6a
Sometimes mossy at the start.
FA. R.Thomas 9.2009

5 Full Metal Jacket .... 1 star 6a+
The wall and bulge to a lower-off at the upper diagonal break.
FA. G.Gibson, R.Thomas 5.2010

6 Any Old Iron .... 2 stars 6c
A worthwhile route on clean rock. *Photo p.34.*
FA. R.Thomas and team 13.12.1987

7 Rag and Bone .... 2 stars 6b+
The best on the wall, but no giveaway. The lower-wall has some good climbing, but the upper wall is both leaning and powerful.
FA. R.Thomas 7.10.1998

8 Wreckers Ball .... 1 star 6a
Make a hard starting sequence that leads to another tricky section just before the break and lower-off.
FA. R.Thomas 21.5.2010

9 Knackers Yard .... 1 star 6a+
A line of two halves. The upper wall is steep but has good holds. *Photo opposite.*
FA. R.Thomas 1998

10 Landfill Tax .... 1 star 6a
Climb to the midway break and then make some steep moves on good holds to the lower-off.
FA. R.Thomas, D.Emanuel 6.2010

Taff's Well West

Matt Woodfield is beginning the steep upper wall of *Knackers Yard* (6a+) - *opposite*. The Outer Pit at Taff's Well West offers up a good number of mid-grade routes that combine technical lower walls with pumpy finishes on pockets and finger slots. This wall is also rain-proof in the summer months due to the dense tree canopy that overhangs it. Photo: Mark Glaister

⓫ Sustainable Development.... 5c
The tricky lower wall leads to the break before a couple of steep pulls gain the lower-off. Quite tough.
FA. R.Thomas 2.10.2009

⓬ Industrial Salvage 5c
The short line up the blank open groove.
FA. R.Thomas, D.Emanuel 6.2010

⓭ Adit Again 4c
Very short pitch to shared lower-off below small overhang.

⓮ Old Drifter 5a
A short line to shared-lower off with *Adit Again*.

Gilwern East

Grade Spread | 14 | 53 | 42 | 7 | -

Gilwern East is composed of two old limestone quarry workings, set high up on the edge of moorland overlooking the Usk Valley and Black Mountains. The two quarries are very different in nature, the Main Walls and Gilwern-in-the-Woods section having an escarpment ambience whilst Tyla Quarry is much more in line as to what a quarry should look like. Although not high there are lots of climbs in the 5th and 6th grades which are well bolted and very popular. The quarries are exposed to wind and rain, but are good spots in warm weather, having pleasant bases and expansive outlooks. It is worth noting that Gilwern West can be reached in 10 minutes or so by continuing along the track from Tyla Quarry.

Approach
From the A465 turn off and head south on the B4246 following signs to Blaenavon. Continue up the hill to Keeper's Pond, then turn right onto a minor road and follow it for 1.6km to parking just before where the road is closed and two blocked-off tracks lead onto the moor and a communication mast.
Main Walls and Gilwern-in-the-Woods - Take the right-hand track for 450m to a footpath sign on the right side of the track. Follow the path downhill and after it cuts back left near a wall continue for 100m and then take the left-hand path where it forks. Continue over a stile and arrive at the base of the Main Walls. The In-the-Woods crag is a further 250m on from the Main Walls.
Tyla Quarry - Take the right-hand track for 750m and the quarry comes into view on the left. There is no access direct from Gilwern village to the north.

Conditions
High and exposed to the elements but sheltered from westerly winds. Seepage can be a problem during wet periods. A very good place to head for in hot weather as it catches a breeze and gets shade in the afternoon.

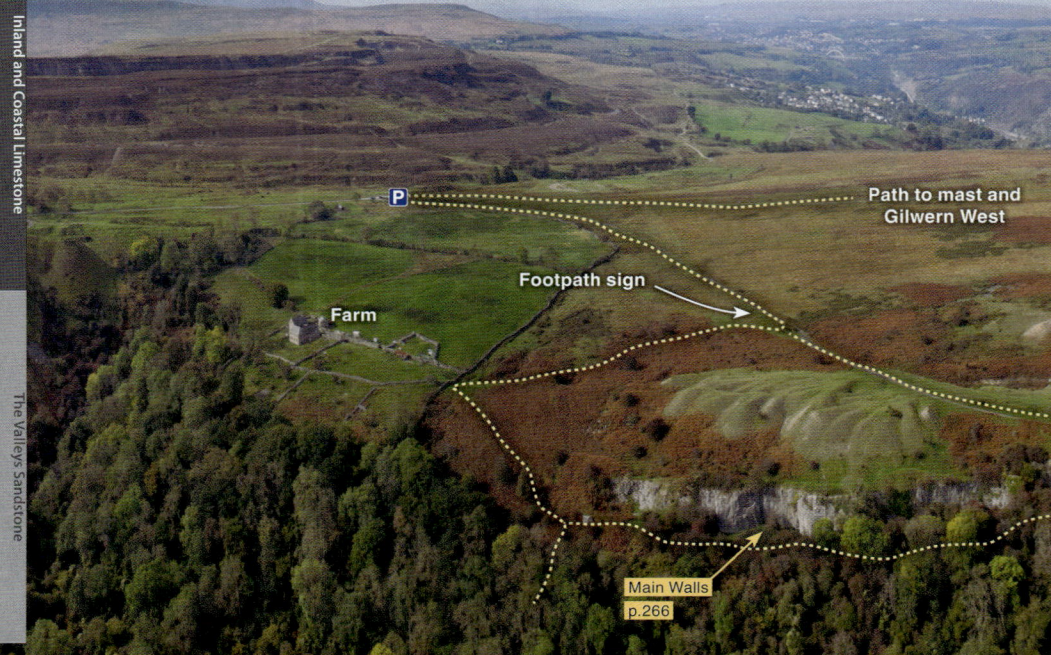

Gilwern East 251

Gilwern East 253

Matt Woodfield on the delightful *Black Knight's Rein* (6a) - *p.254* - at the Main Crag. Gilwern East is a collection of compact walls of excellent limestone that yields some intensely technical and fingery climbs across the low and mid-grades. The Main Crag has a fantastic outlook and a flat grassy base. Photo: Mark Glaister

Gilwern East — Main Crag

Main Crag

A series of good walls composed of excellent compact limestone that give some intense and fingery pitches. The cliff has a peaceful setting, beautiful outlook and a very pleasant grassy base. The lines have been well thought out and bolted, and, although close together, are generally independent of each other.

Approach (map and overview p.251) - Take the path and once over the stile the crag comes into view ahead.

Conditions - The wall faces east and gets morning sun. Seepage can be a problem in the central section.

1 Blossom 6b
A tight but worthwhile line on the far left of the crag.
FA. M.Davies 14.5.2019

2 Bring out the Blossom... 5c
Link *Blossom* to *Bring Out the Crimp*.
FA. M.Davies 14.5.2019

3 Bring out the Crimp .. 6a+
The arete and groove with a tricky start.
FA. P.Blackburn 2012

4 All the Pies Arete .... 6b+
Climb the short steep arete with difficulty. Good moves.
FA. P.Blackburn, P.Tucker 2012

5 Cheapskate .... 6b+
Use the bolts of *Black Night's Rein*. Head left from the corner past a small overhang and finish direct.
FA. P.Blackburn, P.Tucker 2013

6 Black Night's Rein 6a
Good with varied moves. Climb the groove before making a nifty pull rightwards and up onto a ledge. Finish more easily up the crozzly wall and then leftwards to gain the lower-off.
Photo p.252.
FA. P.Tucker, P.Blackburn 2012

7 Direct Start (Black Night's Rein)
.... 6b
Use the bolts on *Black Nights Rein*. Pull blindly and strenuously up to the ledge on *Black Night's Rein*. Finish via that route.
FA. P.Blackburn 2012

8 Grey Wall .... 6a+
A diagonal line moving out right from *Black Night's Rein*.
FA. M.Crocker 15.4.2007

9 The Slytherin 7a
Technical moves up the wall and overlap with the aid of vague side-pulls. Using the large hold out left reduces the grade to **6c**.
FA. P.Blackburn 2014

10 Microwaves 6c
Reachy and thin climbing directly up the wall and delicate groove above.
FA. P.Tucker 2012

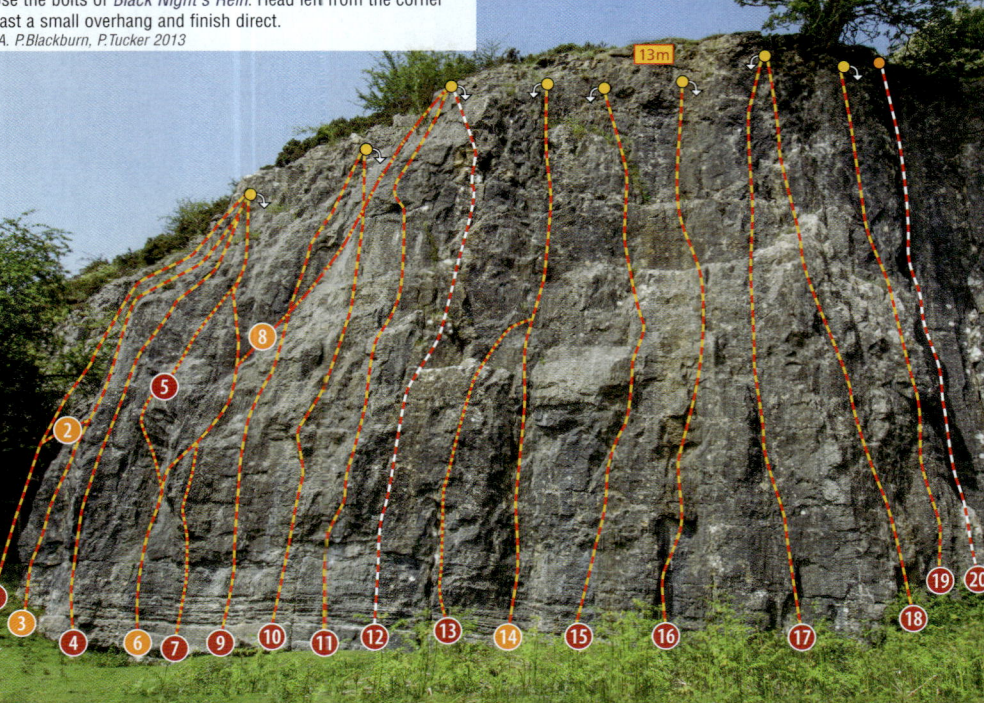

Main Crag **Gilwern East** 255

11 Litiginous/Fergie's Folly
.... 6b+
Thuggish moves lead to easier climbing and a steep finish.
FA. M.Crocker 15.4.2007. Originally climbed as a trad climb but then bolted and re-named Fergie's Folly.

12 Thorn in my Side..... E2 5c
A trad climb. Steep bold moves lead to steadier climbing where the rock needs care.
FA. P.Tucker, P.Watkins 1987/88

13 Quakering 6c
The direct start to *Mr Softy* requires a long reach.
FA. P.Blackburn, P.Tucker 2013

14 Mr Softy .... 6a+
Climb the tricky corner and wall to a ledge on the left. Steep climbing on good holds leads to the lower-off.
FA. P.Blackburn, P.Tucker 2012

15 Pearlescence .... 6b+
Perplexing climbing up the wall and groove.
FA. P.Tucker, P.Blackburn, A.Ledley 2012

16 Talulah Dream.......... 6b+
Small edges lead up the wall to a crucial hold in the groove on the right. Finish steeply up the wall above.
FA. A.Ledley, P.Tucker, P.Blackburn 2012

17 In the Groove 6c
Intricate climbing leads to a good hold in the groove. Continue steeply to ledges. Finish more easily up the wall.
FA. P.Blackburn, M.Marder 2014

18 One Step Beyond 6b
Delicate and slightly bold moves up and leftwards across the slabby wall lead to an easier finish.
FA. P.Blackburn, P.Tucker 2012

19 Reach for a Peach....... 6b+
Start via the water-worn feature to a stiff pull up the mini-pillar to halfway ledges. Balancy moves lead in turn to a stretch to a small flake which unlocks the finish
FA. P.Blackburn, P.Tucker 2013

20 What's the Craic E1 5b
A trad climb. Ascend the chimney and crack. Difficult to protect until the crux, where a good nut placement protects the steep pull up the finishing crack.
FA. P.Blackburn, P.Tucker 2012

21 Petering Out .... 6b+
Climb the crack-line just right of the off-width of *What's the Craic* to a steep finish. Use the first three bolts of *The Golden Tower* and avoid bridging into *What's the Craic*.
FA. P.Blackburn, P.Tucker 2012

22 The Golden Tower.... 6c
A difficult and sequency climb that wends its way up the indefinite pillar. A sharp tufa 'ear' proves crucial to accessing the final moves.
FA. P.Blackburn, P.Tucker 2012

23 Rich and Filthy E4 5c
Climb the water-worn tube via some wide bridging. Continue steeply up and leftwards to finish as for *The Golden Tower*.
FA. M.Crocker 15.4.2007. Previously known as Half Pipe Dream when it was mistakenly bolted - bolts now removed.

24 Magic Carpet........... 6b+
An improbable but rewarding climb that transports you magically and steeply through an area of hanging rock while still giving solid support. Step right near the top.
FA. P.Blackburn, P.Tucker 2012

25 Original Start (Life on Planet Earth)
.... 6c
A sequence of steep and sketchy moves lead up and right into *Life on Planet Earth*. Unfortunately can suffer from seepage.
FA. P.Tucker 2012

26 Life on Planet Earth......... 6b+
Ascend the corner to a taxing move which accesses the steep upper section that is best climbed with care. Stay left of the large holds on *The Plumb*.
FA. P.Tucker, P.Blackburn 2012

Gilwern East — Main Crag

27 The Plumb — 5b
The longest route at the crag heads directly up a pillar on large spaced jugs and stuck-on holds. A fun pitch. Can be climbed direct at **6a**.
FA. P.Blackburn, P.Tucker 2012

28 Asteroids — 5a
Climb on good holds past some large conglomerate blocks and up the final wall. Can be climbed on left of bolts at **6a**.
FA. P.Tucker, P.Blackburn 2012

29 Scorpion — 6a+
A stiff pull directly past the overhang leads to engaging climbing up the groove to the ledge. All that awaits is the sting in the tail!
FA. P.Blackburn, P.Tucker 2013

30 Thug Life — 6c
Start right at the back of the cave on the left and make some reachy moves out to the lip - high first bolt. Thug your way around the lip until under a bolt, then finish straight up, joining *Garden of Eden* at its third bolt.
FA. J.Jones 30.8.2016

31 Garden of Eden — 6a+
An athletic pull onto the slab below the groove leads to more delicate climbing up the open groove and another slab above.
FA. P.Tucker, P.Blackburn 2012

Main Crag **Gilwern East** 257

32 Superposition .... 7a+
Packs a lot of climbing into a short distance. Using a complex series of moves on edges and pinches, gain the midway break via a long reach. Finish more easily. Difficult to on-sight.
FA. P.Tucker 2012

33 Wall of Balls E4 6a
Technical moves of fine rock past a peg.
FA. M.Crocker 15.4.2007. Previously known as Sidewinder when it was mistakenly bolted.

34 Firepower .... 7a+
A steep and powerful sequence using an edge on the right, a small pocket and a series of rounded holds, will hopefully propel you to the top.
FA. P.Tucker 2013

35 Crackatoa E2 5c
A trad route. Climb the twin cracks with adequate protection to a hard move or two to reach a ledge.
FA. P.Blackburn, P.Tucker 2012

36 Talking Hands .... 6b+
Harder than it looks with confusing moves to the large ledge. The key is to make the rounded side-pull work somehow. Difficult to on-sight but very worthwhile.
FA. P.Blackburn, H.Brown, C.Gill 2014

37 Hand in Pocket 6b
Steady climbing to the pocket before steep blind pulls transport you to the top. A nice pitch.
FA. P.Blackburn, P.Tucker 2012

38 Inch Pinch 6c
Good steep climbing requiring the right sequence. Ascend sharp pockets to a good finger slot in the overhang. Swing right on small footholds and then levitate up the hanging groove. It can get a little dirty.
FA. P.Blackburn, P.Tucker 2012

39 The Imp .... 7a+
Takes a direct line up the middle of the blank wall, technical and fingery. Finish as for *Dolphin Snoggin'*.
FA. J.Jones 30.8.2016

40 Dolphin Snoggin' 6a
The corner is best lay-backed before steep climbing leads leftwards to the lower-off.
FA. P.Blackburn, P.Tucker 2013

41 Periscope .... HVS 5a
Climb the wall 5m to the right of the bolts of *Dolphin Snoggin'* and finish up some suspect rock to belay at the large tree.
FA. P.Tucker 2013

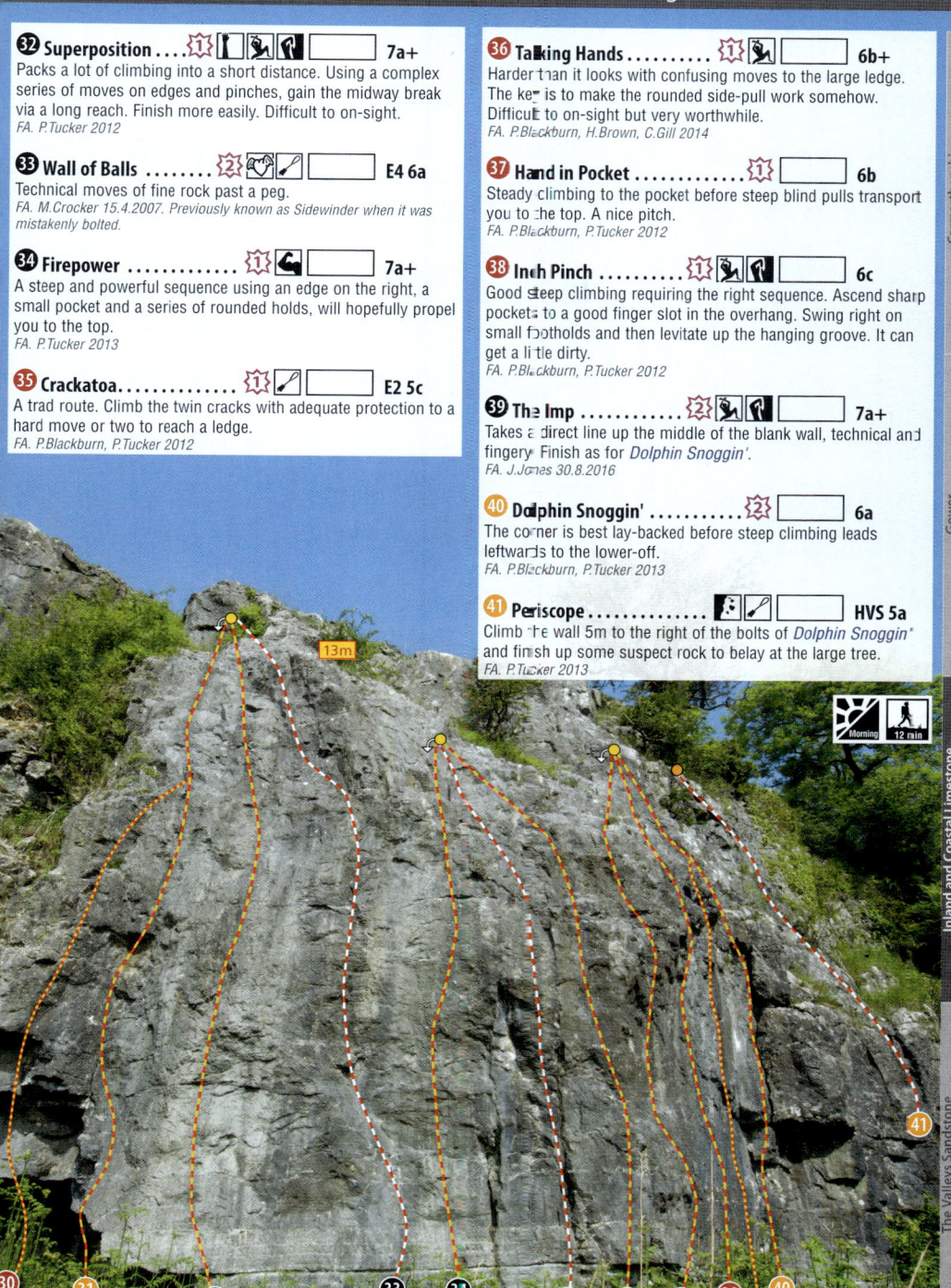

Gilwern East — Main Crag

42 Picnic Time For Teddy Bears 6b+
Just right of *Periscope* is an isolated short wall. A bouldery sequence past a couple of bolts gains a ledge and lower-off.
FA. M.Davies, G.Percival, G.Jenkin 3.7.2018

43 A Sip Full of Sap 5b
This route is the first on the wall 50m right of *Picnic Time For Teddy Bears*. Follow the short groove to a shared lower-off.
FA. M.Davies 18.4.2018

44 Mysteries of the Kingdom 6c
Climb the difficult steep wall left of a rock scar to a lower-off shared with *A Sip Full of Sap*.
FA. G.Percival 3.7.2018

45 Profound and Hidden 6c
Tricky moves are needed to gain a thin crack high on the wall.
FA. G.Percival 3.7.2018

46 Darkness into Light 6c
A tough start up the flared groove.
FA. G.Percival 3.7.2018

47 Sap is Rising 5c
A good pitch on the right-hand side of the wall. Handy if the routes further left are busy.
FA. M.Davies, G.Percival, G.Jenkin 3.7.2018

Matt Woodfield inching his way up the line of slopers encountered on *The White Stuff* (6a) - *p.261* - at the Gilwern-in-the-Woods section of Gilwern East. The climbs are less frequented than those to be found at the Main Crag but are worth the extra couple of minutes of approach. The style of the routes is similar being extremely intense technical wall climbs
Photo: Mark Glaister

Gilwern East — Gilwern-in-the-Woods

Gilwern-in-the-Woods

Beyond the Main Crag the escarpment continues as a broken and vegetated cliff for some distance and then becomes cleaner and more open. The various walls have some subtle lines that provide some neat and well-bolted climbing.

Approach (map and overview p.251) - Continue for 250m along the crag base path from the Main Crag. The path can be a bit overgrown and trousers are recommended.

Conditions - The walls face east and get morning sun. Seepage can be a problem and where shaded by the trees the faces will take a little time to dry after rain.

1 Orange Blorenge Blancmange 6a
The left-hand line is a pleasing pitch that goes leftwards past the midway bulge.
FA. G.Percival 3.7.2018

2 The Welsh are Coming... 6b
Move up the wall and past the overlaps to reach a ledge. Easier climbing on the upper wall remains.
FA. G.Percival, J.Parrott 7.6.2018

3 Vanity of Small Differences... 6c
Excellent sequency climbing passing the right-hand end of the low overlaps. Some tricky to see holds.
FA. G.Percival 18.4.2018

4 Crimpa-Lean Sheet... 7b+
Hard technical moves on small and unhelpful holds.
FA. G.Percival 19.6.2018

5 Mystery Rawl Wall... 7a
A hard bouldery lower wall. Move into the upper section of *Crimpa-Lean Sheet* to finish.
FA. G.Percival 4.5.2018

6 The Two Hundred Year Echo 6a+
A short hard start leads into a flared groove. Finish rightwards on sloping holds. Worth tracking down.
FA. M.Davies, G.Percival, G.Jenkin 12.2.2018

7 God Bless Asia Bibi... 7a+
High standard sequency wall climbing.
FA. G.Percival 5.4.2018

8 Throw in the Kitchen Towel 6c+
Utilising the sloping hold at the second bolt is the key to unlocking the sequence.
FA. G.Percival 18.4.2018

9 The Woodsman... 7a
Thin pulls on the lower wall gain the much easier upper groove.
FA. G.Percival 4.5.2018

10 Iron to Defeat Napoleon. 6a+
Excellent moves up the thin crack and bald wall above
FA. M.Davies, G.Percival, G.Jenkin 12.2.2018

11 The White Stuff Left-hand 6b+
After the start, keep to the left of the bolt line of *The White Stuff*.

Gilwern-in-the-Woods **Gilwern East**

12 The White Stuff....... 6a
Take a right-trending line up the lower wall and then head up direct to the lower-off. Slopers galore. *Photo p.259*.
FA. G.Jenkin, G.Percival 12.2.2018

13 Rompa Stompa...... 6b
Good and challenging climbing up the vague open groove.
FA. M.Davies, G.Percival 5.4.2018

14 Book End Rib........... 6c
Climb a hard rib to start.
FA. G.Percival, M.Davies 18.4.2018

15 Bristol Viking Raider 5b
The flake-crack on the right-hand side of the wall. At its end make a runout traverse left to a lower-off.
FA. G.Percival, M.Davies 18.4.2018

16 The Remains of the Day......... 6a
Wall left of the groove of *The Sweetest Flight*. A fallen tree has covered this line at the time of publication.
FA. G.Percival, M.Davies 5.4.2018

17 The Sweetest Flight............ 5c
The corner in the centre of the wall. A fallen tree has covered this line at the time of publication
FA. M.Davies, C.Lindley, B.Mullan 17.7.2018

Gilwern East — Tyla Quarry - Upper Tier

Tyla Quarry - Upper Tier

Initial impressions of the Upper Tier are a bit under-whelming compared with the other Gilwern crags, however on closer inspection the routes have plenty of interest and the potential to rack up some mileage.

Approach (map and overview p.251) - From the parking take the right-hand track for 750m and the quarry is on the left.

Conditions - Although high up and exposed to the elements the quarry has an easterly aspect and might provide a sheltered alternative if the west facing crags are too windy. Seepage in places after rainy spells.

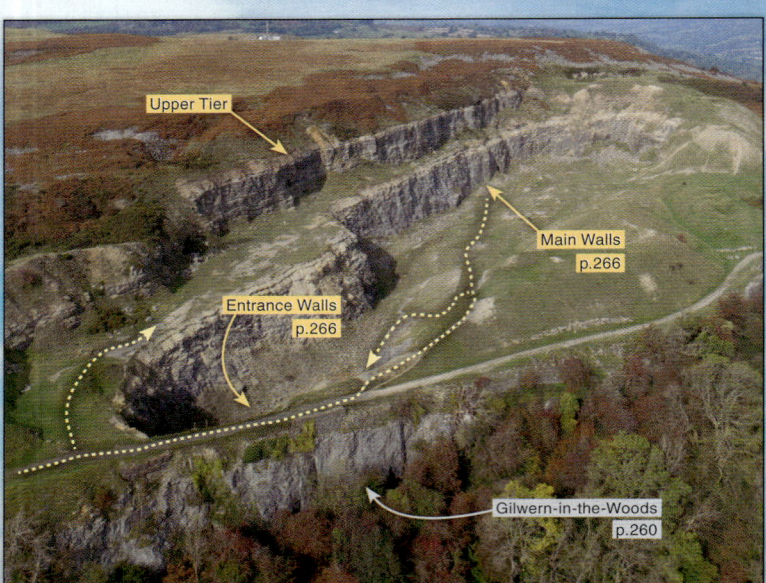

Upper Tier
Main Walls p.266
Entrance Walls p.266
Gilwern-in-the-Woods p.260

Tyla Quarry - Upper Tier — Gilwern East

1 Put Your Back Into It 5c
The first line on the wall is a good introduction. The overhang is the meat of the climb that is overcome on surprisingly good holds. The bolts are just where you need them.
FA. G.Jenkin, Y.Jones 14.4.2019

2 Don't Laugh at my Scone. 5b
The overhang and headwall are the main event on this line.
FA. G.Jenkin, Y.Jones 14.4.2019

3 The Great Satan 5c
Good holds all the way directly up the wall and horizontal breaks to a lower-off of the right.
FA. G.Jenkin 22.6.2019

4 Pretty Picture Book 5c
The breaks and walls are not too hard to pass if you have a bit of reach to spare!
FA. G.Jenkin, D.Grange 19.6.2018

5 Purple Sue 5b
An enjoyable climb - one of the best in this quarry. Climb the left edge of the square-cut cave then head diagonally rightwards above the cave to end at a perched ledge and lower-off.
FA. D.Grange, G.Jenkin 25.5.2023

6 Look Again. .... 6a+
A steep and fairly burly pitch that takes on the right side of the cave. Shared lower-off with *Purple Sue*.
FA. G.Jenkin, D.Grange, C.Connern, Y.Jones 16.6.2024

7 Remember to Breathe 6b+
A very difficult sequence up the lower wall defines this line. The moves maybe harder now than when originally climbed as the loss of a crucial foothold has been reported.
FA. G.Jenkin, G.Percival 19.6. 2018

8 Chill to the Bone............ 6b
Climb to the right of the bolts and follow the line directly to the lower-off. The difficulties are low on the pitch and things ease considerably above.
FA G.Jenkin, G.Percival 12.2.2018

9 Chill to the Touch .... 6b+
Follow *Chill To The Bone* before an interesting and well-bolted rightward line leads to the *Hot To The Touch* lower-off.
FA. G.Jenkin, D.Grange 6.6.2023

10 Hot to the Touch............ 6c
The crux mid-height wall is reach dependant problem.
FA. G.Percival 3.7.2018

11 All in for the Draws 5c
Overcome the initial difficult bulge then proceed amiably up and right to finish at the lower-off of *Fromage not Farage*.
FA. G. Jenkin, D.Grange 31.5.2023

12 Fromage not Farage.......... 3c
Balance up the breaks and walls.
FA. G.Jenkin, M.Davies 15.4.2019

13 Dodgy Foot Syndrome 4a
A pleasant juggy pitch on the far right side of the wall.
FA. G.Jenkin, M.Davies 15.4.2019

Gilwern East — Tyla Quarry - Upper Tier

14 Seeking Sunshine — 6a
The wall left of the arete taken direct is a fun little pitch.
FA. G.Jenkin, G.Percival 18.4.2018

15 The Pervasive Grey — 6a
The severely undercut arete is a brief but exhilarating outing. Start up *Seeking Sunshine* and pull out right onto the arete just above the overhang. *Photo opposite*.
FA. G.Jenkin, G.Percival 18.4.2018

16 When Will You Dry? — 5c
The wander up the wall right of the arete.
FA. G.Jenkin, G.Percival 18.4.2018

17 Mass Civil Disobedience or Mass Extinction — 5c
Tricky wall climbing where a reach will be an advantage.
FA. M.Davies, G.Jenkin 15.4.2019

18 Watch Out, Watch Out, the Wiki Wonkers Are About — 5c
Start up a small corner, and then take the wall above direct.
FA. M.Davies, G.Jenkin 15.4.2019

19 There is a Renaissance Man In Toulouse — 5a
The line of slim corners and grooves are furnished with some unstable rock.
FA. G.Jenkin, D.Grange 16.6.2018

20 The Tremenal Tremors — 5c
The flake and leaning wall are well bolted. The hardest climbing is to be found at the start and approaching the lower-off.
FA. G.Jenkin, D.Grange, D.Sargeant 15.6.2018

Gilwern East

21 **Four Star Root** 5c
The thin crack is an enticing little line and climb.
FA. J.Evans, D.Meek 3.8.2022

22 **Pan narrans** 6b
A pleasing and popular pitch that climbs the clean face and breaks to a lower-off on the right.
FA. G.Jenkin, G.Percival 5.4.2018

23 **(d) rock** .... 6a+
Worth a look. Head right of the initial overhang and then continue up the excellent wall above on some decent holds.
FA. G.Jenkin, D.Grange 15.6.2018

John Adams on *The Pervasive Grey* (6a) - *opposite* - at Tyla Quarry, Gilwern. Photo: Mark Glaister

Gilwern East — Tyla Quarry - Entrance Walls

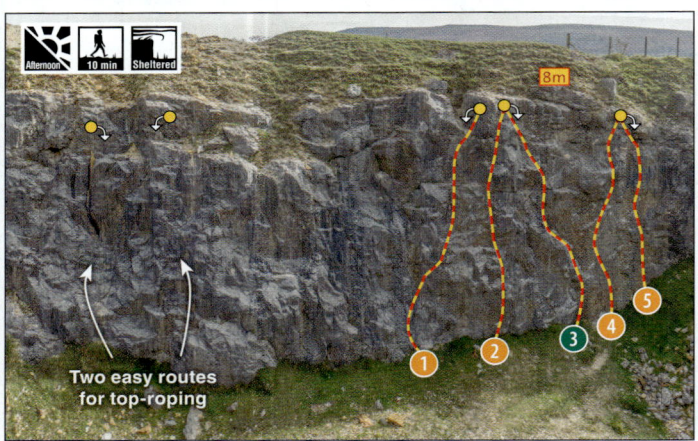

Tyla Quarry - Entrance Walls
A short wall with a handful of bolted lines.
Approach (map and overview p.251) - From the parking, take the right-hand track for 750m and the quarry comes into view on the left. Enter the lower quarry and double back leftwards and the wall is on the left
Conditions - Sheltered and sunny in the afternoon.

1 Bhaktapur 5a
Execute a tricky start and then drift rightwards to the lower-off.
FA. G.Jenkin, G.Percival 3.7.2018

2 Lo Manthang 5c
The direct line via a difficult final projecting nose.
FA. G.Jenkin, G.Percival 3.7.2018

3 Back from the Berbers 4c
The leftward leading ramp-line is an awkward obstacle.
FA. G.Jenkin, G.Percival 3.7.2018

4 Evening Class .... 6a+
A fingery wall and bulge prove to be the best hereabouts.
FA. G.Percival 26.8.2017

5 Musical Groove 6a
The techy wall and upper groove.
FA. G.Percival 26.8.2017

6 Riding Bareback 4b
This line is between the Entrance Wall and the left end of the Main Walls. The bolted line is a good little easier pitch.
FA. G.Percival 16.2.2018

7 Riding Horseless 3a
Use the *Riding Bareback* bolts and take the groove to the right.
FA. M.Davies 14.5.2019

Tyla Quarry - Main Walls
A long low wall with some interesting lines on rock of variable quality. Wear a helmet at all times as stones do occasionally fall from the terrace above.
Approach (map and overview p.251) - From the parking take the right-hand track for 750m and the quarry comes into view on the left. Enter the quarry and the wall is directly ahead.
Conditions - Seepage in places after rainy spells.

8 Gap in the stairs 4a
An easy angled line on the face 30m left of the start of the bulk of the climbing.
FA. J.Lewis 11.8.2024

9 Left Cheek 3c
The left-hand line to a shared lower-off.
FA. J.Lewis 15.8.2024

10 Butthole 3c
Climb directly to the shared lower-off past the butthole!
FA. I.Tattersall 15.8.2024

11 Claire's Cyntaf 2a
Trend leftwards to the shared lower-off.
FA. C.Lineham 15.8.2024

12 Lost Credentials 4b
Climb up ledges with a couple of awkward steps.
FA. G.Gibson 3.6.2018

13 No Credentials 5b
Move right from low on *Lost Credentials* and follow a rib.
FA. G.Gibson 3.6.2018

14 Take the Mantel 5c
The short wall via a mantel onto a tiny ledge.
FA. G.Percival, G.Jenkin 12.2.2018

15 A Lovely Day 5b
Move into a groove and head right to finish as for *Plus One*.
FA. G.Jenkin, Y.Jones 23.6.2018

16 Plus One 5c
The smooth wall and a rockover reach easier moves.
FA. G.Percival, G.Jenkin 12.2.2018

Tyla Quarry - Main Walls **Gilwern East** 267

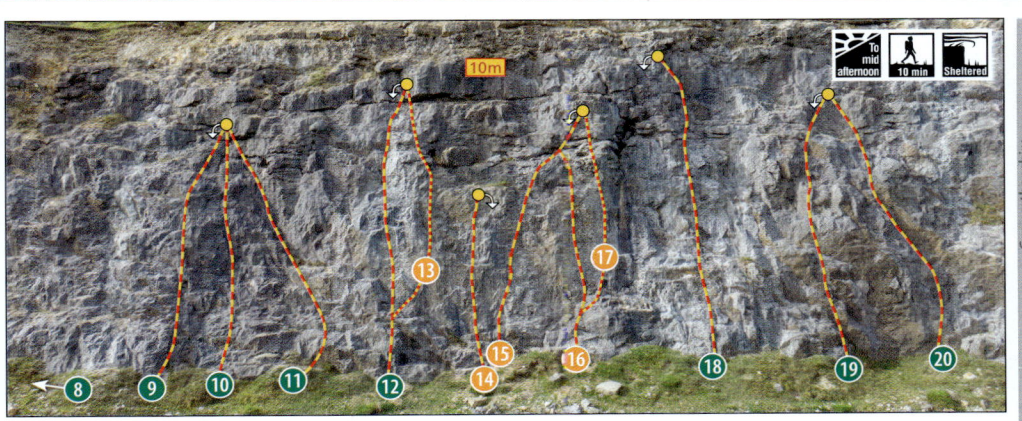

17 Dry-line 5c
A more direct take on *Plus One* via a wall and bulge.
FA. G.Percival, G.Jenkin 12.2.2018

18 Out Of Bulk 4b
The wall to the right of a corner has some reasonable climbing.
FA. G.Gibson 3.6.2018

19 The One that Wasn't There 4a
The direct line though the steps up to the shared lower off.
FA. R.Charnley 15.8.2024

20 The One that is There Somewhere 4c
Move up to a hidden jug and then the ramp and stepped wall.
FA. J.Wilkinson 15.8.2024

21 My Timeline 5c
The wall above the low grassy ledge.
FA G.Gibson 3.6.2018

22 My Naughty Valentine 5c
A difficult lower wall accesses easier ground above
FA. M.Davies, G.Percival 16.2.2018

23 Timeliness 5b
A pleasant wall climb. Weave around to find the best line.
FA. G.Gibson 3.6.2018

24 The Tumble 6a
Spiral up the rib passing holes.
FA. G.Percival, M.Davies 16.2.2018

25 Your Dinner is Ruined 5b
Stay on line above half-height to avoid some poor rock.
FA. D.Grange, G.Jenkin 25.9.2018

26 Too Hot In Chang Mai 4c
A steady and reasonable pitch finishing direct up a slab.
FA. G.Jenkin, G.Percival 16.2.2018

27 Quarry Goggles 5b
Another line similar to its left-hand neighbour.
FA. G Jenkin, G.Percival 16.2.2018

28 Saving Obscurity 5c
Wall on slightly fragile rock.
FA. G.Gibson 3.6.2018

29 Lost Obscurity 5c
The final line is also not on the soundest of rock.
FA. G.Gibson 3.6.2018

Gilwern West

Grade Spread 8 59 35 8 -

The western crags of Gilwern are a very popular destination for those searching out climbing in the 5th and 6th grades. The crags are all quarried, and on the developed sectors the rock is usually reliable although the less travelled lines still have friable sections.
The approach is now longer than in the past due to the road that passes the cliffs being closed because of a landslip (and looks like it is unlikely to reopen). The rockfall that has closed the road occurred between the Tyre and Ivor Biggun sectors and although this has not altered the climbs, careful attention should be paid to further instability developing.

Conditions
High and very exposed to the elements. Seepage can be a problem during prolonged wet spells. A good place to head for in hot weather as it is high up and catches a breeze.

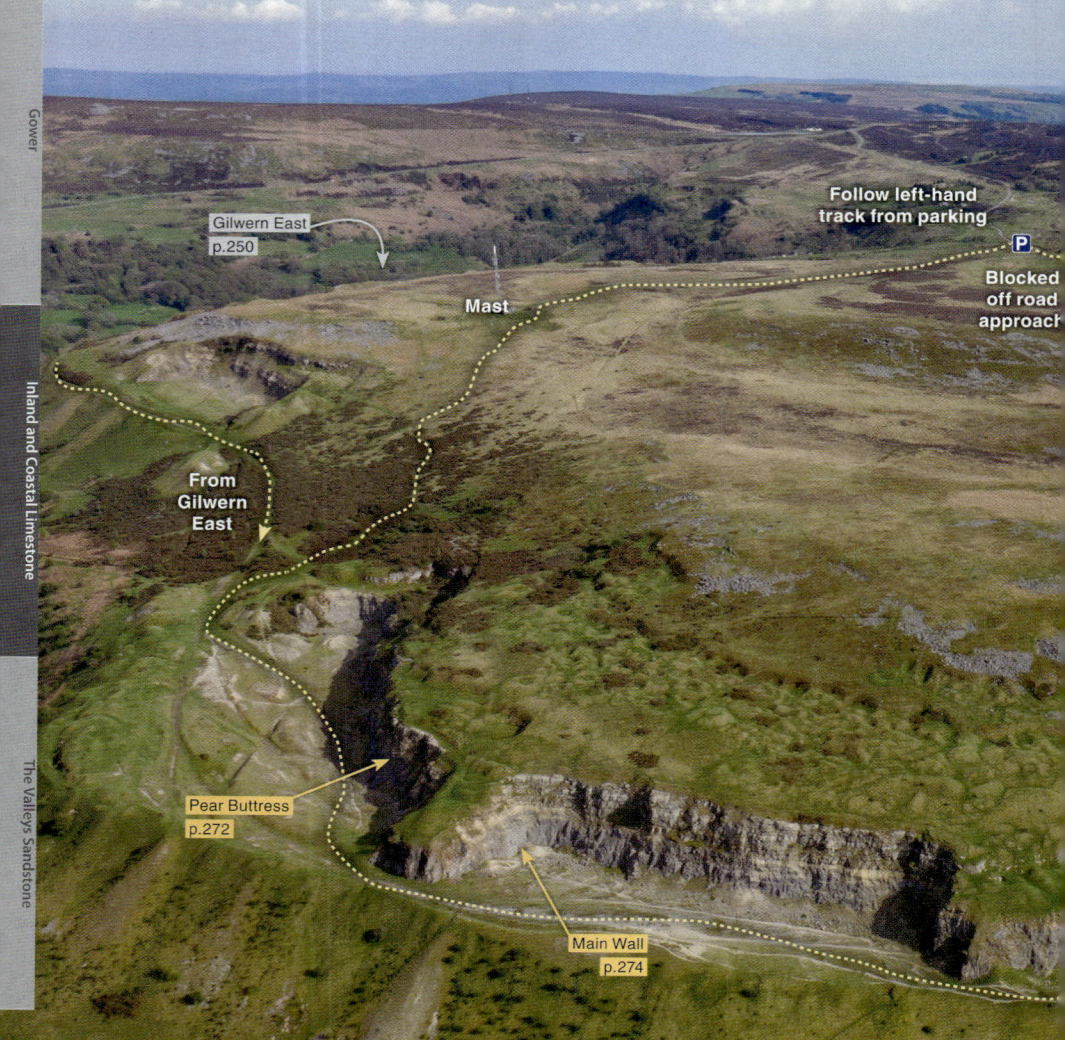

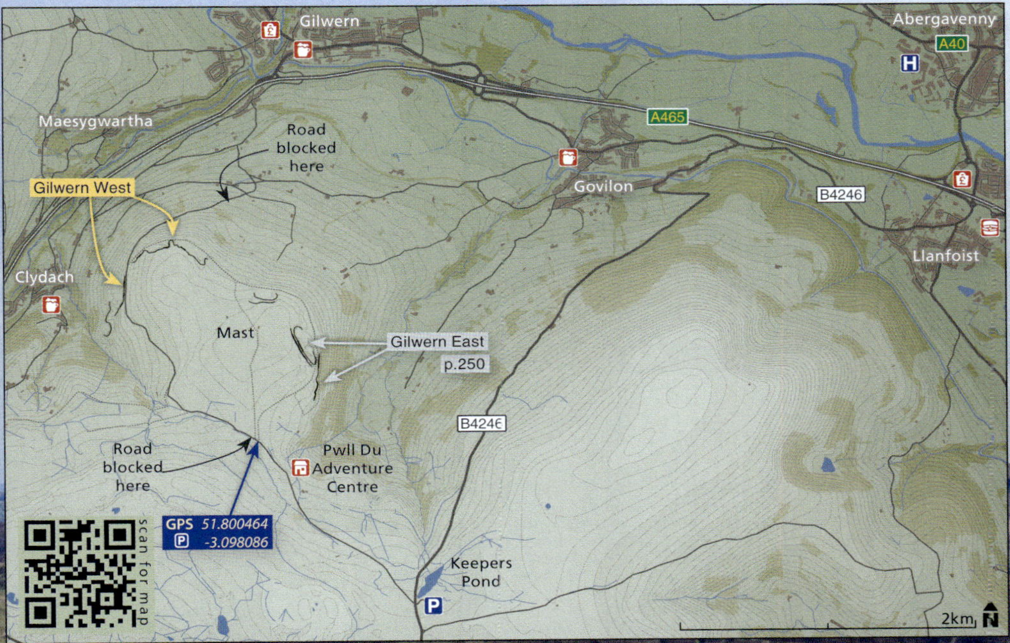

Gilwern West 269

Approach
From the A465 turn off at the Abergavenny junction and head south on the B4246 following signs to Blaenavon. Continue up the hill to Keeper's Pond, then turn right onto a minor road and follow it for 1.6km to parking just before where the road is closed and tracks leads onto the moor and a communication mast. Follow the left-hand track towards the mast and head left past it on a small path that heads down to the track that runs under the quarries/crags. Go left and the various sectors are encountered from here.
Alternatively (and slightly longer) follow the blocked-off road to where paths lead off left and right to the various sectors.

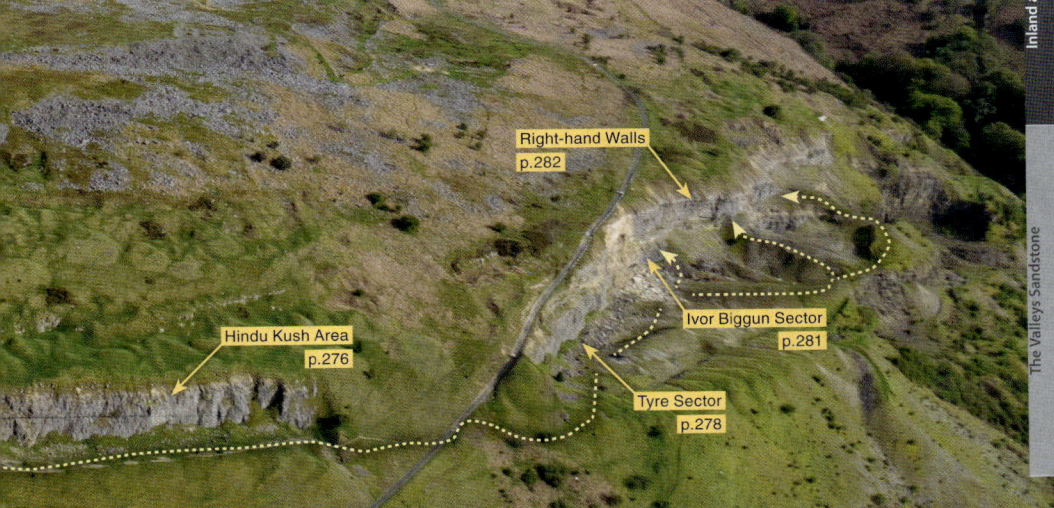

Gilwern West 271

Bethan Cox getting to grips with the superb flowstone holds on *Pwll Du Crack* (6a) - *p.275* - on the Main Wall the finest section of cliff at Gilwern West. This is one of the most popular climbing destinations in the region having plenty of easier and mid-grade routes. The crag, like many others featured in this guidebook, has been the focus of a rebolting program. Photo: Mark Glaister

Gilwern West — Pear Buttress

Pear Buttress

Two compact buttresses that might prove to be useful if the other crags are busy. The routes are short but pack in the moves and most are reasonably bolted. Some of the first bolts are high and a clip-stick will be useful.

Approach (map and overview p.269) - After dropping down from the moor to the track the wall is at the far end of the first quarry encountered.

Conditions - Shady but quick drying. Seepage may occur but the rock does dry quickly after rainfall.

❶ Wayne Fell in Do Do 4c
The narrow rib to a lower-off just left of an old chain. Weave about to find the easiest line. It is a drainage line and dirt is sometimes washed down the line at the top.
FA. P.Tucker, H.Jones 3.2012

❷ Jetison Bilge 5a
The crack, initially sharing bolts with *Wayne Fell in Do Do*. Move right near the top to a lower-off. It is a drainage line and dirt is sometimes washed down the line at the top.
FA. P.Tucker, P.Blackburn 3.2012

❸ Fruitless Pair .... 6b+
Climb direct up smooth rock to the right of the crack that features a tough bouldery sequence to start.
FA. P.Tucker, P.Blackburn 3.2012

❹ La Poire 6b
Start up a tiny right-facing corner and then take the face above rightward to finish.
FA. P.Blackburn, P.Tucker 3.2012

❺ Posh and Becs 6c
The wall direct passing a tiny orange niche.
FA. P.Tucker, P.Blackburn 3.2012

❻ Apples and Pairs 6a
Follow a series of blind corners moving leftwards above them to a shared lower-off with *Posh and Becs*.
FA. P.Blackburn, P.Tucker 3.2012

❼ Welcome to Sport Mountain 4b
The first route on the narrow buttress 25m right of the main buttress.
FA. M.Davies 22.7.2019

❽ Florence Nightingale 3b
The groove to the right of *Welcome to Sport Mountain*.
FA. M.Davies 22.7.2019

❾ Iron Bolt Hill 4a
The right arete of the *Florence Nighting Gale* groove.
FA. M.Davies 22.7.2019

Daniel Sadler on the technical wall climbing encountered on *Under a Blood Red Sky* (6a) - *p.277* - at the Hindu Kush Area, Gilwern West. This section of the crag is typical of many hereabouts being only around 10m in height but packing in tricky moves from the first to last.
Photo: Mark Glaister

Gilwern West — Main Wall

Main Wall

The left-hand side of the main area is composed of a fine wall of flowstone which, although not very tall, offers some sustained and enjoyable pitches. The right-hand side is less appealing but the climbs are a bit more challenging than first appearances might suggest.
Approach (map and overview p.269) - This wall is between Pear Buttress and the Hindu Kush Area.
Conditions - The area is high up and exposed to the elements. Seepage may occur but the rock does dry quickly. It gets the sun from mid-afternoon onwards.

❶ Jug Fest 5a
An enjoyable little line that starts on the far left of the wall and heads up and right and then back left on good flowstone.
FA. B.Gregory, P.Bowen 4.2007

❷ Black Tide 5b
Climb stuck-on holds onto a black slab. Move left at the top. Care is needed with the rock in places.
FA. P.Blackburn 4.10.2016

❸ Porcellena 5c
The groove. A steady start leads to a tricky move up the corner. Care with the rock is needed in the upper half.
FA. P.Blackburn 2.10.2016

❹ Destination Brynmawr .. 6a
Climb up and right into a steep right-leaning corner. Make a strenuous pull to gain a flake and finish on sometimes dirty holds to a lower-off on the right.
FA. B.Gregory 2005

❺ Tea Leaves 6b
The left-hand arete of the flowstone face has some testing moves in its upper half where a couple of pulls up right gain better holds. Climbing the line direct is closer to **6c**.
FA. B.Gregory, B.Brewer 2.2007

❻ Battle of the Bulge 6c
The direct line up the smooth face and bulge to a lower-off.
FA. B.Gregory, B.Brewer 2.2007

❼ Nose Job .... 6c+
Climb the steep calcite wall with a hidden pocket high up.
FA. P.Blackburn 6.2016

❽ Flow Job 6b
An excellent piece of flowstone face climbing from start to finish.
FA. P.Tucker, P.Bowen 2004

❾ All Things Bright and Beautiful
.... 6a+
Climb up before making a hard sequence rightwards to more reasonable holds. Continue on still interesting ground to the top.
FA. P.Tucker, P.Bowen 2004. Wrongly named Christian Broke My Flake.

❿ Diagnosis Made Easy . 7a
Bouldery moves on a tight line. Climb directly up to and over the bulge onto the upper thin wall.
FA. B.Gregory, B.Brewer 2007

Main Wall **Gilwern West** 275

11 Pwll Du Crack 6a
Good climbing up the steepening line of weakness on some excellent holds. *Photo p.270.*
FA. P.Bowen 2004

12 Go With the Flow 6a
A worthwhile line with flowing moves up the slight rib between *Pwll Du Crack* and *There's No Business Like Flow Business*.
FA. P.Tucker, P.Bowen 2004

13 There's No Business Like Flow Business
.... 5c
Climb the fine drape of flowstone. Slightly escapable.
FA. P.Tucker, P.Bowen 2004

14 The Brexit Legacy 6a
Climb the calcite pillar using hidden pockets. Avoid the short corner to the right at this grade.
FA. P.Blackburn, H.Charles 7.2016

15 Should I Stay .... 6b+
The first line on the right-hand wall. Climb the arete between the short corner and the groove of *Article 50*.
FA. P.Blackburn, P.Tucker 2016

16 What, Still No Bolts ..... 6c+
The groove direct between *Should I Say* and *Should I Go*.
FA. M.Crocker 14.2.2012. Retro-bolted and also known as Article 50.

17 Should I Go .... 6b+
Climb the shallow scoop right of the *Article 50* groove until a stretch up and right to a good hold provides the key.
FA. P.Blackburn, P.Tucker 15.6.2016

18 Sailing to Freedom............. 5c
Climb directly to a pocket and then up the crack above it.
FA. P.Blackburn, H.Charles 8.2016

19 Whatever Floats Your Boat 6a
A delicate step left leads to a groove and finish.
FA. R.Hayes, P.Bowen 2007

20 A Paddock Full of Ponies . 5c
Climb the steep wall with stuck on holds to easier ground.
FA. R.Hayes, P.Bowen 2007

21 On White Horses .... 6a+
The faint groove with a short but tricky sequence. Stay strictly in the groove. Using any holds on other lines drops the grade.

22 Crack Me Up................. 4c
Climb the crack direct.
FA. R.Hayes, P.Bowen 2007

23 All Aboard My Dinghy ... 5b
An appealing line that follows the square-cut rib.
FA. R.Hayes, P.Bowen 2007

24 Rounding the Mark 5c
The short wall and awkward step over the bulge. Contains more climbing than first appears.
FA. P.Blackburn, H.Charles 8.2016

A low-level bouldering traverse of the wall starting to the left of Jug Fest and finishing at All Aboard my Dingy is **f5**.

Gilwern West — Hindu Kush Area

Hindu Kush Area

A long low crag that has a number of good little pitches that are technical and sustained. This makes for more of an experience than might first be anticipated. The rock is good and the crag base is flat and grassy.

Approach (map and overview p.269) - This is the wall encountered on the approach before the closed road is reached.

Conditions - Exposed to wind and rain but the face is quick drying. It gets the sun from mid-afternoon onwards.

1 Health Freak 5b
Move up the initial groove with one difficult move. Finish up the short steep wall and final arete. *Photo inside back cover*.
FA. P.Blackburn 25.2.2017

2 Cod Liver Oil 6b
Make some intricate moves up left before heading back rightwards to a lower-off. More involved than it first appears.
FA. B.Gregory, P.Bowen 2007

3 Glucosamine and Chondroitin
.... 6c
Climb directly up the wall to the bulge and pull through it on crimps. Short but intense climbing.
FA. B.Gregory, P.Bowen 2007

4 Green Energy .... 7a+
A very tight eliminate line. The black scoop direct between *Glucosamine and Chondroitin* and *Fuelled by Pies*. Utilises the bolts of *Glucosamine and Chondroitin* for protection.
FA. P.Tucker 2000s

5 Fuelled by Pies ...... 7a+
Thin and complex pulling and undercutting up the wall just left of *Johnny Takes a Tumble*.
FA. B.Gregory 2007

6 Johnny Takes a Tumble .. 6a
Climb the crack and traverse left to shared lower-off. Can be muddy on the finishing holds.
FA. B.Gregory, P.Bowen 2007

7 The House that Jack Built 6a
The wall and overhang avoiding the crack of *Johnny Takes a Tumble*.
FA. P.Blackburn 8.4.2017

Hindu Kush Area **Gilwern West**

8 Snap Crackle 'n' Pop 6a
A good pitch that has a difficult start. Above things gradually ease. *Photo p.19*.
FA. L.Jones, B.Hayes 8.9.2007

9 White Noise 5a
Follow the faint thin crack on good holds to a shared lower-off with *Snap Crackle 'n' Pop*.
FA. J.Steer, B.Hayes 8.9.2007

10 The Road to Nowhere 5a
Head up a flowstone wall using a series of hidden finger holds and delicate steps.
FA. P.Blackburn 18.3.2017

11 Back, Crack and Sack 5a
Follow the crack-line to the overlap and then move up rightwards to a lower-off.
FA. J.Steer, B.Hayes 8.9.2007

12 Take me up the Hindu Kush .. 5c
An easy start leads to a hard move to finish.
FA. B.Hayes, J.Steer 8.9.2007

13 To Dai or not to Dai. 5c
Relatively easy climbing leads to one hardish move.
FA. P.Bowen, D.Williams 8.9.2007

14 Brittle Biscuit 4c
Avoiding the crack pushes the grade up to 5c.
FA. D.Williams, P.Bowen 8.9.2007

15 Tad 5a
The first of three short climbs. Follow a line directly just right of the line of bolts.
FA. P.Blackburn 14.1.2017

16 Smidgen. 5b
The middle short line begins under a small overhang. Pass the overhang via a dynamic move.
FA. P.Blackburn 14.1.2017

17 Scintilla 5c
Thin and delicate moves lead to better holds.
FA. P.Blackburn 7.1.2017

18 Under a Blood Red Sky .. 6a
Thoughtful climbing requiring delicate footwork. *Photo p.273*.
FA. B.Hayes, J.Steer 8.9.2007

19 The Event Horizon 6a
Climb the wall avoiding the corner on its right.
FA. P.Blackburn 20.5.2017

Gilwern West — Tyre Sector

Tyre Sector

A long low wall of quarried rock that has a lot of climbs in the 6th grade and a number a notch in difficulty higher and lower. All the routes are worth doing but some loose holds are in evidence on the less travelled lines. This is a very pleasant spot which has been cleared of tyres illegally dumped from the road above. The face receives sun from mid-afternoon and is a lovely spot on a summers evening.

Approach (map and overview p.269) - Walk down a short path from the closed road to arrive at the base of the crags and the first climbs.

Conditions - Exposed to the elements but a very pleasant location on warm afternoons and evenings.

❶ Coming Unstuck 6b
A hard bouldery start leads to delicate sustained climbing on fragile concretions.
FA. G.Gibson 19.7.2017

❷ I'm Stuck, I'm Off 6b
Climb the wall on its left-hand side. Pleasantly sustained with a bit of a reach for the belay
FA. G.Gibson 19.7.2017

❸ Stig of the Dump .... 6a+
The short but worthwhile wall on mostly good holds.
FA. G.Gibson 19.7.2017

❹ Stickle Brick 5c
Straightforward climbing on the left-hand side of the next buttress.
FA. G.Gibson 19.7.2017

❺ Stick it up 'em .... 6a+
The wall is climbed on stuck-on holds and rugosities.
FA. G.Gibson 19.7.2017

❻ Stick it to 'em .... 6a+
Similar to the previous line via a shallow scoop.
FA. G.Gibson 22.6.2017

❼ Evostick 4b
The right-hand side of the wall is a nice pitch. Stay left on the best rock.
FA. G.Gibson 22.6.2017

Tyre Sector **Gilwern West** 279

8 William James Memorial Route
.... 6c+
The enticing wall to the right of the tree. Follow the rib to a bulge. Pass the bulge rightwards to an easier finish.
FA. G.Percival 25.8.2017

9 Rubber, Blubber 6c
A super little pitch that features some tricky to read technicalities and varied moves up the slim pillar.
FA. G.Gibson 22.7.2017

10 Tyre and Brimstone 6a
Intricate face climbing on accommodating holds.
FA. G.Gibson 22.6.2017

11 Funeral Tyre .... 6a+
The brown drainage streak with unobvious moves low down.
FA. G.Gibson 22.7.2017

12 Tyred Out .... 6a+
The slabby face steepens gradually to a fingery finale. Care with some holds needed midway.
FA. G.Gibson 22.7.2017

13 Retyred 5b
The superb little crackline/jug-fest to the right is a very good pitch at the grade.
FA. G.Gibson 22.6.2017

14 Too Tyred? .... 6b+
Fingery and sequency climbing up the face just right of *Retyred*. Finish as for *Retyred*.
FA. G.Gibson 22.7.2017

Gilwern West — Tyre Sector

15 Walls Have Ears — 7a
A highly technical, varied and sustained pitch.
FA. P.Blackburn 1.7.2017

16 Pirelli Times — 7c
Desperate and very reachy moves just above the second bolt.
FA. G.Gibson 5.7.2017

17 Don't Worry be Snappy — 7b+
After some hard starting moves make big moves up and left of a bolt to a layaway. Head back right to finish up a rib.
FA. G.Percival 12.9.2017

18 Dim Tipio Anghyfreithlon — 7b
The fine open groove to the left of *It's Been a Goodyear*.
FA. G.Percival 7.9.2017

19 It's Been a Goodyear — 6c+
Climb the intricate wall on side-pulls to better holds.
FA. G.Gibson 5.7.2017

20 Dunlop Special — 6b+
A fingery and long move above a ledge.
FA. G.Gibson 5.7.2017

21 Retread — 6b
A great piece of sustained face climbing.
FA. G.Gibson 5.7.2017

22 Remoulded — 6c
Pass an overlap utilising some undercuts and crimps.
FA. G.Gibson 5.7.2017

23 Tyre Times — 6c
A complex series of moves on side-pulls and edges.
FA. G.Gibson 5.7.2017

24 Locking Nut — 6c+
Long moves through a bulge then a hard move left and up.
FA. G.Gibson 17.7.2017

25 Onto the Canvas — 5b
Good face moves if slightly short-lived.
FA. G.Gibson 5.7.2017

26 Bald Patch — 5b
Face climbing heading leftwards near the top.
FA. G.Gibson 5.7.2017

27 Mal Alignment — 5b
An easy start leads to steeper moves. Care needed with the rock.
FA. G.Gibson 17.7.2017

28 Get Tracking — 6a
Gradually increasing delicate difficulties up the slight rib.
FA. G.Gibson 17.7.2017

29 Wear and Tear — 5b
A good face route at the grade.
FA. G.Gibson 17.7.2017

30 Majorca With Tyres — 5b
Good face climbing moving rightwards near the top.
FA. G.Jenkin, D.Grange, C.Jameson 17.6.2019

31 Wheel and Tyre — 6a
Climb the steady face to some pushy finishing moves.
FA. G.Gibson 17.7.2017

32 Rimmed — 6a+
A bouldery initial wall gains an easy groove.
FA. R.Thomas, G.Gibson 19.7.2017

33 Torque Wrench — 6b
The face direct on some sloping holds.
FA. R.Thomas, G.Gibson 19.7.2017

34 Running Hot, But Cool in the Zone — 5b
Head up the arete and then up to a slot close to the top.
FA. G.Jenkin, D.Grange 17.6.2019

Ivor Biggun Sector **Gilwern West** 281

Ivor Biggun Sector
The tallest section of crag at Gilwern that is very close to where a landslip has occurred. Assess the danger of further instability before embarking on the climbs.
Approach (map and overview p.269) - Walk past the Tyre Sector to where the landslip marks the left edge of the Ivor Biggun Sector.
Conditions - Exposed to the elements but a very pleasant location on warm afternoons and evenings.

❶ Ivor Biggun 5c
1) 5c, 12m. A difficult wall gains a ledge system and rope that leads to a bolted belay.
2) 5c, 13m. Move onto a block and then head out to, and up the left-hand bolted line to a lower-off.
FA. M.Davies 7.2018

❷ Everybody Wants One ... 5c
1) 5c, 12m. *Ivor Biggun* pitch 1.
2) 5c, 12m. Begin as for *Ivor Biggun* pitch 2 but follow the right-hand bolted line to a lower-off.
FA. M.Davies, G.Percival, P.Tucker 18.4.2019

❸ Pimp My Ride 6c
Bouldery moves up the flakes.
FA. G.Jenkin, D.Grange 18.9.2018

❹ Your Wheels ain't Fly .... 6a+
Some of the moves need a bit of figuring out.
FA. G.Jenkin, D.Grange 18.9.2018

Gilwern West — Right-hand Walls

Right-hand Walls

All the right-hand walls require care when approaching, moving along the base and belaying The first sector is a wide horizontally banded wall that has a number of bolted routes along its full length. The lines are prone to being dirty, loose and have seen little attention since they were established. The next sector is another horizontally banded wall that features a topping overhang which provides some hard finishes. Again the lines are prone to being dirty and see little traffic. The final sector is a small compact wall at the far end of the escarpment.

Approach (map and overview p.269) - Each sector has its own short approach. All involve moving up ledges to the base of the wall and bolted belay options - needs care in places.

Conditions - Exposed to the elements. Many of the lines are dirty and loose.

1 The Slow Lane 6a
Climb the narrowing corner and short headwall.
FA. G.Percival, G.Jenkin, P.Tucker 20.8.2018

2 Middle Lane Hogger 6c
Pumpy jug pulling up the ragged crack. Finish on the right.
FA. G.Percival, P.Tucker 20.8.2018

3 Fast and Furious 7b
Thin crimpy pulls on calcite and edges up the leaning wall.
FA. G.Percival 3.10.2018

4 Riding Shotgun .... 6a+
Sustained and varied with a hard start.
FA. G.Jenkin, D.Grange 5.10.2018

5 Drive-by Shooting 6a
The faint crack-line.
FA. G.Jenkin, G.Percival 27.9.2018

6 Driven 2 Destruction 6a
Another pitch of sustained climbing.
FA. M.Davies, G.Percival 17.9.2018

7 Junk Yard Jete .... 6c+
Climb just left of the low overhang.
FA. G.Percival 13.9.2018

8 Chassis Chase 7a
Overcome the low roof and then make gigantic spans up the steep ground above.
FA. G.Percival 13.9.2018

9 Need for Speed 7b
Make some reachy pulls to pass the low overhangs and then make progress above on conglomerate holds.
FA. G.Percival 27.9.2018

10 Mystery Trad Route X .... 6c+
The mid-height brown calcite streak sporting two old pegs.
FA. G.Percival 27.9.2018

Right-hand Walls Gilwern West

⑪ Hurry, Muttley! Huttley! . 6c
The left-hand line that has a punishing finale at the top overhang.
FA. G.Percival 13.9.2018

⑫ Wacky Races .... 6b+
Juggy pulling up the lower wall gains the top overhang which provides a tough ending.
FA. G.Percival 13.9.2018

⑬ As High as a Kite .... 6a+
Head up on big holds to the high roof and pull leftwards and then back right to pass it.
FA. M.Davies, G.Percival 3.10..2018

⑭ The Driverless Flightless Car 5c
Ascend direct to the right end of the upper overhang.
FA. M.Davies, G.Percival 3.10..2018

⑮ Crash Test Dummy .... 6b+
The first line on this section of wall is on good holds, but the rock is unreliable.
FA. G.Percival 17.9.2018

⑯ Brunette .... 7a+
The middle line of the trio on this section of the wall features a hard lower sequence.
FA. G.Percival 17.9.2018

⑰ Caramel Wall .... 6c+
The exposed wall on the right.
FA. G.Percival 7.9.2018

⑱ The Final Countdown .... 6a+
The left-hand line with tough moves midway.
FA. G.Percival, G.Jenkin, D.Grange 13.9.2018

⑲ The Final Fantasy 5c
Juggy climbing to a hard finish.
FA. G.Percival, G.Jenkin, D.Grange 13.9.2018

⑳ The Book of Revalations 4c
The wall just to the left of the groove/corner.
FA. G.Percival, G.Jenkin, D.Grange 13.9.2018

Witches Point

Grade Spread | 3 | 19 | 36 | 21 | 3

Witches Point is one of the jewels in the crown of hard sport climbing in South Wales. The setting is stunning - an idyllic position above a magnificent 'blue flag' sandy surf beach; in the summer months it takes on a holiday atmosphere. All of the cliffs have good rock and the variety of climbing style ranges from powerful to technical and sustained. The only drawbacks are that it is tidal and conditions can be frustrating in humid warm weather.

Approach
From the A48 Bridgend bypass, take the B4265 southwards to St. Brides Major. Drive through the village and turn right towards Southerndown (ignore earlier signs for Southerndown). Turn left by the Three Golden Cups pub and follow the road down a steep hill to Dunraven Bay car park (fee). The cliff is on the left-hand side of the beach. A walk across the beach reaches the crag in 5 minutes.

Tides
The crag is accessible for around 4 hours either side of low tide. However the base of many of the routes are above the high tide level during calm sea conditions. The exception is Witches Cave which is only accessible for 2 hours on either side of low tide.

Conditions
The cliff is northwest-facing, keeping it out of the sun for most of the day. This provides welcome shade during hot summer weather but also makes it a good evening venue at other times. Seepage can occur in the winter months and early spring, but once dry, it remains so for long periods of time. Conditions can be frustrating in humid warm weather before any sun comes onto the faces.

Access
Dogs are not allowed on the beach in the summer.

Sam Clarke on *Methuselah* (8a) - *p.288* - at the Stone Wings Cliff, Witches Point. This cliff is the premier spot for hard routes at Witches Point with plenty on offer in the upper grades and a handful of worthwhile easier routes on its right-hand side. Photo: Elis Rees

Witches Point

Martyn Richards on the popular *Staple Diet* (7b) - p.289 - at the Stone Wings Cliff. Get the tides and conditions right and the climbing here will not disappoint, its variety of styles and beachside location making it a fine destination for teams of varying abilities and those who like some apres-climbing watersports. Photo: Mark Glaister

Witches Point — Stone Wings Cliff

❶ Crime Slunk Scene 7b
A fun pitch that features a short powerful sequence based on the roof crack. A long extender on the fourth bolt is very helpful.
FA. W.Calvert, 9.7.2021

❷ Liassic Lark 7a
A super little jamming crack with a tough bulge. It can be greasy early in the season. Above the bulge step right to a lower-off.
FA. R.Thomas 8.1994

❸ In Search of Bedrock .... 7a+
The natural continuation to *Liassic Lark* that moves left from its lower-off to climb a steep groove system and headwall.
FA. R.Thomas, G.Gibson 16.7.1994

❹ Help, Help Me Rhondda 7c
A steady start leads to a desperate fingery sequence through the mean-looking bulge.
FA. E.Travers-Jones 8.1993

❺ The Dai Vinci Coed ... 7c+
From the first jug on *Help, Help Me Rhondda* move right slightly then up to the overlap on undercuts and side-pulls. From a good undercut, move right to a pod and make a hard fingery traverse back left before moving up to the lower-off.
FA. R.Lamey 26.6.2013

❻ Methuselah 8a
Follow *The Dai Vinci Coed* and move right into *This God is Mine*. Instead of pulling over the bulge to easy ground, make a wild series of moves right across a sloping rail into *Masada*. Finish up this. Photo p.285.
FA. D.Pickford, 7.8.2016

❼ This God is Mine .... 7b+
A classic of its type. Sustained climbing up the thin crack-line which proves to be tough all of the way to the lower-off.
Photo p.11.
FA. G.Gibson R.Thomas 6.8.1994

❽ Masada .... 8a+
The ascent of the smooth-looking wall requires imagination, ability and endurance. The wall beneath the first overlap is climbed direct, not by stepping out of the crack.
FA. E.Travers-Jones 1995

❾ Stone Wings E5 6a
The antithesis of its neighbours. Brutal jamming combined with hard-earned gear placements.
FA. P.Littlejohn, S.Robinson (1pt) 27.7.1979
FFA. G.Gibson, R.Thomas 19.6.1994

Stone Wings Cliff

A superb wall which is overhanging on its left-hand side and contains a line-up of sustained and pumpy routes. Further right it has some delicate face routes at easier grades. The rock is of the highest quality but can suffer seepage in its central section well into the warmer months.

Approach (map and overview p.284) - Walk across the beach when the tide is out.

Conditions - The walls face northwest and get late afternoon/early evening sun. This is not a good venue if it is humid.

Stone Wings Cliff **Witches Point**

⑩ The Uninvited Guest.. 7b+
The wall right of *Stone Wings* has a hard crux to reach the square-cut groove. From the top of the groove finish up the top section of *Stone Wings* crack. Three large cams are needed for the crack.
FA. G.Gibson, R.Thomas 2.7.1994

⑪ Mr.T. 8a+
Start just right of *The Uninvited Guest*. Follow a thin seam with difficulty to join *Stone Wings*, make crux moves left to join *Masada* at its twin glued jugs and then move left and up to join *This God is Mine*. Go left to the pod on *The Dai Vinci Coed* and finish along its fingery traverse.
FA. M.Richards, A.Sharp 7.9.2013

⑫ Super Size Me 7c+
Climb *Staple Diet* to where it is possible to traverse left to a bottomless groove. Make an improbable rock up to a series of crimps. Above, a hard-to-read section gains the ledge and lower-off.
FA. S.Rawlinson 3.8.2013

⑬ Staple Diet 7b
A stamina workout up the hanging groove and crack. Never technical, always thuggy. *Photo p.286*.
FA. G.Gibson, R.Thomas 1.6.1993

⑭ Tragic Moustache 7a
A hard start over a bulge, then easier moves to a bulging finale.
FA. G.Gibson, R.Thomas 5.6.1993

⑮ Five O'Clock Shadow 6c+
Climb a boulder problem to a big flake and ramp. Continue up the awkward wall and faint rib to the V-groove in the roof. Finish up this with difficulty.
FA. R.Thomas, G.Gibson 30.5.1996

⑯ Magic Touch 6b
An excellent diagonal face climb. Step up and left onto a shelf. Follow a rising traverse leftwards across the face to a lower-off above and right of *Staple Diet*.
FA. P.Littlejohn (without bolts) 5.6.1979

⑰ Pelagic Mush 6a+
A nice little line up the face to the right of *Five O'Clock Shadow*.
FA. R.Thomas, G.Gibson 30.5.1993

⑱ Sideburn 6b+
A short hard section requiring a long reach.
FA. R.Thomas 4.6.1993

⑲ Spear the Bearded Clam 6b
A hard lower section.
FA. R.Thomas 1998

⑳ Slurp the Savoury Oyster 5c
The final line on this section of the cliff.
FA. R.Thomas 1998

Witches Point — Dunraven Cliff

Dunraven Cliff

A large section of cliff that has an impressive central wall cut by ramps and grooves in its upper reaches. On either side are shorter and steeper sections of crag - the Tufa Terrace and the Tufa Gantry (that are awkward to approach).

Approach (map and overview p.284) - When the tide is out, make an easy stroll across the beach to the central section of the cliff. To reach the Tufa Terrace, scramble carefully up rungs and grass. To access The Gantry climb one of the lower lines. Tufa Terrace and The Gantry can be accessed from above but the approach down steep grass slopes is insecure and dangerous in the wet.

Conditions - The walls face northwest and get late afternoon/early evening sun. This is not a good venue in humid weather. Seepage can be a problem.

❶ **Tuffa King Hard** 7a
Far left line on the Tufa Terrace.
FA. R.Thomas, N.O'Neill 1998

❷ **Tufa Joy** 7a
A hard start is followed by a powerful finish rightwards.
FA. G.Gibson, R.Thomas 5.7.1993

❸ **Tufa at the Top** 7a
A gem of a route taking the 'sexual' tufa. Harder than it looks.
FA. R.Thomas, G.Gibson 6.6.1993

❹ **It's Tufa at the Bottom** .. 7a+
Appropriately named and not all over until the belay. Begin on the right.
FA. G.Gibson, R.Thomas 3.7.1993

❺ **Tufa Tennis** .... 6c+
A pleasant companion route on the 'bobbles' to the right.
FA. R.Thomas, G.Gibson 3.7.1993

❻ **PCB** 6a
The first line on the left of the lower main wall is short and starts halfway up the grassy gully leading to Tufa Terrace.
FA. D.Emanuel 2009

❼ **Croeso I Gymru** ...... 6b+
Pleasant climbing and tricky in its top half.
FA. M.Crocker, R.Thomas 23.8.1986

❽ **The World-v-Gibson** .. 7a
A technical crux low down and sustained climbing above.
FA. M.Crocker, R.Thomas 23.8.1986

❾ **Straining at the Leash** ... 7b
A hard bouldery crux that packs a punch.
FA. G.Gibson, R.Thomas 15.5.1993

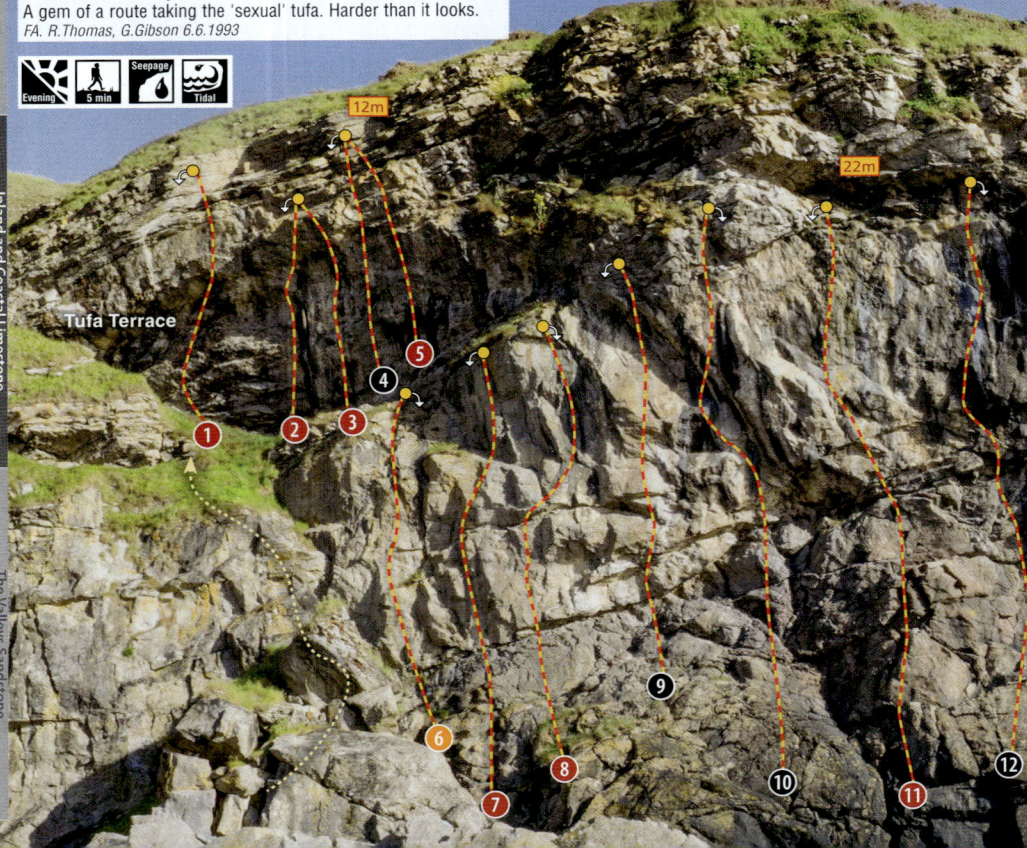

Dunraven Cliff **Witches Point**

10 Leave it to the Dogs ..... 7a+
Good and hard. Sustained climbing up the groove and arete.
FA. G.Gibson, R.Thomas 12.10.1993

11 There's Life in the Old Dog Yet
.... 6c+
A short, sharp crux in a fine position gains easier climbing.
FA. R.Thomas, G.Gibson 16.5.1993

12 Plus ça Change 7b
The centre of the wall via a prominent flake with a trying crux.
FA. G.Gibson, R.Thomas 30.5.1993

13 Hanging by a Thread 6c
One of the classics of the grade in South Wales. Superb and sustained climbing.
FA. R.Thomas, M.Learoyd 8.1986

14 Edge-More 7c
A short, hard and fingery crux that includes a bolt-on hold.
FA. G.Gibson, R.Thomas 3.7.1994

15 Edge-Hog .... 7b+
The leaning arete and powerful bulge in a fine position.
FA. G.Gibson, R.Thomas 11.7.1993

16 Grow-Up! 7c
A steep line through the centre of the bulges and roofs.
FA. M.Crocker 14.5.1994

17 Pasty = Man Boobs 4c
The left-hand bolted line on the slab below the Tufa Gantry.
FA. D.Emanuel 2009

18 Young Gifted and Beige 4a
The right-hand bolted line on the slab below the Tufa Gantry.
FA. D.Emanuel, R.Thomas 2009

19 The Overlook .... 7b+
A very powerful series of heel-hooks and rotations. Tape your hands up for this one, or get some crack gloves!
FA. G.Gibson 15.5.1994

20 Anchors Away .... 6b+
A tricky bulge in a good position.
FA. R.Thomas, G.Gibson 15.5.1994

21 Cast Adrift 6c
Technical climbing on dinks.
FA. R.Thomas, G.Gibson 11.7.1994

22 Broken on the Rocks 6b
A short pleasant wall.
FA. R.Thomas, G.Gibson 11.7.1994

23 Marooned 6b
A single hard move on the right-hand side of the wall.
FA. R.Thomas, G.Gibson 11.7.1994

Witches Point — Folded Walls

Folded Walls

The most recently developed section of Witches Point is a geologically varied crag with routes that reflect this characteristic.

Approach (map and overview p.284) - When the tide is out, make an easy stroll across the beach to the cliff.

Conditions - The walls face northwest and get late afternoon/early evening sun. This is not a good venue in humid weather. Seepage can be a problem.

1 Gwyll 6a
Start in the back of the narrow black zawn. Climb up and out into the light, then steeply up the rolling wall.
FA. R.Thomas A.Rosier 20.7.2018

2 Blaidd Den .... 6a+
Start inside the narrow black zawn. Steeply pass the left side of the fang and continue more easily to the lower-off.
FA. R.Thomas, N.O'Neill, E.Rees 8.2018

3 Bryn Serth 6b
Begin in the narrow black zawn. Steep jug hauling but keep away from the loose/wedged block at the top by moving right using jams.
FA. R.Thomas, R.Phillips 15.7.2018

4 Sand in the Vaseline . 7a+
The series of overlaps.
FA. G.Leyshon 8.2018

5 Gwylan LLwglyd 5b
The left arete of the chimney moving right at the top to a shared-belay.
FA. R.Thomas G.Ashmore 8.2018

6 Cachau Hwch 5b
The left-hand line up the classic folded wall above the platform.
FA. R.Thomas, R.Phillips 1.8.2017

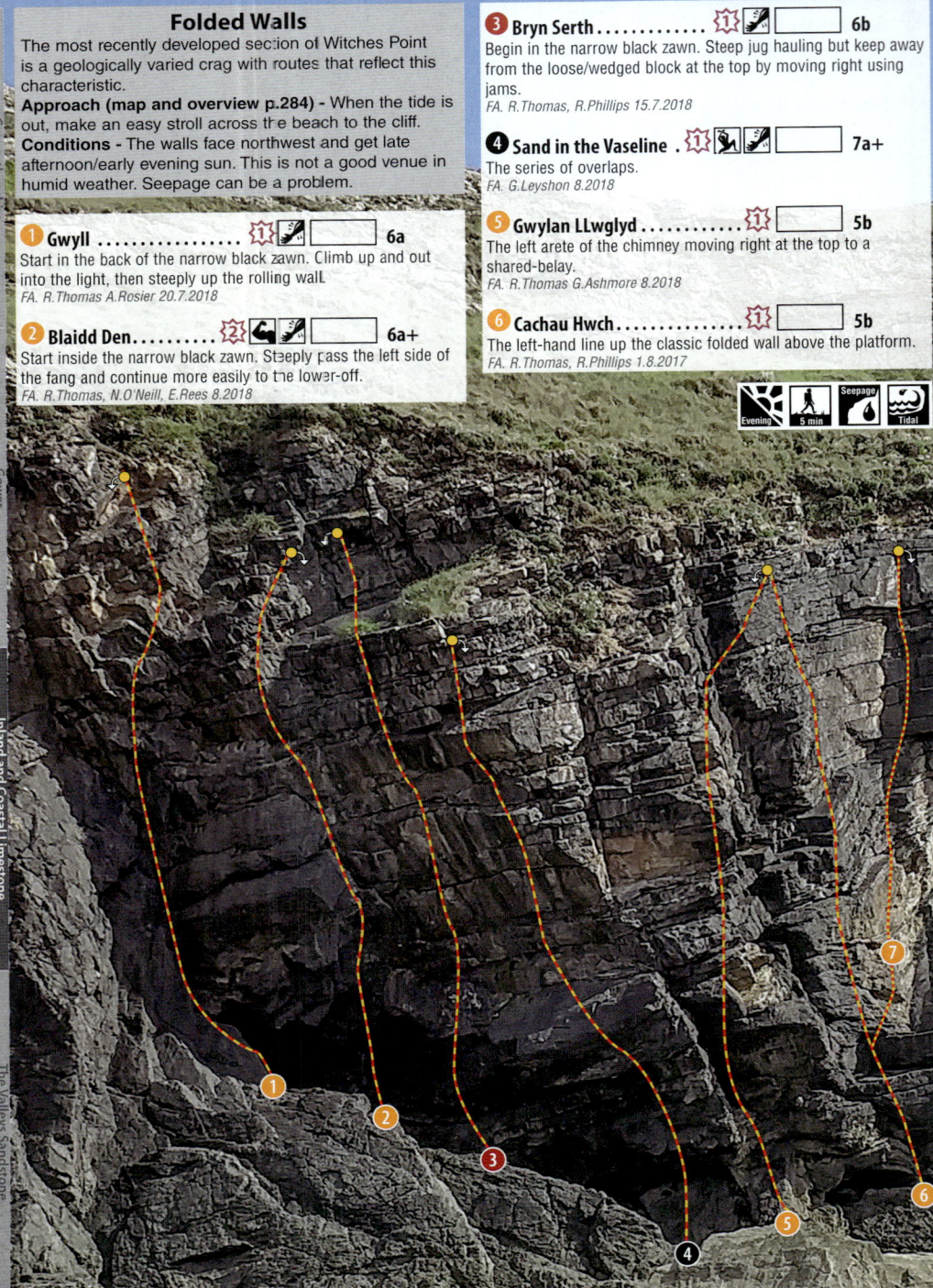

Folded Walls **Witches Point**

7 Mewn Cachiad............ 5b
Start up *Cachau* and climb the crack and black slab on the right.
FA. R.Thomas R.Phillips 31.7.2017

8 Diawl Bach............... 6b+
Start on the platform and tackle the steep prow and arete above.
FA. R.Thomas, G.Davis 1.8.2017

9 Drewgi 5b
The chimney and corner crack from the bottom of the tight syncline.
FA. R.Thomas, G.Davis 2.8.2017

10 Pwdin Blew .... 6a+
The wall between the corner and a crack-line.
FA. R.Thomas 9.2017

11 Twll Tin.................. 6b
The centre of the wall right of the crack-line to a shared lower-off with *Coc Oen*.
FA. R.Thomas, R.Phillips 6.2018

12 Coc Oen.................. 6b
Start up a short corner and then finish up the wall above to a shared lower-off with *Twll Tin*.
FA. R.Thomas, E.Travers-Jones 5.7.2017

13 Wnco Mwnco .... 6b+
Start off a narrow shelf right of *Coc Oen*. A tricky entry gains the steep headwall.
FA. R.Thomas, R.Phillips 30.8.2017

14 Onco Fonco 6b
A coral slab leads to steep slopers and the mid-way ledge. Finish up the wall above.
FA. R.Thomas, G.Ashmore 10.9.2017

15 Hen Gi.................... 6a+
A steep crozzly start and then walls and ledges reach the shared lower-off with *Triciau Newydd*.
FA. R.Thomas, E.Travers 5.7.2017

16 Triciau Newydd 5b
Bulge, wall and ledges to a lower-off shared with *Hen Gi*.
FA. R.Thomas, E.Travers-Jones 8.2017

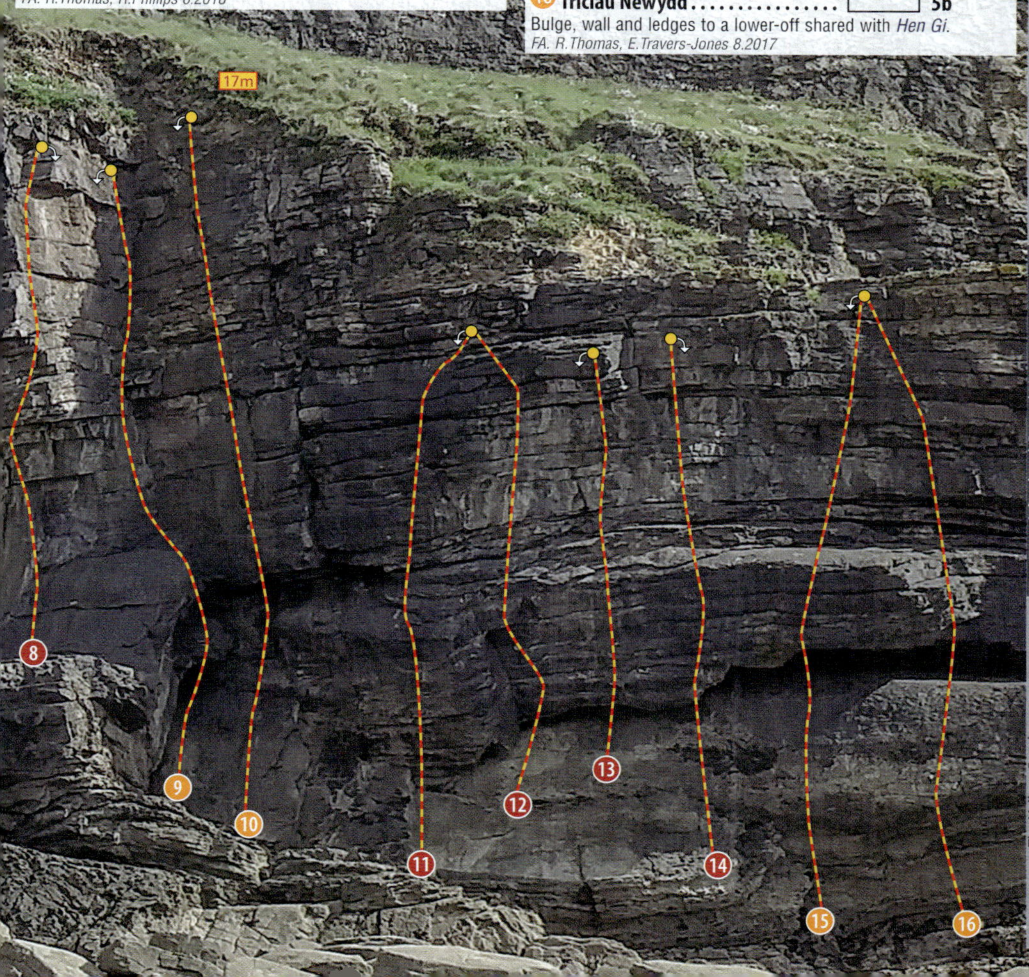

Witches Point — Witches Cave

Witches Cave

Just before the tip of Witches Point is a wide shallow cave topped by a vertical white and black wall. Either side are shorter overhanging walls. There are lots of pitches here but they see far less attention than elsewhere on Witches Point due to the tidal restrictions and the difficulty in finding good conditions, nevertheless the better lines are worth tracking down.

Approach (map and overview p.284) and Tides - An easy stroll across the beach, when the tide is out, gains the ledges below the crag. The crag is accessible for around 2 hours on either side of low water. However the ledges below the crag are exposed for plenty of time in calm seas and it is possible to climb out from one of the far right-hand lines and walk over the top of the headland back to the car park.

Conditions - The crag faces northwest and gets late afternoon/early evening sun. Not a good venue in humid weather and seepage can be a problem.

❶ **Fatman and Nob In** 3c
The wall just right of the corner to a lower-off.
FA. R.Thomas 2010

❷ **Gay Batman** 5a
The gently leaning wall to a shared lower-off with *Fatman and Nob In*.
FA. D.Emanuel 2009

❸ **Robin's Yoghurt Supper** 5b
Climb the wall to the left of the corner and capping overhang to a shared lower-off.
FA. D.Emanuel, R.Thomas, R.Philips 28.6.2009

❹ **Abra-Ker-Fucking-Dabra** 6a
Interesting climbing. Climb up to the hanging corner and move out right to clear the capping roof.
FA. D.Emanuel 2009

❺ **Sorcerer's Assistant** .. 6a+
Follow the undercut nose and roof stack to the right of the corner on big holds.
FA. R.Thomas 2009

❻ **Magic Circle** 6b
Powerful pulling through the large double overhangs.
FA. R.Thomas, R.Phillips, G.Leyshon 2009

❼ **Smoke and Mirrors** ... 6b
A wild route taking in some very steep ground.
FA. R.Thomas, R.Phillips 2009

❽ **Great Expectorations** 6b
Take the multiple roof stack to meet and finish up a groove in the upper wall.
FA. R.Thomas, E.Travers-Jones 18.6.2013

❾ **Phlegmatic Solution** . 6c
Take the roof stack just left of the rockfall and then swing right onto the upper wall - a difficult finish awaits.
FA. R.Thomas, E.Travers-Jones, M.Jordan 20.7.2013

Witches Cave **Witches Point** 295

There has been a small rockfall below the roof.

⓾ Evil Ways 7b
Climb up to the roof and, utilising a foot-lock, pull onto the upper wall. Finish up the technical wall.
FA. M.Crocker 19.7.1986

⑪ Evil K'nee Full .... 7a+
Impressive. Move up to the overhang and reach for a good hold at the lip. Pull onto the upper wall and climb up a faint rib to a hard move up for a sharp edge. Finish at a lower-off above.
FA. R.Thomas, G.Ashmore 2.9.1996

⑫ Willie the Pimp ... 6c+
Follow *Thin LIzzy* until above the lip of the cave and then foot traverse left across the roof. Move up into a niche and climb diagonally left to a lower-off.
FA. E.Travers-Jones 18.8.2014

⑬ White Witch E5 6b
Continue the traverse of *Willie The Pimp* to finish up *Evil K'nee Full*. The old fixed gear is no more, but some of the bolts on the face may suffice.
FA. M.Crocker, R.Thomas 19.7.1986

⑭ Thin Lizzy .... 6c+
Make powerful moves past the low roof to below a corner. Take the technical crack leftwards to the roof, then move left to a 'V' groove. Finish up the groove taking care with some flakes.
FA. R.Thomas, G.Royle 19.7.1986

⑮ Wrasse Wipe 6c
Start up *Thin Lizzy* and then continue up the corner.
FA. R.Thomas 24.6.2009

⑯ Wrrasseputin's Hypodermic Typewriter
.... 6c
Make some steep moves on sharp holds, then finish up the wall above to a shared lower-off with *Thin Lizzy*.
FA. D.Emanuel, R.Phillips 28.6.2009

⑰ Didymo Clogs yer Tackle
.... 6b
Start with a big reach to the first good hold - easier above.
FA. R.Thomas, N.O'Neill 2007

⑱ Fishermen Pump Their Rods .. 6a+
Similar sharp pulling on steep ground.
FA. R.Thomas, M.Hirst 2007

⑲ Wrasse Bandit .... 6b+
Tough stuff through the overhang and bulge.
FA. R.Thomas, G.Ashmore 2006

⑳ Sore Wrasse 6c
The hardest of the shorter steep lines hereabouts.
FA. G.Ashmore, R.Thomas 2006

㉑ Wrassetafarian .... 6b+
The short overhanging wall where the overhangs start to fade.
FA. G.Ashmore 13.7.2009

㉒ Little Wrasse Cull 6a
A boulder problem start leads to easy ground.
FA. R.Thomas, M.Jordan 7.2013

㉓ The Bedraggled Trousered Misogynist
.... 5c
Knob pulling at its finest!
FA. R.Thomas, N.O'Neill 8.2013

Temple Bay

| Grade Spread | 3 | 43 | 28 | 1 | - |

On the eastern side of the headland at Witches Point is a collection of tidal low walls. These contain a number of short sport routes in a pleasant seaside environment. The style of climbing varies from thin technical walls to overhanging faces and juggy roof stacks. Although not in the same class as the best on offer at Witches Point, there is plenty here to keep those after a bit of mileage busy, the grade range is friendly and the beach is superb.

Approach

From Dunraven Bay, walk through the gates in the wall and along the track for 650m, past some unusual walled gardens on the right, until the cliff top is reached. Go right on a path and in a short distance go through a gate on the left. Follow a path up and then down to a stone wall. A path goes left steeply down to the beach from where the Temple Bay crags are easily reached. This is the best approach to use on a first visit. At low tide the crags can be accessed by walking around the headland. Also a ramp between the First and Second Inlet allows easy access up and down from the fisherman's ledges on the top of the headland, but it is not easy to locate from above on first acquaintance.

Tides

The crags are tidal and are accessible for around 3 hours either side of low tide. With careful planning a long day of climbing is possible by working along the cliff line toward the headland as the tide falls, and then as the tide comes in work your way back again.

Conditions

The crags face due south and get lots of sun. They are sheltered from a northwesterly wind. The bases of the routes dry quickly once the tide has retreated although the caves can be damp if there is no breeze.

Rosy Klinkenberg on *Descarte's Dithers* (5c) - *p.303* - at the Cave Inlet, Temple Bay. Temple Bay presents a long line of low tidal crags that offer plenty of routes which vary in style from thin fingery walls to strenuous stacked overhangs as pictured here. Photo: Mark Glaister

Temple Bay — Sea Walls and First Inlet

Sea Walls

A long, low wall of sea battered rock that holds some short but punchy routes on good rock.

Approach (map and overview p.296) - The wall is tidal and can be climbed on for around 2 hours either side of low tide. The wall extends to the very end of the headland.

Conditions - The base of the cliff takes a little time to dry once the tide has gone out.

1 Royle Headache .... 6c+
Head up past the roof to gain and climb the hanging offwidth.
FA. R.Thomas, G.Royle 1987

2 Jilter's Wall .... 6b+
The overhang and white wall to a lower-off shared.
FA. R.Thomas G.Royle 1987

3 Flintstoner .... 7a+
The bulge to the right of a crack
FA. R.Thomas, G.Royle 1987

4 The Inexorable March of Time 6b+
A hard start relents at a good hold and the upper wall.
FA. R.Thomas, G.Davies 1987

5 Aristophanes Plays with Time 6c
At the right end of the undercut section are some black chert lumps. Devise and execute the sequence of slaps and pulls to reach the break and continue directly up the wall.
FA. R.Thomas, G.Davies 1987

First Inlet

A compact wall of excellent rock with some tough little lines, most of them having very fingery starts. The rock is excellent. A couple of the lines top out.

Approach (map and overview p.296) - The inlet is tidal and can be climbed on for around 3 hours either side of low tide. The inlet is the compact wall of bolted lines towards the headland, just beyond an easy-angled ramp that leads up to the fisherman's ledges above the cliff.

Conditions - The base of the cliff takes a little time to dry once the tide has gone out.

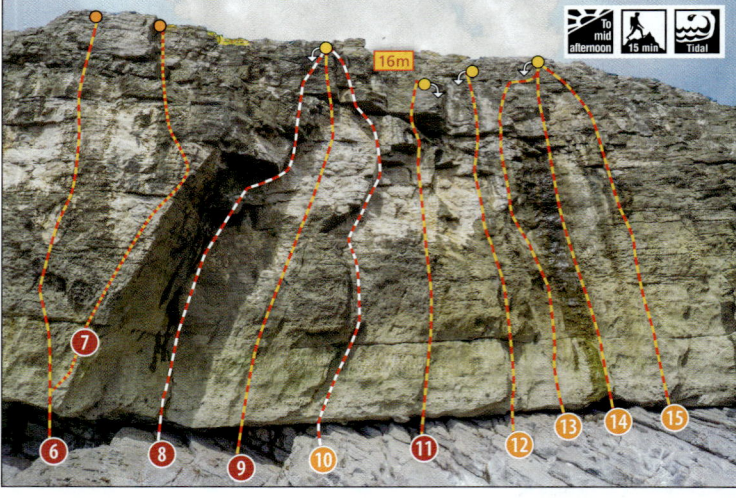

6 Long Awaited 6c
The wall left of the right-leaning arete with the crux low down on some super sharp holds.
FA. R.Thomas, G.Royle 1988

7 Fools Rush In .... 6c+
The wall and right-leaning arete starting up *Long Awaited*.
FA. R.Thomas, G.Royle 10.1988

8 Lasting Impressions .. E3 5c
The leaning corner.
FA. M.Learoyd, R.Thomas, S.Robinson, D.Meek 21.9.1986

9 Dross of 86 .... 6b
A perplexing start to pass the lower bulge gains good holds.
FA. R.Thomas, R.Phillips 2010

10 Life and Soul .... HVS 5a
The series of slim corner cracks.
FA. D.Meek, S.Robinson 21.9.1986

11 Sixty Eight Plus One 6b
The wall to a final difficult move to gain the lower-off.
FA. R.Thomas, E.Travers-Jones 2011

Temple Bay 299

⑫ Blow Me, Another One... ★1 🚶 ▢ 6a
A good pitch with a hard start leading to easier ground.
Photo this page.
FA. R.Thomas, R.Phillips 2011

⑬ Matt of the Iron Gland ★1 🅟 🚶 ▢ 6a+
A thin start gains much better holds and a steep wall to finish.
FA. R.Thomas, R.Phillips 2010

⑭ Wreckers Bay............ ★2 🚶 ▢ 6a+
The gold-coloured wall on comforting pockets heads up to a steep finish.
FA. R.Thomas, G.Ashmore 2010

⑮ Surly Temple........ ★1 🅟 🚶 ▢ 6a+
The wall left of the ledge on the right, again with a hard start.
FA. R.Thomas 1986

Bridget Glaister on the golden-coloured rock of *Blow Me, Another One* (6a) - *this page* - at the First Inlet, Temple Bay. The Inlet is home to some enticing lines on superb rock. Photo: Mark Glaister

Temple Bay — Second Inlet

Second Inlet

A series of short, but intense and sharp pitches. The rock is very good but it will take its toll on soft skin.

Approach (map and overview p.296) - The inlet is tidal and can be climbed on for around 3 hours either side of low tide. Walk along the beach until the wall is seen next to a big boulder that sits on the rock platform. The easy ramp that leads up to the fisherman's ledges above the cliff is just to the left.

Descent - Some routes have belay bolts set back from the edge - use a long sling to set up a lower-off. This can be set up and retrieved by an easy scramble up to the fisherman's ledges on the left. The other routes have lower-offs in place.

Conditions - The base of the cliff takes a little time to dry out once the tide has gone out.

1 Themis is Out of Order ... 6a+
The leftmost bolted line of the wall is a tricky number.
FA. R.Thomas, E.Travers-Jones 23.11.2014

2 Alchemy of Error ... 6a
Climb the leaning wall to a big jug and less steep face above.
FA. R.Thomas, R.Phillips 25.3.2015

3 OW! ... 7a
A very sharp experience, with the hardest moves low down.
FA. E.Travers-Jones, R.Thomas 23.11.2014

4 300 Spartans ... 6b
Climb the compact prow on its left-hand side.
FA. R.Thomas, G.Ashmore 5.2013

5 Sliced up at Thermopylae ... 6a
The right-facing groove is very sharp.
FA. R.Thomas, E.Travers-Jones 23.9.2014

6 Sharpshitter ... 6c
Short two bolt line left of *Minsir*.
FA. R.Thomas, N.O'Neill 8.2016

7 Minsir ... 6c
The groove and burly bulge to a lower-off on the ledge above.
FA. E.Travers-Jones, G.Ashmore 12.10.2014

8 Leonidas' Last Breakfast ... 6a+
The wall just to the right of the groove of *Minsir*.
FA. R.Thomas, E.Travers-Jones 16.9.2014

9 Tip Ripper ... 6c
A hard bouldery start. Undercut, bridge, crimp and lurch to a shared lower-off with *Achilles Hasn't A Foot to Stand On*.
FA. R.Thomas 2013

10 Achilles Hasn't a Foot to Stand On ... 6b+
Opposite the boulder is a shallow arete with a tiny 'tooth' of rock at the base. Follow the arete and face above.
FA. R.Thomas, E.Travers-Jones 2011

11 Euclid's Theorem ... 6a
Climb the wall to the right of the shallow arete of *Achilles Hasn't a Foot to Stand On.* Shared lower-off.
FA. R.Thomas 2011

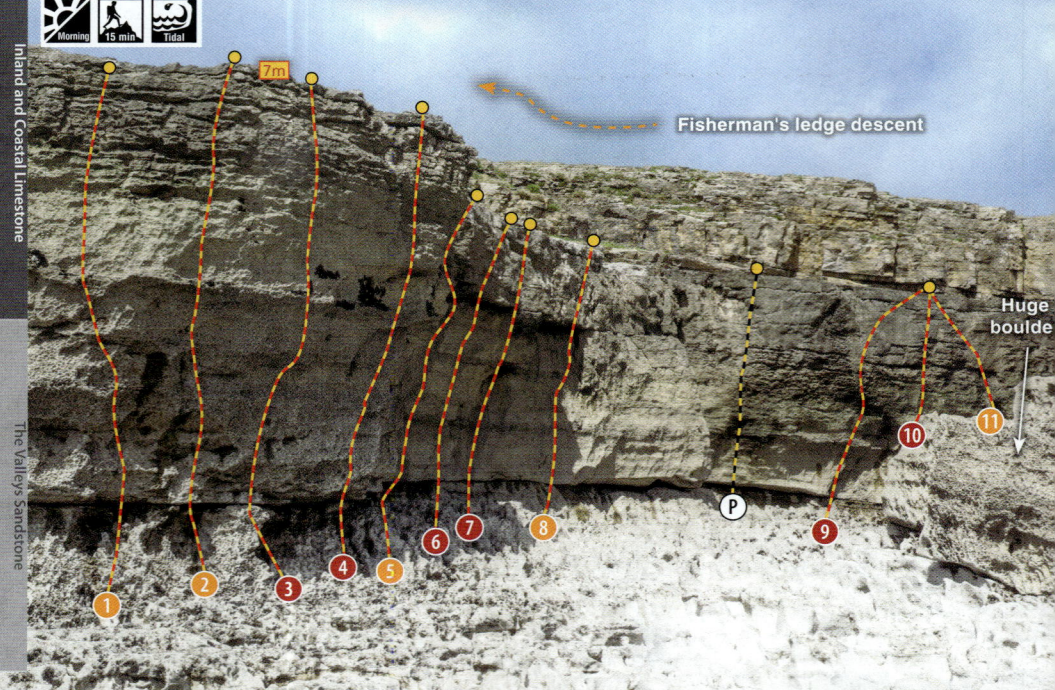

Second Inlet Temple Bay

12 Gift of the Gods .... 6b+
The fingery wall with just one bolt. Walk off.
FA. G.Ashmore 4.8.2011

13 Gods of Long Ashton 6a
The left-hand thin crack. Shares bolts with the next line.
FA. R.Thomas 2011

14 The Dark Force of Glamorgan .... 6a+
The right-hand crack. Shares bolts with the previous line.
FA. R.Thomas 2011

15 It's all Greek to me 5c
Juggy barnacle-encrusted pulling. Use a long sling on bolts on the ledge for a lower-off.
FA. R.Thomas 2011

16 One Less for the Spoiler 4c
The arete. Use a long sling on bolts on the ledge for a lower-off.
FA. R.Thomas 1987

17 Medusa Spares No Head .... 6a+
The left-hand line has a tricky finish.
FA. R.Thomas, E.Travers-Jones, G.Ashmore 12.10.2014

18 Prometheus Bound 5c
FA. R.Thomas, G.Ashmore 9.2014

19 Oceanus Aches 6a
FA. R.Thomas, E.Travers-Jones, G.Ashmore 9.2014

20 Dodecanese Dalliance 5b
FA. R.Thomas, G.Ashmore, E.Travers-Jones 10.2014

Temple Bay — Cave Inlet

Cave Inlet

These two good sections of cliff are dotted with caves and offer well-bolted routes with some exhilarating lines. Many of the routes take steep ground with good juggy rails that favour long arms and short legs.

Approach (map and overview p.296) - The Cave Inlet is tidal and can be climbed on for around 3 hours either side of low tide. Walk along the beach until the wall is encountered.

Descent - Most of the routes have lower-offs. Routes 1 and 2 and 10 to 12 have belay bolts set back from the edge - use a long sling to set up a lower-off. This can be set-up and retrieved by an easy scramble up to the fisherman's ledges on the left.

Conditions - The caves can be damp if the sun has not been out or the weather is humid.

❶ The Barnacle Bill........ 6b
The steep, short and crusty hanging arete. Long sling needed for lower-off.
FA. R.Thomas, R.Phillips 30.9.2014

❷ Canaan Grunts .... HVS 4c
The barnacle-encrusted chimney is trad. Walk off or use a long sling on the lower-off of *The Barnacle Bill*.
FA. R.Thomas, N.O'Neill 4.7.2014

**❸ Hundred Years of Reflection
.... 6b+**
Upside down barnacle pulling leading to the ledge of *Zacchaeus Repents* - finish up direct to a chain lower-off.
FA. R.Thomas, N.O'Neill 8.2014

❹ Dulce et Decorum est.... 6b+
Make very steep moves from the right-hand side of the cave around and onto the wall before joining and finishing as for *Hundred Years of Reflection*.
FA. E.Travers-Jones, R.Thomas 23.9.2014

❺ Zacchaeus Repents...... 6b+
Move up and then out left to steep rib and ledge. Head up and back right to a shared lower-off with *Chargeable Event*.
FA. R.Thomas 2011

❻ Chargeable Event....... 6a
Up the barnacles to some fun steep moves and a lower-off in the corner.
FA. R.Thomas 2011

❼ Lips off my Shofarot. 6a+
Climb easily up the lower wall and make a powerful pull up into the hanging corner. Finish up the corner via technical bridging.
FA. R.Thomas, R.Phillips, R.Leyshon 2011

❽ Lane Discipline .... 6a+
Head up the easy lower wall, from where steep and committing moves are needed to pass the overhang.
FA. R.Thomas, R.Phillips, R.Leyshon 26.4.2014

❾ Hogging the Mid Lane... 6b
Good juggy climbing taking the line just left of the upper cave, with one long move.
FA. R.Thomas, E.Travers-Jones 8.3.2014

❿ Life in the Slow Lane .... 6b+
Steep stuff up the left-hand overhanging arete.
FA. R.Thomas, G.Ashmore 12.4.2012

⓫ Quiet Flows the Jordan 5b
Steep climbing up the right-hand side of the cave.
FA. R.Thomas 2011

⓬ Sultan's Spring 5c
The wall needs a leg-up or jump for the first holds.
FA. R.Thomas 1987

Cave Inlet Temple Bay 303

13 Blowing the Ram's Horn .... VS 4c
The slim corner is trad.
FA. R.Thomas, G.Royle 1986

14 Climb a Sycamore Tree .... HVS 5a
Move easily up to a hanging arete and then steeply up this to finish via ledges.
FA. R.Thomas 1987

15 Tumbledown .... HS 4b
Start up *Climb a Sycamore Tree* and then take the ramp right.
FA. R.Thomas 1986

16 Consequentialist Perfectionism HVS 5a
Make some steep but juggy pulls to ledges.
FA. R.Thomas 1987

17 Converted Traditionalist 5b
Short, sharp jugs over roof lead to ledgy section.
FA. R.Thomas, A.Rosier, M.Tocek 26.11.2018

18 Perverted Exhibitionist .. 6a
Very steep and pumpy but on good jugs.
FA. R.Thomas, A.Rosier, M.Tocek 26.11.2018

19 Nietzche's Niche 5c
Spectacular climbing. Short and pumpy moves passing a couple of overhangs. *Photo p.305*.
FA. R.Thomas, R.Phillips 8.2012

20 Inverted Mentalist ...... 6b+
Pull through the wide roof via a sea of jugs.
FA. A.Rosier, R.Thomas 20.11.2018

21 Reverted Revisionist . 6a+
Similar in style and quality to *Nietzche's Niche*.
FA. R.Thomas, E.Travers-Jones 28.7.2012

22 Raft of the Medusa ..... 6c+
Rightward variation finish to *Reverted Revisionist* across the rail in the horizontal roof to the lower-off of *Calypso Cannibal*.
FA. A.Rosier 26.11.2018

23 Cannibal Calypso 7a
Bridge up the left side of the cave to a ledge. Step right and head straight up to the roof. From a horn at the back of the roof, break out left across the horizontal roofs to a lower-off.
FA. A.Rosier 26.11.2018

24 Swinging the Lead 6c
The right-hand finish to *Cannibal Calypso*.
FA. A.Rosier, R.Thomas 22.11.2018

25 Diverted Existentialist .... 6a+
Prickly wall and stepped roof on the right edge of the cave.
FA. R.Thomas, N.O'Neill 10.2019

26 Cartesian Dualism 5b
Climb just left of the leaning prow and right of the cave.
FA. R.Thomas 2012

27 Descartes' Dithers ... 5c
The leaning prow is a good outing. *Photo p.297*.
FA. R.Thomas 2012

28 Archimedes Screws ...... 6a+
Wild moves over the big overhangs.
FA. R.Thomas 2012

29 The Burning Glass 6b
Power up direct after the first overhang.
FA. R.Thomas, E.Travers-Jones 10.2012

30 Siege of Syracuse 6b
Break right from *The Burning Glass* steep pitch taking a series of rails and overhangs on good but spaced holds. A fine climb.
FA. R.Thomas, G.Ashmore 23.8.2012

Long Wall

A compact short wall of lower-grade lines that are the first/last to be climbable on a falling/rising tide.

Approach (map and overview p.296) - The Long Wall is tidal and can be climbed on for around 3 hours either side of low tide. This is the first wall of stratified rock with bolted lines encountered on the approach.

Descent - Routes 6 to 10 have belay bolts set back from the edge - use a long sling to set up a lower-off. This can be set up and retrieved by an easy scramble up to the fisherman's ledges on the left. The cliff top path is easily gained from the ledges above the climbs.

Conditions - The base of the cliff takes a little time to dry out once the tide has gone out.

❶ Socrates Sucks............ 6a
Climb the left-hand side of the arete avoiding the ledges on the left. The roof at the start is tough.
FA. R.Thomas 2011

❷ Kant Hooks 4c
Not as easy as it looks, better (and a bit harder) if done direct without reaching out to the right. Nice climbing.
FA. R.Thomas 2011

❸ Rude Buoys .... HS 4a
Climb straight up the wall avoiding easy ground on the right.
FA. J.Gallacher, M.Moore 23.6.2015

❹ Sartre Flies .... M
The right-leading line of ledges is an easy way to get to the top.
FA. R.Thomas 2011

❺ Sartre's Underlay .... VS 4c
A direct line, with no protection, crossing *Satre Flies*.
FA. R.Thomas 8.1987

❻ The Carpetbagger.......... 4c
The first bolted line right of the ledges of *Sartres Flies*. Two bolts and a thread which can be backed up with a mid-sized nut.
FA. R.Thomas 5.1987

❼ Fermat's Last Theorem 5b
The wall past glue-in bolts.
FA. R.Thomas 2011

❽ Orestes' Suffering....... 6a+
A sharp and hard starting sequence.
FA. R.Thomas 2011

❾ Electra's Revenge 5c
Past some threads high up.
FA. R.Thomas 2011

❿ Probing Proctologist .... 6a+
The final line on the right. Climb left of the bolts at the grade.
FA. R.Thomas, R.Phillips 8.2012

⓫ Heading for a Sea of Tears 5c
A right-to-left girdle finishing as for *Sartre Flies*. A good outing when the tide is in.
FA. N.O'Neill, R.Thomas 2012

Bridget Glaister negotiating some typical Cave Inlet stacked overhangs on *Nietzche's Niche* (5c) - *p.303* - at Temple Bay. Photo: Glaister Collection

Castle Upon Alun

An old quarry located in a tranquil setting that has a number of its walls developed. The majority of the well established climbing is on a steep slab of excellent well-bolted limestone and offers some hard, thin and fingery routes. If the wall has not been climbed on regularly some of the climbs become dirty and will probably need a brush.

Approach

If you are approaching from Bridgend, turn left off of the B4265 into the village of Ewenny (signed Corntown). Follow the road past a shop and go right at a fork towards Wick. Follow the road keeping right at another fork to a small junction by a house. Turn right here and go down the lane to a parking spot on the right just before a ford. Cross the ford and walk along the road to a viaduct. 200m beyond the viaduct a cobbled track on the right leads uphill to a gate. 30m beyond the gate take a vague path on the right. The path contours around the wooded hillside below a small escarpment, and passes a fence to arrive at the top of the wall. Walk down rightwards to gain the base of the quarry. An alternative parking spot is at a small pull-in just beyond the viaduct.

Conditions

The Main Slab sees little sun, whilst the Opposite Walls get sun until mid afternoon. The crags dry fairly quickly as the quarry is sheltered and takes little seepage, however if humid the Main Slab should be avoided. Some of the climbs may need a clean unless they have seen regular traffic (especially on the Main Slab).

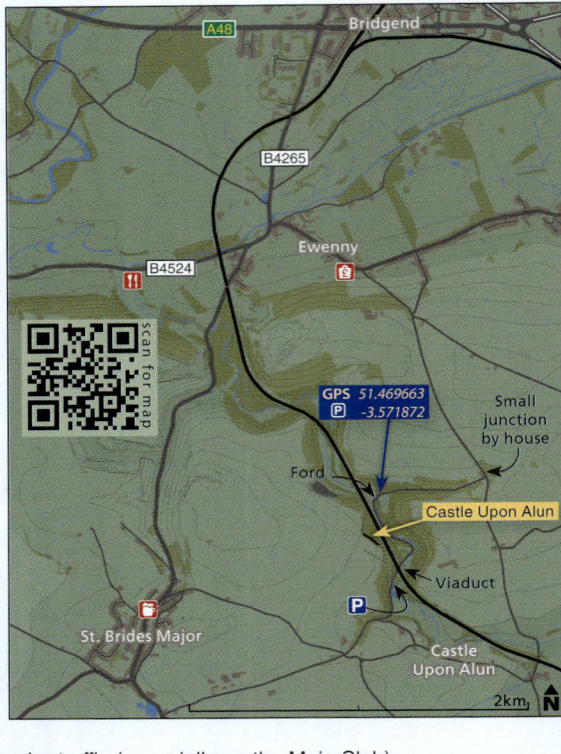

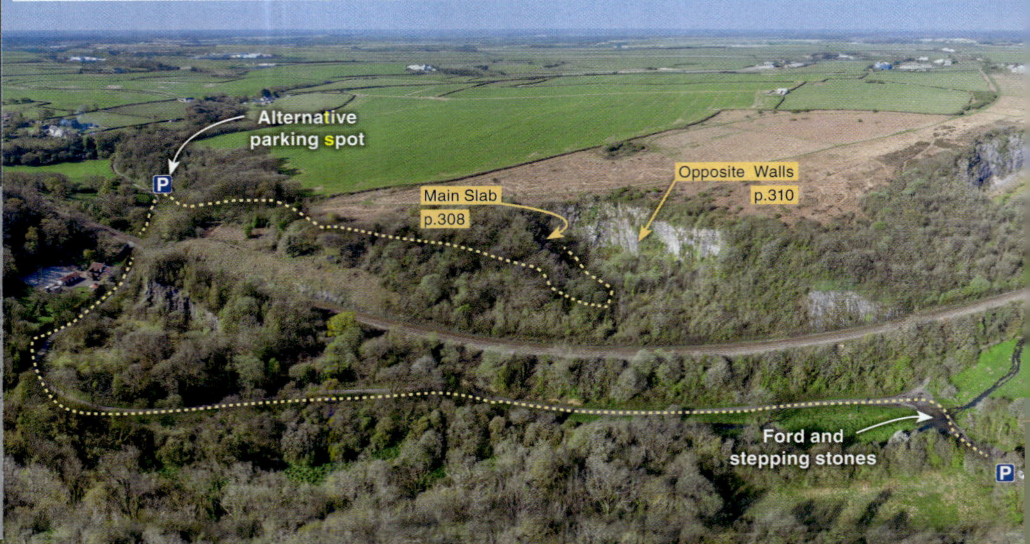

GPS 51.469663, -3.571872

Castle Upon Alun

Jay Astbury inching up the sustained and intricate *A Freem of White Horses* (6b) - *p.308* - on the Ma n Slab at Castle Upon Alun. Photo: Mark Glaister

Castle Upon Alun — Main Slab

Main Slab
A steep slab that has some worthwhile and fingery lines.
Approach (map and overview p.306) - The approach is down the right-hand side (looking out) of the crag.
Conditions - The slab has a shady aspect and sees little sun. Humidity can be a problem.

❶ Jump on the Gravy Train 4c
The first short bolted line on the left.
FA. R.Thomas 8.2016

❷ Off the Rails 4c
Stay on the line to avoid a small amount of shattered rock.
FA. R.Thomas 2005

❸ The Fat Controller 5c
Climb the wall just left of an arete directly behind the tree.
FA. R.Thomas 2005

❹ Scrape the Bottom of the Barrel . 5c
The blocky corner moving right over the roof.
FA. R.Thomas, E.Travers-Jones 28.7.2016

❺ Eugene Genie 7a
Follow the initial line of bolts with a thin start and hard finish.
FA. E.Travers-Jones 1995

❻ Cordoba Express . 6c+
Start up *Eugene Genie* and, at its first bolt, move up and right to a jug. From the jug finish direct on still tricky ground.
FA. R.Thomas 1995

❼ Matalanafesto 6c
A direct start to *Cordoba Express* past two bolts.
FA. G.Ashmore 29.5.2005

❽ Barry Freight .... 6b+
A thin initial sequence gains some better holds that allow a fairly direct line to be followed on the upper wall.
FA. R.Thomas 1995

❾ A Freem of White Horses . 6b
A good pitch when clean. Move up to a shallow hole and then make fingery pulls up the wall on edges and pockets.
Photo p.307.
FA. A.Freem pre -1991

❿ California Freeming .. 6b
An excellent exercise. Reasonable holds lead to a well-defined slot. Reach for a crack and finish direct to a lower-off.
FA. A.Freem pre-1991

⓫ Pubic Enema .... 6b+
Climb direct to a poor crack that leads to a square-cut groove.
FA. R.Thomas 1995

⓬ Freeming of Jeannie . HVS 5a
Climb the right-leaning thin crack and finish by moving into the bolt line of *Branch Line*.
FA. A.Freem pre-1991

⓭ Branch Line 6a
Thin climbing at the start. Unfortunately this line gets dirty.
FA. R.Thomas 1995

Main Slab Castle Upon Alun

14 Feed the Five Thousand.. 6c
Climb up and through the first alcove.
FA. R.Thomas 25.5.2017

15 Maris Piper are Best......... 6c
Head through the second alcove above the second step on the slope below the face. A stiff pull onto the steep slab above the alcove leads to a shared lower-off.
FA. R.Thomas, R.Phillips, G.Leyshan 24.5.2017

16 Anal Retention 6c
Up and right of the alcove at the base of the crag is a white section of rock. Climb this by technical moves.
FA. R.Thomas 1995

17 Banal Pretention 6c
Gain a slot by a technical sequence and continue with difficulty.
FA. R.Thomas 1995

18 Bottom Rail......... 6b+
Start as for *The Trainspotter* and traverse top of *Branch Line*.
FA. R.Thomas G.Davies 26.7.2016

19 The Trainspotter........ 6b
A tricky start gain slightly easier ground above.
FA. R.Thomas 1995

20 Trolley Service Suspended ... 6b
Make a difficult mantelshelf move to gain widely spaced holds.
FA. R.Thomas, M.Hurst 13.8.2016

21 Weak Lemon Drink.......... 6b+
A difficult start is followed by a dyno for a big triangular pocket.
FA. R.Thomas 1995

22 In The Sidings 6a
The last vertical line on the wall at the top of the bank.
FA. R.Thomas, G.Davies 26.7.2016

23 Top Rail 6b
Start as for *In The Sidings* and then make a rising hand traverse left, finishing at a lower-off in a small corner.
FA. R.Thomas, E.Travers-Jones 8.2016

Line of rusty old bolts

Castle Upon Alun — Opposite Walls

Opposite Walls

On the other side of the quarry from the slab is a series of tall vegetated walls. Some of the lines have now become overgrown but many are still regularly climbed and remain clean.

Approach (map and overview p.306) - Walk along a path from the Main Slab to below the first routes.
Conditions - The walls receive sun until mid afternoon.

There are two loose bolted lines on the left (not described)

1 Freeming at the Gusset 6a
The left side of the wall, passing some large orange scars.
FA. R.Thomas 9.2016

2 Freempie 5c
Takes the short wall, ledge and final layback of *Freeming at the Gusset*.
FA. R.Thomas, E.Chapman 15.9.2016

3 Galena Puts Lead in your Pencil 2 5c
The rib and crack to a lower-off right of a high roof.
FA. R.Thomas, G.Ashmore 31.8.2016

4 Plum Bob 1 5b
An easy start leads to a short groove.
FA. R.Thomas, G.Ashmore 31.8.2016

5 Burton Line 1 5b
The groove to the right of *Plum Bob*, starting direct via a rail.
FA. R.Thomas, E.Chapman, J.Wollacot 1.9.2016

6 Joys of Fatherhood .... 6a+
The wall left of the crack followed by *Quadcam of Solace*.
FA. D.Emanuel 2017

7 Quadcam of Solice 1 5b
Follow the left-trending crack-line.
FA. R.Thomas, D.Emanuel 17.9 2016

8 Crack Liqour .... 1 6b+
The crack in the short wall just right of *Quadcam of Solice*.
FA. R.Thomas, R.Phillips G.Leysham 23.9.2016

9 The Freem Team 5b
Gain and climb the right arete of the pillar.
FA. R.Thomas, R.Phillips G.Leysham 23.9.2016

Opposite Walls **Castle Upon Alun** 311

10 Sticky Fingers 4c
Start as for the following then step left to a layback crack.
FA. R.Thomas, N.O'Neill, R.Phillips 9.9.2016

11 Fickle Finger of Fate............ 4c
The groove to a tree/sling lower-off on the right.
FA. R.Thomas, N.O'Neill 7.9.2016

12 Knuckle Down 4a
The groove to a lower-off on the right shared with *Ring Finger*.
FA. R.Thomas, N.O'Neill 4.10.2016

13 Ring Finger 4c
Climb a shattered groove, avoiding a loose block at the top.
FA. R.Thomas, N.O'Neill 4.10.2016

14 Finger Flicking Good 5c
The layback crack to a shared belay with *Fingertip Mistress*.
FA. R.Thomas, R.Phillips 4.10.2016

15 Fingertip Mistress 6a
Gain and climb the crack left of the roof of *Knee Trembler*.
FA. R.Thomas, R.Phillips 4.10.2016

16 Knee Trembler 6b
Start up *Bush Trimmer's Corner* and then take the overhangs to its left.
FA. R.Thomas, E.Travers-Jones 25.9.2016

17 Bush Trimmer's Corner....... 5c
The slim open corner at the far right of the terrace.
FA. R.Thomas, R.Phillips G.Leyshon 23.9.2016

18 Licence to Drill .... 6c+
The left-hand side of the steep wall, passing the large geode.
FA. A.Rosier 13.11.2016

19 For Your Arms Only 7b
The left-hand shot hole, bearing right to a undercling in the headwall. Make a big move to a crystal pocket at the apex.
FA. A.Rosier 13.11.2016

20 Dyno Another Day 7a
The centre of the wall is a little snappy to start. Fine pocket pulling on the headwall accesses a dynamic finish.
FA. R.Thomas 21.10.2016

21 Out of Pocket.................. 6c
Steep pocket cranking right of *Dyno Another Day*.
FA. R.Thomas, R.Phillips 10.11.2016

22 Cold Finger .... 6b+
The crack and subsidiary arete/ramp.
FA. R.McAllister, A.Rosier 30.11.2016

Costa del Major

| Grade Spread | 6 | 44 | 20 | 6 | - |

An extensive horizontally banded limestone sea-cliff that has numerous sport pitches across the grades. Most of the cliff is mildly tidal during calm weather apart from Stout Point where more care is needed as access is quickly cut-off. Seepage can be a problem on some of the routes but once this recedes the faces dry rapidly after rain. The climbing is generally on the steep to very steep side and on good holds - if you can reach them! There is loose rock and a helmet should worn by leader and belayer.

Approach
Enter the village of Llanwit Major and follow signs for its town centre and then the beach. On exiting the village, park in a lay-by near a small stone bridge. Walk a little further along the road and then go left to Rosedew Farm. At the farm go straight on along a track/footpath to the cliff top and stile. Turn left and after 125m locate a down-climb descent past ledges and a steep wall to the beach (there are bolts in place for an abseil/belay if the down-climb is deemed too risky). All the various sectors are approached from this point.

Conditions
The crag catches the sun and is usually sheltered from the wind down at sea-level. Seepage can be persistent particularly so at Stout Point.

Tides
Most sections are accessible for four hours either side of low tide but Stout Point has a shorter window of around 2 hours either side of low tide.

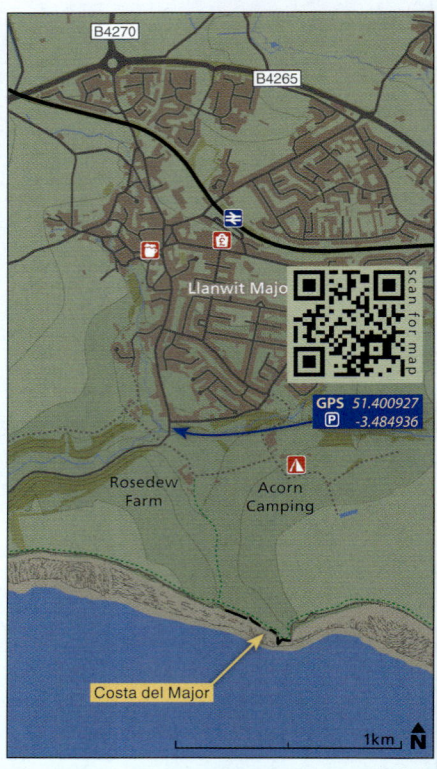

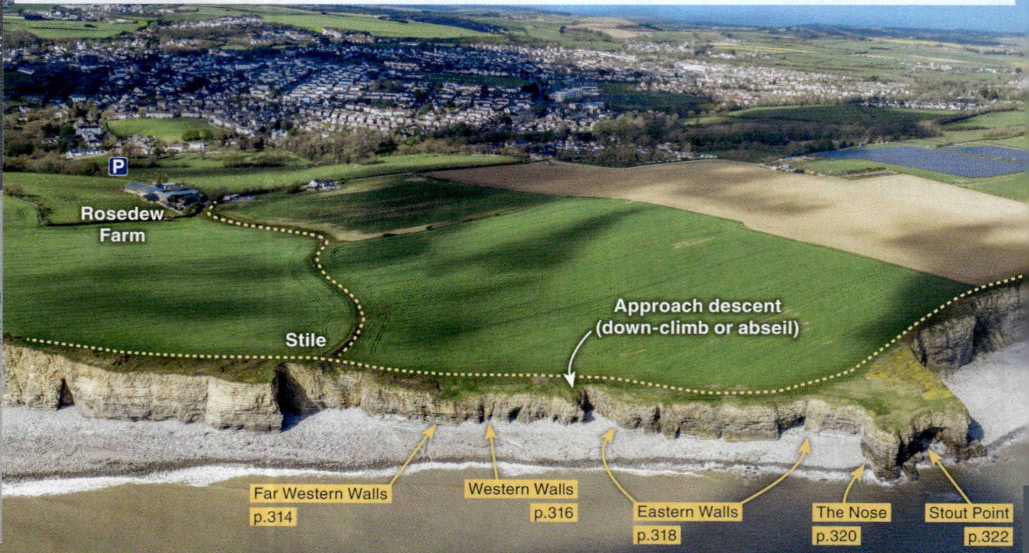

Costa del Major 313

Sun, sea and a stiff neck are more than likely on the menu at the super steep cliffs of the Costa del Major. Here Matt Lawrence is doing battle with *Operation Midnight Climax* (7a) - *p.323* - at the Stout Point section of crag.
Photo: Eben Muse

Costa del Major — Far Western Walls

Far Western Walls
Lots of closely packed pitches that allow for some quick ticks in the mid-grades

Approach (map and overview p.312) - From the beach at the base of the descent, walk right (facing out) for 100m to the sector.

Tides - The routes are accessible for around 4 hours either side of low tide during calm sea conditions.

Conditions - Sunny but seepage can be persistent on some of the lines.

❶ Wonder Girl .... 6a+
Ascend the steep lower section and then climb directly past a roof and finish up the exhilarating headwall.
FA. S.Morton, A.Seren 8.9.2020

❷ Arizona Ted .... 6b+
Similar to *Wonder Girl* and on the same good rock.
FA. R.Thomas, Gandalf, T.Roberts 6.2022

❸ Czech this Out 6b
The walls and overhangs. Avoid the dodgy block on the left.
FA. R.Thomas, Gandalf, G.Torrance 22.6.2022

❹ Pilsen Power 6a
Overcome the low roof and then head up before traversing up leftwards to the lower-off of *Czech this Out*.
FA. R.Thomas, Gandalf, E.Chapman 22.6.2022

❺ Break Stuff 6a
Begin up the steep mini buttress and then follow a line of holds leftwards across the wall to a lower-off.
FA. T.Williams, S.Rawlinson 2020

❻ Gimme a Break 5b
Climb the first steep section of *Break Stuff* and then head directly up the headwall.
FA. T.Williams, S.Rawlinson 2020

❼ Dreaming of Cleaner Thing's 4c
A good pitch on nice holds. Start to the right of the mini buttress and move up steep ground to the headwall.
FA. S.Rawlinson, T.Williams 2020

Far Western Walls Costa del Major

8 Smash and Grab 6b
Start to the left of a shallow recess. A tough start could be off putting but better holds do follow. Unfortunately this line is often dirty as it is under a drainage line.
FA. S.Rawlinson, T.Williams 2020

9 Up and Under 6a
Begin just right of the shallow recess at head height. A stiff quick pull leads to better holds.
FA. S.Rawlinson, T.Williams 2020

10 Simple Arithmetic 6a
Climb to, and up, the small corner.
FA. R.Thomas, E.Chapman 2022

11 F*c*orisation 5c
The overhangs and wall to a shared lower-off.
FA. R.Thomas, E.Chapman 5.5.2022

12 Algie's Bra .... 6a+
The left-hand side of the roof to a shared lower-off with *Trigonometry*.
FA. R.Thomas, E.Chapman 2020

13 Trigonometry .... 6a+
Follow triangular jugs up onto the short head-wall.
FA. S.Rawlinson, R.Thomas 2020

14 Calculus .... 6a+
The right-hand side of the roof and depression to a lower-off on the left shared with *Trigonometry*.
FA. R.Thomas, E.Chapman 2020

15 Sums it Up 6a
The left side of roof to shared lower-off by large block.
FA. R.Thomas, E.Chapman 2020

16 Simultaneous Equations 5b
Take on the right-hand side of the roof to a shared lower-off.
FA. R.Thomas E.Chapman 2020

17 Lolo's Geode 5c
The slim pillar passing a crystal pocket.
FA. G.Torrance, R.Evans, 12.2020

Western Walls

More pitches in the 5th and 6th grades based on steep horizontally banded walls and overhangs.

Approach (map and overview p.312) - From the base of the descent walk right (facing out) and the sector is immediately encountered.

Tides - The routes are accessible for around 4 hours either side of low tide during calm sea conditions.

Conditions - Sunny but seepage can be persistent on some of the lines.

❶ **Crystal Balls.................** ☐ 5b
The arete left of the yellow slab.
FA. R.Thomas, E.Chapman 2020

❷ **Lolo's Ammonite...............** ☐ 5b
A short pitch to a lower-off below the ammonite roof.
FA. G.Torrance, R.Evans 1.12.2020

❸ **Pulling on Puppies..........** 🚩 ☐ 6b
Follow the juggy overhanging arete.
FA. R.Evans, E.Rowley 6.12.2020

❹ **Grasp the Devils Toenail........** ☐ 5a
The yellow wall to the right of the chimney.
FA. E.Chapman, R.Thomas 2020

❺ **The Devils in the Detail........** ☐ 5a
The corner in the upper half of the face has a steep start.
FA. R.Thomas, E.Chapman 2020

❻ **Devil of a Time.........** 🚩 ☐ 6a
Short and steep passing three overhangs.
FA. R.Thomas, G.Ashmore 2020

❼ **Devil's Playground......** 🚩 ☐ 5b
A steep outing to a shared lower-off on the right.
FA. R.Thomas, E.Chapman 2020

❽ **Devil's Spawn...............** 🚩 ☐ 4c
Short and sweet.
FA. R.Thomas, G.Ashmore 2020

❾ **Cam Slut...................** 🚩 ☐ 4b
Romp up the cave sidewall via a shallow corner.
FA. R.Thomas, Gandalf 7.2022

❿ **Pretty Pussy...............** 🚩 ☐ 6a
Pull directly over the high roof.
FA. R.Thomas, E.Chapman 2021

⓫ **Squatting Dog.............** 🚩 ☐ 5a
Overcome the mid-height roof on its left and finish at the lower-off shared with *Pretty Pussy*.
FA. R.Thomas, E.Chapman 10.2020

⓬ **Crouching Tiger, Hidden Badger**
.... 🚩 ☐ 5b
Fun wall climb on jugs up the scooped wall.
FA. S.Rawlinson, R.Thomas 2020

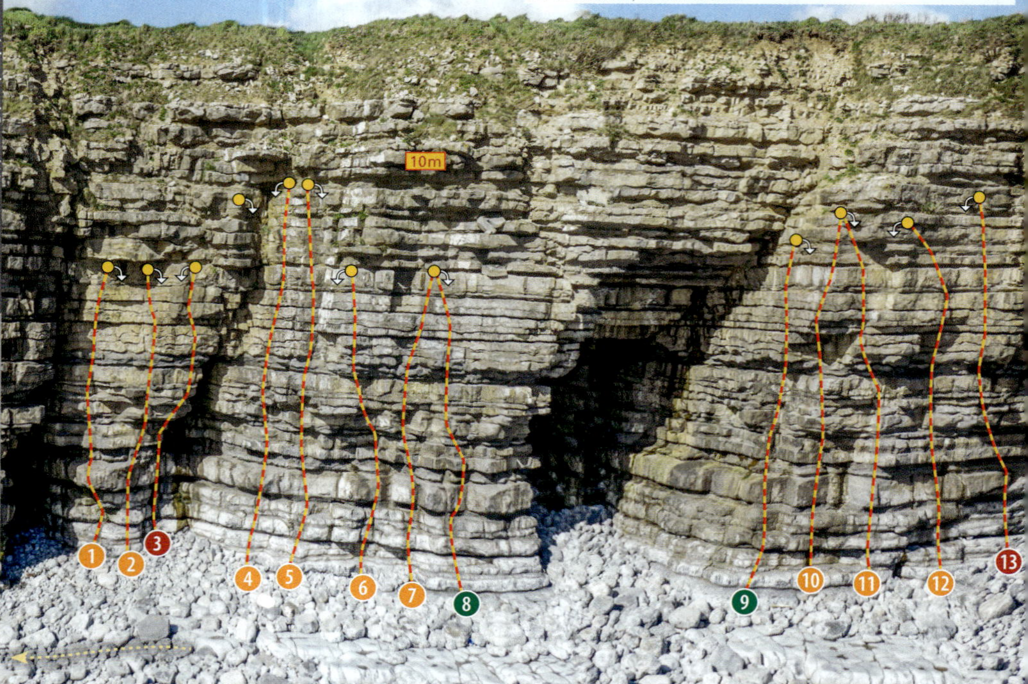

Western Walls Costa del Major

13 Busy Beaver ⭐ 6b
The stack of overhangs right of *Crouching Tiger, Hidden Badger*.
FA. R.Thomas, G.Ashmore 11.2020

14 Lola ⭐⭐ 6b+
Steep ground laced with jugs.
FA. R.Evans, G.Torrance 1.12.2020

15 Showgirl 6b+
Steep jugs lead to a rockover leftwards. Continue above to a shared lower-off with *Lola*.
FA. R.Evans, G.Torrance 26.11.2020

16 Cock-a-doodle 6b
A steep and reachy start gains more steep pulling above.

17 Cock's Crow ⭐ 6a+
The roof and hanging groove.
FA. R.Thomas, M.Woodfield 11.2022

18 Strutting Cock 6a
Steep groove on left side of the wall.
FA. R.Thomas, G.Ashmore 2020

19 Broody Hen 5b
Climb the wall to the left of some jutting blocks to a shared lower-off with *Strutting Cock*.
FA. R.Thomas, G.Ashmore 2020

20 Peasant Phucker 5c
The blocky rib and wall above it to a lower-off.
FA. R.Thomas, E.Chapman 2020

21 Pheasant Plucker ⭐ 6b
Climb up the right-hand side of the cave before trending leftwards to a shared lower-off with *Peasant Phucker*.
FA. R.Thomas, G.Ashmore 2020

22 Ground Bait 6a
The corner to a high overhang and lower-off above it.
FA. R.Thomas, E.Chapman 8.2021

23 Old Repro Bait ⭐ 5c
Walls and overlaps to a shared lower-off.
FA. R.Thomas, E.Chapman 7.2021

24 Mash yer Bait 5a
The left-facing corner in a band of sharp calcite crystal.
FA. R.Thomas, M.Jordan 25.7.2021

25 Dont Swallow the Bait Mate 6b+
Steep stuff passing many overhangs.
FA. R.Thomas, E.Chapman 9.2020

26 White Bait 6b+
A pumpy excursion up left side of cave.
FA. R.Thomas, E.Chapman 9.2020

27 Mister Bait ⭐ 6a
The right wall of the cave. Short but steep.
FA. R.Thomas, E.Chapman, M.Weale 9.2020

28 Jail Bait 6a
A steep juggy romp follows a tough start.
FA. R.Thomas, E.Chapman, M.Weale 9.2020

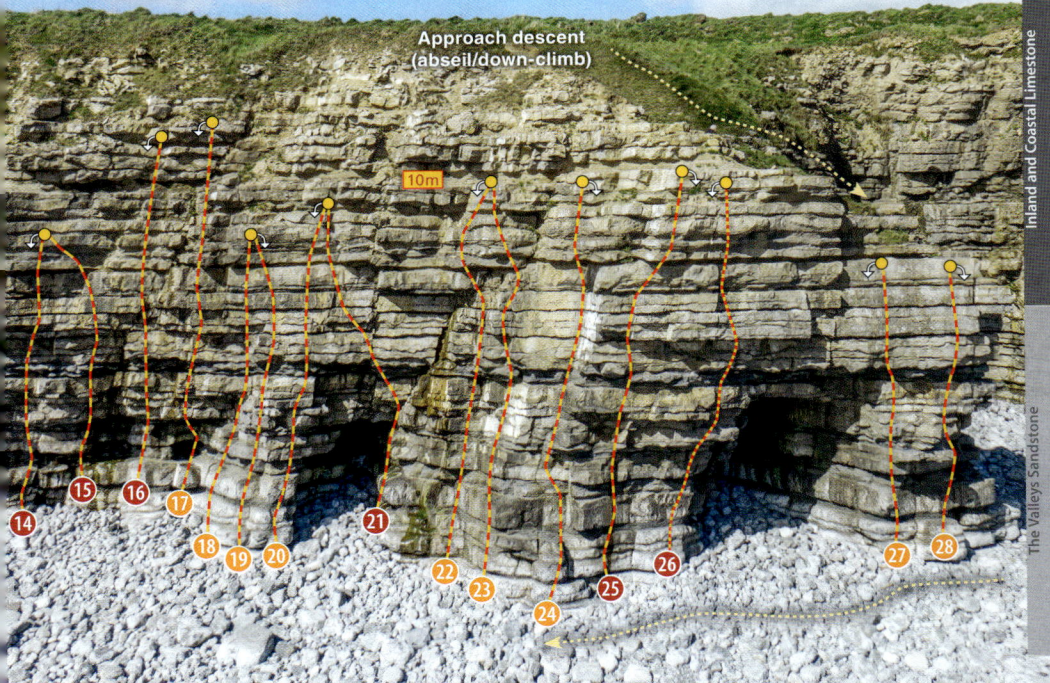

Costa del Major — Eastern Walls

Eastern Walls

A variety of sectors with a collection of mid-grade routes. Take care not to get stranded on the ledges under the right-hand routes once the tide starts to come in.

Approach (map and overview p.312) - From the base of the descent, the routes are on the opposite wall. Another cluster of routes is 100m along the beach.

Tides - The routes are accessible for around 4 hours either side of low tide during calm sea conditions.

Conditions - Sunny but seepage can be persistent on the left-hand side of the Eastern Walls.

1 Robbin' Dog 4c
The wall opposite the descent has a steep start.
FA. R.Thomas, E.Chapman 4.2021

2 Runt of the litter .... 6a+
The groove with black thread at the start.
FA. R.Thomas, R.Joseph 2021

3 Stranded Dogfish .... 6b+
Flail onto the prominent block and then over the steep roof.
FA. R.Thomas 3.2021

4 Dog's Blocks 5c
Climb the blocky groove to a shared lower-off.
FA. R.Thomas 7.1.2021

5 Pining Dog .... 6b+
The pillar left of a damp chimney/cave. An easy stroll to an awkward move to gain a ledge.
FA. R.Evans, G.Torrance 1.12.2020

6 Filthy old Bitch 6b
The banded wall right of the damp chimney/cave.
FA. R.Thomas, G.Ashmore, M.Hirst 4.2021

7 Damp Bitch 5c
The right side of the banded wall.
FA. R.Thomas, G.Torrance 1.12.2020

8 Dog with Two Ticks 5c
40m right of *Damp Bitch* is a high corner near damp streaks.
FA. R.Thomas, S.Cann 4.2022

9 Bastard Wing .... 6a+
Another 60m along the beach. Amble up the lower wall but take good care not to stall on the steeper upper section.
FA. R.Thomas, E.Chapman 9.2020

10 Waiting in the Wings 6a
Follow the thin calcite seam to a steeper upper section.
FA. FA. R.Thomas, N.O'Neill 8.2020

Costa del Major 319

Aaron Martin tackling the typical bands of horizontally-bedded limestone on the route *Wing Commander* (6b) - *this page* - at the Eastern Walls, Stout Point. Photo: Carl Ryan

11 Wings of Derision .... 6a+
The faint corner steepening towards the top.
FA. R.Thomas, N.O'Neill 8.2020

12 Wingman 6a
Take rounded breaks to a small roof and final mantel.
FA. R.Thomas, E.Chapman 8.2020

13 Wing Commander 6b
A steep start on good jams eases above. The lower-off is on the sidewall to the right. *This page*.
FA. R.Thomas, E.Chapman 2020

Costa del Major — The Nose

The Nose
A set of well positioned routes on the protruding nose which is a bit more tidal than the other walls to the left.

Approach (map and overview p.312) - From the base of the descent, turn left (looking out) and walk along the beach to the protruding headland and raised ledges from where the routes begin.

Tides - The routes are accessible for around 4 hours either side of low tide during calm sea conditions.

Conditions - Sunny but more exposed to the wind.

1 You Nose it's Fun 5b
The left-hand route off of ledges. An outrageous voyage on jugs, passing a small roof and high corner.
FA. R.Thomas, G.Torrance 8.2021

2 S'not on your Nellie 4c
The hanging corner on the left side of The Nose gained via a short roof.
FA. R.Thomas, G.Ashmore 3.2021

3 Nose Job 5c
The hanging groove.
FA. R.Thomas, E.Chapman 2.2021

4 S'not Yours .... 6a+
Climb the left wall of the *Septum* corner. Tricky finishing moves. *Photo p.23*.
FA. R.Thomas, E.Chapman 2.2021

5 Septum 5c
The dominating corner.
FA. R.Thomas, E.Chapman 2.2021

6 S'not Right 6a
The right wall of the *Septum* corner requires some steep pulls to reach the lower-off.
FA. E.Chapman 6.3.2021

7 Nosey Parcour 4c
Weave through the roofs beginning up *S'not Right*. *Photo opposite*.
FA. R.Thomas, E.Chapman 3.2021

Stout Point p.322

Joe Jones stretching out between the big holds on the well-positioned *Nosey Parcour* (4c) - *opposite* - at The Nose on the Costa del Major. This section has been the focus of development in the area and now has lots of routes in the lower grades and some much harder fayre in the cave of Stout Point. Photo: Carl Ryan

Costa del Major — Stout Point

Stout Point

An extremely steep venue that has a handful of very hard lines in its central section and some slightly less brutal lines on the margins. Seepage is a problem and access tidal so judging conditions and the timing of approach requires some investigation before visiting.

Approach (map and overview p.312) - From the base of the descent walk left (facing out) for around 100m and around the headland (tidal) to reach the crag.

Tides - The routes are accessible for around 2 hours either side of low tide during calm sea conditions.

Conditions - South facing but severely overhanging and as a consequence nearly always in the shade. Seepage is a major problem.

Stout Point — Costa del Major

❶ Operation Midnight Climax .. 🌀 ☐ **7a**
Begin from the ledge on the left of the cave. An easy start is followed by a long move and sterner and steeper ground above *Photo p.313*.
FA. S.Rawlinson 8.2020

❷ Stout Devout .... 🌀 ☐ **7b**
An interesting route. Climb the hanging arete to a hard pull to gain the big hole. Disorientating moves lead to a lower-off.
FA. R.Lamey 28.6.2020

❸ Homodeus .... ☐ **6b+**
A short steep pitch past some stepped roofs to a shared lower-off with *A Bit Shifty*.
FA. S.Rawlinson 8.2020

❹ A Bit Shifty .... 🌀 ☐ **6c+**
Break out left after the second bolt on *Dystopian Days*.
FA. R.Lamey 8.2020

❺ Dystopian Days .... 🌀 ☐ **7a+**
From the back of the cave super-steep climbing takes you through the strata breaks to a heart breaking final move.
FA. S.Rawlinson 8.2020

❻ Ben's Route .... 🌀 ☐ **7c+**
Climb direct past the lower overhangs then loop right after the final hard roof into *Day in, Day Stout*. Once the lip is reached follow this back left with difficulty until the bolts lead upwards to a lower-off.
FA. B.West 8.2020

❼ Day In, Day Stout .... 🌀 ☐ **7c+**
Grovel through a tricky move low down to easier climbing and some big powerful moves at the top.
FA. R.Lamey 8.2020

❽ Stout Bout .... 🌀 ☐ **7c+**
Begin up *Empire of the Midnight Sun* and link into *Day in, Day Stout*. The crux is right where you (don't) want it.
FA. R.Lamey 7.7.2020

❾ Empire of the Midnight Sun .. 🌀 ☐ **7b**
Fantastic climbing which takes a short but varied journey through some funky terrain. Quite a stretchy in a few places.
FA. S.Rawlinson 8.2020

❿ Apache .... 🌀 ☐ **6c+**
Brilliant climbing, start on the clean wall on the right hand side of the cave and make steady progress up steeper and steeper terrain.
FA. S.Rawlinson 8.2020

⓫ Species .... 🌀 ☐ **6b**
Start of the high ledge on the right hand side of the cave. Easy climbing leads to a roof and the belay.
FA. S.Rawlinson 8.2020

The Valleys Sandstone

Catrin Rose on the wall and rounded rib of *Slipping Into Luxury* (6b+) - *p.469* - at Llanbradach Quarry. This is one of the largest sandstone quarries in the South Wales Valleys and has many routes spread across its various walls. Photo: Marsha Balaeva

The Valleys Sandstone

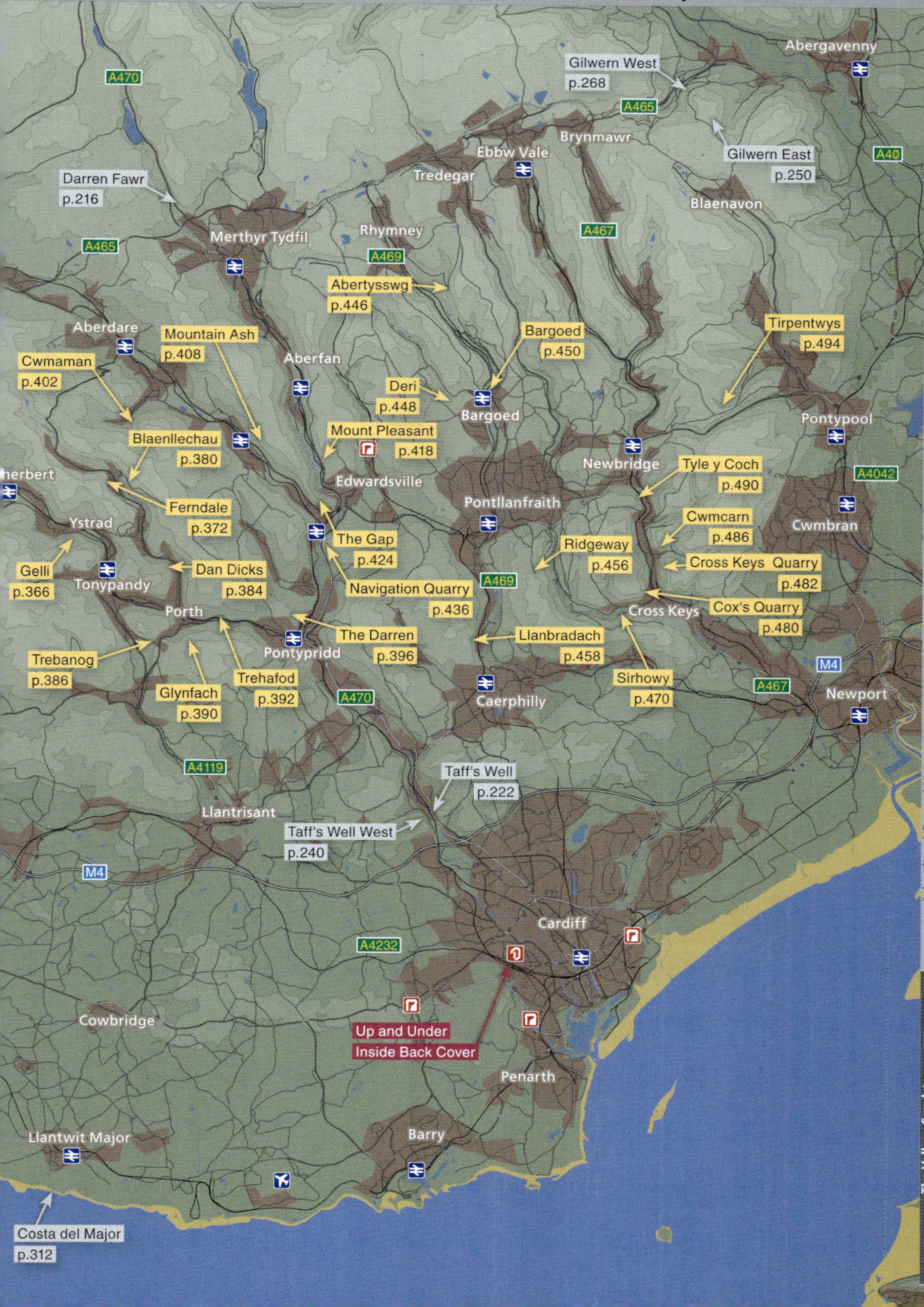
Gilwern West
p.268
Abergavenny
A470
A465
Brynmawr
Ebbw Vale
Gilwern East
p.250
A40
Tredegar
Darren Fawr
p.216
Blaenavon
Rhymney
A467
A465
Merthyr Tydfil
A469
Abertysswg
p.446
Aberdare
Mountain Ash
p.408
Bargoed
p.450
Tirpentwys
p.494
Cwmaman
p.402
Aberfan
Deri
p.448
Bargoed
Pontypool
Mount Pleasant
p.418
Blaenllechau
p.380
Newbridge
Tyle y Coch
p.490
A4042
herbert
Edwardsville
Pontllanfraith
Ferndale
p.372
Cwmcarn
p.486
Ystrad
Cwmbran
The Gap
p.424
Ridgeway
p.456
Cross Keys Quarry
p.482
Gelli
p.366
Dan Dicks
p.384
Tonypandy
A469
Navigation Quarry
p.436
Cross Keys
Cox's Quarry
p.480
Porth
The Darren
p.396
Llanbradach
p.458
Trebanog
p.386
Pontypridd
M4
Trehafod
p.392
Sirhowy
p.470
A467
Newport
Glynfach
p.390
A470
Caerphilly
A4119
Taff's Well
p.222
Llantrisant
Taff's Well West
p.240
M4
Cardiff
A4232
Up and Under
Inside Back Cover
Cowbridge
Penarth
Barry
Llantwit Major
Costa del Major
p.312

Carmarthenshire
Gower
Inland and Coastal Limestone
The Valleys Sandstone

Craig Cwm

Grade Spread | 2 | 28 | 27 | - | -

A long line of natural and quarried crags located in a tranquil rural setting. Craig Cwm has been developed with both sport and traditional routes but the majority are mid-grade sport routes. The climbing is technical and fingery and, although short, the routes pack in the difficulties.

Approach
From the M4, exit at junction 45 and follow signs to Clydach and then the village of Craig cefn-parc. Follow the road through the village and then on to a cattle grid. The parking is in a lay-by 250m back down the road from the cattle grid. You can turn beneath the crag after dropping kit off. DO NOT block the cattle grid, gates or bridleway. Walk up the road past the cattle grid to a boulder next to the road, then head uphill a short way to the crag. If there are more than two cars, plan ahead, park in the village and share a car, or climb elsewhere.

Conditions
The crag is exposed to the elements and set just below moorland but does get the sun in the morning and useful shade on hot days.

Access
The crag is on open access land next to several farms and small holdings that are worked daily. Please park considerately and be polite to any local residents.

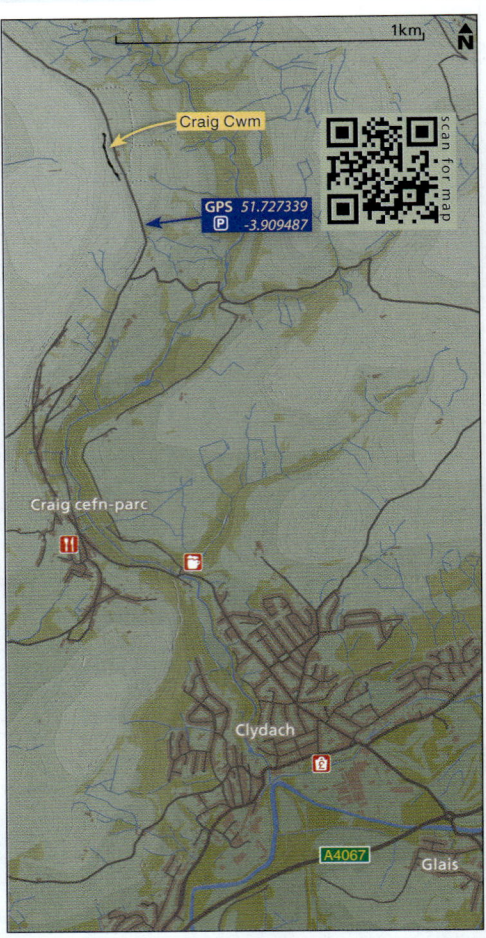

GPS 51.727339 / -3.909487

Aaron Martin on the fine scooped slabs of *Gwyn's Road* (6b) - *p.333* - at the Left-hand Bay, Craig Cwm. Photo: Carl Ryan

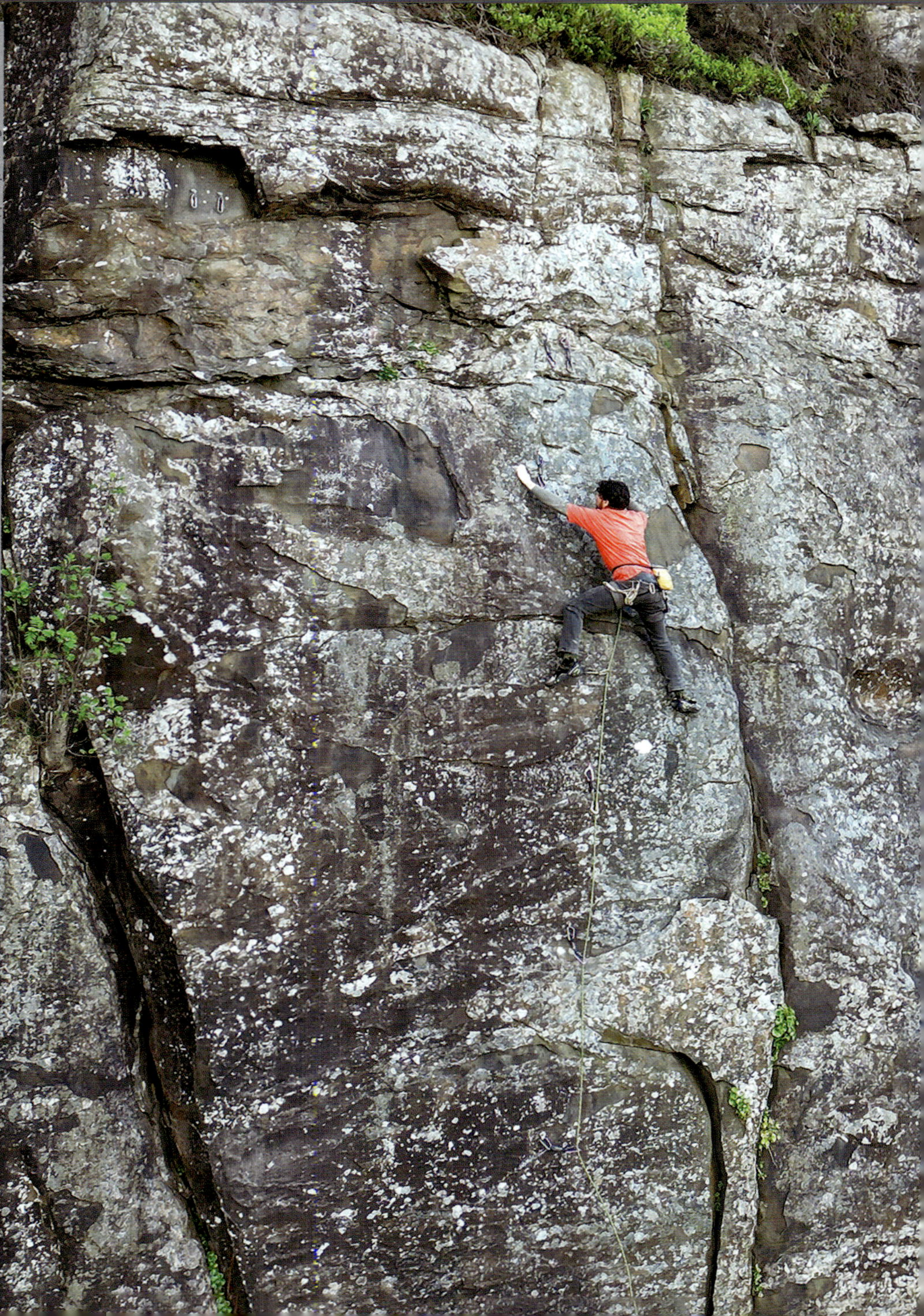

Craig Cwm 331

Joe Jones travelling *On the Road* (6c) - *p.333* - at Craig Cwm, an outlier located away from the traditional sandstone venues. It is made up of a series of isolated buttresses that are on the edge of an area of exposed moorland blessed with fine views. Photo: Carl Ryan

Craig Cwm — Left-hand Bay

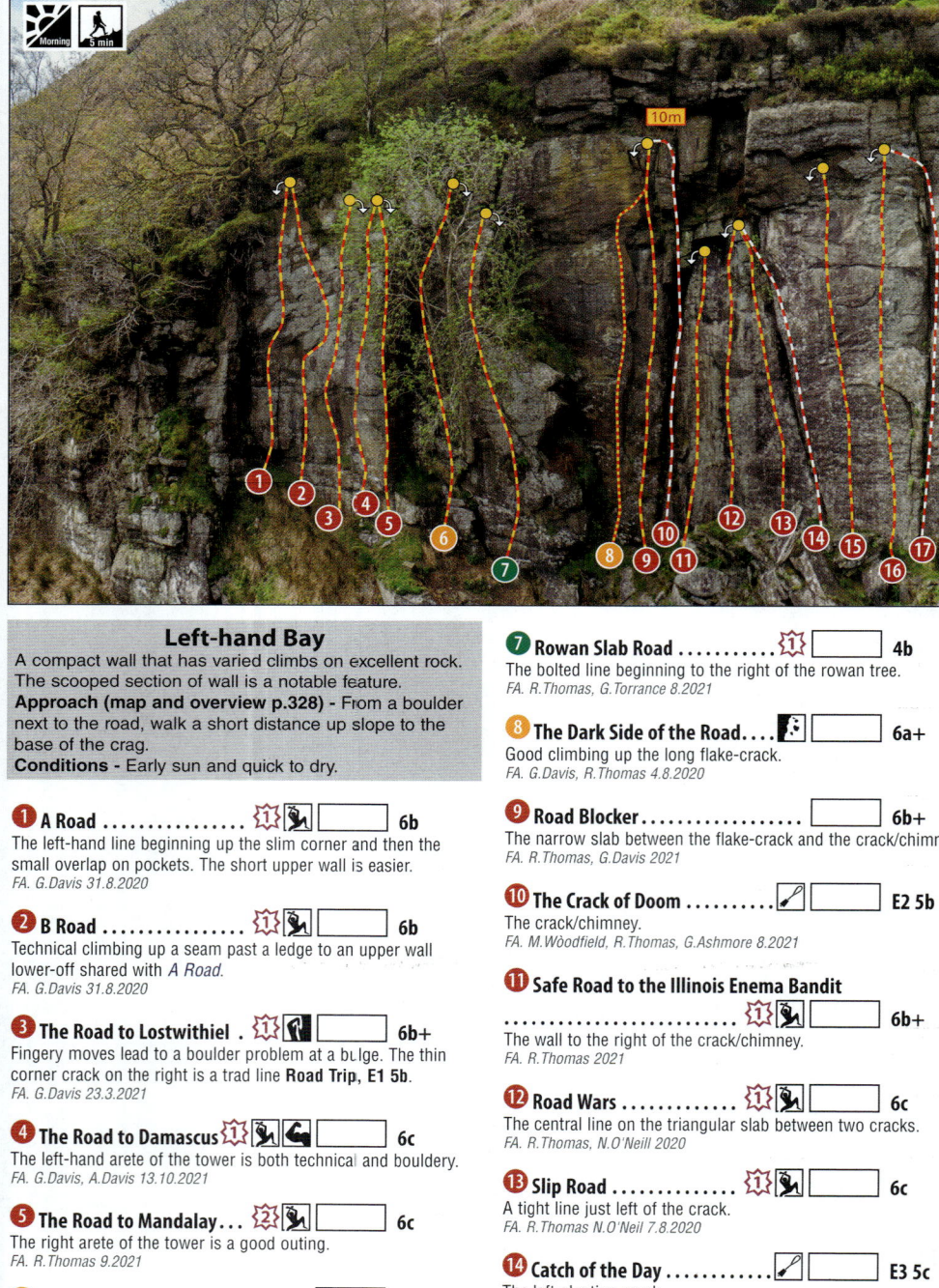

Left-hand Bay

A compact wall that has varied climbs on excellent rock. The scooped section of wall is a notable feature.

Approach (map and overview p.328) - From a boulder next to the road, walk a short distance up slope to the base of the crag.

Conditions - Early sun and quick to dry.

1 A Road 6b
The left-hand line beginning up the slim corner and then the small overlap on pockets. The short upper wall is easier.
FA. G.Davis 31.8.2020

2 B Road 6b
Technical climbing up a seam past a ledge to an upper wall lower-off shared with *A Road*.
FA. G.Davis 31.8.2020

3 The Road to Lostwithiel . 6b+
Fingery moves lead to a boulder problem at a bulge. The thin corner crack on the right is a trad line **Road Trip, E1 5b**.
FA. G.Davis 23.3.2021

4 The Road to Damascus 6c
The left-hand arete of the tower is both technical and bouldery.
FA. G.Davis, A.Davis 13.10.2021

5 The Road to Mandalay... 6c
The right arete of the tower is a good outing.
FA. R.Thomas 9.2021

6 Road to Ruin 5c
The bolted line to the left of the rowan tree.
FA. R.Thomas 3.9.2021

7 Rowan Slab Road 4b
The bolted line beginning to the right of the rowan tree.
FA. R.Thomas, G.Torrance 8.2021

8 The Dark Side of the Road.... 6a+
Good climbing up the long flake-crack.
FA. G.Davis, R.Thomas 4.8.2020

9 Road Blocker................. 6b+
The narrow slab between the flake-crack and the crack/chimney.
FA. R.Thomas, G.Davis 2021

10 The Crack of Doom E2 5b
The crack/chimney.
FA. M.Woodfield, R.Thomas, G.Ashmore 8.2021

11 Safe Road to the Illinois Enema Bandit
.... 6b+
The wall to the right of the crack/chimney.
FA. R.Thomas 2021

12 Road Wars 6c
The central line on the triangular slab between two cracks.
FA. R.Thomas, N.O'Neill 2020

13 Slip Road 6c
A tight line just left of the crack.
FA. R.Thomas N.O'Neil 7.8.2020

14 Catch of the Day E3 5c
The left-slanting crack.
FA. M.Woodfield 4.2021

Left-hand Bay **Craig Cwm**

15 Closed Road 6c
Quality edge climbing just right of the left-slanting crack.
FA. R.Thomas, N.O'Neill 2020

16 On the Road 6c
The wall left of the trad crack. *Photo p.330.*
FA. R.Thomas 2020

17 Pillar of the Community E1 5b
The straight crack.
FA. M.Woodfield, R.Thomas 2020

18 Gwyn's Road 6b
The wall/slab and scoop immediately right of the crack.
Photo p.329.
FA. R.Thomas, M.Woodfield 2020

19 Road Kill .... 6b+
The appealing technical slab passing a couple of scoops.
FA. R.Thomas, M.Woodfield 2020

20 Lone Road 5c
Scoop and wall passing a grassy ledge on its left.
FA. R.Thomas, M.Woodfield 2020

21 Side Road 6a
Branch off rightwards from *Lone Road* to a high lower-off.
FA. R.Thomas, N.O'Neill 2020

22 Flyover 6a
The left-hand line at the top of the steep ramp.
FA. M.Woodfield 2021

23 Expressway .... 6a+
The right-hand line at the top of the steep ramp has a hard start.
FA. M.Woodfield 2021

24 Back Road 5a
The left-hand side of the short arete.
FA. R.Thomas, G.Davis 2020

25 Anaphylactic Arete 6b
The blunt arete right of *Back Road* on its right-hand side.
FA. G.Ashmore, R.Thomas 12.9.2020

26 Gordon Sumner's Coccyx . 7a
The front of the buttress via some snatchy moves to a trickier than expected finish.
FA. G.Ashmore, T.Dhallu 30.5.2021

27 Apoplectic Arete .... 6c+
The left side of right arete.
FA. G.Ashmore, R.Thomas 23.3.2021

28 High Road 6b
Good climbing up the undercut slab.
FA. R.Thomas, N.O'Neill 2020

29 Low Road .... 6a+
The narrow rib to the right of the rounded of chimney.
FA. R.Thomas, N.O'Neill 2020

30 By Road 6a
The wall to the right starting low on the rib.
FA. R.Thomas, N.O'Neill 2020

Craig Cwm — Right-hand Walls

Right-hand Walls

A series of narrow buttresses and walls spread out across the hillside to the right of the Left-hand Bay. Although short, the lines are well bolted, pack in the moves and lots can be ticked in a short time.

Approach (map and overview p.328) – Walk right from the Left-hand Bay.

Conditions – All the walls and buttresses get early sun but are exposed to the elements.

1 Bee Gone 6b
The wall left of the short square-cut arete.
FA. R.Thomas 4.4.2021

2 Buzz Off .... 6b+
Short but intense bouldery style climbing up the arete.
FA. R.Thomas 3.2021

3 I'll Bee Damned .... 6a+
The wall on the right-hand side of the arete.
FA. R.Thomas, E.Muse 27.3.2021

4 Woke Anglo Saxon Protestants 6c+
The wall to with a blind and tricky finish directly up the headwall.
FA. G.Ashmore, G.Davis 31.3.2021

5 Drone On .... 6b+
The arete at the right-hand end of the wall.
FA. R.Thomas, G.Ashmore 5.2021

6 Beeching Closure 6b
Wall to the right of the vegetated corner starting off of a tottering ledge.
FA. R.Thomas, G.Davis 5.2021

7 Lost Branch Line 6b
Tackle the left arete of the sentry-box chimney to a lower-off shared with *Beeching Closure*.
FA. R.Thomas, E.Chapman, N.O'Neill 5.2021

8 Under the Axe 5c
The wall right of the sentry-box chimney.
FA. R.Thomas, G.Davis 2021

9 Filthy Commoner 5b
The creaky and grubby wall left of a rotting tree.
FA. R.Thomas 5.2021

10 Cwm Moaner .... 6a+
Short wall and mantel-shelf onto a ledge.
FA. R.Thomas G.Ashmore 31.3.2021

11 Cwm on Then .... 6b+
The bouldery micro arete is far easier for the tall.
FA. R.Thomas G.Ashmore 2021

12 Common Cold 5c
The chimney. Take care with blocks at mid-height and above.
FA. R.Thomas, E.Chapman 2021

13 Common Ground .... 6a+
The left wall of the arete is more awkward than it looks.
FA. R.Thomas, G.Ashmore 31.3.2021

14 In Direct 4b
The left-hand route features a tricky reach to finish.
FA. S.Jacob, M.Woodfield 28.11.2022

15 Neighbourhood Watch 5a
The right-hand route heads up the line of steep flakes.
FA. M.Woodfield, S.Jacob 28.11.2022

16 Loopy Loo 6a
An overhanging start to *Sad Mad Professor*.
FA. R.Thomas 5.2023

17 Sad Mad Professor .... 6a+
Left arete of the 'big tree block'.
FA. R.Thomas 5.2023

Right-hand Walls Craig Cwm 335

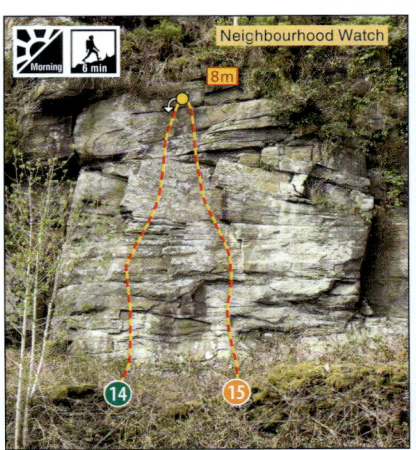

18 Common Deviation .... 6a+
The centre of 'big tree block'.
FA. R.Thomas 5.2023

19 Leering Tower of Pizza .... 6a+
Take on the slim side of the pillar beginning at its base. No sneaking in from the chimney at this grade.
FA. R.Thomas, N.O'Neill 3.2023

20 Pain in the Arse 5b
Right of the deep ivy-choked chimney.
FA. R.Thomas, E.Rees, N.O'Neil 8.6.2023

21 Common Slattern 5b
To the right of the wide rounded crack.
FA. R.Thomas, G.Ashmore 2023

22 Looey Goes Cuckoo ...... 6a+
Follow the short crack, roof and wall.
FA. R.Thomas 5.2023

23 Sciatica Shuffle 5b
A steep start leads to easier ground at mid-height.
FA. R.Thomas, E.Rees, N.O'Neil 11.6.2023

24 Bearded Commoners .... 6a+
A steep but shortish route starting on a raised ledge.
FA. R.Thomas, E.Rees, N.O'Neil 5.2023

25 Swansong 5b
The wide rib to the right of a crack.
FA. R.Thomas, N.O'Neil, E.Rees 6.2023

26 Curtain Call 5b
The wall left of an oak tree to a roof crack.
FA. R.Thomas, E.Rees, N.O'Neil 6.2023

27 Nick's Dripping Pipe 5b
Left of the horizontal oak beyond the ivy curtain.
FA. R.Thomas, N.O'Neil, E.Rees 11.6.2023

336 Dyffryn

Grade Spread | 1 | 27 | 17 | - | -

A quiet crag, set high above the Neath Valley, with some short climbs on generally good rock. The routes are mostly fingery and technical and, what they lack in length, they make up for in intensity - a great place to brush up on technique and build up finger strength.

Approach

From the M4 at Junction 43, drive north on the A465. Turn off after 3km, signed to Neath, and take the first exit. At the next roundabout, take the second left (the first is to Tesco) and continue to a double mini-roundabout. Go right up the hill and continue past two more mini roundabouts, some speed humps and the Clydach Hotel on the right. Just after a church, make a sharp turn left onto a narrow lane. Drive down the lane for 40m and park in the small Dyffryn Woods car park on the right. Follow the path through the woods and up a track for 1.6km and the crag will appear next to the track after a final turn right.

Dyffryn 337

Conditions
The crag is sheltered from westerlies and dries quickly. Nettles on the right side can be a problem and a stick to bash them down is useful. It gets the sun until midday.

Access
Please park carefully as described - **no access is allowed by vehicle to the crag**. No camping or fires at the crag.

Jay Faulkner on *Leave it to Me* (7a) - *p.339* - at Dyffryn. The crag is situated high on the edge of the Neath Valley and presents as a compact edge of quarried sandstone. There are a lot of climbs here in the mid-grades that follow a good variety of features consisting of narrow walls, cracks, corners and bulges. Photo: Rhys Allen

Dyffryn Left

Left

The left end of the quarry has a number of smart little routes that are both fingery and tricky to read - especially if not chalked up. The rock on the whole is solid and clean. A good place to give the fingers a workout.

Approach (map and overview p.336) - The first wall and shady bay.

Conditions - Sunny, sheltered and quick to dry.

1 Sub Prime Market 4b
The small slabby wall 50m to the left of the quarry to a single bolt lower-off.
FA. R.Thomas, G.Ashmore 2008

2 Serendipity 5c
Follow the line marked by a bolt and pegs.
FA. R.Thomas 2007

3 Enigma 6b
The crimpy rippled wall to the left of a crack is good.
FA. R.Thomas 2007

4 Who Dunnit 6a
The crack and niche is an awkward exercise.
FA. R.Thomas 2007

5 You Dunnit 6b
The compact walls and bulges to the right of the crack are tackled via some positive horizontal slots.
FA. G.Gibson 2007

6 Pocket Battleship 6a
A fine pitch up the rounded rib on positive but hard to see edges and a pocket.
FA. R.Thomas 2007

7 Light Cruiser .... 6a+
Take the wall and steep thin headwall just to the right of the arete of *Pocket Battleship*.
FA. R.Thomas 2007

8 Dirty Deeds 5c
Climb the wall and headwall just to the left of the blocky crack. There is a low peg, but the line is fully bolted.
FA. R.Thomas 2008

9 Get Your Fist In 5c
Climb the wall and then the wide crack.
FA. R.Thomas 2008

Left Dyffryn

⑩ Leave it to Me 7a
Follow the arching groove and wall above it. *Photo p.337*.
FA. M.Hirst 2007

⑪ Flue Liner 6a
When dry the rounded chimney corner gives a good exercise in three-dimensional movement.
FA. R.Thomas 2007

⑫ Pot Black .... 6b+
A nice thin wall climbing just to the right of the *Flue Liner* chimney.
FA. R.Thomas 2007

⑬ Slab Happy 6b
The slabby wall to the right of *Pot Black*.
FA. R.Thomas 2007

⑭ Repetitive Strain Inquiry 6a+
Climb to and up the arete right of *Slab Happy*.
FA. R.Thomas 2007

⑮ Porno Text King 6b
Follow the wall and right-hand side of the pillar.
FA. R.Thomas 2007

⑯ Silent Mode 6a
The low overlap and short wall.
FA. F.Thomas 2007

⑰ Rotters Club 5c
Start below a very strange looking initial bolt. Climb the small right-facing corner to a lower-off under the upper overhang.
FA. F.Thomas 2007

⑱ Bad Bad Boy 6b
Start below another strange looking first bolt. Climb the wall to the overhang and pull up left onto the steep wall to finish.
FA. F.Thomas 2007

⑲ Down the Drain 5b
The left-hand crack-line.
FA. F.Thomas 2008

⑳ Our Man from Hyder 5b
The right-hand crack.
FA. F.Thomas 2008

㉑ Mind Like a Sewer .... HVS 5a
The rightward-curving crack at the end of the wall is trad.
FA. M.Jordan, N.Ruddock 2007

Dyffryn Right

Right

The right-hand side of the quarry continues the theme of short intense pitches, but these see less traffic due to the dense carpet of nettles in the summer. A nettle-whacker is a useful addition to the equipment list.

Approach (map and overview p.336)
Conditions - Sunny in the morning.

1 Off to Oz 5b
The slabby wall on the far left past two pegs - old lower-off.
FA. R.Phillips 2007

2 Ed's Triumph 5c
Climb straight up to the old lower-off shared with *Off to Oz*.
FA. E.Rees 2007

3 Nick's Dilemma 6a
The thin crimpy wall to a final bulge.
FA. R.Thomas 2007

4 Playing Away .... 6a+
Climb the seamed wall of blind cracks and grooves.
FA. R.Thomas 2007

5 A Bit of Nokia on the Side 6b
Follow the curving grooves to a bulge and headwall. Big staples.
FA. R.Thomas 2007

6 Barbara 6b
The broken looking line to a short upper groove.
FA. G.Gibson 2007

7 Milky White 6a
The parallel seams sometimes hold grass.
FA. R.Thomas 2007

8 Why Did I Bother .... 6b+
Inch up the slightly rounded rib.
FA. R.Thomas 2007

9 Predictive Text 6b
The wall just right of *Why Did I Bother* is a good pitch.
FA. R.Thomas 2007

10 Baggle Brook Affair 5b
A pleasant little slab, passing a pocket leads to a short corner.
FA. R.Thomas 2007

11 Nifty Fingers 6a
The slabby wall to a break and then the leaning red wall above to finish.
FA. R.Thomas 2007

Right **Dyffryn** 341

12 Lip Service .... ☐ 6a
Climb over broken overlaps and ledges to the upper red wall.
FA. R.Thomas 2007

13 Family Day .... 🎉 ☐ 6b
The low overhang and grooves up the red wall to a lower-off above a grassy ledge.
FA. R.Thomas 2007

14 Affairs of Man .... ☐ 6b
The wall/corner to a bulge and steep headwall above.
FA. R.Thomas 2007

15 Supply on Demand .... ☐ 6b
Take a steep wall to a notch in a bulge that is passed on pockets.
FA. R.Thomas 2007

16 Demolition Gang .... ☐ 6a
The overhang and easy upper groove/corner.
FA. R.Thomas 2008

17 Birthday Bulge .... 🧗 ☐ 5b
A line of weird fixed gear past a tree. Has suffered a rockfall and now looks to be in a loose state.
FA. G.Evans 2007

18 Ed's Folly .... 🎉 ☐ 6a
The wall behind the tree gives a pleasant pitch.
FA. R.Thomas 2008

19 Memory Man .... ☐ 6b
Start by bridging up a chimney and then break left via a hidden hold.
FA. R.Thomas 2008

20 Gathering Gloom .... ✋ ☐ 6a+
Take the wall right of the *Memory Man* chimney with a long reach to finish.
FA. R.Thomas 2008

21 Ockers Delight .... ☐ 6b
Start at a bulging nose and go up the wall to a fine finish over the overhang.
FA. R.Thomas 2008

22 Nick to the Rescue ...... 🎉 🧗 ☐ 6c
The line out of the cave to a juggy finish.
FA. R.Thomas 2008

23 Damp Digits .... ☐ 6a+
Climb up the right-hand side of the cave.
FA. R.Thomas 2009

24 Straight and Narrow .... ☐ 6a+
The wall to the right of the cave.
FA. R.Thomas 2009

Abbey Buttress

Grade Spread | - | 7 | 15 | 4 | -

An interesting spot that is set high above the vast industrial complex of Port Talbot and the M4. Despite this, it is actually a pleasant place to climb and the routes are well worth a look. A visit could easily be combined with one of the other crags in the area, or as a perfect stopping off point on the way to or back, from Gower or Pembroke.

Approach
Leave the M4 at junction 40 and follow the signs for Port Talbot. At a T-junction, turn left onto the A48 and follow it for 700m and turn left onto Incline Road (this changes to Inkerman Row). Pass under the motorway bridge and park on the right before the bungalow. Take the track/footpath just left of the bungalow and, after 100m, go right on a path that contours the slope. After 300m a path heads steeply up left through dense gorse to the quarry.

Conditions
The cliff is extremely open and exposed to any westerly or southwesterly winds. This does mean it dries quickly. The crag receives sun on its walls in the afternoon. A small number of the climbs are occasionally covered with dust/soil due to small mud slides from above one section of the cliff identified on the topo.

Access
Do not park in front of the bungalow or on any of the verges. If the parking on the road is full go back under the bridge and park.

Abbey Buttress 343

Rob McAllister on the aptly named *GAZ 316* (6b+) - *p.344* - at Abbey Buttress. This is an old quarry which sits just above the M4 and overlooks the massive industrial steel complex at Port Talbot, however the crag itself is a pleasant spot. It is also a very convenient venue to call in at on the way to or from other areas. Photo: Carl Ryan

Abbey Buttress

Approach (map and overview p.342) - A path leads up through dense bushes.

1 Community Spirit — 5c
Climb a technical wall past a ledge to gain a corner.
FA. R.Thomas, G.Ashmore 23.3.2016

2 Tired of Waiting — 6a+
After a direct start take the edge of the slab just left of *Ta-Ta Tata*. No straying off route at this grade.
FA. R.Thomas N.O'Neill

3 Ta-Ta Tata — 6a
Take the twisting groove and arete past a muddy ledge.
FA. D.Emanuel 4.2016

4 CND — 5c
The corner and wall, joining and finishing as for *Ta-Ta Tata*.
FA. R.Thomas 23.3.2016

5 Bone Hard Start — 6a
The wall and arete above the 'Bone and Anne' graffiti.
FA. N.O'Neill, R.Thomas 10.3.2016

6 Anne's Stiff Entry — 6a
The right-hand finish to *Bone Hard Start*.
FA. R.Thomas, N.O'Neill 10.3.2016

7 Closed Shop — 6b+
The left-leading ramp gains a series of cracks on the upper wall.
FA. R.Thomas, J.Bullock, G.Evans, L.Moran 26.10.1986

8 Restrictive Practices — E3 5c
Start up *Closed Shop* and take a thin crack and wall on the right.
FA. R.Thomas, G.Royle 30.9.1986

9 GAZ 316 — 6b+
The wall past the mid-height break above the GAZ graffiti.
Photo p.343.
FA. R.Thomas, D.Emanuel 13.3.2016

10 Crack Basher — E3 5c
The long snaking crack-line provides superb climbing.
FA. R.Thomas, G.Royle 28.9.1986

11 Sign of the Times — 7a
The crack, flake and another crack on the left at the top.
FA. R.Thomas (1pt) 9.1986. FFA. M.Crocker 18.10.1986

12 PR Job — 7a
The line of hollow flakes and cracks.
FA. M.Crocker, R.Thomas 18.10.1986

13 Urban Development — 7a+
The wall and finger-crack to a thin pull left to join *PR Job*.
FA. R.Thomas, G.Royle (1pt) 1986. FFA. M.Crocker 18.10.1986

14 Fe 500 — 7a+
The continuation above the finger-crack of *Urban Development*.
FA. E.Travers-Jones 15.3.2016

Abbey Buttress 345

15 Writings on the Wall . . . . **6b+**
The hanging groove and leaf of rock.
FA. G.Royle, R.Thomas 9.1986

16 Stump Stroker . . . . **6c+**
The steep hanging corner and leaning final wall passing a stump.
FA. R.Thomas, N.O'Neill 28.4.2016

17 Split the Equity . . . . **6b+**
The steep flake-line and corner above a small cave.
FA. R.Thomas, G.Royle, J.Bullock 4.1988

18 Hot Mill **7b**
A tough testpiece via a very shallow leaning groove.
FA. R.Thomas, J.Bullock 1995

19 Pig Iron . . . . **6c+**
The hard-to-read pillar right of *Hot Mill* to a shared lower-off.
FA. R.Thomas, N.O'Neill 2009

20 High Jinx **6b**
Start as for *Pig Iron* then move right to the crack and a sting in the tail on the final arete.
FA. R.Thomas, E.Travers-Jones 15.3.2016

21 Mud Lark Crack **6a**
The line of bolts below *High Jinx*. Can be a bit dirty.
FA. R.Thomas, D.Emanuel 19.3.2016

22 Schmisse . . . . **6c+**
Move up to a bolt and swing onto the arete. Climb the groove above via some technical moves.
FA. D.Emanuel 19.3.2016

23 Industrial Relations **E1 5b**
The corner and crack-line in the tower.
FA. G.Royle, R.Thomas 9.1986

24 Chain Reaction **6b**
The slab, gnarly groove and final arete.
FA. R.Thomas, G.Ashmore 17.3.2016

25 Cold Rolled . . . . **6c+**
The isolated steep slab on the right. Delectable technicalities.
FA. R.Thomas 1995

26 Nether Edge **7b**
Not in Sheffield! The short arete with a desperate rockover.
FA. E.Travers-Jones 1997

Pen Pych

Grade Spread | - | 2 | 7 | 3 | -

A stunningly positioned crag that has a small selection of reasonable pitches which are well worth the walk up to it. This is a superb beauty spot that has a particularly picturesque waterfall as a backdrop, as a consequence it can be busy with sight-seers in good weather.

Approach
From Treherbert at the head of the Rhondda Valley, follow signs to Blaencwm and the Pen Pych Woodland Park. Park at the far end of the car park and take the footpath out from the parking and follow it all the way to the crag that is next to the waterfall.

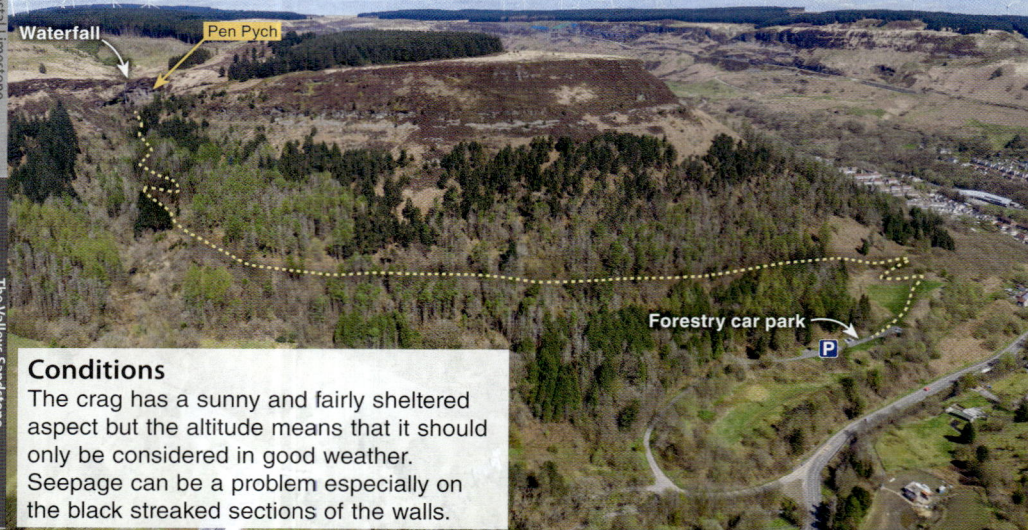

Conditions
The crag has a sunny and fairly sheltered aspect but the altitude means that it should only be considered in good weather.
Seepage can be a problem especially on the black streaked sections of the walls.

Pen Pych 347

❶ Pychy Blinders .... 7b+
The far left-hand line, equipped with some large glue-in bolts.
FA. M.Richards, A.Sharp 5.2019

❷ The Big Pychture 6c
The bolted line just to the left of the crack-line of *Pen Pychtures*.
FA. G.Gibson, R.Thomas 2018

❸ Pen Pychtures .... 6a+
The crack-line and loose continuation corner.
FA. G.Gibson, R.Thomas 8.2018

❹ Pychture Postcards ... 7b
Attain the left leading ramp and then proceed up the tough upper wall.
FA. G.Gibson 8.2018

❺ No More Heroes .... 6c+
The central black streak is a high quality pitch that features a hard-to-onsight crux.
FA. G.Gibson 8.2018

❻ New Hormones ...... 7b+
Tackles the left-hand side of the overlap on the right side of the wall.
FA. G.Gibson 8.2018

❼ Cwm Fly With Me .... 6b+
A steep start gains a slab below a roof. Move right to clear the roof and finish up a chimney.
FA. R.Thomas, G.Ashmore 7.2019

❽ Cwm by 'ere 6c
The leaning arete is extremely steep but luckily not too long. The initial bolt is high and is best stick-clipped.
FA. R.Thomas 7.2019

❾ Cwm Sluts .... 6c+
Ascend the leaning sidewall and then reach around the arete and locate a hidden hold. Move up past a block and then onward past a roof and finish up the wall above a ledge. Avoid the flake on the right.
FA. R.Thomas, G.Gibson 8.2018

❿ Cwm Bach Again .... 6b+
A worthwhile outing. Ascend the overhanging arete to meet even steeper juggy roof. Above the roof difficulties ease.
FA. R.Thomas, D.Davies 7.2018

⓫ Cwm Bach to Me .... 6b+
Climb the hanging groove to a very good hold. Tackle the protruding flake, above which is the finishing ledge.
FA. R.Thomas, D.Davies 14.7.2018

⓬ Bach in the Day 6a
Overcome a steep start just right of a crack. Continue past a bulge to a ledge and shared lower-off.
FA. R.Thomas, D.Davies 13.7.2018

Space Mountain

Grade Spread | 1 | 9 | 24 | 6 | -

A large crag with a lot of good sport routes in the 6a to 7a+ grade span. The environment is superb being high up at the head of the Rhondda Valley. The routes are well bolted and the majority steep and well cleaned.

Approach   Map p.346

From Treherbert at the head of the Rhondda Valley, follow signs to Blaencwm and park at the end of the road in the bus turning area. From the bus stop shelter take the path to an open area with sheds and stables. Pass these on their right and head for the right-hand corner of the various stables and locate a stream. Follow the path next to the stream for 100m to a small wooden bridge. 20m beyond the bridge head steeply up a small path which meets a crossing of various paths. Go across and follow the level path for 10m before taking a faint path on the left uphill. The path is steep and cairned after the initial section and leads to the crag.

Conditions

The crag has a sunny and fairly sheltered aspect and does not seep badly, but the altitude makes this a crag to only head for in good weather.

Access

There is bird restriction on the right end of the crag from 1st March to 31st July.

Space Mountain

Wooden foot-bridge

GPS 51.675926   -3.565876

Bus turning circle

Space Mountain 349

Marsha Balaeva on *Galactus* (7a+) - *p.354* - one of a number of excellent long grade 7s at Space Mountain.
Photo: Matt Hartnell (Balaeva collection)

Space Mountain 351

Al Rosier on *Slayers Gate* (7a) - *p.356* - at Space Mountain. The cliff is set high up at the head of the Rhondda Valley and is one of the area's larger crags that is peppered with walls and stacked overhangs. Photo: Cat McKenna

Space Mountain — Left Wing

Left Wing

The Left Wing is a steep wall split by some cracks and a band of overhangs at mid-height

Approach (map p.346, overview p.348) - This is the first crag reached at the end of the approach path.
Conditions - Slightly shaded by trees but generally the face has a sunny aspect and is clean.

❶ Puny Earthling 6c
Move up the narrow black wall and pull past the stacked overhangs onto the headwall. Climb up and then rightwards to the lower-off.
FA. A.Rosier, W.Calvert, R.McAllister 15.6.2020

❷ Absolutely Vabulous .... 6a+
Head up a red wall to a niche in the band of overhangs. Follow the crack in the headwall above to a lower-off.
FA. R.Thomas 2022

❸ Jungle Jizz Formula ..... 6a+
Take the jamming crack of a variety of dimensions to where it fades on the headwall. Finish at a lower-off just above.
FA. R.Thomas, Gandalf 2022

❹ The Rocketeer .... 6b+
A tough and tricky pitch. Climb up to and over the lower roof to a slab. Follow the slab to a second roof and pass this with difficulty to reach a lower-off.
FA. R.McAllister, A.Rosier 12.7.2020

❺ Super-Dimensional Love Gun
.... 6a+
A good pitch of sustained interest. Start at the right end of the lower wall. Make a rising leftwards traverse to a lower-off.
FA. A.Rosier, W.Calvert 7.7.2020

❻ Beast and the Harlot .  7a
Pull past the low roof using a large flake and then proceed up the wall to an overhang. Overcome this and make hard moves to a finishing jug and lower-off.
FA. W.Calvert, A.Rosier 31.8.2020

❼ Sidewinder .... 6c+
Head up the wall left of the short arete passing a number of overlaps via some difficult and technical sequences.
FA. W.Calvert, R.McAllister 15.8.2020

❽ Black Thought.......... 6b
Climb the short arete and then the slab above left of the bolts.
FA. W.Calvert, A.Rosier 30.7.2020

Rob McAllister midway up *Beyond the Black Rainbow* (7a) - *p.356* - on the Right Wing at Space Mountain. The crag environment is superb and it is a fine spot for those operating in the mid-grades. Photo: Alan Rosier

Space Mountain — Main Cliff

❶ Cybernetic Sex Samurai — 7a
A fine climb up the stepped arete, finishing on its right side.
FA. A.Rosier, W.Calvert

❷ Operation Moonshot — 6c
Short but worthwhile. Begin at a short thin crack and then climb the black and orange vertical wall.
FA. A.Rosier, N.Goile 12.9.2020

❸ Termight — 6b
The orange corner-crack to finish at a mid-height lower-off.
FA. A.Rosier, C.Wyatt 16.9.2020

❹ Nemesis the Warlock — 7a
Exhilarating climbing through the steep ground above *Termight*.
FA. A.Rosier, C.Wyatt 16.9.2020

❺ Pumpelstiltskin — 7a
A bouldery start leads to a technical arete, short slab and groove. Continue up steep overhanging ground passing a small cave to a lower-off. Can be finished at the *Nemesis the Warlock* lower-off which adds a few good moves.
FA. R.McAllister, A.Rosier 1.8.2020

❻ Saffron of Mars — 7a
The logical link of *Pumplestiltskin* into *Nemesis the Warlock*.
FA. A.Rosier, C.Wyatt 15.7.2021

❼ War of the Worlds — 7a+
A long involved pitch that takes a rightward line starting as for *Pumplestiltskin* and finishing up *Altered Carbon*.
FA. A.Rosier 12.6.2022

❽ Four-oh-Four — 7a+
From the large half-height coal pocket on *Galactus*, follow the vague arete right of the *Pumplestiltskin* upper groove to a cave. Move right up the headwall to finish at the lower-off of *Galactus*.
FA. A.Rosier 1.9.2022

❾ Galactus — 7a+
Superb climbing up the wall left of the leaning boulder and then a series of coal pockets through the steepest section of the cliff.
Photo p.349.
FA. A.Rosier, W.Calvert 1.9.2020

Main Cliff

An impressive cliff with good routes in the 6b to 7a+ range. The face is open and clear of trees giving this section a pleasant ambience. The climbs are littered with grooves, corners and overhangs of all dimensions.
Approach (map p.346, overview p.348) - Walk right for 50m from where the approach path meets the base of the cliff.
Conditions - The face has a sunny aspect and is clean.

Main Cliff **Space Mountain** 355

❿ Altered Carbon .... 7a+
Move off of the leaning boulder into the corner and immediately move right to the rib. At the third bolt go back left across the wall using a good crack to below the roof. The substance of the route involves passing two big bulges with one particularly tough move. High in the grade. *Photo p.37*.
FA. A.Rosier 18.7.2020

⓫ One Small Step 6b
The technical groove to a mid-height lower-off.
FA. A.Rosier, R.McAllister 1.8.2020

⓬ One Giant Leap 7b
The continuation above *One Small Step* up the roof and arete.
FA. A.Rosier, N.Goile 12.9.2020

⓭ Asthmanaut 6c
Left side of nose is spectacular with excellent varied climbing.
FA. R.McAllister 20.3.2021

⓮ Celestial Annihilation .... 7a+
The series of overhang-capped corners on right-hand side of the nose. Some awkward moves, a layback crack and then a delicate sequence past an overhanging nose reach a groove. Easier climbing leads to a final tricky section before the lower-off.
FA. R.McAllister 16.9.2021

⓯ Hands, Face...Space! .... 6c+
Follow the orange groove to below a roof. Continue past the roof to a huge slot and holds out to its left, below the blank orange headwall. A reach to a hidden slot at the back of the left arete leads to larger holds and a lower-off on the right.
FA. R.McAllister, B.Gregory 4.9.2020

⓰ Guided by the Science 7a
Mantel onto a block and then reach over a roof and onto the face above. Thin technical moves left to an arete lead to a rest. A rockover gains easier face climbing and a lower-off.
FA. R.McAllister 31.8.2020

Space Mountain — Right Wing

Right Wing

The roof capped wall and arete right of the Main Cliff has some excellent pitches.
Approach (map p.346, overview p.348)
Conditions - Sunny open and quick-drying.
Access - No climbing from 1st March to 31st July due to nesting birds.

1 Nuns and Soldiers............ 6b
Start left of a chimney. The thin lower wall ends at a good hold. Enter a small groove which leads to a slab and lower-off.
FA. W.Calvert, R.McAllister 11.4.2021

2 Pearls of Lutra................ 4b
Climb the slab rightwards, starting at rounded flake.
FA. W.Calvert 27.3.2021

3 Unwind the Chainsaw .... 6b+
The fingery wall to a shared lower-off with *Pearls of Lutra*.
FA. W.Calvert, R.McAllister 5.4.2021

4 Doom-Stack................ 6a
The chimney and wide overhanging corner crack
FA. A.Rosier 8.4.2021

5 Biological Jiu-Jitsu....... 6c
Follow the corner/groove to a roof, then step leftwards across a slab to finish at a lower-off above the roof.
FA. R.McAllister 5.4.2021

6 Beyond the Black Rainbow
.... 7a
The wall and thin crack starting in the cave. *Photo p.353*.
FA. R.McAllister, A.Rosier 24.4.2021

7 Achilles Last Stand....... 6c
A good looking line with short-lived difficulties. Climb the right-hand side of square arete, swapping to its left side near the top.
FA. A.Rosier, R.McAllister 17.4.2021

8 Slayers Gate.......... 7a
The orange wall, soaring groove and arete. *Photo p.350*.
FA. A.Rosier 8.6.2021

9 The Dunning-Kruger Effect
.... 6c
Break out right from the base of the groove on *Slayers Gate* and move past a black bulge to the base of the upper wall. Tricky cross-through moves leftwards gain the lower-off.
FA. A.Rosier 8.4.2021

Bloc

A huge block sits in front of the crag. It is a very pleasant spot with some nice easier bolted lines.
Approach (map p.346, overview p.348) - The block is in front of the Right Wing.
Conditions - Quick drying and partly shaded by trees.
Access - No climbing from 1st March to 31st July due to nesting birds.

10 Voyager 2 .... 5b
The left-hand bolted line.
FA. A.Rosier 28.3.2021

11 Church of the Cosmic Skull 5c
The slabby central bolted line.
FA. A.Rosier, R.McAllister 18.8.2020

12 General Sherman and the Pink Cougar
.... 5b
The right-hand line of bolts on the Bloc (passing *General Sherman* en-route).
FA. A.Rosier, R.McAllister 18.8.2020

13 Outta Space .... 6b+
The right arete of the bloc. Start on the right side of the arete and layback the arete. Top out on the right side of the arete and scramble out rightwards.

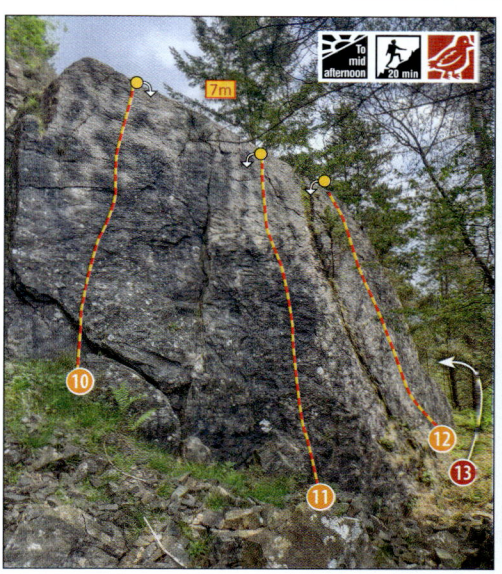

Terrace Wall

A tall vertical wall tucked away at the right-hand end.
Approach (map p.346, overview p.348) - The base can be accessed from either side of the Bloc.
Conditions - Quick drying and sunny.
Access - No climbing from 1st March to 31st July due to nesting birds.

14 Luna Dust to Half Height .... 6a+
The left-hand bolt line to a lower-off on the mid-height terrace.
FA. C.Wyatt, A.Rosier 20.3.2021

15 Luna Dust 6b
From the lower-off on the mid-height terrace continue up leftwards to a rest in a small niche. From the niche climb the pillar on the right to a cleaned area of rock. The lower-off is on the left to avoid slightly suspect blocks.
FA. C.Wyatt 15.4.2021

16 Luna Shadow 6a
The right-hand bolted line to the mid-height terrace and lower-off.
FA. C.Wyatt, J.Westwood 3.4.2021

358 Treherbert Quarry

Grade Spread 2 | 21 | 11 | 3 | -

High above the small town of Treherbert, at the head of the Rhondda Valley, lies an excellent little quarry. The quarry is nicely situated with some fine climbing on good quality rock with routes mainly in the range from 5c to 7a+.

Approach Map p.346

From the main road - A4061 - that runs thorough Treherbert turn onto Station Road and park at the railway station. Cross over the railway line and go left for 100m to where a stream flows down from the right. Walk up to another track just above, cross the stream and then go right, up a gradually steepening track to a bench. Take a path on the left up through woods and when the edge of the quarry is reached, take a faint path left to below the first walls.

GPS 51.672641 -3.536053

Treherbert Quarry 359

Conditions
The altitude and aspect of the quarry means that this is really only a warm weather venue, but the walls dry quickly and don't suffer from seepage. It gets limited sun from mid-afternoon onwards, except the Back Crag which sees the sun until mid-afternoon. It catches the wind and can be a good spot to head for if the midges at other venues are out and about.

Enjoying some steep pulling on the exposed pillar of *Terry Forkwit* (6b) - *p.364* - at Treherbert Quarry. Photo: Glaister Collection

Treherbert Quarry

Tom Skelhon high above the town of Treherbert on the fantastic arete of *Nosepicker* (7a) - *p.363* - at Treherbert Quarry. Many of the best climbs at the crag follow walls and exposed leaning pillars that are above the tree-line and have the added attraction of exposure not often experienced at many of the sandstone crags. Photo: Mark Glaister

Treherbert Quarry — Main Wall

Main Wall

A long and indistinct section of cliff that has some reasonable pitches, and is worth tracking down once the best elsewhere has been sampled. A couple of routes have been lost to rockfall since the last Rockfax guidebook - *Little Big Ego* and *Biffa Bacon*.

Approach (map p.346, overview p.358) - The first lines are at the far left end of the quarried wall, whilst the others require a short scramble up to the base of the crag.

Conditions - Fairly shady but the ribs get the sun earlier.

❶ Spoilt Bastard 6a
The tall arete on the far left is a good line and has some fine positions.
FA. R.Thomas, G.Ashmore 22.6.2014

❷ Uncle Eddie Meets the Modern Parents
.... 6a+
Move over the low bulge with some difficulty and continue up the front of the narrow wall to a hard ending. Some of the rock needs care near the finish.
FA. R.Thomas 8.6.2014

❸ Norman's Knob 6b
The face starting to the left of a chimney. A good first half.
FA. R.Thomas 2014

❹ Tally Whore! 5c
Climb the chimney formed by the huge boulder next to the main wall before moving left onto the face.
FA. D.Emmanuel 2014

❺ Student Grant.................. 6a
Climb the wall and arete to the left of a thin crack. Move rightwards at the top to a lower-off.
FA. R.Thomas, R.Phillips 20.8.2014

❻ Johnny Fartpants 6b
Avoiding the block, follow the wall left of the fist-crack into the chimney then bridge up the right wall to a lower-off.
FA. R.Thomas, E.Travers-Jones 28.9.2014

❼ Submerged by Blubber E2 5b
A trad crack and roof.
FA. M.Crocker, R.Thomas 1989

❽ Scrotal Scratch Mix............. 6a
The bolted crack and roof.
FA. R.Thomas, R.Phillips 7.8.2014

❾ Rowan Jelly 5c
The arete gives a fine line that is steep to get going.
FA. R.Thomas, R.Phillips 7.10.2013

Rhondda Pillar **Treherbert Quarry**

Rhondda Pillar

This fine buttress juts out from the main bulk of the crag and provides a small number of good pitches. One of the best bits of rock in the valley although the shady side can get a bit green at times.

Approach (map p.346, overview p.358) - The prominent square-cut buttress as the cliff line bends around to the main quarried basin.

Conditions - Very exposed to the elements. The routes on the right get the sun in the afternoon but the rest only get evening sun.

⑩ Mint Sauce Dressing..... 6a+
The alternative start to the arete of *Rowan Jelly* is short but intense with hard-to-spot holds.
FA. R.Thomas, R.Phillips 7.10.2013

⑪ Lamb Leer Disease E2 5c
The very appealing left-trending thin crack to a lower-off gets technical near the finish.
FA. M.Ward, M.Crocker 31.12.1988

⑫ Bizarre Geetar.... E3 6a
The left side of the arete. Step left from the boulder and climb the wall and then arete past two sets of pegs. Move right to the Lower-off of *Nosepicker*.
FA. M.Crocker, M.Ward 31.12.1988

⑬ Nosepicker............. 7a
The well-defined arete is tricky to get going on but eases after half-height. *Photo p.360*.
FA. M.Crocker, R.Thomas 2.7.1989

⑭ Thumbsucker........ E5 6a
The finger-crack doesn't quite make it to the floor but is one of the best trad lines on the sandstone.
FA. M.Crocker, M.Ward 31.12.1988

⑮ Nailbiter.................. 6c+
The wall to the right of *Thumbsucker*.
FA. M.Crocker, R.Thomas 2.7.1989

Treherbert Quarry — The Leaning Towers

1 **Drinks at 'The Dog and Hammer'.** 5c
The wall left of the wide chimney.
FA. R.Thomas 2014

2 **Billy the Fish** .... HVS 4c
The wide corner chimney.

3 **Clock Sucker** 4c
Take the arete on the right of the chimney.
FA. R.Thomas, G.Ashmore 10.2013

4 **Crock Licker** .... 6b+
The main arete of the tower is a cracking outing that maintains its interest to the final holds.
FA. R.Thomas, G.Ashmore 10.2013

5 **Terry Forkwit** 6b
The centre of the leaning face is climbed on generally good but slightly spaced holds. *Photo p.359*.
FA. R.Thomas, G.Ashmore 24.3.2014

6 **Norbert Colon Meets the Fat Slags**
.... 6a
The right-hand arete of the tower to finish at the *Terry Forkwit* lower-off.
FA. R.Thomas, D.Emanuel 18.5.2014

7 **Buster Gonads.** 5c
The first of the shorter bolted lines on the walls to the right of the leaning tower.
FA. R.Thomas, D.Emanuel 18.5.2014

8 **A Fish Called Rhondda** 5c
The line of bolts left of the break. Named after a chip shop down in the valley.
FA. R.Thomas, G.Ashmore 26.6.2014

The Leaning Towers

The series of tower-like buttresses first encountered on the approach. The routes, although not of any great height, are pretty steep and pack in the moves.

Approach (map p.346, overview p.358) - The first buttress is just off of the main approach - a low wall that is actually a detached block.

Descent - Walking off is easy. Some of the shorter routes have bolts on top of the crag that can be used as a belay or to set up lower-offs.

Conditions - The routes are exposed to the elements, but get the afternoon sun.

Belay bolts on top of the crag. Lower-offs best arranged with long slings.

Back Crag **Treherbert Quarry**

9 Crescent Wanker............. 5c
The first line of bolts right of the break.
FA. R.Thomas, R.Phillips 7.10.2013

10 OMG She's a Star............ 5c
The centre of the wall via some good moves and rock.
FA. R.Thomas, R.Phillips 7.10.2013

11 The Day the Drill Conked Out 5b
The arete is one of the better shorter routes hereabouts.
FA. R.Thomas 25.9.2013

12 Burning Brush................. 6b+
Take the wall just to the right of the arete.
FA. R.Thomas 25.9.2013

Back Crag

Tucked away from the main quarry is this steep wall which is worth a look and gets the morning sun.
Approach (map p.346, overview p.358) - Continue up the approach path behind the main quarry and then go left on a small path that leads down to the base of the wall.
Conditions - Back Crag gets the sun from first thing and is sheltered from the wind.

13 The Thin Drum 4c
The long rib to the left of the main section of the crag.
FA. R.Thomas 14.4.2014

14 Gallow's Step................... 5c
Start on a block and move up and out right to climb the arete.
FA. R.Thomas, E.Jones 23.4.2014

15 Grunter Ass .... 6b+
Climb direct up the wall to join and finish as for *Gallow's Step*.
FA. R.Thomas, G.Leyshon 21.5.2014

16 Lynch 'em................. E5 6a
The slightly impending slim groove-line with little gear.
FA. M.Crocker, R.Thomas 2.7.1989

17 Exterminate all Bolt Thieves
.... E4 6a
Climb past one high peg above a bad landing.
FA. M.Crocker, R.Thomas 2.7.1989

18 String 'em Up 5a
The arete before moving left to a lower-off.
FA. R.Thomas, G.Ashmore 14.4.2014

19 Seb Eats Shite .... 6a+
Care needed with the rock at the start.
FA. R.Thomas, G.Ashmore 14.4.2014

20 Coprophagic Canine......... 6a+
Take care with the rock at the start.
FA. FA. R.Thomas, G.Ashmore 21.4.2014

21 The Faecal Finger of Fate .... 6a+
The wall direct on pockets.
FA. FA. R.Thomas, G.Ashmore 21.4.2014

22 Double or Squits.............. 6a+
Move off of a block and ascend the blunt rib without deviation
FA. FA. R.Thomas, G.Ashmore 21.4.2014

Gelli

Grade Spread | 9 | 27 | 16 | 1 | -

Above the town of Gelli is a long, quarried crag on the upper level of a series of bays. This provides lots of pitches in the 5th and 6th grades. The outlook is excellent and the base of the crag clean and pleasant, although the start of the approach is a bit uninspiring, being up a dirty track next to some dilapidated sheds and stables. The routes are well bolted, clean and the rock is reasonable - a good spot on a summer afternoon.

GPS 51.642430 -3.477553

Conditions
The quarry is very exposed and is shady for much of the time, although it does get the late afternoon and evening sun in summer. There is no chance of climbing if it is raining.

Approach
From Tonypandy on the A4058, drive past ASDA and turn left at the traffic lights onto the B4223 signed to Gelli. Follow the road for 2.5km to a left turn onto a blocked-off road and park, just before or after it where the main road widens. Walk up a track on the left of the blocked-off road, past dilapidated sheds, and then on steep paths before heading leftwards to the top quarry level where the climbing is located.

Aaron Martin on *Ladyboy's Cage* (6a) - *p.370* - at Gelli. The photo illustrates well the technical and fingery wall climbing often encountered hereabouts. Photo: Carl Ryan

Gelli

Approach (map and overview p.366) - Walk to the very top level of the quarry workings and the developed walls are to the left.

1 Jockey Club 6a
The first line on the left-hand side of the crag to a lower-off.
FA. R.Thomas, G.Ashmore, E.Travers-Jones 5.6.2013

2 Horses Bolted 6b
The wall and difficult overlap to a shared lower-off.
FA. R.Thomas, N.O'Neill 4.7.2013

3 Fools on Horses .... 6a+
The short steep black wall on some tricky to read holds.
FA. R.Thomas, G.Ashmore 8.2012

4 Free Lunch 6c
The line of glue-in bolts has a technical and bouldery start
FA. O.Burrows, H.Watchorn 22.5.2013

5 Stable Boy's Breakfast ... 6b
The short wall right of *Free Lunch* is a brief but worthwhile exercise. The start is the hard bit.
FA. R.Thomas, G.Ashmore, E.Travers-Jones 5.6.2013

6 Green Arete .... HS 4a
The arete has a loose finish. Not recommended.
FA. G.Lewis 1989

7 KES .... VS 4c
The wall to the right of the arete. Finish as for *Green Arete*.
FA. M.Learoyd 1989

8 Kestrel for a Knave 4c
Climb the easy-angled wall to the right of *KES*.
FA. R.Thomas 17.6.2013

9 Joey's Full Pint .... S 3c
The grubby corner.
FA. G.Tucker 2003

10 Mr Farthing .... S 4a
The crack right of *Joey's Full Pint* behind the rowan tree.
FA. R.Thomas 17.6.2013

11 Miss Halfpenny 4b
The red tower to the same belay as *Mr Farthing*.
FA. R.Thomas 17.6.2013

12 Feeling Lucky .... 6a+
The short rounded rib left of the Y-crack of *Wot No Metal*.
FA. R.Thomas, E.Rees 29.5.2012

13 What No Metal E1 5c
The Y-crack to the right of the arete is not bolted but there is a shared lower-off on the ledge that it finishes on.
FA. R.Thomas, G.Royle 1989

14 Little Treasure 6b
The concave wall to the right of the Y-crack of *Wot No Metal*.
FA. M.Learoyd, R.Thomas 1989

15 Toil .... HVS 5a
The thin crack-line just left of the larger grassier crack.
FA. G.Lewis 1989

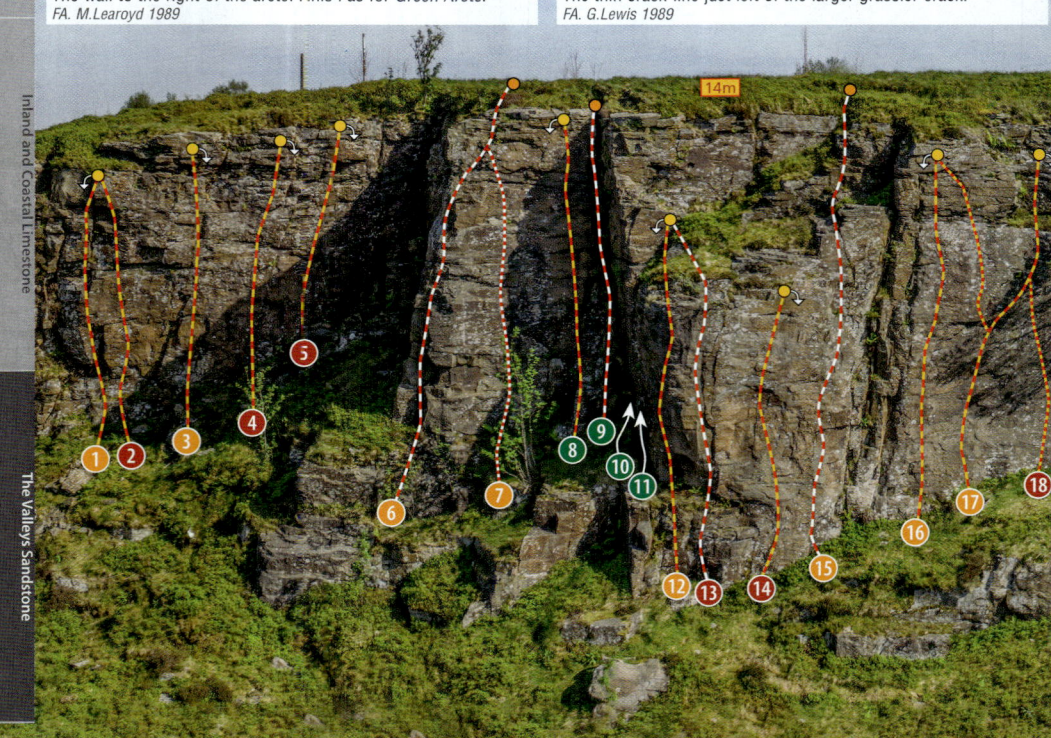

16 My Little Pony's on the Job ... 1 star ... 5c
Climb the wall just right of the large grassy crack.
FA. R.Thomas, R.Phillips, G.Leyshon 5.2012

17 Galvanised ... 2 stars ... 6a+
The flake-crack gives a good pitch. A direct variation is also possible finishing at the lower-off of *My Little Pony's on the Job*.
FA. R.Thomas, M.Learoyd, G.Royle 1989

18 Long Forgotten ... 1 star ... 6b+
A very hard initial section. The holds on *Galvanised* at the start are out of bounds.
FA. R.Thomas, G.Royle 1989

19 Hoarse Trader ... 4c
The arete right of a pine tree in a crack.
FA. R.Thomas, E.Rees 29.5.2012

20 Marinated Goat Cheese ... 1 star ... 4a
Climb just right of *Hoarse Trader*.
FA. R.Thomas, E.Rees 29.5.2012

21 Squeezing the Curd ... 1 star ... 5a
A short pitch below *Marinated Goat Cheese*. Either continue up *Marinated Goat Cheese* or walk off.
FA. R.Thomas, N.O'Neill 2012

22 The Babcock Test ... 1 star ... 6b
A short thin climb between the cracks is a tough exercise.
FA. R.Thomas, N.O'Neill 2012

23 Little Toad ... 6b
The narrow pillar right of *Babcock Test*.
FA. R.Thomas 5.2022

24 Titanium Man ... E1 5b
The crack right of the chimney has a loose block at the start.
FA. G.Royle, R.Thomas 1989

25 Ranga ... 1 star ... 7a+
The face left of *Cigarillo*. No arete or crack at this grade.
FA. F.Hammatt 1.8.2020

26 Cigarillo ... 1 star ... 6b
The crack. The lower-off is set back on the finishing ledge.
FA. M.Learoyd 1989

27 Tobacco King ... 1 star ... 6c+
The wall right of the cracks of *Cigarillo*. Stay off the flake to the right at this grade.
FA. M.Learoyd, L.Foulkes, R.Thomas 1990

28 Down Under ... 2 stars ... 4c
The eye-catching slab is a very pleasant climb.
FA. R.Thomas, M.Learoyd, L.Foulkes, G.Royle 1989

29 Fingers in the Fish ... 2 stars ... 5c
The right-hand side of the *Down Under* slab and arete.
FA. R.Thomas, N.O'Neill, Gandalf 5.2022

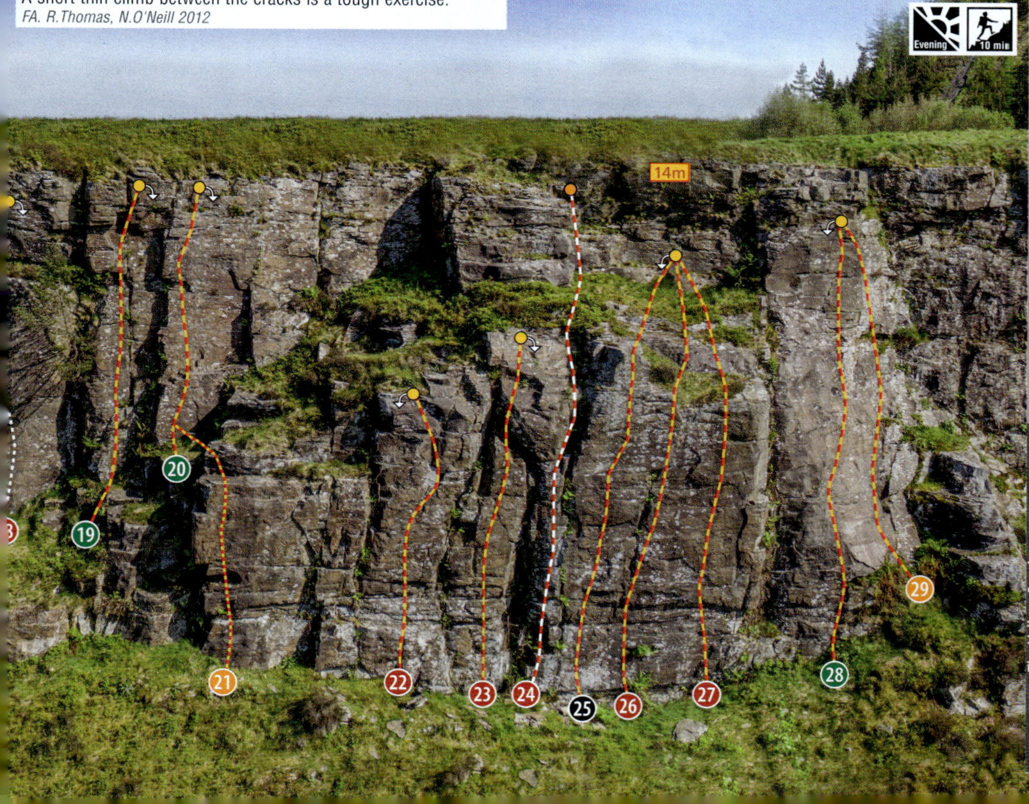

Gelli

30 Working to a Budget 4c
The two short stepped walls.
FA. R.Thomas 26.5.2013

31 Hung Like a Donkey 6a
Climb the pleasing wall starting just to the right of a tree stump.
FA. R.Thomas G.Ashmore 22.5.2013

32 All Talk .... 6a+
A difficult route with a tricky move off a finger jam. Finish by moving left to a shared lower-off with *Hung Like a Donkey*.
FA. R.Thomas, D.Emanuel 5.2012

33 Talking Hoarse 5c
The shallow groove has a difficult start.
FA. R.Thomas, D.Emanuel 15.5.2012

34 Little Taff .... 6a+
Follow the thin crack-line.
FA. R.Thomas, M.Learoyd, L.Foulkes, G.Royle 1989

35 Stubborn as a Mule 5b
Climb the steepish crack to the right of *Little Taff*.
FA. R.Thomas, G.Leyshon, R.Phillips 3.6.2013

36 Hoarse Whisperer 6b
The wall right of the crack of *Stubborn as a Mule*.
FA. R.Thomas 2012

37 A Little Something I Prepared Earlier 6b
A good and sustained wall pitch left of the corner.
FA. R.Thomas, M.Learoyd, L.Foulkes 1989

38 Something that Came up Much Later 4a
The corner has cleaned-up and been fully bolted.
FA. R.Thomas, E.Rees, D.Emanuel 29.5.2012

39 Unearthed .... HS 4b
The slab and crack moving left to a lower-off.
FA. R.Thomas 1989

40 Ladyboy's Cage 6a
The large unstable flake right of the arete. *Photo p.367*.
FA. D.Emanuel, E.Rees 29.5.2012

41 Worzel Budgie Spunker .... 6b+
Thin crack climbing to a shared lower-off. Rockfall may have altered the climb and grade.
FA. D.Emanuel 2012

Gelli

42 Talking Shop — 6a
Climb the crumbly arete to a shared lower-off with *Hoarse Breather*. Keep away from very loose ground to the left.
FA. R.Thomas, G.Leyshon 6.2012

43 Snorting Horse — E1 5a
The left-to-right ascending crack. Clipping the surrounding sea of bolts is not allowed if you are tradding!
FA. R.Thomas, M.Learoyd, G.Royle 1989

44 Hoarse Breather — 6a
The wall above the ledge on good holds.
FA. R.homas, G.Leyshon 6.2012

45 Worzel Cloaca Sniffer — 6a+
Good pumpy climbing to a lower-off at the top of the flared chimney, or head out right to a lower-off (on *Empty Talk*) which ups the grade to **6b**.
FA. R.Thomas, G.Leyshon 24.7.2012

46 Empty Talk — 6a
A worthwhile steepish little number.
FA. R.Thomas, N.O'Neill 20.5.2012

47 Gilding the Lily — 6a
From the right-hand side of the raised ledge, move up to a small block roof and gain pockets in the wall above.
FA. R.Thomas, G.Ashmore 24.4.2013

48 Polishing the Turd — 5b
Climb direct to a shared lower-off with *Gilding the Lily*.
FA. R.Thomas, G.Ashmore 15.5.2013

49 Ice Station Gelli — 6a+
The crack that can be a little floral at times.
FA. M.Learoyd 1989

50 One in Her Eye — 6b+
The wall passing a hard section above the second bolt - pumpy above. There is a block en-route that should be treated with care.
FA. R.Thomas, N.O'Neill 8.2012

51 Send in the Specials — 6a+
Gain the higher grassy ledge and then move left and climb the wall above.
FA. R.Thomas, G.Royle, M.Learoyd 1989

52 Hole in One — 5c
A poor line on the far right starting from the high grassy ledge.
FA. G.Lewis 1989

Following the track up and right to a bay gains an isolated line.

53 Donkey Work — 6a+
The short wall on staple bolts.
FA. R.Thomas, R.Phillips, R.Leyshan 22.5.2012

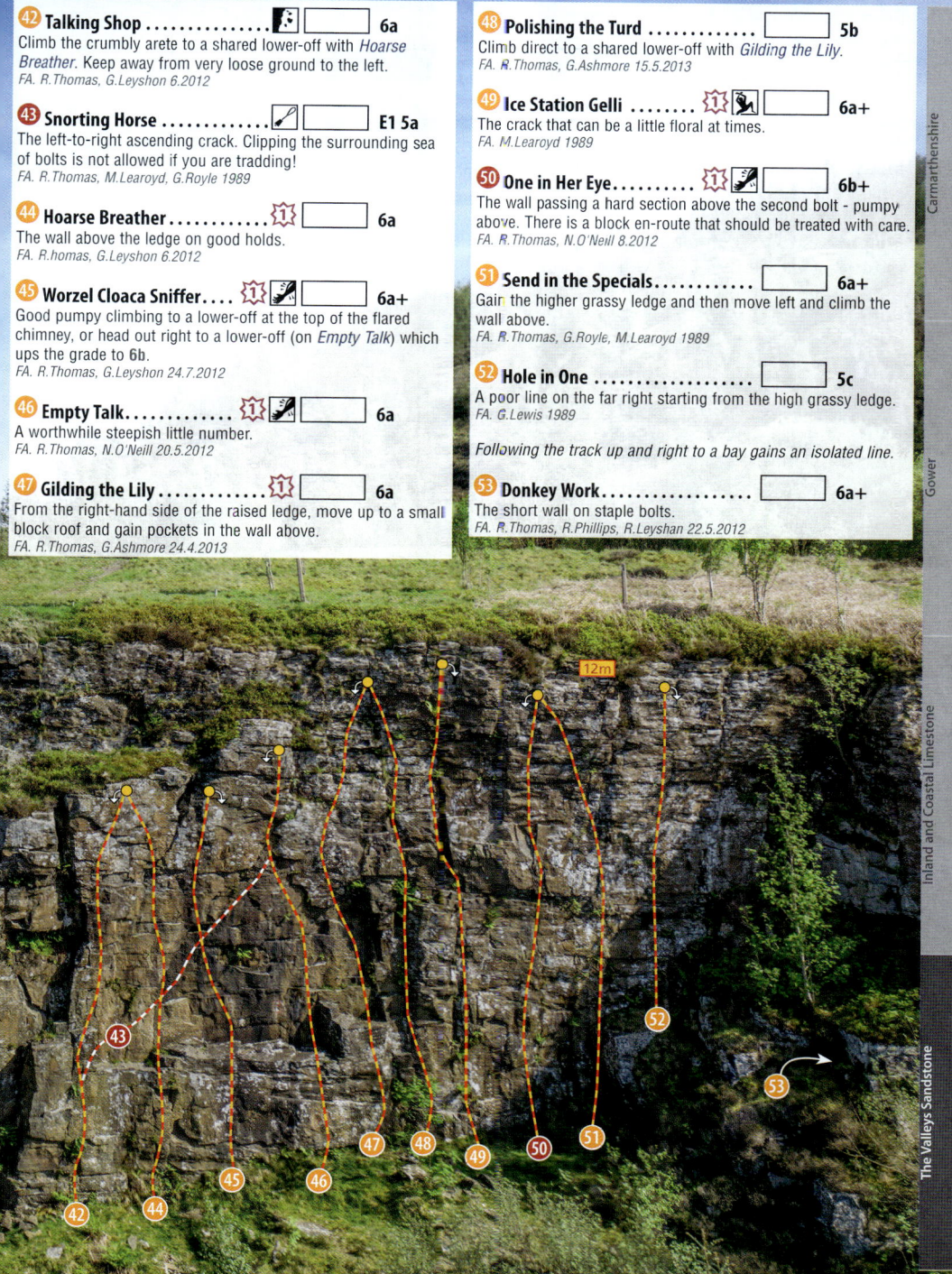

Ferndale

Grade Spread 3 | 25 | 29 | 3 | -

Ferndale quarry is located high above the valley that heads north from Porth. The crag has some reasonable faces that are well bolted, in pleasant surroundings and with an open outlook. The climbing is worthwhile, if little travelled. Ferndale faces east and gets the morning sun whilst across the valley Blaenllechau is west facing and picks up plenty of sun later in the day - combining a visit to both crags is easy. Ferndale Lower is a small quarry with a number of fairly easy to approach routes, useful for a quick hit.

Ferndale

Approach
From Porth, take the A4233 to Ferndale. In the middle of Ferndale the road dog-legs. At the dog-leg turn left and go up the road, to a bridleway sign on the left just past the last house on the left. Park just beyond on the roadside and walk back to the bridleway. Follow this uphill to a metal gate on the left. Go through the gate and take the right-hand path for 60m before breaking right up a faint path. Follow this up the steep hillside to below the Right Quarry. The Main Quarry is 100m to the left.

For Ferndale Lower head up the grass bank 20m left of the garages on the opposite side of the road from the parking. After 10m pick up a vague path that heads up rightwards to the quarry.

Conditions
The quarries faces east, and get the sun in the morning. They are fairly sheltered from a westerly wind. Seepage is a problem after rain and during the winter months.

Eben Muse sampling the technical wall climbing encountered on *Nine Green Bottles* (6c) - *p.377* - one of the standout pitches at Ferndale. Photo: Katherine Woolley

Ferndale — Main Quarry

Main Quarry

A long and fairly extensive section of the quarry with sections of tall walls interspersed by vegetation and a small number of trad lines

Approach (map and overview p.372) - Walk left once the quarry is reached.

Conditions - Sun in the morning but high and exposed.

1 Euphonic Wall 5c
The left-hand side of the tower. Top out as no lower-off.
FA. A.Rosier, R.McAllister 14.1.2018

2 Morning Glory .... 6a+
The front face of the tower has a delicate finish.
FA. A.Rosier, R.McAllister 14.1.2018

3 Afternoon Delight 5c
The right edge of the towers front face.
FA. A.Rosier, R.McAllister, T.Hoddy 25.3.2018

4 Creep 'n' Crawl 6a
The upper wall provides the meat of the route.
FA. A.Rosier, R.McAllister, T.Hoddy 25.3.2018

5 No Bridge Too Far 6a
Climb left of the chimney avoiding the temptation to bridge across it!
FA. R.Thomas, G.Gibson 6.8.2018

6 No Benefits 6a
The right side of the chimney to a shared lower-off.
FA. R.Thomas, G.Gibson 6.8.2018

7 Just Good Friends .... 6b+
The thin crack starting halfway up the gully.
FA. A.Sharp, P.Lewis 18.4.1989

8 Fashion Victim 5b
The left-hand edge of the wall to a shared lower-off.
FA. R.Thomas, R.Phillips 2018

9 Culture Vulture 6b
The rounded arete and wall above. Harder if started direct.
FA. A.Sharp, P.Lewis 15.4.1989

Main Quarry **Ferndale**

⑩ Bucket of KFC and Two One Armers
.... 6b
The slab and layback crack is a very nice pitch.
FA. A.Sharp 2010

⑪ Vat of Tikka Masala and an Orange Seagull
.... 6a+
The crack-line moving left at the top to shared lower-off.
FA. R.Thomas, R.Phillips 4.8.2018

⑫ Frank's Shake's a Limp One ... 5c
The right edge of wall, using the groove in places.
FA. R.Thomas 2018

⑬ Race You up the Wallbars ... 7a+
A thin sequence starting just left of the initial bolt.
FA. A.Sharp, P.Lewis 8.4.1989

⑭ Rhondda Ranger 7a
The slabby wall just to the left of the thin crack of *Silent Movies*.
FA. M.Richards, A.Sharp 26.5.2010

⑮ Silent Movies .... HVS 5a
The striking finger-crack. Abseil descent from the belay tree.
FA. A.Sharp, P.Lewis 1.4.1989

⑯ Talking Box! .... 6b+
The blackened slab to the right of the *Silent Movies* crack.
FA. G.Gibson 2018

⑰ Fernilicious 6b
The line to the right of *Talking Box!*.
FA. G.Gibson 2018

⑱ Fern's Cottons 6a
The short corner and flake on the right side of the terrace.
FA. G.Gibson 2018

⑲ Sperm Bank 6b
The left line on the front end of the rib.
FA. A.Rosier, R.McAllister, T.Hoddy 25.3.2018

⑳ Eurotrash 5c
The front of the pillar is a good climb.
FA. G.Gibson 2018

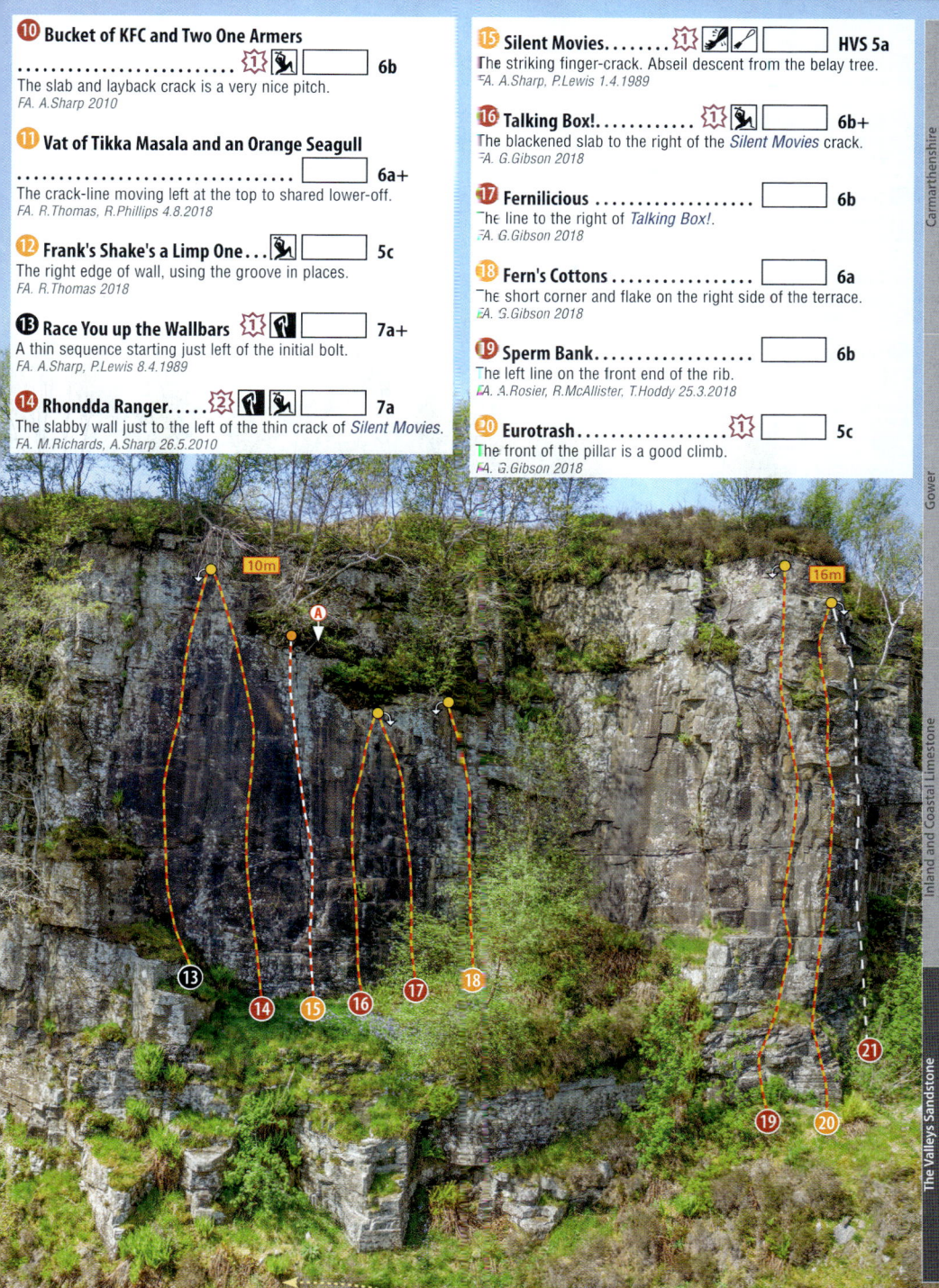

Ferndale — Main Quarry

21 Totally Auburn 6b
The line right of *Eurotrash* that follows the arete on its left.
FA. G.Gibson 2018

22 Balancing Blondine 5c
Tackle the middle of the slab.
FA. G.Gibson 2018

23 Turf Accountancy 4c
The right-hand side of the slab.
FA. G.Gibson 2018

24 Sod Off 5b
The left-hand side of the narrow wall to shared belay.
FA. R.Thomas, E.Travers-Jones 7.10.2018

25 Sod's Law 4c
Right arete of the wall
FA. R.Thomas 9.2018

26 Rhondda Born 6b
Climb ledges left of the long arete, to a big rattly hold Climb the blank looking section to finish up a crack.
FA. P.Lewis, A.Sharp, P.Harding 15.4.1989

27 Anteater's Arete 5c
The long arete, starting from the deck
FA. R.McAllister, A.Rosier 21.6.2018

28 Phogeys Wall 7a
Climb the large flake and technical wall above it on small holds past the right-hand end of the overlaps. Move left under the final big roof and gain the lower-off above.
FA. A.Rosier, S.Pack 26.6.2018

29 Physical Presents 7b
Start up *By Appointment Only*, and at a big staple bolt, take the wall on the left via difficult moves to a shared lower-off.
FA. A.Sharp, P.Lewis 8.1.1989

Main Quarry **Ferndale**

30 By Appointment Only ... 6c+
A neat pitch. Start underneath a niche below a small roof midway up the wall. Climb up to the roof and move over it and up the wall direct to the top.
FA. A.Sharp, P.Lewis 1.4.1989

31 Nine Green Bottles ... 6c
The right-hand side of the wall to a shared lower-off. Start by coming in from the right. *Photo p.373*.
FA. P.Lewis, A.Sharp 8.4.1989

32 Oral Challenge ... 6b+
Climb the wall moving right near the top to the lower-off.
FA. A.Rosier, R.McAllister, T.Hoddy 25.3.2018

33 Prick Test ... 6b
The wall and narrow corner to a shared lower-off..
FA. A.Rosier, R.McAllister 26.4.2018

34 Gojira ... 5c
The long corner and sharp fin above it.
FA. A.Rosier, R.McAllister 25.3.2018

35 One Size Fits All ... 7a
Line of chipped holds just right of the corner of *Gojira*.
FA. T.Foster 18.4.1989

36 Hypnothighs ... 6b
The slim corner in the centre of the wall.
FA. A.Rosier, R.McAllister, T.Hoddy 25.3.2018

37 La Digue ... 6c
The wall left of the crack has some difficult technicalities.
FA. M.Crocker R.Thomas 15.1.1989

38 Seashells in the Seychelles ... E1 5b
The crack.
FA M.Crocker, R.Thomas 15.1.1989

39 Gregoire's Island Lodge ... 6a+
The wall right of the crack.
FA. M.Crocker, R.Thomas 15.1.1989

Ferndale — Right-hand Quarry

Right-hand Quarry
This quarry is much smaller than the Main Quarry. The rock is good and moves testing. The lower-offs are single bolt.
Approach (map and overview p.372) - The quarry is directly above where the approach path meets the floor of the working.
Conditions - The faces get sun from first thing but seepage maybe a problem after periods of wet weather.

1 S.A.D. 5b
First micro route is at the far left end of the quarry.
FA. R.Thomas 9.1.2019

2 Another Jewell .... 6b+
Climb up to and utilise the hanging flake.
FA. G.Gibson 1.2019

3 Gem Them 6a
Tackles the very slim groove.
FA. G.Gibson 1.2019

4 A Little Garnett 6b
The pillar is a worthwhile little exercise.
FA. G.Gibson 1.2019

5 Opal Fruits 6b
Ascend the very edge of the wall.
FA. G.Gibson 1.2019

6 Our Jade 6a
The wall below an oak tree.
FA. G.Gibson 1.2019

7 Big Jim 6b
Follow the left-hand side of arete.
FA. R.Thomas, E.Chapman, S.Cann 9.2018

8 Bolts and Torque 6b
The blunt arete next to the tombstone.
FA. R.Thomas, N.O'Neill 9.2018

9 Netsky - No Beginning 6c
Just right of the large boulder. Climb the left side of the wall via edges, side-pulls, undercuts, slopers and pockets.
FA. W.Calvert 1.9.2018

10 Wallop 69 .... 6b+
The flake. High first bolt, clip-stick highly recommended.
FA. R.Thomas, N.O'Neill 18.4.2019

Lower Quarry — Ferndale

Lower Quarry

A small quarry that is easy to reach and secluded, although not far above the town. There is a wide selection of styles on offer ranging from wide cracks to highly technical aretes and walls.

Approach (map and overview p.372) - Head up the grass bank 20m left of the garages on the opposite side of the road from the parking. After 10m pick up a vague path that heads rightwards to the quarry. The approach can be a bit overgrown especially the grassy bank.

Conditions - The faces get sun from first thing but seepage maybe a problem after periods of wet weather.

11 Taken to the Cleaners ... 5c
Start with some hand jamming.
FA. R.Thomas, N.O'Neil 9.10.2018

12 Omerta 6a
The steep wall immediately left of an arete has tricky start.
FA. A.Rosier, R.McAllister 13.5.2018

13 Laid to Rest .... 7b+
The right-hand side of the perched arete is a bouldery pitch.
FA. A.Rosier, D.Howard 26.7.2018

14 Beyond the Wizard's Sleeve .. 6b+
The central offwidth corner-crack and roof.
FA. R.McAllister, A.Rosier 27.5.2018

15 Angle Grindr 6c
The right wall of the corner-crack.
FA. R.McAllister, A.Rosier 14.7.2018

16 Calamity of Conscience .. 6b+
The egg-shaped bulge of the front face of the tower.
FA. A.Rosier, O.Burrows 21.3.2020

17 Backdoor Girl 4c
The narrow pillar to a shared lower-off.
FA. R.Thomas, G.Ashmore 28.9.2018

18 Slip in the Tradesmen's Entrance
.... 5c
The wall left of the arete, keeping out of the groove on the left.
FA. R.Thomas, G.Ashmore 28.9.2018

19 Pucker Up 6a
The arete has a difficult move to pass the first bolt.
FA. R.Thomas 28.9.2018

20 Back Passage 6a
The crack and red wall right of the arete.
FA. R.Thomas, N.O'Neil 9.10.2018

21 Going Through the Motions .. 6b
A thin start to pass the green bulge is very tricky if vaguely damp.
FA. R.Thomas 2018

Blaenllechau

Blaenllechau is a compact quarry that has some good lower-grade routes. The rock is solid, well bolted and the base of the crag pleasant and quiet. Take care following the approach description as the path from the road is easily missed.

Approach

From Porth, take the A4233 to Ferndale. In the centre of Ferndale the road dog-legs. At the dog-leg, turn right to Blaenllechau. Go up into the village and, at the shops, use a turning circle to make an extremely tight right turn onto Blaenllechau Road. Go up the road and park near the last houses. Walk up the road to the first (small) crash barrier and, 10m further on, go down a faint vegetated path onto the top of the grassy spoil heaps. Walk along these to the quarry. This approach can be extremely overgrown and an alternative is to walk up the road for a further 200m to a locked gate. Go through the broken wall just right of the gate and follow the quarry side of the fence which leads to the base of the quarry.

Conditions

The quarry faces west and gets the sun from midday onwards. However, the hillside is high above the valley floor and exposed to westerly winds. The faces dry quickly and seepage is not too much of a problem.

Blaenllechau

Tamar River on *Cock and Ball Story* (6b+) - *p.383* - located on the set of bijou buttresses and walls at Blaenllechau. Photo: Katherine Woolley

Blaenllechau

Approach (map and overview p.380) - Walk down from barrier and along top of grassy spoil heap to quarry.

On entering the quarry, the first routes are found on a tall buttress on the left.

① Dirtbag Arete 6b
The wall left of the arete finishing on the left-hand side of the arete itself.
FA. R.Thomas, E.Travers-Jones 6.2011

② Electrolux .... HVS 4c
Climb the groove and wall to a shared lower-off.
FA. S.Coles 8.2.1992

③ Dicky Dyson 5c
The striking arete to the right of the *Electrolux* groove.
FA. R.Thomas, R.Phillips 6.2011

④ Dust Devil 5a
The wide groove and right edge of the wall above.
FA. R.Thomas, E.Rees, N.O'Neill 6.2011

⑤ Suction Power 4a
The grassy and run-out staircase leading to the tree.
FA. G.Ashmore 6.2011

Blaenllechau 383

The next set of routes are a little further on, the first lines being on a short rounded slab.

❻ Raspberry Ripple .... 🕮 1 ▢ 4c
Climb the left edge of slab via a blunt arete.
FA. R.Thomas, E.Rees, N.O'Neill 6.2011

❼ Ripple Slab .... 🕮 1 ▢ 3a
As the name says. A nice little exercise.
FA. E.Rees, R.Thomas, N.O'Neill 6.2011

❽ Fairy Godmother .... 🕮 1 ▢ 4c
The far left line on this bit of the crag.
FA. R.Thomas, G.Ashmore 5.2011

❾ Fairy's Liquid.............. 🕮 1 ▢ 4c
Climb just right of *Fairy Godmother* to a shared lower-off.
FA. R.Thomas, G.Ashmore 5.2011

❿ Fairy Ring .... 🕮 1 ▢ 6c
Climb direct without deviation onto the ledge on the left of the very thin seam.
FA. R.Thomas, N.O'Neill 6.2011

⓫ Away With The Mixer .... 🕮 2 ▢ 6b+
The central flake-line of the wall.
FA. P.Lewis, A.Sharp 22.10.1988

⓬ Away with the Fairies ...... 🕮 1 ▢ 6c
Climb the very thin seam.
FA. P.Lewis, A.Sharp 22.10.1988

⓭ Fair Enough .... ▢ 4c
Take the corner-crack to a ledge and lower-off. Care needed with some of the rock.
FA. R.Thomas, E.Rees, N.O'Neill 6.2011

⓮ Hands that Do Dishes.......... ▢ 4c
The standalone arete. The interest is in the initial moves if climbed direct.
FA. R.Thomas 6.2011

⓯ Leaky Ball Cock .... 🕮 1 ▢ 5a
Good moves up the stepped left arete.
FA. Ro.Thomas, E.Rees 28.5.2011

⓰ Cock and Ball Story......... 🕮 1 ▢ 6b+
The central bolt-line. *Photo p.381*.
FA. G.Ashmore, R.Thomas 28.5.2011

⓱ Plumbing the Depths........ 🕮 1 ▢ 7a
The right-hand line has some perplexing moves.
FA. G.Ashmore, R.Thomas 28.5.2011

Dan Dicks

Grade Spread - 2 8 4 -

Dan Dicks is a useful local crag that gets lots of early sun and is only a quick step from the parking. However, it does have a restriction because of nesting birds, so is only really an option from August to October.

Approach
From Porth, take the A4233 towards Ferndale/Maerdy, and after about 1km turn left into Ynyshir by a footbridge. Turn right at the next junction and drive into the village. 100m after the Station Hotel, turn left and then sharp right into a dead-end road. Go up the road to a steep track on the left between the terraced houses (opposite a bench), and park considerately on the road. Walk up the track and take a path that goes straight on at the bend. Follow the path leftward and then right to the quarry.

Conditions
The quarry is low lying and faces southeast, receiving plenty of sun until early afternoon.

Access
There is sometimes a bird restriction from 1st March to 31st July - check the BMC RAD.

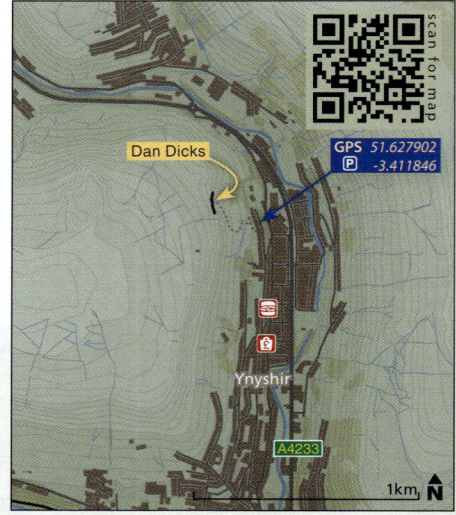

GPS 51.627902 -3.411846

Dan Dicks

1 Steely Dan 7b
The wall and slab with some very thin moves midway.
FA. M.Richards, A.Sharp 9.2009

2 Rhod Above the Bridge 6b
The long corner groove finishing on the left - move right to gain the lower-off.
FA. D.Morris, A.Sharp 9.2009

3 Road Whore 7a
Climb the groove of *Rhod Above the Bridge* and finish direct.
FA. A.Sharp 9.2009

4 Banjo Versus the Pigeon 6b
Climb *Rhod Above the Bridge* and finish on the right.
FA. D.Morris 9.2009

5 Catch the Pigeon 6b
Follow the arete just right of *Rhod Above The Bridge*.
FA. D.Morris, A.Sharp, P.Lewis 9.2009

6 Tricky Dickie Takes a Sickie .... 7b+
At the first bolt of *Catch the Pigeon*, step right and climb the blank wall without drifting back into *Catch the Pigeon*.
FA. M.Richards, A.Sharp 10.2009

7 The Corner .... HVS 5a
The full-height corner holds plenty of vegetation.
FA. J.Harwood, A.Sharp 4.1991

8 Dan'ds-Inferno 6b
Climb the arete to the right of *The Corner*.
FA. A.Sharp, P.Lewis 9.2009

9 Sweet Whistling Geronimo ... 7a
Start up the narrow corner and finish up the fine arete.
FA. A.Sharp, D.Morris 7.2009

10 Dixienormous .... 7a+
Climb the wall to the right of *Sweet Whistling Geronimo* and finish up the arete as for *Sweet Whistling Geronimo*.
FA. M.Richards, A.Sharp 9.2009

11 Dan Dix 6a
The wall 16m to the right of *Dixienormous*.
FA. A.Sharp, P.Lewis 4.1991

12 Whistle Dixie .... 7a+
The bolted line up the left side-wall.
FA. A.Sharp 9.2009

13 Speechless 6c
The thin crack in the right wall.
FA. A.Sharp, D.Morris 8.2009

14 Pre Nups .... 6b+
Climb the right arete, moving left to a shared lower-off with *Speechless*.
FA. M.Richards, A.Sharp 8.8.2009

Access - There is sometimes a bird restriction from 1st March to 31st July due to nesting birds. Check on the BMC RAD to see if the ban is in force.

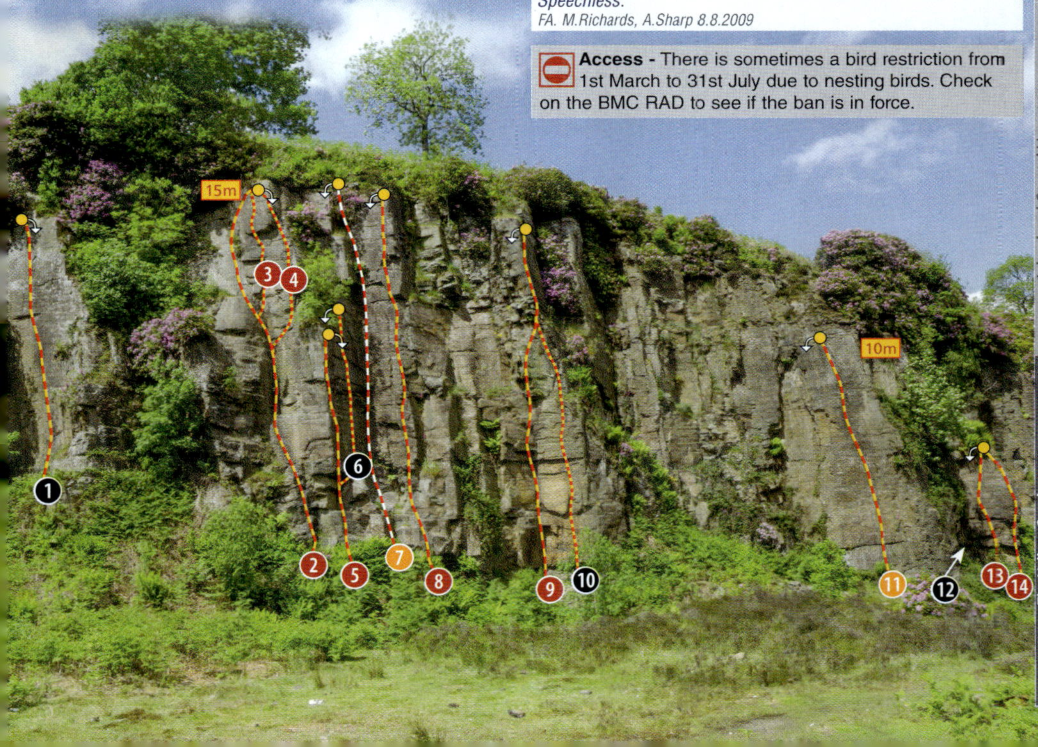

Trebanog

Grade Spread | 1 | 6 | 9 | 1 | -

Trebanog is a small edge of partially quarried rock that sits close to the village in an exposed position. The rock is excellent and has both trad and sport pitches, all of which are relatively popular given their modest height. The rock is good, well-weathered sandstone that dries out very quickly. There are lots of lower-grade trad lines here, but the sport pitches described here are well worth a quick visit.

Approach
From the A4058 in Porth, turn towards Trebanog at some lights. Continue for about 1.5km to the traffic lights on the A4233 in the middle of Trebanog. Turn right towards Edmondstown and the crag is on the right after 200m, just above the road. Park on the street and walk up the short grass slope to the base. The majority of the sport routes are to the left.

Conditions
Open and exposed to the wind, but gets plenty of sun. It dries quickly and does not seep.

- Banog's Barmy Army p.388
- Firewater p.389
- Stiff Little Pinky p.389

Conor White on the lower moves of *Banog's Barmy Army* (7a) - *p.388* - one of a number of fine short sport pitches at Trebanog. This is a really good crag to head for if short of time as it is only a stone's throw from the parking. Photo: Eben Muse

Trebanog

Approach (map and overview p.386) - Walk up the short slope from the road to the base of the crag and the first sport lines described are towards the left end of the crag.

❶ March of Progress 7b
The featureless wall has a tough crux sequence. Using holds in *For Your Hands Only* reduces the grade.
FA. A.Sharp, P.Lewis 1990

❷ For Your Hands Only .. 6c
The central crack-line is an excellent little route. It shares the bolts of other lines.
FA. A.Sharp 1984

❸ Banog's Barmy Army 7a
A good pitch. Stand up on a low ledge, move right and climb to the upper overhang. Swing left past the overhang to jugs.
Photo p.387.
FA. A.Sharp, P.Lewis 1990

❹ Grab Some Tree and Follow Me 7a
Start just to the left of the corner. No bridging across to the corner at this grade. Make difficult moves to the break and then continue over the overhang and up the wall direct to finish.
FA. A.Sharp 1991

❺ On yer Bike Turbo Tits 6b
The leaning wall left of the arete and high roofs. No stepping across left or onto ledges on the right at this grade.
FA. R.Thomas 2023

❻ Hurley's Burly Arete .... 6a+
The arete. No bridging out onto the slab on the right or scuttling left at this grade.
FA. R.Thomas 12.2023

❼ The Blaggard's Wet Pocket ... 6a
The arete and wall left of a shallow corner. Straying off-piste strictly forbidden and be sure to use the pocket.
FA. R.Thomas, Gandalf 11.2023

❽ Firewater 6b
The blank looking wall to the left of a niche in the centre of the wall is a popular pitch.
FA. A.Sharp 1984

❾ Hair of the Dog 7a
Climb direct up from the central niche to finish at the same lower-off as *Firewater*.
FA. A.Sharp 1983

❿ Pete of Lancs 6c
The direct line between *Hair of the Dog* and *Ethanol*.
FA. G.Davis 2017

Banog's Barmy Army

Trebanog 389

11 Ethanol 6c
Climb the wall and move left to the lower-off of *Hair of the Dog*.
FA. J.Harwood (trad) 26.3.1990

12 Ethanol Direct Finish .... 6c+
Climb *Ethanol* then head straight up (instead of traversing left) via a thin layaway to the top.
FA. J.Harwood (trad) 26.3.1990

13 WPC 6a
Climb to the right of some thin cracks and make a long reach for the top break.
FA. R.Thomas, Gandalf 25.11.2023

14 Jilly Wizz 4c
Head up to the short roof and left side of the arete above. A must for the aspirant sport climber's first outdoor lead.
FA. R.Thomas, Gandalf 11.2023

15 Stiff Little Pinky 6a
The flakes left of a small pink splash of paint. Finish at a single bolt lower-off.

16 My Little Pinky 5b
Begin just left of a small pink paint splash.
FA. R.Thomas, N.O'Neill 2024

17 Pink Stink 5b
Climb right of the pink paint splash.
FA. R.Thomas, N.O'Neill 2024

Glynfach

Grade Spread | - | 5 | 5 | 1 | -

A small quarried crag set high above the valley with expansive views. The quarry is quiet and has good rock, with some worthwhile climbs which are intense and well bolted.

Approach Map p.386
Follow the A4058 out of Pontypridd towards Porth. At the Rhondda Heritage Park and Hotel roundabout, continue in the direction of Porth and take the third right (signed to Porth Town Centre). Take the third left by a Chinese take-away onto River Terrace, and continue uphill over a metal railed bridge and bear immediately left onto Cross Street. Follow this until it bends right and park. A path leads up onto the hillside - where various paths lead steeply to the quarry.

Conditions
The crag is high up and exposed, but gets plenty of sun and dries out fairly quickly.

GPS 51.606597 -3.405246

Glynfach 391

① Fach Roo .... 6a+
On the far left of the quarry is a short steep line on good rock.
FA. R.Thomas 17.4.1999

② Hot Fuss 6a
Climb the awkward wide crack to a ledge on the left and then head up the face to the left of the arete.
FA. A.Sharp, M.Richards 30.8.2010

③ Killer Arete .... 6b+
A wild ride that takes on the overhanging side of the arete on surprising holds. Climb the awkward crack as for *Hot Fuss*, then swing right and climb the wall just right of the arete. *Photo p.41.*
FA. A.Sharp, P.Lewis 22.7.1990

④ Turn off the Sun 7a
Climb *Killer Arete* to its third bolt and then head right to finish at the lower-off of *Moses Supposes His Toeses Were Roses*.
FA. A.Sharp, M.Richards 30.8.2010

⑤ Dai Hard 7b
Start right of *Killer Arete* and move up to a hard move that gains the edge of a flake. Finish up the steep ground above.
FA. G.Ashmore 29.4.1999

⑥ Moses Supposes His Toeses Were Roses
.... 6c
The wall to the left of the corner direct passing a flake midway.
FA. P.Lewis, A.Sharp 22.7.1990

⑦ Nervous Nineties 7a
Follow *Moses Supposes His Toeses Were Roses* to a thin break above the midway flake. Make a hard move right, then go directly up. No bridging into the corner at this grade.
FA. A.Sharp, P.Lewis 22.7.1990

⑧ Fach Roo Too .... 6a+
The bolted line just to the right of the corner.
FA. R.Thomas 1993

⑨ Psychotherapy 7a
The neat little wall passing a couple of bolts.
FA. A.Sharp, P.Lewis 22.7.1990

To the right are a couple of thin cracks - both VS 4c.

⑩ Yak's Back 5c
The bolted line just to the right of the two thin cracks.
FA. G.Henderson, J.Obradovic 22.7.1990

⑪ Little Kurd 6a
The bolted line on the far right.
FA. R.Thomas, E.Travers-Jones 1999

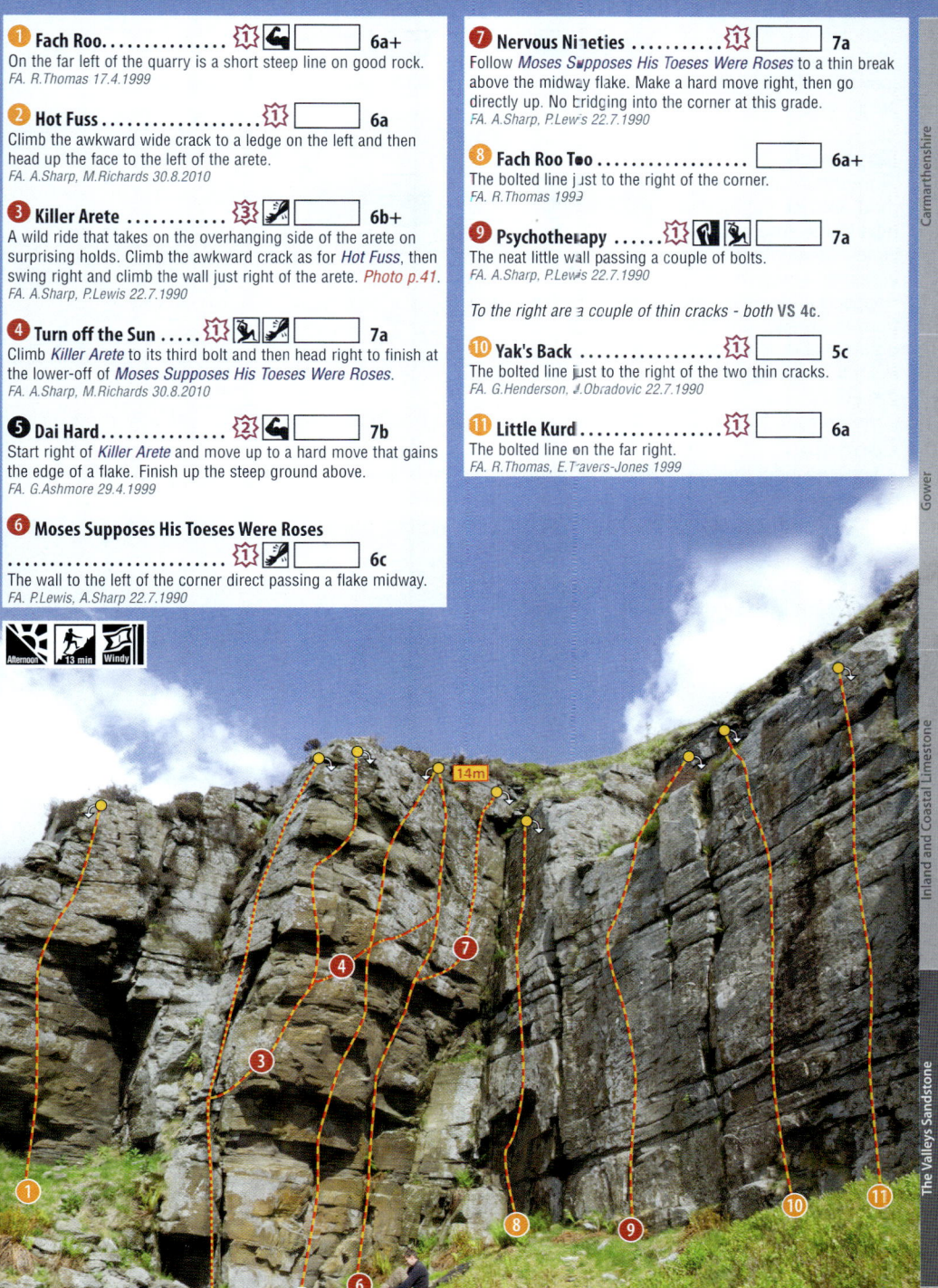

Trehafod

Grade Spread - 7 12 - -

Trehafod is a small crag with a limited number of short but fairly good lines. It is handy for a quick hit if passing, or an evening workout for the fingers. Its sunny aspect and quiet roadside location (coupled with the possibility of dry climbing in light rain) makes it a useful standby if all other crags nearby are out of condition.

Approach
From the A4058 Pontypridd to Porth road, exit for Trehafod at a roundabout next to the Rhondda Heritage Park and Hotel. Drive into the village and, just after crossing a large metal bridge, turn left opposite a funeral directors (about 100m from the railway station parking). Go under a bridge and park immediately on the left. The crag is just up the road on the right.

Conditions
A sunny aspect and quick drying. In light rainfall, there is a possibility of climbing here as the dense vegetation on top of the cliff gives some shelter.

Trehafod 393

Ben Tiffin setting up for the final thin pulls to reach the lower-off on the crag must-do route *Discount Included in the Price* (6a+) - *p.395* - at Trehafod. A small venue made up of a series of compact walls, however it is roadside and set in a quiet area with a pleasant outllook. Photo: Mark Glaister

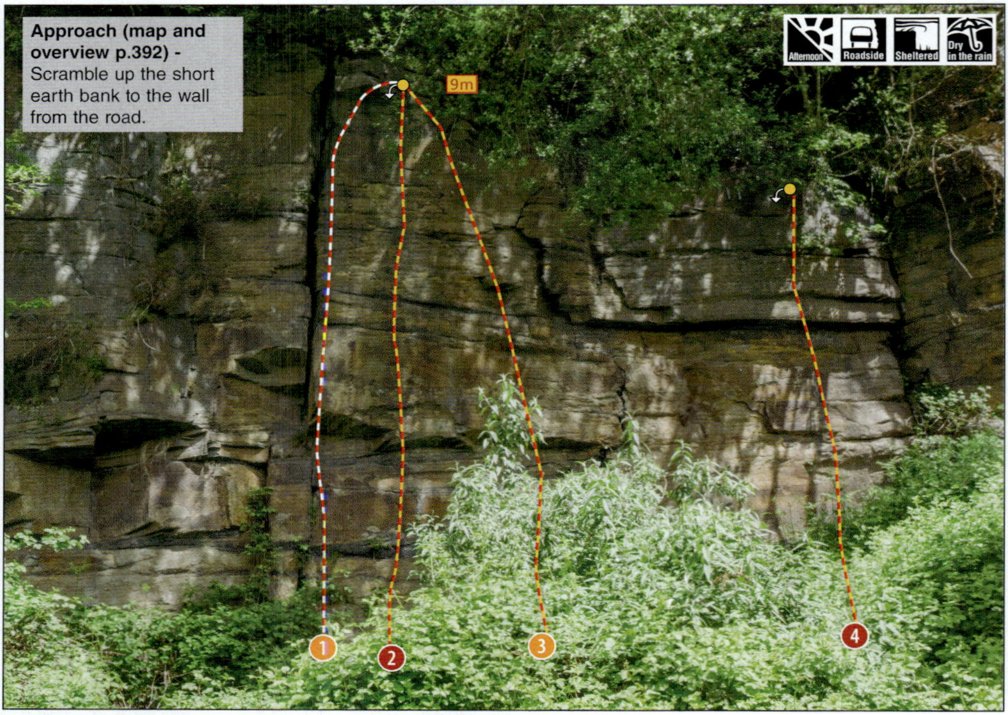

Trehafod

Approach (map and overview p.392) - Scramble up the short earth bank to the wall from the road.

1 Roaches Revisited .... HVS 5b
The off-width crack on the left-hand side of the wall.
FA. C.Evans 1992

2 Beauty School Drop-out . 7a
The wall right of the off-width climbed direct is thin and sustained. Using the crack edge reduces the grade to 6c.
FA. A.Sharp, P.Lewis 2.1992

3 Earl of Porth .... 6a+
The wall just right of *Beauty School Drop-out* is a good little outing and well travelled.
FA. A.Sharp, P.Lewis 12.2008

4 Guto Nythbran 6b
A bouldery thin pull past the small overlap gives the crux.
FA. A.Sharp, P.Lewis 1.2009

5 Elf and Safety 6c
Pull over the low overhang at a crack.
FA. A.Sharp, P.Lewis 27.12.2008

6 Rave Crave/Rhubarb . 7a
Make a dyno to pass the low overhang and take the wall above via more hard climbing.
FA. C.Evans, A.Sharp 1992

7 Meg (a) Skater Girl from Gelli 6a
The right side of the overhang past a groove and wall.
FA. A.Sharp, P.Lewis 27.12.2008

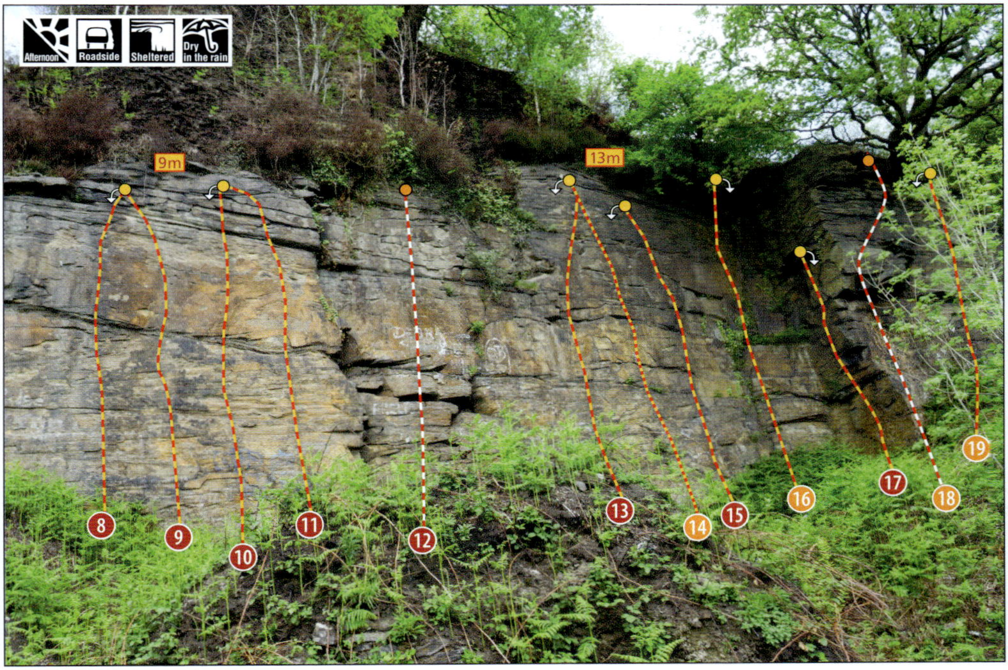

Trehafod

8 Missing Link — 6b+
The wall past pockets. Shares the first bolt with *Demi Moore*.
FA. C.Evans 1992

9 Demi Moore — 7a
Nice wall climbing past a pocket.
FA. A.Sharp, P.Lewis 1992

10 Gorki's Zygotic Mynci — 6c+
Very good and feels longer than it appears.
FA. C.Evans 1992

11 Just Another One-Move Wonder — 6b+
The clue is in the name. The crack to the right is out of bounds.
FA. A.Sharp 1992

The loose off-width is Nasty Norman, VS 4c.

12 Sniffing Deborah's Pocket — E2 5c
Climb to the ledge and continue up the wall above past an old bolt and a peg.
FA. C.Evans, R.Chard 1992

13 Cenotaph Norm Carter — 6b
The right-trending line to finish at the lower-off of *Discount Included in the Price* has a hard initial wall. Step right near the top to avoid poor rock.
FA. C.Evans, R.Chard 1992

14 Discount Included in the Price — 6a+
Worth stopping by for. It has plenty of climbing and is no pushover. Finish direct on thin crimps. *Photo p.393*.
FA. C.Evans 1992. FA. (New finish) A.Sharp, P.Lewis 12.2008

15 Baldy Walks to Ponty — 6b
The direct line to the right has some tough moves.
FA. L.Ashton 1992. FA. (Direct) A.Sharp, P.Lewis 12.2008

16 Rhondda Leader — 6a
The final bolted line on the main face.
FA. A.Sharp, P.Lewis 1.2009

17 Michelle Pfeiffer — 6c
To the right is a leaning wall with a thin crack in it.
FA. A.Sharp, P.Lewis 8.2.1992

18 Beef Curry and Chips — HVS 5b
Climb the arete on its right-hand side.
FA. C.Evans, A.Sharp, P.Lewis 8.2.1992

19 Saga Louts — 6a+
The wall direct.
FA. A.Sharp, P.Lewis 1.2009

The low-level traverse starting from Meg (a) Skater Girl from Gelli is Sir Kit, f6A+.

The Darren

Hidden away in the woods high above Pontypridd is this compact quarry that has some good strenuous pitches which are well equipped and on good rock. The walls see little in the way of sunlight and are heavily shaded by tree cover, and as a consequence take time to come into condition. Once dry the Terminal Overhanging Wall stays dry in light rain.

Approach
The approach through Pontypridd is quite complicated. From the large roundabout in the centre, take the exit signed to the town centre. Follow this road and turn left towards Graigwen just after a pedestrian crossing. Follow the road as in winds gently uphill and eventually round to the left dropping down to a T-junction. Turn right and follow the road steeply up the hill for 1km to a right into Whiterock Avenue. Follow this then take the first left into Whiterock Close and then left again into Lanwood Road. Park 50m down this road, next to a path between two bungalows on the left. Follow the path rightwards behind the bungalows and, at a 'keep out' sign, contour left on a smaller path to the quarry.

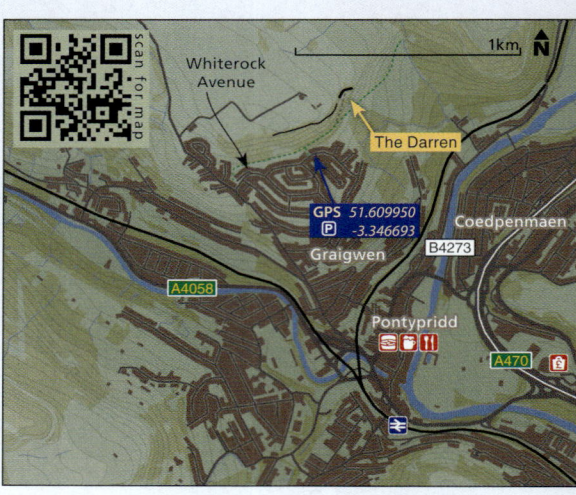

Conditions
Both of the main walls described are shaded by trees and get little sun and the Terminally Overhanging Wall can take a little time to dry after the winter months. However, once dry it can be climbed on in light rain. The B.A.T. Wall takes little seepage and dries much more quickly, but does not stay dry in the rain.

Dean Howard on *Slapstan* (7b+) - *p.398* - at The Darren. The main event hereabouts is the Terminally Overhanging Wall that has the dual role of giving the visitor some fine high-end objectives and also as a popular training venue which has spawned a good number of link-ups. Photo: Elis Rees

The Darren — The Terminally Overhanging Wall

The first quarried bay has a couple of short bolted climbs.

❶ Striking Twelve 6c
The thin wall on the left-hand side of the small quarry.
FA. A.Sharp, P.Harding, T.Foster 23.4.1989

❷ My New House .... 6b+
The line of old bolts up the steep slab at the back of the bay.
FA. G.Ashmore, R.Lawrence 2.5.1992

❸ Behind the Bike Sheds... 6b
A mossy slab on the right edge of the small quarry.
FA. T.Foster 23.4.1989

The Terminally Overhanging Wall

The Terminally Overhanging Wall is a tall overhanging wall, covered in vertical cracks and overlaps. A well-regarded training venue. To the right is another lesser wall (The B.A.T. Wall) which is set at a gentler angle and has some slightly easier lines.

Approach (map and overview p.396) - The main wall is just beyond the first bay.

Conditions - The Terminally Overhanging Wall gives shelter from light rain, and is a good venue in warm weather. The B.A.T. Wall gets some morning sun, but dries quickly and takes little seepage.

❹ The Short Sharp Manic Depressive
.... 6c
The left arete of the inset corner.
FA. A.Sharp, M.Richards, J.Williams 1994

❺ Lotta Bottle Direct 7a
The thin crack to the right. A start via Smack is available at 6c+.
FA. A.Sharp 1983. FA (Direct) P.Lewis 9.6.1990

❻ Smack 6c
The right-hand arete of the inset corner.
FA. A.Sharp 1989

❼ Morganstown Sam ...... 6a+
The bolted slab on the left side of the rib.
FA. R.Thomas, S.Caan 13.4.2019

❽ Capstan .... 7b+
The left arete of the wall, taken on its right-hand side. Brilliant.
FA. A.Sharp 1997

❾ Slapstan .... 7b+
From the fourth bolt on Capstan move rightwards to a pocket, and then make powerful moves straight up to a slopey jug. Traverse rightwards again to join and finish up Round Are Way. Photo p.397.
FA. S.Marsh, A.Sharp 5.7.2023

❿ The Basildon Slapper .... 7b+
A big pump. Head up between the arete and the cracks via a series of small overlaps.
FA. A.Sharp 5.1997. FA. (After a rockfall) M.Richards 9.2014

⓫ Night Train .... 7b+
At the fourth bolt of The Basildon Slapper, traverse to Round Are Way and at the hanging flake move right to the niche of Rise. Go right into and finish as for Sharpy Unplugged.
FA. M.Richards 21.8.2014

⓬ Round are Way ...... 7a+
Move up to the overhang. Head left and then up steep ground right of the crack/niche.
FA. A.Sharp, P.Lewis, J.Harwood 8.5.1997

⓭ Rise 7b
Start up Round Are Way and follow the discontinuous thin crack-line, oblong niche and layaway with hard moves just above half-height and big moves above.
FA. T.Forster, P.Harding 1990

The Terminally Overhanging Wall — The Darren

14 Sharpy Unplugged ... 7b+
The classic of the wall with brilliant climbing all the way to the lower-off.
FA. A.Sharp 10.5.1997

15 Enter the Darren ... 6c+
Climb up the tricky slab to gain and follow the crack past a couple of overhangs to a lower-off
FA. P.Lewis, A.Sharp 24.6.1989

The Terminally Overhanging Wall - Link-ups
The Terminal Overhanging Wall has a number of link-ups that give plenty of scope for the cognoscenti to squeeze as much out of the crag as possible. These are listed with grades, descriptions and user comments on the **UKC database.**

The Darren — B.A.T Wall

B.A.T Wall

To the right is another lesser wall (The B.A.T. Wall) which is at a gentler angle and has some slightly easier lines.
Approach (map and overview p.396) - The face is opposite The Terminally Overhanging Wall
Conditions - The B.A.T. Wall gets some morning sun, but dries quickly and takes little seepage.

❶ **Gutted** 6b
Slabby and pleasant with a few good moves.
FA. A.Sharp 1999

❷ **Sorry Lorry Morry** 6b
A good pitch up the flared corner/groove and thin crack.
Photo opposite.
FA. A.Sharp, P.Lewis 8.1.1989

❸ **Juvenile Justice** .... 7a+
A bald slab with tiny holds at the crux and a very trying sequence to match.
FA. A.Sharp, P.Lewis 7.1.1989

The Darren — 401

④ Boulevard de Alfred Turner (1926) .... VS 4b
The deep-set groove, moving right at the tree to a thin crack.
FA. G.Lewis, H.Griffiths 1981

⑤ Andrew the Zebra .... 6a+
Take the difficult bulge and crack to a lower-off.
FA. G.Lewis, C.Heard, S.Robinson 1981

⑥ Calling Card .... 6c+
The groove to the right is deceptively hard, from the ledge continue up the wall as for *Andrrew The Zebra*.
FA. T.Penning, J.Harwood, P.Lewis, A.Sharp 12.6.1990

⑦ Shaken not Stirred ...... 6c+
Short and to the point. Climb the wall right of a large flake-crack.
FA. A.Sharp, J.Harwood, P.Lewis 15.1.1989

⑧ Madame-X 7a
The arete at the right-hand end of the wall.
FA. A.Sharp, J.Harwood, P.Lewis 15.1.1989

Al Murray approaching the final wall of *Sorry Lorry Morry* (6b) - *opposite* - on the B.A.T Wall at The Darren. Photo: Keith Sharples

Cwmaman

Grade Spread - 14 9 6 -

Cwmaman is hidden high up at the back of the Dare Valley. It is a fine little quarry in a decent setting and contains some good routes. There are two sections of crag, both of which receive the sun for some of the day. The Main Wall is a clean sheet of almost perfect sandstone and has some of the area's best sport routes. The Right-hand wall has a gentler atmosphere with routes in the lower grades.

Approach

From the A470, take the A4059 through Mountain Ash towards Aberdare. Turn left at a roundabout towards Aberaman and at a T-junction turn right (again signed to Aberaman). Follow the road and take the first left, (almost back on yourself) for Cwmaman. Follow this road to a T-junction and turn left into Jubilee Road. Follow this road for 1 mile and just after the Shepherd's Arms take the third left. Take the next left which goes down a short steep hill and around a left-hand bend. Continue up this for 100m and park. Take a small road on the left (signed footpath and bench) to twin cottages. From here follow the upper of two paths on the left for 100m to a telegraph pole. Continue for 15m and take a small path on the right steeply uphill to the quarry.

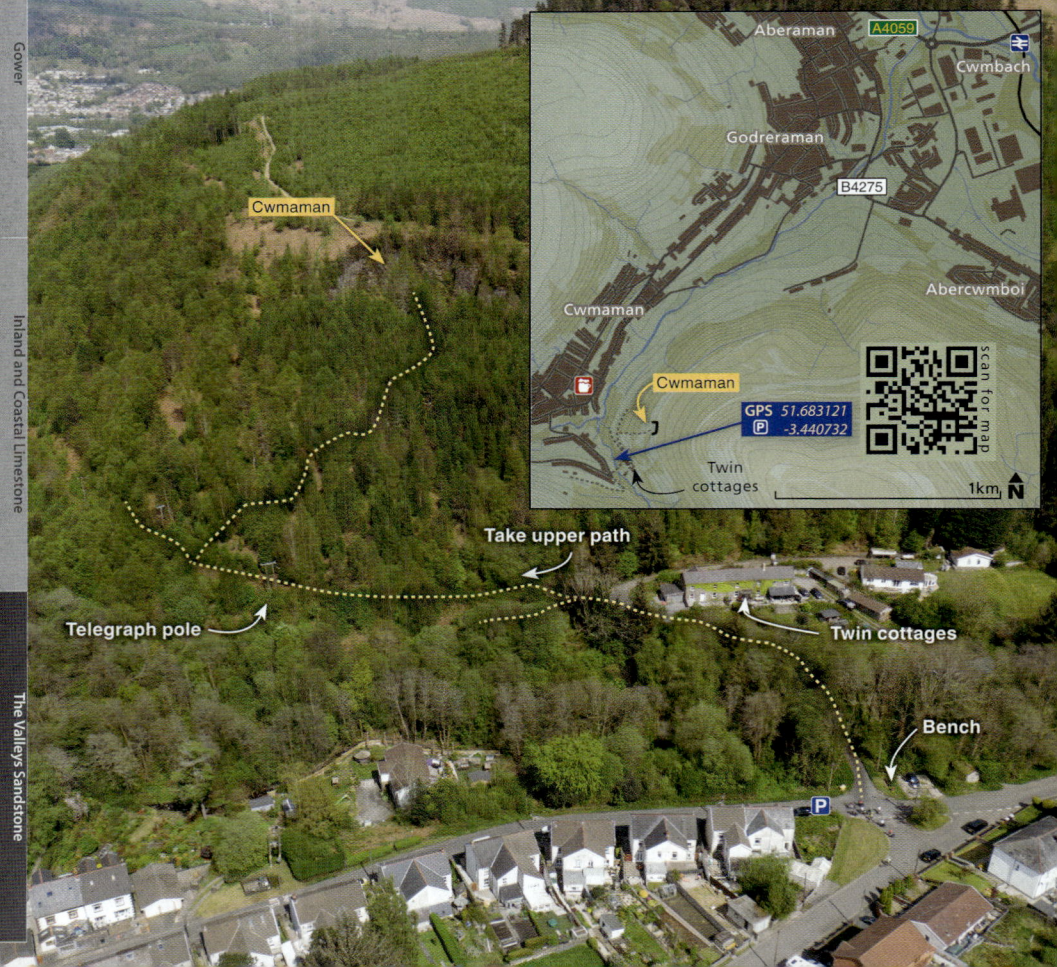

Cwmaman

Conditions
The Main Wall sees the sun for most of the day whilst the other walls get sun in the afternoon. The Main Wall dries quickly, but can suffer some seepage towards its right-hand side well into early summer and for this reason a couple of its routes can remain a little dirty.

Aaron Martin captured perfectly demonstrating the fingery and technical nature of the wall climbing encountered on many of the Valleys sandstone quarried faces. The route is *Mother of Pearl* (7b) - *p.404* - on Cwmaman's Main Wall. Photo: Elis Rees

Cwmaman Main Wall

Main Wall

A fine south-facing wall of compact vertical sandstone that has a handful of good fingery pitches. The setting is very pleasant, being both quiet and away from any roads.
Approach (map and overview p.402) - The Main Wall is on the left when entering the quarry.
Conditions - The wall gets plenty of sun and is sheltered from westerly winds. It can get hot in summer but does receive some shade in the evening. There is a bit seepage at the very base of the wall that can affect a number of the starts.

❶ 30' is the new 20' .... 6c+
The crimpy wall just to the right of the corner.
FA. S.Delaney, G.Jones 26.4.2010

❷ Good Tradition 6b
The left-hand side of the wall gives a pleasant but intense pitch.
FA. A.Sharp, P.Lewis 5.11.1988

❸ A Clear Head and a Blow Lamp
.... 6c
The crack-line is stern. Boulder out the initial move and continue up still tough ground to the top. Move left to the lower-off.
FA. A.Sharp, P.Lewis 5.11.1988

❹ A Clear Conscience and a Blow Job
.... 6c+
A good extension to *A Clear Head and a Blow Lamp*. Move right on edges and then on up to a lower-off on the right.
FA. A.Sharp, P.Lewis 5.11.1988

❺ Maybe Tomorrow .... 7b+
The direct start to *A Clear Conscience and a Blow Job*.
FA. A.Sharp 1995

❻ Mother of Pearl... 7b
The centre of the wall gives one of the original classics of the area. The mid-section is particularly thin. *Photo p.403.*
FA. A.Sharp, P.Lewis 5.11.1988

❼ Two for Tuesday .... 6c+
The crack-line is much better than it looks, but can be dirty.
FA. A.Sharp, P.Lewis, J.Harwood 8.5.1989

❽ The World is my Lobster
.... 6c+
The left edge of the higher wall via a small overlap low down.
FA. A.Sharp, P.Lewis, J.Harwood 8.5.1989

❾ Propaganda...... 7a+
Classic climbing of its genre left of centre on the main wall. Top of the grade. *Photo opposite and p.6.*
FA. A.Sharp, P.Lewis 7.11.1988

❿ Science Friction... 7b
A fine route up the centre of the wall. Similar to *Propaganda* but with a harder start.
FA. A.Sharp, P.Lewis 5.11.1988

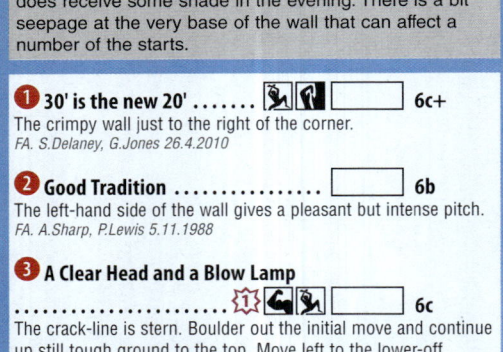

Cwmaman

11 La Rage ..... 7b+
The wall just right of centre suffers seepage and has one very hard move.
FA. A.Sharp, P.Lewis 16.5.1989

12 Innuendo 7b
The right-hand line is rarely dry and is very hard when it is.
FA. M.Crocker, R.Thomas 18.5.1989

13 The Numbers Game 7a
A traverse of the wall. Start up *Good Tradition* and traverse the high break to the mid-way broken corner, then move up to the next horizontal break. Follow the break right to meet and finish up *Innuendo*.
FA. A.Sharp, P.Lewis 16.5.1989

Jen Stephens moving fast on the crimps on *Propaganda* (7a+) - *opposite* - at Cwmaman. The Main Wall is the showpiece of the quarry and has some superb wall climbs that will expose any suitor lacking the required finger strength. The other walls offer lines of reduced difficulty but also lesser quality. Photo: Mark Glaister

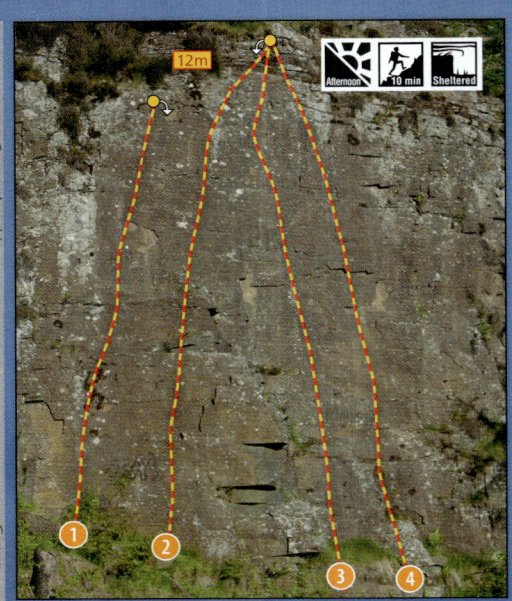

Zoo Time Wall

A small wall just to the right of the Main Wall with four fairly popular easier lines.
Conditions - The wall gets the sun in the afternoon and is fairly sheltered.

1 Looking for Leather 1 5b
The first line on the left-hand side of the wall.
FA. M.Jordan, N.Jordan 12.6.2010

2 Instead of This 1 5c
The wall past the prominent ledge. A pig-tail lower-off.
FA. G.Gibson, R.Thomas 16.6.1990

3 Circus Clowns 1 6a
Climb the central line of the trio that end at the pig-tail lower-off.
FA. R.Thomas, G.Leyshon 6.2010

4 Zoo Time 1 6a
The clean section of the wall to the right gives good climbing. Finish at the shared pig-tail lower-off.
FA. R.Thomas, G.Gibson 16.6.1990

Right-hand Wall

A good wall with a handful of quality pitches on its far right. Some of the rock is suspect so care is required.
Approach (map and overview p.402) - The Right-hand Wall is the first area encountered on the approach.
Conditions - The wall gets afternoon sun and is fairly sheltered.

5 Cilly Arete 1 6a
The lone arete with a vegetated slope leading up to it.
FA. G.Lewis, S.Delaney 20.4.2010

6 Sam Sparrow 1 5c
The left-hand bolt-line up the broken looking wall.
FA. G.Lewis, S.Delaney 3.2010

Carmarthenshire
Gower
Inland and Coastal Limestone
The Valleys Sandstone

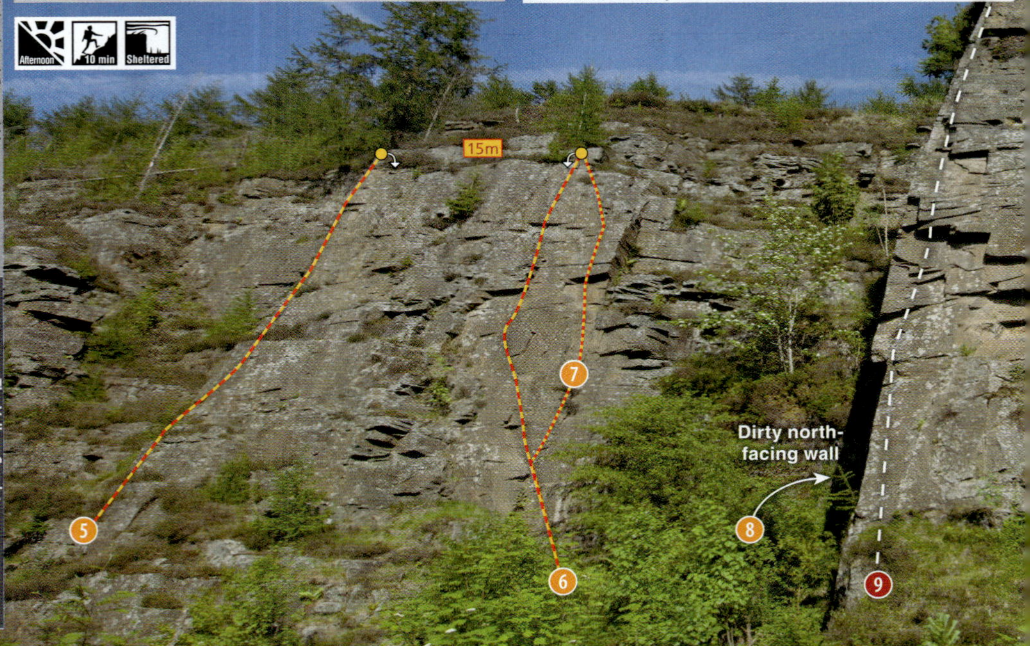

Right-hand Wall **Cwmaman** *407*

7 Alys Rook 5b
The right-hand line of bolts moving out of *Sam Sparrow*. The direct start goes at **6c**.
FA. G.Lewis, S.Delaney 3.2010

8 Spam Javelin 5b
The wall to the left of the prominent arete of *Pork Sword* is very dirty but does have one sport line on it.
FA. R.Thomas, E.Travers-Jones 1990

9 Pork Sword 6b
The arete taken on its right-hand side has very hollow rock.
FA. R.Thomas 15.3.1998

10 Turkey Twizzler .... 6a+
The line just right of the arete of *Pork Sword* passing through the loose niche has hollow rock above.
FA. R.Thomas, N.Jordan, M.Jordan 2010

11 Anniversary Walk 6a
The wall right of the low niche of *Turkey Twizzler* is a good introduction to this section of the face. Good moves.
FA. R.Thomas, M.Crocker 13.11.1988

12 The Forgotten Route 5c
Climb direct to a lower-off below a grassy niche close to the top.
FA. G.Lewis, S.Delaney 1.9.2009

13 Hey Mister 6a
A good wall pitch that finishes just right of a grassy niche.
FA. R.Thomas, M.Crocker 13.11.1988

14 Buff the Happy Lamp. 6b
A strange line but with decent climbing. The original started more directly but now a tree is in the way. Climb *Yank the Plank* and make thin moves up left to join *Hey Mister* before following a rising line to finish at the lower-off of *Anniversary Walk*.
FA. R.Thomas, P.Hadley 8.1999

15 Yank the Plank 6a
A pleasing little pitch.
FA. R.Thomas, P.Hadley 8.1999

16 Evil Ways 6a
The right-most line on the wall has a tough move near the finish.
FA. P.Hadley, Thomas 8.1999

Mountain Ash

Mountain Ash quarry is in the shape of a bowl and provides a welcome retreat from any harsh weather. There is a good mixture of climbing styles and grades, ranging from short and desperate fingery testpieces through to some long and slabbier walls. There are enough routes here to pack a lot into a short session.

Approach
When approaching from the south on the A470, take a left turn at the main roundabout at Abercynon. Follow the A4059, signposted Aberdare, into the town of Mountain Ash, 2km after the Cynon Business Park. Turn right into Mary Street, and after 100m go right into Newton Villas and park (or back on the approach road if all spaces are full). Walk up a dirt track directly ahead to an open area at the end of the track. A path on the left zig-zags up steeply to meet another path. Go right on this path to enter the quarry in 60m.

Conditions
This is a very sheltered venue with walls that face in all directions. The right-hand wall does suffer a bit of dampness after rain and through the winter months, but there is plenty to do here in dry weather. The cliff takes little in the way of seepage.

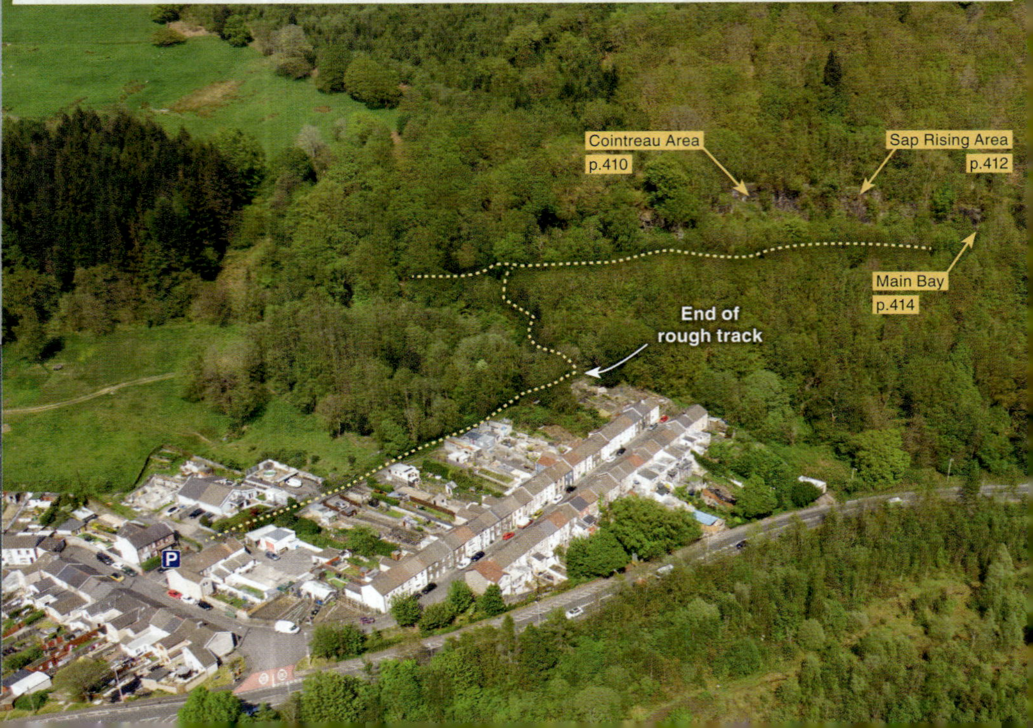

GPS 51.677757 -3.367689

- Cointreau Area p.410
- Sap Rising Area p.412
- Main Bay p.414
- End of rough track

Mountain Ash

Marti Hallett on *Fatal Reflection* (6b) - *p.412* - at Mountain Ash. This line is one of a trio of very good sustained mid-grade routes that take on the full height of the wall. Photo: Mark Glaister

Mountain Ash — Cointreau Area

1. What's the Arc de Triomphe for Then? — 6a
The slab on the left has a single tough move.
FA. J.Williams 1992

2. The Old Firm — 6b+
The centre of the wide rib and upper wall. Big glue-in bolts.
FA. C.Evans 1992

3. Coggars Lane — 6b+
Climb up the pillar and through the overhang.
FA. C.Evans, P.Green 1992

4. Outspan — 7a+
Quality climbing with a bold start and fingery climbing above.
FA. M.Crocker, R.Thomas 25.9.1988

5. Hot Cross Guns — 7b+
Sustained climbing that links the start of *Outspan* to the upper section of *Ripe and Ready*.
FA. M.Richards, A.Sharp 14.4.2009

6. Ripe 'n Ready — 7b+
A 'fingernail' desperate up the centre of the wall, or just a pure dyno - you choose.
FA. M.Crocker, R.Thomas 27.10.1988

7. Pastis on Ice — 7a+
The prominent arete gives a test of finger strength and ingenuity.
FA. M.Crocker 25.9.1988. FA. (Direct) E.Travers-Jones 23.5.1995

8. Cointreau — 7a+
The orange wall gives a sandstone classic.
FA. M.Crocker, J.Harwood 17.4.1994

9. Choice Cut — E2 5c
The thin crack from ledges high on the right.
FA. P.Donnithorne, A.Price 7.11.1988

10. Blacker than Black — 6c+
A desperate problem. Jump down onto the last bolt to lower-off.
FA. M.Crocker, J.Harwood 17.4.1994

11. Branch Manager — 6c+
Typical of these walls, more of an extended boulder problem.
FA. R.Thomas 31.3.1996

12. Totally Stumped — 6c
Desperate moves via a vague scoop.
FA. R.Thomas 21.3.1995

13. Molybdenum Man — 6c
The excellent little arete. Surprisingly hard.
FA. M.Crocker, R.Thomas 27.10.1988

14. Ferndale Revisited — 7b
Another desperate boulder problem from bottom to top.
FA. A.Sharp, P.Lewis 22.4.1989

15. Dusk — 7a+
Marginally easier than its left-hand neighbour.
FA. E.Travers-Jones 21.3.1995

16. I Came — 6a+
Slabby moves up the left side of the slab and the short headwall.
FA. R.Thomas 22.3.1995

17. S'not Yours — 5c
A short but worthwhile pitch with a tricky thin start.
FA. R.Thomas 22.3.1995

Cointreau Area
Three walls that are the first encountered on entering the quarry. The high orange-coloured wall of smooth rock with the route *Cointreau* is the best here. Below it is a low wall of compact sandstone with some short but testing little lines. All three sections are clean and dry quickly.
Approach (map and overview p.408) - The first climbable wall on entering the quarry.

Cointreau Area Mountain Ash

18 He Sawed 5a
A short, relatively easy slab.
FA. R.Thomas 22.3.1995

19 Conkered .... 6a+
Further right of a chimney is line with a single bolt.
FA. R.Thomas 22.3.1995

Mountain Ash — Sap Rising Area

Sap Rising Area

A good couple of walls with four longer routes and some worthwhile shorter pitches. An open aspect means that the walls get plenty of sun, although seepage can be a problem on the bottom walls of the longer lines.

Approach (map and overview p.408) - Easily identified a short distance on from the Cointreau Area.

❶ Bring Back the Birch 5b
A pleasant slab that has a single hard move.
FA. R.Thomas 22.3.1995

❷ Under the Axe 6b
A short blunt rib and sharp V-groove.
FA. R.Thomas 22.3.1995

❸ No Barking up this Tree 5b
A single hard move.
FA. R.Thomas, P.Donnithorne 23.3.1995

❹ A Sight for Saw Eyes .... 6a+
The dyno is at the start. The rest is easier.
FA. R.Thomas, P.Donnithorne 23.3.1995

❺ Carpet Bombing 5c
The wall left of the prominent arete has two bolts and requires a long clip-stick as the first is well above the ground.
FA. N.White 1995

❻ Tragedy E1 5a
The arete is an eye-catching but very bold proposition.
FA. M.Crocker, M.Learoyd, R.Thomas, P.Lewis 9.10.1988

❼ More than a Feeling ..... 6b+
Fingery pulls and laybacking up the right-hand side of the arete. The start is particularly thin on footholds. *Photo p.415.*
FA. A.Rosier 17.7.2014

❽ The Future Holds 7b
A complicated sequence with a trying finish. Quite popular.
FA. M.Crocker, 16.10.1988

❾ Aphrodite's Curse .... 6a+
The slab/wall to the right of the corner and high left arete is a long and very sustained pitch.
FA. R.Thomas, Gandalf 10.2023

❿ Fatal Reflection 6b
A very good single pitch that has a thin start and less demanding but fine climbing above. Start on the boulder left of the low roof of *Rising Sap*. Climb the slab/wall and blunt arete high up. *Photo p.409.*
FA. R.Thomas, S.Cann, E.Chapman, Gandalf 4.2022

⓫ Rising Sap .... 6b+
A super route. A long pitch finishing up a flying arete. The start is a bit easier for the tall and very thin for everyone else.
FA. R.Thomas 1995

⓬ Weeping Stump 5b
Follow the groove, exit left and continue to finish up the right side of the finishing arete.
FA. R.Thomas, G.Tucker, N.Goile, A.Rosier 3.7.2008

Mountain Ash

Sap Rising Area

413

Mountain Ash — Main Bay

Main Bay

The final area in the quarry is an impressive collection of right-angled corners which are home to some excellent routes. Once dry the walls stay in good condition, but get less sun than the other parts of Mountain Ash.

Approach (map and overview p.408) - A series of bays and raised terraces 50m right of the Rising Sap Area.

❶ Attrocities .... 6b+
The left-hand side of the shady, right-facing wall.
FA. A.Rosier, R.McAllister 9.7.2014

❷ No Chips Round Here. 7b
The steep wall right of *Attrocities*, moving rightwards and finishing direct. The original route, **A Clip Round the Ear, 7a+** finished leftwards to the *Attrocities* lower-off.
FA. G.Ashmore 12.7.1995. FA. (ACatE) A.Sharp, P.Lewis 3.3.1991

❸ Constantinople 5c
The corner of the shady, right-facing wall to the right of *No Chips Round Here*.
FA. G.Lewis 2016

❹ Helmet Man's Day Off 5a
The left-hand line on the slab right of the corner.
FA. M.Hirst 13.7.1995

❺ Ant Frenzy 5b
The centre of the slab right of the corner.
FA. M.Hirst 13.7.1995

❻ Homebase 5c
Just before the start of the terrace at the left end of the Main Bay is an arete. Climb this to a shared lower-off.
FA. G.Lewis, G.Barker 1989

❼ Cymru Euro 2016 .... 5a
The shallow corner right of *Homebase*.
FA. G.Lewis, L.Elgar 2016

Having dispatched the fingery starting moves Marti Hallett continues up the less tricky rib of *More Than a Feeling* (6b) - *p.412* - in the Main Bay at Mountain Ash. Photo: Mark Glaister

Mountain Ash — Main Bay

8 Little Polvier 5a
The corner on the left side of the terrace.
FA. G.Lewis, A.Keward 1989

9 Double Bore .... 6b+
The groove and wall left of *Slap Happy's* left-trending thin crack.
FA. A.Sharp, P.Lewis 28.3.2009

10 Slap Happy .... 6c+
The left-trending crack moving right at the top.
FA. A.Sharp, P.Lewis 11.4.1991

11 Sport for All .... 7b+
The very blank-looking face to the right is not all it appears.
FA. A.Sharp, P.Lewis 31.3.1991

12 Sporting Supplement ... 6b
Fine climbing via the shallow scoop.
FA. P.Lewis, A.Sharp 13.4.1991

13 Sunday Sport.............. E3 5c
The flake-line with an old peg.
FA. A.Sharp, P.Lewis 16.4.1991

14 The Abdominal Showman .... 7a+
The flake-line just left of the corner. Desperate if climbed direct.
FA. A.Sharp, P.Lewis 13.4.1991

15 A Certain Peace.......... 6b+
The short wall and arete is a worthwhile pitch that has a perplexing sequence to reach the second ledge.
FA. R.Thomas, M.Crocker 27.10.1988

16 Misadventure 7a
The fine wall to the right gives a pitch worth seeking out.
FA. R.Thomas 12.7.1995

17 Mountin' Ass Crack ...... 6b+
The narrow crack-line just right of *Misadventure*.
FA. A.Rosier 15.7.2014

18 A Far Cry from Squamish . E4 6a
The diagonal crack-line has been cleaned up. Can be linked into *The Theory and Practice of Glue Sniffing*.
FA. M.Crocker 22.7.1990 (Link - R.Thomas, P.Hadley 1999)

19 The Theory and Practice of Glue Sniffing
.... 6c+
Branch out left from *Jet Lagged* at 5m via a rib and corner.
FA. G.Ashmore 12.7.199

Main Bay **Mountain Ash** 417

20 Jet Lagged 6c
The wall above a bouldery crux start.
FA. M.Crocker 22.7.1990

21 Sennapod Corner .... HVS 5a
Speaks for itself really. Gets a star if it is clean.
FA. P.Thomas 1970

22 Whiter than White Wall .. 7a+
The clean-looking wall has a particularly trying crux.
FA. M.Crocker, M.Ward 21.5.1988

23 A Load of Rubbish E2 5b
The first series of cracks gives a worthwhile pitch.
FA. A.Richardson 1984

24 Valleys Initiative 7a
One of the better routes in the vicinity. A climactic finale.
FA. A.Sharp, J.Harwood 4.10.1991

25 Ain't as Effical E3 5c
The next to last crack-line is often a little dirty.
FA. M.Crocker, M.Ward. G.Jenkin 21.5.1988

26 Grave Concern .... 6a+
The crack-line.
FA. R.Thomas, E.Rees 1998

27 Final Plot .... 6a+
Climb the wall to crux moves that access the small ramp.
FA. R.Thomas, E.Rees 1998

28 Parabola .... 6a+
The slab and roof over to the right.
FA. A.Rosier, N.Goile 4.7.2015

Mount Pleasant

Grade Spread | 1 | 42 | 15 | 2 | -

A two tier quarry that has plenty of routes in the mid grades. The variety of climbing on offer is broad ranging from slabs to overhangs and most other features in between. The setting is quiet and apart from the ever-present fly tipping it is a place worth checking out especially once the sun comes around in the afternoon.

Approach
Parking is available near the memorial seen on entering Mount Pleasant from the south. Walk back along the road for 400m and just beyond the average speed camera take a track on the left that leads up through the wood to the quarry.

Conditions
Sunny from midday and sheltered. The lesser travelled lines may need some cleaning.

Access
In the past there have been times when the landowner has asked climbers to move on - however this has not happened for a long time and now seems not to be pro-actively enforced. In the unlikely event you should be asked to leave please be polite and report to the BMC.

Lower Tier — Mount Pleasant

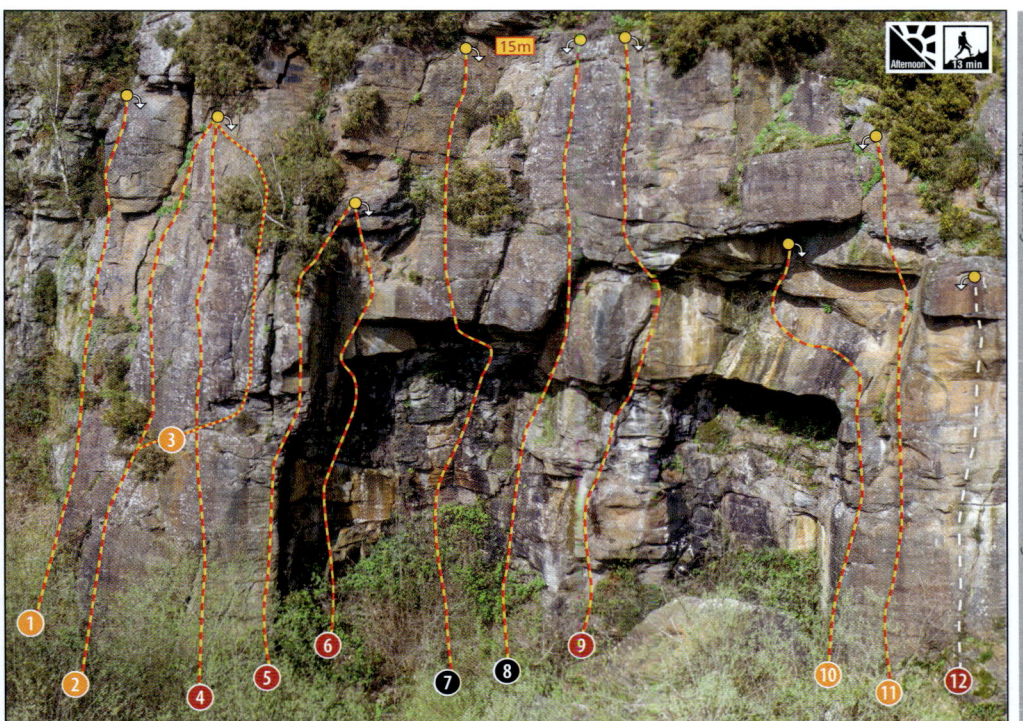

Lower Tier
A wide, low section of crag offering a good number of varied climbs across the grades.
Approach - Walk across to the base from the end of the approach track.
Conditions - Sunny and sheltered but can seep.

1 Monkey Business .... 6a+
A rambling but worthwhile route up left-hand side of the slab to a tough bulge and arete.
FA. R.Thomas 2009

2 Flidington Rex 5a
Climb the slab and then layback the groove.
FA. K.Davies, D.Emanuel 9.2.2008

3 Big Bad Baboon 5c
Start up *Flidington Rex* and at a horizontal break traverse rightwards to a crack. Climb the crack and move rightwards to a small tree before finishing up a corner.
FA. D.Emanuel, K.Davies 16.2.2008

4 Orangutanarium 6b
Monkey up a crack to a ledge and follow the bolt line up the featureless face above, passing a small bulge to a lower-off.
FA. D.Emanuel 2008

5 Cone Penetration Test ... 6b+
Take a line of pockets up the arete to reach a tree and lower-off.
FA. R.Thomas 2008

6 Remediation Required .. 6b
The corner to the right of *Cone Penetration Test* is much better than it appears.
FA. R.Thomas 2009

7 Fisty Nuts .... 7b+
The hard to ignore jam crack through the large roof.
FA. G.Gibson 2009

8 Phill's a Bit Wrong But...
.... 7b
The wall below the hanging groove and continuation above.

9 Fistula 7a
A superb route that tackles the twisting crack and easier but fine headwall above it.
FA. R.Thomas, D.Emanuel 2010

10 Rabbit Proof Fence .... 6a+
Follow the line of staples right of the cave past an overhang to a lower-off at the lip of a second overhang.
FA. R.Thomas, N.Jordan, M.Jordan 6.6.2008

11 Uluru .... 6a+
The pocketed groove passing a roof on its right. A little loose at the start.
FA. D.Emanuel 2008

Mount Pleasant — Lower Tier

12 Cox 2 Inhibitor .... 6b+
Climb direct via pockets and a tricky bulge.
FA. R.Thomas 2008

13 Proton Pump 6a
A shallow groove and hard to read final bulge.
FA. R.Thomas 2008

14 Voltarol Vigour 6a
The staple line just to the right of the corner.
FA. R.Thomas 2008

15 Sucking Dicks' Lowfenac 5c
Ascend the slab left of a corner.
FA. R.Thomas 2008

16 Co-Codamol Crunch 5c
Climb to the same lower off as *Sucking Dicks' Low Fenac*.
FA. R.Thomas 2008

17 Tramadol Trip .... 6a+
Take the pockets in a faint groove left of a slanting crack.
FA. R.Thomas 2008

18 Paracetamol Punch 6b
Follow pockets to a slab and then tackle the bulge above.
FA. R.Thomas 2008

19 Ed Less 6a
Use a deep pocket to surmount the low overhang and then continue up the slab above.
FA. R.Thomas 16.4.2008

20 Cut Throat .... 6a+
The line just left of *Guillotine* to the lower-off of *Ed Less*.
FA. R.Thomas 2008

21 Guillotine 5a
The left-facing corner above an earth bank.
FA. D.Emanuel 2009

22 Final Cut 6b
Head up left to a pocket, then go right to further pockets before a tricky move reaches the slabby arete.
FA. R.Thomas 2009

Lower Tier **Mount Pleasant** 421

㉓ Primal Cut 6b
The short wall to an awkward last move to reach the lower-off above a ledge
FA. G.Gibson 2009

㉔ Razor Strop 6b
Left of the vegetated section.
FA. R.Thomas 2008

㉕ The Poddling............. 6a
Climb the scooped wall, fin and central crack.
FA. D.Emanuel 2009

㉖ Ed More 5a
The delicate rounded slab and left wall of a dirty crack.
FA. E.Rees 2008

㉗ Aqua Mule Show........ 5a
Surmount a smooth slab and gain a large ledge. Trend right to a lower-off.
FA. D.Emanuel, K.Davies 21.5.2008

㉘ Known Only Unto God ... 6a+
An easy start leads to a hard finale and lower-off.
FA. G.Gibson 2008

㉙ Oolacunta 6a
A friable start reaches the rounded rib above.
FA. D.Emanuel, K.Davies 25.6.2008

㉚ Uber Gruppen Fuhrer........... 4a
Climb to a ledge, traverse right onto the face and follow the line of bolts to a lower-off.
FA. D.Emanuel, K.Davies 24.6.2008

A short distance right and hidden by trees is the Drift Mine Wall, home to a couple of bolted lines.

㉛ Daddy's Little Lemon Licker 6a
From right of the mine entrance, trend leftwards to the lower-off.
FA. D.Emanuel 2009

㉜ Homme de L'elephant 5c
Right most line of staples, on the Drift Mine Wall.
FA. D.Emanuel, R.Thomas, K.Davies 2008

Mount Pleasant — Upper Tier

Upper Tier

Lots of lines in the 5th and 6th grade that get plenty of sun and dry quickly.

Approach (map and overview p.418) - From the end of the approach track walk across to the left end of the lower tier and then on up to the terrace that runs beneath the Upper Tier from where all the routes begin.

Conditions - Sunny and sheltered but can seep.

1 Polari Cartso 5c
The first bolted line passing to the right of a sling around a tree.
FA. D.Emanuel, R.Thomas 11.2008

2 Rhondda Tan 5a
The slab with a horizontal breaks.
FA. D.Emanuel, R.Thomas 11.2008

3 Steroid Vest 6a
Another slab with horizontal breaks.
FA. D.Emanuel, R.Thomas 11.2008

4 Back to Black 5c
The wide crack - still a little loose and eliminate.
FA. D.Emanuel, R.Thomas 11.2008

5 Johnny Bionic 5c
The finger jamming vertical crack to a slab.
FA. D.Emanuel, R.Thomas 11.2008

6 Slabadabadoo 5b
The slab to a huge lower-off ring.
FA. D.Emanuel, R.Thomas 11.2008

7 Fisting the Night Away 5c
The winding crack-line.
FA. D.Emanuel, R.Thomas 11.2008

8 Paul Prefers Pretty Pussy 6b
The crack and arete. Has a peg low down.
FA. R.Thomas 2009

9 Monkey Stole My Face ... 6a+
Jam up the steep crack and continuation slab.
FA. D.Emanuel, R.Thomas 2009

10 Balls of Damocles 6b
Head up a V-groove and gain the thin slab above.
FA. R.Thomas 2008

11 Boy George V .... 6a+
Surmount the giant egg and gain a ledge. Shared lower-off with *Dream of Wet Rabbits*.
FA. R.Thomas 2009

12 Dream of Wet Rabbits 5c
The right side of the corner/groove to a shared lower-off.
FA. D.Emanuel, R.Thomas 2008

13 Rent Boys and Radiators ..... 6a+
Approach the long and shattered vertical shot hole with care.
FA. R.Thomas 2008

14 We Like Damp Beaver 6b
The long face and breaks.
FA. R.Thomas, D.Emanuel 2009

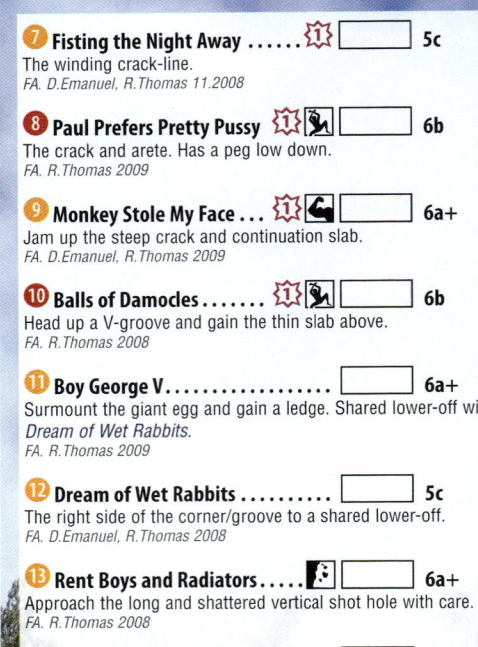

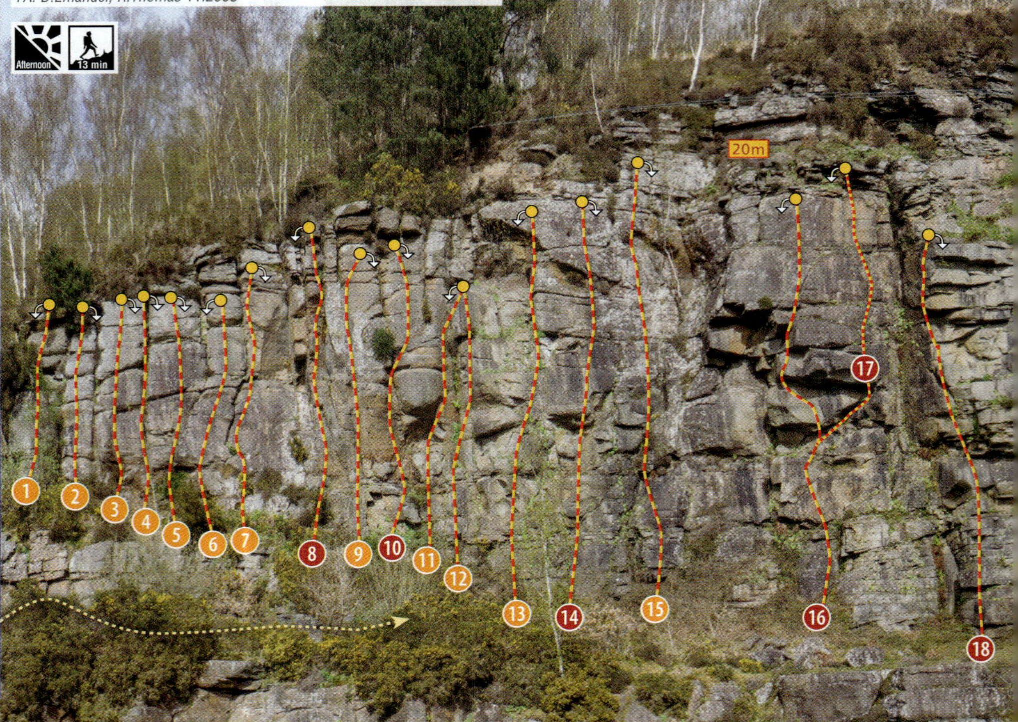

Upper Tier **Mount Pleasant** 423

⑮ Hot Little Minx .... 6a+
Bolted line left of a corner with a tree in it.
FA. R.Thomas, D.Emanuel 13.6.2009

⑯ The Pleasant Mount .... 6c+
The left side of the wall via the technical hanging scoop.
FA. G.Gibson 1.5.2009

⑰ Mounting at the Edge .... 6b+
Head out rightwards from *The Pleasant Mount* at bolt two.
FA. G.Gibson 2.5.2009

⑱ Man in a Honda Over Yonder in Rhondda
.... 6b
Follow the long stepped arete to a hard-to-clip lower-off.
FA. G.Gibson 2.5.2009

⑲ Poke Her Face 6a
A delicate exercise up the blunt rib.
FA. G.Gibson 2.5.2009

⑳ Over the Top 6a
Climb the wall and then move left to the lower-off.
FA. R.Thomas 5.2009

㉑ Bull Camp .... 6a+
The shallow groove and slab.
FA. R.Thomas 6.2009

㉒ I Love Valley Girls .... 6a+
As for *Bull Camp*, then swing right and climb on poor rock.
FA. S.Delaney 20.9.2009

㉓ Henry Allingham 5a
Climb the left-hand groove to the roof, then move out right and make an exposed mantel moves to finish.
FA. G.Lewis, S.Delaney 1.4.2009

㉔ Harry Patch 6a
Climb to a ledge and up the crack-line to left of *Chloe's Crack*.
FA. G.Lewis, S.Delaney 11.3.2009

㉕ Chloe's Crack 5a
Climb onto a ledge, move right and follow the cleaned crack to a lower-off in the overhanging top-out.
FA. S.Delaney, G.Lewis 11.3.2009

㉖ Emiliano Mercado del Toro 5c
The arete.
FA. S.Delaney, G.Lewis 1.4.2009

㉗ Bonaroo Lally Tappers 5c
The slabby face to the left of the final arete in the quarry.

㉘ Meat Fly vs the Custard Cannon .. 6a
Right of the final arete in the right of the quarry. Climb deep crack and hand traverse to finish up slab above.

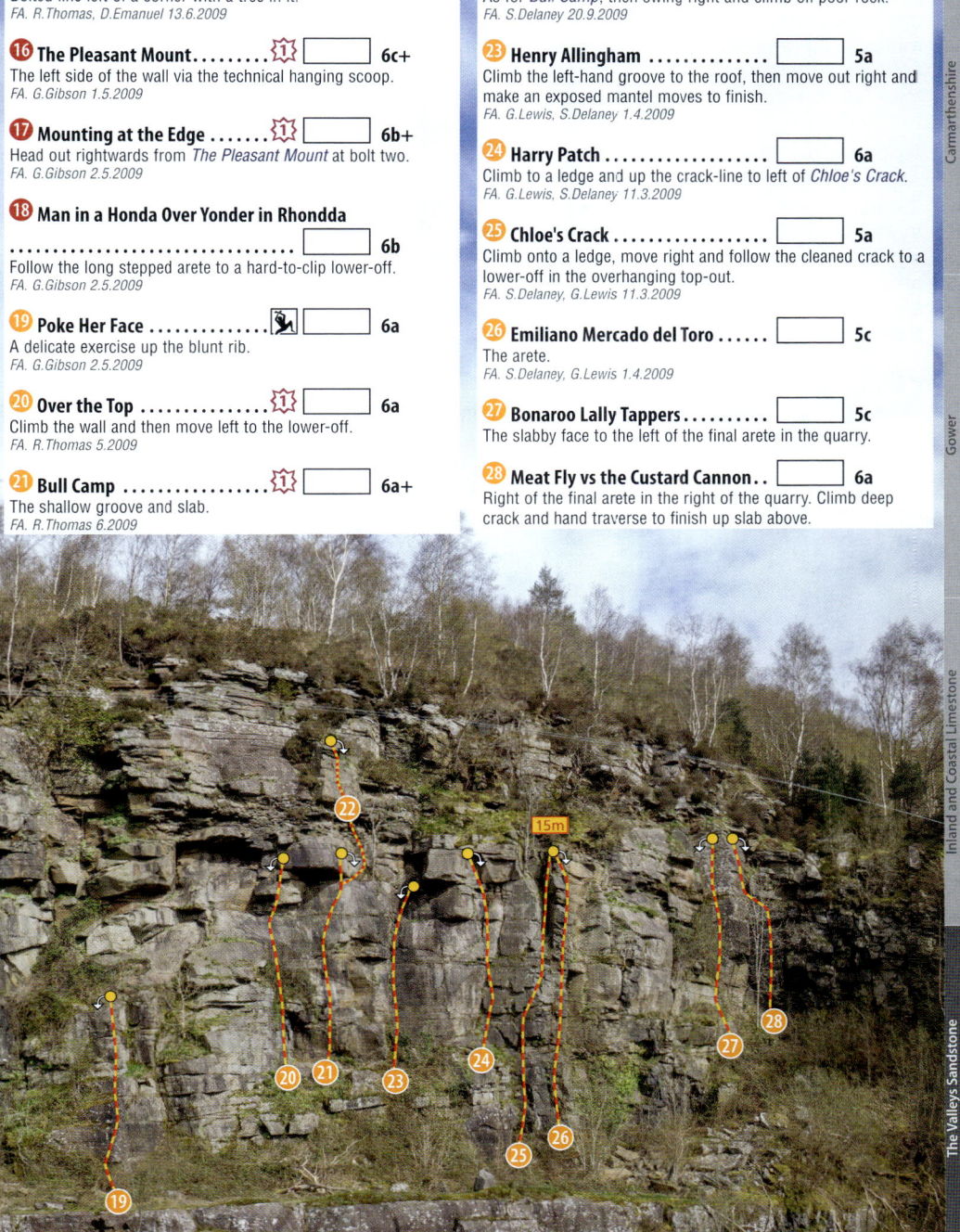

The Gap

| Grade Spread | 1 | 26 | 31 | 10 | - |

The Gap is one of the original and best known of the sandstone climbing areas in South Wales, although nowadays others have overtaken it in popularity. Sitting high on a hill overlooking the A470 Cardiff to Merthyr Tydfil road, it has a nice open aspect and plenty of routes at all grades that are well equipped. The majority of the routes are wall climbs, with the hardest featuring sustained sequences on thin edges. There are plenty of routes in the lower 6s including a few smart crack-lines.

Approach   Map p.418

At the large roundabout on the A470 when travelling from Cardiff, turn right, signposted Ystrad Mynach (A4059), or left when approaching from Merthyr Tydfil. At the next roundabout, turn left (A4054) towards Quakers Yard. On entering the village, and just before a pelican crossing, take the first left over a narrow bridge across the river. From here the road ascends steeply through a built-up area until the A470 is recrossed on a bridge. Take the first right immediately beyond the bridge and after 1km the cliff will be seen on the left. Parking is readily available below the quarries.

Conditions

The cliff is very open and dries relatively quickly, although it does take seepage in the winter. Due to its exposed nature it is best avoided in windy or cold conditions. The crag gets very little sun except first thing in the morning, which makes it the ideal venue in hot weather. Midges can be a problem in very humid and calm weather.

Salmon Running, Bear Cunning (7a) - *p.431* - on the Main Wall at The Gap. A short approach and shady climbing make The Gap a fine warm weather venue or somewhere for a couple of hours after work. Photo: Keith Sharples

The Gap

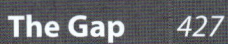

Zac Moss and Dan Bradford on the popular crack climb *Rattle Those Tusks* (6b) - *p.431* - on the Main Wall at The Gap. Although predominately a wall climbing destination The Gap also has a small number of long and fully bolted crack climbs. Photo: Mark Glaister

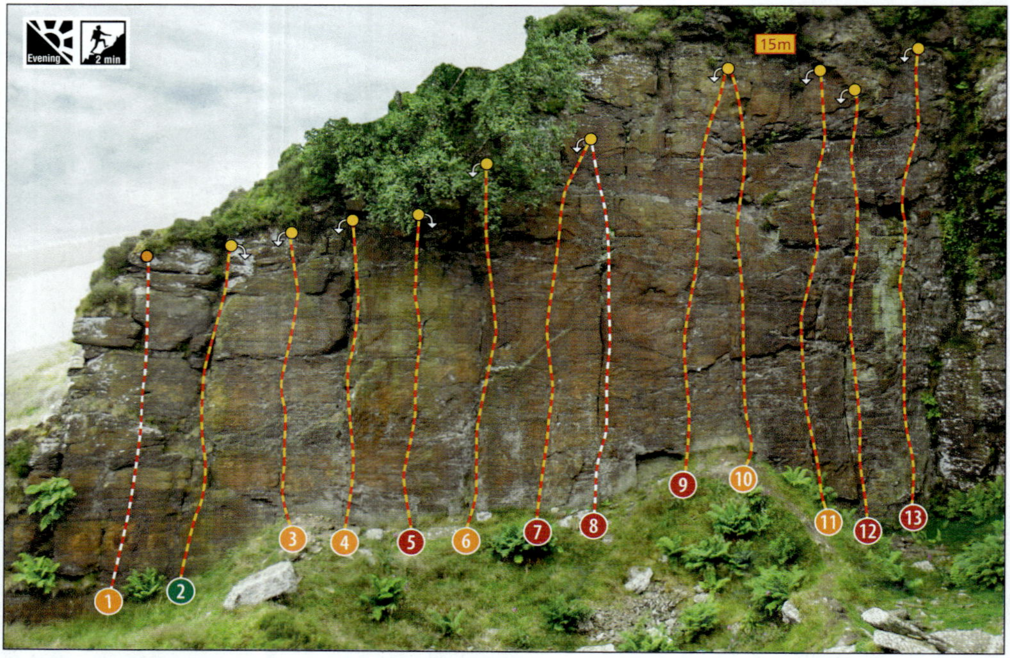

The Gap — Left Wall

Left Wall
A pleasant section of the crag that is home to a number of intense and fingery sport routes on good rock.
Approach (map p.418, overview p.424)
Conditions - The wall faces north and only receives evening sunshine in mid-summer. It dries relatively quickly, but suffers from a little seepage towards its right-hand side.

1 As it Was .... VS 4c
The short wall just to the right of the arete.
FA. R.Thomas 1994

2 Jack's Crack 4b
The wide crack.
FA. M.Jordan, J.Jordan 2020

3 Kabuto Mushi .... 6a+
Tough thin crimping up the short narrow wall.
FA. R.Thomas, E.Travers-Jones 1993

4 Duster 5b
The crack right of Kabuto Mushi.
FA. M.Jordan, J.Jordan 2020

5 Yikes 6c
A problematic wall on small holds. Thankfully the difficulties are short lived.
FA. M.Crocker, R.Thomas, M.Learoyd 25.3.1990

6 Muster 6a
The crack below the tree.
FA. M.Jordan, J.Jordan 2020

7 So Uncool 6c
A fingery start leads to balancy and sustained moves up the ramp above.
FA. G.Gibson, R.Thomas 6.2.1993

8 Just Hanging Around E1 5b
The fine traditional crack-line is well worth the effort, or it can be handily top-roped from the lower-off of So Uncool.
FA. R.Thomas, G.Royle 1990

9 Bluster 6b
Start on top of the mound and follow the left-hand line of bolts to a shared lower-off.
FA. R.Thomas 1993

10 Fluster .... 6a+
The right-hand line of bolts starting on top of the mound is similar to Bluster, though not as tricky at the start.
FA. R.Thomas 1993

11 Marlin on the Wall ..... 6a+
The 'marlin' adds a new dimension to the word protection - the old hook was once used as a piece of protection. Good climbing.
FA. R.Thomas 1993

12 Don't Blame Me 6b
A pleasant line which tackles the wall on edges and incuts.
FA. M.Hirst 2005

13 Sumo no Shiro .... 6b+
Climb the wall to a shallow small cave and pull out onto the headwall. Can be a bit green and damp.
FA. R.Thomas, E.Travers-Jones 1993

Jake Luther on the regional testpiece *Encore Magnifique* (7b+) - *p.431* - at The Gap. This wall and those to its left were developed over three decades ago and offer up some incredibly thin wall climbing that still requires much effort on the part of most suitors even today. Photo: Keith Sharples

The Gap — Main Wall

Main Wall
A fine wall of excellent sandstone, seamed with grooves and small overlaps towards its left. To the right, it forms a gently leaning wall of compact rock split by long cracks and covered in matchstick-edge crimps.

Approach (map p.418, overview p.424)

Conditions - The wall faces northeast and gets early morning sun, making it an ideal summer venue. It dries very quickly.

1 Canine League .... 6a+
Through the roof right of the corner. Good climbing when dry.
FA. R.Thomas, S.Coles 22.9.1994

2 Sleeping Dogs Lie .... 6b+
A classic of its type through the centre of the roofs.
FA. R.Thomas 1993

3 Don't Bark Yet 7a
The bulge and wall finishing over the overlap.
FA. M.Hirst 2004

4 Smack My Bitch Up ...... 6b+
The right-hand side wall of the corner has good moves.
FA. R.Thomas, M.Hirst 2004

5 Generation Bitch 6b
Start up *Generation Gap* and climb direct.
FA. R.Thomas 2004

6 Generation Gap 5c
A pleasant pitch starting up the left-hand edge of the pillar and taking the right-hand line of bolts.
FA. G.Royle, R.Thomas 1993

7 Mister Faraday 6a
A stubborn start leads to the upper section of *Generation Gap*.
FA. R.Thomas 1993

8 Poker in the Eye .... 6a+
Take the roof and storm the walls above.
FA. R.Thomas 1993

9 Grout Expectations 6a
An easier line past an overlap and up a groove.
FA. R.Thomas 1993

10 Shackles of Love .... 6a+
Climb the crack, wall and shallow groove.
FA. R.Thomas 1993

11 Fill That Gap 6b
The corner crack is a decent line now that a massive flake has been removed. Jamming ability will be an asset. *Photo p.435*.
FA. R.Thomas 2021

12 Ring of Confidence 6b
The low-level flakes and wall on the right to the top.
FA. R.Thomas 1993

Main Wall **The Gap** 431

13 Get Flossed .... 7a+
A tough start to the last route. Keep direct for the tick.
FA. G.Gibson, R.Thomas 18.6.1994

14 Loctite .... 7b+
Desperate fingery climbing on thin edges. Eases off above, just!
FA. A.Sharp, P.Lewis 15.7.1989

15 Land of the Dinosaurs ... 6b
The crack gives a sport route with a traditional feel.
FA. R.Thomas, G.Davies, M.Learoyd 1990

16 A Momentary Lapse of Reason
.... 7b+
A stern test of fingertip strength. Climb straight up the wall between the cracks.
FA. T.Forster, P.Harding 6.1989

17 Rattle Those Tusks 6b
The long crack and upper roof is a classic challenge.
Photo p.426.
FA. R.Thomas, M.Learoyd 1990

18 Mad at the Sun .. 7c
One of the sandstone's hardest. Start up *Leave it to Me* and make a thin traverse left out onto the face. Finish over the roof.
FA. M.Crocker, R.Thomas 8.4.1990

19 Leave it to Me 6c
The shallow groove and short headwall above the start of *Mad at the Sun* is a worthwhile and varied line.
FA. M.Hirst 2007

20 Salmon Running, Bear Cunning
.... 7a
The right-hand side of the arete. *Photo p.425*.
FA. P.Lewis, A.Sharp 17.6.1990.

21 John West 7b
Short direct finish to *Salmon Running, Bear Cunning*.
FA. E.Travers-Jones 1992

22 Anything You Can Do . 7b
The excellent open wall has a clearly defined crux sequence through the tiny overlap.
FA. A.Sharp, P.Lewis 17.4.1990. FA. (Finish) G.Gibson 28.6.1992

23 Encore Magnifique ... 7b+
A sandstone classic up the centre of the wall. Continuously interesting moves on excellent stone. *Photo p.429*.
FA. M.Crocker, R.Thomas 25.3.1990

24 Pleasant Valley Sunday
.... 7b
Typical of the wall with an unusual crossover crux. Linking into *Encore Magnifique* is a worth while alternative, also **7b**.
FA. A.Sharp, P.Lewis 18.7.1989. Direct start G.Gibson 1992.

Right Wall

The right-hand side of the quarry is a little more open with a small selection of routes.
Approach (map p.418, overview p.424) - A quick stroll up the hill from the parking area and the wall is up on the right.
Conditions - The wall dries quickly after rain.

❶ **One Track Mind** 7a
The fine arete is one of the best on the sandstone.
FA. A.Sharp, P.Lewis 11.7.1989

❷ **Greased Balls**........... 6b
The left wall of the corner is popular when in condition.
FA. R.Thomas 1994

❸ **Full Bag** 6b
The groove and crack right of the corner.
FA. R.Thomas, M.Learoyd 1990

❹ **Controlled Emission** 6c
A gem of a pitch that features some intricate face moves.
FA. P.Donnithorne, E.Alsford 1993

❺ **Sperm Wail** .... 7a+
The smooth-looking wall with a testing middle section. Watch out for the worrying fourth clip.
FA. M.Crocker, R.Thomas 11.4.1990

❻ **Scrotum Oil** 6c
The fine wall with good moves between positive holds.
FA. R.Thomas 1994

❼ **Naked Truth**............. 6a
The long crack-line needs care with the rock to start.
FA. R.Thomas, G.Gibson 12.8.1990

❽ **Barefaced Cheek**............ 6a+
A rather crumbly experience in its current form.
FA. R.Thomas 2021

❾ **Has the Fat Lady Sung?** 6b
Climb the short wall and face above the ledge to a lower-off. Take care with a block close to the top.
FA. R.Thomas 8.2009

Right Wall — The Gap

10 Pick up the Pieces 6a+
The slim wall proves better than it looks.
FA. R.Thomas 1991

11 Retro Butt In 5c
Begin left of the cave. Gain and climb just right of the corner until it is possible to step out right to a crack and lower-off.
FA. R.Thomas 1992

12 Butt Hole Scoundrels 6b+
Head for the grubby hole left of the white paint splodges. Crank through the roofs to join and finish up the arete of *Perfect Scoundrels*.
FA. R.Thomas 1993

13 Butt Hole Left Deviant 6b
Follow *Butt Hole Scouderels* and then move left to finish as for *Retro Butt In*.
FA. R.Thomas 1992

14 Perfect Scoundrels 6c
The alcove, roof and rib gives a good varied mix of moves.
FA. T.Fenning, P.Lewis, A.Sharp 1990. FA. (Direct) G.Gibson 18.6.1994

15 Butt Out 5c
Start on the right-hand side of the cave. Climb past some dubious rock onto a grassy ledge, then up the headwall.
FA. R.Thomas, M.Hirst 2004

16 Per Rectum 5b
The rib on the right-hand side of the cave and the wall above the ledge.
FA. R.Thomas, M.Hirst 2004

17 Stool Sample 5c
The short pillar. Shares staple bolts with *Per Rectum*.
FA. N.O'Neill, R.Thomas 2005

18 As It Is 5c
The blunt arete.
FA. R.Thomas 1994

19 Turd Strangler 6c
The short fingery wall.
FA. M Hirst, R.Thomas 2004

20 Dai Horrea 6b
Start a little higher up the slope. Steep moves to gain the belay.
FA. R.Thomas, M.Hirst 2004

21 Final Analysis 6b
Begin at a hole in the rock. Climb direct to a ledge using a finger pocket and then move left to join and finish as for *Dai Horrea*.
FA. R.Thomas 2018

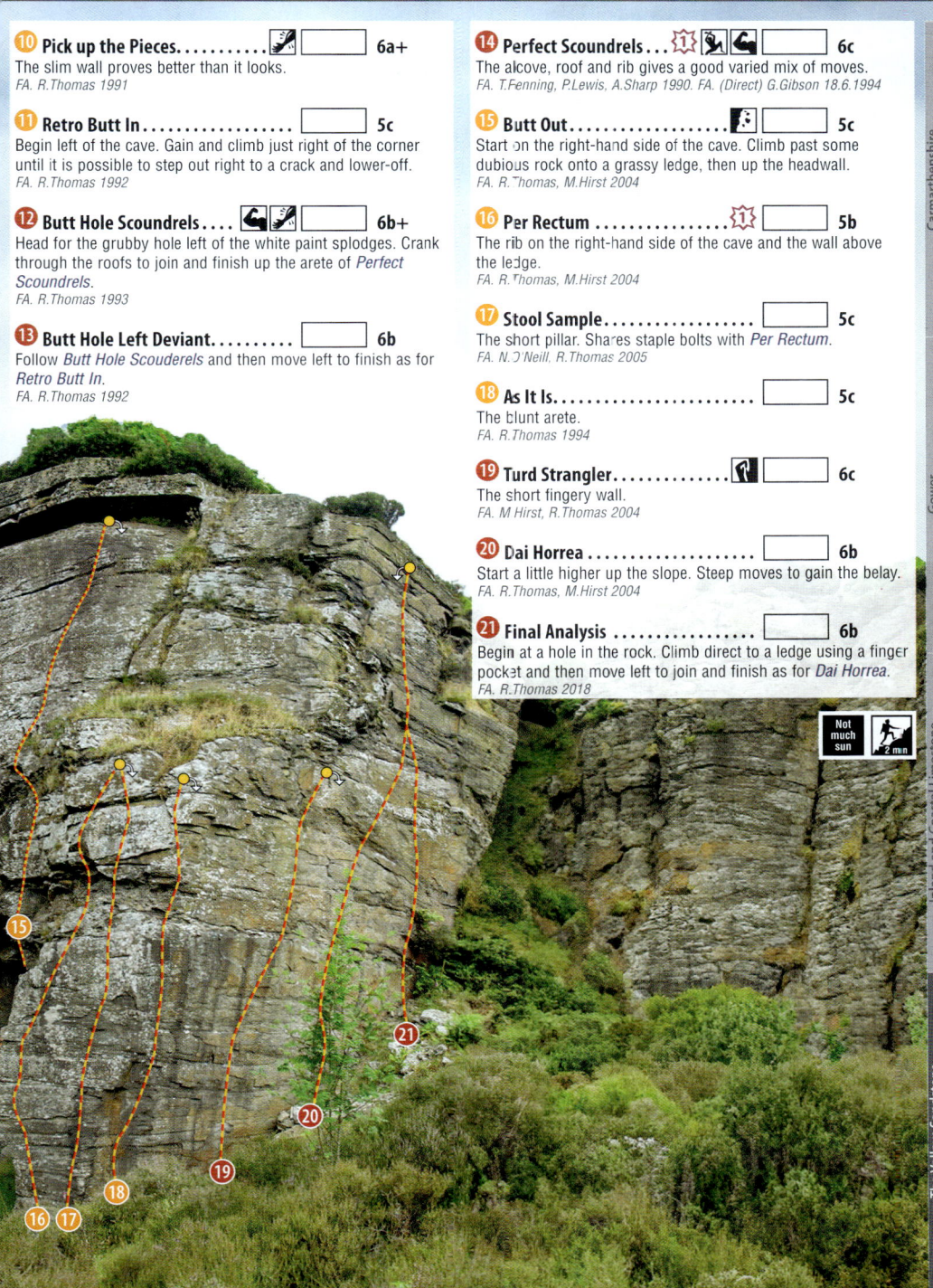

The Gap — Upper Quarry

Upper Quarry

A smaller quarry with some bolted lines between the older trad lines which (mainly) follow the cracks.

Approach (map p.418, overview p.424) - From the parking, walk up the dirt track on the right and the quarry is on the left as it levels out.

Conditions - The quarry faces northeast and gets only limited early morning sunshine. The walls dry quickly after rain, but it is a little more exposed than the Main Quarry.

1 Newton's Apple 6a
A nice little pitch up the wall between the big cracks.
FA. R.Thomas, G.Royle 1990

2 It's a Sine .... 6a+
The slabby wall to the left of the nasty looking corner on good rock.
FA. R.Thomas 5.5.1995

3 Scared Seal Banter ... 7a+
A good route that has some hard and complex sequences.
FA. M.Crocker, R.Thomas, M.Learoyd 4.3.1990

4 The Mastic Mick 6c
The overlap, large hole and wall above to the left of the big off-width crack.
FA. M.Crocker, M.Learoyd 4.3.1990

5 The Grout of San Romano 6c
The wall to the right of the big off-width crack is hard at the start and only slightly less pressing above.
FA. M.Crocker 4.3.1990

6 Listen to Uncle 6b
The wall left of the arete of *The Godfather*.
FA. R.Thomas 2018

7 The Godfather .... 6a+
Climb the good looking arete with some balancy moves, to pass a smooth ledge and make steeper moves to finish.
FA. G.Lewis, H.Griffiths 1990

8 Up Yours 6a
The juggy rib on less quarried rock.
FA. R.Thomas, M.Learoyd 1990

9 Mortar Life 6a
A short wall to the right. Top out as there is no lower-off.
FA. R.Thomas 1992

10 Shorter Life 5a
The wall to the right of *Mortar Life*. Top-out as there is no lower-off.
FA. J.Harwood 2005

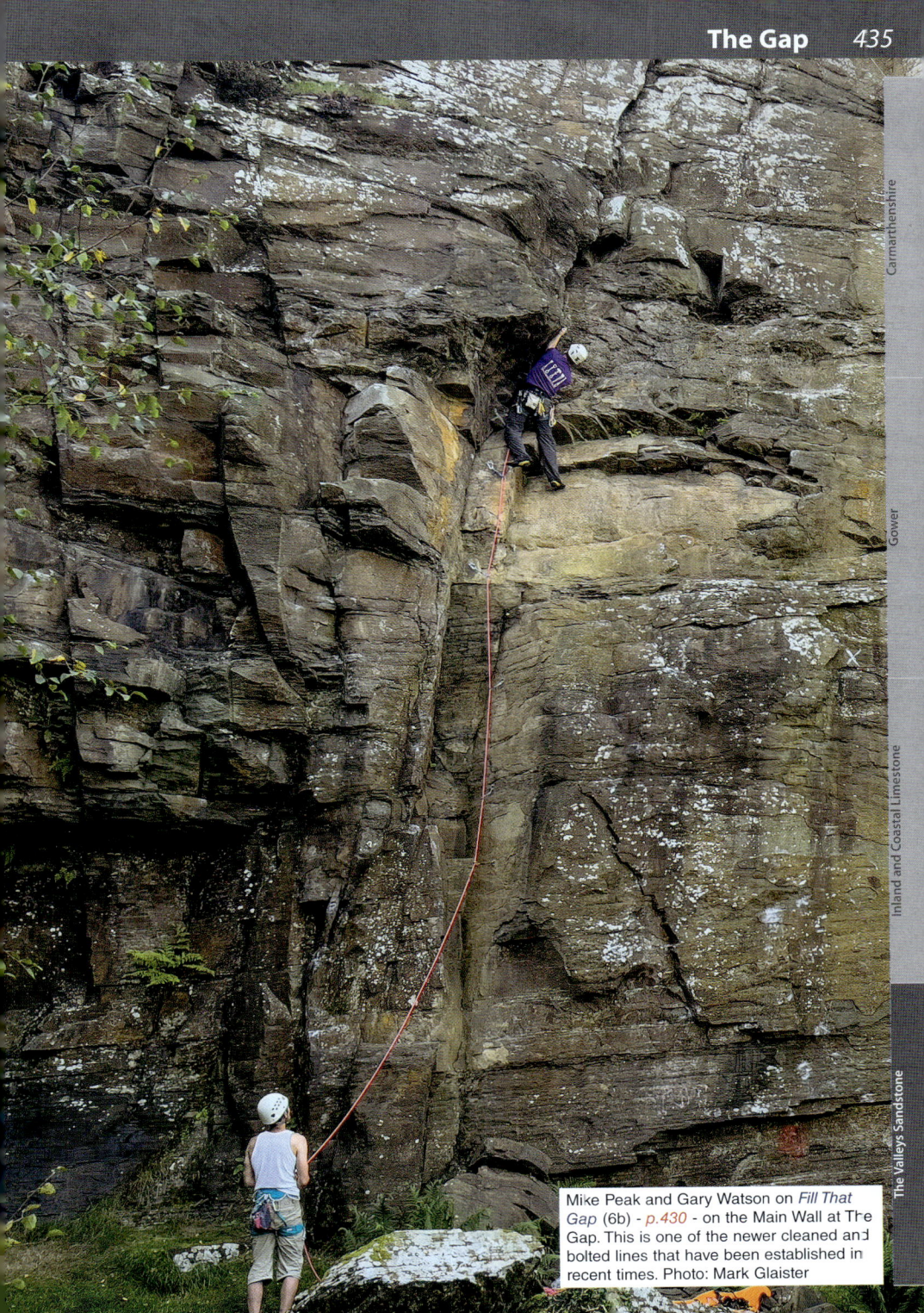

Mike Peak and Gary Watson on *Fill That Gap* (6b) - *p.430* - on the Main Wall at The Gap. This is one of the newer cleaned and bolted lines that have been established in recent times. Photo: Mark Glaister

Navigation Quarry

| Grade Spread | 4 | 17 | 25 | 5 | - |

Navigation Quarry is a very pleasant and popular climbing venue located on moorland high above the valley. The quarry presents a rectangular bay with its main feature being a fine vertical wall of high quality sandstone that is well weathered and provides predominately tremendous wall climbing. The quarry is a very good destination for those seeking out climbs in the 6th grade but there are some easier and harder lines that are worth tracking down. The quarry is situated well away from road noise and has a sunny aspect and very clean and open base for relaxing between climbs. Navigation quarry is a reliable spot to head for during cool weather as it is a sun trap although it does suffer from seepage during wet periods.

Approach
If travelling north on the A470 from Pontypridd, turn off towards Abercynon on the B4275. Continue straight on at the roundabout and at the traffic lights. Continue for 100m to parking on the right, just before the Navigation House pub, or down the road opposite the pub.
If travelling south on the A470 from Merthyr Tydfil, go east on the A472 from the large roundabout just north of Abercynon to another roundabout, and then south on the A4054 towards Cilfynydd. At the first set of traffic lights go right across the A470 then right again at the next lights to the parking by the Navigation House pub.
Walk back up to the traffic lights and turn left over the A470. At the next lights cross the main road and go through a gate to a path. Follow this for 300m to where another path cuts back left. Follow this path uphill for 100m to where another path branches back right, and follow this path for 500m until the quarry can be seen on the left.

Navigation Quarry 437

Conditions
The quarry faces southwest, gets plenty of sun and is fairly sheltered, making it a possible year-round venue. Seepage does occur, but the rock dries quickly after rainfall.

Access
There is a restriction due to nesting birds from March 1st to August 1st. This is a variable restriction and applies only to a small section of the crag - see BMC RAD.

Jen Warner enjoying some of Navigation Quarry's finest face climbing on *Black Magic* (6b) - *p.442* - at its Central Wall. Photo: Mark Glaister

Seweryn Osypiuk and Juliana Werner on the fine wall climbing of The *Relaxed Ladybird* (6c) - *p.442* - at Navigation Quarry. Photo: Mark Glaister

Navigation Quarry

① Leftover 5a
The left-hand side of the unattractive left wall past a loose and vegetated section.
FA. G.Lewis 2000s

② Threadsearch 4a
Left-hand short easy line.

③ Octopod 3c
Right-hand short easy line.

④ Gold Block 5c
Climb just to the left of the corner with two possible finishes.
FA. G.Lewis, M.Learoyd 1984

⑤ How I Wrote Elastic Man .... 7a+
Starting from the ledge below the upper wall climb the very thin fingery wall on the left.
FA. G.Ashmore, G.Morris 28.10.2017

Approach (map and overview p.436)

Navigation Quarry

6 The Elastic Retreat ... 6c+
From a belay on a high ledge (reached via routes below), climb the wall and overhang past a bolt.
FA. G.Barker 7.1989

7 Half Man, Half Machine.. 6b
The black groove - often dirty - and the right-leading line above the bulge to a lower-off.
FA. A.Rosier 18.3.2012

8 Bootylicious ... 5c
Make a steep couple of moves to reach the pocketed slab and follow it to a lower-off.
FA. A.Rosier, R.McAllister 21.9.2017

9 Rockover Beethoven 6a
Climb the thin black slab to a lower-off.
FA. R.Brewer 1988

10 The Bolt Fund Blues ..... 6b+
Climb the slab and high notch to the right of *Rockover Beethoven*. Finish direct and belay on double staples located 3m back from the edge of the crag.
FA. A.Rosier, R.Giles 27.9.2007

11 Where Did You Get that Bolt ... 7a
The wall via a dyno to a slot. Finish up *Good Sweat and Jeers*.
FA. A.Sharp, P.Lewis 11.2.1989

12 Good Sweat and Jeers ... 6a+
Climb to a tiny cave feature and then up the slab above to an overlap. Move right into *Blood, Sweat and Beers* and finish up it.
FA. R.Thomas 8.12.2017

13 Blood, Sweat and Beers.. 6b
A good route up the slab, fingery overlap and juggy headwall.
FA. A.Rosier 27.9.2007

14 Squash Match 6a
Start as for *Blood Sweat and Beers*. Follow a left-trending line to gain the grassy ledge. Go left and then boldly follow the right-trending ramp up the final wall.
FA. G.Lewis, M.Learoyd, L.Foulkes 1983

15 Squash Match Direct . 6a
A fine link-up that gives a much safer finish. Climb *Squash Match* to join and finish as for *Bolt Fund Blues*.
FA. A.Rosier 13.6.2006

16 Greeny .... 6a+
The bolted line beginning at the 'GREENY' graffiti.
FA. G.Lewis, G.Barker 1989

17 Death Match 5c
The corner and headwall.
FA. A.Rosier, P.Rogers 13.6.2005

18 Death Twitch 6a
The rounded rib and headwall is a good pitch.
FA. R.Thomas 1987

19 Fly Me to the Moon ..... VS 4c
The cracks and headwall. A well-travelled trad line.
FA. G.Lewis, S.Blackman 1982

20 A Blank Abstract 7a
The thin slab to a finish up the headwall.
FA. G.Ashmore, R.Lawrence 10.1.1992

Navigation Quarry

21 Man or Mouse 7b
The excellent thin slab eases with height.
FA. A.Sharp, P.Lewis 11.2.1989

22 Craxsploitation ...... 6b+
Sustained slabby and blind crack manoeuvres all the way, a very good pitch and one of the best at the grade here.
FA. A.Rosier et al 25.2.2018

23 Let Me Play Among the Stars
.... E2 5c
Climb to and up the right-hand crack (two bolts). Finish up the wall above. The start has lost a large flake and is now bold.
FA. G.Lewis, S.Blackman, C.Heard 1982

24 Deus Ex Machina 6c
Good climbing. A tough start above the low overlap gains easier but interesting ground.
FA. A.Rosier 24.3.2012

25 Black Magic 6b
Start up the thin crack. A fine climb with continual interest.
Photo p.437.
FA. A.Foster 1988

26 The Relaxed Ladybird 6c
A good varied pitch with a steep finish past an overlap.
Photo p.438.
FA. A.Rosier 13.8.2007

27 Great Expectations... 6c+
Hard moves interspersed with good rests up the blank face.
FA. M.Learoyd, G.Lewis 4.11.1988

28 Western Front Direct 7a
A tremendous sport route that features a hard pull over the overhang and is topped off with a technical face crack.
FA. M.Crocker, R.Thomas 29.10.1988

29 Eastern Bloc Rock .... 7a+
The three small overhangs right of *Western Front Direct*.
FA. M.Crocker, R.Thomas 29.10.1988

30 Dry Entry 5c
A shorter pitch to mid-height. Can be used as an alternative start to *Goblin Girl*.
FA. R.Thomas 15.10.2017

31 Goblin Girl .... 6b+
A long pitch left of the corner that has all the difficulties concentrated in its upper reaches.
FA. G.Barker, G.Lewis 2.7.1989

Navigation Quarry

32 Evening Light 6b
Climb the lower buttress - straightforward climbing but runout - to below the headwall of much better rock. Climb the arete and move rightwards to finish.
FA. G.Lewis, H.Griffiths 1984

33 Save a Mouse Eat a Pussy .... 6c+
Start up a small corner and then climb easily to below the upper slab. From a borehole, climb up onto the slab and follow the thin and technical scoop above to easier ground and the top.
FA. G.Lewis, G.Barker 6.1989

34 Mouse Trap .... 6b+
Follow *Save a Mouse Eat a Pussy* to below the upper slab. Move up onto the slab and follow the bolted line rightwards to the top.
FA. G.Lewis, P.Jones 15.8.1992

35 The Owl and the Antelope E2 5c
Climb to an overhung ledge at the start of the right-trending line of overhangs. Move up to a niche and climb the wall above rightwards to the top, passing two horizontal cracks.
FA. G.Lewis, C.Heard, M.Learoyd 1983

36 On Jupiter and Mars E1 5b
A fine feature of the buttress that follows the right-trending line of overhangs. Start up *The Owl and the Antelope*.
FA. G.Lewis, S.Blackman 1982

37 Over the Moon E4 5c
Head up right over a roof and then go leftwards to meet *On Jupiter and Mars*. Move right and pull over the overhang onto the headwall. Step right and finish up the exposed arete.
FA. A.Rosier, G.Lewis 3.4.2008

38 Crash Landing 6a
The slab and groove gives some pleasant technical climbing.
FA. G.Lewis, R.Renshaw 1983

39 Ol' Blue Eyes 6c
Climb to and over a prominent bulge via a bouldery move and then up the easier wall to a lower-off.
FA. G.Barker, M.Kidd 6.1989

40 Heart Throb 6b
Climb up to a corner and follow it to its end. Move left onto slabby ground to finish.
FA. G.Lewis, D.Hart 15.1.1989

41 Ewe Flock Wit .... 6a+
Ascend the wall and traverse left below a tree to the upper slab.
FA. R.Thomas 17.9.2017

42 Ram Raider .... 6a+
The left-leading corner and slab above.
FA. A.Rosier, R.Thomas 19.9.2017

43 Spring Lamb Mantel 6b
Start up *Ram Raider* then break right to a mantel and ledge leading to an easier upper wall.
FA. R.Thomas, A.Rosier, R.McAllister 21.9.2017

44 Feeling Sheep 7b
A short bouldery crux.
FA. G.Ashmore 18.10.1997

45 Baaaaad to the Bone ..... 6b+
White bulge to lower-off. Continuing above the ledge on the green coloured bolts is 5a.
FA. A.Rosier 24.9.2017

46 Tupping Time 4c
The corner gains a ledge. Finishing on the left is 4c. Finishing up the red groove is 5c and good. The right-hand finish is 5b.
FA. R.Thomas, A.Rosier, R.McAllister 21.9.2017

Navigation Quarry

47 Stainless Steel Association 4c
On the right is a sunless wall. This is the first bolted line.
FA. R.Thomas, G.Leyshan, R.Phillips 8.10.2017

48 Stainless Steel Incorporation .... 6a+
From the first bolt of *Stainless Steel Association* launch out right to gain the flat hold then straight up to shared belay on the left.
FA. R.Thomas 10.2017

Access - A variable restriction only applies to routes near where the bird nests. See BMC RAD for details.

49 Micro Incorporation .... 6b+
Boldly gain the flat hold via the arete, then continue as for *Stainless Steel Incorporation*.

50 Alco-Troll 6a
The bolt-line up the left-hand side of arete.
FA. F.Rosier, R.Giles 1.3.2008

51 Principles of Rock Mechanics, Part 1
.... 7a
Takes the right-hand side of the arete.
FA. F.Rosier 5.3.2008

Abertysswg

A compact section of wall perched high above a large quarry working, way up at the head of one of the central valleys. The selection of lines is limited but the climbing is varied and well bolted. This is an exposed spot and not the place to go during inclement weather, but could be a place to escape the midges as it picks up a breeze in warm weather. There is potential here for some new routes.

Approach
Follow the A4049 all of the way up the Rhymney Valley, past New Tredegar to Rhymney itself and then follow signs to the village of Abertysswg. Go through the village and after 600m at a sharp left-hand hairpin bend park on the track that leads off of it. Walk along a path to the left of the track and then steeply up the side of the quarry next to woods and then just before the top of the quarry traverse right a short distance to reach the base of the cliff. The crag can also be approached from the quarry floor which is reached by walking along the track from the parking. From the track pick a way up the scree to the base of the crag.

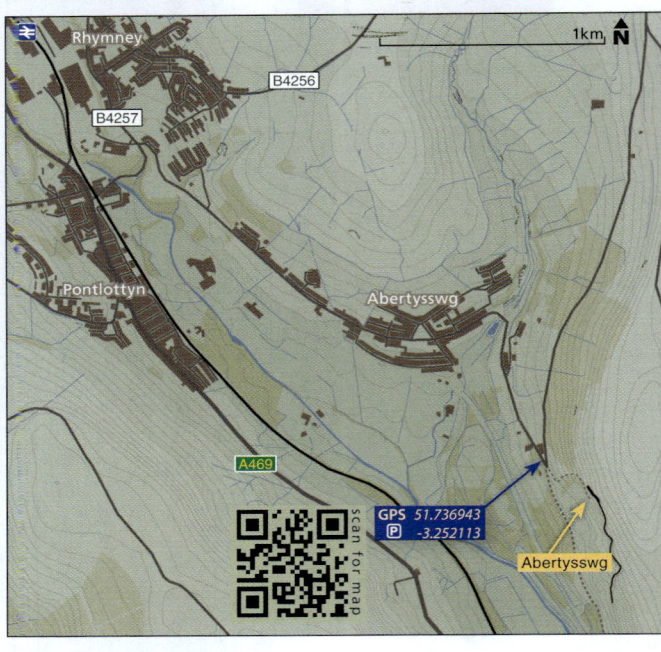

Conditions
Very exposed to the elements but it has a sunny aspect and will dry rapidly after rain.

Abertysswg 447

1 Flock Ewe 5c
The wall left of the wide crack on the first tower reached on the approach.
FA. R.Thomas, G.Ashmore 11.3.2012

2 Ewe Knows I Loves Ewe .. VS 4b
The wide rattly chimney crack in the middle of the tower.
FA. R.Thomas, R.Phillips 2014

3 Chuck Prince Goes Dancing ... 6b+
The left-hand route on the gully wall.
FA. G.Ashmore 13.3.2012

4 Boring Bristolian Benefits Beneficiary...
.... 7a+
Reach the arete from the left and finish directly up the it via some difficult moves.
FA. G.Ashmore 13.3.2012

5 Jimmy Cayne's Reefer .... 6c+
The wall left of the arete to gain a left-trending seam.
FA. G.Ashmore 16.4.2012

6 Warren Spector vs Rector
.... 7b+
Climb up the problem arete to below the roof. Move along the lip of the roof using an unlikely heel hook, then pull up into the crack with difficulty. Finish up easier ground.
FA. G.Ashmore, R.Thomas 15.5.2015

7 Hung for a Sheep 6c
A tough fingery direct start to *Lambs to the Slaughter*.
FA. R.Thomas, G.Ashmore 2012

8 Lambs to the Slaughter 6a
Climb a flake-crack and then head left to gain the crack that leads all of the way to the top and a lower-off..
FA. R.Thomas, G.Ashmore 11.3.2012

9 Sheepish Looks .... 6a+
Start as for *Lambs to the Slaughter* but continue straight up to separate lower-off.
FA. R.Thomas, G.Ashmore 13.4.2012

10 Mutton Dressed as Lamb ..... 6a+
Climb straight up the right-hand side of wall to a shared lower-off with *Sheepish Looks*.
FA. R.Thomas, G.Ashmore 16.4.2012

11 Good Shepherd 5b
Right arete of wall.
FA. R.Thomas, R.Phillips 2014

Deri

Deri is a steep wall of compact rock, tucked away in the hills above the town of the same name. It is not too far from Bargoed Quarry and a visit to both on the same day could be easily combined, if finger strength is not depleted! The main attraction at Deri is the steep wall of grade 7s which, once clean, gives some excellent sustained pitches.

Approach   Map p.450

Take the A469 to Bargoed and drive past the station to a junction below a big viaduct. Turn left (signed to Deri) and continue to another left turn (also signed Deri). Once in the village, turn left over the river and, just beyond at a sharp right-hand bend, head straight on up a steep road. Go up this narrow road for 600m and turn left at a cattle grid. Follow the single track road for 1500m, past a farm, and down into a wooded dip. A little way up the road is some limited space to pull off and park. Walk back down to the wooded dip and go over a stile at a signpost. Walk downstream and, after 200m, a faint path contours off right to a fence. Step over and pick up another faint path that quickly leads to the quarry.

Conditions

The crag is shady and fairly high up, but well sheltered from the wind. The main wall is steep enough to allow climbing in light rain. Seepage does occur after prolonged rainfall.

Access

A restriction because of nesting birds is in place from 1st March to 30th June.

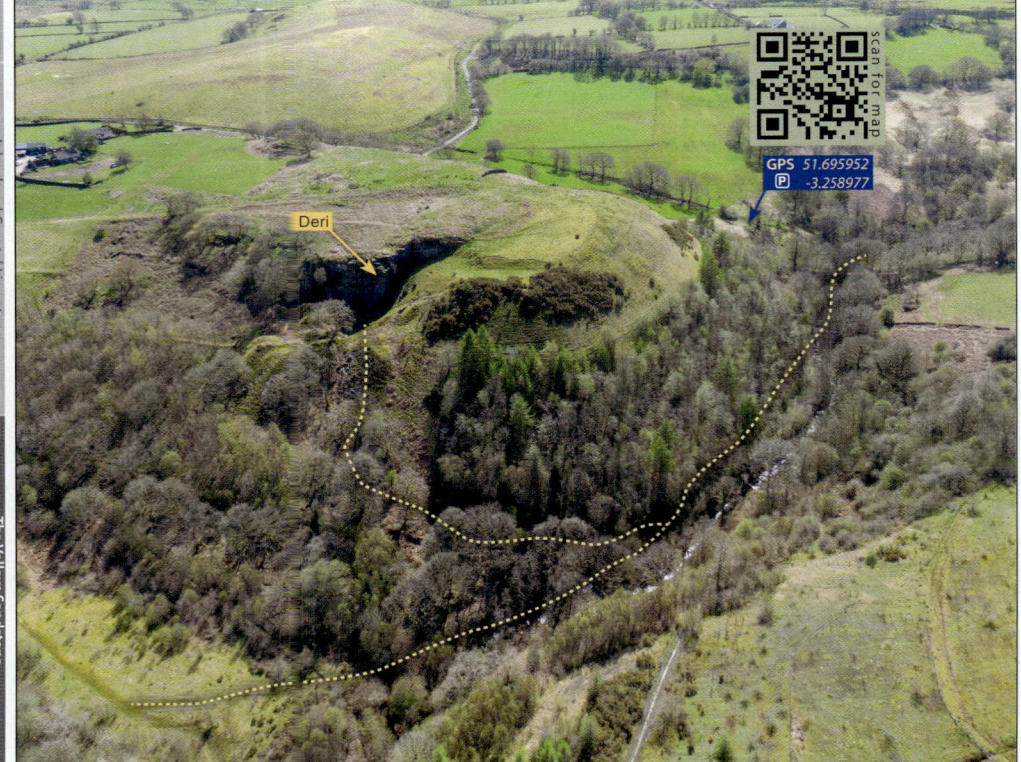

Deri

1. Ace in the Hole — 5c
The short wall on the left of the crag.
FA. R.Thomas, G.Gibson 4.9.1994

2. Two of a Kind — 7a+
The short wall with a scoop above a starting overhang.
FA. G.Gibson 4.9.1994

3. Mine's a Pair — 6b+
A steep start to the corner/groove.
FA. G.Gibson 8.10.1994

4. Joker in the Pack — 6c
The wall to the left of the arete of *House of Cards*.
FA. R.Thomas, G.Gibson 4.9.1994

5. House of Cards — 7a
The left-hand side of the main arete.
FA. G.Gibson, R.Thomas 1.9.1994

6. Kicking Ass and Taking Names — 7a
The main arete on its right-hand side is a fine line and climb.
FA. A.Sharp, P.Lewis, T.Foster, P.Harding 27.3.1989

7. Chattery Teeth — 7a+
Excellent moves up the blank wall to a shared lower-off.
FA. G.Gibson, R.Thomas 8.10.1994

8. Olympic Doctor — 7a+
Hard sequences at the start and finish.
FA. A.Sharp, P.Lewis 1993

9. Deri Made — 6c
The flared crack, wall and break to a final hard move.
FA. R.Thomas, G.Gibson 1.9.1994

10. Steroid John — 6c+
A pumpy pitch up the wall to the right.
FA. P.Lewis, A.Sharp 1993

11. Coffee Shop — 7a
Hard to start and a blind finish. There is a lone bolt to the right.
FA. G.Gibson 1.9.1994

12. Full Dog — 7b
The blunt arete is loose at the start. Still to be re-equipped.
FA. G.Gibson, R.Thomas 1.9.1994

13. Menage a Chien — 7a+
Link *Mister Foothold* into *Full Dog*. Good climbing.
FA. M.Crocker, R.Thomas 13.5.1989

14. Mister Foothold — 7a
The wall, groove and slot to a pumpy headwall on hidden jugs.
FA. A.Sharp, P.Lewis 1993

15. Troilism Trouble — E2 5c
The jamming crack left of the dirty corner. Good when clean.
FA. R.Thomas, M.Crocker 13.5.1989

16. The Toiler — 6b+
Left of the stapled corner crack with a steep start.
FA. R.Thomas, D.Emanuel 2015

17. Dia Monde — 6a
Right most of several (bolted project lines) on the slab.
FA. D.Emanuel, R.Thomas 2016

Access - No climbing 1st March to 30th June because of nesting birds. See UKC and BMC RAD.

Bargoed

Grade Spread | - | 6 | 19 | 2 | -

Bargoed is a compact quarried wall with some worth while wall climbs which are of a fingery and technical nature. The routes are well equipped, and the rock is generally reliable and clean. This is a good spot for those looking for some good grade 6s with extremely quick and easy access.

Approach
Follow the A469 past Bargoed railway station and downhill to a large viaduct on the left. Don't go under the viaduct but continue up the hill for 100m and turn left into a lane - Quarry Row. Drive past the houses and continue for 100m to parking on the right. The crag is just a short walk through the trees on the right. Do not park in sight of the houses.

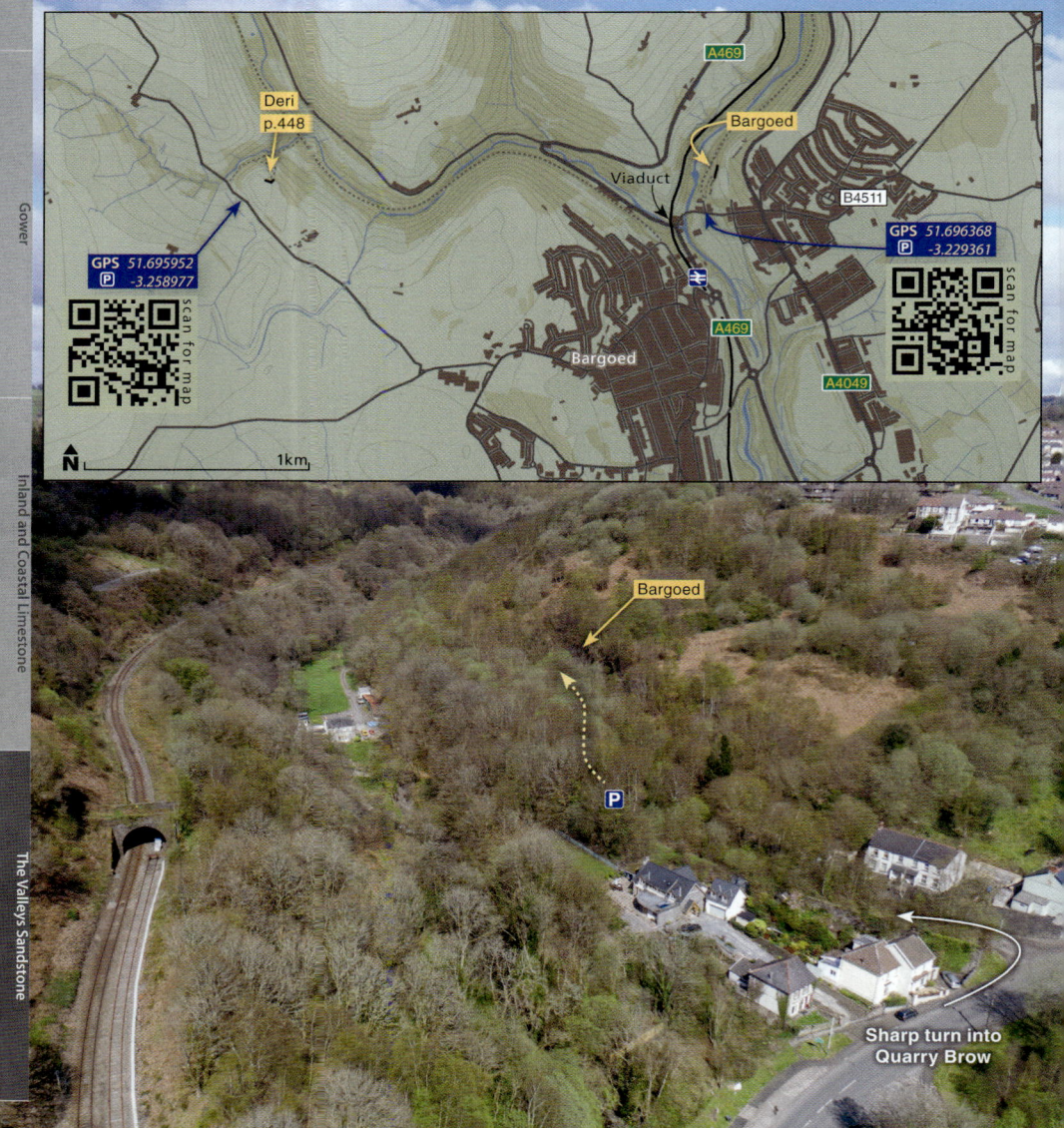

Bargoed 451

Conditions
The cliff is set amongst trees, west facing and sheltered. The rock is clean and dries fairly quickly, although some sections do seep.

Access
Park considerately - do not park in sight of the houses. No camping or fires.

Tom Skelhon on the fingery lower wall of *Lyddite* (7a+) - *p.455* - at Bargoed. Photo: Mark Glaister

Bargoed

Charlotte Macdonald nearing the top of *Hawk's Cheap* (6a+) - *p.455*. Bargoed is a good choice of crag if short of time as the parking is very close to the cliff. The routes are either side of the prominent arete in the middle of the crag and the wall to its right are those to head for on a first visit. Photo: Mark Glaister

Bargoed

① **Gift Wrapped at Bargoed** 5c
The awkward slab on the far left.
FA. L.Jay 2011

② **Ianto's Bargoed Bumblers Blind Spot**
.... 6a+
Climb past staples and a bolt.
FA. R.Thomas, G.Ashmore, E.Travers-Jones 14.9.2013

③ **Bargoed Bushwhacker**... 6b
Technical moves up the pockets and flakes to a shared lower-off.
FA. R.Thomas, G.Ashmore 13.10.2011

④ **Bargoed Sideshow** 6a
Move up ledges and continue past a red niche.
FA. R.Thomas, D.Emanuel 7.10.2011

⑤ **Meat Seeking Missile** 6b
The right-trending line above some ledges.
FA. D.Emanuel 2012

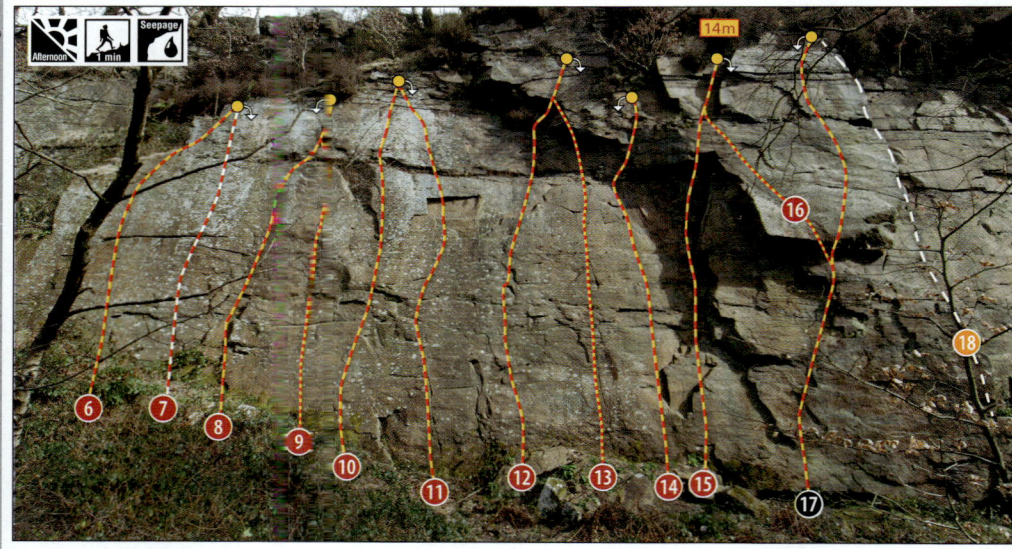

⑥ **Simply Simian** 6b
A sneaky undercut at the coal break helps gain good footholds.
FA. R.Thomas, D.Emanuel 9.2011

⑦ **Mr. Gorrilla's Got a Big Nose** ... E3 6b
Hard wall climbing passing a slot at mic-height.
FA. M.Crocker, R.Thomas 4.3.1989

⑧ **Super Strung Direct** ..... 6b+
The left-hand start to the original line joins it near the top.
FA. R.Thomas, A.Rosier 11.9.2011

⑨ **Super Strung Out at Bargoed**
.... 6b
Climb up to a hole near the top and a lower-off just above.
FA. R.Thomas, D.Emanuel 2011

⑩ **Bringing the Brane Theory to Bargoed**
.... 6b
Climb the wall right of the high scoop passing a ledge.
FA. R.Thomas, G.Ashmore 1.9.2011

⑪ **Bargoed Blow Job**. 6b
The large flake on this line is unstable. Avoid.
FA. R.Thomas, E.Travers-Jones 4.9.2011

⑫ **Beavers at Bargoed** .. 6b
A hard start on pockets and edges gains the final overhang.
FA. R.Thomas, G.Ashmore 1.9.2011

Bargoed 455

⑬ Balthazaar's Ball Sac Bulges Beholding Bouncing Bargoed Booties 6b
The slab has a thin and difficult initial sequence.
FA. R.Thomas, A.Rosier 9.2011

⑭ House Training Catwoman ... 6b
Hollow flakes left of the corner. Finish over the overhang.
FA. D.Emanuel, R.Thomas 10.2011

⑮ Pepperatzi 6b
The corner, overhang and groove is a good line.
FA. L.Foulkes, M.Learoyd 1989

⑯ Twenty One Ounces Of Blow .. 6b+
Pull out left over the overlap. Follow the left arete to an awkward swing left at a pocket and finish up the *Pepperatzi* groove.
FA. G.Ashmore 1.9.2011

⑰ Blowing for Tugs......... 7a+
Direct up the front of the pillar via a hard bouldery rockover.
FA. A.Sharp, P.Lewis, J.Harwood 29.1.1989

⑱ Groping for Jugs 6a
The superb central arete moving onto the left side at the top.
FA. G.Ashmore, R.Thomas 1.9.2011

⑲ Hawk's Cheep .... 6a+
The corner has good moves. *Photo p.452.*
FA. P.Lewis, A.Sharp, J.Harwood 29.1.1989

⑳ Brittania 6b
The wall passing a small square niche via a very thin pull.
FA. A.Rosier, R.Thomas 26.9.2011

㉑ Beware the Burly Butcher of Bargoed .... 6b+
A left-trending line with a long undercut move and thin cracks.
FA. R.Thomas, G.Ashmore 8.8.2011

㉒ Our Man in Bargoed.. 6c+
Climb direct above the start of *Beware the Burly Butcher...*
FA. A.Sharp, P.Lewis, J.Harwood 29.1.1989

㉓ Lyddite .... 7a+
Thin fingery wall to a well positioned upper arete. *Photo p.451*
FA. G.Ashmore 4.9.2011

㉔ Black Dog............. 6b+
Gain the ramp, move up a few metres and then step left. Climb the groove and crack above to finish.
FA. A.Sharp, P.Lewis, J.Harwood 29.1.1989

㉕ Up For Grabs .... 6b+
From the ramp of *Black Dog*, move right and up past overhangs to a lower-off on the ledge.
FA. M.Learoyd, L.Foulkes 1989

㉖ Bored of Brackla Becomes Benefactor of Bargoed 6c
The wall right of the *Black Dog* corner has a hard start.
FA. G.Ashmore 6.8.2011

㉗ Bargain Basement Bargoed 6a
The final bolted line up the wall to a shared lower-off.
FA. R.Thomas, G.Ashmore 8.2011

Ridgeway

Grade Spread - 3 6 - -

An old quarry with a small number of climbs, the best being on the vertical dark wall at the far end of the working. Good for a quick hit of grade 6 wall pitches only a couple of minutes from the parking.

Approach
From the A472 Ystrad Mynach to Blackwood road at a roundabout take the exit to Bryn Meadows Golf Club and follow it for 2km to a lay-by on the right and park here (there is more parking near a cattle grid a little further up the road if necessary). Just up the road from the lay-by locate a gap in the hedge on the right that leads to a ruined building. Take a path to the right of the ruined building that quickly accesses the quarry.

Conditions
Sheltered and sunny in the morning but fairly high up so not a good place in the cooler months.

Ridgeway 457

❶ Geotechnique .... 6b+
The left arete of the wall starting half way up the banking.
FA. A.Rosier 13.3.2010

❷ Powered by Cheese and Ham . 6a
Tackle the crack that begins just right of the tree.
FA. B.Danby 12.9.2010

❸ Spacebats .... 6c+
Ascend the wall between the cracks.
FA. R.McAllister 10.9.2010

❹ Analogue Kid .... 6a+
Follow the diagonal crack to its end and then the wall above.
FA. A.Rosier 13.3.2010

❺ Kill the Superheroes .... 6b+
Begin up *Analogue Kid* and climb direct up the bolted line.
FA. A.Rosier 13.3.2010

❻ Wee Wyllie Wonka 6a
The twin cracks and high corner on the far right of the slab.
FA. R.Thomas 17.3.2011

❼ Yo Momma .... 6b+
Start at the graffiti 'BONEY' and climb the leaning orange wall, close to its left arete.
FA. A.Rosier 12.9.2010

❽ Chasing Dragonflies 6b
The central line on the leaning wall.
FA. A.Rosier 21.3.2010

❾ Shotgun Party 6b
A short sharp route on the right side of the leaning wall. Bridging out into the loose and vegetated corner is off-route.
FA. A.Rosier 21.3.2010

Grade Spread | 3 | 7 | 63 | 16 | -

Llanbradach quarry is the second largest sandstone quarry in southeast Wales and has the number of routes to match. It also has the biggest routes on sandstone to date - two-pitch routes up to a height of 50m. However, Llanbradach is not a place for those of an unadventurous nature as the wooded lower quarry is a bit of a jungle and the walls are dominated by vegetation, apart from the Expansionist Wall which penetrates the tree canopy. The Upper Tier has some very good long pitches that are well worth the slightly longer approach walk.

1km
N
Llanbradach
A469
scan for map
GPS 51.599545
P -3.232359
Llanbradach
Large roundabout
Bedwas
A468
Caerphilly

Conditions

The lower quarry is heavily vegetated and will be humid in warm weather and takes time to dry after wet weather, it is very sheltered, although this means it can be midgy. The Upper Tier is more open especially toward the right-hand end.

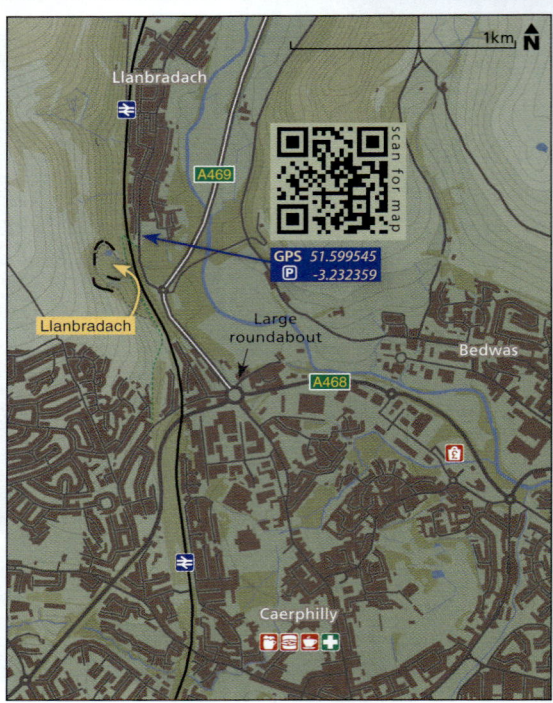

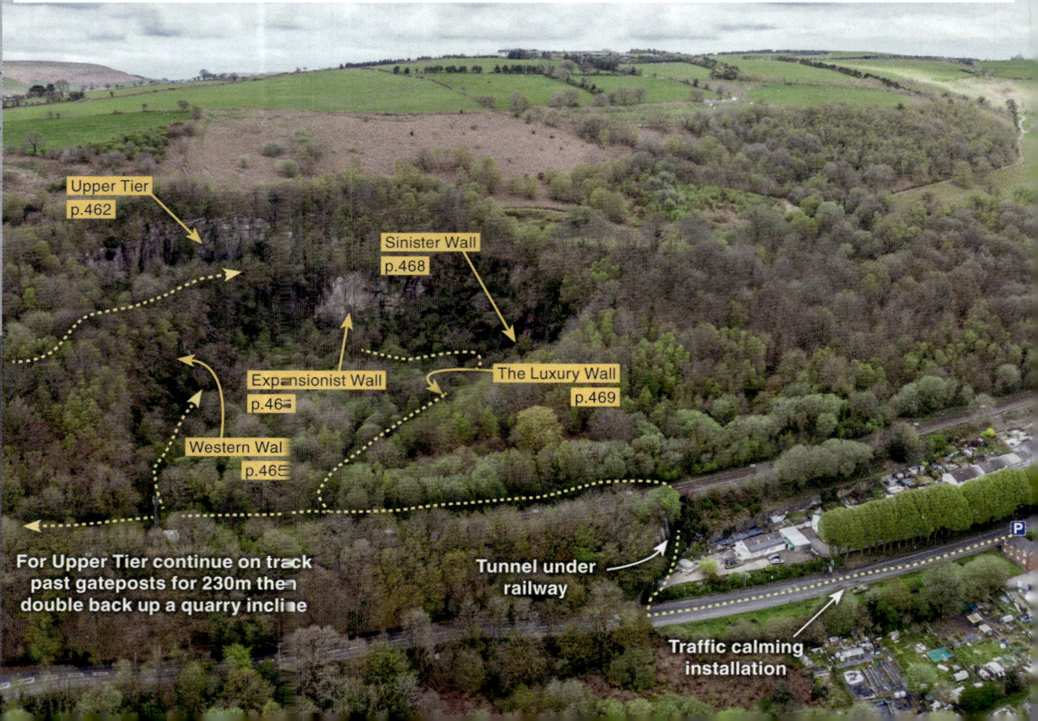

Upper Tier
p.462
Sinister Wall
p.468
Expansionist Wall
p.46
The Luxury Wall
p.469
Western Wal
p.46
For Upper Tier continue on track past gateposts for 230m then double back up a quarry incline
Tunnel under railway
Traffic calming installation
P

Llanbradach

Approach
From a large roundabout on the Caerphilly ring road, head north on the A469 signed to Llanbradach. Turn left at the next roundabout (this is the southern roundabout signed to Llanbradach if approaching from the north). Around 300m from the roundabout a quarry track can be seen leading off to the left and under a railway bridge. Park at the roadside 150m further on, just beyond the traffic calming installation on the edge of the village. Go back to the quarry track and walk up it under the railway. Turn left onto a flat, wide path alongside the railway. Walk along the track for 100m to a narrow path on the right that leads through trees to a pond on the right-hand side of the quarry, from where all of the areas apart from the Western Wall and Upper Tier can be reached. To reach the Western Wall, walk a little further and take a vague path on the right which leads quickly to the crag. To reach the Upper Tier, continue along the wide track next to the railway line to some gateposts. Walk a further 230m along the track and pick up a gentle quarry incline that cuts back right. Follow a path up this and on to the bottom of the Upper Tier.

Eugene Travers-Jones on the impressive wall climbing to be had on *Roaring Forties* (6b+) - *p.463* - at the Upper Tier, Llanbradach Quarry. Photo: Aaron Martin

Rhys Evans pulling around the final overhang onto the headwall of *Dirty as a Dog* (6b) - *p.463* - at the Upper Tier, Llanbradach. This massive quarry working has a number of walls and buttresses which have been developed over the years but the biggest and best is the Upper Tier featured here. However its popularity has ebbed and flowed over the decades. In recent times however the Upper Tier has undergone a big clean up that has once again revealed the numerous well-equipped impressive faces and aretes. Photo: Mark Glaister

Llanbradach — Upper Tier

Upper Tier

The upper tier of Llanbradach offers well equipped lines in a variety of styles in the mid-grades. All of the best lines are clean and well-bolted.

Approach (map and overview p.458) - Follow the track past the lower quarry entrance to gate posts. Walk another 230m and cut back up rightwards via an old quarry track to the left-hand end of the tier.

Conditions - The wall faces east and gets the sun until just after midday.

The first route on the Upper Tier is on a smaller section of wall to the left and not shown on the topo.

❶ Roraima 6c
The centre of the isolated tower. Not shown on the topo.
FA. R.Thomas, G.Gibson 23.3.1997

❷ Three Men in a Goat 6c
The left-hand of three routes from a small terrace keeping out of the crack on the left.
FA. R.Thomas, M.Hirst, G.Ashmore 2.4.1997

❸ Once Bitten .... 6b+
The centre of wall. Pleasant after the crux start from the ledge.
FA. R.Thomas, M.Crocker 1991

❹ Twice Shy 6a
The easier right-hand line of the wall. Pleasant.
FA. R.Thomas, G.Gibson 23.3.1997

❺ Hollow Feeling 6b
The short arete.
FA. M.Learoyd, R.Thomas 1991

❻ Sermon on the Mount 6c
Start as for *Hollow Feeling* then say a prayer and launch from the hollow flakes onto small solid edges.
FA. R.Thomas, G.Davies 1991

❼ Practice What You Preach E3 5b
A bold traditional route up the centre of the wall.
FA. M.Crocker, R.Thomas 1991

❽ Pampered 6b
The left arete of the slabby wall is a good pitch.
FA. R.Thomas 14.4.1997

❾ You Change Me .... 6c+
The centre of the slabby wall direct, swinging right from the arete to the belay.
FA. M.Crocker 1991

❿ Nappy Rush 6b
An exciting and impressive wall climb on positive holds.
FA. R.Thomas 1997

⓫ Torch the Earth ...... 7b+
Fierce technical face climbing.
FA. M.Crocker, R.Thomas 27.1.1991

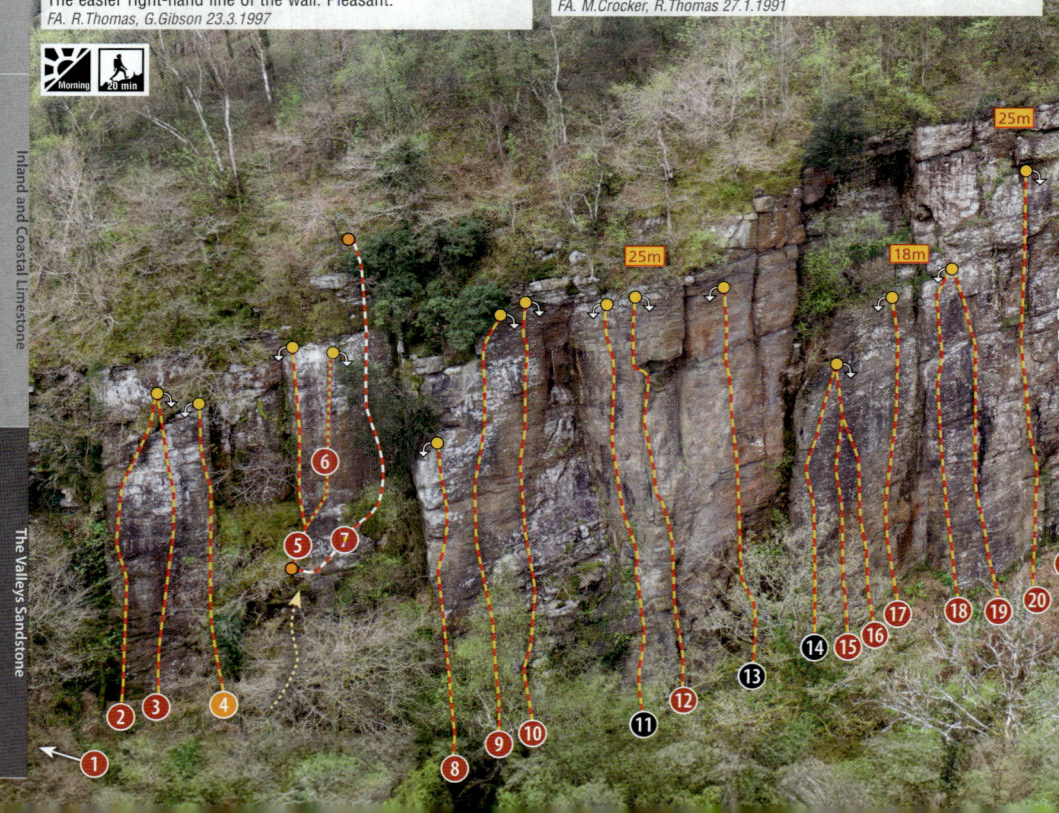

Upper Tier **Llanbradach** 463

12 Dirty as a Dog 6b
The impressive crack-line to a high roof and final short wall.
Photo p.460.
FA. R.Thomas, G.Royle, M.Learoyd 27.1.1991

13 Desert Storm .... 7a+
An intimidating, sustained line with a tricky move near the top.
FA. M.Crocker, R.Thomas 27.1.1991

14 Twenty Second Chance .. 7a+
Features a desperate start up the rounded arete.
FA. M.Crocker, R.Thomas 26.1.1991

15 Sixty Seconds Go See 7a
Hard starting moves lead to some fine face climbing above.
FA. M.Crocker, R.Thomas 26.1.1991

16 Roaring Forties ...... 6b+
Good wall climbing finishing via a crack and shallow groove.
Finish as for *Sixty Seconds Go See*. *Photo p.459.*
FA. R.Thomas, J.Bullock 1989

17 Between the Lines ... 6b+
The right-hand line on the wall.
FA. R.Thomas, G.Royle 1991

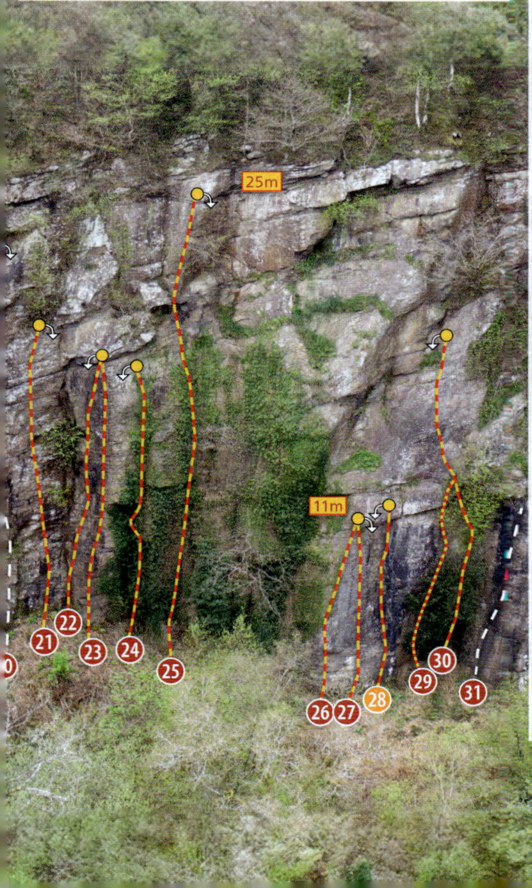

18 The Missing Quarter ..... 6b+
The blunt rib to the first lower-off (above is a ledge and poor rock).
FA. R.Thomas, E.Rees 1998

19 Scoo .... 6b+
The shallow groove system to a shared lower-off with *The Missing Quarter*.
FA. M.Learoyd, R.Thomas 1989

20 Dandelion 6b
To the right is a slim corner groove before the corner proper.
Climb this to a lower-off below the roof.
FA. M.Frost, R.Thomas 8.4.1997

21 Burdock 6b
The wall just left of the main angle of the bay.
FA. M.Frost 6.6.1997

22 Blinded By Puppies 6c
Bridge the corner until at the second bolt, then climb up the face on the right to a shared lower-off with *Blinded by Love*.
FA. Gareth Alf 16.10.2022

23 Blinded by Love .... 6b+
A superb sustained outing on the stepped arete.
FA. R.Thomas, G.Royle, M.Learoyd 1991

24 The Laughing Policeman .... 6b+
The crack and groove system starting up a difficult rib. It suffers from seepage low down, hence the line is on the rib on the right at the start. Overgrown with ivy at time of writing.
FA. R.Thomas, G.Gibson 13.7.1997

25 Fair Cop .... 6b+
The crack, wall and flying arete. A long sustained pitch with an 'out there' finish. Overgrown with ivy at time of writing.
FA. R.Thomas, G.Gibson 24.5.1997

26 Attitude Test 7a
The blunt and desperately technical low-level arete.
FA. M.Crocker 1991

27 The Merthyr Infill 6c
A short, technical and worth while wall.
FA. G.Gibson 23.3.1997

28 Blue Bell .... 6a+
The shallow groove with an awkward bulge.
FA. G.Gibson, R.Thomas 18.5.1997

29 Sand Together 6c
A blunt rib with a short steep section. Move right below the overhang into *Red Herring*.
FA. G.Gibson 18.5.1997

30 Red 'erring .... 6c+
The steep pink wall, overhang and rounded finale.
FA. G.Gibson, R.Thomas 18.5.1997

Llanbradach — Upper Tier

31 Plaque Attack .... 6b+
Technical climbing up the angled face.
FA. G.Gibson, R.Thomas 23.3.1997

32 Incidentally 6b
The arete of the angled face moving left to a shared lower-off.
FA. G.Gibson, R.Thomas 23.3.1997

33 Cop the Lot 7a
The narrow groove and blunt rib on the other side of the dirty groove has a hard finish.
FA. G.Gibson 24.5.1997

34 The Caerphilly Cop Out .. 6c+
The blunt rib via a long reach and short difficult face.
FA. G.Gibson 24.5.1997

35 I Am what I Am 6b
The shallow groove and open face. Excellent face climbing with a crux finish.
FA. G.Gibson, R.Thomas 24.5.1997

36 You are What You Is ..... 6b+
The central line of the open face has a hard start and fine face climbing above.
FA. G.Barker, R.Trevitt 1989

37 Is it What You are That Is? 6c
The right arete of the wall with a low crux and sportingly bolted middle section.
FA. G.Gibson, R.Thomas 18.5.1997

38 The Brush Down 7a
A long line on the far right. Follow the left-hand line of bolts. Overgrown by ivy at time of writing.
FA. G.Gibson, R.Thomas 10.9.2008

39 The Brush Off 7a
Start up *The Brush Down* but take the right-hand bolt line. Overgrown by ivy at time of writing
FA. G.Gibson, R.Thomas 10.9.2008

40 My Little Routy Wooty .... 6a+
A line on the far right. Overgrown by ivy at time of writing Not shown on the topo.
FA. G.Gibson, R.Thomas 10.9.2008

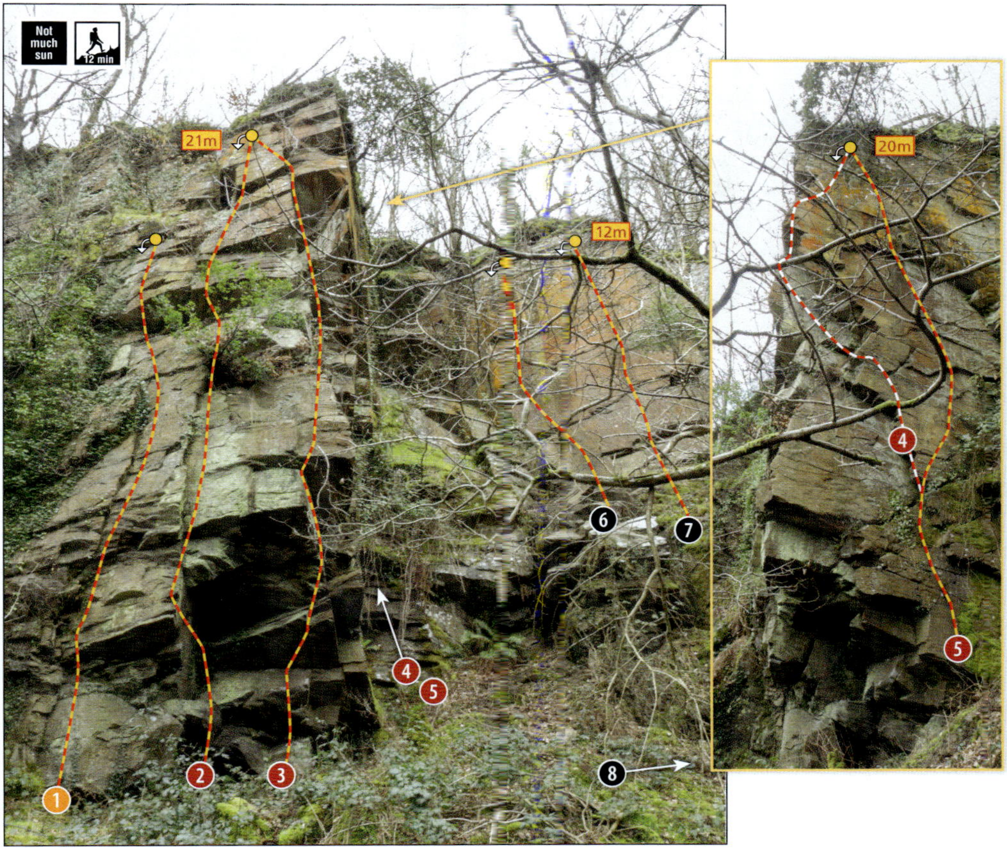

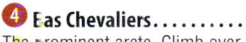

Western Wall

A small section of crag with a handful of routes and one of the best finger-wreckers in the area. These routes may need cleaning, but the gear is good.

Approach (map and overview p.458) - Take the less defined second path off of the main track and the buttress is the first on the left.

Conditions - The buttress faces north and gets very little (if any) sun except on late mid-summer evenings. There is no seepage but the rock can feel damp in humid weather conditions.

1 Horn of Plenty .... 6a+
The groove and short wall above.
FA. R.Thomas, 3.5.1998

2 Magellan's Straight .... 6b+
The short overhang, groove and centre of the tower above.
FA. R.Thomas 7.5.1998

3 Maurice Chevalier........... 7a
Pull right under the overlap to climb the groove and face above.
FA. G.Ashmore 5.4.1999

4 Eas Chevaliers.............. E3 5c
The prominent arete. Climb over the lower roof and up a short smooth wall.
FA. M.Crocker, R.Thomas 26.11.1988

5 Mouton Dagger......... 1 6c
Take the centre of the wall. Excellent moves when clean.
FA. R.Thomas 1.5.1999

The next two lines start from a ledge below the orange wall.

6 Hush Money................ 7a+
The left arete of the smooth-looking wall.
FA. M.Crocker 11.12.1988

7 Contraband 3 7c
Brilliant technical face climbing up the centre of the wall.
FA. M.Crocker, M.Ward, R.Thomas 11.12.1988

The next line is on an isolated face 100m to the right.

8 Boston Strangler 1 7b
The narrow rectangular face.
FA. M.Crocker 1990

Carmarthenshire
Gower
Inland and Coastal Limestone
The Valleys Sandstone

Llanbradach — Expansionist Wall

Expansionist Wall

In the centre of the quarry lies its largest section of cliff. The lower walls provide a series of pitches with a friendly feel to them, whilst the upper section has a handful of routes with a significantly bigger feel to them. The upper wall is difficult of access but the best approach is via routes on the lower walls.

Approach (map and overview p.458) - Take the path into the lower quarry and skirt around the base of the wall past the Sinister Wall. The first three routes are on the left, up a steep slope. The routes on the impressive upper wall are reached by pitches on the lower section, plus one of two connecting pitches.

Conditions - The wall faces east, is sheltered and receives the sunshine until about 1pm. It dries quickly and, apart from a little seepage in its lower half (most of which can be avoided), provides an ideal venue in many weather conditions.

This is the tall vertical wall on the left reached via a steep slope below the main crag.

1 Amnesia 7a
The first line on the left of the wall to the right of a tree growing out of a crack high on the wall.
FA. G.Gibson 5.5.1996

2 Insomnia 6c
The central line of the wall that features a hard move to gain a ledge. Go careful with the final flake-crack.
FA. G.Gibson 5.5.1996

3 Acatalepsia . . . . 6a+
The wall just left of the right-facing fake/crack.
FA. R.Thomas 3.6.1996

4 Sub-Contraction 7a
The left arete of the wall has a single desperate move.
FA. G.Gibson 7.4.1996

5 Simple Addition 6c
A flat wall peppered with pockets.
FA. R.Thomas, G.Gibson 5.4.1996

6 Post Expressionist 6b
A good pitch up the centre of the wall via a prominent flake. Can be used to reach *The Caerphilly Contract* and *Little White Lies*.
FA. R.Thomas, G.Gibson 31.3.1996

7 Too Keynes by Half 6c
A fine little route up the right edge of the wall. Care is needed with the initial holds. Can be used to reach *Caerphilly Contract* and *Little White Lies*.
FA. R.Thomas, G.Gibson 5.4.1996

8 Falling Freely . . . . 7a+
A left-trending pitch up the prominent red wall. Fingery and on good rock. Any wetness at the start can be avoided.
FA. G.Gibson 17.3.1996

9 Splashdown . . . . 6c+
The prominent left-slanting groove exiting right to a lower-off. Take care at the start.
FA. G.Gibson, G.Ashmore 16.3.1996

Expansionist Wall **Llanbradach** 467

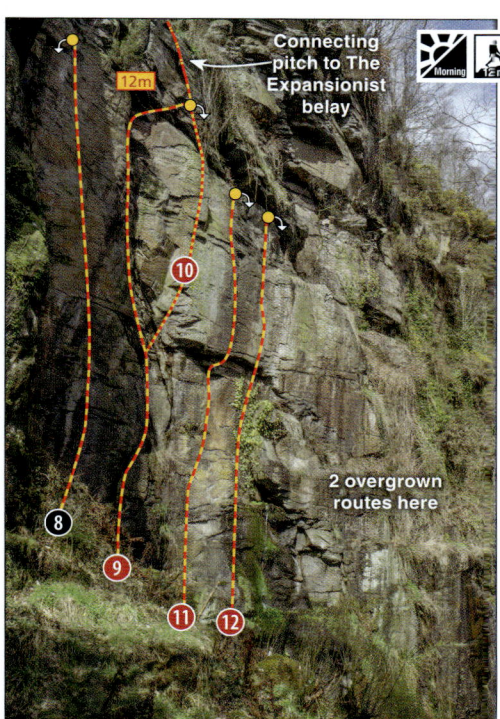

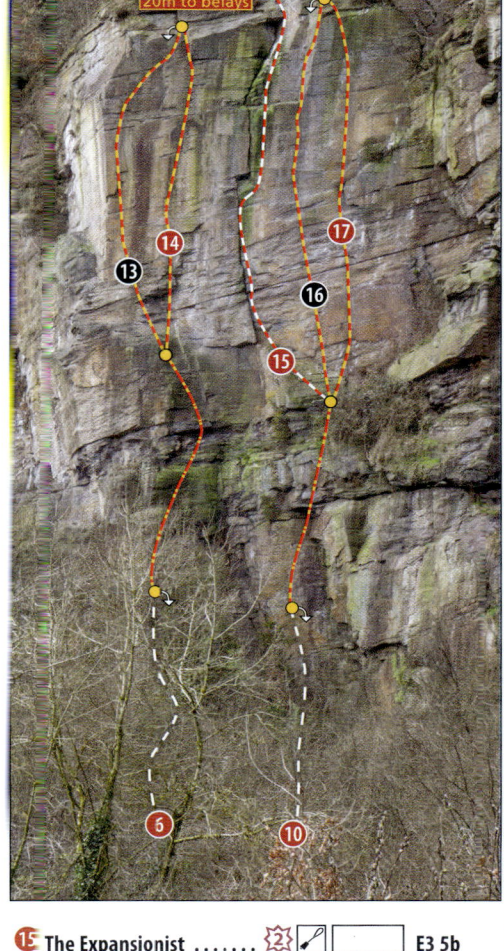

🔟 Total Recoil .... 6b+
A varied route with a short crux wall. There is a link pitch from this to the *The Expansionist* and routes to the right.
FA. G.Gibson, R.Thomas 16.3.1996

⓫ Cascade .... 6c+
A technical sequence leads through the overlap.
FA. G.Gibson 3.2.1996

⓬ Sphagnum 45 .... 6b
The groove and wall above the spring.
FA. G.Gibson 5.4.1996

Three routes to the right; **Right of Spring, 6b, Splash it on all Over, 6c** *and* **Bathtime, 6b** *are now overgrown.*

The upper wall has a number of routes in an impressive and quite intimidating position. They are best reached by Post Expressionist *or* Total Recoil *and a connecting pitch.*

⓭ The Caerphilly Contract
.... 7b+
The magnificent upper arete provides a classic route with a well defined crux section. Easier for the tall.
FA. M.Crocker, R.Thomas, M.Ward 6.11.1988

⓮ Little White Lies .... 6c+
The easier wall to the right of *The Caerphilly Contract* is not quite so fine but still worth the effort.
FA. M.Crocker, R.Thomas 27.11.1988

⓯ The Expansionist E3 5b
The striking central crack-line gives a brilliant pitch. The first pitch fell down so start up *Total Recoil*.
FA. P.Littlejohn, J.Harwood, C.Horsfield 25.5.1978

⓰ Grit Box .... 7a+
One of the finest wall pitches in the area. The crux is at the start - the rest just majestic cranking.
FA. G.Gibson 5.4.1996

⓱ Giant Sand............. 7a
The right-hand line on this wall is worth doing if you have made the effort to get up here in the first place.
FA. G.Gibson, R.Thomas 31.4.1996

Llanbradach — Sinister Wall

Sinister Wall

A compact wall split into two sections, the right-hand being more overhanging than the left. Both walls give some nice routes mostly on small edges and pockets.

Approach (map and overview p.458) - From the Luxury Wall, continue on the path and bear right after 50m to the wall that can be seen amongst the trees.

Conditions - The wall faces southeast and gets sunshine until mid-afternoon. Unfortunately it does suffer seepage during the winter months.

❶ Bringeth yon Leach .. 7a+
The first line on the wall involves some extreme crimping.
FA. G.Gibson 2009

❷ Food for Parasites .... 7a+
The hardest on this section of wall and a true test of finger strength and technique.
FA. R.Thomas, G.Royle 12.6.1996

❸ The Host 6c
Climb just left of the central streak utilising a few flaky holds. Finish on the left.
FA. R.Thomas 1.7.1996

❹ Giving it all Up 7a
The centre of the wall has a crux at half-height.
FA. R.Thomas, G.Gibson 5.5.1996

❺ Dreaming in Colour .. 7a
A superb sustained and fingery sequence is needed to solve the problem posed by the wall to the left of the arete.
FA. R.Thomas, G.Gibson 28.4.1996

❻ Letters of Life 6c
The left-hand side of the blunt arete with one difficult move.
FA. R.Thomas, G.Gibson 28.4.1996

❼ Overleaf 6b
The wall above the ledge gained from *Dreaming in Colour* with a wobbly 'leaf'.
FA. R.Thomas, G.Gibson 19.6.1996

❽ The Evil Eye 7a
The cracks and wall past the 'eye' to a difficult slab.
FA. G.Gibson 28.4.1996

❾ In Blood, of Life, of Sin? . 7a+
An excellent fingery wall climb, with a dynamic crux.
FA. G.Gibson 28.4.1996

❿ Abbattoir and Costello
.... 7b+
The centre of the black wall. Intricate, sustained and steep.
FA. G.Gibson 29.6.1996

⓫ Sinister 7b
The final route of the wall has a low crux and a finger stamina test above.
FA. G.Gibson, R.Thomas 4.5.1996

⓬ Snapper 6c
From the top of *The Evil Eye*, straightforward climbing leads upwards in a superb position.
FA. G.Gibson 29.6.1996

⓭ Shadow of the Sun ... 7a
A super little route on the isolated wall to the left.
FA. R.Thomas, G.Gibson 29.6.1996

⓮ Save Our NHS .... 7b+
Pull through the green scoop and make a couple of moves on poor rock to gain a shakeout jug, then finish up the steep wall.
FA. T.Williams 2020

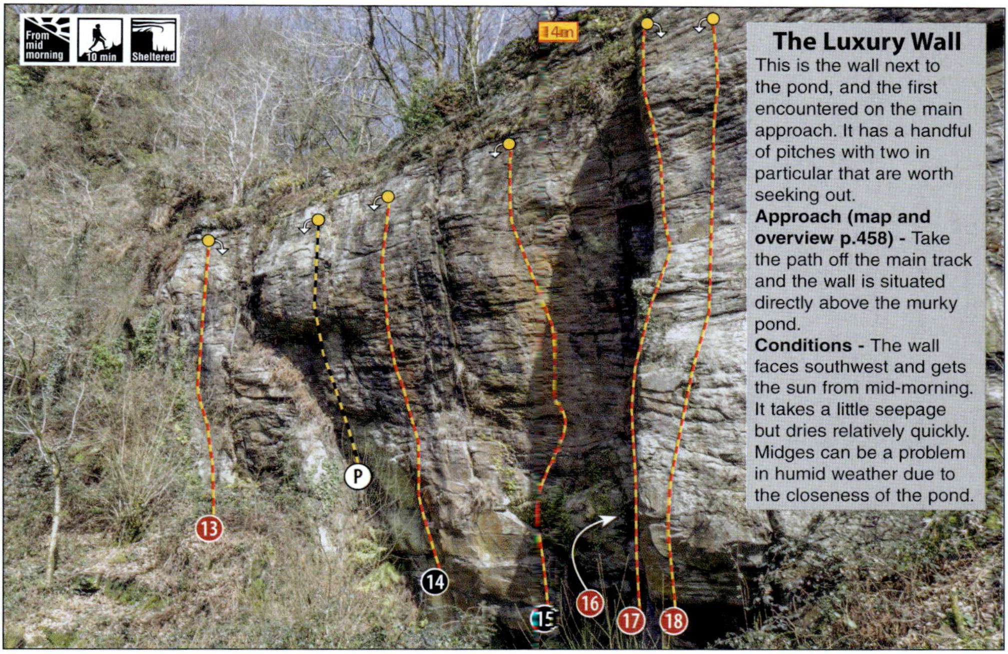

The Luxury Wall

This is the wall next to the pond, and the first encountered on the main approach. It has a handful of pitches with two in particular that are worth seeking out.

Approach (map and overview p.458) - Take the path off the main track and the wall is situated directly above the murky pond.

Conditions - The wall faces southwest and gets the sun from mid-morning. It takes a little seepage but dries relatively quickly. Midges can be a problem in humid weather due to the closeness of the pond.

15 Slip into Something Sexy 3 stars ...... 7a+
The fine wall gives an excellent exercise in fingery wall climbing.
FA. M.Crocker, R.Thomas 12.11.1988

16 Slipped .... 6c+
The corner, utilising the right wall.
FA. A.Rosier 2009

17 Slipping into Luxury 2 stars ...... 6b+
Technical face climbing on 'dinks' and pockets up the wall between the corner and arete gains a mid-height ledge on the rib. Finish up the rib. Very pleasant. *Photo p.324*.
FA. M.Ward, G.Jenkin, M.Crocker 6.11.1988

18 The Slap of Luxury ... 1 star 7a
The right-hand side of arete and wall has a butch start and a technical finish.
FA. R.Thomas, G.Gibson 30.3.1996

19 The Luxury Gap 7a
The centre of the wall above a ledge. Surprisingly technical.
FA. G.Gibson 30.3.1996

20 Internal Reflection 6a
A decent easier route.
FA. R.Thomas, G.Gibson 30.3.1996

21 Gladness 4c
The groove has some poor rock.
FA. R.Thomas, G.Gibson, D.Emanuel 2009

22 Madness 6b
The bulge and poorer upper wall.
FA. R.Thomas, G.Gibson 2009

23 Sadness 5a
The groove system.
FA. G.Jenkin, R.Thomas 6.11.1988

24 Blandess 4c
Climb past some unreliable rock.
FA. G.Gibson, R.Thomas, D.Emanuel 2009

25 Badness 4a
Climb on poor rock up sloping ledges.
FA. G.Gibson 2009

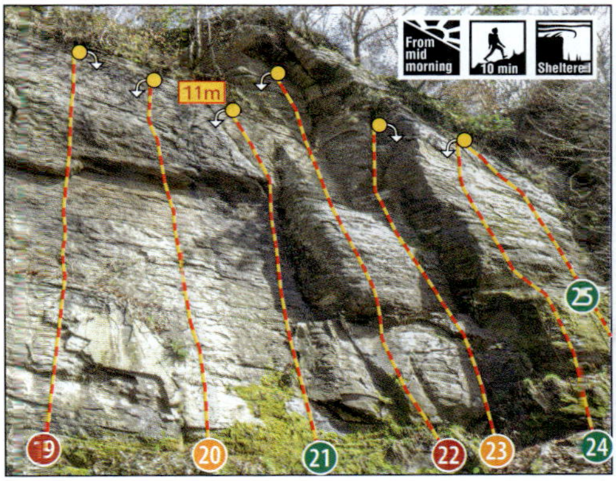

Carmarthenshire
Gower
Inland and Coastal Limestone
The Valleys Sandstone

Sirhowy

Grade Spread — 27 | 35 | 7 | —

Sirhowy is one of the finest chunks of quarried sandstone in the area, made even better because of its tranquil setting with little in the way of road traffic noise or onlookers. It also has its own picnic area complete with bench and tables! The best climbing is on The Rust Curtain with its brilliant line-up of fingery wall climbs, whilst the Western Wall has plenty of excellent (slightly) easier climbing on some of the best rock around.

Approach
From junction 28 on the M4, take the A467 dual carriageway north to the fourth roundabout. Take the first left at this roundabout, which leads directly into the Sirhowy Country Park. Park at the end, next to the crag. The barriers to the park occasionally close early, but the times for closure are posted on the notice board at the entrance. Park outside the barrier if staying later than the locking up time. Alternatively, in the middle of Wattsville, turn off the main road onto Hafod Tudor Terrace. After 50m turn left under a tunnel and continue downhill and turn right. In 200m a large parking area is reached on the left. Walk a short way further on the road and then go left over a bridge to arrive in the parking area next to the crag.

Conditions
The crag faces west and receives afternoon and early evening sun although the tree canopy is dense in summer. It dries relatively quickly except in the winter months when seepage is present. Sirhowy can be a perfect venue in warm weather.

Access
This crag changed ownership in 2023, and although an attempt by the local area to purchase it was unsuccessful, funds raised are now being used to re-equip the crag.

The Rust Curtain

One of the cleanest walls on the sandstone crags, offering some fierce and fingery face climbing with a very pleasant ambiance.

Approach - A simple stroll from the parking places.
Conditions - The wall takes relatively little seepage outside the winter months. The face picks up sun from mid afternoon and dries quickly.

① The Waco Kid 6b
The first bolt line on the far left of the wall.
FA. A.Rosier 29.8.2016

② Gott in Himmel 7a
A short fingery and desperate exercise. *Photo p.473*.
FA. R.Thomas, S.Coles 9.5.1996

③ King Krab 7a
The girdle traverse is a strenuous undertaking - long quickdraws and double ropes are required. Head up *Gott in Himmel* and then stretch up and across rightwards into the break of *Butcher Heinrich*. Follow the break rightwards to the end of the wall. Finish up *Aedan's Arete*.
FA. A.Rosier, W.Gregory 28.6.2008

④ Butcher Heinrich 7b
Superb, technical face climbing on micro holds.
FA. M.Crocker, R.Thomas 1989

⑤ Strange Little Boy 7a
A tight filler-in line between two older routes.
FA. A.Rosier 29.8.2016

⑥ Strange Little Girl 6c
A fine pitch up the crack-line. A good introduction to this section of the crag.
FA. F.Thomas, M.Crocker 1989

⑦ King Ada 7b
Quality wall climbing with a frustrating crux and perhaps the best move on the wall. Moving into *Strange Little Girl* at the break gives a decent **6c**.
FA. G.Gibson, R.Thomas 7.4.1996

⑧ Skanderbeg 7b
A good clean wall pitch with the difficulties lower down. There is a direct start at **7b+**.
FA. M.Crocker, R.Thomas 11.6.1989. FA. (Start) O.Burrows 15.10.2016

⑨ King Zog .... 7a+
Excellent climbing. Start up a flake. Finish slightly left via a desperate move to pass the 'smooth band'.
FA. M.Crocker, R.Thomas 11.6.1989

⑩ Face .... 7b+
One of the best here with a reachy start, an overlap and a technical finale.
FA. G.Gibson, R.Thomas 6.4.1996

⑪ Mawr, Mawr, Mawr 7a
Tackle the intermittent crack-line direct. *Photo p.479*.
FA. G.Gibson, R.Thomas 6.4.1996

Sirhowy — The Rust Curtain

12 The Crimson King 7a
Climb the wall finishing leftwards to the same lower-off as *Mawr, Mawr, Mawr*. Hardest at the start.
FA. G.Gibson, R.Thomas 6.4.1996

13 Sunstone 7a
The wall behind a tree stump has a fingery start and finale.
FA. A.Rosier 27.7.2007

14 VIP Lunge .... 6c+
The wall just right of the tree stump has a trying start.
FA. R.Thomas, G.Gibson 6.4.1996

15 Hostility Suite 6c
The wall just to the left of the prominent arete.
FA. R.Thomas, G.Gibson 6.4.1996

16 Aedan's Arete .... 6a+
The right-hand arete of the wall.
FA. A.Rosier 24.7.2007

17 Brucifer .... 6a+
Climb through the left-hand side of the slim overlap.
FA. A.Rosier 14.5.2005

18 Take Your Pants to Heaven 6c
Climb the crack up and over the roof.
FA. A.Rosier 21.5.2005

19 Gouge the Unknown .... 6c+
The thin wall under the right-hand side of the roof.
FA. R.Thomas 2007

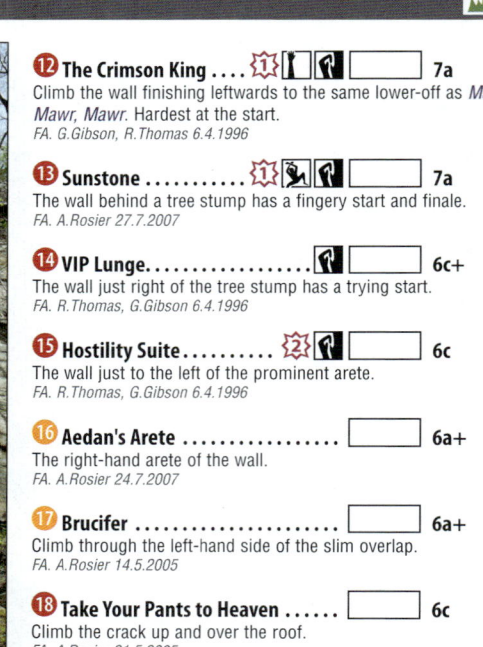

Sirhowy 473

Kieran Keavy on *Gott in Himmel* (7a) - *p.471* - at Sirhowy's Rust Cutain. The Rust Curtain is one of South Wales most popular venues that has a fabulous selection of wall climbs.
Photo: Eben Muse

20 Knickerless in Hell .... ☐ 6b
A steep wall and groove to a large lower-off.
FA. R.Thomas 2007

21 Holey Moses .... ☐ 6a
Easier moves through the overlap's right-hand side.
FA. P.Wardman 15.5.2005

22 Where the Arc is It? .... ☐ 5c
Up a shield then left to the lower-off of *Holey Moses*.
FA. P.Wardman 15.5.2005

23 The Big Squeeze .... ☐ 5c
Climb over a small overlap then direct up the wall.
FA. R.Thomas 2019

24 Temples of Cwmaman .... ☐ 5a
Climb the wall to a small roof.
FA. A.Rosier 15.5.2005

25 Arch of the Last Craven Ant ..... ☐ 5c
Climb past a loose flake to a short arete.
FA. R.Thomas 2007

Sirhowy

Emmie Chadwick on *Queens of the Stone Age* (6b+) - *p.476* - at the Western Wall, Sirhowy. The Western Wall is a great companion to the nearby Rust Curtain having another selection of popular lines but at a lower level of difficulty. The rock has a more natural appearance and is less steep which gives climbs that succumb to good technique rather than pure pulling power. In recent times the whole crag was put up for sale and a local led campaign crowd-sourced a significant amount of money that would of been enough to buy the site. However technical problems meant that a deal could not be completed. Nevertheless the new owner of the site has been very positive about climbing continuing, and the crag is now being re-equipped, new signs installed and the area tidied up. Photo: Sam Parsons

Sirhowy — Western Wall

Western Wall

An excellent venue that has good rock and plenty of interesting routes which are generally easier than on The Rust Curtain. The base of the cliff is a pleasant spot to relax between climbs.

Approach (map and overview p.477) - Walk a short distance along the base of the crag from the Rust/Dust Curtain walls.

Conditions - This wall needs time to dry out.

❶ Queen Bee — 5c
The slightly fragile curving corner on the far left of the wall.
FA. R.Thomas, G.Ashmore 27.9.2013

❷ A Poxy Queen — 6b
A bouldery pitch. Make a long move to a reinforced protruding square-cut hold and then mantel onto the ledge above. Move right and finish up the interesting wall.
FA. R.Thomas, G.Ashmore 27.9.2013

❸ Slip into the Queen — 6b+
A similar but slightly harder version of *A Poxy Queen* avoiding the glued-on rail. Finishes as for *A Poxy Queen*.
FA. R.Thomas, E.Travers-Jones 29.9.2013

❹ Little Queen — 5c
A good pitch. Move left up ledges and then climb the steep crack using some off-balance moves.
FA. A.Rosier, R.McAllister 30.6.2013

❺ Sheer Heart Attack — 7a+
An intense bit of finger work up the steep wall above a ledge.
FA. A.Rosier, R.McAllister 10.7.2013

❻ Deaf as a Post — 7a+
From the ramp, make a big move past an overlap to a crack. At its top, move left and up to good holds. Alternatively, follow the direct finish to the lower-off of *Killer Queen*.
FA. M.Crocker, R.Thomas 1989

❼ Killer Queen — 7a
Climb ledges and a crack to a tricky wall.
FA. A.Rosier, R.Thomas 2.7.2013

❽ Queens of the Stone Age — 6b+
Teeter up the right-leading ramp and climb the sustained wall above it. Good moves from start to finish. *Photo 474*.
FA. A.Rosier, R McAllister 25.6.2013

❾ Drag Queen — 6a+
Start up the ramp of *Queens of the Stone Age* but continue up the groove at its end. Lots of interesting moves. *Photo opposite*.
FA. A.Rosier, R.McAllister 30.6.2013

❿ Raving Queen — 6b+
Nip up the thin crack and make a tricky sequence to get on the sloping ramp of *Drag Queen*. Finish up this.
FA. A.Rosier, R.McAllister 30.6.2013

⓫ The Queen is Dead — 6b
Climb up past a shot-hole and continue up the smart wall above.
FA. A.Rosier, R.McAllister 30.6.2013

⓬ Drama Queen — 5c
The unattractive corner on the right-hand side of the wall.
FA. R.Thomas, A.Rosier, R.McAllister 10.7.2013

John Warner enjoying perfect conditions on *Drag Queen* (6a+) - *opposite* - at the Western Wall, Sirhowy. Photo: Mark Glaister

Sirhowy Upper Tier

Upper Tier

This was the last section of Sirhowy to be developed. It is comprised of a set of walls seamed with cracks. Not of the same quality as the rest of the crag but worth a look if the other areas are busy.

Approach (map and overview p.470) - Walk a little further on along the base of the cliff from the Western Walls and then head up the bank.

Conditions - Catches little sun.

1 Budda's Watching 5b
The sandwiched wall past ledges.
FA. A.Rosier, R.Heirene 16.3.2016

2 Providence .... 6b+
The arete just right of *Budda's Watching*.
FA. A.Rosier, O.Burrows, J.Williams 26.5.2016

3 Psilocybic 6c
The crack and face in the centre of the wall right of the corner.
FA. A.Rosier, O.Burrows 10.9.2015

4 Zeitgeist E2 5c
The fine looking crack left of the arete takes plenty of gear.
FA. A.Rosier, R.McAllister 3.9.2015

5 Forgotten Ground 6a
Climb just to the right of the arete to a shared lower-off.
FA. A.Rosier, R.McAllister 9.7.2015

6 Approaching the Nadir 6a
The left-leaning crack joining *Forgotten Ground* at the top.
FA. A.Rosier, R.McAllister 25.6.2015

7 Hooker with a Penis .... 6a+
The finger-crack and face to a move left to a shared lower-off.
FA. A.Rosier, R.McAllister 25.6.2015

8 Lateralus 6b
Pass the tricky overlap and step right beneath the lower-off before a hard move gains the top of the wall.
FA. A.Rosier, R.McAllister 11.6.2015

9 Rosetta Stoned 6a
Skirt overlaps on their right to finish at a shared lower-off.
FA. A.Rosier, R.McAllister 17.6.2015

10 Stinkfist 6a
The corner-crack.
FA. A.Rosier, R.McAllister 30.6.2015

11 Intension .... 6b+
The narrow groove in the centre of the buttress.
FA. A.Rosier, R.McAllister 25.6.2015

12 Third Eye 6b
The arete of the buttress. Try not to bridge.
FA. A.Rosier, R.McAllister, N.Goile 28.6.2015

13 The Grudge 6c
The left-hand crack in the buttress is a tricky number. Go right to a shared lower-off with *Jambi*.
FA. A.Rosier 17.6.2015

14 Jambi 6c
The twisting right-hand crack of the buttress is hard low down.
FA. A.Rosier, R.McAllister 17.6.2015

15 Prison Sex 5c
The chimney to a shared lower-off with *Jambi*.
FA. A.Rosier, R.McAllister 30.6.2015

16 The Outsider 5c
The jamming crack in the tower. Shared lower-off with *Jambi*.
FA. A.Rosier, R.McAllister 30.6.2015

Corie Jones on *Mawr, Mawr, Mawr* (7a) - *p.471* - at the Rust Curtain, Sirhowy. Photo: Amy Chitty

Cox's Quarry

The climbing is on a small wall of excellent rock set at the base of a massive quarry working. Although the number of pitches is small the climbing is excellent and well-bolted. The setting is tranquil and the face is set in an open sheltered glade.

Approach
From junction 28 on the M4, take the A467 dual carriageway north to the fourth roundabout. Take the third exit and then the first left turn (signposted for an industrial estate). Park immediately, opposite a forestry commission track on the right. Walk up the forestry track for 600m and lookout for a steep path on the left. Follow the path uphill until it levels out and continue through the quarry entrance and on to the crag which is at the far end of the working.

Conditions
The wall is clean and very sheltered but this may hinder drying during wet weather.

Access
There maybe restrictions that apply to other sections of the quarry - check the BMC RAD.

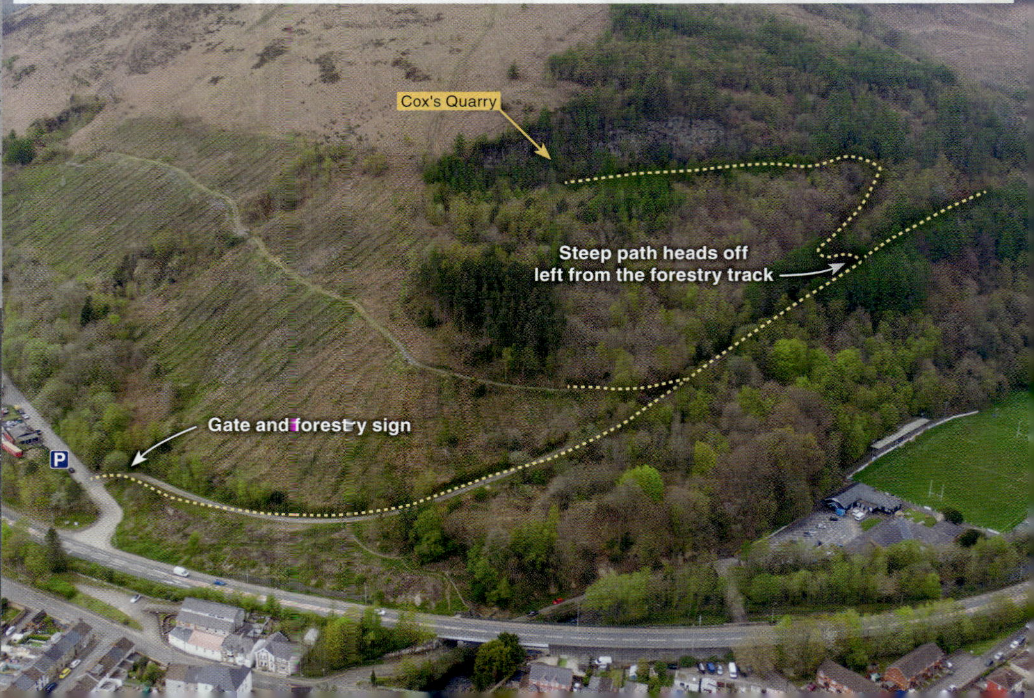

GPS 51.618217 -3.133212

Cox's Quarry

Steep path heads off left from the forestry track

Gate and forestry sign

Cox's Quarry 481

1 Coxs Yucca — 5c
The very short crack on the far left-hand side of the wall to a shared lower-off on the right.
FA. R.Thomas 2022

2 Cox Bloc — 6a
The squat wall to a shared lower-off on a block.
FA. R.Thomas 2022

3 Thieving Coxs — 6b+
The wall left of the wide crack.
FA. R.Thomas 2022

4 Boner's Crack — 5b
The wide crack in the middle of the wall.
FA. D.Emanuel, R.Thomas 1.2017

5 Hands off Cox — 6b+
The short fingery red wall right of the crack is excellent.
FA. R.Thomas, D.Emanuel 2017

6 On with Cox — 6c+
The crimpy red wall finishing at the lower-off on the nose.
FA. Gandalf, R.Thomas 2017

7 Sox on Cox — 6c+
Start as for *On with Cox*. Move right at the first bolt and then up the centre of the wall to a steep finish over the nose.
FA. Gandalf, R.Thomas 4.2023

8 Smears on Cox — 6c
Start at the undercut right arete. Make bouldery moves interspersed with good shake-outs.
FA. Gandalf, R.Thomas 4.2023

Cross Keys Quarry

| Grade Spread | 7 | 14 | 9 | 1 | - |

A very convenient series of closely spaced buttresses that have a number of good low and mid-grade lines. Although close to houses it is a secluded spot that is for the most part clear of the tree canopy, has a sunny aspect and is very sheltered.

Approach
Take the A467 north from Crosskeys to a roundabout with a huge mountain bike sculpture in its centre. Take the exit to Cwmcarn and then the third left onto Sillver Street. After 100m go left onto North Road and continue along it to where the houses on the right turn from terraces to detached. Park here with care as it is a busy residential road. Go up a short steep road between the terrace and detached buildings and at the top go right for 40m and pick up a path that heads back left and then up the slope to quickly gain the base of the crag.

Conditions
The crags has a low-lying, sunny aspect and is open and quick drying.

The Left Walls and First Buttress — Cross Keys Quarry

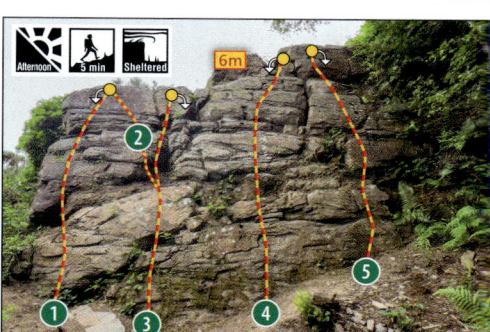

The Left Walls and First Buttress
The low walls on the left have some short well-bolted low grade lines whilst the First Buttress is a more substantial tower that is easily viewed from the approach path.
Approach - Each buttress is easily accessed on a path.
Conditions - Very sheltered and open.

❶ The Key is in the Name 3a
First climb on the left bolted for younger ones and novices.
FA. F.Rocke 9.5.2024

❷ Beagle Banter 3b
The line right of *The Key is in the Name* to a shared lower-off.
FA. F.Rocke 9.5.2024

❸ Powered by Pepsi 3b
Climb the start of *Beagle Banter* but continue straight-up.
FA. F.Rocke 9.5.2024

❹ Cuddles Small but mighty 4a
Needs traffic but goes, watch out for loose rock and mud.
FA. N.Rocke 9.5.2024

❺ Hugo Hugs are the Best 4a
The less clean line on the right side of the wall.
FA. N.Rocke 9.5.2024

❻ Rock Out with Your Lock Out 6a
An eliminate with a tricky start and finish.
FA. N.Rocke, L.James 20.4.2024

❼ Lock Stock and Two Broken Holds 6a
Layback to a shared lower-off with *Rocking With Your Lock Out*
FA. N.Rocke 20.4.2024

❽ Safe Cracker 5c
The face via a tree root and mantelshelf is an eliminate.
FA. N.Rocke 20.4.2024

❾ Lookout Post 6a
The bolted line left of the ramp and then onto the face.
FA. J.King 8.5.2024

❿ Escape Through the Roof . . . . . 6a+
Shares the first bolt with *Cock Lock*. Move left past the low roof and onto the ramp. Overcome the second roof and finish out left.
FA. J.King 8.5.2024

⓫ Cock Lock . . . . 6a+
Right of the left arete passing a protruding rectangular block.
FA. = Thomas 1999

⓬ Pick Locks . . . . 6b+
The bolted pillar and wall right of the full-height crack-line.
FA. = Thomas 1999

⓭ Skeleton Key 6b
Clip the initial bolt of *Pick Locks* and climb the wall direct.
FA. = Thomas 1999

⓮ Lockup . . . . 6a+
Ascend the right arete of the buttress beginning up the slope.
FA. = Thomas 1999

Cross Keys Quarry — Second Buttress and Right-hand Walls

Second Buttress and Right-hand Walls

Two substantial sections of crag that allow plenty to be climbed in a short space of time.

Approach (map and overview p.482) - Each buttress is easily accessed on a path.

Conditions - Very sheltered.

1 Cagophilist .... 6a+
The left-hand side of the arete. Start right of some tree stumps.
FA. G.Jones 25.5.2024

2 Kleidariaphobia .... 6c+
The left arete passing a couple of small overhangs.
FA. N.Rocke, G.Jones 10.5.2024

3 Five Lever .... 6b+
Wall to the right of the arete and left of a wide crack.
FA. R.Thomas, G.Ashmore 1999

4 Locksmith 5c
The wide crack..
FA. N.O'Neill, R.Thomas 1999

5 Petersman 6c
Wall to the right of the wide crack of *Locksmith*.
FA. R.Thomas, N.O'Neill, G.Davies 8.5.2024

6 The Right Combination 5c
The line left of the slab has a tricky start.
FA. N.Rocke 8.5.2024

7 She's a Key-per 5c
Slabby with a tricky direct start on thin crimps.
FA. D.Foster 8.5.2024

8 Lock 'n' Roll 4b
Direct up face of slab *She's a Key-per*.
FA. D.Foster 8.5.2024

9 Lock to the Top 5c
Climb the corner and roof above it.
FA. N.Rocke 8.5.2024

Second Buttress and Right-hand Walls — Cross Keys Quarry

⑩ Lock Sucker 6c
The left arete of the narrow face.
FA. Gandalf, G.Jones 10.5.2024

⑪ Radovan Karadijc .... 7a+
The short red face between the aretes.
FA. G.Ashmore 17.10.1999

⑫ Lockdown .... 6b+
The right-hand arete right of the narrow face.
FA. R.Thomas 2024

⑬ Lock Out 4b
The slim slab above a ledge to a shared lower-off.
FA. R.Thomas 2024

⑭ Are You Feeling Locky ? ...... 6a+
Climb to the right of a tree. No use of the crack at this grade.
FA. N.Rocke 8.5.2024

⑮ Lock Don't Drop .... 6b+
An eliminate up the narrow face between the cracks.
FA. J.King 24.4.2024

⑯ Knob Lock .... 6a+
The wall right of the curving crack.
FA. R.Thomas 2024

⑰ Deadbolt 6b
The far right-hand line up the face on some small fragile holds to a shared lower-off.
FA. R.Thomas 2024

Cwmcarn

Grade Spread — 13 13 — —

Cwmcarn is an old quarry that has a good number of bolted lines which are quick to approach. The first routes encountered are the best and follow strong corner and arete features. In summer the dense tree cover gives the place a rather gloomy feel but when the leaves are off of the trees and the sun is out the character is more pleasant and allows the faces to get the sun.

Approach
Take the A467 north from Crosskeys to a roundabout with a huge mountain bike sculpture in its centre. Take the third exit to Cwmcarn and then go immediately left signed to Cwmcarn Village. After 500m turn right (just before a pub) onto Park Street and then left to Tribute Avenue and park. Take a path on the left at the bend past sheds and then a path up through the woods to the quarry.

Conditions
A viable destination in the cooler months when the leaves are off of the trees and the sun is out. Sheltered but will take time to dry after rain.

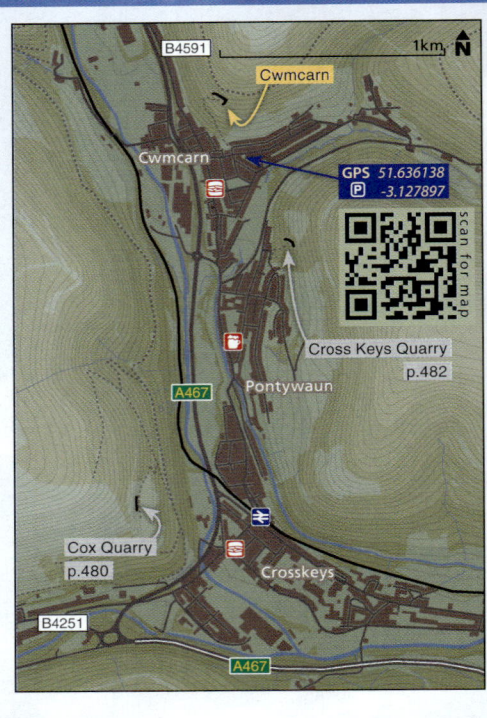

Main Wall Cwmcarn

Main Wall
The best of the routes are on the left of this section of the quarry. All of the wall has been cleaned in the past but vegetation has returned on some of the lines.
Approach - The first wall seen on entering the quarry.
Conditions - Best when the sun can penetrate the tree canopy. Can take time to dry once wet.

1 Endosperm 5b
A line up the slab on the left when entering quarry.
FA. N.O'Neill R.Thomas 29.7.2016

2 Jiffy's Twitter Spat .... 6a+
A short but steep wall left of a thin crack.
FA. A.Rosier, M.Wright 20.5.2016

3 Archaeopteryx 6a
The long corner and bulge left of *Terrordactyl* to a lower-off.
FA. R.Thomas, G.Ashmore 5.1.2017

4 Terrordactyl.................. 6a+
One of the best hereabouts. Follow the arete to some crux moves left around a bulge at the top.
FA. A.Rosier 26.7.2016

5 The Phill.................... 6b+
A fine line up the tall tower easily view when entering the quarry.
FA. M.Wright, A.Rosier 20.5.2016

6 Pig in a Cage 5b
A pleasant sustained pitch up the corner.
FA. A.Rosier, R.McAllister 12.5.2016

7 Tweaking Lats.............. 6a
The arete. Deviating left at the crux reduces the grade.
FA. R.Thomas M.Wright 6.5.2016

8 Feeling Totally Hacked Off!...... 6a
The corner that can gather some vegetation towards the top.
FA. R.Thomas, A.Rosier 25.5.2016

9 Clint Yeastwood 5a
The corner with a ledge at two thirds height.
FA. A.Rosier, A.J.Rosier, C.Wyatt 4.6.2016

10 Take the Rap for Beating the Crap 6b
Bolts reported as loose. The central tower to a ledge then the short headwall above.
FA. R.Thomas N.O'Neil 8.5.2016

Cwmcarn — Main Wall

⓫ Nick's Line 6b
Climb the groove on the left-side of the central tower with a tough move right to the arete at mid-height.
FA. N.O'Neill, R.Thomas 8.5.2016

⓬ Eyeful Tower .... 6b+
From the ledge reached via some rungs head up the central tower on improving rock.
FA. A.Rosier 4.5.2016

⓭ Polyphemus .... 6b+
Start up the rungs of *Eyeful Tower* and from the right end of the ledge climb the tower to the right of some unstable blocks. Do not use the blocks.
FA. A.Rosier 15.5.2016

⓮ Crimson .... 6c+
Head up easy ground to a good ledge at mid-height. Move left and climb the wall with difficulty via a big flat hold and pinch above to a finish on large holds.
FA. M.Wright, R.Thomas 5.4.2016

⓯ Auf Wiedersehen Mate 6b
Begin as for *Crimson* and from the mid-height ledge climb the cracks between *Crimson* and the corner on the right to finish at a shared lower-off with *Crimson*.
FA. A.Rosier 26.7.2016

⓰ Pus in my Boots 6a
Move up and left to the arete of the narrow buttress from where a series of 'step-ups' reach some slightly harder technical moves before the lower-off.
FA. R.Thomas, M.Wright, R.McAllister 17.5.2016

⓱ Yellow Tower .... 6b+
Start as for *Pus in my Boots* and continue direct up the narrow buttress passing a streak of yellow paint. Needs another bolt to protect moves above the ledge.
FA. M.Wright, R.Thomas 5.4.2016

⓲ Like it then Lump it .... 6b+
Begin just right of *Yellow Tower* and carefully move left under the roof to a good undercut and ledge. Using surprisingly good holds climb to a final ledge and lower-off.
FA. R.Thomas, M.Wright 23.5.2016

⓳ Sour Grapes 5c
The arete is better and harder if started to the right of the bolts.
FA. A.Rosier, R.Thomas 25.5.2016

⓴ Cwmcarnage 6b
The green cracks.
FA. A.Rosier, R.Thomas 25.5.2016

Upper Tier

Located up on a high ledge to the right of the Main Wall is this rather unappealing section of the quarry that holds some short but tough pitches.

Approach (map and overview p.486) - Enter the quarry and walk right and up to the ledge from where all the routes start.

Conditions - The wall sees little in the way of sun. Can take time to dry once wet.

1 The Terrace Gardener.......... 6a+
Start at the left-hand end of the terrace. Make a tricky start up the cracks which then lead to a tree and lower-off.
FA. R.Thomas, M.Wright 16.5.2016

2 Bramble Pitt Gets Hammered ... 6a+
Climb the short lower wall to the mid-height horizontal break and finish via the small roof above.
FA. R.Thomas, M.Wright 16.5.2016

3 Corneal Abrasion 6b
Make bouldery moves to good jugs and then progress up the groove and overlap to a lower-off.
FA. R.Thomas M.Wright 4.5.2016

4 Stumbling Block Project ..... 6a+?
Route has changed since block has fallen. Move up to a rock scar and continue to a lower-off.
FA. R.Thomas 17.7.2016

5 Lisa Likes 67 .... 6b
Follow the diagonal crack to the roof, pull over it and finish up the short headwall.
FA. R.Thomas, M.Wright, A.Rosier 3.5.2016

6 Drop Knee at 67? 6b
Pull over the roof utilising an elegant "drop knee" or pull hard, swear a lot and flail upwards. An excellent short problem on sound rock.
FA. R.Thomas, M.Wright 6.5.2016

Tyle y Coch

Grade Spread | 8 | 2 | 9 | 3 | -

Tyle y Coch quarry is set in a pleasant quiet dell on the hillside between Abercarn and Newbridge. It has a sheer main wall of quality sandstone plus another wall with some easier offerings.

Approach
From the A467 turn off towards West End and follow the road into the village and past The Crown pub. Continue out of the village and after around 500m park in a large lay-by on the left. Walk back 20m and at a telegraph pole nip up the steep bank and follow a path left to a low tunnel under the disused railway line. The quarry is on the other side of the tunnel.

Conditions
The quarry gets morning sun but there is a dense tree canopy. Seepage does occur and the Main Wall takes time to dry out; once dry the Main Wall is steep enough to allow climbing in the rain.

GPS 51.656414 -3.137216

Access
The cliff is on private land and a notice is posted stating that climbing is prohibited, although no reports of climbing being prevented have been reported. The issue is to do with civil liability - please leave if asked and report any information to the BMC and Rockfax. The inclusion of the quarry in this book implies no right of access to climb there.

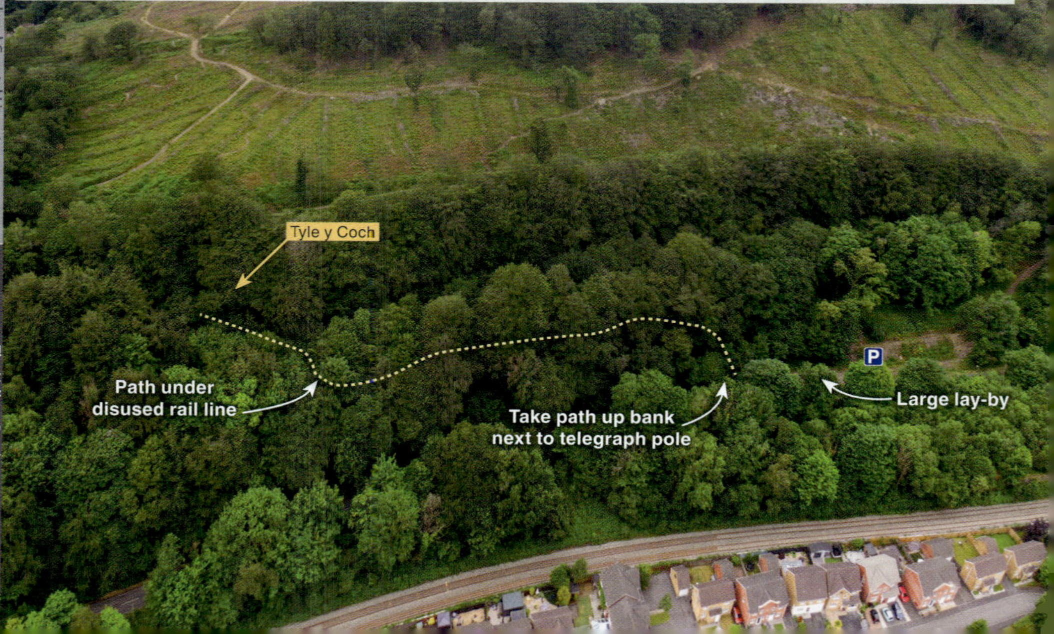

Ollie Burrows on *Mislivings* (7a) - *p.493* - at Tyle y Coch. The Main Wall is a compact section of quarried sandstone that is split by some long thin crack-lines and crossed by slim overlaps that give a choice selection of routes. The only drawback is that in mid-summer the tree canopy is so dense that it can be a rather gloomy spot but an excellent venue if hot. Photo: Alan Rosier

Tyle y Coch — Main Wall

Main Wall

The Main Wall is tall and compact split by lots of thin cracks and crossed by some overlaps. This is a good spot for those after tough lines in the mid-grades.

Approach (map and overview p.490)

Conditions - Very shady due to the dense tree canopy in summer and suffers quite badly from seepage - best to have a plan B as it can be wet when least expected. Once dry it gives sheltered climbing in the rain.

Access - The crag is on private land and climbing is not allowed by the landowners.

❶ Y Caled Caled 7c
Steep line 20m to the left of the main wall. Excellent when clean.
FA. M.Wright 20.9.2016

❷ Rump and Scoop 6a
The arete to the left of the large corner is worthwhile.
FA. J.James, S.Abbott, W.Gladwin 8.10.2000

❸ Root Canal .... 6a+
The large corner is a bit of a struggle right until the end.
FA. J.James, T.Williams 23.7.2000

❹ Belly Up 7b
The vague crack via a hole and a difficult and fingery finale.
FA. G.Gibson 16.9.2001

❺ A Cleft Stick 7a
Climb the left fork of the thin Y-crack in the lower wall and then continue via an overlap and tricky sequence on the headwall.
FA. G.Gibson, R.Thomas 23.9.2001

❻ The Pink Lady .... 6c+
The centre of the wall trending right via an incipient crack-line.
FA. G.Jenkin, G.Gibson 16.9.2001

❼ Paradise Row 7a
An excellent wall climb both sustained and technical.
FA. G.Gibson, R.Thomas 23.9.2001

❽ Fairies Wear Boots ...... 6c+
A fine pitch. The long thin snaking crack gives a great outing. The lower-off is just above the second overlap.
FA. A.Rosier, B.Gregory, R.McAllister 16.8.2013

❾ The Four Minute Tyle . 7b
A direct line with a hard start and finish.
FA. G.Percival 17.9.2014

❿ Peachy .... 6b+
Climb the tough lower wall past a jutting hold and a borehole.
FA. J.James, W.Gladwin 14.7.2000

⓫ Mislivings 7a
A peculiar left-trending line to a final bulging finish. Start up *Peachy* and go left with feet under the overlap. *Photo p.491*.
FA. J.James, W.Gladwin 22.6.2001

⓬ The Big Tissue .... 6b+
The overlap to the left of the arete, starting with a tough mantel move and finishing up a thin wall.
FA. J.James, W.Gladwin, D.Jones 13.5.2001

⓭ Cheeky Arete .... S 4a
The arete with a single peg in place.
FA. S.Abbott, J.James, W.Gladwin 14.5.2000

Minor Wall Tyle y Coch

Minor Wall
The Minor Wall is the first wall seen on entering the quarry. It is a little off-putting but has some easier lines that do get traffic. The bolts are being replaced on this section of the crag.

Approach (map and overview p.490)

Conditions - Very shady due to the dense tree canopy in summer and suffers quite badly from seepage. If planning a visit it is best to have a plan B as it can be wet when least expected. Once dry is gives sheltered climbing in the rain.

Access - The crag is on private land and climbing is not allowed by the landowners.

14 Bore Hole 3c
Climb the line of borehole strikes on the left of the wall.
FA. W.Gladwin, J.James 16.7.2000

15 The Ring 3c
Climb the tiny corner line and go direct above.
FA. W.Gladwin, J.James 16.7.2000

16 Mal Culo 4c
Head out right from *The Ring* to a slab and finish over an overhang.
FA. W.Gladwin, J.James, J.Keyhole 7.5.2000

17 Buen Culo 4b
Climb a steep wall to easier angled ground above.
FA. W.Gladwin, S.Abbott, J.James 13.5.2000

18 Suppose a Tree 4c
Start up the corner and move left before climbing to a lower-off that is just above a small roof.
FA. W.Gladwin, J.James 8.7.2000

19 High Moon 6b
A good little pitch up the face sandwiched between the arete and the corner.
FA. J.James, W.Gladwin 12.1999

20 Enema of the Affair ..... 6c+
The arete via some perplexing manoeuvres.
FA. J.James, W.Gladwin 14.5.2000

21 Jumping Jack Flash 4c
The short orange wall.
FA. S.Abbott, J.James, W.Gladwin 14.5.2000

22 Lily of the Valleys 3c
The final easier-angled line.
FA. S.Abbott, J.James, W.Gladwin, D.Jones 4.2.2001

Tirpentwys

Grade Spread | 2 | 16 | 11 | 1 | -

Tucked away at the end of a quiet valley is this pleasant quarried crag. The rock is generally solid and the climbing fairly sustained and pumpy with a good supply of crimps, jugs and cracks available. The base of the cliff is flat and grassy and in good weather this is a lovely place to relax between climbs.

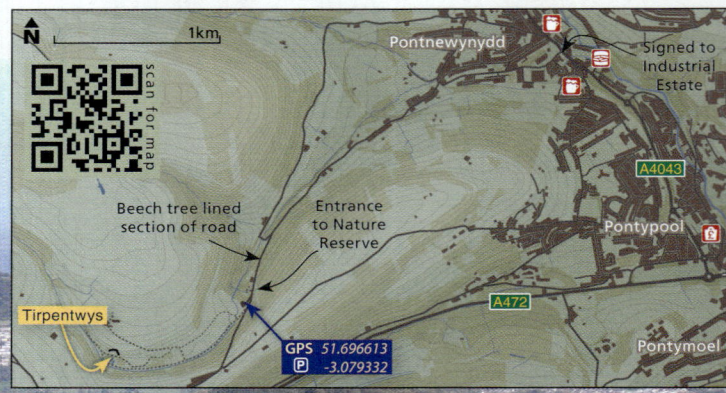

Approach
From the A4043 Pontypool/Blaenavon road turn off into the Pontnewynydd Industrial Estate and drive straight through it to a T-junction. Turn left and continue to where the road becomes lined with ancient beech trees. A further 150m further on is the entrance to Tirpentwys Nature Reserve - park here. Just beyond the entrance to the Nature Reserve is another gated tarmac/gravel track - follow this for 650m until it bends to the right. Go straight on following another gravel track for 300m until a wooden footbridge on the left is encountered. Continue for 50m further along the track, cross a small drainage ditch on the right and go over a fence to reach the crag.

Conditions
The quarry faces southwest and gets sun for much of the day. It is very sheltered and dries quite quickly, making it a possible year-round venue. Seepage can become a problem after prolonged periods of rainfall.

Tirpentwys

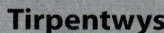

Access
There have been no recorded access issues after the crag has recently passed into new ownership, however old signs prohibiting climbing are still in place. If in the unlikely event you are asked to leave please do so politely and report any information to the BMC access representative and Rockfax.

Jen Stephens on the extremely popular *Supertramp* (7a) - *p.499* - at Tirpentwys. Photo: Mark Glaister

Jay Astbury beginning the initial sequence onto the headwall of the thin *Hail Mary* (7a) - *p.500*. Tirpentwys has a great deal to recommend it, being set in a quiet valley and having the luxury of an open grassy base from which to watch the goings on and relax between routes. Photo: Mark Glaister

Tirpentwys — Main Wall

Main Wall

The main wall has a few well-trodden shorter lines on its left margin. It gradually gains height and steepness to the right culminating in a tall wall seamed with thin cracks that has a number of very good routes.

Approach (map and overview p.494)

Conditions - The wall gets plenty of sun apart from the tree shaded short wall on the left.

1 Shrew 5b
The wall via a ledge and crack with a tricky bulge.
FA. J.Steer, D.Williams 24.3.2008

2 Yank My Chain 4b
The central line up a ramp is a straight-forward climb that passes a peculiar metal fixing.
FA. D.Williams, J.Steer 24.3.2008

3 Paw Me 4c
Climb the right-hand side of the wall via a ledge.
FA. J.James, P.Bowen 24.3.2008

4 By Default Line 5b
The corner-crack gives a traditional feeling sport climb.
FA. P.Bowen, J.James 24.3.2008

5 The Brown Dirt Cowboy .... 6a+
The first line on the larger wall has a brittle band with some good but unnerving holds.
FA. P.Bowen 6.4.2008

6 Where There's Muck There's Brass 6a
The pillar past a dirty band on good but awkward to use holds, especially at the start.
FA. P.Bowen 6.4.2008

7 Mucky Ducky .... 6a+
A technical start and easier wall above a ledge.
FA. G.Gibson 5.2009

8 Lets Get Down and Dirty .... 6a+
A short sequence of very hard moves from the ledge.
FA. P.Bowen, B.Hayes 9.4.2008

Main Wall **Tirpentwys** 499

9 Dirty Deeds Done Dirt Cheap 6b+
Hard moves above the ledge.
FA. P.Bowen 6.4.2008

10 Choosey Suzie 6b+
The pillar has a technical section low down.
FA. G.Gibson 5.2009

11 Lundy Boy 6b
Pumpy jug-pulling marks out the quality of this line.
FA. J.James, P.Bowen 5.4.2008

12 Supertramp 7a
The leaning headwall is superb. Difficulties increase as height is gained, particularly after the large mid-height pocket.
Photo p.28 and p.495.
FA. L.Jones 6.4.2008

13 Strawberry Jam 7b+
The crack-line in the upper half of the face gives a stern test of ability from bottom to top.
FA. B.Gregory 14.4.2008

14 The Cragmeister 6b+
The central line of the face has a testing jamming crack after a steep, juggy start.
FA. B.Gregory 24.3.2008

15 Rocky 6a
Tackle the sandy-coloured bulge with good blocky holds above.
FA. B.Hayes, J.James 4.4.2008

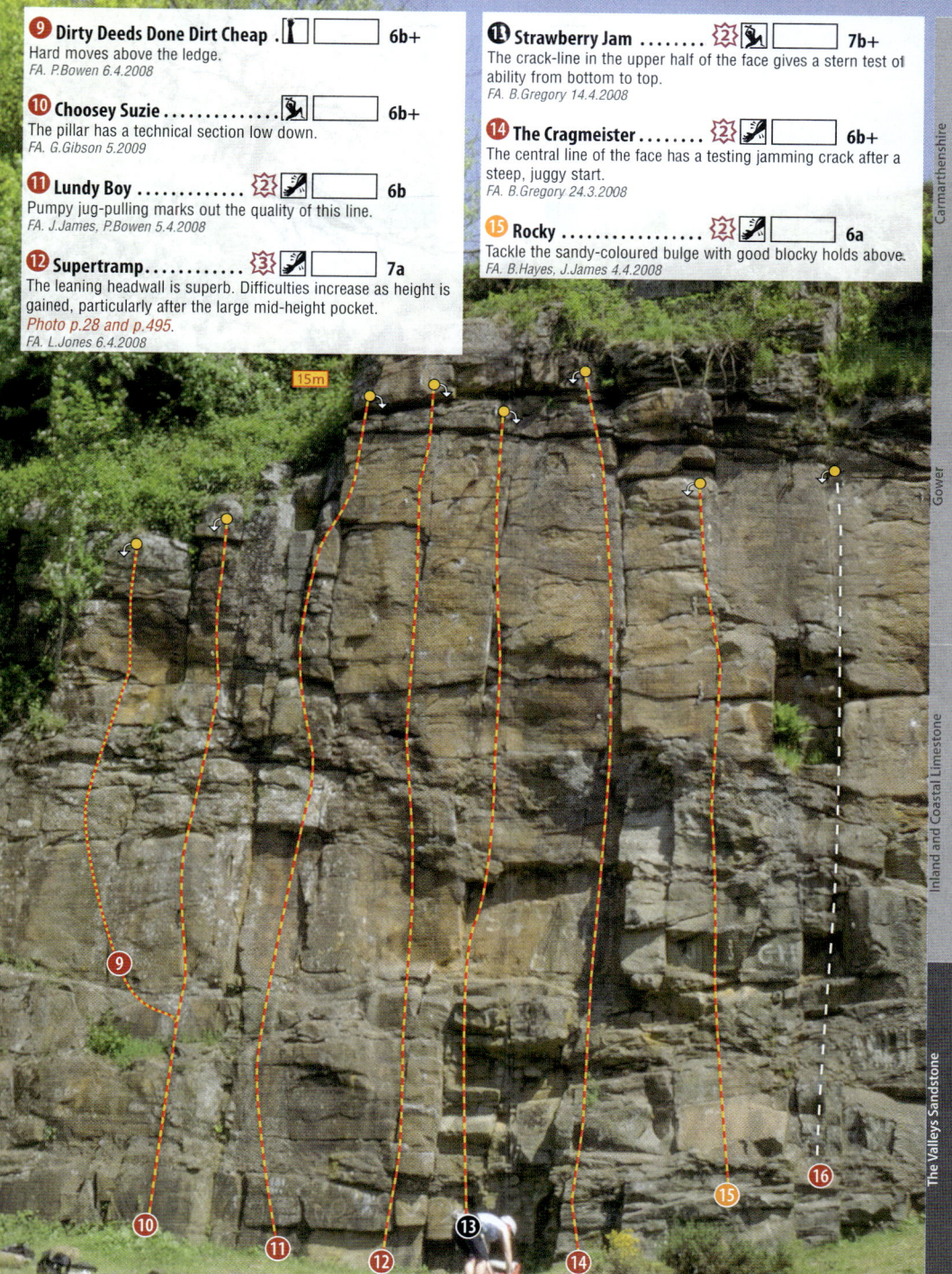

Tirpentwys — Main Wall

16 The Tactless Teacher …… 6b
Enjoyable climbing. An easy start leads to a fingery finale.
FA. L.Jones, B.Hayes 5.4.2008

17 Hail Mary …… 7a
An easy start with crimpy face climbing above. *Photo p.496.*
FA. B.Gregory 24.3.2008

18 Twisted Logic …… 6b+
The lower wall, laced with pockets, leads to a difficult climax via a rockover on the left.
FA. L.Jones, B.Hayes 6.4.2008

19 Leading Edge …… 6a
The right-hand arete and wide crack.
FA. P.Bowen, B.Hayes 5.4.2008

20 Mental Mantels …… 6a
Start up *Leading Edge* and move right The wall above the ledge providing the crux.
FA. P.Bowen, J.Steer 24.3.2008

Right Wall Tirpentwys

㉑ Diamond Dog 6b
A good pitch with plenty of varied moves. Gain the line from the right.
FA. J.James, J.Steer 24.3 2008

㉒ The Chimney Finish ..... 6a+
An awkward and slightly bold start up the blank groove and pockets gains better holds above. Continue more steeply and step left to finish.
FA. P.Bowen, J.Steer 24.3.2008

㉓ Flakes and Chips ..... 6b+
Taking the wall direct past the bolts gives a fingery little number with three hard moves. It can be climbed on the left or right.
FA. P.Bowen, J.James 4.4.2008

㉔ Ledge and Braces 5a
The wall above the raised platform is slabby. Keep the bolt runners on your left.
FA. P.Bowen, J.James, B.Hayes 4.4.2008

Right Wall
The small buttress to the right also has a number of bolted pitches.

❶ Fledgeling .... 6a+
The short hard wall.
FA. R.Thomas, G.Gibson 5.2010

❷ The Yolk's on You 6b
The arete has a hard pull on small holds to get going and another higher up.
FA. R.Thomas, G.Gibson 5.2010

❸ You've Had Your Chicks 6a
An easy groove leads the way to a problematic pull.
FA. G.Gibson, R.Thomas 2.2010

❹ Crumlin Towards England 5a
The juggy wall from the left side of the grassy ledge.
FA. G.Gibson, R.Thomas 5.2010

❺ Crumlin at the Seams 6a
The thin crack above the grassy ledge.
FA. G.Gibson, R.Thomas 5.2010

❻ Crumlin at the Edges 6a
The right arete above the grassy ledge.
FA. G.Gibson, R.Thomas 5.2010

South Wales Sport Climbs — Route Index

Stars	Grade	Route	Photo	Page
	6a	16KN Working Load		135
	6c+	30' is the new 20'		404
*	6b	300 Spartans		300
	6a	3D Dog		71
*	6c+	4th Dimensional Melodies		193
**	7b+	Abbatoir and Costello		468
	7a+	Abdominal Showman, The		416
	5b	Above Holy Sister		127
	6b+	Above the Stupid		58
	6a	Abra-Ker-Fucking-Dabra		294
*	6a+	Absolutely Vabulous		352
**	6c	Academy Awards		215
	6a+	Acatalepsia		466
	5c	Ace in the Hole		449
*	6b+	ACE Inhibitors		73
	6b+	Achilles Hasn't a Foot to Stand On		300
	6c	Achilles Last Stand		356
○○○	8b	Achilles' Wrath	16	84
	6b	Adam Hussein's Nan		247
	4c	Adit Again		249
**	7b+	Adrift on Dirac's Sea		69
***	E2	Adulteress, The		102
	6a+	Aedan's Arete		472
	6b	Affairs of Man		341
	5c	Affluenza		248
*	5c	Afternoon Delight		374
	E3	Ain't as Effical		417
*	7a+	Air Display		195
○○○	8a+	Air Show	77	84
	4b	Al Perchino		96
***	6b+	Al-Tikrit		120
	6a	Alchemy of Error		300
	6a	Alco-Troll		445
	6a+	Algie's Bra		315
*	5b	All Aboard My Dinghy		275
*	6a+	All For Nothing		63
	3a	All Hands on the Sea Cocks		92
	5c	All in for the Draws		263
	6a	All of a Quiver		182
*	6c	All Sand Together		463
	6a+	All Talk		370
*	7b+	All that Glitters is not Gold		189
*	6b+	All the Pies Arete		254
	6a+	All Things Bright and Beautiful		274
	6b	All's Well		247
	6b	Alpha Blocker		73
**	7a+	Altered Carbon	37	355
*	5b	Alys Rook		407
	5b	Amblimance		133
	7a	Amnesia		466
*	6b+	Amritsar		185
	6b	Anal Gesia		153
*	6c	Anal Retention		309
	6a+	Analogue Kid		457
	6b	Anaphylactic Arete		333
*	6b+	Anchors Away		291
	5b	Andre Marriner		91
	6a	Andrew the Zebra		401
	6c	Angel of Mons		236
*	6c	Angle Grindr		379
*	5c	Angry Pirate		226
*	7a	Angst of Anti-Fashion, The		126
	6a	Anne's Stiff Entry		344
	6a	Anniversary Walk		407
*	6b	Anoek Clear Missile		153
*	6b	Anonymous Bosch		161
*	6c	Anonymous Flare		153
	6a+	Another Cupid Stunt		58
*	6b+	Another Jewell		378
	5b	Ant Frenzy		414
*	6a+	Anteater's Arete		376
**	6c	Any Old Iron	34	248
**	7b	Anything You Can Do		431
***	6c+	Apache		323
***	6a+	Aphrodite's Curse		412
	6c+	Apoplectic Arete		333
	6a	Apples and Pairs		272
	6a	Approaching the Nadir		478
	6a	Apricot Jam		187
*	7a	Aptitude Test		463
*	5a	Aqua Mule Show		421
*	6c	Arab Spring		135
	5c	Arch of the Last Craven Ant		473
*	6a	Archaeopteryx		487
	6a	Archie		157
	6a+	Archimedes Screws		303
*	6a+	Are You Feeling Locky ?		485
*	6c	Aristophanes Plays with Time		298
**	6b+	Arizona Ted		314
	8b	Armada		84
**	7b	Arwen		126
	6a+	As High as a Kite		283
	5c	As it is		433
	VS	As it Was		428
*	7b+	As You Were!		103
	7a	Ashes to Ashes		193
	6b+	Aspidistra		180
	6b+	Ass in the Hole		239
***	6c	Asset Manager		61
	5a	Asteroids		256
	6c	Asthmanaut		355
	5c	Atomic Wedgie		104
	5b	Atraumen		90
*	E5	Attrition		83
	6b+	Attrocities		414
	7c+	Au		189
	6b	Auf Wiedersehen Mate		488
**	6a+	Aur of Glory		189
	6a	Aur of Need		189
	6c	Away with the Fairies		383
	6b+	Away With The Mixer		383
	E1	Axe, The		105
	6c+	Ay, Caramba		129
	6b	B Road		332
	6b+	Baaaaad to the Bone		444
	6c	Babcock Test, The		369
*	6c+	Baby Bouncer		152
	6b+	Baby Going Boing Boing		152
	6a	Bach in the Day		347
	5b	Back Chimney		188
	4c	Back from the Berbers		266
*	6a	Back Passage		379
	5a	Back Road		333
	6a	Back to Black (Mount P)		422
***	7c+	Back to Black (Trial Wall)		102
*	5a	Back, Crack and Sack		277
	4c	Backdoor Girl		379
*	6b	Bad Bad Boy		339
**	7a+	Badger's Out!		68
	4a	Badness		469
*	5b	Baggle Brook Affair		340
	6c	Balancing Blondine		376
	5c	Bald Patch		280
*	6b	Baldy Walks to Ponty		395
	6b	Balls of Damocles		422
*	6b	Balthazaar's Ball Sac Bulges Beholding		
		Bouncing Bargoed Booties		455
	6c	Banal Pretention		309
	6b	Banjo Versus the Pigeon		385
**	7a	Banog's Barmy Army	387	388
	6b	Barbara		340
	6b	Bareback Rider		149
	6a	Barefaced Cheek		433
	6b	Bargain Basement Bargoed		455
	6b	Bargoed Blow Job		454
	6b	Bargoed Bushwhacker		454
	6a	Bargoed Sideshow		454
	6a	Barnacle Bill		92
	6b	Barnacle Bill, The		302
	6c	Barnacles at Dawn		52
	6b+	Barry Freight		308
	6a	Barzan Lost His Head		120
	E3	Bas Chevaliers		465
*	4c	Basil Brush		171
**	7b+	Basildon Slapper, The		398
**	7b+	Basilica		209
	6a+	Bastard Wing		318
	6a+	Bathroom Blitz		135
**	6c	Battle of the Bulge		274
	3b	Beagle Banter		483
	6a+	Bearded Commoners		335
*	7a	Beast and the Harlot		352
*	6b	Beat A Block, Ha!		73
	6a+	Beautiful People, The		107
*	7a	Beauty School Drop-out		394
	6a	Beavers at Bargoed		454
**	7b+	Becalmed on Dirac's Sea		69
	6b	Bedlam		109
	5c	Bedraggled Trousered Misogynist		295
	6b	Bee Gone		334
	6b	Beeching Closure		334
	HVS	Beef Curry and Chips		395
*	7b	Beer Coracle		69
*	7a+	Before Planck's Time		67
	6b	Behind the Bike Sheds		398
	6c	Bella Donna		159
*	6b	Bellerophon		193
**	7b	Belly It Up		492
*	7c+	Ben's Route		323
*	6a+	Bending Sickle		161
***	7a+	Berlin	198	213
***	7b	Berlin Extension		213
	6a	Bermuda Tentacles		226
	6a	Besetting Fears		97
	6b	Best Possible Taste		58
**	6a+	Beth		123
**	6b+	Between the Lines		463
	6c+	Beware of Poachers	205	206
**	6b+	Beware the Burly Butcher of Bargoed		455
*	7a	Beyond the Black Rainbow	353	356
	6b	Beyond the Fringe		175
	6b+	Beyond the Wizard's Sleeve		379
	5a	Bhaktapur		266
	5c	Big Bad Baboon		419
	6b+	Big Ears Takes Flight		204
*	6b	Big Jim		378
*	6c	Big Pychture, The		347
	5c	Big Squeeze, The		473
**	E6	Big Time, The		213
	6b	Big Tissue, The		493
	HVS	Billy the Fish		364
*	6c	Biological Jiu-Jitsu		356
	5b	Birthday Bulge		341
	6b	Bit of Nokia on the Side, A		340
	6c+	Bit Shifty, A		323
**	6b	Bitch		71
	6c	Bitter End		247
*	E3	Bizarre Geetar		363
**	6c	Black Adder	81	80
	6b+	Black Dog		455
*	7a	Black Friday		107
**	6b	Black Magic	437	442
*	6a	Black Night's Rein	252	254
○○○	8a	Black Pearl, The		213
	5a	Black Sea Shanty		92
*	6b	Black Thought		352
	6b	Black Tide		274
**	7b+	Black Wall		103
○○	8a+	Black Wall Direct		103
	6c+	Blacker than Black		410
***	6c+	Blackman's Pinch	74	102
***	6a	Blaggard's Wet Pocket, The		388
*	6a+	Blaidd Den		292
	4c	Blandess		469
*	7a	Blank Abstract, A		441
**	6b	Blank Dark Thirty		65
**	6b+	Blinded by Love		463
*	6c	Blinded By Puppies		463
	6b+	Blockbuster (Third Sister)		132
*	5c	Blockbuster (Trial Wall)	100	105
***	6a+	Blockiness		86
	6a+	Blood Spunker		72
	6a	Blood, Sweat and Beers		441
○○	8a	Bloody Sport Climbers		213
	6b	Blossom		254
	6b+	Blow Me Down (Thar)		114
*	6a	Blow Me, Another One	299	299
	5c	Blow Up		114
*	7a+	Blowing for Tugs		455
	6a+	Blowing the Horn		124
	VS	Blowing The Ram's Horn		303
**	6c+	Blue Sky Day, A		219
*	6b	Bluster		428
*	6b	Bob's Birthday Party		205
*	6c	Bob's Your Uncle		137
	5c	Bodice Ripper		128
	6c	Bold as Brass		186
*	7a	Bolder Boulder		138
*	6b+	Bolt Fund Blues, The		441
	6b	Bolts and Torque		378
*	6b	Bolus Feed		64
	7b	Bonacci's Sequence		62
	5c	Bonaroo Lally Tappers		423
*	6a	Bone Hard Start		344
	5b	Bonehead		204
	5c	Boner's Crack		481
	6a	Boney King of Nowhere Direct, The		244
	6b	Bongo Bongo Land		220
	6c	Book End Rib		261
**	4c	Book of Revalations, The		283
	7c	Bootneck		83
	5c	Bootylicious		441
	4b	Border Control		91
	3c	Bore Hole		493
	6c	Bored of Brackla Becomes Benefactor of Bargoed		455
	6a	Bored of Toad Hall		90
	7a+	Boring Bristolian Benefits Beneficiary		447
	6b+	Bosom Pals		114
*	7b	Boston Strangler		161
*	6b	Bottom Drawers	93	88

Route Index — South Wales Sport Climbs

Stars	Grade	Route	Photo	Page
*	6b+	Bottom Rail		309
	VS	Boulevard de Alfred Turner (1926).		401
*	6a	Bowen Arrow		182
**	6a	Bowen to the Inevitable		183
	6a+	Boy George V		422
	6a+	Bramble Pitt Gets Hammered		489
*	6a	Branch Line		308
	6c+	Branch Manager		410
*	7a	Brass Farthing		140
**	6c+	Brazilian Blend		215
	6b+	Bre-X		187
*	6a	Break Stuff		314
**	6c	Breakout		215
*	6b+	Breccial Motion		180
	4b	Brexit Exit		185
	6a	Brexit Legacy, The		275
	5b	Bring Back the Birch		412
*	6a	Bring out the Blossom		254
*	6a+	Bring out the Crimp		254
*	7a+	Bringeth yon Leach		468
*	6b	Bringing The Brane Theory To Bargoed		454
*	7a	Bristol Beat		245
*	5b	Bristol Viking Raider		261
	6b	Brittania		455
*	4c	Brittle Biscuit		277
*	6b	Broken on the Rocks		291
*	6a	Brood Mare		149
	5b	Broody Hen		317
	6a+	Brown Dirt Cowboy, The		498
	6a+	Brucifer		472
	7a+	Brunette		283
*	7a	Brush Down, The		464
*	7a	Brush Off, The		464
*	6b	Bryn Serth		292
*	6b	Bucket of KFC and Two One Armers		375
*	5c	Buckets of Bubbly		102
	5b	Budda's Watching		478
	4b	Buen Culo		493
*	6b	Buff the Happy Lamp		407
*	4c	Bulbus Tara		232
	6a+	Bull Camp		423
**	7b+	Bull Fighter		179
*	6a	Bull Market		61
*	6b	Burdock		463
*	6c+	Burn After Reading		60
	6b+	Burning Brush		365
**	6b	Burning Glass, The		303
*	5b	Burton Line		310
*	5c	Bush Trimmer's Corner		311
*	5c	Buster Gonads		364
*	6b	Busy Beaver		317
**	7b	Butcher Heinrich		471
*	6a	Butcher's Slab		112
	6b	Butt Hole Left Deviant		433
	6b+	Butt Hole Scoundrels		433
	5c	Butt Out		433
	5c	Butterball		114
	3c	Butthole		266
	6b+	Buzz Off		334
**	6c+	By Appointment Only		377
*	5b	By Default Line		498
	7a	By Proxy		208
	6a	By Road		333
*	6b+	Bye Bye Eddy		189
*	6b+	Bye Dad		95
	5b	Cachau Hwch		292
**	7b+	Caerphilly Contract, The		467
*	6c+	Caerphilly Cop Out, The		464
	6a+	Cagophilist		484
*	6b+	Calamity of Conscience		379
	6b	Calcitaclone		111
*	6b+	Calcite Crack'n Up		111
*	6b+	Calcite Crunch		111
*	6b+	Calcite Punch		111
	5b	Calcitron		111
*	6a+	Calculus		315
*	6b	California Freeming		308
*	6c	Call a Spade a Spade		211
*	6c+	Calling Card		401
*	4b	Cam Slut		316
**	6c+	Camino Del Roy, El		215
	6c	Can the Can		244
*	5b	Can't Swallow That		107
	HVS	Canaan Grunts		302
*	6a+	Canine League		430
	4b	Caninia		169
*	7a	Cannibal Calypso		303
***	7b+	Capstan		398
oo	8a	Captain Barbarcssa		213
**	7b	Captain Hook		195
*	6b+	Captain Jacque Hoff		90
	6c+	Caramel Wall		283
*	6b	Carbon Copy		115
*	6b+	Carbon Dating		115
*	6b	Carbon Era		115
*	4b	Carbon Light		115
*	6b	Carbon Times		115
	6a	Carbonate		115
	5c	Carboniferous		115
	6b	Carpet Bombing		412
*	4c	Carpetbagger, The		304
	5b	Cartesian Dualism		303
*	6c+	Cascade		467
**	5b	Cash in the Attic		96
	6a+	Cast Adrift (Telpyn P)		51
*	6c	Cast Adrift (Witches P)		291
	6a	Cast Me Away		88
*	4b	Catapult		91
	E3	Catch of the Day		332
*	6b	Catch the Pigeon		385
	6c+	Catching Fire		89
	6b	Cauldron of Satyr		153
	4a	Ceasg		94
*	6b	Celestial Annihilation		355
**	7b	Celestial Being		237
*	6b	Cenotaph Norm Carter		395
*	6b	Central Deviator		67
*	6b	Central Integrator		65
*	6b+	Cerbat Mustang		148
*	6b+	Certain Peace, A		416
*	5b	Ch Cha Cha, La		129
*	6b	Chain Reaction		345
***	7a+	Chattery Teeth		449
	6b+	Cheapskate		254
*	4b	Checking Lichen		104
*	5b	Checkpoint Checkout		91
	S	Cheeky Arete		493
	6b	Cheese Sandwich		188
**	5c	Cheesy Flaps		197
**	6b+	Cheesy Rider		202
	4c	Chemical Ali		120
	7a	Chicken Licken		172
*	7b	Chilean Flame Flower		137
*	7b+	Chilean Flame Thrower		136
	6b	Chill to the Bone		263
*	6b+	Chill to the Touch		263
	6c+	Chimney Finish, The		501
*	6c+	Chinese Whispers		245
**	7b	Chiropractor		163
**	7c	Chives of Freedom	201	213
	5a	Chloe's Crack		423
*	6b	Chock a Block		145
	E2	Choice Cut		410
*	6b	Choosey Suzie		499
	7a	Christendom		236
	6b	Chubby Loving		114
*	6b+	Chuck Prince Goes Dancing		447
	5c	Church of the Cosmic Skull		357
	6b	Cigarillo		339
*	6a	Cilly Arete		406
*	6a	Cinders Catch		39
	4b	Cino, El		91
*	6a	Circus Clowns		406
	6b	CJD		235
	6a	Clair de Lune		245
	2a	Claire's Cyntaf		256
*	6c	Clampetts, The		191
*	6b	Clapham Injunction		190
*	6c	Clear Conscience and a Blow Job, A		404
*	6c	Clear Head and a Blow Lamp, A		404
	4a	Cleft a bit		168
*	7a	Cleft Stick, A		492
*	4b	Cleftomaniac		168
	HVS	Climb a Sycamore Tree		303
	6a	Clint Yeastwood		487
**	6c	Clip Joint		163
*	4c	Clock Sucker		364
*	6c	Closed Road		333
	6b+	Closed Shop		344
	6a+	Clot Thickens, The		89
	5b	CND		344
*	7a	Co-Codamol Crunch		420
	6b	Coc Oen		293
*	6b+	Cock and Ball Story	381	383
	6b	Cock Lock		483
	6b	Cock-a-doodle		317
*	6a+	Cock's Crow		317
*	6c	Cocky Black Chauffage		85
*	6b	Cod Father		50
	6b	Cod Liver Oil		276
	7a	Coffee Shop		449
	6b+	Coggars Lane		410
***	7a+	Cointreau		410
	6b+	Cold Finger		311
*	6b	Cold Inconvenience		144
*	6c+	Cold Rolled		345
*	6b	Coming Unstuck		278
	5c	Common Cold		334
	6a+	Common Deviation		335
	6a+	Common Ground		334
*	5b	Common Slattern		335
	5c	Community Spirit		344
	6a	Concrete Cows		90
*	6b+	Condenser		150
	6b+	Cone Penetration Test		419
*	5a	Confidential - Lower Wall, LA		231
	7a	Confidential, LA		231
	7a	Conglomeration		191
**	7b	Connard Canard		171
	6b	Connect One		204
*	6a+	Connecticut Connection - Lower W.		231
**	7a+	Connecticut Connection, The	229	231
	HVS	Consequentialist Perfectionism		303
**	6c+	Constant Gardener, The		195
	5c	Constantinople		414
	6a+	Continued Nursing Care		64
***	7c	Contraband		465
**	6c	Controlled Emission		432
	5b	Converted Traditionalist		303
**	7a	Cool Crux Clan, The		195
*	7a	Cop the Lot		464
	6a	Copper Bottom		186
	6a+	Copperopolis		187
	6a+	Coprophagic Canine		365
	6c+	Cordoba Express		308
	6b	Corneal Abrasion		489
	HVS	Corner, The		385
*	6b+	Cox 2 Inhibitor		420
*	6a	Cox Bloc		481
	5c	Coxs Yucca		481
***	E3	Crack Basher		344
*	6b+	Crack Liqour		310
	4c	Crack Me Up		275
	E2	Crack of Doom, The		332
	E2	Crackatoa		257
	6b+	Cracker Barrel		89
*	6a	Cradle Snatcher		152
**	6c+	Cragmeister, The		499
*	5b	Crash and Dash		61
	6a	Crash Landing		444
	6b+	Crash Test Dummy		283
	6a	Crass Word Pizzle		94
*	7a	Crawling Chaos, The		238
**	7a+	Crawling King Snake		176
	6b+	Craxsploitation		442
*	6c	Creaming Dream, The		247
	6b+	Credit Squeeze	57	60
*	6a	Creep 'n' Crawl		374
	6b+	Creme de Rockfall		202
	6b+	Creme de Roquefort		202
	5c	Crescent Wanker		365
	6c	Crest of a Wave		54
*	6c	Crib Biter		149
***	7b	Crime and Punishment		103
**	7b	Crime Slunk Scene		288
	6c+	Crimes of Fashion		228
*	6b+	Crimp Paddle		94
	7b+	Crimpa-Lean Sheet		260
*	6c+	Crimson		488
*	6a	Crimson King, The		472
	5b	Crinoid Crimper		111
	6c	Crock Block		193
*	7a	Crock Licker		364
**	7c	Crock of Gold		214
	6b	Croeso I Gymru		290
	6b+	Crooked Little Pinky		246
*	7a+	Cross Country Boot Call		71
*	5c	Cross Incontinents		85
	7b+	Cross the Rubicon		193
**	5b	Crouching Tiger, Hidden Badger		316
	6a	Crumlin at the Edges		501
	6a	Crumlin at the Seams		501
	5a	Crumlin Towards England		501
	5a	Crusty Barnacles		226
	6b	Crystal Balls		316
	4a	Cuddles Small but mighty		483
*	6c	Cujo		205

Carmarthenshire · Gower · Inland and Coastal Limestone · The Valleys Sandstone

South Wales Sport Climbs — Route Index

Stars	Grade	Route	Photo	Page
*	6b	Culture Vulture		374
*	5a	Cunning Little Fox		171
*	5c	Cure for Crabs		51
	5b	Curtain Call		335
	6a+	Cut Throat		420
	6a+	Cut Through the Crap		58
	6b+	Cwm Bach Again		347
	6b+	Cwm Bach to Me		347
*	6c	Cwm by 'ere		347
	6b+	Cwm Fly With Me		347
	6a+	Cwm Moaner		334
	6b+	Cwm on Then		334
**	5c	Cwm Sluts		347
	6b	Cwmcarnage		488
*	7a	Cybernetic Sex Samurai		354
	5a	Cymru Euro 2016		414
	6b+	Cynical		113
*	6b	Czech this Out		314
	6b	D'ya Hear Ma Dear		235
*	6a+	(d) rock		265
	6a	Daddy's Little Lemon Licker		421
	HVS	Daft Nutter		63
**	6c	Daggers	227	234
**	7b	Dai Hard		391
	6b	Dai Horrea		433
***	7c+	Dai Vinci Coed, The		288
	5c	Dai's Route		144
**	7a+	Daisy Chainsaw		221
*	5c	Damp Bitch		318
	6b+	Damp Cod Piece		50
	6a+	Damp Digits		341
	6a	Dan Dix		385
*	6b	Dan'ds-Inferno		385
	6b+	Dan's Dihedral		221
	6b	Dandelion		463
	7a	Dandelion Slab, The		209
	7a+	Danny La Rue		215
	4a	Dark Art of Banana Magic, The		239
	6a+	Dark Force of Glamorgan, The		301
**	7b+	Dark Matter		245
	6a+	Dark Side of the Road, The		332
*	6c	Darkness into Light		258
**	6c	Daughters of Lear, The		131
***	5a	Dawson's Corner		95
**	5b	Dawsons Creek		95
**	7c+	Day In, Day Stout		323
	5b	Day the Drill Conked Out, The		365
	6b+	Day the Sky Fell in, The		173
*	7b	De-Regulators, The		206
*	7a	Dead Man's Shoes		54
	6b	Deadbolt		485
	6c	Deadly Nightshade		204
*	7a+	Deaf as a Post		476
*	5c	Death Match		441
	6a	Death Twitch		441
	6c	Debauching Deborah		141
	6a+	Debbie Likes it Wet		138
*	7a	Debbie Reynolds	133	138
	6c+	Deborah		141
**	6c	Decades Apart		193
*	6b	Decimus Maximus		236
*	5b	Deflated Dickhead, The		203
	7a	Demi Moore		395
	6a	Democratic Republic of Maesteg		204
	6c	Demolition Gang		341
	6c	Dental Detour		188
	7a	Dental Floss Tycoon		140
*	6b	Dentist's Chair		140
***	7b+	Department of Correction		139
*	6c	Depression Cherry		221
**	7b+	Deputy Dawg		139
**	6c	Deri Made		449
***	7a+	Desert Storm		463
*	5a	Destination Brynmawr		274
*	6c	Deus Ex Machina		442
*	6c+	Devil May Care		112
*	6a	Devil of a Time		316
	6a+	Devil's Brew		153
*	5b	Devil's Playground		316
*	4c	Devil's Spawn		316
*	4b	Devilment		113
*	5a	Devils in the Detail, The		316
	6a	Dia Monde		449
*	7a	Diagnosis Made Easy		274
*	6b	Diamond Dog		501
	6b+	Diawl Bach		293
°°	6b	Dicky Dyson		382
	6b	Didymo Clogs yer Tackle		295
**	7c	Digitorum Brevis		246
*	6c	Digue, La		377
	7b	Dim Tipio Anghyfreithlon		280
***	E9	Dina Crac		211
°°°	8a	Dinasty		213
*	6b	Direct Start (Black Night's Rein)		254
	6b+	Dirt Box		153
	6b	Dirtbag Arete		382
*	6b	Dirty as a Dog	460	463
*	5c	Dirty Deeds		338
	6b+	Dirty Deeds Done Dirt Cheap		499
*	6b+	Dirty Drawers		88
	5c	Dirty Innuendo		89
*	6a+	Discount Included in the Price	393	395
*	6c	Dish the Dirt		58
	5c	Dishonourable Discharge		72
	6a+	Dismal Differentiator		65
**	7a	Disraeli's Curl		64
	7a	Disraeli's Curl Direct		64
	4b	Dissertation Distraction		239
*	6a+	Diverted Existentialist		303
*	6b	Diving for Pearls		53
*	7a+	Dixienormous		385
	5b	Dodecanese Dalliance		301
*	4a	Dodgy Foot Syndrome		263
**	7b+	Doesn't Matter		245
	6c+	Dog Head		69
	6a	Dog Leg		70
*	5c	Dog with Two Ticks		318
*	6b	Dog Wuff		70
	5c	Dog's Blocks		318
	6a	Doggy Bag		70
*	6b	Doggy Style		70
	6a+	Doggy Style Deviant		70
*	6a	Dolphin Snoggin'		257
	6a+	Donkey Work		371
	6b+	Dont Swallow the Bait Mate		317
*	6a	Doom-Stack		356
**	6c+	Double Dutch		197
*	6b+	Double Bore		416
	6c	Double or Squits		365
	6c	Down and Out in Paris and London		221
*	5b	Down in One		107
	5c	Down the Drain		339
**	4c	Down Under		369
*	7a	Down Under Deborah		141
	7a+	Dr Van Steiner		214
	6a+	Dr. Finger Blaster		220
	6a+	Drag Queen	477	476
	6c	Drama Queen		476
*	6c	Dream Academy		215
	6b	Dream of Wet Rabbits		422
	5c	Dreaming in Colour		468
**	4c	Dreaming of Cleaner Thing's		314
	5b	Drewgi		293
	6b+	Drill Your Own		111
*	7a	Drilling Beyond the Sea		129
*	7a	Drilling Fields, The		161
*	5c	Drinks at 'The Dog and Hammer'		364
	6a	Drive-by Shooting		282
***	5c	Driven 2 Destruction		282
	5c	Driverless Flightless Car, The		283
	5c	Drone On		334
*	6b	Drop knee at 67?		489
	6b	Dross of 86		298
*	6b+	Dulce Et Decorum Est		302
	6b	Dumbfounded Dunderhead, The		204
	6b+	Dunlop Special		280
	6c	Dunning-Kruger Effect, The		356
*	7c	Durbin Two, Watson Nil		211
*	7a+	Dusk		410
**	7a+	Ducky Lucky		173
*	5a	Dust Devil		382
*	5c	Duster		428
*	7b+	Dynamo Kiev		153
*	7a	Dyno Another Day		311
*	7a+	Dystopian Days		323
*	6b+	Each Way Nudger		211
	6a	Amount of Fun to be had by a Bear with a Broken Baculum, The		73
*	6a+	Earl of Porth		394
*	5a	Easter Rising		173
**	7a+	Eastern Bloc Rock		442
	5b	Eat My Shorts		129
*	6a	Ed Less		420
*	5a	Ed More		421
*	6a	Ed's Folly		341
*	5c	Ed's Triumph		340
***	7b+	Edge-Hog		291
	7c	Edge-More		291
**	7b+	Eel Lips		191
*	7a	Ego Sanction, The		55
	4c	Egret		157
	4c	Eirwyn		156
*	4a	Ejit		155
*	6c+	Elastic Retreat, The		441
	5c	Electra's Revenge		304
	HVS	Electrolux		382
*	6a	Electrum		186
	6a	Elephantacino		91
*	6c	Elf and Safety		394
	6c+	Elfin Mermaid		191
*	6b+	Elysium		155
	5c	Emiliano Mercado del Toro		423
**	7b	Empire of the Midnight Sun		323
*	6a	Empty Talk		371
*	7b	Empty Your Pockets		138
***	7b+	Encore Magnifique	429	431
	5b	Endosperm		487
**	5c	Enema Affair, The	135	137
*	6c+	Enema of the Affair		493
*	5c	Enigma		338
	6a	Enter the Darren		399
**	7a+	Eowyn		126
	5b	Erewhon		155
	6a+	Escape Through the Roof		483
	6b	Escapement		161
	6c	Escaping Chaos		238
	6c	Ethanol		389
	6c+	Ethanol Direct Finish		389
*	6a	Euclid's Theorem		300
*	7a	Eugene Genie		308
	7b+	Eugene's High Point		208
	6c+	Euler's Number		62
*	5c	Euphonic Wall		374
°°°	8b	Euro Fighter		84
	5c	Eurotrash		375
*	6a+	Evening Class		266
*	6b	Evening Light		444
*	5a	Evening Primrose		173
*	6a	Event Horizon, The		277
*	5c	Everybody Wants One		281
*	7a	Evil Eye, The		468
***	7a+	Evil K'nee Full		295
*	6a	Evil Ways (Cwmaman)		407
	7b	Evil Ways (Witches P)		295
	4b	Evostick		279
	6a+	Ewe Flock Wit		444
	VS	Ewe Knows I Loves Ewe		447
*	6a	Excavation Left		160
	5c	Excavation Right		160
	E3	Expansionist, The		467
	6a+	Expressway		333
	E4	Exterminate all Bolt Thieves		365
*	6b+	Eyeful Tower		488
**	7a+	EZ PZ		123
	5c	F*c*orisation		315
***	6a+	F*uc*ose	27	123
***	7b+	Face		471
	5c	Fach Roo		391
	5c	Fach Roo Too		391
**	7a+	Fade to Black		175
	6a+	Faecal Finger of Fate, The		365
	6b+	Fair Cop		463
	4c	Fair Enough		383
*	6c+	Fairies Wear Boots		492
*	4c	Fairy Godmother		383
*	5c	Fairy Ring		383
	4c	Fairy's Liquid		383
	7a+	Falling Freely		466
*	6b	Family Day		341
	6a+	Family Values		210
*	6a+	Fanny's Your Aunt		137
*	E4	Far Cry from Squamish, A		416
	5b	Fashion Victim		374
	7b	Fast and Furious		282
	5c	Faster! Pussycat		248
	6c+	Fastest Horse in Town, The		221
	7c	Fat Controller, The		308
*	4b	Fat End of the Veg		108
	7b	Fata Morgana		283
*	6b	Fatal Reflection	409	412
	6a+	Father Confessor		112

Route Index — South Wales Sport Climbs — 505

Stars	Grade	Route	Photo	Page
	3c	Fatman and Nob In		294
**	6c+	Fats Waller		80
**	7a+	Fe 500		344
*	6a+	Fear Inoculum		219
*	6c	Feed the Five Thousand		309
**	7a	Feeling Good is Good Enough		218
*	6a+	Feeling Lucky		368
	7b	Feeling Sheep		444
	6a	Feeling Totally Hacked Off!		487
	5b	Fermat's Last Theorem		304
	6a	Fern's Cottons		375
*	7b	Ferndale Revisited		410
	6b	Fernilicious		375
**	6b	Feud For Thought		183
	4c	Fickle Finger of Fate		311
*	6b	Fiesta	22	137
	VS	Fiff and Faff		106
*	5c	Filial Duty		95
	6b	Fill That Gap	435	430
	5b	Filly Buster		149
	5b	Filthy Commoner		334
*	6b	Filthy old Bitch		318
*	6b	Filthy Snatch		153
∞∞	8a	Fin		193
	5b	Fin End of the Wedge, The		104
	6b	Final Analysis		433
	6a+	Final Countdown, The		283
*	6b	Final Cut		420
	5a	Final Draft		128
	5c	Final Fantasy, The		283
	6a+	Final Plot		417
	5c	Finger Flicking Good		311
**	5c	Fingers in the Fish		369
	6a+	Fingertip Mistress		311
**	7b+	Fings Ain't What They Used To Be		208
*	7a+	Firepower		257
*	6b	Firewater		388
	6a+	First Handout		86
	5b	First Order		185
	5c	First Step To Enlightenment, The		209
	5c	Fish Called Rhondda, A		364
	6b	Fisherman's Tackle, A		51
	6a+	Fishermen Pump Their Rods		295
	6a	Fishmonger		50
***	4c	Fistful of Tenners		96
	5c	Fisting the Night Away		422
	7a	Fistula		419
**	7b+	Fisty Nuts		419
*	6b+	Five Lever		484
	2c	Five O'Clock Shadow		289
**	6b+	Flakes and Chips		501
	7a+	Flaming Fingers		136
	6a+	Fledgeling		501
	5a	Flidington Rex		419
	7a+	Flintstoner		298
**	7b+	Float Like a Butterfly, Sting Like a Bee		69
	3b	Florence Nightingale		272
	6b	Flock Ewe		447
	5b	Flounder		97
**	6b	Flow Job		274
	6a	Flue Liner		339
**	6a+	Fluster		428
*	6b	Fly		180
	VS	Fly Me to the Moon		441
	6a	Flyover		333
**	5b	Foam Under Sister		130
**	7a+	Food for Parasites		468
	6b+	Fool		188
*	6a+	Fools on Horses		368
**	6c+	Fools Rush In (Temple B)		298
*	4c	Fools Rush In (Utopia A)		155
	6a	Footsie		106
	5b	For Cod's Sake		51
	4a	For Fonting Friends		239
*	E1	For King Trad Prawn		179
	HVS	For the Love of Ivy		206
	6c	For Ye Who Has Sinned		113
**	7b	For Your Arms Only		311
*	6c	For Your Hands Only		388
	6b	Forgiveness		112
	6a	Forgotten Ground		478
	6a	Forgotten Route, The		407
	5c	Fought to the End		95
**	7b	Four Minute Tyle, The		492
*	5c	Four Star Root		265
**	7a+	Four-oh-Four		354
**	7b	Fowl Play		172
*	7a	Foxy Lady		172
	5c	Frank's Shake's a Limp One		375
	4b	Frappacino		91
*	6c	Free Lunch		368
	6a+	Freeloaders Arete		109
**	6b	Freem of White Horses, A	307	308
	5b	Freem Team, The		310
	6a	Freeming at the Gusset		310
	HVS	Freeming of Jeannie		308
	5c	Freempie		310
*	7a	French Undressing		137
	5c	Frisky Foal		148
	5c	Fromage Frais		202
*	3c	Fromage not Farage		263
	6b+	Fruitless Pair		272
*	7a+	Fuelled by Pies		276
*	6b	Full Bag		432
	7b	Full Dog		449
	6a+	Full Metal Jacket		248
	6a+	Funeral Tyre		279
**	7b	Future Holds, The		412
**	7b	G.L.C SAF		247
	6a	Gaddafi Groove		135
	6c	Gafsa		135
***	7a+	Galactus	349	354
	5c	Galena Puts Lead in your Pencil		310
	5c	Gallow's Step		365
	6a+	Galvanised		369
	6b+	Games of Ambivalence		239
	4a	Gap in the stairs		266
	6a+	Garden of Eden		256
	6b	Gary's Talking Climbs		177
	6a+	Gathering Gloom		341
	5a	Gay Batman		294
	6b+	GAZ 316	343	344
	6b+	Gaze Over By There		234
*	6c+	Geef onze fietsen terug		197
	5c	Geez Louise		89
	6a	Gem Them		378
	6c+	Gemini Spunk Wizard and His Sexually Active Teapot		134
	5c	General Sherman and the Pink Cougar		357
	6b	Generation Bitch		430
	6a	Generation Gap		430
***	6c+	Genghis Khan		232
	6a	Gentleman's Relish		183
**	6a	Gentleman's Retreat		183
	6c+	Gentlemen Prefer Bolts		183
	5c	Geoff's Nutcracker		190
	6b+	Geotechnique		457
	6a	Get Down on This		235
	7a+	Get Flossed		431
	2c	Get Out Claws		63
	6c+	Get Thee Hence		235
	6a	Get Tracking		280
	6a	Get Your Cod Out		51
	5c	Get Your Fist In		338
*	E6	Giant Killer		231
**	7a	Giant Sand		467
	6b+	Gift of the Gods		301
	6a	Gift Wrapped at Bargoed		454
	5a	Gilded Cage		189
	6a	Gilding the Lily		371
	5b	Gimme a Break		314
	5c	Ginny		131
	6c	Giraffacino		91
	E4	Girdle Traverse		195
	7b	Give it Some Belly		247
	6c	Give it Some Wellie		247
	6a	Give the Dog a Bone		71
	7a	Giving it all Up		468
	4c	Gizzard Puke		67
	6c+	Gladius		221
	4c	Gladness		469
**	7b	Gladstone's Deficit		67
**	7a	Glamdring		156
	6a	Glenys Encounters Her First Limp Member		245
**	6c	Glucosamine and Chondroitin		276
	6c	Glug, Glug, Glug		53
	7a	Gnasher		140
	6a	Go With the Flow		275
	6b+	Goblin Girl		442
**	7a+	God Bless Asia Bibi		260
	6a+	Godfather, The		434
	6c	Godot		156
	6c	Gods of Long Ashton		301
	6c	Going Down On Deborah		141
	6b	Going Through the Motions		379
	6a	Gojira		377
	5c	Gold Block		440
	6c	Gold Digger		189
*	7a+	Gold Rush, The		189
	6a+	Gold Teeth in Them Thar Hills		190
	6a	Golden Boy		189
∞∞	8b	Golden Eagle		176
*	3b	Golden Gate		187
	5c	Golden Hour		189
*	5b	Golden Plover		187
	4b	Golden Snitch		187
	6a	Golden String, The		62
*	6c	Golden Tower, The		255
**	7b	Golden Wonder		189
	4c	Goldfish		187
	6a+	Golgotha		236
**	6b	Good Gear, Good Cheer		235
	7a	Good Shepherd		447
	5c	Good Ship Venus		90
	6a+	Good Sweat and Jeers		441
	6b	Good Tradition		404
***	6c+	Goose in Lucy	167	171
	7a	Gordon Sumner's Coccyx		333
*	7a	Gorilla Warfare		187
	7a	Gorilliant		211
	6c+	Gorki's Zygotic Mynci		395
*	8a	Gott in Himmel	473	471
	6c+	Gouge the Unknown		472
*	6a	Gower Gold		185
	6a	Gower Power		185
	7a	Grab Some Tree and Follow Me		388
	6a+	Grainger Man		124
	5a	Grasp the Devils Toenail		316
	6a+	Grated Expectations		153
	5a	Grave Concern		417
	6a+	Grazed and Transfused		89
	6b	Greased Balls		432
	6c+	Great Expectations		442
**	6b	Great Expectorations		294
	5c	Great Satan, The		263
	HS	Green Arete		368
	7a+	Green Energy		276
	5c	Green Shoots of Recovery		61
	6a+	Greeny		441
	6a+	Gregoire's Island Lodge		377
	6a+	Grey Wall		254
***	7a+	Grit Box		467
**	5a	Groovy Baby		132
**	E2	Groovy Tube Day		214
	6a	Groping for Jugs		455
	6a	Ground Bait		317
	6a	Grout Expectations		430
**	6c	Grout of San Romano, The		434
*	7c	Grow-Up!		291
	6c	Grudge, The		478
	6b+	Grunter Ass		365
	7a	Guided by the Science		355
*	5b	Guillible Troubles		150
	5a	Guillotine		420
∞∞	8a+	Gunshow		84
	6c+	Guth's Gut		149
	6b	Guto Nythbran		394
	6b	Gutted		400
**	6b+	Gwest y Gymru 7 Inch Mix		234
	5b	Gwylan LLwglyd		292
	6a	Gwyll		292
**	6b	Gwyn's Road	329	333
	6b+	Gypsy Eyes		172
	8a	H1N1		455
**	7a	Hail Mary	496	500
	7a	Hair of the Dog		388
	7a	Half Man, Half Machine		441
	6b	Hand in Pocket		257
	6a+	Hand Shandy/Make a Splash		86
	6b+	Hands Off Cox		481
	4c	Hands that Do Dishes		383
**	6c+	Hands, Face...Space!		355
	6a+	Hanger Them High		190
***	5c	Hanging by a Thread		291
	7a	Hant, The		103
*	7a+	Happy Valley		138
	6c+	Hard Prawn		179
***	7b+	Harlem		214
**	6c	Harriet Harman and the Lehman Sisters		134
	6a	Harry Patch		423
	6b	Has the Fat Lady Sung?		433
	6b+	Hatchet Man		105
	7c	Hawaiian Chance		214
*	7a	Hawk's Cheep	452	455
	6b	Haworth Lassies, The		130
**	7c+	Hayabusa		213
	5a	He Sawed		411
	5c	Heading for a Sea of Tears		304
	6a	Heading South		61
	5b	Health Freak	Inside back cover	276
	6b	Heart Throb		444
	6a	Heavenly		237

Carmarthenshire

Gower

Inland and Coastal Limestone

The Valleys Sandstone

South Wales Sport Climbs — Route Index

Stars	Grade	Route	Photo	Page
*	6c+	Heavens to Murgatroyd	1	9
	8b	Hector Protector		4
	8a+	Hector Protector Right-hand Start		5
	8a	Hector Rejector		4
∘∘∘	8b+	Hell Dagger		4
	8b	Hellshow		4
	5a	Helmet Man's Day Off	4	4
**	7c	Help, Help Me Rhondda	2	8
∘∘∘	8b	Helvetia	39	4
	6a+	Hen Gi	2	3
	5a	Henry Allingham	4	3
	6b+	Herding Cats	2	0
*	6a	Hey Mister		
	6b	High Jinx	1	5
*	6b	High Moon	4	3
*	6b	High Road	3	3
*	6a	Hirsuit Ulvula	2	2
*	6a	Hoarse Breather	2	1
	4c	Hoarse Trader	1	9
*	6b	Hoarse Whisperer	2	0
	6b	Hogging the Mid Lane	2	2
**	5b	Holds May Spin	78	6
	5c	Hole in One	2	1
*	6b	Holey Moses	1	3
	6b	Hollow Feeling	4	2
**	4c	Holy Sister	1	7
	5c	Homebase	4	4
	6a	Homme de L'elephant	2	1
	6b+	Homodeus	2	3
	5b	Honeybucket Supreme	2	8
	6a+	Hook, Line and Stinker		1
**	6a+	Hooker with a Penis	4	8
*	7a	Hooker, The	1	3
	6a+	Horn of Plenty	4	5
*	5c	Horse Flavoured Shadows		7
	6b+	Horse Wessel	1	8
	6b	Horses Bolted	5	8
*	6c	Host, The	4	8
**	6c	Hostility Suite	4	2
	7b+	Hot Cross Guns	4	0
*	6b	Hot Flush	1	5
	6a	Hot Fuss	3	1
	6a+	Hot Little Minx	4	3
*	7b	Hot Mill	5	5
	5b	Hot off the Press	1	8
	6c	Hot to the Touch	5	3
	7a	House of Cards	4	9
	6a	House that Jack Built, The	2	6
	6b	House Training Catwoman	4	5
	7a+	How I Wrote Elastic Man	4	0
*	6a+	Howdy Partner	1	9
	6b	Howling Hadrons	2	5
	6b	Hubble, Rubble	1	3
	4a	Hugo Hugs are the Best	4	3
	6a	Hullabaloo		4
	6c+	Humidor	1	0
	6b+	Hundred Years of Reflection	3	2
	6c	Hung for a Sheep	4	7
	6a	Hung Like a Donkey	1	0
***	6a+	Hung Over	143	1
	6a+	Hurley's Burly Arete	3	8
	6c	Hurry, Muttley! Huttley!	2	3
	7a+	Hush Money	4	5
**	7c+	Hydraulic Lunch	1	1
	6a+	Hypertension		3
	6b	Hypnothighs	3	7
*	7b+	Hypocritical Mass	1	5
**	6b	I Am what I Am	4	4
	6c+	I Bolt, Therefore I Am	1	1
	6a	I Came	1	0
	6a	I Conkered	4	1
*	6c	I Don't Want to Dance	1	1
	6a+	I Love Valley Girls	4	3
**	7a+	I.K.M.E.N.K.	1	7
	6a+	I'll Bee Damned	3	4
	6b	I'm Alright Jack	2	1
	7b+	I'm Spartacus	2	7
*	6b	I'm Stuck, I'm Off		
	6a+	Ianto's Bargoed Bumblers Blind Spot	4	4
*	7a+	Ice Cream Sunday	2	7
	6a+	Ice Station Gelli	3	1
**	6b	Id-iot	2	5
	6a	Illegal Congress	2	0
**	7a+	Imp, The	2	7
***	8c	Importunity	1	6
	4b	In Blood, of Life, of Sin?	4	8
	4b	In Direct	3	4
	7a+	In Search of Bedrock	2	8
*	6c	In the Groove	2	5
	6a	In The Sidings	3	9
	6c	Inch Pinch (Gilwern E)	2	7
*	7a	Inch Pinch (Trial Wall)		103
*	6b	Incidentally		464
	7b+	Incidentally X		215
	E1	Industrial Relations		345
	5c	Industrial Salvage		249
	6b+	Inexorable March of Time, The		298
*	7a+	Inflated Roundhead, The		203
	6a	Innocents Abroad		55
*	7b	Innuendo		405
*	6a+	Insatiable Appetite		123
*	6b+	Insider Dealer		61
	6c	Insomnia		466
*	5c	Instead of This		406
*	6b+	Intension		478
**	6b+	Intensity of Spring, The		219
	6a	Internal Reflection		469
	6b+	Inverted Mentalist		303
*	6c	Invincible		220
	4a	Iron Bolt Hill		272
*	6a+	Iron to Defeat Napoleon		260
	6c	Is it What You are That Is?		464
*	6a+	Isambard's Bums		188
	6c	It Stinks		129
**	7a+	It's a Black World	241	245
*	6a+	It's a Sine		434
	5c	It's all Greek to me		301
	6c+	It's Been a Goodyear		280
*	6a	It's Hero Time		129
	5c	It's Not All Over		114
	6b+	It's Oh So Quiet		109
*	7a+	It's Tufa at the Bottom		290
	5c	Ivor Biggun		281
	4b	Jack's Crack		428
*	6b+	Jaded Locals		161
	6c	Jail Bait		317
	6c	Jambi		478
*	6a+	Jap's Eye		197
	6c	Jesus Wept		236
	6c	Jet Lagged		417
	5a	Jetison Bilge		272
***	7a+	Jezebel		193
	6b	Jiffy's Twitter Spat		487
*	4c	Jilly Wizz		389
	6b+	Jilter's Wall		298
*	6c+	Jimmy Cayne's Reefer		447
	5c	Jockey Club (Fetlock Zawn)		149
	6a	Jockey Club (Gelli)		368
	S	Joey's Full Pint		368
	7b	John West		431
*	6b+	John's Route		86
	5c	Johnny Bionic		422
	6b	Johnny Fartpants		362
	6a	Johnny Takes a Tumble		276
	6c	Joker in the Pack		449
***	7a	Joy de Viva	169	173
	6b	Joys of a Tethered Goat		65
	6b	Joys of Fatherhood		310
	6a+	Jubilee Step Sister		127
*	5a	Jug Fest		274
	5c	Juice Runs Down My Leg		67
*	4a	Julie's Delight		155
	4c	Jump on the Gravy Train		308
*	7a	Jump Over My Shadow		191
***	7a	Jump the Sun		175
*	7a	Jump to Conclusions		163
	4c	Jumping Jack Flash		493
	6b+	Jungle Jizz Formula		352
	6c+	Junk Yard Jete		282
	5b	Just 2 Mohs		111
	6b+	Just Another One-Move Wonder		395
	6b+	Just Good Friends		374
*	E1	Just Hanging Around		428
*	7c	Just in Time		213
*	6b	Just One Cornetto	118	123
	7a+	Juvenile Justice		400
*	6a+	Kabuto Mushi		428
	4c	Kant Hooks		304
	6b+	Keelhaul		54
	7b+	Kennelgarth		208
	VS	KES		368
∘∘	8a	Kestrel		176
	4c	Kestrel for a Knave		368
	3a	Key is in the Name, The		483
	4b	Kickback Tar		92
*	7a	Kicking Ass and Taking Names		449
	6b+	Kill the Superheroes		457
***	6c	Killer Arete	41	391
*	7a	Killer Queen		476
**	7b	'King Ada		471
	5b	King Cnut		186
**	7a+	King George verses the Suffragettes		85
	7a	King Krab		471
	6a	King Louie		187
**	7a	King Prawn	49	53
***	7a+	King Zog		471
*	6b	King's Shilling, The		90
**	7a+	Kings of New York		231
	6b	Kings of New York - Lower Wall		231
	6a	Kipper Ripper		51
*	5c	Kiss the Gunner's Daughter		226
*	7a+	Kitchener's Nabla		65
*	5c	Kitten		169
	6c+	Kleidariaphobia		484
*	6a+	Knackers Yard	249	248
	6a	Knee Jerk		62
*	6b	Knee Trembler		311
	6b	Knickerless in Hell		473
	6a+	Knob Lock		485
	6a+	Known Only Unto God		421
	4a	Knuckle Down		311
∘∘	6a	L'Enigma et le Renard		171
	6a+	Labrynthitis		64
**	7a	Lack Toes Intolerant		122
	6c	La Doux Parfum de la Lingerie Utilisé		88
	6a	Ladyboy's Cage	367	370
*	7b+	Laid to Rest		379
**	E2	Lamb Leer Disease		363
	6a	Lambs to the Slaughter (Abertwssygy)		447
	6c+	Lambs to the Slaughter (Trial Wall)		110
*	6a	Lamisil		90
*	6b	Land of the Dinosaurs		431
	6a	Landfill Tax		248
	4a	Landlubber		94
*	6a+	Lane Discipline		302
	5a	Lara		94
*	E3	Lasting Impressions		298
*	6b	Lateralus		478
	7b+	Laughing Boy		152
	6b+	Laughing Policeman, The		463
*	6a	Leading Edge		500
*	5a	Leaky Ball Cock		383
*	7a	Leave it to Me (Dyffryn)	337	339
*	6c	Leave it to Me (Gap)		431
*	7a+	Leave it to the Dogs		291
	5a	Ledge and Braces		501
*	6b	Ledger (Free Luncher's)		145
	4c	Ledger (Watch House)		159
	6a+	Leering Tower of Pizza		335
	3c	Left Cheek		266
	6b+	Left Line		106
*	6b	Left Wing Rebolt		163
**	7b	Leftist Gold		189
	7a	Leftism		137
	5a	Leftover		440
	6a	Lemon Soul		95
	6a+	Leonidas' Last Breakfast		300
**	2c	Leopard Cannot Change His Spots, A		168
	2c	Leopard Cub		168
	4b	Leopard Prints		168
	7a+	Less is More		58
**	E2	Let Me Play Among the Stars		442
	6a+	Lets Get Down and Dirty		498
*	6c	Letters of Life		468
**	7a	Liassic Lark		288
	5c	Liber Noctis		220
	6c+	Licence to Drill		311
	HVS	Life and Soul		298
*	6b+	Life in the Slow Lane		302
	6b+	Life on Planet Earth		255
	6c+	Life Without Porpoise, A		106
*	6c	Life's Too Short		152
*	6a+	Light Cruiser		338
*	6c+	Like a Scorpion		134
*	6b+	Like it then Lump it		488
	3c	Lily of the Valleys		493
	6a+	Limonite		187
*	7c	Line of Duty		139
	6c	Lip Service		341
	6a+	Lips off my Shofarot		302
	6b	Lisa Likes 67		489
	6b	Listen to Uncle		434
**	7a	Listing Badly		60
**	6b+	Litiginous/Fergie's Folly		255
	6b	Litter Runt		70
*	6b	Little Garnett, A		378
	6a	Little Kurd		391
*	7a	Little Miss Lover		172
	5a	Little Polvier		416
	5c	Little Queen		476
	6a+	Little Shrimp		50

Route Index — South Wales Sport Climbs

Stars	Grade	Route	Photo	Page
**	6b	Little Something / Prepared Earlier, A		370
*	6a+	Little Taff		370
	6b	Little Toad		369
*	6b	Little Treasure		368
	5c	Little White Dove		156
**	6c+	Little White Lies		467
	6a	Little Wrasse Cull		295
	6c+	LMN SQZY		122
	5c	Lo Manthang		266
	6a+	Load of Bullocks		152
	E2	Load of Rubbish, A		417
	7b	Lobster Bisque		52
*	4b	Lock 'n' Roll		484
*	6b+	Lock Don't Drop		485
	4b	Lock Out		485
	6a	Lock Stock & Two Broken Holds		483
*	6c	Lock Sucker		485
	6b	Lock to the Top		484
	6b+	Lockdown		485
*	6c+	Locking Nut		280
	5c	Locksmith		484
*	5c	Lockup		483
**	7b+	Loctite		431
**	6b+	Lola		317
*	6c	Lolo's Ammonite		316
*	5c	Lolo's Geode		315
*	5c	Lone Road		333
**	7b+	Loneliness of the Long Distance Runner, The		195
*	6c	Long Awaited		298
*	6b+	Long Forgotten		369
	6a+	Looey Goes Cuckoo		335
*	6a+	Look Again		263
**	7a	Look Over Yonder		234
*	5b	Looking for Leather		406
	6a	Lookout Post		483
	6a	Loopy Loo		334
	6b	Lost Branch Line		334
	4b	Lost Credentials		266
	6b	Lost in Translation		131
	5c	Lost Obscurity		267
	7a	Lotta Bottle Direct		398
*	6c	Loud and Prowed		186
*	5b	Lovely Day, A		266
	5a	Low on the Hardness Scale		111
*	6a+	Low Road		333
*	6c	Lucas Numbers		62
**	6c+	Lucky Lizzy		171
*	6b	Lundy Boy		499
	7a	Lungworms		238
	7a	Luthien		126
	7a	Luxury Gap, The		469
**	7a+	Lyddite	451	455
	E5	Lynch 'em		365
*	5b	Ma Maid's Mermaid		91
	5c	Ma Moule Don't Like U Laffin		53
*	7a+	Ma's Strict		215
**	7c	Mad at the Sun		431
*	7a	Madame-X		401
	6b	Madness		469
	6b+	Magellan's Straight		465
**	6b	Magic Carpet		255
**	6b	Magic Circle		294
**	6b	Magic Touch		289
	5b	Majorca With Tyres		280
	5b	Mal Alignment		280
	4c	Mal Culo		493
	6b+	Malopolski		148
	6b	Man Down		124
	6b	Man in a Honda Over Yonder in Rhondda		423
*	6c+	Man Machine		71
*	7b	Man or Mollusc		53
**	7b	Man or Mouse		442
	6a+	Man Up		124
*	6b	Mandiba		156
**	6b	Mannequins of Horror		221
*	6c	Mano a Mano		124
*	7b	March of Progress		388
	5a	Mare Tranquilis		245
*	4a	Marinated Goat Cheese		369
***	7a+	Marine Layer		83
	6a+	Marinieri		91
*	6a+	Mariposas, Las		130
*	6c	Maris Piper are Best		309
*	6a	Marlin on the Wall		428
**	7a	Marmalade Skies		171
	6b	Marooned		291
*	6b+	Mary Hinge's Close Shave		73
∞∞	8a+	Masada		288
	5a	Mash yer Bait		317
	5c	Mass Civil Disobedience		

Stars	Grade	Route	Photo	Page
		or Mass Extinction		264
*	6c	Mastic Mick, The		434
	6c	Matalanafesto		308
*	6a+	Matt of the Iron Gland		299
	6c	Matt's Ice Bucket Challenge		235
	6b	Maud		180
	7a	Maurice Chevalier		465
***	7a	Mawr, Mawr, Mawr	479	471
	6c	Maximus Extensicus		237
	7b+	Maybe Tomorrow		404
*	6c+	McGoohan Loses Six		73
*	4b	Me Harty's		92
	6c	Meat and Two Veg		108
	6a	Meat Fly vs the Custard Cannon		423
	6b	Meat Seeking Missile		454
	6a+	Medusa Spares No Head		301
*	6c+	Meduseld		185
	6c	Meg (a) Skater Girl from Gelli		394
*	5c	Mega Mix		234
	6a	Megalodon		226
***	7a	Melting Man	233	232
*	7a	Melty Man Cometh, The		231
*	6b	Memory Man		341
	E2	Men From Boys		55
*	7a+	Menage a Chien		449
	6c	Mental Mantels		500
*	6b	Mental Message		55
**	7c	Merlin		177
	6b	Mermaid's Footwork, A		97
**	7a	Mermaid's Tale, A		95
*	6b	Merthyr Infill, The		463
	6c	Meteor Storm		155
∞∞	8a	Methuselah	285	288
	6c	Mewn Cachiad		293
	5a	Michelinia		155
*	6c	Michelle Pfeiffer		395
	6b+	Micro Incorporation		445
**	6c+	Microwaves		254
**	6c+	Midas Touch, The		189
	6c	Middle Lane Hogger		282
	6a	Milking the Snake		72
	6a	Milky White		340
*	7a	Millennium Thug, The		191
**	7b	Million Destinies, A		246
	6c	Minchkins, The		177
	HVS	Mind Like a Sewer		339
	5b	Mine's a Pair		449
	6a	Mini the Minx		89
*	7a	Minnesota Nice		232
**	7b+	Minnesota Spice		232
	4c	Minnie Me		110
	5b	Minnie You		110
*	6c	Minsir		300
*	7a	Mint Sauce Dressing		363
**	7a	Misadventure		416
***	7a	Mislivings	491	493
*	6b	Miss Alto		206
	4b	Miss Halfpenny		368
**	6c	Miss You		197
	6b+	Missing Link		395
*	6b+	Missing Quarter, The		463
*	7a+	Mistaking Cassini's Identity		63
	6a	Mister Bait		317
*	6a	Mister Faraday		430
	6c	Mister Foothold		449
*	6c+	Mister Polite Good		197
*	6b+	Moirai		130
*	6b	Molasses		123
	6c	Molybdenum Man		410
*	7b+	Momentary Lapse of Reason, A		431
*	5c	Monica's Dress		107
**	7b	Monkey Business		419
*	6a+	Monkey Stole My Face		422
	6c	Moonage Daydream		218
	7a	More More More		58
*	6b+	More than a Feeling	415	412
	6c	More than Enough		58
*	7a+	Moreland		58
	5a	Morfa, Morfa, Morfa		60
	6a+	Morganstown Sam		398
*	6a+	Morning Glory		374
∞∞∞	8b	Mortal Kombat	211	
	6a	Mortar Life		434
	6c	Morticia		206
*	6c	Moses Supposes His Toeses Were Roses		391
*	6c	Moshe Dayan Is Coming To Get You		135
**	7b	Mother of Pearl	403	404
***	7c+	Motion Sickness		173
	6a	Moule Mariniere		53
*	6b+	Mountin' Ass Crack		416
*	6b+	Mounting at the Edge		423

Stars	Grade	Route	Photo	Page
**	6b+	Mouse Trap		444
	6c+	Mouton Dagger		465
	S	Mr Farthing		368
*	6a+	Mr Potato Head		203
*	6a+	Mr Softy		255
	E3	Mr. Gorrilla's Got a Big Nose		454
∞∞	8a+	Mr.T		289
*	6b	Mubarak		35
**	7c	Muchas Maracas		214
	6b	Mucky Ducky		498
	6a	Mud Lark Crack		13
*	7a	Munsterosity	207	206
	6c	Musical Groove		266
*	5c	Mussel Man		53
	6a	Muster		428
*	E4	Mutiny Crack		82
*	7c	Mutton Dressed As Lamb		447
	6b+	Mutton Geoff		10
*	6a+	My Blue Bell		463
	6b	My Inheritance		53
	5b	My Little Pinky		389
*	5c	My Little Pony's on the Job		369
*	6a+	My Littlle Routy Wooty		464
*	5c	My Naughty Valentine		267
*	6b+	My New House		398
	6a	My Slice of Pie		63
*	5c	My Timeline		267
	6c	Mysteries of the Kingdom		258
*	7a	Mystery Rawl Wall		260
*	7a	Mystery Trad Route X		283
**	5c	Nailbiter		363
	6a	Naked Truth		433
	5b	Names from Roger's Profanisorous		96
	6b	Napier's Bones		65
***	6b	Nappy Rush		462
	4a	Naughty Corner, The		94
	6b	Naughty Step Direct Start, The		97
	6a+	Naughty Step, The		97
	6a+	Nazi Sheep		220
	7b	Need for Speed		282
	5a	Neighbourhood Watch		334
**	7a	Neil Kinnock's Last Stand		244
**	6b+	Nematode		44
**	7a	Nemesis the Warlock		354
	7b	Nervous Nineties		391
	7b	Nether Edge		345
*	6c	Netsky - No Beginning		378
*	5a	Never Out Fox the Fox		70
	7a	New Day Today		237
*	7b+	New Hormones		347
	6a+	New Zawn		41
	6a	Newton's Apple		434
	5c	Nia Miss		63
*	5c	Nice Groove		53
**	6c	Nick to the Rescue		341
	HVS	Nick's Corner		09
	6a	Nick's Dilemma		340
	5b	Nick's Dripping Pipe		335
	6b	Nick's Line		488
	5c	Nietzche's Niche	305	303
	6a	Nifty Fingers		340
	7b+	Night Train		398
*	6a+	Nil By Mouth		64
**	6c	Nine Green Bottles	373	377
	6c	Ninetails		69
	6c+	Ninja Worrier		221
	5b	No Barking up this Tree		412
**	6c	No Beer, No Fear		335
	6a	No Benefits		374
	6a	No Bridge Too Far		374
**	7b	No Chips Round Here		414
	5b	No Credentials		266
**	6b+	No Epoxy au Oxley		72
	5c	No Father Day		94
**	6c+	No More Heroes		347
*	7a+	No Rest for the Wicked		63
	5a	No Tar		92
	5b	Noah's Arse		62
*	6b	Noisiness		109
	5c	Non Binary		61
***	6a	Norbert Colon Meets the Fat Slags		364
**	7a	Normal Norman	242	247
	6a+	Norman's Knob		362
	5c	Nose Job (Costa del M)		320
*	5c	Nose Job (Gilwern W)		320
***	7a	Nosepicker	360	363
	4c	Nosey Parcour	321	320
***	7c+	Nostradamus		95
**	6c+	Not My Fault!		235
	6b	Nothing in it		73
*	6c	Nouveau Cuisine		23

South Wales Sport Climbs — Route Index

Stars	Grade	Route	Photo	Page
*	7a	Numbers Game, The		405
	6b	Nuns and Soldiers		356
	6a	Oceanus Aches		301
	6b	Ockers Delight		341
	3c	Octopod		440
	6a+	Off at a Tangent		63
***	6b	Off the Peg		145
	4c	Off the Rails		308
	6b	Off to Oz		340
**	6c	Oh Man		124
	6a	OK Squire		109
	6c	Ol' Blue Eyes		444
	5a	Old Drifter		249
*	6b+	Old Firm, The		410
*	5c	Old Repro Bait		317
	7a+	Old Slapper		193
*	7a+	Olympic Doctor		449
	6a	Omerta		379
*	5c	OMG She's a Star		365
*	E1	On Jupiter and Mars		444
**	6c	On the Road	330	333
*	6a+	On White Horses		275
*	6c+	On With Cox		481
**	6b	On yer Bike Turbo Tits		388
*	6b+	Once Bitten		462
	6a	Once Upon a Time		244
	6b	Onco Fonco		293
**	7b	One Giant Leap		355
*	6b+	One in her Key		371
	4c	One Less for the Spoiler		301
**	6b	One More for Me		123
	7a	One Size Fits All		377
	E3	One Small Step (Rams)		195
*	6b	One Small Step (Space M)		355
	6b	One Step Beyond		255
	6b	One Step in the Shade		159
	6b+	One that is There Somewhere, The		267
	4c	One that Wasn't There, The		267
	4a	One Ton Depot		83
***	7c	One Track Mind		432
*	7a	Onto the Canvas		280
	5b	Oolacunta		421
	6a	Opal Fruits		378
	6b	Open Groove		235
*	6b	Open Roads		206
***	6b+	Open Wide Please	121	140
**	7a	Operation Midnight Climax	313	323
*	6c	Operation Moonshot		354
	5a	Operation Seaman		92
	6b+	Oral Challenge		377
*	6a	Orange Blorenge Blancmange		260
**	6b	Orangutanarium		419
	6a+	Orestes' Suffering		304
*	6c	Organised Chaos		231
	6c	Original Start (Life on Planet Earth)		255
**	7b	Orion		183
	6b+	Oumuamua		220
	6a	Our Jade		378
	5b	Our Man from Hyder		339
*	6c+	Our Man in Bargoed		455
	7a+	Out Come the Freaks		208
	4b	Out Of Bulk		267
**	6c	Out of Pocket		311
	4c	Out of the Pit		228
	6c	Outsider, The		478
**	7a+	Outspan		410
	6b+	Outta Space		357
***	7c+	Outta Time		213
*	E4	Over the Moon		444
	6a	Over the Top		423
*	6b	Overleaf		468
*	7b+	Overlook, The		291
	7a	OW!		300
***	E2	Owl and the Antelope, The		444
	6a+	Ox-Over Moon		153
*	7a	Oyster Party		52
	5c	P.E.G Feed		64
*	5c	Paddock Full of Ponies, A		275
	5a	Page Turner		128
*	5b	Pain in the Arse		335
∘∘∘	8a	Palace of Swords Reversed	32	171
	6c	Palgrave		185
	6a	Palm		244
**	7b+	Palm Springs		246
	6b	Pampered		462
	6a+	Pan narrans		265
	7c	Panorama		137
	4c	Pantomime Riposte		187
**	6c	Par 3		86
	6a+	Parabola		417
*	6b	Paracetamol Punch		420
**	7a	Paradise Row		492
*	7c	Parlour Français		180
	7b	Parlour Games		180
**	6a+	Parlour Vous le Sport		183
	7a+	Party Animal		246
	6c	Paso Fino		148
	7a+	Pastis on Ice		410
*	4c	Pasty = Man Boobs		291
	6b	Paternal Love		95
	6b	Paul Prefers Pretty Pussy		422
	4c	Paul's Penchant for Pretty Pussy Poses Problems for the Prudes of Pontypridd.		228
	4c	Paw Me		498
	6a	PCB		290
**	6b+	Peachy		492
	6b	Peacock Guys, The		124
	6b+	Pearlescence		255
	4b	Pearls of Lutra		356
	5c	Peasant Phucker		317
***	7c	Pegasus	181	183
	6a+	Pelagic Mush		289
	6a+	Pen Pychtures		347
*	5c	Penny Falls		187
	6b	Penumbra		159
	6b	Pepperatzi		462
	6a	Per Rectum		433
	6b+	Perfect Prude		72
	6c	Perfect Scoundrels		433
	HVS	Periscope		257
*	7c	Persistent Offender		138
	5a	Peruvian Marching Powder		133
*	6a	Pervasive Grey, The	265	264
	6a	Perverted Exhibitionist		303
	6c	Pete of Lancs		388
*	6b+	Petering Out		255
	6c	Petersman		484
	6b	Pheasant Plucker		317
	6b	Phelan Man		124
	6c	Philandering Fillipino		190
*	6b+	Phill, The		487
	7b	Phill's a Bit Wrong But....		419
**	6c	Phlegmatic Solution		294
*	7a	Phogeys Wall		376
**	7b	Physical Presents		376
	6b+	Pick Locks		483
	6a+	Pick up the Pieces		433
	6b+	Picnic Time For Teddy Bears		258
	6b	Pied Noir		107
*	5b	Pig in a Cage		487
	6c+	Pig Iron		345
	4c	Pilgrim		234
	E1	Pillar of the Community		333
*	6b	Pillars of the Earth		102
	6a	Pilsen Power		314
	6c	Pimp My Ride		281
*	5c	Pinch a Minch		177
*	7a+	Pinch is On, The		60
	6c	Pinheads		203
*	6b+	Pining Dog		318
*	6c+	Pink Lady, The		492
	5b	Pink Stink		389
		Pioneers of the Hypnotic Groove		
***	7b		25	171
	7c	Pirelli Times		280
	6b	Pis En Lit		210
	6a+	Plankwalk		54
	6b+	Plaque Attack		464
	6b+	Play the Joker		238
	6a+	Playing Away		340
	6a	Playing the Pink Oboe	125	124
	6c+	Pleasant Mount, The		423
**	7b	Pleasant Valley Sunday		431
	5b	Pleiades		131
	5b	Plum Bob		310
	5b	Plumb, The		256
	7a	Plumbing the Depths		383
	6b+	Plumper Romp		114
	7b	Plus ça Change		291
	5c	Plus One		266
	6b	Pneuma		220
	6a	Pocket Battleship		338
	5c	Pocket Universe		149
	6b	Poddling, The		421
	6b	Poire, La		272
	6c	Poke Her Face		423
*	6b	Poker in the Eye		430
	5c	Polari Cartso		422
	6c	Polishing the Turd		371
	6b+	Polynomial		185
	6b+	Polyphemus		488
	7b	Popped In, Souled Out		137
	5c	Poppin' in the Poop Deck		226
	5c	Porcellena		274
	6b	Pork Sword		407
	6b	Porno Text King		339
*	6c	Posh and Becs		272
	6b	Post Expressionist		466
	6b+	Pot Black		339
	4b	Pot Boiler		128
	5c	Pothead		203
**	7b+	Poultry in Motion		173
	7b	Pour Marcel		215
		Powder of the Leopard Skin Leg Warmers, The		168
**	7b+	Power Struggle		173
*	6c	Power Vacuum		135
*	6a	Powered by Cheese and Ham		457
	3b	Powered by Pepsi		483
**	7c	Powers That Be		213
*	6b	Poxy Queen, A		476
*	7a	PR Job		344
	E3	Practice What You Preach		462
	6a	Prawn Cock Tale		179
*	6b+	Prawn Star		179
*	6b	Prawnsite		179
**	7a+	Pray for the Cray		52
	6b+	Pre Nups		385
*	6b	Predictive Text		340
*	5c	Pretty Picture Book		263
	6a	Pretty Pussy		316
*	6b	Prick Test		377
	6a+	Prim		130
	6b	Primal Cut		289
	7a	Principles of Rock Mechanics, Part 1		445
**	7b	Prison Bitch		138
	5c	Prison Sex		478
	3b	Probate Pending		96
	6a+	Probing Proctologist		304
	6c	Profound and Hidden		258
	6c	Prometheus Bound		301
*	7a	Promises		228
***	7a+	Propaganda	6, 405	404
	7a	Proton Pump		420
	6b+	Providence		478
	6c	Psilocybic		478
	7a	Psychotherapy		391
	6b+	Pubic Enema		308
	7a	Pucker Up		379
*	7a	Pugsley		206
	6a+	Pulling Back		149
	6a	Pulling on Puppies		316
*	7a+	Pump Action		163
	6a	Pump and Dump (Bosco's Gulch)		186
	6a+	Pump and Dump (Morfa B)		61
	6a	Pump My Bilge		92
*	7a	Pumpelstiltskin		354
*	6c	Puny Earthling		352
	4b	Pure Cino		91
*	6b+	Purgatory		156
	5b	Purple Sue		263
	6a	Pus in my Boots		488
*	7a	Puss Off		211
	5c	Put Your Back Into It		263
	6a+	Pwdin Blew		293
**	6a	Pwll Du Crack	270	275
*	7b	Pychture Postcards		347
*	7b+	Pychy Blinders		347
	5a	Pysgodwibblywobbly		96
	5b	Quadcam of Solice		310
	6c	Quakering		255
***	7b	Quantum of Lydon's Feelings		68
***	7b	Quantum of Lydon's Future		68
	5b	Quarry Goggles		267
	7a	Quartz Bicycle, The		246
	5c	Queen Bee		476
	7b	Queen is Dead, The		476
	6b+	Queens of the Stone Age		476
	6b+	Quest for the Origins of Place Holder Notation, The		64
	6b+	Question of Rabbits, A		63
**	6c	Quiet Earth, The		219
	5b	Quiet Flows the Jordan		302
	4a	R2 Sucking D2 Licking Deep Inside a Half-Cooked Chicken		239
	6a+	Rabbit Proof Fence		419
	7a+	Race You up the Wallbars		375
	7a+	Radovan Karadjic		485
	6c+	Raft of the Medusa		303
	7b+	Rag and Bone		248
**	7b+	Rage, La		405
*	7b	Rain Dance		195
	6b+	Rainbow's End		219
*	7a	Raindogs		246

Route Index — South Wales Sport Climbs 509

Stars	Grade	Route	Photo	Page
*	6a	Ram Bam Thank Ewe Lamb		124
*	6a	Ram Raider		444
*	6b	Ram Raiders		124
	5a	Ramp It Up		132
**	7b	Rampage		195
*	6c+	Rancho La Cha, Cha, Cha		237
*	7a+	Ranga		369
	4c	Raspberry Ripple (Blaenllechau)		383
	4b	Raspberry Ripple (Watch House)		159
***	7b	Rat on a Hot Tin Roof		209
**	6b	Rattle Those Tusks	426	431
*	7a	Rave Crave/Rhubarb		394
***	7a+	Raven, The	177	177
*	7b+	Ravenclaw		177
*	6b+	Raving Queen		476
*	5b	Razor Strop		421
*	6b+	Reach for a Peach		255
*	6a	Reaction Series		183
	5a	Recurring Nightmare		63
*	6c+	Red 'erring		463
	6b	Red Organised Man, The		231
**	6b+	Red Square	224	231
*	6b+	Red Wall		220
*	7c	Regulators, The		206
*	7a	Reign of the Deer		191
**	6c	Relaxed Ladybird, The	438	442
	6a	Remains of the Day, The		261
	6b	Remediation Required		419
*	6b+	Remember to Breathe		263
*	6c	Remoulded		280
*	6c+	Renaissance		195
	6a+	Rent Boys and Radiators		422
*	6b+	Repentance Arete		112
*	6c+	Repentance Arete Direct		112
*	6a+	Repetitive Strain Inquiry		339
***	7b+	Resisting Arrest		138
*	E3	Restrictive Practices		344
*	6b	Retread		280
*	5c	Retro Butt In		433
***	7b	Retrobution	1	103
*	5b	Retyred		279
*	6a+	Reverted Revisionist		303
*	5c	Reynard		170
	6b	Rhod Above the Bridge		385
	6b	Rhondda Born		376
	6a	Rhondda Leader		395
**	7a	Rhondda Ranger		375
	6b	Rhondda Tan		422
	E4	Rich and Filthy		255
	6b	Richter Scale, The		54
*	6c	Rictus Grin	217	219
	5c	Ride on the Chocolate Unicorn, A		239
**	7a	Ride the Funky Wave, Babe		195
	6b+	Ridiculous is the Burden of Genius		129
*	4b	Riding Bareback		266
	3a	Riding Horseless		266
	6a+	Riding Shotgun		282
	3c	Right Carfuffle		161
*	5c	Right Combination, The		484
	6a	Rikes Raggy		129
	6a+	Rimmed		280
	4c	Ring Finger		311
*	6b	Ring of Confidence		430
	3c	Ring, The		493
*	7b+	Ripe 'n Ready		410
*	3a	Ripple Slab		383
**	7b	Rise		398
	5b	Rise and Shine		160
***	6b+	Rising Sap		412
	HVS	Roaches Revisited		394
	6b+	Road Blocker		332
**	6b+	Road Kill		333
	6c	Road to Damascus, The		332
*	5a	Road to Eldorado, The		211
*	6b+	Road to Lostwithiel, The		332
**	6c	Road to Mandalay, The		332
*	5a	Road to Nowhere, The		277
	5c	Road to Ruin		332
*	6c	Road Wars		332
*	7a	Road Whore		385
*	6b	Road, A		332
**	6b+	Roaring Forties	459	463
**	7a+	Rob Roy		202
	4c	Robbin' Dog		318
*	5b	Robin's Yoghurt Supper		294
**	6b+	Rock Bottom		145
	6a	Rock Out with Your Lock Out		483
**	6b+	Rocketeer, The		352
*	6a	Rockover Beethoven		441
**	6b	Rocky		499
*	6b	Rompa Stompa		261
*	6a+	Root Canal		492
	6c	Roraima		462
***	7b+	Rose-Line		209
*	6a	Rosetta Stoned		478
	6b	Rosie		126
**	7b+	Rotbeest		197
	5c	Rotters Club		339
*	7a+	Round are Way		398
	6b	Rounding the Mark		275
	5c	Rowan Jelly		362
*	4b	Rowan Slab Road		332
*	6b+	Royal Flush		239
	6c+	Royle Headache		298
*	6c	Rubber, Blubber		279
	5b	Rubble Escalator		72
*	6a+	Rudaceous Ramble		180
	6b	Rude Buoys		304
	3b	Rugosa		169
*	6b+	Rum Thieves		80
	6a	Rump and Scoop		492
**	5c	Running Hot, But Cool in the Zone		280
*	7a	Running Man, The		206
	6a+	Runt of the litter		318
**	7b+	Rush Hour		179
	6c	S.A.D		378
**	4c	S'not on your Nellie		320
**	6a	S'not Right		320
*	6a+	S'not Yours (Costa del M)	23	320
*	6a+	S'not Yours (Mountain A)		410
**	6b+	Saboo		463
	HVS	Sad Little Nutter		63
	6a+	Sad Mad Professor		334
*	6b	Saddle Sores		149
	5a	Sadness		469
*	5c	Safe Connection		55
	5c	Safe Cracker		483
*	6b+	Safe Road to the Illinois Enema Bandit		332
**	7a	Saffron of Mars		354
	6a+	Saga Louts		395
	5c	Sailing to Freedom		275
**	7b+	Salem's Lot		214
*	7b+	Salisbury's Crowd		67
	5c	Sallies of Youth		214
*	7a	Salmon Running, Bear Cunning	425	431
	5c	Salty Dog		71
ooo	8a	Salva Mea		171
	5b	Sam Can Do It		190
	5c	Sam Sparrow		406
*	4c	Sand Eel		51
*	7a+	Sand in the Vaseline		292
	6b	Sand Man		86
**	7b+	Sangreal		209
	7b+	Sangria Finish		209
	5c	Sap is Rising		258
	M	Sartre Flies		304
	VS	Sartre's Underlay		304
	3c	Savant		239
	6c+	Save a Mouse Eat a Pussy		444
**	7b+	Save Our NHS		468
	5c	Saving Obscurity		267
*	7a+	Scared Seal Banter		434
*	6b	Scarface		145
	5c	Scarfish		96
	6b	Schengen		91
*	4b	Schmills and Boon		128
	6c+	Schmisse		345
	5c	Sciatica Shuffle		335
*	7b	Science Friction		404
	5c	Scintilla		277
	6b	Scintillate		112
***	6a+	Scissor Sister		127
	5c	Scooby Two Tokes		128
***	4b	Scooby Doo		128
	6b	Scorpion		256
**	7a+	Scram		237
	5c	Scrape the Bottom of the Barrel		308
	6a+	Scraping the Barrel		202
*	7a+	Scream for Cream		247
	6a+	Screaming Lampshades		204
	5c	Scrotal Scratch Mix		362
*	6c	Scrotum Oil		432
	5c	Scurvy Dog		94
*	4c	Scurvy Rubber Ducky...Aaar!		226
	4b	Scuttle		96
	5c	Sea Fairer		53
	5a	Sea Shanty Rib		92
*	7b+	Seagull Stuka Strike		69
	5b	Seaman in the Groove		92
	5c	Seaman Limbo		92
	5a	Seaman's Sea Shanty		92
	E1	Seashells in the Seychelles		377
	6a+	Seb Eats Shite		365
	5b	Secret Drawers		88
*	7b	Security Plus		247
	6a	Seeking Sunshine		264
***	6b+	Selling Short		61
	6a+	Send in the Specials		371
	HVS	Sennapod Corner		417
***	7c+	Senser		93
	5c	Septum		320
	5c	Serendipity		338
	6c	Sermon on the Mount		462
	6b	Serpent's Tooth	12	31
	6a	Seven Deadly Sins, The		413
**	7b	Seven Thirty at Arras		68
	6c	Sh**storm		22
	6a	Shackles of Love		430
*	6c	Shadow Master		59
**	7a	Shadow of the Sun		468
**	6c+	Shaken not Stirred		401
***	7b	Sharktopus vs Megapotamus		226
***	7b	Sharp Cereal Professor, The		214
	6c	Sharpshitter		300
***	7b+	Sharpy Unplugged		399
	5c	She's a Key-per		484
**	7a	She's Slipping Away	59	60
	6a	Sheepish Looks		447
**	7a+	Sheer Heart Attack		476
**	7b	Shellin' Out		53
	6c	Shining Dawn		189
	6c	Short Sharp Manic Depressive, The		398
**	6b	Short Sharp Sock		67
	5a	Shorter Life		434
	6b	Shotgun Party		457
*	6b+	Should I Go		275
*	6b+	Should I Stay		275
	6b+	Showgirl		317
	5b	Shrew		498
*	7b+	Siberian Husky		208
	6a	Sid Snot		58
	6a	Side Road		333
	6b	Sideburn		289
	6c+	Sidewinder		352
**	6b	Siege of Syracuse		303
	6a+	Sight for Saw Eyes, A		112
	7a	Sign of the Times		344
	7b	Signal Crayfish		50
	E1	Silent Echo		138
	6a	Silent Mode		339
	HVS	Silent Movies		375
**	7a	Silver Sixpence	Cover	140
	6c	Silver Surfers Sermon		67
	6c	Simple Addition		466
	6c	Simple Arithmetic		315
	E2	Simple Simon		190
	6b	Simply Simian		454
	5b	Simultaneous Equations		315
	6a+	Sin Bin		112
	4c	Sin Sear		112
	6b	Sinbad		113
**	7c	Singularity		245
**	7b	Sinister		468
**	7a+	Sink or Swim		247
**	7a+	Sinner Man		113
	6b	Sinus		113
*	5b	Sip Full of Sap, A		258
*	7b	Sister Bliss		136
*	5c	Sister Mary's Blessed Finger		137
**	7a	Sister of Mercy		126
	5c	Sisters of Pain		127
*	6b	Sixty Eight Plus One		298
	6a+	Sixty Seconds Go See		463
**	7b	Skanderbeg		471
	7a+	Skedaddle		193
	6b	Skeleton Key		483
	6b	Skin Ed		203
***	7c	Skull Attack		103
oo	8a+	Skylark		177
	6b	Slab Happy		339
	5b	Slabadabadoo		422
	6a+	Slabasaurus		226
*	6c+	Slab Happy		416
*	7a	Slap of Luxury, The		469
*	7b+	Slapstan	397	398
	7a	Slayers Gate	350	350
*	6b+	Sleeping Dogs Lie		430
	6a	Sliced up at Thermopylae		300
	5c	Slip in the Tradesmen's Entrance		379
**	7a+	Slip into Something Sexy		469
*	6b	Slip into the Queen		476
	6c	Slip Road		332

South Wales Sport Climbs — Route Index

Stars	Grade	Route	Photo	Page
	6c+	Slipped		469
*	6b	Slippery Lip Trip, The		238
**	6b+	Slipping into Luxury	324	469
**	6b	Slot Machine		186
	6a	Slow Lane, The		282
*	7b	Slurp the Savoury Oyster		289
	7a	Slytherin, The		254
	6c	Smack		398
*	6b+	Smack My Bitch Up		430
	6a	Small Fry		51
	6a	Smart Keas		63
	6b	Smash and Grab		315
***	7c	Smashed Rat		209
*	6c	Smears on Cox		481
	5c	Smeaton's Stump		90
*	4c	Smeghead		204
	5b	Smidgen		277
**	6b	Smoke and Mirrors		294
	6a	Snap Crackle 'n' Pop	19	277
*	6c	Snapper		468
	6c+	Snatch		191
*	6b	Snatched from the Cradle		152
	E2	Sniffing Deborah's Pocket		395
	E1	Snorting Horse		371
*	6b+	Snuffle Hound		71
	6c	So Uncool		428
*	6c	Soapy Dahl		71
**	6a	Soapy Dog		71
*	6a	Socrates Sucks		304
	5b	Sod Off		376
	4c	Sod's Law		376
*	6a+	Soft Prawn		179
*	6a+	Soil and Shuvel		153
	6a	Solanum		159
*	4a	Something That Came Up Much Later		370
*	6b+	Somewhere in Her Smile She Knows		97
***	6c	Sophie's Wit Tank		72
*	6a+	Sorcerer's Assistant		294
	6c	Sore Wrasse		295
*	6b	Sorry Lorry Morry	401	400
	5c	Sour Grapes		488
*	6c	South East Wall		126
	3b	South East Wall (of the Pinnacle)		245
*	6a+	Southeast Wall		137
	6b	Southwest Guru		204
	6c+	Sox on Cox		481
	6c+	Space Cowboys		237
	6c+	Spacebats		457
***	6c	Spades of Glory		102
	E4	Spain		214
	5b	Spam Javelin		407
	5b	Spear the Bearded Clam		289
*	6b	Species		323
*	6c+	Spectre of Love		54
	6c	Speechless		385
	6b	Sperm Bank		375
*	7a+	Sperm Wail		432
	6b	Sphagnum 45		467
*	6a+	Spic'n Span		107
	6c	Spider		180
**	6a	Spit it Out		107
	6b	Spit'n Polish		107
	6c	Spittle and Spume		106
	6c+	Splashdown		466
*	6b+	Split the Equity		345
	6a	Spoilt Bastard		362
*	7b+	Sport for All		416
	5b	Sport Girl		161
∞	8a	Sport Wars (Dinas R)		213
*	6a	Sport Wars (Watch House)		160
*	6b	Sporting Supplement		416
	5b	Sportsman		161
	5c	Sprats from the Captain's Table		51
*	6b	Spring Lamb Mantel		444
*	6a	Spunk Welded		72
*	6a	Squash Match		441
	6a	Squash Match Direct		441
*	6b+	Squash the Squaddie		206
	5a	Squatting Dog		316
	6c	Squeal Like a Hog		191
	4c	Squeeze for Cream		246
	6c	Squeeze that Lemon		62
	5a	Squeezing the Curd		369
*	6c+	St. Vitus's Dance		161
*	6b	Stable Boy's Breakfast		368
*	4c	Stainless Steel Association		445
	6a+	Stainless Steel Incorporation		445
*	5c	Stalag Luft		239
*	6c+	Stallions' Beans		149
	6a+	Stand at Ease		122
*	6c	Standing on a Beach		191
***	7b	Staple Diet	286	289
**	6b	Starke Reminder, A		189
	5c	Starmageddon		220
**	7c	Starter for Ten		191
	5c	Starting Block		135
*	7a	Stay Hungry		246
	7b	Steely Dan		385
	6a	Stepped Corner		112
	6c+	Steroid John		449
	6a	Steroid Vest		422
*	6a+	Stick it to 'em		278
	6a+	Stick it up 'em		278
*	5c	Stickle Brick		278
	4c	Sticky Fingers		311
	7a+	Sticky Tissue Issue		88
	6a	Stiff Blow, A		114
*	6a+	Stiff Little Pinky		389
	6a+	Stig of the Dump		278
***	7b+	Still Life		213
*	7a+	Still Nifty at Fifty		180
	6c	Stingray		95
	6a	Stinkfist		478
	6b	Stinking of Fish		197
	7a	Stoeipoesje		197
**	E5	Stone Wings		288
*	6b+	Stonewall		145
	5c	Stool Sample		433
**	7c+	Stout Bout		323
*	7b	Stout Devout		323
	6a+	Straight and Narrow		341
	6b	Straight as a Dai		67
*	7b	Straining at the Leash		290
*	6b+	Straining Pitch		163
	6b+	Stranded Dogfish		318
	7a	Strange Little Boy		471
***	6c	Strange Little Girl		471
	7b+	Strawberry Jam		499
	6c+	Stray Bullets		237
*	7a	Stray Cats		210
*	7b+	Streaming Neutrinos		245
	6c	Striking Twelve		398
	5a	String 'em Up		365
*	6c	Stroke of Good Luck		72
	6a+	Stroking the Lizard		72
	6b	Strongbow Flyer, The		80
	6a	Strutting Cock		317
*	6c+	Stuart's Line Left Finish		82
*	5b	Stubborn as a Mule		370
	6c+	Stuck On You		177
**	6c	Stuck up Bitch		72
	6b	Stud Farm		149
	6a	Student Grant		362
*	6a+	Stumbling Block Project		489
**	6c	Stump Stroker		345
	4b	Sub Prime Market		338
	7a	Sub-Contraction		466
	E2	Submerged by Blubber		362
*	7b+	Subversive Body Pumping		213
	5c	Sucking Dicks' Lowfenac		420
	6b+	Suffering Succotash		129
**	7b+	Sugar Bullets		237
*	5c	Sultan's Spring		302
*	6b+	Sumo no Shiro		428
	6a	Sums it Up		315
*	6b	Sunni Daze		120
	E3	Sunday Sport		416
*	7a	Sunstone		472
*	7c+	Super Size Me		289
*	6b+	Super Strung Direct		454
*	6b	Super Strung Out at Bargoed		454
	6a+	Super-Dimensional Love Gun		352
	7a+	Superposition		257
*	7a	Supertramp	28, 495	499
	6b	Supply on Demand		341
*	6b+	Support Your Local Sheriff		139
	4c	Suppose a Tree		493
*	6a	Suppose I Try		153
*	6a+	Surly Temple		299
∞∞	8b+	Surplomb de Ray	171	
	7a	Sustainable Development		249
	7a	Sverige		215
	5b	Swansong		335
	7a	Sweet Whistling Geronimo		385
	5c	Sweetest Flight, The		261
	6c+	Swim With The Sharks		175
	6c	Swinging the Lead		303
	6b	Synthesizer Slab		113
	6a	Ta-Ta Tata		344
	6a	Table Scraps		70
*	6b	Tactless Teacher, The		500
	5a	Tad		277
**	5c	Taffy Duck		247
*	5c	Take me up the Hindu Kush		277
	5c	Take the Mantle		266
	6b	Take the Rap for Beating the Crap		487
	6c	Take Your Pants to Heaven		472
	5c	Taken to the Cleaners		379
	7b+	Talk About False Gods		237
*	6b+	Talking Box!		375
*	6b+	Talking Hands		257
*	5c	Talking Hoarse		370
	6a	Talking Shop		371
	5c	Tally Whore!		362
	6b+	Talulah Dream		255
	6c	Tapping the Keg		202
**	6b+	Tarus Bulbous		232
	6a+	Tasty Protein Supplement		58
	7a	Taxi to the Ocean		53
**	6b	Tea Leaves		274
	6c	Technitis		208
	6c+	Tedium of a Long Distance Redpointer		67
	S	Teen Prawn		179
*	6c+	Teenage Kicks		152
	6a	Teenage Rampage		132
	5b	Telefunken U47		197
	HVS	Telpyn Corner		53
	5a	Temples of Cwmaman		473
*	6b	Termight		354
	6a+	Terrace Gardener, The		489
	6a+	Terrordactyl		487
***	6b	Terry Forkwit	359	364
	6b+	Tha'r She Blows		114
*	6b+	Thankless Child		130
	6a	Them's Be Barnacles, Them's Be		92
*	6a	Themis is Out of Order		300
	6c+	Theory and Practice of Glue Sniffing		416
*	5a	There is a Renaissance Man In Toulouse		264
**	6c+	There's Life in the Old Dog Yet		291
	5c	There's No Business Like Flow Business		275
*	6a+	They Killed Kenny		129
*	6b+	Thieving Coxs		481
	6a	Thieving Little Parasites		80
	4c	Thin Drum, The		365
*	6c+	Thin Lizzy		295
*	7a	Thinner		206
	6b	Third Eye		478
	6c+	This ain't Pretty		80
***	7b+	This God is Mine	11	288
*	6b+	This Vicar's Tea Party		95
	3b	Thorn		160
	E2	Thorn in my Side		255
*	7b+	Thousand Bomber Raid		68
*	6c+	Thousand Yard Stare		206
**	6b	Threadbare		144
	4a	Threadsearch		440
*	6c	Three Men in a Goat		462
*	7a+	Three Minute Hero		141
*	6b+	Three's the Charm		219
*	6c+	Throw in the Kitchen Towel		260
	6c	Thug Life		256
***	E5	Thumbsucker		363
*	6a	Tickety-Boo	161	160
**	6c+	Tidal Rush		61
	6c+	Tidy as Matt's Toolbox		235
	7c+	Tiger Cut		209
	5b	Timeliness		267
	6a	Tinkers Dog		248
	6c	Tip Ripper		300
*	6a+	Tired of Waiting		344
	4c	Tirpentwys Style		234
	E1	Titanium Man		369
*	5c	To Dai or not to Dai		277
*	6c+	Tobacco King		369
	HVS	Toil		368
	6b+	Toiler, The		449
*	6b	Tom		156
	5b	Tom Foolery		155
*	4c	Too Hot In Chang Mai		267
	6c	Too Keynes by Half		466
**	7a	Too Many Fingers		163
	6b+	Too Tyred?		279
	5c	Top Drawer		88
*	5c	Top Rail		309
*	7b+	Torch the Earth		462
	6b	Torque Wrench		449
	7b	Tortilla Flats		215
	6a+	Tory-ectomy		113
	6b+	Total Recoil		467

Route Index — South Wales Sport Climbs

Stars	Grade	Route	Photo	Page
*	6b	Totally Auburn		376
**	7c	Totally Clips		195
*	6c	Totally Radish		211
*	6c	Totally Stumped		410
	7a+	Touch and Go		163
*	6b	Touching The Rusty Ring		131
	VS	Tough Carapace		52
*	6b+	Tower of Ecthelion		132
*	6b+	Tower of the Serpent		221
	6b+	Towers of Curon		104
	4c	Toxic Assets		61
	6a	Toxic Badger Dust		226
	6c+	Toxicology		153
*	6c	Trad Man V2		161
	E1	Tragedy		412
*	7a	Tragic Moustache		289
***	7b	Trailblazer		247
	6b	Trainspotter, The		309
	6a+	Tramadol Trip		420
	5a	Transgressor's Corner		112
*	6b+	Tread Gently		160
	6a	Trebanog Calling		231
*	5c	Tremenal Tremors, The		264
	6c	Tremors		54
*	4b	Trevena Fish Hotel, The		96
*	7a	Tribulations		103
	5b	Triciau Newydd		293
*	4b	Tricksy or Treaty		135
	7b+	Tricky Dickie Takes a Sickie		385
	4a	Tricky Treat		135
*	6a+	Trigonometry		315
*	6b+	Triple Sigh		175
	5b	Triton Left		97
	5b	Triton Right		97
	E2	Troilism Trouble		449
*	6b	Trolley Service Suspended		309
	8c	Tsunami		85
*	7a	Tufa at the Top		290
	7a	Tufa Joy		290
*	6c+	Tufa Tennis		290
	7a	Tuffa King Hard		290
	6a	Tumble, The		267
	HS	Tumbledown		303
	4c	Tupping Time		444
	6c	Turd Strangler		433
	4c	Turf Accountancy		376
	6c+	Turing's Sum		65
**	7c	Turkey Lurking	165	173
	6a+	Turkey Twizzler		407
*	7a	Turn off the Sun		391
	4a	Turtle Apocalypse		94
*	6a	Tweaking Lats		487
*	7a	Twelve Inch Version!, The		234
*	6b+	Twenty One Ounces Of Blow		455
*	7a+	Twenty Second Chance		463
*	6a	Twice Shy		462
***	6c	Twilight World		137
**	6c	Twisted Logic		500
	6b	Twll Tin		293
	6c+	Two for Tuesday		404
	6a+	Two Hundred Year Echo, The		260
*	6a+	Two Nans and a Grandpa		133
	7a+	Two of a Kind		449
	4b	Two Tokes on the Bong		128
*	6a	Tyre and Brimstone		279
	6c	Tyre Times		280
	6a+	Tyred Out		279
	4a	Uber Gruppen Fuhrer		421
	5c	Ugly Cousin		127
	5a	Ugly Lovely Climb		133
	5a	Ugly Stepsister		126
**	6c+	Ulrika Ka Ka Ka		235
***	7c	Ultimatum	147	146
	6a+	Uluru		419
	6b+	Umbra		159
*	6a	Uncle Eddie Meets the Modern Parents		362
*	6a	Under a Blood Red Sky	273	277
∞	8a	Under Arrest		138
*	7a+	Under Attack		103
	5c	Under the Axe (Craig C)		334
	6b	Under the Axe (Mountain A)		412
	6a+	Under the Mattress		96
∞	8a	Underdog		138
*	7a+	Underling, The		131
*	6b	Underling's Underling, The		131
	6b+	Underneath the Larches		152
	HS	Unearthed		370
	6a+	Unholy Alliance		171
**	7b+	Uninvited Guest, The		289
*	6b	Unleashed		71
**	6c+	Until it Sleeps		175
	6b+	Unwind the Chainsaw		356
	6a	Up and Under		315
*	6b+	Up For Grabs		455
	6a	Up Yours		434
	6c+	Uprising		135
**	7a+	Urban Development		344
	4a	Ursula		94
	5a	Utopia		155
*	6c+	Valley Uprising		138
	7a	Valleys Initiative		417
	6c	Vanity of Small Differences		260
	6a	Vat of Tikka Masala and an Orange Seagull		375
	HS	Veg? Ina		108
	5a	Vegazzle		108
	4c	Vegemite		108
	6a	Veginismus		108
∞∞∞	8a	Vennerne		84
*	7a+	Vera Figner's Lost List		68
	6c	Vibrant Thing		220
	6c+	VIP Lunge		472
	7a	Vitamin Z		215
***	6c	Vladimir and the Pearl	46	52
*	7a+	Voice From The Pulpit		177
	6a	Voltarol Vigour		420
	5b	Voyage of the Zawn Treader		141
	5b	Voyager 2		357
*	5b	Vulpes Vulpes		171
*	4c	Vulpix		171
	6b+	Wacky Races		283
	6b	Waco Kid, The		471
*	6c+	Wages of Sin		113
*	5b	Wait for the Fat Lady's Thong		115
	6b+	Wait Here Please		156
*	6a	Waiting in the Wings		318
*	6b+	Wake, The		204
**	E4	Wall of Balls		257
*	6b+	Wallop 69		373
	7a	Walls Have Ears		280
*	7a	Wandelende tak		197
**	7a+	War of the Worlds		354
	6a	Warmth of Man, The		239
**	7b+	Warren Spector vs Rector		447
*	5c	Watch Out, Watch Out, The Wiki Wonkers Are About		264
***	7b	Watchmen		209
*	6c	Water		135
*	6b+	Waxing Lyrical		73
***	7c+	Way of the Warrior		177
	4c	Wayne Fell in Do Do		272
	6b	We Like Damp Beaver		422
	6b+	Weak Lemon Drink		309
	6b+	Weaponized Funk		220
	5b	Wear and Tear		280
	6a	Wedge Dew Bin		104
	6a	Wedge-egade Master		104
	5c	Wedgling		104
	6a	Wee Wyllie Wonka		457
	5b	Weeping Stump		112
	4b	Welcome to Sport Mountain		272
	6b	Welsh are Coming, The		260
***	7a	Western Front Direct		142
**	7b	Wet Afternoon		234
*	E1	What No Metal		368
	6c+	What, Still No Bolts		275
	6a	What's the Arc de Triomphe for Then?		110
*	E1	What's the Craic		155
	6c	What's Up Doc		29
	6a	Whatever Floats Your Boat		75
	6a	Wheel and Tyre		280
**	7a+	When I'm 64		80
	7a+	When Push Comes To Shove		11
	7b	When Push Comes to Shove (Direct)		11
	5c	When Will You Dry?		64
	7a	Where Did You Get that Bolt		41
	6c+	Where Has Stu Gone?		82
	5c	Where the Arc is It?		73
**	7b+	Where the Fox That?		73
	6a	Where There's Muck There's Brass		98
	6b+	Whetstone		105
	4a	Whispering Whelks		92
	7a+	Whistle Dixie		385
	6b+	White Bait		217
	5a	White Noise (Gilwern W)		277
**	6c+	White Noise (Trial Wall)		109
	6b+	White Stuff Left-hand, The		260
	6a	White Stuff, The	259	261
	E5	White Witch		235
*	7a+	Whiter than White Wall		417
	6b	Who Dunnit		38
	6b+	Why Did I Bother		240
***	7b+	Wide Eyed and Legless		138
**	6b	Wierd and Wayward		130
*	6c	Wij zitten nog in een sneeuwstorm		197
*	6b	Will of the People		220
**	6c+	William James Memorial Route		279
**	6c+	Willie the Pimp		295
*	6c+	Wing Commander		319
	6a	Wingman		319
*	6a	Wings of Derision		319
*	7a	Wisdom		140
*	5a	Wisdom of Age		182
*	5a+	Wish Bone		186
*	5a	Wittle Thieving Lankers		80
*	6b+	Wnco Mwnco		293
**	6c+	Woke Anglo Saxon Protestants		334
*	6a	Wonder Girl		314
*	6b+	Wonderful Land		107
*	7a	Woodsman, The		260
	4c	Working to a Budget		370
**	7b+	World in Action		136
*	7a	World is my Lobster, The		404
*	6b	World Without End		102
	7a	World-v-Gibson, The		290
*	6b+	Worzel Budgie Spunker		370
*	6a+	Worzel Cloaca Sniffer		371
*	6a+	WPC		389
*	6b+	Wrasse		51
	6b+	Wrasse Bandit		295
*	6c	Wrasse Wipe		295
*	6c	Wrasseputin's Hypodermic Typewriter		295
	6b+	Wrassetafarian		295
*	7a+	Wreckage		60
	6a	Wreckers Ball		248
**	6a+	Wreckers Bay		299
**	7b	Wrecking Ball	83	82
	6b	Wristlock		73
*	6a	Writings on the Wall		345
	4b	Wynne		160
	6a	Xanadom		155
	5b	Xanadu	157	155
	7c	Y Caled Caled		492
	6a+	Y'All Come Back Now		191
*	5c	Yak's Back		391
	4b	Yank My Chain		498
	6a	Yank the Plank		407
*	5a	Yar!		226
	6b+	Yellow Tower		488
	6c	Yikes		428
	6b+	Yo Momma		457
	6b	Yolk's on You, The		501
**	6b+	You are What You Is		434
*	6b+	You Change Me		432
	6b	You Dunnit		338
***	7a	You Never Can Tell		246
**	5b	You Nose it's Fun		320
	6a+	You Sane Bolter		64
	6a	You've Had Your Chicks		501
*	6c	Young Fire, Old Flame		193
*	4a	Young Gifted and Beige		291
	6a	Your Dinner is Ruined		267
**	7b+	Your Future, Our Clutter!		58
*	6a+	Your Wheels ain't Fly		251
**	7c	Z-Cars		69
	6b+	Zacchaeus Repents		302
**	7c+	Zealot		102
	E2	Zeitgeist		478
	6a	Zero Inclination		63
	6b	Zeuwit		50
	6a	Zoo Time		406
∞∞∞	8a	Zulu Wall		146

South Wales Sport Climbs — General Index and Map

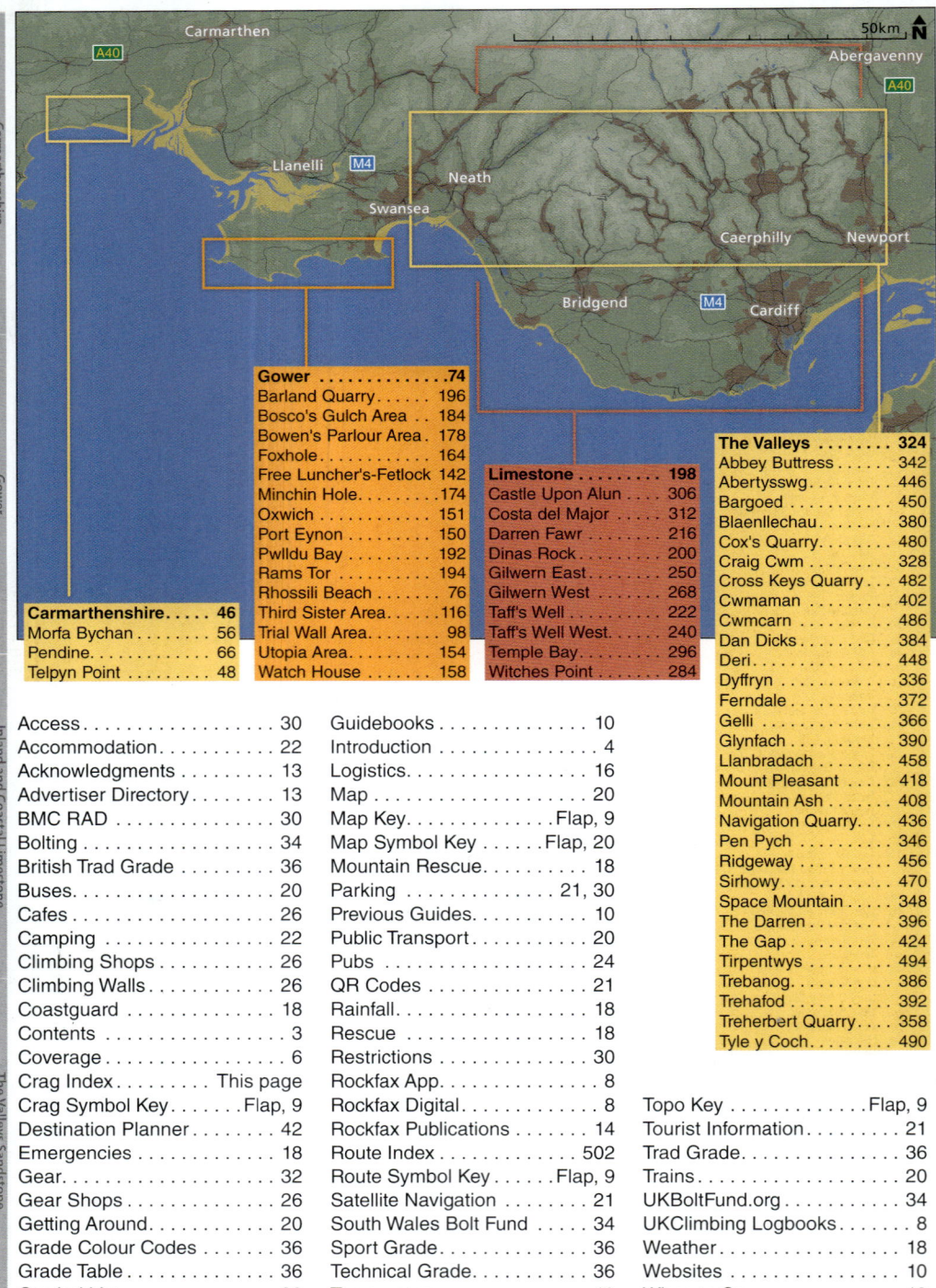

Gower 74
Barland Quarry 196
Bosco's Gulch Area .. 184
Bowen's Parlour Area . 178
Foxhole 164
Free Luncher's-Fetlock 142
Minchin Hole 174
Oxwich 151
Port Eynon 150
Pwlldu Bay 192
Rams Tor 194
Rhossili Beach 76
Third Sister Area 116
Trial Wall Area 98
Utopia Area 154
Watch House 158

Limestone 198
Castle Upon Alun 306
Costa del Major 312
Darren Fawr 216
Dinas Rock 200
Gilwern East 250
Gilwern West 268
Taff's Well 222
Taff's Well West 240
Temple Bay 296
Witches Point 284

Carmarthenshire .. 46
Morfa Bychan 56
Pendine 66
Telpyn Point 48

The Valleys 324
Abbey Buttress 342
Abertysswg 446
Bargoed 450
Blaenllechau 380
Cox's Quarry 480
Craig Cwm 328
Cross Keys Quarry ... 482
Cwmaman 402
Cwmcarn 486
Dan Dicks 384
Deri 448
Dyffryn 336
Ferndale 372
Gelli 366
Glynfach 390
Llanbradach 458
Mount Pleasant 418
Mountain Ash 408
Navigation Quarry .. 436
Pen Pych 346
Ridgeway 456
Sirhowy 470
Space Mountain 348
The Darren 396
The Gap 424
Tirpentwys 494
Trebanog 386
Trehafod 392
Treherbert Quarry .. 358
Tyle y Coch 490

Access	30	Guidebooks	10
Accommodation	22	Introduction	4
Acknowledgments	13	Logistics	16
Advertiser Directory	13	Map	20
BMC RAD	30	Map Key	Flap, 9
Bolting	34	Map Symbol Key	Flap, 20
British Trad Grade	36	Mountain Rescue	18
Buses	20	Parking	21, 30
Cafes	26	Previous Guides	10
Camping	22	Public Transport	20
Climbing Shops	26	Pubs	24
Climbing Walls	26	QR Codes	21
Coastguard	18	Rainfall	18
Contents	3	Rescue	18
Coverage	6	Restrictions	30
Crag Index	This page	Rockfax App	8
Crag Symbol Key	Flap, 9	Rockfax Digital	8
Destination Planner	42	Rockfax Publications	14
Emergencies	18	Route Index	502
Gear	32	Route Symbol Key	Flap, 9
Gear Shops	26	Satellite Navigation	21
Getting Around	20	South Wales Bolt Fund	34
Grade Colour Codes	36	Sport Grade	36
Grade Table	36	Technical Grade	36
Graded List	38	Temperature	18
		Topo Key	Flap, 9
		Tourist Information	21
		Trad Grade	36
		Trains	20
		UKBoltFund.org	34
		UKClimbing Logbooks	8
		Weather	18
		Websites	10
		When to Go	18